The Who's Who of
CARDIFF CITY
1899-2006

The Who's Who of
CARDIFF CITY
1899-2006

DB PUBLISHING

First published in Great Britain in 2006 by The Breedon Books Publishing Company Limited Breedon House, 3 The Parker Centre, Derby, DE21 4SZ.

Paperback edition published in Great Britain in 2012 by The Derby Books Publishing Company Limited, 3 The Parker Centre, Derby, DE21 4SZ.

This edition published in Great Britain in 2013 by DB Publishing, an imprint of JMD Media Ltd

A catalogue record for this book is available from the British Library.

ISBN 978-1-78091-151-9

Printed and bound by Copytech (UK) Ltd, Peterborough

Contents

Acknowledgements

I should like to express my thanks to the following organisations for their help:

Cardiff City Football Club, and in particular Tony Dilloway, and Richard Shepherd, who has also very kindly loaned many of the photographs in the book; The Football League; *The Lancashire Evening Post* (who have also provided a number of photographs), Cardiff Central Reference Library and the libraries of Haverfordwest, Carmarthen and Swansea and The British Newspaper Library.

Thanks also to a number of individuals both locally and farther afield who have provided information on different players.

Dean Hayes
May 2006

Important Notice

Publishers Acknowledgements

We would like to thank David Walters and Richard Shepherd for all their help with the picture research.

Preface

The Complete Who's Who of Cardiff City Football Club covers a biographical history of every player to have represented the Bluebirds in a Football League match, a total of 811 individuals. This book features not only the well-known names in City's past but also those less famous players to appear for the club, researched down to every last man, whether they played four or 400 matches.

Piecing together information from numerous sources and slowly identifying a career from birth to death (where applicable) is in many ways like a huge jigsaw. Gathering information on City's stars, past and present, is a lifetime's work; players will come and go and facts will continue to be unearthed in an attempt to obtain a comprehensive biography. In a text with such a huge amount of data, I have tried hard to eradicate mistakes. Football writing in the past has been prone to error, many carried through the years from volume to volume. While every care has been taken it is maybe inevitable in a work containing so much material that errors have slipped through the net.

This book is a text that will give nostalgic pleasure, reviving memories. It is also, though, a historical research document for present and future generations – a history of the 'Men who made the Bluebirds'.

Dean P. Hayes
Pembrokeshire
May 2006

ABRAHAM Gareth John

Central-defender

Born: Merthyr Tydfil, 13 February 1969.
Career: Cardiff City 1987. Hereford United 1993.

Welsh Cup winner 1991–92.

■ Tough-tackling centre-half Gareth Abraham captained Cardiff City's youth team to Welsh Cup glory in 1986–87

before making an unhappy first-team debut the following season in a 3–0 defeat at Wrexham. Three days later, on his home debut, he scored in a 3–1 defeat of Darlington. However, they were his only appearances in a season City won promotion from the Fourth Division. A regular in the Bluebirds side for the next couple of seasons, which ended with the club returning to the League's basement, he was then in and out of it prior to a move to Hereford United in January 1993. He spent a couple of seasons at Edgar Street before joining Merthyr Tydfil, where he not only played but was also groundsman.

ABRAM Robert Lawrence (Lol)

Left-half/inside-left

Born: Banks, 14 May 1889.
Died: 1966.
Career: Southport Central. Colne Town. Stockport County 1907. Heart of Midlothian 1911. Chelsea 1914. Cardiff City 1920. Southport 1921.

■ Lol Abram played for both Southport Central and Colne Town before beginning his League career with Stockport County, when Fred Stewart was the Hatters boss. After a spell north of the border with Heart of Midlothian, Abram joined Chelsea prior to the outbreak of World War One. During the hostilities he 'guested' for Southport Central, Stockport and Hearts, his former clubs, before returning to Stamford Bridge for the resumption of League football. In June 1920, after scoring seven goals in 44 games for the Pensioners, he joined City on a free transfer but made just one appearance – in a goalless home draw against Clapton Orient in the first League game at Ninian Park. He wasn't called upon again and returned north to end his career at Haig Avenue.

ADAMS Darren Steven

Forward

Born: Newham, 12 January 1974.
Career: Danson Furness. Cardiff City 1994. Woking (loan) 1996. Aldershot. Dover Athletic.

Welsh Cup finalist 1993–94.

■ Hailed as a great investment when signed from non-League Danson Furness early in 1994, he made his debut as a substitute, coming off the bench to replace Tony Bird in a goalless home draw against Barnet. Possessing superb pace for a striker, he kept his place for the next game and scored City's opening goal in a 5–1 defeat of Wrexham. Adams, who appeared in six different numbered outfield shirts that season, had a disappointing 1994–95, and, although he found the net more frequently the following season, he was loaned out to Woking. On leaving Ninian Park he joined Aldershot, later playing for Dover Athletic.

ADAMS Robert James (Bob)

Goalkeeper

Born: Coleford, 28 February 1917.
Died: 1970.
Career: Chepstow. Cardiff City 1932. Bristol Rovers 1934. Millwall 1935. Bristol City 1936.

■ Goalkeeper Bob Adams was a 16-year-old amateur when he made his Cardiff debut – keeping a clean sheet in a 2–0 defeat of Southend United in February 1933. He spent two seasons at Ninian Park as deputy to Tom Farquharson, and although he played more often in 1933–34 City finished bottom of the Third Division South, and he was on the receiving end of some heavy defeats, including Bristol City (home 1–5) and Brighton & Hove Albion (away 0–4). At the end of that season he left to play for Bristol Rovers, later moving on to Millwall where he made his last League appearance prior to a spell with Bristol City.

ADLAM Leslie William (Les)

Right-half

Born: Guildford, 24 June 1897.
Career: Guildford United. Oldham Athletic 1922. Queen's Park Rangers 1931. Cardiff City 1933.

■ Wing-half Les Adlam had played for Guildford United prior to joining Oldham Athletic in 1922. Over the next 10 seasons Adlam missed very few matches and in 1929–30 was ever present as the Latics just missed out on promotion to the top flight behind Blackpool and Chelsea. For much of his time at Boundary Park the Latics were a struggling club, though Adlam was one of the club's most consistent players, appearing in 279 League games. On leaving Oldham he had a couple of seasons with Queen's Park Rangers, but by the time he joined Cardiff City in 1933 Les Adlam was past his best and made very little impression.

AINSWORTH Gareth

Midfield

Born: Blackburn, 10 May 1973.
Career: Blackburn Rovers. Northwich

Victoria. Preston North End 1992. Cambridge United 1992. Preston North End 1992. Lincoln City 1995. Port Vale 1997. Wimbledon 1998. Preston North End (loan) 2002. Walsall (loan) 2002. Cardiff City 2003. Queen's Park Rangers 2003.

Division Two Promotion 2002–03.

■ A fast and skilful winger, he joined Preston North End from Northwich Victoria in January 1992, this after completing a YTS contract with his home-town team Blackburn Rovers. After just a handful of games for North End, he joined Cambridge United but was soon back at Deepdale. In 1993–94 he helped Preston reach the play-offs, but in October 1995 he left Deepdale a second time to play for Lincoln City. In two seasons at Sincil Bank he was the club's leading scorer and Player of the Year, while in 1996–97 he won selection for the PFA Division Three team. Port Vale then paid £500,000 for his services, and his displays for the Valiants led to Wimbledon paying £2 million for him in November 1998. Dogged by a groin injury, he rarely got the chance to prove his worth in the Premiership, and after loan spells with Preston and Walsall he joined Cardiff City in a short-term deal to boost their challenge for the play-offs. He then moved to Queen's Park Rangers but spent most of his first season with the club on the treatment table.

AITKEN Fergus McKenna (Fergie)

Winger

Born: Glasgow, 5 June 1896. Died: 1989.

Career: Petershill. Benburb. Third Lanark. Bury 1919. Blackburn Rovers 1921. Cardiff City 1922. Birmingham 1922. Southport 1923. Bradford Park Avenue 1926.

■ Having played football for Petershill, Benburb and Third Lanark, winger Fergie Aitken came south of the border to play for Bury. He was a regular member of the Shakers side in the first two seasons after World War One, when the Lancashire club came close to winning promotion to the First Division. He then had a brief spell with Blackburn Rovers before joining Cardiff. Struggling to make any impact, he appeared in just two games before returning to the north-west with Southport. Here he fared much better – four goals in 78 games – before ending his career with Bradford Park Avenue.

AIZLEWOOD Mark

Central-defender

Born: Newport, 1 October 1959. Career: Cromwell FC 1975. Newport County 1975–76. Luton Town 1978. Charlton Athletic 1982. Leeds United 1987. Bradford City 1989. Bristol City 1990. Cardiff City 1993. Merthyr Tydfil.

Welsh Cup finalist 1993–94.

■ Mark Aizlewood followed his elder brother Steve to Newport County, making his League debut as a 16-year-old schoolboy after getting permission

from his headmaster to play! After establishing himself as a first-team regular, he was transferred to Luton Town for £50,000, and during his stay at Kenilworth Road he helped the Hatters win promotion. In November 1982 another £50,000 deal took him to Charlton Athletic. He was the Addicks Player of the Year in 1984–85 and 1985–86, but he was stripped of the captaincy and suspended for 14 days for making a rude gesture to the crowd after being barracked. It came as no surprise when he was later allowed to join Leeds United for a fee of £200,000. Taunts from the terraces caused him to react the same way again, so he was transferred to Bradford City, but, after one season at Valley Parade, he was on the move again, this time to Bristol City. After playing a major role in the Robins FA Cup run of 1991–92, he was released and joined Cardiff City. In a season in which the Bluebirds just avoided relegation to the Third Division, he scored in the games against Reading and Exeter City and won the last of his 39 Welsh caps. Midway through the following campaign he left the Bluebirds to become player-coach at Merthyr Tydfil and had a spell coaching Newport before becoming involved in media work.

ALEXANDER Neil

Goalkeeper

Born: Edinburgh, 10 March 1978. Career: Edina Hibs. Stenhousemuir 1996. Livingston 1998. Cardiff City 2001.

Division Two Promotion 2002–03.

■ After playing Scottish junior football for Edina Hibs, goalkeeper Neil Alexander signed for Stenhousemuir, where his performances alerted Livingston, whom he joined in the summer of 1998. In his first season at Livingston he helped the Livi Lions win the Second Division Championship, and then in 2000–01 he helped the club win promotion to the Scottish Premier League. In the close season he joined Cardiff City, the Bluebirds paying £200,000 for his services, and he went on to become the club's only ever present in the 2001–02 season. His displays between the posts for City led

to him being called up by Scotland manager Berti Vogts for the tour to the Far East, where he sat on the bench in all three matches. The agile 'keeper grew in confidence the following season and finished on a high with three successive clean sheets for the Bluebirds in the Second Division play-offs. He still earned a regular place in Berti Vogts's Scotland squad but was left frustrated as he was still waiting for a first cap by the end of the season. The 2003–04 campaign proved to be a disappointing one for Neil Alexander as, midway through the season, he lost his place to Martyn Margetson and spent the remainder of the campaign on the bench. After starting the following season as the club's third-choice 'keeper, he eventually returned to the side, and it was his outstanding performances that were massively significant in the club's survival. In 2005–06 Alexander was ever present and his displays throughout the campaign showed him to be one of the top 'keepers outside of the top flight, earning him international recognition for Scotland.

ALLAN Alexander (Sandy) Begg

Centre-forward

Born: Forfar, 29 October 1947.
Career: Rhyl. Cardiff City 1967. Bristol Rovers 1970. Swansea City (loan) 1973.

■ Sandy Allan was spotted by Cardiff manager Jimmy Scoular playing for Rhyl in the Cheshire League. Although he was given an early chance in Division Two, he found himself low down the pecking order, with Bobby Brown, Brian Clark, Norman Dean and John Toshack all blocking his way at one time or another. However, he does hold one City record – that of scoring a headed hat-trick in the European Cup-Winners' Cup match against Mjondalen at Ninian Park in October 1969, when City won 5–1 in the second leg. Although he was a prolific scorer at reserve-team level, he was allowed to join Bristol Rovers for a moderate fee and did well for them before having a brief loan spell at Swansea prior to emigrating to Australia.

ALLCHURCH Ivor John

Inside-forward

Born: Swansea, 16 December 1929.
Died: 10 May 1997.
Career: Plasmarl. Swansea City 1947. Newcastle United 1958. Cardiff City 1962. Swansea City 1965. Worcester City. Haverfordwest. Pontardawe.

Welsh Cup winner 1963–64, 1964–65.

■ Ivor Allchurch was known as the 'golden boy' of Welsh football. He was one of the most gifted players ever to emerge from Wales. During the course of 1950–51 Allchurch, who won his first full cap against England at Roker Park, became the youngest Swansea player to have appeared in all 42 League matches. The following season he was selected to play for the Welsh League against the Irish League, scoring two and creating three in an easy win at Windsor Park. First Division clubs were now beginning to take an interest in the blond youngster, and Wolves made an abortive £36,000 offer for him. Allchurch was a fixture in the Welsh team, missing only a handful of games through injury. One of his best games for Wales was against a combined United Kingdom side for the

75th anniversary of the FA of Wales, when he scored twice in a 3–2 win. For Swansea Allchurch netted seven hat-tricks, including four goals in a 5–0 win over Sunderland in August 1958. After he had appeared for Wales in the 1958 World Cup Finals in Sweden, he received great praise from the world's press, and it was obvious that he would soon get the chance to show what he could do in the top flight. Newcastle United signed him for £28,000 in October 1958, and he made a great start for the Magpies, scoring twice in a 3–1 win over Leicester City. When he arrived on Tyneside, Newcastle were struggling and the Welsh international was assigned to a striker's role, where his creative talents were largely wasted. Newcastle were relegated to the Second Division, and in August 1962 Allchurch returned to South Wales for a fee of £18,000 to play for Cardiff City. Allchurch scored on his Bluebirds debut in a 4–4 draw against, ironically, Newcastle United. He was the club's leading scorer in 1963–64 and 1964–65, netting one of the best hat-tricks ever seen at Roker Park in September 1963, as City drew 3–3 with Sunderland, and then in April 1965 netting a treble in the South Wales derby as Cardiff beat Swansea 5–0. In May 1966 Allchurch played his 68th and last game for Wales in Chile, a record that stood for 20 years until broken by Joey Jones. He then moved back to Swansea, and in 1967–68, after being awarded the MBE for his services to Welsh football, he was the Swans leading scorer with 21 goals, including a hat-trick against Doncaster Rovers. At the end of that season the 38-year-old played non-League football for Worcester City, Haverfordwest and Pontardawe, turning out until past his 50th birthday, before finally hanging up his boots.

ALLEN Brynley William

Forward

Born: Gilfach Goch, 23 March 1921.
Career: Gilfach Welfare. Swansea City 1939. Cardiff City 1945. Newport County 1947. Cardiff City 1948. Reading 1949. Coventry City 1950.

Division Three South Champions 1946–47.

Ivor Allchurch

■ Although on the books of City's rivals Swansea, Bryn Allen 'guested' for the Bluebirds during World War Two. His transfer to the Ninian Park club was eventually made permanent, and he made his Football League debut in a 2–1

defeat at Norwich City on the opening day of the 1946–47 season. That season he went on to score 17 goals in 39 League games for Cardiff, including a hat-trick in a 6–2 home win over Northampton Town, as the Bluebirds went on to win the Third Division South Championship. He had played in just two games at the start of the following season when he was transferred to Newport County. He spent just under a year at Somerton Park before he returned to Cardiff. In 17 League games he scored five goals, including four in a five game spell midway through the 1948–49 season. At the end of that campaign Allen left Ninian Park for a second time to play for Reading. He later joined Coventry City, where his form was such that he won two full caps for Wales.

ALLEN Christopher Anthony

Left-winger

Born: Oxford, 18 November 1972.
Career: Oxford United 1991. Nottingham Forest 1996. Luton Town (loan) 1997.

Cardiff City (loan) 1998. Port Vale 1999. Stockport County 1999. Slough Town.

■ An England Under-21 international, he began his career with Oxford United and while at the Manor Ground scored for the Endsleigh League XI against the Italian Select. Able to operate on the left-wing or as a central striker, he was a regular scorer for Oxford. In February 1996 he went on loan to Premiership club Nottingham Forest but, although he scored on his debut, the clubs couldn't agree a fee. He eventually moved to the City Ground for a fee of £300,000 in the summer of 1996. Unable to win a regular place, he had a loan spell with Luton prior to arriving at Ninian Park, also on loan, but he was disappointing, the Bluebirds fans expecting more from the speed king. Freed by Forest in March 1999, he joined Port Vale but couldn't settle and moved to Stockport County on a monthly contract. Released after one season, he then played non-League football for Slough Town.

ALSTON Adrian

Forward

*Born: Preston, 6 February 1949.
Career: Safeways, Australia. Luton Town 1974. Cardiff City 1975. Tampa Bay Rowdies.*

*Division Three runners-up 1975–76.
Welsh Cup winners 1975–76.*

■ The brother of Alex Alston, the Preston North End forward, he emigrated to Australia, where he played for the Safeways club. While 'Down Under', he played for the Australian national side, who qualified for the 1974 World Cup Finals in West Germany. His goalscoring exploits for Safeways persuaded Luton Town to give him a chance in the Football League. After one season at Kenilworth Road, Jimmy Andrews paid £20,000 to bring him to Ninian Park. He scored two goals on his debut as the Bluebirds beat Chesterfield 4–3 in a seven-goal thriller at Ninian Park. Later in that 1975–76 season, Alston became the first post-war Cardiff player to score a hat-trick in the FA Cup, when the Bluebirds beat Exeter City 6–2 in a first-round tie. In the final game of the campaign he scored the

only goal as Cardiff beat Bury at Gigg Lane to clinch promotion to the Second Division. After failing to reproduce that season's form in Division Two, he left Ninian Park to play in the NASL for Tampa Bay Rowdies, where an injury curtailed his career.

ANDERSON Frank (Ernie)

Left-half

*Born: Scotland, 1896.
Career: Distillery. Clydebank. Cardiff City. Stockport County 1920. Cardiff City 1921. Aberdare Athletic 1922.*

■ Wing-half Ernie Anderson played his early football for Distillery before returning to his native Scotland to play for Clydebank. His performances impressed Cardiff manager Fred Stewart, who signed him for the Ninian Park club. Unable to break into the club's first team, he moved to Stockport County where, in 1920–21, he found the net three times in 24 games. He rejoined City for the start of the following season but appeared in just one game – a 1–0 home defeat at the hands of Oldham Athletic – before moving on to finish his career with Aberdare Athletic.

ANDERSON Reginald S.

Inside-right

*Born: London, 1914.
Died: 1942.
Career: Dulwich Hamlet. Cardiff City 1938.*

■ An England amateur international and prolific scorer for Dulwich Hamlet,

inside-forward Reg Anderson was brought to the club by Sir Herbert Merrett. This skilful player scored on his Cardiff debut in a 4–1 home win over Notts County in April 1939. Retained as an amateur for the 1939–40 season, Sgt Observer Anderson RAF lost his life on an operational flight in April 1942.

ANDERSON William John

Winger

*Born: Liverpool, 24 January 1947.
Career: Manchester United 1964. Aston Villa 1967. Cardiff City 1973. Portland Timbers.*

*Welsh Cup winner 1972–73, 1973–74.
Welsh Cup finalist 1974–75. Division Three runners-up 1975–76.*

■ Willie Anderson was understudy to George Best at Manchester United for four seasons, and though in that time he appeared in only 12 first-team games two were major Cup semi-finals. In January 1967 he was transferred to Aston Villa for a fee of £20,000. An ever present in seasons 1967–68 and 1970–71, his best season goalscoring wise was 1971–72 when he scored 16 goals in 48 League and Cup matches. He won a League Cup runners'-up medal in 1971 and a Third Division Championship medal the following season. Bluebirds boss Jimmy Scoular had expressed an interest in Anderson in 1971, but he had to wait until February 1973 before getting his man for £60,000. During his time at Villa Park Anderson had scored 36 goals in 231 games. He became hugely popular with the Bluebirds faithful, and his best season was, without doubt, 1975–76 when the club won promotion as runners-up to Hereford United in Division Three. Terrorising defences on both flanks, he laid on chances galore for the likes of Tony Evans and Adrian Alston. In 1977 he left Cardiff and signed for his former Villa teammate Brian Tiler at Portland Timbers in the NASL.

ANDREWS George

Centre-forward

*Born: Dudley, 23 April 1942.
Career: Vono Sports. Luton Town 1960.*

Lower Gornal Athletic. Cardiff City 1965. Southport 1967. Shrewsbury Town 1969. Walsall 1973.

■ Rejected by Luton Town, George Andrews was playing in the West Midlands with Lower Gornal Athletic when he came to the attention of Cardiff City manager Jimmy Scoular in October 1965. Within days of putting pen to paper, Andrews had made his first-team debut in a 2–1 home defeat by Portsmouth. A week later he scored his first goal for the club in another 2–1 reversal at Bolton Wanderers. Andrews soon settled in and showed an ability to score goals, particularly from close range. Forming a good strike force with George Johnston and Terry Harkin, he netted 20 League and Cup goals in 1965–66 and had found the net six times in 12 games at the start of the following season, when he lost his place to the recently signed Bobby Brown. Transferred to Southport for £6,000, he had three good years at Haig Avenue, scoring 41 goals in 117 games before moving on to Shrewsbury Town. He continued to score with great regularity at Gay Meadow, finding the net 49 times in 124 League games. In 1973 he finally arrived at Walsall, and in four years at Fellows Park the Dudley-born striker, who enjoyed an excellent League career in the lower Divisions, took his tally of goals to 149 in 443 games.

ARDLEY Neal Christopher

Midfielder

Born: Epsom 1 September 1972.
Career: Wimbledon 1991. Watford 2002. Cardiff City (loan) 2005.

■ A strong-tackling midfielder who is not easily beaten, Neal Ardley began his career with Wimbledon, and though he made his debut in a 2–1 win at Aston Villa in April 1991 it was 1992–93 before he was able to establish a regular place in the Dons side. He scored in his first two full games in the Premiership, and although he then lost his place to Paul Miller he returned to net two goals in the 5–2 destruction of Oldham Athletic. His form led to him winning the first of 10 England Under-21 caps when he was selected to play against Poland. The scorer of a number of

spectacular goals, one of his best was a 40-yard free-kick, which caught Neville Southall off guard in the match against Everton, and towards the end of that 1996–97 season he netted another 40-yard goal against Chelsea! Very much part of Wimbledon's playmaking and dead ball operations, he was devastated when the club lost their top-flight status, but he continued to be a regular and scored 26 goals in 301 League and Cup games when he left to play for Watford, initially on weekly terms. He was responsible for laying on four of Watford's goals in their remarkable 7–4 defeat of Burnley and over the next couple of seasons proved to be the Vicarage Road club's most consistent player. He joined the Bluebirds on loan in March 2005, appearing in the last eight games of the season. Not only did a number of his crosses lay on vital goals for other players, but he also found the net in the match against Leicester City, when his delightful free-kick beat former England 'keeper Ian Walker. He continued to be an important member of the Cardiff side in 2005–06, where his experience helped City in their quest to be among the leading sides in the Championship.

ASHTON Roger William

Goalkeeper

Born: Llanidloes, 16 August 1921.
Died: 1985.
Career: Wrexham 1945. Cardiff City 1948. Bath City. Newport County 1949.

■ Unable to make the grade with Wrexham, goalkeeper Roger Ashton joined Cardiff City in April 1948. After a couple of impressive displays in the club's reserve side, he replaced Danny Canning for the final game of the 1947–48 season, a 2–1 defeat of Barnsley at Oakwell. Although Canning then joined Swansea, the Bluebirds signed Phil Joslin from Torquay United, and, still finding his first-team opportunities limited, he moved to non-League Bath City. He was later given another chance at League level by Newport County and spent the second-half of the 1949–50 season playing for the Somerton Park club.

ATTLEY Brian Robert

Defender/midfield

Born: Cardiff, 23 August 1955.
Career: Cardiff City 1973. Swansea City 1979. Derby County 1982. Oxford United 1983. Gresley Rovers. Stapenhill.

Welsh Cup finalist 1974–75. Division Three runner-up 1975–76.

■ The nephew of Len Attley, an inside-forward who represented Cardiff City briefly in the mid-1930s, he graduated through the Ninian Park club's reserve sides to make his first-team debut against Blackpool in March 1975. The following season he helped the Bluebirds win promotion to Division Two, scoring the only goal of his Cardiff career at Port Vale. Used as a utility player, his best role seemed to be at full-back, though there were many games when he was used in midfield. Never an automatic choice, he left Cardiff to join Swansea in February 1979, John Toshack paying £25,000 for his signature. He won promotion with the Swans twice, ending in the First Division. After failing to make the line-up in Swansea's first match in the top flight, he figured in only four more matches before a similar fee took him to Derby County. During his time at the

Baseball Ground he had a loan spell with Oxford United, but, having had little success in Peter Taylor's regime at the club, he moved into non-League football with Gresley Rovers.

ATTLEY Leonard J. (Len)

Inside-left

Born: Cardiff, 1910.
Career: Cardiff City 1934. Yeovil and Petters United.

■ Uncle of Brian, a utility defender with the Bluebirds in the 1970s, he was recruited from junior football. A skilful inside-forward, he made a goalscoring debut, helping Cardiff beat Millwall 3–1, but in two seasons with the Ninian Park club he only made spasmodic appearances. Released at the end of the 1935–36 season, he moved into non-League football with Yeovil, giving the Glovers several seasons' service.

BADDELEY Lee Matthew

Central-defender

Born: Cardiff, 12 July 1974.
Career: Cardiff City 1991. Exeter City 1997.

Division Three Champions 1992–93.

■ Central-defender Lee Baddeley made his debut for his home-town club in the opening game of the 1991–92 season, when he came on as a substitute for Gareth Abraham in the match against Lincoln City. Capped twice for the Wales Under-21 side, it was 1993–94 before he established himself as a regular member of City's first team, and, though he always seemed to be suffering with head injuries, he still managed to appear in 164 League and Cup games for the Bluebirds – his only goal coming in a 3–0 home win over Brighton in November 1994. Finding himself third or sometimes fourth choice in the pecking order for a central-defensive role, he left Ninian Park in February 1997 and joined Exeter City. Initially, he struggled to make an impact due to a long-standing hamstring injury and then, on recovering, found himself in and out of the side so decided to retire.

BAILLIE James (Jim)

Right-half

Born: Hamilton, 8 June 1902.
Career: Derry Celtic. Cardiff City 1926. Fulham 1930. Dundee United 1931.

■ Signed from Scottish junior club Derry Celtic, wing-half Jim Baillie had the unenviable task of trying to get into the Bluebirds first team with the likes of Fred Keenor, Billy Hardy, Harry Wake and George Blackburn all ahead of him in the pecking order. After just a handful of appearances spread over two seasons, Baillie joined Fulham but later returned north of the border to play for Dundee United, helping them win promotion to the Scottish First Division.

BAIRD Ian James

Forward

Born: Rotherham, 1 April 1964.
Career: Southampton 1982. Cardiff City (loan) 1983. Newcastle United (loan) 1984. Leeds United 1985. Portsmouth 1987. Leeds United 1988. Middlesbrough 1990. Heart of Midlothian 1992. Bristol City 1993. Plymouth Argyle 1995. Brighton & Hove Albion 1996.

■ A robust striker, Ian Baird's aggression often got him into trouble with referees. An England Schoolboy international, he started out with Southampton but came to Cardiff City on a loan spell midway through the 1983–84 season. Though he scored a goal every other game for City – 6 in 12 appearances – they were all scored away from Ninian Park! Saints were prepared to sell him to Cardiff, but the club dithered over the price and, after returning to The Dell, in stepped Leeds United. After two years at Elland Road, he joined newly-promoted Portsmouth to play First Division football, an FA tribunal setting the fee at £285,000. Hard-up Pompey sold him back to Leeds, but, after Lee Chapman's arrival, Baird moved on to Middlesbrough before playing north of the border for Hearts. He returned to England in July 1993 with Bristol City, before further moves saw him play for Plymouth Argyle and Brighton & Hove Albion prior to him going to Hong Kong.

BAKER Colin Walter

Wing-half

Born: Cardiff, 18 December 1934.
Career: Cardiff Nomads. Cardiff City 1953.

Welsh Cup winner 1955–56, 1958–59, 1963–64, 1964–65. Welsh Cup finalist 1959–60. Division Two runner-up 1959–60.

■ Colin Baker, who won the first of his seven full international caps for Wales against Mexico in the 1958 World Cup Finals in Sweden, was one of the greatest wing-halves in the history of Cardiff City. Joining the Ninian Park club from Cardiff Nomads, he made his League debut in a 2–2 draw at home to Sheffield Wednesday on the final day of the 1953–54 season, later replacing his namesake Billy Baker in the side on a permanent basis. After winning a regular spot in the 1955–56 season, Baker missed very few games over the next 10 terms and in 1961–62 was ever present. Although he was not a prolific scorer, finding the net on just 19 occasions during his Bluebirds career, he did come close to scoring a hat-trick in the 5–1 home win over Charlton Athletic in January 1960. He had scored two of Cardiff's goals when his long-range shot took a wicked deflection and hit the foot of the Addicks 'keeper's

post. Colin Baker very rarely suffered from injuries, but he was the injured player who had to come off when David Summerhayes became the club's first substitute in the opening match of the 1965–66 season against Bury. In later years Baker, along with Derek Tapscott, ran the Ninian Park club's lottery.

BAKER William George

Left-half

Born: Penrhiwceiber, 3 October 1920. Career: Troedrhiw. Cardiff City 1938. Ipswich Town 1955. Ton Pentre.

Division Three South champions 1946–47. Welsh Cup finalist 1950–51. Division Two runner-up 1951–52.

■ A former coalminer, Billy Baker had trials with a number of clubs, including Arsenal and Wolverhampton Wanderers, before joining Cardiff City

in the summer of 1938. He made his debut for the Bluebirds at outside-right in a 2–0 home win over Northampton Town in February 1939 but had only made three appearances when World War Two intervened. After appearing in 22 wartime fixtures in 1940–41, Baker went to fight for his country but was captured by the Japanese and was a prisoner of war for almost four years. When League football resumed in 1946–47, Baker was converted to wing-back, and over the next nine seasons he

went on to make 324 first-team appearances. In 1948 Baker, a regular 12th man for Wales, made his full international debut in a 2–0 defeat of Northern Ireland. In 1951–52 he was instrumental in helping the Bluebirds win promotion to the First Division – his only goal in that campaign coming in the 3–0 home win over rivals Swansea Town. Billy Baker was the only Cardiff City player to have played before World War Two and enjoyed a lengthy career after it. He severed his ties with the Ninian Park club in June 1955 when he signed for Ipswich Town. He spent two seasons at Portman Road before returning to Wales to play non-League football for Ton Pentre.

BALLSOM William George

Right-back/centre-half

Born: Trealaw, 30 October 1912. Died: 1983. Career: Tunbridge Wells Rangers. Gillingham 1935. Cardiff City 1938.

Welsh Cup finalist 1938–39.

■ Lanky defender George Ballsom was with Porth in the early 1930s before playing for Tunbridge Wells Rangers. His strong tackling and good use of the ball prompted Gillingham to give him his chance at League level, and he was a member of their side for three seasons. When the Gills failed to be re-elected to the Football League in 1938, Ballsom returned to South Wales to join Cardiff City. Taking over from Arthur Granville, Ballsom became the club's first choice right-back and appeared in 34 of the 1938–39 season League games. Retained for the aborted 1939–40 campaign, he later drifted into the local non-League football scene.

BANNON Paul Anthony

Forward

Born: Dublin, 15 November 1956. Career: Nottingham Forest 1975. Bridgend Town. Carlisle United 1979. Darlington (loan) 1983. Bristol Rovers 1984. Cardiff City (loan) 1984. Plymouth Argyle (loan) 1984.

■ Dublin-born forward Paul Bannon had failed to establish himself with Nottingham Forest and moved into

non-League football with Bridgend Town prior to joining Carlisle United in February 1979. After several useful seasons, including helping the Cumbrian outfit win promotion to Division Two in 1981–82, Bannon signed for Bristol Rovers, this after he had a loan spell with Darlington. Unable to hold down a regular place in the Eastville side, he came to Ninian Park on loan but had a very disappointing time in what was a very poor Cardiff team. He then went on loan to Plymouth Argyle before ending his career back with Bristol Rovers.

BARBER Keith

Goalkeeper

Born: Luton 21 September 1947. Career: Dunstable Town. Luton Town 1971. Swansea City 1977. Cardiff City (loan) 1978.

■ Goalkeeper Keith Barber played non-League football for Dunstable Town before joining his home-town club, Luton Town. Having established himself as the Hatters first choice 'keeper, he helped them win promotion to the First Division in 1973–74. Although he couldn't prevent their relegation the following season, he went on to appear in 158 games for the Kenilworth Road club before leaving to play for Swansea

City. During his time at Vetch Field he had a brief loan spell with Cardiff City. The second of his two appearances for City was back at Kenilworth Road and, much to his chagrin, the Hatters smashed seven goals past him!

BARKER Christopher Andrew

Defender

Born: Sheffield, 2 March 1980.
Career: Alfreton. Barnsley 1998. Cardiff City 2002.

Division Two promotion 2002–03.

■ Possessing a cultured left-foot and good passing ability, Chris Barker started out with Barnsley where, after his first full season with the club, 1999–2000, he won the club's Young

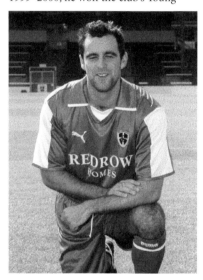

Player of the Year award. When Barnsley manager Dave Bassett brought in Matteo Corbo it was felt that Barker wouldn't be a regular, but he saw off that challenge and continued to play in every game following the appointment of new manager Nigel Spackman. At the end of the season he became the first player to win the Barnsley Young Player of the Year award on two occasions. Continuing to produce some committed displays at left-back, he had played in 130 games for the Oakwell club before dropping a Division to sign for the Bluebirds for £600,000. However, following a good first season, he jumped straight back up with promotion via the play-offs. Making the left-back spot his

own at the end of the season, he was a regular in the City side in 2003–04, but this strong, versatile player is still looking to register his first goal for the club. In 2005–06 the tough-tackling left-back missed very few games and was one of the successes of the Cardiff back four as they defied the pundits who felt they may well lose their Championship status.

BARNARD Leigh Kenneth

Midfield

Born: Worsley, 29 October 1958.
Career: Portsmouth 1976. Peterborough United (loan) 1982. Swindon Town 1982. Exeter City (loan) 1985. Cardiff City 1989.

■ Midfielder Leigh Barnard worked his way up through the ranks at Fratton Park to become a regular member of the Portsmouth side, helping the south-coast club win promotion to the Third Division in 1979–80. The following season he suffered a series of injuries and lost his place in the Pompey side. After a loan spell with Peterborough United, he joined Swindon Town, soon establishing himself as an important member of the Robins side. During his time at the County Ground, he helped Swindon win the Fourth Division Championship in 1986–87 and then the following season win promotion to Division Two. Following a loan spell at Exeter, Barnard, who had scored 21 goals in 217 League games, joined Cardiff in October 1989. Although the Bluebirds were relegated to the Fourth Division, Barnard had a very promising season, scoring eight goals in 35 games, including three in successive high-scoring games towards the end of the campaign. He had another season with Cardiff before returning to Swindon to work as the club's commercial officer.

BARNETT Albert

Left-back/left-half

Born: Altrincham, 1893.
Career: Macclesfield. Glossop 1913. Cardiff City 1914. Aberdare Athletic 1924. Fordsons.

Division Two runner-up 1920–21.

■ Able to play in a variety of positions,

Albert Barnett began his League career with Glossop, but after one season he moved into the Southern League with Cardiff City. A regular member of the side in the seasons either side of World War One, he made his Football League debut for the Bluebirds in a goalless draw at Bristol City. The Robins were Cardiff's opponents when Barnett scored what was his only goal for the club in a 1–0 win. However, after that season his first-team appearances were few and far between, and he eventually left the club to continue his career with Aberdare Athletic, later playing for Fordsons.

BARTLETT John

Right-back

Born: South Wales, 1914.
Career: Cardiff City 1933.

■ Locally-born right-back John Bartlett appeared in just one League game for the Bluebirds, a 4–0 reversal at Queen's Park Rangers in the club's disastrous re-election season of 1933–34. Deemed to be at fault for two of the goals, he returned to the reserves before parting company with the club at the end of the season.

BARTLETT Kevin Francis

Forward

*Born: Portsmouth, 12 October 1962.
Career: Portsmouth 1980. Fareham
Town. Cardiff City 1986. West Bromwich
Albion 1989. Notts County 1990. Port
Vale (loan) 1992. Cambridge United
1993.*

*Division Four runner-up 1987–88.
Welsh Cup winner 1987–88.*

■ Speedy forward Kevin Bartlett began
his career with his home-town club
Portsmouth but, being unable to make
much impression, drifted into non-
League football with Fareham Town.
Cardiff City manager Frank Burrows
signed Bartlett in September 1986, and
he made a sensational debut by scoring
twice in a 4–0 win over Taff Well in a
third-round Welsh Cup tie. Three days
later he repeated the dose in a 3–0
defeat of Cambridge United. In 1987–88
he scored 12 goals in 37 League games,
as City won promotion to Division
Three, and was finding the net with
great regularity the following season
when he was transferred to West
Bromwich Albion. On leaving the
Hawthorns, he had a prolific spell with
Notts County before following a loan
spell with Port Vale. He ended his first-
class career with Cambridge United.

BASSETT William Edward George (Billy)

Centre-half

*Born: Brithdir, 8 June 1912.
Died: 1977.
Career: Aberaman Athletic.
Wolverhampton Wanderers 1933. Cardiff
City 1934. Crystal Palace 1945.
Porthmadoc.*

■ Centre-half Billy Bassett had been on
the books of both Aberaman Athletic
and Wolverhampton Wanderers before
arriving at Ninian Park in the summer
of 1934. Signed by City manager Ben
Watts-Jones, he made his debut on the
opening day of the 1934–35 season as
the Bluebirds beat Charlton Athletic
2–1. Though he was a virtual ever
present until the outbreak of World War
Two, Billy Bassett's only goals for the
club came in that first season against
Bournemouth and Bristol City. Those
were disappointing times for City as
they struggled for much of Bassett's
time with the club, but the strong-
tackling pivot was outstanding. During
the war years he served with the Welsh
Guards, but, having joined Crystal
Palace just prior to the start of the
hostilities, he returned to Selhurst Park
and made 70 League appearances. On
leaving Palace, he returned to South
Wales to become player-manager of
Porthmadoc.

BATER Philip Thomas

Full-back

*Born: Cardiff, 26 October 1955.
Career: Bristol Rovers 1973. Wrexham
1981. Bristol Rovers 1983. Brentford
1986. Cardiff City 1987.*

*Division Four runner-up 1987–88.
Welsh Cup winner 1987–88.*

■ Though he was born in Cardiff, Phil
Bater slipped through the Ninian Park
club's net as Bristol Rovers took him on
as an apprentice prior to signing
professional forms. Rovers had just
gained promotion to Division Two
when the 18-year-old Bater made his
League debut. Able to play in either full-
back spot, he soon became a fixture in
the Pirates team, and over the next
seven seasons he made 212 League
appearances. Following Rovers'
relegation, Bater left Eastville, joining

Wrexham for £50,000. Installed as the
Robins club captain, he couldn't prevent
their relegation to Division Three, and
the following season saw no
improvement as Wrexham tumbled into
the Fourth Division. With financial
restraints starting to bite, Bater was sold
to his old club for just £10,000. He went
on to take his total of first-team
appearances for Bristol Rovers to 353
before leaving to play for Brentford.
Within a year he had moved on to
Cardiff City but had a disastrous debut
against one of his former clubs,
Wrexham – not only did the Bluebirds
lose 3–0, but Bater earned unwanted
notoriety by being sent off on his debut
– the first man to do so in the club's
history! On hanging up his boots, he
returned to Bristol to work as a
landscape gardener.

BEADLES George Harold (Harry)

Forward

*Born: Llanllwchaiarn, 28 September
1897.
Died: 1958.
Career: Newton. Liverpool 1920.
Graysons. Liverpool 1921. Cardiff City
1924. Sheffield Wednesday 1925.
Southport 1926. Workington. Dundalk.*

FA Cup finalist 1924–25.

■ Harry Beadles played for local club
Newtown before, during World War
One, serving with the Royal Welch
Fusiliers, where he came under the
influence of George Latham. He saw
action in Turkey and was awarded the
Serbian Gold Medal for gallantry. After
the war, he joined Liverpool, playing
just a handful of games in the sides that
won the League Championship in the
consecutive seasons of 1921–22 and
1922–23. Unable to hold down a regular
place, he moved to Cardiff City,
replacing Joe Clennell who had joined
Stoke. After making his City debut in a
1–1 draw at Spurs, Beadles proved quite
a prolific scorer, finding the net with
great regularity. One of his strikes came
in the FA Cup quarter-final defeat of
Leicester City, and he was in the Cardiff
side that lost in the 1925 Final to
Sheffield United. During his two
seasons at Ninian Park, Beadles won

two full caps for Wales, but in 1926 he signed for Southport. He proved a prolific scorer for the Haig Avenue club, topping the goalscoring charts in each of his three seasons with the club. He later became captain and coach of Dundalk in the Irish League before severing all connections with the game and going into hotel management in Liverpool.

BEARE George

Winger

Born: Southampton, 2 October 1885. Died: 1970.
Career: Shirley Warren. Southampton. Blackpool 1908. Everton 1910. Cardiff City 1914. Bristol City 1921. Cardiff City 1922. Oswestry Town.

Division Two runner-up 1920–21.

■ After starting his career with his home-town team, Southampton, winger George Beare went north to play for Blackpool. His performances for the Seasiders led to Everton signing him in 1910. A virtual ever present in three

seasons with the Toffees, Beare had scored 19 goals in 118 games when he left to join Cardiff City in 1914. After a season of Southern League football, Beare played in a number of friendly matches during the war years, and in November 1916 he scored a hat-trick in a 4–0 win against an International Army XI. Following another season of Southern League football in 1919–20, Beare made his Football League debut

for City in a 1–1 draw at West Ham United in October 1920 and went on to appear in 23 games that season before leaving to end his career with Bristol City.

BEECH Christopher

Left-back

Born: Congleton, 5 November 1975. Career: Manchester City 1992. Cardiff City 1997. Rotherham United 1998. Doncaster Rovers 2002.

FAW Invitation finalist 1997–99.

■ Chris Beech signed for the Bluebirds from Manchester City prior to the 1997–98 season, without having appeared for the then Maine Road club. He remained an ever present throughout Cardiff's Third Division campaign but was surprisingly given a free transfer at the end of the season. A speedy left wing-back, he was among 11 players freed by City, and part of the reason for his departure was City's terrible record of having finished in the bottom four twice in the last three seasons. Beech then joined Rotherham United but injuries hampered his progress at Millmoor, and he spent most of his time in the reserves, captaining them to the Pontin League Division One Championship. Beech remained with the Millers until December 2002 when he left to play for Doncaster Rovers, helping them return to the Football League in 2002–03 before later being placed on the transfer list.

BELL Gary

Left-back

Born: Stourbridge, 4 April 1947. Career: Lower Gornal Athletic. Cardiff City 1966. Hereford United (loan) 1974. Newport County 1974. Bridgend Town.

Welsh Cup winner 1969–70, 1970–71, 1972–73. Welsh Cup finalist 1971–72.

■ Gary Bell was spotted playing as an out-and-out left-winger for West Midlands League side Lower Gornal Athletic but was given his debut at left-half in a match against Wolverhampton Wanderers at Molineux in September 1966. It proved to be a disastrous first match for the Stourbridge-born player

as he conceded two penalties in a 7–1 mauling! It was Jimmy Scoular who converted Bell into a left-back, but it wasn't until 1968–69 that he established himself as a first-team regular and formed an outstanding full-back partnership with Dave Carver. He was ever present in 1970–71 when the Bluebirds finished third in Division Two and missed just one game in two other seasons. After losing his place to Freddie Pethard, he went on loan to Hereford United before signing for Newport County. Bell, who had played in 265 League and Cup games, was a virtual ever present in the Newport side, making 126 League appearances for the Somerton Park club. On parting company with County, he went into Welsh League football with Bridgend Town and other such clubs.

BELLAMY Gary

Central-defender

Born: Worksop, 4 July 1962. Career: Chesterfield 1980. Wolverhampton Wanderers 1987. Cardiff City (loan) 1992. Leyton Orient 1992.

■ Gary Bellamy first played League football for Chesterfield, where he made 207 first-team appearances and helped the Spireites win the Fourth Division Championship in 1984–85. He joined

Wolves in the summer of 1987 for a bargain fee of £17,000 and soon established himself in the Molineux club's defence. In his first season with Wolves he helped them win the Fourth Division title and was a member of the side that beat Burnley in the Final of the Sherpa Van Trophy. In 1988–89 Bellamy won a Third Division Championship medal and continued to be a mainstay of the Wolves side until towards the end of the 1991–92 season, when he had a loan spell with Cardiff City. Appearing in nine games, only two of which were lost, Bellamy helped the Bluebirds to finish ninth in Division Four but then returned to Molineux before joining Leyton Orient. The vastly experienced defender served Orient well for four seasons but was released in the summer of 1996.

BENNETT David Anthony

Winger

Born: Manchester, 11 July 1959.
Career: Manchester City 1978. Cardiff City 1981. Coventry City 1983. Sheffield Wednesday 1989. Swindon Town 1990. Shrewsbury Town (loan) 1991.

Welsh Cup finalist 1981–82. Division Three runner-up 1982–83.

■ Winger Dave Bennett started his Football League career with Manchester City. He had scored nine goals in 52 League games and appeared in the 1981 FA Cup Final replay against Spurs when Cardiff City paid £120,000 to take him to Ninian Park, where he played alongside his brother Gary. In their first season together the Bluebirds were relegated, but in 1982–83 he was instrumental in the club winning promotion back to Division Two at the first attempt. Though he provided a continuous stream of chances for Bob Hatton and Jeff Hemmerman, he netted 12 goals himself. However, in the close season, Bennett, who had scored 19 goals in 85 games for City, joined Coventry for £120,000, a figure fixed by an independent tribunal. Bennett was a first-team regular at Highfield Road for five seasons and in 1987 won an FA Cup-winners' medal as the Sky Blues beat Spurs 3–2. Bennett scored one and set up another as Coventry won their

first major honour. On leaving Highfield Road, Bennett, who had scored 33 goals in 208 first-team outings, played for Sheffield Wednesday, Swindon Town and Shrewsbury Town before leaving the League scene.

BENNETT Gary Ernest

Central-defender

Born: Manchester, 4 December 1961.
Career: Ashton United. Manchester City 1979. Cardiff City 1981. Sunderland 1984. Carlisle United 1995. Scarborough 1996. Darlington 1997.

Welsh Cup finalist 1981–82. Division Three runner-up 1982–83.

■ Gary Bennett, brother of Dave, began his career with Ashton United before joining Manchester City in September 1979. Unable to break into the Maine Road club's first team, he joined Cardiff City on a free transfer two years later. A versatile player, he found his best position in defence, though it was 1982–83 before he established himself fully at Ninian Park. During that

promotion-winning season he scored a number of vital goals, but he was eventually transferred to Sunderland for £65,000 in July 1984. Within two minutes of his debut for the north-east club he had scored past England 'keeper Peter Shilton! The following season he was at centre-half in the League Cup Final defeat by Norwich City, and in 1987–88, when the club won the Third Division Championship, he was the only member of the Sunderland side to be selected for the annual PFA XI. A virtual ever present in 11 seasons at Roker Park, he scored 24 goals in 463 games before moving to Carlisle United. Hampered by injuries during his time at Brunton Park, he switched to Scarborough. After a hugely successful Indian summer, he then joined Darlington as the player-coach, a position he held when he decided to retire.

BENNETT Michael Richard

Midfield

Born: Camberwell, 27 July 1969.
Career: Charlton Athletic 1987. Wimbledon 1990. Brentford 1992. Charlton Athletic 1994. Millwall 1995. Cardiff City 1996. Cambridge City. Leyton Orient 1997. Brighton & Hove Albion 1998. Canvey Island.

■ A right-sided midfielder who could also play at right-back, Mickey Bennett worked his way up through the ranks at Charlton Athletic before making his League debut for the Addicks. A £250,000 fee took him to Wimbledon, but he failed to win a regular place and 18 months later Brentford paid just £60,000 to take him to Griffin Park. A former England Youth international, he later had a second spell with Charlton before joining Millwall. Injuries decimated his season, and he was released in the summer of 1996. Joining Cardiff on non-contract terms, he opened his scoring account against Rochdale, and he had just won over the fans when he was surprisingly released just before Christmas. Following a spell with non-League Cambridge City, he came back into the League with Leyton Orient before joining up with Brighton & Hove Albion. Following Mickey Adams's decision to release him, he went to play for Canvey Island.

BEST Thomas Hubert

Centre-forward

Born: Milford Haven, 23 December 1920. Career: Merthyr Tydfil. Chester City 1947. Cardiff City 1948. Queen's Park Rangers 1949. Hereford United 1950.

■ Playing his early football for Welsh League team Merthyr Tydfil, the son of a West Indian father and Welsh mother, he carried the nickname 'Darkie' due to his mixed-race features at a time when black footballers were a rarity. On leaving Merthyr, he joined Chester and it was from the then Sealand Road club that Cardiff signed him in 1948. Though he made his debut in a 2–0 defeat at West Bromwich Albion in October of that year, it wasn't until later in the season that he got an extended run in the side. Indeed, he netted in five consecutive games as City lost just once in 14 matches to finish fourth in Division Two. He continued to find the net in the early part of the 1949–50 season, but such was the competition for places that he was allowed to join Queen's Park Rangers. Unable to hold down a regular first-team place with the Loftus Road club, he joined non-League Hereford United where for three seasons he was a prolific scorer.

BIRD Anthony

Forward

Born: Cardiff, 1 September 1974. Career: Cardiff City 1993. Barry Town 1996. Swansea City 1997. Merthyr (loan) 2000. Kidderminster Harriers 2000. St Patrick's Athletic.

Division Three champions 1992–93. Welsh Cup finalist 1993–94.

■ Welsh Under-21 international Tony Bird worked his way up through the ranks at Ninian Park to make his Cardiff City debut as a substitute for Cohen Griffith in a 3–2 win at Walsall in August 1992. Though he only made three starts that season – a campaign in which the Bluebirds won the Third Division Championship – he did score in the 2–1 defeat of Carlisle United. Over the next couple of seasons he found himself in and out of the Cardiff side, though he did make the most of his chances in the fight against relegation in 1994–95. Despite scoring three times in the opening two games of the following season, Bird was one of the first to go in a cost-cutting exercise at the turn of the year and became a prolific scorer for Barry Town in the Konica League, netting 42 goals in 1996–97. In the close season he returned to League action with Swansea City and at one stage was on course to become the first Swans player since Bob Latchford to net 20 goals. After suspension forced him to miss the first three games of the following season, he spent most of his time on the bench. He made enough appearances in 1999–2000 to win a Third Division Championship medal but then left the Vetch to play for Kidderminster Harriers. Here he moved into midfield but spent most of his time at the club on the transfer list and left to continue his career with St Patrick's Athletic.

BIRD Donald William Carlton (Dickie)

Outside-left

Born: Llandrindod Wells, 5 January 1908. Died: 1987. Career: Llandrindod Wells. Cardiff City 1929. Bury 1931. Torquay United 1932. Derby County 1934. Sheffield United 1935. Southend United 1936.

■ Signed from Llandrindod Wells, winger Dickie Bird only had a short spell at Cardiff City, though he did score on his home debut in a 5–1 win over Bury on the final day of the 1929–30 season. Unable to oust Walter Robbins from the City side, he joined Bury but hadn't appeared in their first team when, in June 1932, he moved to Torquay United. Bird produced his best football while with the Devon club before moving back up the Divisions, first with Derby County and then Sheffield United. He joined his last League club, Southend United, in 1936, prior to leaving the game after one season at Roots Hall.

BIRD Ronald Philip

Outside-left

Born: Birmingham, 27 December 1941. Career: Birmingham City 1959. Bradford Park Avenue1961. Bury 1965. Cardiff City 1966. Crewe Alexandra 1971. Gloucester City.

Welsh Cup winner 1966–67, 1969–70, 1970–71.

■ One of the most popular players ever to turn out for the Bluebirds, Ronnie Bird began his career with Birmingham City, but, finding his first-team opportunities limited, he moved to Bradford Park Avenue, where Jimmy Scoular was then the Yorkshire club's player-manager. His exciting wing play helped Park Avenue consolidate their position in the Third Division following their promotion in 1960–61, but after scoring 39 goals in 129 games he left to join Bury. His stay at Gigg Lane was brief, and in February 1966 he teamed up with Jimmy Scoular again, this time at Ninian Park. Popular because of his eccentricities – he could equally score with a vicious left-foot shot or fall over the ball – he soon established himself in the Bluebirds side. In 1966–67 he won a Welsh Cup medal as Wrexham were beaten 4–3 on aggregate and repeated the achievement three seasons later when Chester were defeated 5–0 over two legs. He later won another Welsh Cup medal, but after five seasons at Ninian Park he joined Crewe Alexandra, where he ended his League career prior to a spell in non-League football with

Gloucester City. He later entered management with Ebbw Vale and then Bridgend Town.

BISHOP Raymond John

Forward

Born: Hengoed, 24 November 1955.
Career: Cheltenham Town. Cardiff City 1977. Newport County 1981. Torquay United 1982.

■ A GPO engineer, Ray Bishop was playing non-League football for Cheltenham Town when City manager Jimmy Andrews paid a nominal fee to bring the forward to Ninian Park. He played fairly regularly for four years, with his best season in terms of goals scored being 1979–80 when he shared the leading goalscorer's spot with Gary Stevens – both netting 11 League goals. At the end of the following season, Bishop, who had scored 29 goals in 118 League and Cup games, was allowed to join Newport County after Len Ashurst had offered £10,000 for his services. Things didn't work out for him at Somerton Park, and it wasn't too long before he joined Torquay United. He appeared in 40 games for the Devon club before ending his career.

BLACKBURN George Frederick

Left-half

Born: Willesden Green, 8 March 1899.
Died: 1957.
Career: Hampstead Town. Aston Villa 1920. Cardiff City 1926. Mansfield Town 1931. Cheltenham Town 1932.

Welsh Cup winner 1926–27, 1929–30. FA Charity Shield winner 1927–28. Welsh Cup finalist 1928–29.

■ Signed by Aston Villa from the amateurs of Hampstead Town, he turned professional in December 1920 and made his debut at Bradford City in March the following year. A hardworking left-half, he quickly became established and in 1924 picked up an FA Cup runners'-up medal as Villa were beaten 2–0 by Newcastle United. Also that season he won international recognition, playing for England against France. Having played

in 145 League and Cup games for Villa, Blackburn signed for Cardiff in exchange for Joe Nicholson in the summer of 1926. Making his debut in a seven-goal thriller at Burnley – City lost 4–3 – he became a firm favourite with the Cardiff fans, though he missed out on the 1927 FA Cup Final. He did though win two Welsh Cup medals and a runners-up medal in the same competition. Blackburn, whose only goal for the club came in a 4–2 win over Blackpool in February 1930, had appeared in 119 games for the Bluebirds when, along with Harry Wake, he joined Mansfield Town on the Stags entry into the Football League in the summer of 1931. He later became player-manager of Cheltenham Town before becoming trainer at Birmingham City, leaving in 1946 after they had won the Football League South Championship.

BLAIR Douglas

Inside-forward

Born: Ecclesfield, 26 June 1921.
Career: Blackpool 1939. Cardiff City 1947. Hereford United 1954.

Welsh Cup finalist 1950–51. Division Two runner-up 1951–52.

■ The son of Jimmy Blair, Cardiff City's Scottish international full-back of the

1920s, Doug Blair began his career with Blackpool, but after being unable to break into the Seasiders first team he joined City in the summer of 1947. He immediately became an integral part of the Bluebirds Second Division team. They improved steadily for four years before winning promotion to the top flight in 1951–52. Doug Blair missed very few games in his time at Ninian Park, going on to score 30 goals in 216 League and Cup outings. On leaving Ninian Park, Blair, who had a deceptive body swerve and superb ball control, joined non-League Hereford United, where he ended his playing career in 1957.

BLAIR James (Jimmy)

Left-back

Born: Glenboig, 11 May 1888.
Died: 1964.
Career: Bonnybridge Thistle. Glasgow Ashfield. Clyde 1913. Sheffield Wednesday 1914. Cardiff City 1920. Bournemouth 1926.

Division Two runner-up 1920–21. Welsh Cup winner 1921–22, 1922–23. Division One runner-up 1923–24. FA Cup finalist 1924–25.

■ Jimmy Blair began his career in his native Scotland with Bonnybridge Thistle and Glasgow Ashfield before joining Clyde in 1913. While with the Bully Wee he was a target for several English clubs, being rated as the best full-back in Scottish football at that time. In 1914 Sheffield Wednesday paid Clyde £2,000 for his services, but they did not get the return they hoped for. This, however, was largely due to unfortunate circumstances. Blair had no sooner arrived at Hillsborough than he was injured in a motorcycle accident and suffered another accident soon after that. He had only played in 20 first-team games for the Owls when football was suspended because of World War One, and he returned to Scotland. Wednesday had quite a job persuading him to move south again after the war, for Blair wanted a better deal than the Yorkshire club could offer. When he finally returned he found himself in a side doomed to relegation. In April 1920 he was in the Scotland side beaten 5–4 by England in an epic rain-swept

international at Hillsborough, but seven months later he joined Cardiff City for £3,500. After making his Bluebirds debut in a 4–2 win at Blackpool, he went on to give City six years' service, appearing in 208 League and Cup games. He was in the Cardiff side that lost to Sheffield United in the 1925 FA Cup Final and earned six full international caps for Scotland during his stay at Ninian Park. In 1926 he joined Bournemouth, spending two seasons at Dean Court before hanging up his boots. He returned to Cardiff in a coaching capacity in 1932 before later returning to the licensing trade.

BLAKE Darcy

Midfield

Born: 13 December 1988.
Career: Cardiff City 2005.

■ Midfield Darcy Blake appeared in just three minutes of League football for the Bluebirds after replacing Jeff Whitley after 87 minutes of the Easter Monday clash against Crewe at Gresty Road – a game that ended all-square at 1–1. A member of the academy production line, great things are hoped for the youngster who will wait to get more chances of first-team football next season.

BLAKE Nathan Alexander

Striker

Born: Cardiff, 27 January 1972.
Career: Newport County. Chelsea. Cardiff City 1990. Sheffield United 1994. Bolton Wanderers 1995. Blackburn Rovers 1998. Wolverhampton Wanderers 2001. Leeds United (loan) 2004.

Welsh Cup winner 1991–92, 1992–93. Division Three Champion 1992–93.

■ Nathan Blake started out with Newport County before being taken on as a trainee by Chelsea. He returned to South Wales to his home-town club Cardiff City and made his debut against Bristol Rovers in March 1990. He soon became a regular in the Bluebirds side, playing in defence as well as up front. He netted 11 goals to help City win the Third Division Championship in 1992–93, but rose to national prominence the following season when

his goal knocked Manchester City out of the FA Cup as the Welsh Cup winners reached the fifth round. He had scored 40 goals in 164 outings for Cardiff when Sheffield United paid £300,000 to take him to Bramall Lane. Unable to prevent the Blades from being relegated, he was their leading scorer in 1994–95 prior to making a £1.35 million move to Bolton Wanderers. Although he took time to settle, he formed a prolific strike partnership with John McGinlay but was then unexpectedly allowed to join neighbours Blackburn Rovers for £4.25 million. He suffered a series of niggling injuries at Ewood Park, and as his confidence ebbed away he left to play for Wolverhampton Wanderers for £1.4 million. After a good first season, in which he helped the Molineux club reach the Premiership via the play-offs, he has suffered with numerous injuries, though when fit he is still a valued member of the Welsh squad. He spent most of his time at the Walker Stadium on the bench, and after a brief loan spell with Leeds he was released by the East Midlands club.

BLAKEMORE Ralph G.

Left-back

Born: Cardiff.
Career: Cardiff City 1930. Bradford City 1931.

■ Left-back Ralph Blakemore's only first-team appearance for Cardiff City came on the final day of the 1930–31 season, when the Bluebirds went down 3–1 at home to Bury. With the club relegated to the Third Division South, Blakemore left Ninian Park in the hope of regular first-team football with Bradford City, but his time at Valley Parade saw him dogged by injury and he was forced to retire without appearing for the Yorkshire club's first team.

BLAND William Henry (Harry)

Right-back/right-half

Born: Leeds, 12 January 1898.
Career: Royal Navy. Plymouth Argyle 1927. Arsenal 1933. Cardiff City 1934.

■ Harry Bland was a regular in the successful Plymouth Argyle side of the 1920s when the Pilgrims finished runners-up in the Third Division South on six occasions, prior to becoming champions in 1929–30. He scored two goals in 122 games before leaving to join Arsenal. Unable to break into the Gunners side, he moved to Cardiff, but he was a member of the side that conceded 15 goals against Crystal Palace (1–6) Torquay United (2–5) and Luton Town (0–4). Not surprisingly, he lost his place and was released at the end of that 1934–35 season.

BLENKINSOP Ernest

Left-back

Born: Cudworth, 20 April 1902.
Died: 1969.
Career: Cudworth United Methodists. Hull City 1921. Sheffield Wednesday 1922. Liverpool 1933. Cardiff City 1937. Buxton. Hurst.

■ Ernie Blenkinsop was working at Brierley Colliery when Hull City signed him for £100 and 80 pints of beer! He was transferred to Sheffield Wednesday in December 1922 and over the next 12 seasons went on to appear in 424 League and Cup games for the Owls. He won the first of 26 full caps for England in 1928 when he played in the 3–1 win over Belgium in Antwerp. He later captained England twice against the Scots before losing his place to Arsenal's Eddie Hapgood. Blenkinsop had superb

ball control and was an immaculate distributor of the ball. He won a Second Division Championship medal in 1925–26 and League Championship medals in 1928–29 and 1929–30. Soon after Billy Walker was appointed as Wednesday manager, Blenkinsop was allowed to leave Hillsborough and joined Liverpool for £6,500. It was a decision that angered a good number of Wednesday supporters, who let the new Wednesday boss know that they felt he had made a big mistake. He spent three seasons at Anfield, making 71 appearances, before arriving at Ninian Park in November 1937. He went on to appear in 10 League games that season before being appointed the club's coach for 1938–39. However, following the appointment of Cyril Spiers as manager, he left to play non-League football for Buxton and later Hurst.

BODIN Paul John

Left-back

Born: Cardiff, 13 September 1964.
Career: Chelsea. Newport County 1982. Cardiff City 1982. Bath City. Newport County 1987. Swindon Town 1988. Crystal Palace 1991. Newcastle United (loan) 1991. Swindon Town 1992. Reading 1996. Wycombe Wanderers (loan) 1997. Bath City.

Division Three runner-up 1982–83.

■ Released by Chelsea as a junior, he

joined Newport County but was freed by the Somerton Park club without making a first-team appearance. Bodin joined his home-town team Cardiff City and immediately won a place in the Bluebirds side to face Wrexham on the opening day of the 1982–83 season. After helping City win promotion in his first campaign with the club, he won selection for Wales at Under-21 level. Having spent three seasons at Ninian Park, he was released and joined Bath City. In 1987 he was given another chance to resurrect his League career with Newport County, of all clubs. However, within two months they were wound up, and he joined Swindon Town for £30,000. In his first season at the County Ground he helped the Robins reach the play-offs and 'qualify' for the First Division by beating Sunderland. They were then demoted to the Third Division for their past financial irregularities. Capped 23 times by Wales, he then joined Crystal Palace, the Eagles paying £550,000 for his services. His style of play wasn't suited to the Selhurst Park club, and after a loan spell with Newcastle he rejoined Swindon. A star of the Swindon side that won promotion to the Premiership via the play-offs, he scored the winner from the penalty spot in the play-off final. Although he later suffered successive relegations with the Wiltshire club, he took his tally of goals in his two spells to 40 in 297 games before following spells with Reading and Wycombe Wanderers. He became player-manager of Bath City.

BOLAND William (Willie) John

Midfield

Born: Ennis, Ireland, 6 August 1975.
Career: Coventry City 1992. Cardiff City 1999.

FAW Invitation finalist 1999–2000.
Division Three runner-up 2000–01.
FAW Premier Cup winner 2001–02.
Division Two Promotion 2002–03.

■ Republic of Ireland Under-21 international Willie Boland is a skilful midfielder who rarely wastes the ball. Beginning his career with Coventry City, he was given an opportunity by the

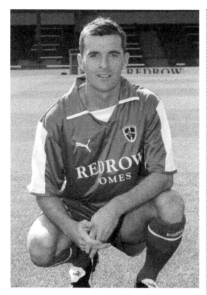

Sky Blues new manager Ron Atkinson but then spent much of his time in the reserves, understudying Kevin Richardson and later George Boateng. Boland turned down an offer to join Dundee United, and in the 1999 close season he joined the Bluebirds. Initially he struggled to adapt to life outside the Premiership and then in his second season at Ninian Park he had the misfortune to break his leg at Barnet. However, once fully fit, he showed his true value with some outstanding displays and played an important role in the Bluebirds' successful promotion campaign. In 2001–02 he was voted Cardiff's Player of the Year as he formed a powerful midfield trio with Mark Bonner and Graham Kavanagh. He had another highly productive campaign in 2002–03 when he was, by far, City's most consistent player, and since then he has continued to show good form. However, despite his efforts he has failed to win a call up for the full Republic of Ireland international side. After helping the club avoid relegation in 2004–05, Boland started the 2005–06 season in fine style but injuries and a loss of form cost him his place in the side.

BOLESAN Mirko

Central-defender

Born: Italy, 6 May 1975.
Career: Sestrese (Italy). Cardiff City 1995.

■ A central-defender, Mirko Bolesan came to Ninian Park as a trialist from the Italian club Sestrese in October 1995. Coming off the bench in the 1–0 home defeat at the hands of Scunthorpe United when replacing Derek Brazil after just two minutes, it proved to be his only appearance for the club before later returning home.

BONNER Mark

Midfield

Born: Ormskirk, 7 June 1974.
Career: Blackpool 1992. Cardiff City 1998. Hull City (loan) 1999. Oldham Athletic 2004.

Division Three promotion 1998–99.
FAW Invitation Cup finalist 1999–2000.
Division Three runner-up 2000–01.
Division Two promotion 2002–03.

■ Midfielder Mark Bonner started out with Blackpool where, after injuries had restricted his appearances in his first couple of seasons with the Seasiders, he became one of the club's successes. His hardworking displays and intelligent forward runs won him many friends as he became an important part of the club's plans. Just when it seemed he would go on to greater things he again missed many matches through injury problems. Bonner was released by Blackpool during the 1998 close season after scoring 15 goals in 220 games and joined Cardiff City on a free transfer. He soon proved himself a gutsy player, but when he lost his place through injury he was allowed out on loan to Hull City. He made a dramatic debut, scoring the winner against Rotherham United before damage to an ankle in a freak training

accident saw him return to Ninian Park. He finished the season as City's first choice in midfield as the Bluebirds were promoted. He was also one of City's few successes in their relegation season of 1999–2000 and was named Cardiff's Most Improved Player. Sadly, injuries hampered his progress the following season, but in 2001–02 he played a major role in the club winning promotion. Since then he has suffered a number of niggling injuries and, after dropping out of favour, joined Oldham Athletic.

BONSON Joseph

Centre-forward

Born: Barnsley, 19 June 1936.
Died: 1991.
Career: Wolverhampton Wanderers 1953. Cardiff City 1957. Scunthorpe United 1960. Doncaster Rovers 1962. Newport County 1962. Brentford 1964. Lincoln City 1966.

Welsh Cup winner 1958–59. Division Two runner-up 1959–60.

■ A one-time schoolboy sprint champion, Joe Bonson was a big, burly centre-forward who began his career with Wolverhampton Wanderers. Considering the wealth of forward talent at Molineux, the young Bonson did well to appear in 10 League games. He had, in 1953–54, scored 48 goals for Wolves in the Birmingham League, 14 in the FA Youth Cup and another four in the Central League. The Bluebirds had just transferred Johnny Nicholls to Exeter City and signed Bonson as his replacement for £7,000. He made a goalscoring debut in a 1–1 home draw against Ipswich Town in November 1957 and that season scored 12 goals in 25 League games. He formed two formidable striking partnerships, first with Ron Hewitt and then, from 1958–59, with Derek Tapscott, following his arrival from Arsenal. Bonson's best season in terms of goals scored was 1959–60 when he netted 18 goals in just 26 matches, including scoring twice in three consecutive games. At the end of that campaign Bonson was exchanged for Scunthorpe United's Peter Donnelly. Bonson, who scored the majority of his goals with his head, netted 11 goals in 52 games for Scunthorpe before playing for a number of clubs – Doncaster Rovers, Newport County, Brentford and Lincoln City. His best spell was at Somerton Park when he scored 47 goals in 99 games.

BOULDING Michael Thomas

Striker

Born: Sheffield, 5 February 1975.
Career: Hallam FC. Mansfield Town 1991. Grimsby Town 2001. Aston Villa 2002. Sheffield United 2002 (loan). Grimsby Town 2003. Barnsley 2004. Cardiff City 2005 (loan). Rotherham United 2005.

■ A former tennis professional, Michael Boulding is a pacy and persistent left-sided attacking player who joined Mansfield Town from the local Sheffield team Hallam in the summer of 1999. Much to the disgust of the Stags supporters, he was used mainly as a substitute, once coming off the bench to turn a 3–1 deficit against Hartlepool into a 4–3 victory. Allowed to join Grimsby Town, he formed a good understanding with Bradley Allen and ended the season as the top scorer. His total of 11 goals included seven in a nine-game spell, including a hat-trick against Burnley. One of the speediest strikers in the game, he joined Aston Villa in the summer of 2002 and scored on his home debut against Zurich in the Intertoto Cup. Unable to force his way into Villa's League side, he joined Sheffield United on loan before rejoining Grimsby. After finding the net on a regular basis and taking his tally of goals to 27 in 74 League games in his two spells, he was sold to Barnsley for £50,000. Much of his time at Oakwell saw him hampered by injuries, and in March 2005 he joined Cardiff on loan. Though he made four appearances as a substitute in the club's successful fight against relegation, his future at the club is uncertain. After not being offered a contract, he left Ninian Park to play football for Rotherham United.

BOWEN Jason Peter

Winger

Born: Merthyr Tydfil, 24 August 1972.

Career: Swansea City 1990. Birmingham City 1995. Southampton (loan) 1997. Reading 1997. Cardiff City 1999.

Division Three promotion 1998–99. FAW Invitation Cup finalist 1999–2000. Division Three runner-up 2000–01. FAW Premier Cup winner 2001–02. Division Two promotion 2002–03.

■ After a couple of outings as a substitute, Jason Bowen made his full first-team debut for Swansea against Cardiff in a 2–1 FA Cup win for the Swans in November 1991. With his speed taking him past defenders and into shooting positions, he became a great favourite with the Vetch crowd. In March 1993 he scored his first hat-trick for the club in a 4–2 defeat of Chester, while a year later helping Swansea win the Autoglass Trophy. He had scored 37 goals in 160 games for the Swans when, in the summer of 1995, he was transferred to Birmingham City for £350,000. The Welsh international suffered from a number of injuries at St Andrew's and, after a loan spell with Southampton, joined Reading. His stay with the Royals was brief, and he returned to South Wales to play for Cardiff City, helping the Bluebirds gain

promotion from the Third Division in his first season at Ninian Park. Although the 1999–2000 season was a disappointing one for City, Bowen ended the campaign as the club's leading scorer with 17 goals. A talented player with pace, movement and good ball control, he was switched to a role just behind the front two, his balance and skill pulling defences apart. Over the next few seasons he wasn't always able to get in as many first-team appearances as he would have liked, and towards the end of the 2003–04 season, after scoring 37 goals in 161 games, he was released.

BOYLE Terence David John

Central-defender

Born: Ammanford, 29 October 1958.
Career: Tottenham Hotspur 1975. Crystal Palace 1978. Wimbledon 1981. Bristol City 1981. Newport County 1982. Cardiff City 1986. Swansea City 1989. Merthyr Tydfil 1990. Barry Town 1992. Ebbw Vale. Inter Cardiff. Cinderford Town.

Division Four runner-up 1987–88. Welsh Cup winner 1987–88.

■ After failing to make the grade with Tottenham Hostpur, Terry Boyle moved across London to play for Crystal Palace. At Selhurst Park he made 26 League appearances and had a short spell on loan at Wimbledon as well as being capped twice by Wales. In fact, the tough-tackling defender scored on his international debut in a 3–1 win over the Republic of Ireland. On leaving the Eagles, Boyle joined Bristol City, playing in 37 League games for the Ashton Gate club before being given a free transfer and joining Newport County to ease the club's financial difficulties. One of the best defenders ever to play for the Somerton Park club, he had appeared in 166 games before joining Cardiff City for £22,000 – a fee fixed by an independent tribunal. Ever present in 1986–87, his first season at Ninian Park, Boyle shared the supporters' Player of the Year award with Alan Curtis. The following season he also played in all the games as the Bluebirds won promotion to the Third Division and won the Welsh Cup, beating Wrexham in the Final. He went on to appear in

101 consecutive League games from his debut and 158 League and Cup matches altogether before leaving to end his League career with Swansea City. He subsequently played for Merthyr Tydfil and Barry Town, whom he helped win the Welsh League and Cup double in 1993–94. He then took up player-manager roles at Ebbw Vale, Inter Cardiff and Cinderford Town.

BRACK Alistair Holland Brack

Full-back

*Born: Aberdeen, 27 January 1940.
Career: Cardiff City 1961. Worcester City 1964.*

■ Highly-rated Scottish-born defender Alistair Brack made just one appearance for City – a 2–1 defeat at home to Middlesbrough in September 1962 – though his displays for the club's reserve side over the next couple of seasons possibly warranted more. Eventually he became dispirited and left Ninian Park to continue his career with non-League Worcester City.

BRAYSON Paul

Forward

*Born: Newcastle, 16 September 1977.
Career: Newcastle United 1995. Swansea City (loan) 1997. Reading 1998. Cardiff City 2000. Cheltenham Town 2002.*

*FAW Invitation Cup finalist 1999–2000.
Division Three runner-up 2000–01.*

■ A player with a natural touch in front of goal, Paul Brayson scored almost 100 goals during two seasons on the staff of Newcastle United, leading to selection for the England Youth side. He couldn't break into the Magpies League side though, and in January 1997 he was loaned out to Swansea City. Although small in stature, he showed lots of promise, claiming five League goals during his spell at the Vetch before a back injury forced his return to St James' Park. He then joined Reading in March 1998, with manager Tommy Burns paying £100,000 for his signature. Though he failed to prevent the Royals being relegated, he was a regular

member of their side until joining Cardiff in March 2000. He soon got off the mark, scoring in a 2–1 win at Oldham and appearing in the FAW Invitation Cup Final. The Bluebirds were impressed by his contribution and the move was made permanent. In 2000–01 Brayson proved to be something of a revelation at Cardiff, netting 15 goals from just 25 starts, helping the club win promotion to Division Two. The following season he was played wide on the left and at times behind the front two. Out of contract, he was unlucky to be released by the Bluebirds and left to play for Cheltenham Town. After a couple of seasons in and out of the Robins side he was again released in the summer of 2004.

BRAZIER Matthew Ronald

Midfield

*Born: Leytonstone, 2 July 1976.
Career: Queen's Park Rangers 1994. Fulham 1998. Cardiff City (loan 1998). Cardiff City 1999. Leyton Orient 2002.*

*Division Three promotion 1998–99.
FAW Invitation Cup finalist 1999–2000.
Division Three runner-up 2000–01.*

■ A midfielder, always full of running, he began his career with Queen's Park Rangers during the Loftus Road club's Premiership relegation season of 1995–96. He established himself as a first-team regular the following season before a series of injuries took their toll, and he was allowed to join Fulham for £65,000 in March 1998. After scoring on his debut at Preston, he fell out of favour, and at the start of the following campaign he joined Cardiff on loan. He proved a huge success during his 11-match stay – it would have been longer had it not been for a back injury – as he scored two memorable goals in the games against Rochdale and Chester City. He then rejoined Fulham, but in the summer of 1999 he was described as the 'People's Signing' after Cardiff had paid £100,000 for his services. City fans were delighted to see him back at Ninian Park, but unfortunately he found it difficult to live up to expectations and there were occasions when he looked somewhat lightweight

in the side. He bounced back the following season until experiencing a lengthy absence through illness. In January 2002 he and Kevin Nugent were surprisingly allowed to join Leyton Orient, and Brazier was a first-team regular until midway through the 2003–04 season when, after trials with Oxford United and Queen's Park Rangers, he was released on a free transfer.

BRAZIL Derek Michael

Central-defender

Born: Dublin, 14 December 1968.
Career: Rivermount Boys Club.
Manchester United 1986. Oldham Athletic (loan) 1990. Swansea City (loan) 1991. Cardiff City 1992. Newport 1996.

Division Three champion 1992–93.
Welsh Cup winner 1992–93.

■ Derek Brazil, who went on to represent the Republic of Ireland at Under-23 and 'B' international level, began his career with Manchester United, but during his five years at Old Trafford he made just a couple of substitute appearances for the Red Devils. Following loan spells with Oldham Athletic and Swansea City, Brazil signed for Cardiff in the summer of 1992. A central-defender who could also play equally well in either full-back position, he helped the Bluebirds win the Third Division Championship in his first season at Ninian Park. Brazil was the mainstay of the City defence for the

next few seasons, especially in the marshalling of the players around him. Eventually injuries began to get the better of 'Brazza' and at the end of the 1995–96 season he was released and joined Newport.

BRIGNULL Philip Arthur

Central-defender

Born: Stratford, 2 October 1960.
Career: West Ham United 1978. Bournemouth 1981. Wrexham (loan) 1985. Cardiff City 1986. Newport County 1987.

■ An England Schoolboy international, centre-half Phil Brignull spent four years at Upton Park, but his only appearance for the Hammers was as a substitute in a goalless draw at Ninian Park in May 1979. On leaving West Ham, he joined Bournemouth, going on to appear in 129 League games for the Cherries before he lost his place through injury. Following a loan spell with Wrexham, he joined the Bluebirds for £9,000 – half the fee being donated by an oil company and the rest from individual donations, including manager Alan Durban! Unable to prevent City's relegation to Division Four, he was a regular in the 1986–87 season before Frank Burrows released him, and he ended his career with Newport County.

BRITTAN Richard Charles (Charlie)

Full-back

Born: Isle of Wight, 7 August 1887.
Died: 1949.
Career: Portsmouth 1903. Northampton Town 1908. Tottenham Hotspur 1911. Cardiff City 1920.

Division Two runner-up 1920–21. Welsh Cup winner 1919–20, 1921–22.

■ Having started his career as a 16-year-old with Portsmouth prior to joining Northampton Town, full-back Charlie Brittan had established himself as possibly the best defender in the Southern League when Spurs signed him in October 1911. During his time with the Cobblers he made five appearances for the Southern League in

inter-League matches. However, at White Hart Lane he was not quite able to live up to his reputation in the higher grade of football and could never be sure of a place in the Spurs team. After putting in a transfer request he returned to the Southern League with Cardiff City where he made a further two appearances for the Southern League, two appearances for the Welsh League and helped the Bluebirds win the Welsh Cup in 1920 and 1922. Having played in 88 Southern League games for Cardiff, Brittan made his Football League debut for the Bluebirds in their inaugural game, skippering the side to a 5–2 win at Stockport County. An influential leader, he lost his place to Jimmy Nelson midway through the 1922–23 season. On hanging up his boots, he pursued a career in business, later going into politics as a member of Cardiff City's Council.

BROCK Kevin Stanley

Midfield

Born: Bicester, 9 September 1962.
Career: Oxford United 1979. Queen's Park Rangers 1987. Newcastle United 1988. Cardiff City (loan) 1994. Stevenage Borough. Yeovil Town. Rushden and Diamonds.

Welsh Cup finalist 1993–94.

■ Although a much sought after schoolboy star, courted by a string of big clubs including Manchester United, Spurs and Everton, Kevin Brock opted to sign for his local club Oxford United. He assisted the Manor Ground club in their rise to the top flight as well as becoming the first lower Division player for many years to be selected for an England side – appearing for the Under-21 XI. His manager Jim Smith rated him highly, and when he left to manage Queen's Park Rangers he took Brock to Loftus Road with him and then on to Newcastle United. A regular at St James' Park for five seasons, he just missed out on promotion in the play-offs of 1990, when he had his best season for United. After not figuring in either Ossie Ardiles's or Kevin Keegan's plans, he was allowed to join Cardiff City on loan. He scored twice in his 14 League outings for the Bluebirds before returning to the

Magpies. After trials with Cambridge United and Stockport County, he moved into non-League football with Stevenage Borough before later playing for Yeovil Town and Rushden and Diamonds.

BROWN Andrew Robert

Inside-left

Born: Coatbridge, 20 February 1915.
Died: 1973.
Career: Cumbernauld Thistle. Cardiff City 1936. Torquay United 1938. Colchester United.

■ Spotted playing in Scottish junior football for Cumbernauld Thistle, Andy Brown spent two seasons with Cardiff City almost entirely in the reserves. He did make two appearances for the City first team before leaving to play for Torquay United in 1938. After appearing for the Plainmoor club either side of World War Two, he wound down his career with a spell at Colchester United.

BROWN James Grady (Jim)

Goalkeeper

Born: Coatbridge, 11 May 1952.
Career: Albion Rovers 1968. Chesterfield 1972. Sheffield United 1974. Detroit Express. Washington Diplomats. Chicago Sting. Cardiff City 1982. Kettering Town. Chesterfield 1983.

■ Jim Brown was a precocious talent, making his Scottish League debut for Albion Rovers as a 16-year-old in 1968. His displays led to a lot of interest south of the border, and in December 1972 Chesterfield paid £4,000 to take him to Saltergate. After two seasons with the Spireites he joined First Division Sheffield United for £60,000. After an impressive first season at Bramall Lane, in which the Blades finished sixth in the top flight, Brown was capped at full international level for Scotland as they drew 1–1 with Romania. Following United's relegation, he spent three seasons playing Second Division football before leaving to play in the NASL with Detroit Express. He subsequently assisted Washington Diplomats and Chicago Sting before, in December 1982, joining Cardiff City. Though the Bluebirds were unbeaten in the three games he played, he lost his place to Eric Steele and left to

play non-League football for Kettering Town. He later rejoined Chesterfield and became one of the few 'keepers to score in a Football League match!

BROWN Robert Henry (Bobby)

Centre-forward

Born: Streatham, 2 May 1940.
Career: Barnet. Fulham 1960. Watford 1961. Northampton Town 1963. Cardiff City 1966.

Welsh Cup winner 1966–67.

■ While playing for Barnet, centre-forward Bobby Brown won England amateur international honours before joining Fulham. His stay at Craven Cottage was brief, and he moved on to Watford in November 1961, where he scored 10 goals in 28 League games. In December 1963 he signed for Northampton Town, scoring consistently for the Cobblers in three years at the County Ground. Cardiff City manager Jimmy Scoular paid £15,000 for his services in October 1966, and even though the Bluebirds were rooted to the foot of Division Two Brown soon got down to the business he knew so well – scoring goals. He netted 15 in 29 League games and at the end of the season City just avoided relegation to the Third Division. In that campaign, he won a Welsh Cup medal, scoring in the first leg of the Final as Wrexham were beaten 4–3 on aggregate. He continued to find the net in 1967–68, but in the Boxing Day game against Aston Villa he injured his knee and never played again. After working in City's lottery organisation, he became involved in Welsh football with Mike Smith, the two of them later entering League management with Hull City.

BROWN Thomas Henry (Tommy)

Outside-left

Born: Darlington, 15 November 1896.
Career: Darlington Close Works. Portsmouth. Spennymoor United. Norwich City. Brighton & Hove Albion 1920. Cardiff City 1921. Bristol City 1922. South Shields 1923. Luton Town 1924. Poole Town 1925.

■ The Darlington-born winger had trials with local sides Darlington Close Works and Spennymoor United before playing Southern League football for Portsmouth and Norwich City. He had joined Brighton & Hove Albion when he made his Football League debut, but in the summer of 1921 he moved to Cardiff City. He had little joy in his one season at the club, making just two appearances – home defeats at the hands of Aston Villa and Oldham Athletic – before spending the rest of his time as understudy to Jack Evans. Released at the end of the 1921–22 season, he signed for Bristol City prior to a return to the North East and South Shields. Here he scored his only League goal before ending his first-class career with Luton Town. Having made only 59 appearances for his five League clubs in six years, he then went to play non-League football for Poole Town.

BUCHANAN John

Midfield

Born: Dingwall, 19 September 1951.
Career: Ross County. Northampton Town 1970. Cardiff City 1974. Northampton Town 1981.

Welsh Cup finalist 1974–75, 1976–77. Division Three runners-up 1975–76.

■ Midfielder John Buchanan played his early football for Ross County in the Highland League before coming south of the border to play for Northampton Town. He soon won a place in the Cobblers first team and in four years at the County Ground scored 25 goals in 114 League games. In October 1974 Buchanan moved to Ninian Park in exchange for John Farrington and made his debut in a 3–2 home win over York City. At the end of that season, the Bluebirds were relegated but bounced back in 1975–76 when a late unbeaten run resulted in the club winning promotion to Division Two. Though Buchanan played all his games in midfield, he topped the club's scoring charts on two occasions with a best of 16 in 1978–79 when City finished ninth in the Second Division. That season saw him score his only hat-trick for the club in a 4–0 home win over Sheffield United. Buchanan left Ninian Park in 1981, after scoring 61 goals in 264 League and Cup games, to see out his career with Northampton Town, for whom he netted 30 goals in 183 League outings during his two spells with the club.

BULLOCK Lee

Midfield

Born: Stockton, 22 May 1981. Career: York City 1999. Cardiff City 2004. Hartlepool United 2005.

■ Midfielder Lee Bullock began his career with York City, and in 1999–2000 his first full season as a professional, his impressive performances were monitored by both Newcastle and Sunderland. A good all-round player, he netted some vital goals for the Minstermen, playing an important part in the Bootham Crescent club's revival. Continuing to make excellent progress, he was a virtual ever present over the next couple of seasons, going on to score 27 goals in 189 games before joining the Bluebirds on loan. The longest-serving player at Bootham Crescent, he stayed at Ninian Park until the end of the 2003–04 season, producing some good performances. In

fact, he scored three goals from four starts before joining City on a permanent basis in the close season. Despite costing a six-figure fee, Bullock was allowed to leave Ninian Park prior to the start of the 2005–06 season and joined Hartlepool United.

BURKE Marshall

Midfield

Born: Glasgow, 26 March 1959. Career: Burnley 1977. Leeds United 1980. Blackburn Rovers 1980. Lincoln City 1982. Cardiff City (loan) 1983. Scarborough 1984. Tranmere Rovers 1984. Northwich Victoria. Colne Dynamoes. Darwen. Bacup. Clitheroe.

■ Marshall Burke celebrated his signing professional forms with a starring role for Scotland in an international youth tournament in France. He was still only 18 when he made his Football League debut for Burnley but it was only in October 1979, when Brian Miller took over as manager, that he enjoyed an extended run in the Clarets side. However, at the end of the 1979–80 season he was one of a number of players released after Burnley had been relegated to Division Three and joined Leeds United. Unable to break into the first team, he moved on to Blackburn Rovers and later Lincoln City. It was while playing for the Imps during the 1982–83 season that he and Cardiff's

Dave Bennett were sent off for fighting! While at Sincil Bank, Len Ashurst brought him to Ninian Park on a month's loan, but after just four League and Cup appearances he rejoined Lincoln. He later had a successful spell in non-League football with Colne Dynamoes and an appearance as a substitute in their historic FA Vase triumph at Wembley in 1988.

BURNS Michael Edward

Forward

Born: Preston, 21 December 1946. Career: Skelmersdale United. Blackpool 1969. Newcastle United 1974. Cardiff City 1978. Middlesbrough 1978.

■ A former England amateur international, Mickey Burns began his career with Skelmersdale United, appearing in the 1967 Amateur Cup Final defeat by Enfield. In 1969 he joined Blackpool, and in his first season at Bloomfield Road his speedy wing play helped the Seasiders win promotion to the First Division. During the club's relegation season of 1970–71, he was their leading scorer, a feat he repeated in 1971–72 when his total of 20 goals included a hat-trick in a 5–0 win over Watford. He also netted the winner in the 2–1 defeat of Bologna in the 1971 Anglo-Italian Final, and when the Seasiders beat Lanerossi Vicenza 10–0 the following season he scored four of Blackpool's goals. Another treble against Luton Town in 1972–73 followed, but in the summer of 1974, after scoring 62 goals in 203 games, he was transferred to Newcastle United for £170,000. Playing just behind the front two for the Magpies, he often found the net as United reached Wembley in 1976 and qualified for Europe the following season. Following the departure of Richard Dinnis as manager, Burns joined Cardiff City as player-coach. It turned out to be a disastrous decision as he never settled, and after just six League appearances he signed for Middlesbrough. An educated individual, Burns was a key promoter of the YTS and football's links with the community. He later became an important member of the PFA staff in Manchester.

BURTON Deon John

Striker

Born: Ashford, 25 October 1976.
Career: Portsmouth 1994. Cardiff City (loan) 1996. Derby County 1997. Barnsley (loan) 1998. Stoke City loan) 2002. Portsmouth 2002. Walsall (loan) 2003. Swindon Town (loan) 2003. Brentford 2004. Rotherham United 2005. Sheffield Wednesday 2006.

■ A striker with skill and finishing ability, he started out with Portsmouth where his progress was held up by poor team performances. Midway through the 1996–97 season he was loaned out to Cardiff City and delighted the fans with a double in the 2–0 home win over Torquay United on his debut, but five games later he was back at Fratton Park. During the close season Burton joined Derby County for £1 million. A member of the Jamaican side that reached France '98, Burton struggled to win a first-team place on his return to Derby, and Jim Smith sent him on loan to Barnsley. On rejoining the Rams he showed a level of consistency only hinted at previously, though he then began to suffer a spate of niggling injuries and missed games. He was then placed on the transfer list, but even so, when pressed into action, he responded enthusiastically, netting some important goals. Loaned out to Stoke City, his goal in the home leg of the play-off semi-final against Cardiff City kept the club's hopes alive, and they eventually went on to win promotion. Burton started the 2002–03 campaign on loan at his former club Portsmouth before being recalled by Derby. He had taken his tally of goals for the Pride Park club to 31 in 143 games when, in December 2002, he signed for the south coast club on a permanent basis. Capped 48 times by Jamaica, he then had loan spells with Walsall and Swindon before being released in the summer of 2004. Deon Burton then joined Brentford and after a good start with the Griffin Park club become hugely popular among the fans, and he finished the 2004–05 season as the club's leading scorer. After a short stay at Rotherham United, he moved to Sheffield Wednesday in the transfer window of 2006 and assisted the club in the end of season fight to stay in the Championship. He also continues to represent Jamaica.

BYRNE Gerald

Midfield

Born: Glasgow, 10 April 1957.
Career: Cardiff City 1975. Weymouth 1979.

■ Glasgow-born defender Gerry Byrne joined the Ninian Park club on junior forms but had to wait almost four years before getting a first-team opportunity. He helped his side keep a clean sheet on his debut in a goalless home draw against Spurs and kept his place for the next eight games. Following a 4–1 home defeat by Luton Town, he lost his place and spent the rest of the season and the early part of the 1978–79 campaign in and out of the side. Lacking just a bit of pace, he eventually drifted into non-League football with Weymouth where he played for a good number of years.

CADETTE Nathan Daniel

Midfield

Born: Cardiff, 6 January 1980.
Career: Cardiff City 1997. Telford United (loan) 1998. Inter Cardiff.

■ After increasingly catching the eye for the reserves and youth teams during the 1997–98 season, he made a handful of first-team appearances as a substitute. Rewarded with a full senior contract at the end of the season, he then spent the entire 1998–99 season on loan to Telford United to gain extra experience. Enthusiastic and willing as he was, he couldn't force his way into the Bluebirds League side and left to play for Inter Cardiff.

CALDER Robert (Bob)

Full-back

Born: Glasgow, 16 June 1909.
Career: Glasgow Rangers. Cardiff City 1933. Bradford City 1934. Newport County 1935. Barrow 1936. Milford United.

■ Signed from Glasgow Rangers, full-back Bob Calder joined Cardiff in readiness for the start of the 1933–34 season. Though he played in the first 37 games of that campaign, it was a disastrous season for the Bluebirds, who finished bottom of the Third Division South. Following manager Ben Watts-Jones's clear out, Calder joined Newport County, but he couldn't hold down a regular place and left to finish his League career with Barrow. He later returned to Wales to play non-League football for Milford United.

CALLAN Dennis

Wing-half

Born: Merthyr Tydfil, 27 July 1932.
Career: Troedyrhiw. Cardiff City 1952. Exeter City (loan) 1954.

■ Having played his early football for Troedyrhiw, he joined the Bluebirds in the summer of 1952 and, over the next few seasons, appeared regularly in the club's Welsh League and Football Combination sides. He was called into the City side for the game against Huddersfield Town at the start of the 1955–56 season, but the Bluebirds lost 2–1 and he returned to the reserves. He then had a spell on loan with Exeter City and, though he was more successful with the Devon club, he still couldn't win a regular place in the side.

CAMPBELL Alan James

Midfield

Born: Arbroath 21 January 1948.
Career: Charlton Athletic 1965. Birmingham City 1970. Cardiff City 1976. Carlisle United 1980. Bromsgrove Rovers.

Division Three runner-up 1975–76. Welsh Cup finalist 1976–77.

■ Midfielder Alan Campbell began his career with Charlton Athletic and, after developing into a schemer of note and appearing in more than 200 games for the London club, joined Birmingham City. At St Andrew's he teamed up well with Johnny Vincent, Trevor Hockey and Malcolm Beard and in 1971–72 helped them win promotion to the First Division. In March 1976, after losing his place to Malcolm Page and having played in 209 games, he was transferred to Cardiff City for £20,000. The Bluebirds certainly got value for money as Campbell appeared in the last 14 games of the 1975–76 season – only one of which was lost – to help them win promotion to Division Two. Campbell proved to be a popular figure with the

City supporters, spending five seasons at Ninian Park. A Scottish Under-23 international, he joined Carlisle United in November 1980 but was dogged by injury, and he left the first-class scene to end his footballing days with non-League Bromsgrove Rovers.

CAMPBELL Andrew Paul (Andy)

Striker

Born: Stockton, 18 April 1979.
Career: Middlesbrough 1996. Sheffield United (loan) 1998. Sheffield United (loan) 1999. Bolton Wanderers (loan) 2001. Cardiff City 2002.

Division Two promotion 2002–03.

■ One of the youngest players ever to play for Middlesbrough, he was still a few days short of his 17th birthday when he came off the bench against Sheffield Wednesday in April 1996. Given further Premiership experience over the next couple of seasons, he was loaned out to Sheffield United. In 1999–2000 he began to receive more frequent call-ups to the 'Boro side and won recognition for England at Under-21 level, scoring on his debut against

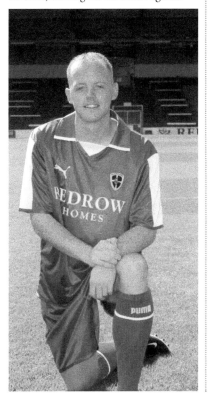

Yugoslavia. However, the following season, with the side struggling, he found it difficult to win a regular place and had a loan spell with Bolton Wanderers. In February 2002 he joined the Bluebirds on loan, and after netting on his debut against Northampton Town he hit seven goals in his first six matches. He quickly became a great favourite with the Ninian Park crowd, and in April he joined the club on a permanent basis. The following season, in the Second Division play-off final against Queen's Park Rangers at the Millennium Stadium, he netted the extra-time winner to clinch promotion for the Bluebirds – it was the first time he had stolen the limelight from record-breaking goalscorer Robert Earnshaw!

CAMPBELL Hugh

Outside-left

Born: Glasgow, 20 January 1911.
Career: Glasgow Rangers. Clapton Orient 1935. Cardiff City 1936. Ballymena. Halifax Town 1937.

■ Having been on the books of Rangers, Glasgow-born winger Hugh Campbell came south of the border to try his luck with Clapton Orient. Unable to make much headway, he joined the Bluebirds, but his only appearance in the City first team was on the final day of the 1936–37 season when Cardiff lost 2–1 at Bristol City. He then had spell in Ireland with Ballymena before returning to see out his career in the Football League with Halifax Town.

CANNING Leslie Daniel (Danny)

Goalkeeper

Born: Pontypridd, 21 February 1926.
Career: Abercynon. Cardiff City 1945. Swansea City 1949. Nottingham Forest 1951. Yarmouth. Newport County.

Division Three South Champion 1946–47.

■ Goalkeeper Danny Canning joined the Bluebirds during the latter stages of World War Two from local side Abercynon. He took over from George

Poland after two games of the 1946–47 season and kept 22 clean sheets in 38 games as Cardiff won the Third Division South Championship. His performances the following season, as he went on to appear in 78 games from his debut, helped City finish fifth in Division Two. Surprisingly allowed to leave Ninian Park, Canning joined rivals Swansea and in 1948–49 helped them win promotion, as champions of the Third Division South. He later had a brief spell with Nottingham Forest before playing non-League football for Yarmouth. He ended his playing days with Newport County but never made their first team.

CARLESS Ernest Francis (Ernie)

Inside-forward

Born: Barry, 9 September 1912.
Died: 1987.
Career: Wolverhampton Wanderers 1931. Barry Town 1931. Cardiff City 1932. Altrincham. Barry Town. Plymouth Argyle 1946.

■ All-round sportsman Ernie Carless seemed to be around the Ninian Park scene on and off for a good number of years. Though he only appeared in one League game – a 3–1 home defeat by Exeter City in November 1932 – he turned up years later to be a cornerstone of City's team during the war years and played against Moscow Dynamo in 1945. After the hostilities, he became groundsman at Ninian Park and later performed the same duties for Plymouth Argyle, for whom he had also made a handful of League appearances. Besides playing cricket for Glamorgan and Devon in the Minor Counties, he also represented Cardiff City at baseball and basketball.

CARLIN William

Midfield

Born: Liverpool, 6 October 1940.
Career: Liverpool 1958. Halifax Town 1962. Carlisle United 1964. Sheffield United 1967. Derby County 1968. Leicester City 1970. Notts County 1971. Cardiff City 1973.

■ One of the game's great personalities,

the diminutive Willie Carlin was jettisoned by his home-town club Liverpool after just a single Anfield outing and joined Halifax Town. In his first season at The Shay the Yorkshire club suffered relegation to the Fourth Division, but he soon became their leading scorer. He later assisted Carlisle United to the Third Division Championship in 1964–65 and spent three seasons at Brunton Park until moving to Sheffield United. After a season in which much of his time was spent involved in the Blades' First Division relegation struggle, he joined Brian Clough's Derby County for a then Rams record payment of £60,000. An inspiration to Derby's rise from the Second Division in 1969 and their fourth placing in the top flight a year later, it came as a great surprise when he was allowed to move to Leicester City in October 1970. In his only season at Filbert Street, he helped the Foxes win the Second Division Championship before Jimmy Bloomfield rather hastily discarded the pint-sized battler. He then joined Notts County and helped them win promotion from the Third Division before finally arriving at Ninian Park in November 1973, where his former Leicester boss Frank O'Farrell was in charge. After making his debut in a 1–0 win over Bolton Wanderers, he was instrumental in sparking City's then annual Second Division survival acts – scoring his only goal against Middlesbrough – before retiring in May 1974.

CARPENTER Richard

Midfield

*Born: Sheerness, 30 September 1972.
Career: Gillingham 1991. Fulham 1996.
Cardiff City 1998. Brighton & Hove Albion 2000.*

Division Three promotion 1998–99.

■ Beginning his career with Gillingham, midfielder Richard Carpenter, a former captain of the club's youth team, was a regular in the Kent side for five seasons, playing 142 games before in September 1996 joining Fulham for £15,000. In his early days with the Cottagers he was most impressive, but following the signing of

Paul Trollope he never made the starting line-up again!

Signed by Cardiff in the summer of 1998 for a fee of £35,000, he played a crucial role in the Bluebirds' promotion campaign in 1998–99, having previously won promotion three times with Gillingham, Fulham and now City. Despite the club's relegation after just one season of Second Division football, Carpenter had a good spell in a midfield holding role alongside Mark Bonner. However, out of contract in July 2000, he joined Brighton & Hove Albion and in his first season with the Seagulls helped them win the Third Division Championship. In 2001–02 he really came into his own as Brighton won the Second Division title. He later went on to win his third promotion with the Seagulls in the narrow play-off victory over Bristol City at the Millennium Stadium.

CARSS Anthony John (Tony)

Midfield

*Born: Alnwick, 31 March 1976.
Career: Bradford City. Blackburn Rovers 1994. Darlington 1995. Cardiff City 1997. Chesterfield 1998. Carlisle United 2000. Oldham Athletic 2000. Huddersfield Town 2003.*

FAW Invitation Cup finalist 1997–98.

■ A left-sided midfielder who failed to make the grade with Blackburn Rovers, he joined Darlington, appearing for them in the 1996 Wembley play-off final. Despite scoring a number of spectacular goals for the Quakers, he was released during the summer of 1997 and signed for Cardiff City. Unable to reproduce his training ground talent in the first team, despite appearing in most of the games in 1997–98, he was given a free transfer the day after playing in the last match of the season – the FAW Invitation Cup Final against Wrexham. He then joined Chesterfield but suffered a broken leg during his early days at Saltergate. He made a full recovery, but at the end of the 1999–2000 season he moved to Carlisle United. His stay at Brunton Park was brief, and he was soon on his way to Oldham Athletic, where he was named the club's Player of the Season for 2000–01. Injuries then

disrupted his progress but he bounced back prior to signing for Huddersfield Town, whom he helped win promotion via the play-offs.

CARVER David Francis

Full-back

*Born: Wickersley, 16 April 1944.
Career: Rotherham United 1962. Cardiff City 1966. Swansea City (loan) 1972. Hereford United 1973. Doncaster Rovers 1974.*

Welsh Cup winner 1967–68, 1968–69, 1969–70, 1970–71. Welsh Cup finalist 1971–72.

■ A strong, well-balanced player with two good feet, David Carver began his League career with his home-town club Rotherham United. After establishing himself in the Millers defence, Carver went on to appear in 83 games before Jimmy Scoular paid £11,000 to bring him to Ninian Park in January 1966. He played his first match in Cardiff colours in a 1–1 draw at Bury and over the next six seasons was a virtual ever present as he and Gary Bell formed a solid combination at full-back. He won Welsh Cup medals in four successive seasons from 1968 to 1971 and was ever present in seasons 1969–70 and 1970–71, when he appeared in 93 consecutive League games. Carver's only goal for the Bluebirds came on 17 October 1970 when he hit one of the goals in a 2–2 draw against Leicester City in a match featured on BBC TV's *Match of the Day* programme. Following a short loan spell with Swansea, he joined Hereford United on a free transfer. Carver later returned to Yorkshire to end his playing days with Doncaster Rovers.

CARVER John William

Full-back

*Born: Newcastle, 16 January 1965.
Career: Newcastle United 1983. Cardiff City 1985. Newcastle Blue Star.*

■ A former Newcastle United reserve, full-back John Carver was taken on a three-month trial at Ninian Park by City manager Alan Durban. Though he impressed on his debut in a 4–1 win at Notts County and looked a more than useful player during his time with the club, he was released in November 1985 after the team had begun to struggle – a campaign which ended in relegation. He then returned to the North East to play for Newcastle Blue Star.

CASHMORE Arthur A.

Forward

Born: Birmingham, 30 October 1893.
Career: Sparkhill Arondale. Bromsgrove Rovers. Manchester United 1913. Oldham Athletic 1914. Darlaston. Cardiff City 1919. Notts County 1921. Darlaston. Nuneaton Town.

Division Two runner-up 1920–21.

■ Arthur Cashmore played local football for Sparkhill Arondale and Bromsgrove Rovers prior to being given his League debut by Manchester United. Unable to win a regular place in the Red Devils First Division side, he moved to nearby Oldham Athletic, and in

1914–15, as the Latics finished runners-up to Everton in the top flight, he scored eight goals in 16 games. His progress at Boundary Park was hampered by injuries, and he moved to play for Darlaston before City signed him for the start of their final season of Southern League football. Having scored on his debut in a 2–1 defeat of Crystal Palace, he was the club's leading scorer with 14 goals in 22 games. A

member of Cardiff's first-ever League XI at Stockport, he was an ever present in the Bluebirds side until the arrival of Fred Pagnam from Arsenal. During that time, he formed a good understanding with Jimmy Gill, netting 11 goals in 26 games plus the winners in FA Cup matches against Brighton and Chelsea. On leaving Ninian Park he played for Notts County before seeing out his career with another spell at Darlaston and finally at Nuneaton Town.

CASSIDY Joseph (Joe)

Forward

Born: Calder, 10 August 1896.
Died: 1949.
Career: Vale of Clyde. Glasgow Celtic 1913. Bolton Wanderers 1924. Cardiff City 1925. Dundee. Clyde. Ballymena. Morton. Dundalk.

■ Scottish international forward Joe Cassidy started his career with Vale of Clyde before joining Celtic in 1913. Though he lost some of his good years to the Kaiser, he was an important member of the Hoops side in the immediate years following the end of the hostilities. During that time Cassidy, who scored 104 goals in 204 Scottish League and Cup matches, helped Celtic win the League title in 1921–22 and the Scottish Cup in 1923, when his goal helped defeat Hibernian. He came into the Football League with Bolton Wanderers, but after one season at Burnden Park he was on the move again – to Cardiff City for £3,800. In only his third game he netted a hat-trick in a 5–2 defeat of Leicester City, but at the end of that 1925–26 season he returned to Scotland to play for Dundee. Before his retirement from the game, 'Trooper', as he was known (who had four children, born in all four countries of the British Isles), saw service with Clyde, Ballymena, Morton and Dundalk.

CASTLE Frederick Richard (Fred)

Centre-forward

Born: Pen-y-Graig, 10 April 1902.
Died: 1982.
Career: Mid-Rhondda United. Cardiff City 1926. Chesterfield 1928. Gillingham 1929. Mid-Rhondda United. Derry City. Doncaster Rovers 1930.

■ Centre-forward Fred Castle had seen service with both Pontypridd and Mid-Rhondda before arriving at Ninian Park in 1926. His first-team chances with City were severely restricted, and, after making his debut in a 5–0 defeat at Newcastle United on Christmas Day 1926, he only made a further two appearances in two seasons with the club. He then moved on to Chesterfield and later Gillingham, and, although he found the net on a fairly regular basis, he was never a regular first-team player. There followed spells with Mid-Rhondda and Derry City before he finished his career with Doncaster Rovers.

CHANDLER Jeffrey George

Winger

Born: Hammersmith, 19 June 1959.
Career: Blackpool 1976. Leeds United 1979. Bolton Wanderers 1981. Derby County 1985. Mansfield Town (loan) 1986. Bolton Wanderers 1987. Cardiff City 1989.

■ Winger Jeff Chandler began his career with Blackpool as a striker, scoring on his League debut in a 2–1 win at Blackburn Rovers in September 1977. His first full season ended in disappointment when the Seasiders were relegated, and in September 1979 he joined Leeds United. It was while with the Elland Road club that Chandler won full international honours for the Republic of Ireland. In October 1981 Bolton Wanderers paid £40,000 for his services and over the next four seasons he was a fixture in the Trotters side. Scoring a number of spectacular goals, his best season was 1984–85 when he found the net on 20 occasions. In the summer of 1985 he joined Derby County, helping the Rams win promotion to Division Two in 1985–86. After a loan spell with Mansfield he rejoined Bolton, and though he suffered damaged knee ligaments he was in the side that won the Sherpa Van Trophy at Wembley. Having scored 48 goals in 211 games in his two spells with the club, he joined Cardiff City for £15,000 in November 1989, but unfortunately injury curtailed his career at Ninian Park after he had appeared in 28 first-team games.

CHARLES Clive Michael

Full-back

Born: Bow, 3 October 1951.
Died: 26 August 2003.
Career: West Ham United 1969. Cardiff City 1974. Portland Timbers 1976.

Welsh Cup winner 1973–74. 1975–76.
Division Three runner-up 1975–76.

■ England Youth international Clive Charles began his career with West Ham United but found his progress at Upton Park was hampered by the Hammers' surfeit of quality defenders. Charles joined Cardiff City on a free transfer just before the transfer deadline in March 1974 and, after helping the Bluebirds draw 2–2 at West Bromwich Albion, played in midfield to help the club avoid relegation. In 1974–75 Clive Charles became the first black player to captain Cardiff City, but towards the end of the season he suffered a spate of injuries which restricted his appearances as the club were relegated. The following

season he helped City win promotion and was still a first-team regular when, midway through the 1975–76 season, he left to play in the NASL for Portland Timbers prior to coaching in Oregon.

CHARLES Melvyn (Mel)

Centre-half/centre-forward

Born: Swansea, 14 May 1935.
Career: Leeds United. Swansea Town 1952. Arsenal 1959. Cardiff City 1962. Porthmadoc. Port Vale 1967. Haverfordwest.

Welsh Cup winner 1963–64.

■ Mel Charles was voted the best centre-half in the 1958 World Cup Finals, but he showed his versatility at international level seven years later by scoring all four goals in a 4–0 defeat of Northern Ireland at Ninian Park. After a trial with Leeds United, he signed for Swansea Town and over the next seven seasons played in 233 League games for the Vetch Field club, scoring 69 goals. Like his brother John, he became very much sought after, and in March 1959 he joined Arsenal for a club record fee of £42,750 plus youngsters Peter Davis and David Dodson. After alternating between centre-half and centre-forward, the multi-gifted Charles's Highbury career was devastated by two cartilage operations. However, in 1961–62 he netted 17 goals in 23 League and Cup

games, including a hat-trick against Blackburn Rovers, but in February of that season he returned to Wales to sign for Cardiff City for £28,500. Mel Charles did well for the Bluebirds, scoring regularly when selected in attack and doing a good job in defence until being displaced by his brother on his return from Italy. He then played non-League football for Porthmadoc in the Welsh League before returning to League action with Port Vale. He later played for Haverfordwest before hanging up his boots.

CHARLES William John

Centre-half/centre-forward

Born: Swansea, 27 December 1931.
Died: 21 February 2004.
Career: Leeds United 1949. Juventus 1957. Leeds United 1962. AS Roma 1962. Cardiff City 1963. Hereford United 1966.

Welsh Cup winners 1963–64. 1964–65.

■ Few would argue with the description of John Charles as the greatest Welsh player of all time. Many Welshmen would go further and describe 'the gentle giant' as simply the greatest player of all time. After leaving school, he joined the Swansea groundstaff, but his stay at the Vetch was brief as Leeds United manager Major Frank Buckley persuaded the young Charles to go to Elland Road. On 8 March 1950 he became the youngest Welshman ever to represent his country when, at the age of 18 years 71 days old, he played against Northern Ireland. As Leeds strived to climb out of the Second Division, Charles was switched from centre-half to centre-forward with devastating effect. In 1953–54 Charles scored 42 goals to become the first Welshman to top the Football League scoring lists. After returning to plug a leaky defence, he was restored to the forward line and in the club's promotion-winning season of 1955–56 he scored 29 goals. In the top flight he continued to score with great regularity, and Leeds were tagged 'Charles United'! In 1957 Italian giants Juventus paid £65,000, a record fee for a British player, to take Charles into Serie 'A'. Within a year a poll by the Italian football paper *Il Calcio Illustra* elected

Charles the best player in the country. Helped by his 28 goals, Juventus won the Championship in his first season at the club and two years later won both the Championship and the Cup. Charles, who won 38 caps for his country, was forced out of Wales's 1958 World Cup quarter-final match with Brazil following the savage treatment he received in the play-off match against Hungary. After five successful years, he returned to these shores to play for Leeds, but life under Don Revie's management was different, and he soon returned to Italy and AS Roma. Injuries hampered his progress, and in the summer of 1963 he signed for Cardiff City for £20,000. By now Charles had slowed down, and at Ninian Park he reverted into a defender's role, though he did score two of the goals in the 5–0 drubbing of Swansea in April 1965. In 1966 he was transferred to Hereford United, for whom he scored 130 goals in 243 appearances. He left Edgar Street in 1971, just before the club achieved their ambition of Football League status, and, after a spell as manager of

Merthyr Tydfil, he became youth coach at Swansea.

CHISHOLM Kenneth McTaggart

Inside-forward

Born: Glasgow, 12 April 1925.
Died: 1990.
Career: Queen's Park 1945. Partick Thistle 1946. Leeds United 1948. Leicester City 1949. Coventry City 1950. Cardiff City 1952. Sunderland 1954. Workington 1956. Glentoran.

Division Two runner-up 1951–52.

■ Ken Chisholm was a fighter pilot during World War Two. He joined Queen's Park in 1945 and the following year turned out for Scotland in a Victory International against Northern Ireland. He left Hampden Park in 1946

for Partick Thistle, and the legendary Major Frank Buckley, manager of Leeds United, signed him in 1948. He stayed at Elland Road for less than a year before moving to Leicester City, with whom he won his only honour, an FA Cup runners'-up medal in 1949. In March 1950 he signed for Coventry City and soon became a great favourite at Highfield Road. In 1950–51, his only complete season with the Sky Blues, he netted 24 goals, most of them before

Christmas. He had scored 10 the following term, but by March 1952 Coventry were struggling to avoid relegation, and in a desperate attempt to revive his ailing side Harry Storer sold him to Cardiff City. He made his debut for the Bluebirds in a disastrous 6–1 defeat at Sheffield United but then proceeded to score eight goals in the last 11 games of the season to help the club end the campaign as runners-up and gain promotion to the First Division. For the next two seasons he was the Ninian Park club's leading scorer, and in October 1953 he netted his only hat-trick for the club in a 5–0 defeat of Charlton Athletic. He later played for Sunderland and Workington before becoming player-manager of Glentoran. Chisholm was one of the players involved in the Sunderland illegal payments scandal of the 1950s. He was suspended sine die for refusing to answer the investigating committee's questions. Subsequently he admitted receiving illegal payments and forfeited his benefit qualification terms.

CHRISTIE Derrick Hugh Michael

Winger

Born: Hackney, 15 March 1957.
Career: Northampton Town 1975. Cambridge United 1978. Reading 1984. Cardiff City 1985. Peterborough United 1986.

■ Speedy winger Derrick Christie began his League career with Northampton Town. He spent five years at the County Ground, scoring 18 goals in 138 games and helping the Cobblers win promotion to Division Three in 1975–76. On joining Cambridge United, Christie spent a similar amount of time with similar statistical returns, 19 goals in 138 games, before moving to Reading. Unable to get into their record-breaking team, he contacted Alan Durban and arrived at Ninian Park in October 1985. After some good displays, he failed to live up to his early promise and was released at the end of that 1985–86 relegation season. He then had a spell with Peterborough United before drifting into non-League football.

CLARK Brian Donald

Forward

Born: Bristol, 13 January 1943.
Career: Bristol City 1960. Huddersfield Town 1966. Cardiff City 1968. Bournemouth 1972. Millwall 1973. Cardiff City 1975. Newport County 1976. Maesteg. AFC Cardiff. Bridgend Town.

Welsh Cup winner 1968–69, 1969–70, 1970–71, 1975–76. Welsh Cup finalist 1971–72. Division Three runner-up 1975–76.

■ The son of former Bristol City favourite Don Clark, he joined the Ashton Gate club in March 1960 and played his first game for the club on the final day of the 1960–61 season against Brentford, a match in which John Atyeo netted a hat-trick in a 3–0 win. Clark came into his own in 1962–63, topping the club's scoring charts with 23 goals. He continued to find the net on a regular basis, and in 1964–65, when the club won promotion to the Second Division, he top scored with 24 goals. This total included 12 in the first eight games of the season. In October 1966, after scoring 93 goals in 220 games, he left Ashton Gate to join Huddersfield Town in exchange for John Quigley. Unable to settle with the Yorkshire club, he was snapped up by Cardiff City manager Jimmy Scoular for the bargain fee of £8,000. He scored twice on his debut as the Bluebirds won 4–3 at Derby County and, forming a formidable partnership with John Toshack, netted 17 League goals in 1968–69. Also that season he won the first of four Welsh Cup medals before being one of three ever presents in 1969–70. That campaign he topped the club's League scoring charts, and in the Welsh Cup against Barmouth and Dyffryn he scored five goals in City's 6–1 win. In 1970–71 he again headed the club's scoring list, but it was his goal that defeated Real Madrid 1–0 in the European Cup-Winners' Cup quarter-final first leg that ensured his place in the club's history! The following season he was City's leading scorer for a third successive term, but in 1972 he and Ian Gibson were somewhat surprisingly allowed to leave and joined Bournemouth for a combined fee of

£100,000. After a year at Dean Court, he had a spell with Millwall before returning to Ninian Park to play for the Bluebirds. In 1975–76 he helped City win promotion to Division Two but, after scoring 91 goals in his two spells, left to play for Newport County. He later had spells as player-manager at Maesteg, AFC Cardiff and Bridgend Town.

CLARK Joseph Walter (Joe)

Outside-left

Born: Willington Quay, 15 February 1890.
Died: 1960.
Career: Hebburn Argyle. Cardiff City 1912. Aberaman Athletic. Southampton 1922. Rochdale 1923.

Division Two runners-up 1920–21.

■ Formerly with non-League Hebburn Argyle, Joe Clark had the unenviable task of being understudy to the legendary Jack Evans in Cardiff City's pre-League days. Despite the club's admission to the Football League, he remained mainly in the reserves, though he did get on the scoresheet in a 3–0 home win over Nottingham Forest in April 1921. Clark, who had impressed

Southampton officials when he'd played against them in an FA Cup tie in 1921, joined the Saints early the following year. However, he failed to perform to the best of his ability and moved on to Rochdale on a free transfer.

CLARKE Malcolm McQueen

Midfield

Born: Clydebank, 29 June 1944.
Career: Johnstone Burgh. Leicester City 1965. Cardiff City 1967. Bristol City 1969. Hartlepool United 1970.

Welsh Cup winner 1967–68.

■ Malcolm Clarke joined Leicester City from Scottish junior club Johnstone Burgh in the summer of 1965. Dubiously distinguished by having had the shortest-ever first-team career with the Foxes – coming on in the 89th minute of his sole League game against Leeds United in September 1965 – he was reported not to have touched the ball during the remainder of play! In August 1967 Cardiff manager Jimmy Scoular signed him on a free transfer, and he soon replaced Gareth Williams when he was sold to Bolton Wanderers. He claimed a goal in the Welsh Cup

Final of 1968 as Cardiff gained an aggregate victory over Hereford United and then aided the Bluebirds with their surprising progress to the semi-finals of the European Cup-Winners' Cup. Injuries then disrupted his progress, and, after being unable to oust Mel Sutton, he joined Bristol City. Unable to make much impact at Ashton Gate, he joined Hartlepool United where he ended his League career.

CLARKE Royston James (Roy)

Outside-left

Born: Newport, 1 June 1925.
Career: Cardiff City 1942. Manchester City 1947. Stockport County 1958. Northwich Victoria.
Division Three South champions 1946–47.

■ Roy Clarke won 22 caps for Wales, yet his first taste of international recognition was as a member of the Welsh Schools Baseball team in 1939!

During World War Two he worked in the coal mines but managed to play for local side Albion Rovers of Newport at the weekends. Cardiff City won the race for his signature in 1942, and his early performances on the left wing were impressive enough to earn him a place in the Wales team for the Victory International of 1946 against Northern Ireland. As it turned out, Clarke played less than one full season of peacetime football for the Bluebirds. His speedy hard-shooting forays down the left flank were a feature of the Cardiff side that won promotion to the Second Division in 1946–47. Towards the end of that season, Manchester City paid £12,000 for Clarke's services. He holds the unique record of playing in three different Divisions of the Football League in three consecutive League games – the last of 39 games for the Bluebirds in the penultimate game of the 1946–47 season. His debut for Manchester City was in their last game of their Second Division promotion-winning season and in the opening game of the 1947–48 campaign in the First Division! While with Manchester City, Clarke helped them reach the 1955 FA Cup Final but missed the big match through injury. The following year, however, he picked up an FA Cup medal after they had beaten Birmingham 3–1. Clarke, who netted 73 goals in 349 games for the Maine Road club, later joined Stockport County before leaving to play non-League football for Northwich Victoria. In 1966 he returned to Maine Road to run the City social club.

CLENNELL Joseph (Joe)

Inside-left

Born: New Silksworth, 19 February 1889.
Died: 1965.
Career: Silksworth United. Seaham Harbour. Blackpool 1910. Blackburn Rovers 1910. Everton 1913. Cardiff City 1921. Stoke 1924. Bristol Rovers 1926. Rochdale 1927. Ebbw Vale. Barry Town. Bangor. Great Harwood.

Welsh Cup winner 1921–22, 1922–23.
Division One runner-up 1923–24.

■ Often described as 'a little demon', Joe Clennell played in junior football in his native North East with the likes of Silkworth United and Seaham Harbour before entering the Football League with Blackpool. In 1910 he moved on to Blackburn Rovers, and following three years at Ewood Park he signed for Everton. On the opening day of the 1914–15 season, Clennell scored a hat-trick as Everton beat Spurs 3–1 at White Hart Lane. He went on to score 17 goals in 41 League and Cup games when the club won the League Championship and reached the semi-finals of the FA Cup. In wartime football Clennell scored 128 goals in 124 games for Everton, including four in a match on five occasions! When League football resumed in 1919 he continued to find the net regularly, netting a hat-trick against Bradford City. In October 1921 Clennell signed for Cardiff City following the Bluebirds' promotion to the First Division. Over the next four years Clennell scored with great regularity with his best season in 1922–23 when he found the net 14 times in the League, including a hat-trick in a 5–1 win at Burnley. After losing his place to Harry Beadles, he joined Stoke before later moving on to Bristol Rovers and Rochdale. He was only staying briefly anywhere at this time, but his affinity with Wales showed through when he became player-manager of Ebbw Vale, then Barry Town and Bangor before going to Great Harwood. He later managed Distillery in the Irish League and coached Accrington Stanley.

COLDICOTT Stacy

Midfield

Born: Redditch, 29 April 1974.
Career: West Bromwich Albion 1992. Cardiff City (loan) 1996. Grimsby Town 1998.

■ Determined, aggressive and totally committed, Stacy Coldicott began his career with West Bromwich Albion, where he produced several competent displays at both right-back and in midfield. Unable to establish himself as a first-team regular, he had a loan spell with Cardiff at the start of the 1996–97 season before returning to the Hawthorns. He had appeared in 127 games for the Baggies, over a third as substitute, when in the summer of 1998 he moved to Grimsby Town. One of a number of former Albion players who followed manager Alan Buckley to Blundell Park, his total commitment endeared him to the Mariners fans. Much of his time with Grimsby was spent fighting relegation battles, but a broken leg at Burnley in 2002–03 cost him his place. He returned to the Grimsby side the following season but was unable to avert a second successive relegation.

COLDRICK Graham George

Defender

Born: Newport, 6 November 1945.
Career: Cardiff City 1962. Newport County 1970.

Welsh Cup winner 1964–65, 1966–67.

■ Welsh Under-23 international defender Graham Coldrick made his first two League appearances for the Bluebirds as a makeshift forward but soon slotted into the City side in a full-back berth. Throughout his time at Ninian Park, Coldrick was dogged by knee injuries – his best season being 1966–67 when his only goals came in successive matches in wins over Norwich City and Birmingham. He

eventually lost his place in the Cardiff side due to the consistency of David Carver and Graham Bell and moved to Newport County for what was then a Somerton Park club record fee of £4,000. A regular in the county side for five years, he clocked up 157 League appearances before hanging up his boots.

COLLINS James (Jack)

Outside-left

Born: London.
Career: Liverpool 1931. Cardiff City 1932. Millwall 1933. Bangor 1934.

■ Left-winger Jack Collins started out with Liverpool but, on being unable to force his way into their League side, joined Cardiff in 1932. Over the course of the 1932–33 season Collins made six appearances for the Bluebirds, spending most of his time in the reserves. In the close season he was allowed to join Millwall, but again he failed to figure in their first-team plans and left to play non-League football for Bangor City.

COLLINS James Henry (Jimmy)

Centre-forward

Born: Bermondsey, 30 January 1911.
Died: 1983.
Career: Tooting and Mitcham. Queen's Park Rangers 1931. Tunbridge Wells Rangers. Rochdale 1933. Stockport County 1934. Walsall 1935. Liverpool 1935. Cardiff City 1937. Aberaman.

Welsh Cup finalist 1938–39.

■ Somewhat on the small side for a centre-forward, Jimmy Collins began his career with Tooting and Mitcham before being given his chance in the Football League with Queen's Park Rangers. He failed to make much of an impact and returned to non-League football with Tunbridge Wells Rangers. He proved to be a prolific scorer with the Kent club and so was given another chance at League level by Rochdale. He later had brief spells with Stockport County, Walsall and Liverpool before signing for Cardiff City in 1937. He scored City's goal in a 1–1 draw at Clapton Orient on the opening day of the 1937–38 season and then netted a hat-trick on his first

appearance at Ninian Park as Torquay United were beaten 5–2. He ended the season as the club's top scorer with 23 goals in 39 League games as City finished 10th in the Third Division South. He headed the scoring charts again in 1938–39 with 18 goals in 36 League games, including his second hat-trick in a 5–3 home win over Watford. He scored four goals in the three League matches that were played in the abandoned season of 1939–40. World War Two brought his Football League career to an end, though he did manage a few games for Aberaman.

COLLINS James Michael

Central-defender

Born: Newport, 23 August 1983.
Career: Cardiff City 2000. West Ham United 2005.

FAW Premier Cup winner 2001–02.

■ Though he started out as a central-defender, he later switched to playing as a striker. Collins made his senior debut when he came off the bench to replace Rob Earnshaw in the closing minutes of the FA Cup first-round tie against Bristol Rovers in November 2000, after the Welsh international had netted a hat-trick. He made a handful more appearances during the season, mostly as a substitute. In 2001–02 the Cardiff coaching staff were unsure for some time whether Collins should be playing in attack or defence, but as all his best performances came at centre-half it seemed that's where his future would lie. The following season he scored two FA Cup goals in the matches against

Tranmere Rovers and appeared for Wales at Under-21 level. In 2003–04 he began to forge an excellent central-defensive partnership with Danny Gabbidon, his form winning him his first full cap against Norway and making him the first player to hold caps at every level for his country. On leaving Ninian Park in the summer of 2005, Collins joined Premiership new boys West Ham United, and in a most successful season the Welsh international helped the Hammers reach the FA Cup Final.

COLLINS William Elvet

Outside-right

Born: Bedwellty, 16 October 1902.
Career: Rhymney Town. Cardiff City 1923. Clapton Orient 1927. Lovells Athletic. Rhymney Town. Llanelly. Newport County 1932. Llanelly. Oakdale Welfare.

■ Winger Elvet Collins arrived at Ninian Park in 1923 after impressing in local League football with Rhymney Town. Due to fierce competition for places, he had to be content with just 13 appearances in the four years he was with the Bluebirds. He then joined Clapton Orient, where he was a first-team regular for a couple of seasons prior to brief spells with Lovells Athletic, Rhymney Town and Llanelly. He then returned to League action with Newport County before having a further spell with Llanelly.

COOPER Kevin Lee

Midfield/winger

Born: Derby 8 February 1975
Career: Derby County 1993. Stockport County 1997. Wimbledon 2001. Wolverhampton Wanderers 2002. Sunderland (loan) 2004. Norwich City (loan) 2004. Cardiff City 2005.

■ After appearing from the bench in a settled Derby County side, he went on loan to Stockport County before joining the Edgeley Park club on a permanent basis. An instant hit with the Hatters with his busy play, manager Gary Megson was forever praising his attitude and commitment and in 1999–2000 he played in all 51 of County's League and

Cup games. Deservedly he won several Player of the Year awards. He had scored 23 goals in 187 games for County when in March 2001 he was sold to Wimbledon for £800,000. Despite finding the net on a more regular basis for the Dons, a year later he was transferred to Wimbledon's promotion rivals Wolves for £1 million. Ensuring that the Molineux club made the play-offs, he then struggled to hold down a regular place and after suffering a number of injuries, had spells on loan with both Sunderland and Norwich City. The 2004–05 season was a similar story and in the close season he was allowed to join Cardiff. An influential member of the City side, he showed great composure on the ball and over the course of the campaign created many goalscoring chances for his colleagues.

CORKHILL William Grant (Billy)

Wing-half

Born: Belfast, 23 April 1910.
Died: 1978.
Career: Northern Nomads. Marine. Notts County 1931. Cardiff City 1938. Notts County 1945.

Welsh Cup finalist 1938–39.

■ Belfast-born wing-half Billy Corkhill played non-League football for Lancashire sides Northern Nomads and Marine before signing for Notts County in 1931. Over the next six seasons Corkhill developed into one of the finest players in the Third Division, and when City manager Bill Jennings brought him to Ninian Park in 1938 his signing was seen as a big step forward by the Bluebirds. Although injuries disrupted his only season with the club, he turned in some outstanding displays in what was the last full campaign before the hostilities. At the end of the war he re-signed for Notts County and in 1950–51 helped them win the Third Division South Championship. He went on to make 264 League appearances for County, one of which was in goal before later managing both Scunthorpe United and Bradford Park Avenue.

CORNER David Edward

Central-defender

Born: Sunderland, 15 May 1966.
Career: Sunderland 1984. Cardiff City (loan) 1985. Peterborough United (Loan) 1988. Leyton Orient 1988. Darlington 1989.

■ England Youth international centre-half David Corner arrived at Ninian Park on a one-month loan only six months after playing for Sunderland in the 1985 Milk Cup Final against Norwich City. He did little to impress in the six games in which he played and returned to Roker Park. He had appeared in 33 League games for the Wearsiders when, following a loan spell with Peterborough United, he signed for Leyton Orient. His stay at Brisbane Road was brief, and he returned to the North East to see out his career with Darlington.

CORNFORTH John Michael

Midfield

Born: Whitley Bay, 7 October 1967.
Career: Sunderland 1985. Doncaster Rovers (loan) 1986. Shrewsbury Town (loan) 1989. Lincoln City (loan) 1990. Swansea City 1991. Birmingham City 1996. Wycombe Wanderers 1996. Peterborough United (loan) 1998. Cardiff City 1999. Scunthorpe United 1999. Exeter City 2000.

■ Unable to hold down a regular place at his first club Sunderland, John Cornforth had loan spells with Doncaster Rovers, Shrewsbury Town and Lincoln City before joining Swansea City for a fee of £50,000 in the summer of 1991. He had the misfortune to break his leg during the early stages of his time at the Vetch but recovered to become the first Swansea captain in the history of the club to lead a team out at Wembley in the Autoglass Trophy Final, where he scored his side's first goal in the penalty shoot-out. His outstanding passing skills led to him winning full international honours for Wales in 1995. In March 1996, following Swansea's relegation, he moved to Birmingham City for £350,000, but, unable to establish himself at St Andrew's, he moved to Wycombe

Wanderers. Following a loan spell with Peterborough, he joined Cardiff City in the summer of 1999. He appeared in 10 League games and in all but two he either started on the bench or was substituted! After an equally brief spell with Scunthorpe, he became Exeter's player-coach before retiring at the end of the 2000–01 season.

CORNWELL John Anthony

Midfield/central-defender

Born: Bethnal Green 13 October 1964. Career: Leyton Orient 1982. Newcastle United 1987. Swindon Town 1988. Southend United 1990. Cardiff City (loan) 1993. Brentford (loan) 1993. Northampton Town (loan) 1994.

■ A product of Frank Clark's junior network, utility player John Cornwell made 227 League and Cup outings for Leyton Orient before joining Newcastle United for £50,000 in December 1987. Though he had the opportunity to develop at a top club, he found it difficult in a side that initially couldn't maintain a promotion challenge, and after a year at St James' Park he moved to Swindon Town. A wholehearted player, he had two years with the Wiltshire club before signing for Southend United. At the start of the 1993–94 season he went on loan to Cardiff City – the five games in which he scored twice were never dull, with a total of 23 goals being scored! There followed further loan spells with Brentford and Northampton Town before he hung up his boots.

COUCH Alan

Midfield

Born: Neath, 15 March 1953. Career: Cardiff City 1970. Barry Town 1973.

■ A member of Cardiff City's successful youth side of 1970–71, midfielder Alan Couch never quite made it at Football League level, playing in just a few games in seasons 1971–72 and 1972–73. City manager Jimmy Scoular released him, and he went to play for Barry Town prior to playing non-League football for many seasons.

COURT Harold John (Jack)

Inside-right

Born: Tir Phil, 13 June 1917. Career: Llanbradach. Cardiff City 1938. Dundee 1946. Swindon Town 1950.

■ Having made his Cardiff debut towards the end of the 1938–39 season in a 1–0 defeat at home to Crystal Palace, the inside-forward's career was cruelly curtailed by the outbreak of World War Two. He remained with the Bluebirds during the early part of the hostilities before later 'guesting' for Arsenal, Plymouth Argyle, Torquay United and Arbroath. After serving in the Army, he rejoined Cardiff for the 1946–47 season but, on being unable to break into the League side, left to play for Dundee. He later returned to the Football League with Swindon Town, finishing his career at the County Ground.

COX Neil James

Defender

Born: Scunthorpe, 8 October 1971. Career: Scunthorpe United 1990. Aston Villa 1991. Middlesbrough 1994. Bolton Wanderers 1997. Watford 1999. Cardiff City 2005.

■ England Under-21 international Neil Cox started out with his home-town club Scunthorpe United before Aston Villa paid £400,000 for his services in February 1991. Though not a regular in the Villa side, he won a Football League Cup-winners' medal in 1994 before in the close season joining Middlesbrough for a club record fee of £1 million. Elected by his fellow professionals to the PFA award-winning side, he helped 'Boro win the First Division Championship in his first season with the club. Showing an eye for goal, he netted after just two minutes of the game against Liverpool to score one of the fastest goals in the Premiership by a defender. A virtual ever present in his time at the Riverside, he left the Teeside club in the summer of 1997 after their disastrous end of season to join Bolton Wanderers. After just two games, he suffered a leg injury which kept him out of action for four months. On his return he scored against his old club Aston

Villa. During his time with the Trotters, Cox produced some wonderful displays, once scoring three goals in five games from his position at right-back. Hugely popular with the Bolton fans, he moved to Watford in November 1999 for a paltry £500,000. After a while, he settled into the Watford style of play, and though manager Luca Vialli put him on the transfer list, and he didn't even have a squad number, he responded with some sterling displays and was later appointed club captain. Continuing to lead by example he had appeared in 248 games for the Hornets when joining Cardiff in the summer of 2005. Though injuries hampered his progress at Ninian Park, he was a most popular acquisition and his efforts to get forward in support of the attack were rewarded with a brace of goals in the 3–0 defeat of Stoke City.

CRAWFORD Andrew

Forward

Born: Filey, 30 January 1959. Career: Filey Town. Derby County 1977. Blackburn Rovers 1979. Bournemouth 1981. Cardiff City 1983. Middlesbrough 1983. Stockport County 1984. Torquay United 1985.

■ Andy Crawford was a sharp, little striker, who had played for Filey Town prior to signing for Derby County in December 1977. Had Colin Addison persevered with him, he might have done well for the Rams, but the County boss accepted a £50,000 bid from Blackburn Rovers. Crawford was the Lancashire club's leading scorer in 1979–80 when they won promotion from the Third Division and had scored 21 goals in 56 games when allowed to join Bournemouth. While with the Cherries he was in another promotion team when David Webb led them from the Fourth Division in 1981–82. On his release from Dean Court, Len Ashurst offered Crawford a trial, and, although he did quite well in his six games, scoring in a 3–1 defeat of Grimsby Town, he was not offered a contract. He then moved on to Middlesbrough and two months later scored against City in a 2–0 defeat at Ayresome Park. Continuing his travels, he had brief spells with both Stockport County and Torquay United.

CRIBB Stanley Roy (Stan)

Outside-left

Born: Gosport, 11 May 1905.
Died: 1989.
Career: Gosport Athletic. Southampton 1924. West Ham United 1930. Queen's Park Rangers 1931. Cardiff City 1932.

■ Gosport-born left-winger Stan Cribb began his career with his home-town club, where his performances alerted Southampton manager Jim McIntyre. He stayed at The Dell for six seasons and earned, among other things, a reputation for being a reliable penalty-taker. Having scored 22 goals in 70 games, he left the Saints for West Ham United but soon joined Queen's Park Rangers. Though he only spent one season at Loftus Road, he netted 13 goals in 28 games, including three consecutive games in which he scored two goals in each. He signed for Cardiff in the summer of 1932, replacing the recently departed Walter Robbins. He scored on his debut in a 4–2 defeat at Reading and then again in his first game at Ninian Park as Bournemouth were beaten 3–0. Despite scoring 11 goals in 28 games, he found himself given a free transfer, and he decided to retire. He later returned to The Dell to scout for Southampton.

CROFT Gary

Full-back/midfield

Born: Burton-on-Trent, 17 February 1974.
Career: Grimsby Town 1992. Blackburn Rovers 1996. Ipswich Town 1999. Wigan Athletic (loan) 2002. Cardiff City 2002. Grimsby Town 2005.

Division Two Promotion 2002–03.

■ Beginning his career with Grimsby Town, Gary Croft developed nominally into a defender but with the versatility to play almost anywhere. During his early days with the Mariners he had the misfortune to miss a League representative game due to suspension, but he made up for that disappointment when he was selected by England for the Toulon Under-21 tournament. In March

1996 Blackburn Rovers, realising his potential, paid £1.7 million for his services. He had just replaced Graeme Le Saux in the Rovers side when he suffered a spate of injuries, including a dislocated shoulder, and, on being unable to win back his place, moved to Ipswich Town for a fee of £800,000. Shortly after his arrival at Portman Road things started to go wrong for him when he received a custodial sentence as a result of motoring offences and became the first professional footballer to play in a League game wearing a 'tag'. Following a loan spell with Wigan, Croft joined Cardiff on similar terms before, in March 2002, the move became permanent. The following season he became an important member of the Bluebirds side that won promotion to the First Division via the play-offs. He missed the start of the 2003–04 campaign after being struck down by appendicitis but after later returning to first-team duties enjoyed a couple of decent runs in the line-up. On being released by the Bluebirds, Gary Croft joined Grimsby Town and has been instrumental in the Mariners pushing for promotion from Division Two.

CROWE Glen Michael

Forward

Born: Dublin, 25 December 1977.
Career: Wolverhampton Wanderers 1996.

Exeter City (loan) 1997. Cardiff City (loan) 1997. Exeter City (loan) 1998. Plymouth Argyle 1999.

■ A determined left-footed striker, Glen Crowe was still a trainee when he made a surprise impact in the final two games of the 1995–96 season for Wolves. After coming off the bench against Reading, he was immediately booked and then started in the game against Charlton, lashing in a superb equaliser to give the Molineux club their first goal in five outings! A Republic of Ireland Under-21 international, he had a loan spell with Exeter City in a bid to sharpen up and his five goals in 10 games helped the Grecians avoid relegation. In October 1997 Crowe had another loan spell, this time with Cardiff City, and scored on his debut in a 1–1 draw with Hartlepool United. On his return to Molineux he found he still couldn't force his way into the first team, and after another loan spell with Exeter City he joined Plymouth Argyle on a free transfer. Most of his appearances for the Pilgrims were made from the bench, and in the close season he moved into the local non-League scene.

CURTIS Alan Thomas

Forward/midfield

Born: Pentre, 16 April 1954.
Career: Swansea City 1972. Leeds United 1979. Swansea City 1980. Southampton 1983. Stoke City (loan) 1986. Cardiff City 1986. Swansea City 1989. Barry Town. Haverfordwest.

Division Four runner-up 1987–88.
Welsh Cup winner 1987–88.

■ A nephew of former Swansea, Manchester City and Wales international Roy Paul, Alan Curtis joined Swansea on leaving school and soon emerged as a player of skill, vision and imagination. He became quite a prolific marksman with the Swans, netting his first League hat-trick against Crewe Alexandra in November 1977, while five months later both Curtis and Robbie James netted trebles as the Swans recorded their biggest-ever League win, defeating Hartlepool United 8–0. Curtis built his reputation as Swansea surged out of the lower reaches of the Football League, and in

May 1979 he joined Leeds United for £400,000, a record for a player from the lower Divisions. Unfortunately injury and a loss of form blighted his time at Elland Road, and in December 1980 he rejoined Swansea. He went on to be an important member of the Swansea side that won promotion to the First Division for the first time in their history. Curtis left the Vetch Field for a second time in November 1983 following the club's relegation from the top flight. He joined Southampton but things didn't work out for him at The Dell, and after a loan spell with Stoke City he returned to South Wales, joining the Bluebirds on a free transfer. In 1987–88 Curtis was instrumental in the club winning promotion to the Third Division and the Welsh Cup, in which he scored one of the goals in a 2–0 win over Wrexham. He continued to be a regular member of the Cardiff side until in the early part of the 1989–90 season he returned to the Vetch for a third spell. He announced his retirement at the end of that season, having scored 96 goals in 364 League games for the Swans. He then joined Barry Town as player-coach before a spell playing for Haverfordwest. He later returned to the Vetch as the club's assistant coach.

CURTIS Ernest Robert (Ernie)

Inside-forward/outside-left

Born: Cardiff, 10 June 1907.
Died: 1992.
Career: Cardiff Corinthians. Cardiff City 1926. Birmingham 1927. Cardiff City 1933. Coventry City 1934. Hartlepool United 1937.

FA Cup winner 1926–27. Welsh Cup winner 1926–27. FA Charity Shield winner 1927–28.

■ After representing Cardiff Boys and Wales as a Schoolboy, Ernie Curtis became an electrician with Cardiff City Corporation, playing amateur soccer in his spare time. Shortly afterwards he was taken on by Cardiff City and was soon capped by Wales at amateur level. After turning professional, he began a highly successful year at Ninian Park, culminating in his appearance for the Bluebirds in the 1927 FA Cup Final. He was, at the time, the youngest player to take part in an FA Cup Final, but he was far from overawed. A few weeks later he added a Welsh Cup medal to his collection when City beat Rhyl 2–0 to round off a fairytale campaign. In October 1927 he won his first full Welsh cap against Scotland at Wrexham and scored in a 2–2 draw. Birmingham

showed an interest in him, and it was with some reluctance that he left Ninian Park for St Andrew's. Because Birmingham wouldn't release him for international matches, Curtis didn't feature in the Welsh side as often as he might have done. In 1933 he moved back to Cardiff but soon found himself in a wages dispute and left the game to become a licensee in Birmingham. Coventry City obtained his release from his contract, resurrecting his career as a player and later player-coach. At the outbreak of World War Two he joined the Royal Artillery and was sent to the Far East. He was captured by the Japanese and from 1941 to the end of the hostilities he was a prisoner of war. In the late 1940s he became Cardiff's trainer and then occupied various positions at the club until retirement.

CURTIS Mark Wayne

Right-back

Born: Neath, 22 February 1967.
Career: Swansea City. Cardiff City 1984. Brecon Corries.

■ Having been released by Swansea City in 1985, full-back Wayne Curtis spent several months on the dole before deciding to apply to Cardiff City for a trial. Bluebirds manager Alan Durban offered him non-contract terms, followed by a contract as he performed well in a struggling City side. However, he failed to impress new manager Frank Burrows, and at the end of the 1986–87 season he left to join Brecon Corries.

DALE Carl

Forward

Born: Colwyn Bay, 29 April 1966.
Career: Bangor City. Chester City 1988. Cardiff City 1991. Yeovil Town 1998.

Welsh Cup winner 1991–92, 1992–93. Division Three champion 1992–93.

■ Carl Dale began his career with Bangor City before joining Chester City for a fee of £12,000 in May 1988. In three seasons with the then Sealand Road club, he scored 48 goals in 139 games, prompting the Bluebirds to pay £100,000 to bring him to Ninian Park. He made his City debut at Crewe in August 1991, scoring the club's goal in a

1–1 draw. Forming a deadly partnership with Chris Pike, he top-scored for the club with 22 goals, but City could only finish ninth in Division Four. After helping the club win promotion in 1992–93 when he scored 11 goals in 35 outings, he struggled with injury for a couple of seasons before being back to his best in 1995–96. During that campaign he scored 30 goals, 21 in the League, including a hat-trick in a 3–2 home win over Doncaster Rovers and nine in the various Cup competitions. Despite not being fully fit in 1996–97, his four goals in the final five games of the season took the club into the play-offs. Again, he suffered with injuries in the 1997–98 season, but Dale, a forward who was always dangerous, even when not completely fit, continued to score. Frank Burrows eventually gave him a free transfer, and, having scored 94 goals in 253 League and Cup games, he moved on to play for Yeovil Town.

DANIEL Raymond Christopher

Left-back

Born: Luton 10 December 1964.
Career: Luton Town 1982. Gillingham

1983. Hull City 1986. Cardiff City 1989. Portsmouth 1990. Notts County (loan) 1994. Walsall 1995.

■ Left-sided hard-tackling full-back Ray Daniel, who won England Youth international honours, began his career with his home-town club Luton Town.

Finding himself in and out of the Hatters side, he had a loan spell with Gillingham before moving on a free transfer to Hull City. He spent three seasons at Boothferry Park, though for part of that time he was sidelined by injury before, in August 1989, Cardiff manager Len Ashurst paid £40,000 for his services. Daniel missed very few games in that relegation season of 1989–90, scoring his only goal for the club in a 3–3 draw with Fulham. He had played in the opening 13 games of the following campaign when City accepted an £80,000 bid from Portsmouth. He was a regular in the Pompey side for a couple of seasons before injuries and a loss of form restricted his appearances. He had a loan spell with Notts County before signing for Walsall where he ended his League career.

DANIEL William Raymond (Ray)

Centre-half

Born: Swansea, 2 November 1928.
Died: 7 November 1997.
Career: Swansea Town. Arsenal 1946. Sunderland 1953. Cardiff City 1957. Swansea Town 1958. Hereford United 1960.

■ After starting his career with Swansea, he joined Arsenal in October 1946 but spent his first five seasons at Highbury in the North London club's reserve side. It was 1951–52 before he made the first team on a regular basis and, although he had broken his wrist, which was set in plaster, he passed a late fitness test to line-up against Newcastle in the 1952 FA Cup Final. Early in the game, Daniel clashed with Jackie Milburn and the partly knitted bone was broken again. The following season he missed just one game as the Gunners won the League Championship on goal average from Preston North End. It was thought that Daniel would be the next Arsenal captain but after yet another disagreement with manager Tom Whittaker he was allowed to leave Highbury in 1953 and joined Sunderland for a record £30,000. Teaming up with fellow international Trevor Ford, he was a virtual ever present in the Sunderland side. But during his time at Roker Park allegations regarding illegal bonuses paid to a number of players were reported to the Football League, and Daniel was one of those suspended. This not only cost him a fine but also restricted his appearances for Wales. In October 1957 he rather surprisingly joined Cardiff City, making his debut in a 2–0 win at Bristol Rovers. Unable to displace Danny Malloy, he moved on to his home-town team Swansea, later playing on a part-time basis for non-League Hereford United, for whom he made a mammoth 317 appearances, scoring 66 goals between 1960 and 1967.

DARLINGTON Jermaine Christopher

Defender

Born: Hackney, 11 April 1974.
Career: Charlton Athletic 1992. Dover Athletic. Aylesbury United. Queen's Park

Rangers 1999. Wimbledon 2001. Watford 2004. Cardiff City 2005.

■ After beginning his career with Charlton Athletic, Jermaine Darlington drifted into non-League football, playing for Dover Athletic and Aylesbury United before the attacking left-wing back was given a second chance at League level by Queen's Park Rangers. Having taken the jump from non-League to Division One in his stride, he became a firm favourite with the Loftus Road crowd and in 1999–2000 was voted the Rangers Players' Player of the Year. Despite playing in a struggling team, he continued to show excellent form and in July 2001 was transferred to Wimbledon for a bargain fee of £200,000. As the Dons pruned their playing staff, Darlington's versatility meant that he got plenty of first-team opportunities, playing in both full-back positions and in midfield. Despite continuing to impress, he was not offered a new contract following their relegation and moved on to Watford. After a season at Vicarage Road, Darlington signed for the Bluebirds, and though injuries have hampered his progress at Ninian Park he did demonstrate speed and vision, attributes which made him a handful in the games in which he played.

DAVIES Albert Bryn (Bryn)

Inside-forward

Born: Cardiff.
Career: Army. Cardiff City 1935. Ipswich Town 1938.

■ Inside-forward Bryn Davies joined the Bluebirds as an amateur in 1935 following Army service. Most of his time at Ninian Park was spent in the reserves, as he made just seven League appearances spread over three seasons. Following Ipswich Town's admission to the Football League in 1938, Davies left Cardiff to join the Portman Road club, and in his only season – his career being terminated by World War Two – he scored seven goals in 32 games.

DAVIES Benjamin E. (Ben)

Goalkeeper

Born: Middlesbrough.

Died: 1970.
Career: Middlesbrough 1910. Cardiff City 1920. Leicester City 1923. Bradford Park Avenue 1924.

Division Two runners-up 1920–21. Welsh Cup winners 1921–22.

■ A tall, slim goalkeeper, his top-flight experience at Middlesbrough was limited by the form of England international Tim Williamson, and in the summer of 1920 he left Ayresome Park to join Cardiff City for their initial season in the Football League. Replacing Jack Kneeshaw, he made his Bluebirds debut against Bristol City in January 1921, keeping a clean sheet in a 1–0 win. Davies kept his place in the side for the remainder of the season, conceding just 12 goals in 19 games as Cardiff won promotion to the First Division. Davies was the club's first-choice 'keeper until

midway through the 1922–23 season when he lost his place to Tom Farquharson. Though he battled hard to regain his place, he couldn't oust the legendary Irishman, and in June 1923 he joined Leicester City. Unable to win a regular place in the Foxes side, he joined Bradford Park Avenue but failed to make a first-team appearance.

DAVIES David Lyn (Lyn)

Goalkeeper

Born: Neath, 29 September 1947.
Career: Cardiff City 1965. Llanelli. Swansea City 1972.

■ Neath-born Lyn Davies had all the attributes for a top goalkeeper when he joined the Bluebirds and in 1965–66 acquitted himself in the 11 games he played. However, one month during the following season absolutely shattered his confidence. Coming into the side in preference to Dilwyn John and Bob Wilson, he found himself on the end of a 7–1 defeat at Wolves, a 5–0 reversal at Charlton, a 1–1 draw with Derby County, a 4–2 defeat by Hull City and another 7–1 mauling at Plymouth Argyle! Also during this horrendous spell, he made his only appearance for the Wales Under-23 side against England at Molineux – not his favourite ground – and had another eight goals blasted past him! He was devastated when he left Ninian Park but rebuilt his career with Llanelli and played three League games for Swansea before returning to local non-League circles.

DAVIES Frederick

Goalkeeper

Born: Liverpool, 22 August 1939.
Career Borough United. Wolverhampton Wanderers 1957. Cardiff City 1968. Bournemouth 1970.

Welsh Cup winner 1967–68, 1968–69, 1969–70.

■ Goalkeeper Fred Davies was spotted by Wolves keeping goal for Borough United, a Llandudno side playing in the Welsh League. He had to wait almost five years before making his League debut for the Molineux club – helping Wolves beat Spurs 3–1 in February 1962. He had, though, been pushed into the big-time the previous Saturday when he played against arch rivals West Bromwich Albion in an FA Cup tie. While with Wolves, he helped them win promotion from Division Two in 1966–67, but in January 1968 Jimmy Scoular paid £10,000 to bring the wholehearted 'keeper to Ninian Park. After making his debut in a 3–0 home defeat of Portsmouth, Davies missed very few games, helping the Bluebirds mount serious promotion challenges in 1968–69 and 1969–70. Allowed to join Bournemouth in the close season, he starred in the Cherries' Fourth Division promotion-winning side of 1970–71. After retiring he became trainer/coach at Dean Court and then followed his good friend John Bond to Norwich, Manchester City, Swansea and Birmingham as coach.

DAVIES Gareth Melville

Central-defender

*Born: Hereford, 11 December 1973.
Career: Hereford United 1992. Crystal Palace 1995. Cardiff City (loan) 1997. Reading 1997. Swindon Town 1999. Chippenham Town.*

■ Welsh Under-21 international central-defender Gareth Davies started his career with his home-town club, Hereford United. A strong, forceful tackler, also capable of playing in midfield, he had played in 111 games for the Edgar Street club when Crystal Palace paid £120,000 for him in the summer of 1995. In his first season at Selhurst Park he was in and out of the Palace side, but midway through the 1996–97 campaign manager Dave Bassett loaned him out to Cardiff City. He scored on his debut in a 2–0 defeat of Hartlepool United and against Scarborough but was then recalled to Selhurst Park by Palace's new manager, Steve Coppell. Still unable to win a regular place, he was transferred to Reading. Initially he proved to be one of Terry Bullivant's best signings, but when he was sacked Davies couldn't impress new boss Tommy Burns. Forced to train on his own until the PFA were called in to settle the dispute, Davies left to play for Swindon Town. Unable to prevent their relegation, he then suffered serious injury problems that required surgery and missed the entire 2000–01 season. Eventually forced to announce his retirement from the professional game, he subsequently joined Chippenham Town.

DAVIES Gareth Robert

Midfield

*Born: Cardiff, 6 October 1959.
Career: Sully. Cardiff City 1986.*

■ A Welsh League player with Sully and a director in his family's printing business, Gareth Davies was engaged by the Bluebirds on non-contract terms. After making his Football League debut

in a 2–0 defeat at Stockport County, he returned to City's reserve team, but failed to make much impression on the professional ranks, making just one further substitute appearance before leaving the club.

DAVIES John Gerwyn

Goalkeeper

*Born: Llandysul, 18 November 1959.
Career: Cardiff City 1977. Hull City 1980. Notts County (loan) 1986.*

■ Welsh-speaking goalkeeper John Davies's chances at Ninian Park were limited due to the fine form of Ron Healey. In two seasons with the club he made seven League appearances and was on the winning side only once. Also in those games the club suffered a couple of heavy defeats. In the summer of 1980 he was transferred to Hull City for £12,000, going on to make 24 appearances for the Tigers as well as spending a period on loan at Notts County.

DAVIES Leonard Stephen (Len)

Forward

*Born: Splott, 28 April 1899.
Died: 1945.
Career: Victoria Athletic. Cardiff City 1920. Thames 1931. Bangor City.*

Welsh Cup winner 1921–22, 1922–23, 1926–27, 1927–28, 1929–30. Division One runner-up 1923–24. FA Cup winner 1926–27. FA Charity Shield winner 1927–28. Welsh Cup finalist 1928–29.

■ On leaving school, Len Davies, one of Cardiff City's greatest-ever players, qualified as a marine engineer and spent some time at sea before returning to soccer and signing for the Bluebirds. At Ninian Park Davies enjoyed a long and illustrious career and was part of the 1927 FA Cup Final winning team. He had earlier suffered the disappointment of being left out of the 1925 FA Cup Final team, who faced Sheffield United. Throughout the 1920s Len Davies was a great favourite, and he remains the only player to score over 100 League goals for the club. During that time he netted

hat-tricks against Bradford City (home, 6–2, in 1921–22) and Chelsea (home, 6–1, in 1922–23), while in 1923–24 he netted all four goals in a 4–2 win at West Bromwich Albion and all four again against Bury at home, winning 4–1, in 1924–25. Ironically, though, he is probably best remembered for the goal he missed rather than those he scored. In 1924 Cardiff required two points from their match with Birmingham to take the First Division title. The Bluebirds were awarded a penalty, which no one was anxious to take. Len Davies stepped up but missed, and the match ended goalless. Cardiff City were left as runners-up to Huddersfield Town. After the match, Davies was inconsolable and he was haunted by the penalty miss for the rest of his life. In 1929 Davies toured Canada with the FAW party, and in one match in Vancouver he hit seven goals against a Lower Mainland XI. He later captained Thames in their last season of League football and played in the 9–2 defeat by Cardiff, which is City's record League win at Ninian Park. Davies then had a spell as player-manager of Bangor City before later working in wartime aircraft production at Speke, Liverpool. Sadly, he died of pneumonia shortly after World War Two, aged 46.

DAVIES Paul Andrew

Forward

*Born: Kidderminster, 9 October 1960.
Career: Oldswinford Town. Cardiff City*

1978. Trowbridge Town. SC Heracles (Holland). Kidderminster Harriers.

■ Signed from non-League Oldswinford Town, Paul Davies failed to bridge the gap into League football, this in spite of a reasonable goalscoring record at reserve level. On leaving Ninian Park, after a couple of first-team appearances, Davies had a spell with Trowbridge Town before spending a year in Holland with SC Heracles of Almelo. He then returned to the UK to join Kidderminster Harriers where he won England semi-professional honours and appeared in the club's FA Trophy-winning side against Burton Albion in 1987.

DAVIES Ronald Thomas

Full-back

Born: Merthyr Tydfil, 21 September 1932.
Career: Merthyr Tydfil. Cardiff City 1952. Southampton 1958. Aldershot 1964.

■ Full-back Ron Davies spent much of his six years at Ninian Park in City's reserve side, though during the early part of 1957–58 he had a run of five games at centre-forward, scoring three goals. In March 1958 he left the Bluebirds and joined Southampton to replace the recently departed Len Wilkins. He played his part in the Saints' rise from the Third Division to becoming a top Second Division outfit. In August 1964, after playing in 161 League games for the south coast club, he moved to Aldershot and spent two seasons at the Recreation Ground before retiring.

DAVIES Stanley Charles (Stan)

Forward

Born: Chirk, 24 March 1898.
Died: 1972.
Career: Chirk. Rochdale. Preston North End 1919. Everton 1920. West Bromwich Albion 1921. Birmingham 1927. Cardiff City 1928. Rotherham United 1929. Barnsley 1930. Manchester Central. Dudley Town.

■ Welsh international forward Stan Davies worked in the coal mines in Chirk for 12 months before he began playing for the local club. When war broke out Davies found himself in France on the Western Front with the Royal Welsh Fusiliers. Wounded at Cambrai, he then joined the Army Signalling School, ending the war with the Military Medal and the Belgian Croix de Guerre. He resumed his football during wartime with Rochdale before joining Preston North End at the end of the hostilities. He failed to settle at Deepdale and moved to Everton. After scoring a hat-trick against Manchester United on the opening day of the 1921–22 season, the Blues surprisingly allowed him to join West Bromwich Albion. In four seasons at the Hawthorns he was Albion's leading scorer – an aggregate total of 77 goals in 147 League games. He spent a season with Birmingham before moving to Cardiff in the summer of 1928. Nicknamed 'Mr Versatility', he could give a good account of himself in any position, but, though he impressed on his debut in a 1–1 draw at Newcastle United, he struggled to get into a City side rooted at the foot of the First Division. On leaving Ninian Park he became player-manager of Rotherham United, but lack of success turned a section of the supporters against him, and he then drifted into non-League football with Manchester City Central and later Dudley Town.

DAVIES William (Willie)

Outside-right

Born: Troedyrhiwfuwch, 16 February 1900.
Died: 1953.
Career: Rhymney. Swansea Amateurs. Swansea Town 1921. Cardiff City 1924. Notts County 1927. Tottenham Hotspur 1929. Swansea Town 1933. Llanelly.

FA Cup finalist 1924–25.

■ Willie Davies played for the village team in Troedyrhiwfuwch before joining Rhymney, for whom he once hit 61 goals in a single season. He was signed by Swansea and filled every forward position before settling down on the right wing. While with the Swans, he won the first of his 17 Welsh caps, but in the summer of 1924 Cardiff took advantage of Swansea's financial plight and brought him to Ninian Park. In his first season he was part of City's FA Cup side and scored a vital goal directly from a corner-kick in the quarter-final against Leicester City to win the match in the dying seconds. A serious chest illness then put him out of action for a year, forcing him to miss the club's 1927 FA Cup Final win, but he came back briefly to first-team action before joining Notts County. He spent two seasons at Meadow Lane prior to signing for Tottenham Hotspur. The fast-raiding winger, who continually popped up in goalscoring positions, spent four seasons at White Hart Lane before winding down his career with Swansea and Llanelly before, in 1938, taking charge of the caretaking department of Pontarddulais schools.

DAVIES Wilfred James (Jim)

Outside-left

Born: Cardiff.
Career: Troedyrhiw. Cardiff City 1938.

■ Winger Jim Davies joined the Bluebirds from Troedyrhiw in November 1938, along with Billy Baker. His only appearance in the club's League side came the following month when he provided the cross for Jimmy Collins to score City's goal in a 1–1 draw at Aldershot. He remained with the club until the outbreak of World War Two, but all his other appearances in a blue shirt were for the reserves.

DEAN Norman

Forward

Born: Corby, 13 September 1944.
Career: Corby Town. Southampton 1963. Cardiff City 1967. Barnsley 1968.

Welsh Cup winner 1966–67. 1967–68.

■ Norman Dean began his career with Southampton, where in 1965–66 he made a great impact, scoring 11 vital goals in the Saints' promotion to Division One. Included in that total was a hat-trick in a 5–2 win over south coast rivals Portsmouth. Signed for Cardiff City by Jimmy Scoular just before the transfer deadline in March 1967, Dean failed to command a regular place at Ninian Park. His greatest achievement came during City's European campaign of 1967–68, when he got into the team because of Bobby Brown's injury and Brian Clark's ineligibility, and scored the winner against Moscow Torpedo in the play-off at Augsburg and netted in both legs of the semi-final against Hamburg. In September 1968 he joined Barnsley, but his career at Oakwell was blighted by injury and a broken leg forced him to miss the entire 1971–72 season. He tried desperately to regain full fitness but was forced into early retirement.

DEIGHTON James (Jack)

Goalkeeper

Born: Liverpool.
Career: Everton 1934. Cardiff City 1935.

■ Unable to make the grade with Everton due to the outstanding form of long-serving goalkeeper Ted Sagar, Jack Deighton arrived at Ninian Park in 1935–36 to contest the number-one jersey with Jack Leckie and George Poland. Though he ended the campaign by playing in the last 11 games, he was not retained and moved into the local leagues, playing for a number of clubs.

DELANEY Mark Anthony

Right-back

Born: Fishguard, 13 May 1976.
Career: Carmarthen Town. Cardiff City 1998. Aston Villa 1999.

Division Three Promotion 1998–99.

■ Mark Delaney was plucked from League of Wales side Carmarthen Town by Cardiff City manager Frank Burrows in the summer of 1998. Although most Bluebirds fans thought his signing was unwise, he soon won them over with some exciting displays. Towards the end of his first season, in which he was selected by his peers for the PFA award-winning Third Division team, Delaney left Ninian Park to join Aston Villa for a fee of £500,000. The Cardiff fans complained bitterly because the club had let him go. He soon established himself as a regular in the Villa side and appeared in the FA Cup Final against Chelsea to crown a fine first full season in the Premiership – a campaign in which he won the first of 26 Welsh caps. Two separate knee injuries then kept him out of the Villa side, and he had

only just returned to first-team action when he sustained a broken right foot playing for Wales against Azerbaijan. He then had a cartilage operation and, shortly after returning to the side, suffered cruciate ligament damage, which brought his 2002–03 season to a premature end. Injuries have continued to hamper his progress at both club and international level for this reliable, defensively composed and strong full-back.

DEMANGE Kenneth John Philip Petit

Midfield

Born: Dublin, 3 September 1964.
Career: Home Farm. Liverpool 1983. Scunthorpe United (loan) 1986. Leeds United 1987. Hull City 1988. Cardiff City (loan) 1990. Cardiff City (loan) 1991. Limerick 1992. Ards 1993. Bohemians 1994. Dundalk 1994.

■ A Republic of Ireland Youth international, winning the Irish Young Player of the Year award as a 17-year-old with Home Farm, he signed a three-year contract with Liverpool, though he never got a League game. He did, though, win full international honours for the Republic of Ireland when he came off the bench against Brazil in Dublin in May 1987. Having spent a brief period on loan with Scunthorpe United, he left Anfield to play for Leeds United and marked his debut with an early goal against Manchester City. Though he looked to have the makings of a fine player, he was surprisingly allowed to leave and joined Hull City for £65,000. In and out of the side at Hull, he was loaned to Cardiff twice, in November 1990 and the following March, making 15 appearances for the struggling Bluebirds. After Hull cancelled his contract he returned to Ireland to join Limerick. Twelve months later, in 1993, he moved north to Ards, later returning to the Republic to play for Bohemians and Dundalk.

DERRETT Stephen Clifford

Full-back

Born: Cardiff, 16 October 1947.
Career: Cardiff City 1965. Carlisle United

1972. Aldershot (loan) 1973. Rotherham United 1973. Newport County 1976. Barry Town. Bridgend.

Welsh Cup winner 1968–69.

■ After working his way up through the ranks at Ninian Park, full-back Steve Derrett made his first-team debut for the Bluebirds in Holland in a European Cup-Winners' Cup match, making his League debut at home to Birmingham City in November 1967. Equally at home at full-back or as a sweeper, where his quick powers of recovery were used to advantage, he won four full caps for Wales, although two of his appearances saw the national side suffer heavy defeats at the hands of Scotland and Italy. Derrett, whose only goal came in a 5–1 defeat at Sheffield United in April 1971, left Cardiff in 1972 to join Carlisle United. Unable to settle at Brunton Park, he had a brief loan spell with Aldershot before moving to Rotherham United. He had quite a lengthy stay at Millmoor before returning to South Wales with Newport County. After a knee injury ended his first-team career, he went into non-League football with Barry Town and later Bridgend. While at Somerton Park he obtained an FA coaching qualification and was appointed assistant warden at a Cardiff youth club. He later worked as a sales representative for a safety equipment firm in Cardiff.

DIAMOND John James (Jack)

Centre-forward

Born: Middlesbrough, 30 October 1910.
Died: 1961.
Career: Bethesda (Hull). East Riding Amateurs. Beverley White Star. Hull City 1931. Newark Town. Shelbourne. Southport 1933. Barnsley 1934. Cardiff City 1935. Bury 1936. Oldham Athletic 1936. Hartlepool United 1938. Hyde United.

■ After beginning his League career with Hull City, where he made just one appearance, he went over to Ireland to play for Shelbourne. After scoring 33 goals in 1932–33, 'Legs', as he was known, named after the notorious American gangster of the period, returned to Football League action with Southport. He scored 28 goals in 48 games for the Sandgrounders, and following a brief spell with Barnsley he joined Cardiff City. Finding himself in and out of the Bluebirds side in 1935–36, he still managed to score a goal every other game – 9 in 18 outings, including a spell of five in six games. Moving on to Bury and later Oldham Athletic where he top scored in 1937–38 with 18 goals in 39 games, Diamond ended his first-team career with Hartlepool United.

DIBBLE Andrew Gerald (Andy)

Goalkeeper

Born: Cwmbran, 8 May 1965.
Career: Cardiff City 1982. Luton Town 1984. Sunderland (loan) 1986. Huddersfield Town (loan) 1987. Manchester City 1988. Aberdeen (loan) 1990. Middlesbrough (loan) 1991. Bolton Wanderers (loan) 1991. West Bromwich Albion (loan) 1992. Glasgow Rangers 1997. Luton Town 1997. Middlesbrough 1998. Altrincham. Hartlepool United 1999. Carlisle United (loan) 1999. Stockport County 2000. Wrexham 2001.

Welsh Cup finalist 1981–82. Division Three runner-up 1982–83.

■ Much-travelled goalkeeper Andy Dibble began his League career with Cardiff City, making his debut on his

17th birthday as the Bluebirds went down to a single goal home defeat by Crystal Palace. Cardiff were relegated that season, but Dibble was the club's first-choice 'keeper the following season, helping his side win promotion at the first attempt. In 1983–84 he played in all but one match, his performances alerting a number of the top clubs. In July 1984 Luton Town paid £125,000 for his services, but his early displays were disappointing and he was loaned out to Sunderland and Huddersfield Town. He returned to help the Hatters win the League Cup Final in 1988 when his save from Nigel Winterburn's penalty helped Luton beat Arsenal 3–2. In June 1988 Manchester City paid £240,000 for him, and although while at Maine Road he made more appearances for the club that he did anywhere else he still had loan spells with Aberdeen, Middlesbrough, Bolton and West Bromwich Albion. In March 1997 he joined Rangers, making his debut in a 1–0 win over Celtic in the Old Firm Derby, helping the Ibrox club record a ninth successive Championship. After that, he had brief spells with Luton and Middlesbrough before playing non-League football for Altrincham. He returned to League action with Hartlepool, Carlisle United and Stockport County before joining Wrexham. As well as inspiring his colleagues at the Racecourse Ground to promotion, he acted as goalkeeping coach to the Robins.

DIXON Cecil Hubert

Outside-right

Born: Trowbridge, 28 March 1935.
Career: Trowbridge Town. Cardiff City 1954. Newport County 1957. Northampton Town 1961.

■ Winger Cecil Dixon joined the Bluebirds from non-League Trowbridge Town in the summer of 1954 and, though he spent three seasons at Ninian Park, much of his time was spent in the club's Combination side. He did get on the scoresheet once – in a 2–1 defeat of Birmingham in November 1955 – but his progress to regular first-team football was blocked by Gordon Nutt, Mike Tiddy and later Brian Walsh. One

of a number of City players to join Newport County, he went on to score 15 goals in 107 League games for the Somerton Park club, before finishing his first-class career with Northampton Town.

DOBBS Gerald Francis

Midfield

Born: Lambeth, 24 January 1971.
Career: Wimbledon 1989. Cardiff City (loan) 1995.

■ Midfielder Gerald Dobbs began his playing career with Wimbledon but having signed professional forms had to wait almost three years before, in April 1992, making his League debut against Nottingham Forest. Over the next few seasons he produced some consistent displays – creating a good impression, especially with his ability to cross the ball from the left touchline. However, he was languishing in the Dons reserve side when, in September 1995, he was loaned out to Cardiff City. Unfortunately, after just four first-team games, he was forced to return to London, having aggravated a previous injury, and spent the rest of the campaign on the sidelines before being released.

DONNELLY Peter

Centre-forward

Born: Hull, 22 September 1936.
Career: Doncaster Rovers 1954. Scunthorpe United 1958. Cardiff City 1960. Swansea City 1961. Brighton & Hove Albion 1962. Bradford City 1965.

■ Centre-forward Peter Donnelly was released by his first club, Doncaster Rovers, after just a handful of first-team outings and joined Scunthorpe United. His impressive form – 19 goals in 39 games – prompted Cardiff manager Bill Jones to offer Joe Bonson in exchange for him. Joining the Bluebirds on their return to the top flight, he proved to be a more than useful, bustling forward, teaming up well with Derek Tapscott and Graham Moore and scoring the winning goal in a 2–1 defeat of Leicester City by charging England 'keeper Gordon Banks into the Canton End goal! Surprisingly allowed to join rivals Swansea, he later played for

Brighton & Hove Albion and Bradford City.

DOWNING Keith Gordon

Midfield

Born: Oldbury, 23 July 1965.
Career: Mile Oak Rovers. Notts County 1984. Wolverhampton Wanderers 1987. Birmingham City 1993. Stoke City 1994. Cardiff City 1995. Hereford United 1995.

■ Nicknamed 'Psycho' by the Molineux faithful following his aggressive displays in midfield, Keith Downing played his early football for Mile Oak Rovers before joining Notts County. Unable to hold down a regular first-team place at Meadow Lane, he moved to Wolves in the summer of 1987, and in his first season he helped the club win the Fourth Division Championship and was a member of the side that won the Sherpa Van Trophy. In 1988–89 he helped Wolves win the Third Division title and continued to be an important member of the side for the next few seasons. Injuries then began to restrict his appearances, and in 1993, after appearing in 228 games, he left to join Birmingham City. After just two games he suffered a serious leg injury and on recovery moved on to Stoke City, where he was later given a free transfer. After a

short spell with the Bluebirds at the start of the 1995–96 season, he left to play for Hereford United, and, though he helped them reach the play-offs, he suffered with a chronic back ailment and had to retire.

DUDLEY Frank Ernest

Inside-forward

Born: Southend, 9 May 1925.
Career: Southend United 1945. Leeds United 1949. Southampton 1951. Cardiff City 1953. Brentford 1953. Folkestone.

■ As a 15-year-old Frank Dudley was only 5ft 4in tall and had no ambitions to be a footballer, but after shooting up another six inches he joined his home-town club Southend United as an amateur trialist, turning professional in October 1945. His versatility for the Roots Hall club attracted the attention of a number of top clubs, and in the summer of 1949 he joined Leeds United. Filling all of the forward positions, he ended his first season at Elland Road as the Yorkshire club's leading scorer. Renowned for his fierce shooting, he joined Southampton, signing for the south coast club on a Leeds–London train. Having proved to be a prolific scorer for the Saints, he joined Cardiff in October 1953, making his debut in a 3–0 reversal at Burnley. He did get on the scoresheet in a 5–0 rout of Charlton Athletic before leaving to continue his career with Brentford. During the course of that 1953–54 season he achieved a remarkable record when his first three League goals were for different clubs in different Divisions – Southampton (Third South), Cardiff City (First) and Brentford (Second). Having scored 118 League goals for his five clubs, he later played non-League football for Folkestone before returning to Southend as the club's youth-team coach.

DURBAN William Alan

Midfield

Born: Bridgend, 7 July 1941.
Career: Cardiff City 1958. Derby County 1963. Shrewsbury Town 1973.

■ Alan Durban joined Cardiff City in September 1958 and made his League

debut a year later in a 2–1 win at Derby County, the club with which he was to make his name. At Ninian Park Durban was a more than useful inside-forward, but after an in-and-out period he was transferred to Derby County for just £10,000. It was certainly money well spent as Durban was one of the few players at the Baseball Ground to survive and play a significant role in the Brian Clough era. Durban had two distinct phases at Derby: first as a goalscoring inside-forward and second as an intelligent midfield player. In his first role he scored 24 goals in 1964–65, going on to score 112 goals in 403 first-team games for the Rams, including four hat-tricks, but there is no doubt that his best days at the club were when he played in midfield. Durban spent 10 years at the Baseball Ground and was a major influence in the team's rise to the First Division and, in 1971–72, its capture of the League Championship. On leaving Derby he joined Shrewsbury Town, later becoming their player-manager. He steered the club out of the Fourth Division and to Welsh Cup success. He later managed Stoke City, taking them into the top flight in 1978–79, and Sunderland, where after three troubled years he was sacked. Six

months later he was appointed manager of Cardiff City, but it turned out to be a bad move. After the Bluebirds suffered relegation in two successive seasons, Durban was dismissed.

DURKAN James (Jack)

Right-back

Born: Bannockburn, 14 July 1915.
Career: King's Park. Cardiff City 1933. Bristol Rovers 1934.

■ Full-back Jack Durkan arrived at Ninian Park from King's Park in 1933, and, though he only appeared in six League games during the club's re-election season of 1933–34, he appeared at both right and left-back. Not retained by the club, he moved on to Bristol Rovers where, at the end of the following season, he left to play non-League football.

DURRELL Joseph Timothy

Outside-left

Born: Stepney, 15 March 1953.
Career: West Ham United 1970. Bristol City 1973. Cardiff City (loan) 1975. Gillingham 1975.

■ Stepney-born winger Joe Durrell worked his way up through the ranks at Upton Park to appear in a handful of League games for West Ham United at the start of the 1970s. Unable to make much headway with the Hammers, he joined Bristol City but again struggled to hold down a first-team place. Cardiff manager Jimmy Andrews took him on loan at the start of the 1975–76 season, and he appeared in two games, being substituted in the second, before returning to Ashton Gate. A quick, tricky, wide man, he later moved to Gillingham where he helped the recently promoted Kent club consolidate their position in Division Three.

DUTHIE John Flett

Wing-half

Born: Fraserburgh, 7 January 1903.
Died: 1969.
Career: Fraserburgh Town. Hartlepool United. Clydebank. Hartlepool United 1923. Norwich City 1924. Queen's Park Rangers 1927. York City 1928. Crystal

Palace 1929. York City 1930. Crewe Alexandra 1931. Aberdeen 1932. Workington 1932. Cardiff City 1933. Caerau.

■ A much-travelled and versatile player, John Duthie played Scottish junior football for Fraserburgh Town before moving south to Hartlepool United in 1922. He had a brief loan spell back in Scotland with Clydebank before rejoining Hartlepool. Though he spent three seasons at the Victoria Ground, he played most of his games in the reserves, until 1924 when he moved to Norwich City. Able to play at either wing-half or inside-forward, Duthie journeyed to Queen's Park Rangers, York City, Crystal Palace and Crewe Alexandra before returning north of the border for a stint with Aberdeen. He joined Cardiff for the start of the disastrous re-election season of 1933–34, but he made little impression, and in the close season he was released and joined Welsh League club Caerau.

DWYER Philip John

Defender

Born: Cardiff, 28 October 1953.
Career: Cardiff City 1971. Rochdale (loan) 1985.

Welsh Cup winner 1972–73. 1973–74. 1975–76.

Welsh Cup finalist 1974–75, 1976–77. Division Three runner-up 1975–76.

■ One of the Cardiff City greats, Phil Dwyer holds the club record for the greatest number of appearances for the Bluebirds, with a total of 573. Never one to shirk a challenge, Dwyer won Under-21 and Under-23 international honours before securing the first of 10 full caps for Wales against Iran in 1978 – a match in which he scored the only goal. A member of the successful Bluebirds youth team of 1971, he made his debut for the Cardiff side in a goalless draw at Orient in October 1972. He held his place for the rest of the season and ended the campaign with his first Welsh Cup medal when Bangor City were beaten over two legs. An ever present in 1973–74, he won another Welsh Cup medal and played in 76 consecutive matches from his debut until injury forced him to miss a game. In 1975–76 he missed just one game – a 4–1 defeat at Hereford – as the Bluebirds won promotion to the Second Division. At the end of that season he won his third Welsh Cup medal, scoring two goals in the first leg against Hereford United in a tie that City won 6–5 on aggregate. Despite a series of niggling injuries, he missed very few games and was ever present in 1983–84. Although the majority of his 573 games were played at full-back or in the centre of defence, he still managed to sore 50 goals. City manager Alan Durban let him leave Ninian Park towards the end of the

1984–85 season, and he joined Rochdale on loan. Hanging up his boots, he joined the South Wales Police Force in Barry.

EADIE James

Goalkeeper

Born: Alexandria, 4 February 1947.
Career: Kirkintilloch Rob Roy. Cardiff City 1966. Chester City (loan) 1972. Bristol Rovers 1973. Bath City.

Welsh Cup winner 1970–71.

■ Easy-going Scot Jim Eadie joined the Bluebirds from his local club Kirkintilloch Rob Roy but had to wait a number of seasons before keeping a clean sheet on his debut in a 2–0 win over Portsmouth in March 1970. The following season he replaced Frank Parsons as City's number-one 'keeper and was outstanding as the club just missed out on promotion to the First Division. The following season he had to make way for Bill Irwin and, after a loan spell with Chester, joined Bristol Rovers. He kept clean sheets in his first five games for the Pirates and in 1972–73 was an underrated factor in Rovers' promotion to the Second Division, once going nearly 700 minutes without conceding a goal. He went on to appear in 204 games for the then Eastville club before ending his career with a spell at non-League Bath City.

EARNSHAW Robert

Forward

Born: Zambia, 6 April 1981.
Career: Cardiff City 1998. Morton (loan) 2000. West Bromwich Albion 2004. Norwich City 2005.

FAW Invitation Cup finalist 1999–2000. Division Three runner-up 2000–01. Division Two promotion 2002–03.

■ During his early days in football, Zambian-born Rob Earnshaw wanted to play international football for the country of his birth. His mother was a Zambian women's international while his uncle played football for a top Belgian club. Having joined Cardiff City, he scored 47 goals for the club's youth team in 1997–98, including a hat-trick in the Midland Bank Welsh Cup

Final against Llanelli. It was from this point that he started to celebrate all his goals with a somersault. Earnshaw's first goal for the full City side came at Hartlepool United on the opening day of the 1998–99 season – a stunning overhead kick. As the season unfolded, he had loan spells with Fulham and Middlesbrough without being called into either club's first team. There followed a further loan spell with Scottish League side Morton, where Earnshaw scored twice in his three games. He finally established himself in the Cardiff side in 2000–01 when he top scored for the Bluebirds with 25 goals, including a hat-trick in the FA Cup against Bristol Rovers and another in the Third Division game with Torquay United. Voted Cardiff's Young Player of the Year, he was also selected for the PFA's Third Division team. Despite suffering from a spate of injuries in 2001–02 he still managed 15 goals. Undoubtedly the highlight of his injury-hit campaign came on his full debut for Wales against Germany at the Millennium Stadium, where he produced an outstanding forward display and scored the game's only goal. The 2002–03 season was a phenomenal one for Earnshaw. He made his first start in the League Cup against Boston United, and, after netting a hat-trick, he went on to score 35 goals in all competitions. In so doing, he broke two of the club's long-standing records – his tally of 31 League goals beat Stan Richards's total of 30 set in the first season after World War Two and his total of 35 in all games broke Hughie Ferguson's record of 32 set in 1926–27. He continued to feature for Wales and was voted into the PFA Second Division team just as the Bluebirds won promotion to the First Division. In the 2003–04 season Earnshaw, who netted a hat-trick in the 4–0 defeat of Scotland, continued to score with great regularity, netting four against Gillingham in a total of 26. He had scored 104 goals in 199 League and Cup games for Cardiff when, in September 2004, he signed for West Bromwich Albion. Although never a regular in the first team, he proved to be a very useful asset when called off the bench and ended the season as the club's top scorer with 14 goals. He also had the distinction of scoring the club's first Premiership hat-trick in a 4–1 win at Charlton Athletic. Nevertheless, he was allowed to join Norwich City after just one season at the Hawthorns and scored the only goal of the game when the Canaries visited Ninian Park towards the end of the 2005–06 season.

ECKHARDT Jeffrey Edward

Central-defender/midfield

Born: Sheffield, 7 October 1965.
Career: Sheffield United 1984. Fulham 1987. Stockport County 1994. Cardiff City 1996. Newport County.

FAW Invitation Cup finalist 1997–98. Division Three promotion 1998–99. Division Three runner-up 2000–01.

■ Utility player Jeff Eckhardt began his League career with his home-town club Sheffield United before, in November 1987, moving to Fulham for a fee of £50,000. Able to play at the back, in midfield or up front, Eckhardt missed very few games over the next seven seasons and had appeared in 268 League

and Cup games, scoring 25 goals, when, in July 1994, he was transferred to Stockport County, also for £50,000. After two seasons at Edgeley Park, Eckhardt moved to South Wales, with Cardiff paying £30,000 for his services. He soon showed himself to be a very determined, hardworking player, who brought much needed steel to a defence that badly needed bolstering. He scored

on his debut in a 1–0 defeat of Brighton and netted another four in City's chase for a play-off place. After missing the first four games of the 1997–98 season through injury, his progress was further hampered by illness and more injuries, though he still netted some crucial goals when he did turn out. Early the following season it looked as if City were prepared to sell him to Hull City, but he earned a new contract when he convinced manager Frank Burrows that he could still do the job in the Second Division. After two more seasons at Ninian Park, City somewhat surprisingly decided not to offer him a new deal. Eckhardt immediately received an offer from another Third Division club and, though he is a qualified chiropodist, he decided to continue playing with Newport County.

EDGLEY Brian Kenneth

Inside-forward

Born: Shrewsbury, 26 August 1937.
Career: Shrewsbury Town 1956. Cardiff City 1960. Brentford 1961. Barnsley 1962. Caernarfon Town. Hereford United.

■ Inside-forward Brian Edgley began his Football League career with his home-town club Shrewsbury Town, going on to score 12 goals in 113 League outings before being signed by Cardiff boss Bill Jones in July 1960. Signed primarily as understudy to Welsh international Graham Moore, he stayed just one season at Ninian Park, his only goal coming in a 3–0 home win over Manchester United midway through that 1960–61 season. He left the Bluebirds to play for Brentford, later ending his League career with Barnsley. He then had a spell with Caernarfon in the mid-1960s before emigrating to South Africa. On his return to these shores, he ended his playing days at Hereford.

EDWARDS George

Outside-left

Born: Treherbert, 2 December 1920.
Career: Swansea City 1938. Birmingham City 1944. Cardiff City 1948.

Welsh Cup finalist 1950–51. Division Two runner-up 1951–52.

■ George Edwards was one of football's outstanding wingers of the 1940s. He began his career as an amateur with Swansea and made his first-team debut towards the end of the 1938–39 season.

Before the outbreak of World War Two he had won a Welsh amateur cap against England. During the hostilities he continued to play for the Swans while studying for a degree at Swansea University. When he was called up to the RAF he was stationed in the Midlands and 'guested' for Coventry City. In 1945–46 he played for Wales in the Victory Internationals, and in October 1946 he won the first of 12 full caps in Wales's 3–1 defeat of Scotland. By now, George Edwards was a Birmingham player, having helped them win the League South title in 1945–46. He also helped the St Andrew's club win the Second Division title in 1947–48 before, midway through the following season, joining Cardiff City for a fee of £12,000. An ideal replacement for Roy Clarke, who had left Ninian Park for Manchester City, he made his debut in a 2–2 draw at Leicester before scoring on his home debut in a 6–1 rout of Bradford Park Avenue. A member of the Bluebirds team that won promotion to the First Division in 1951–52, providing a number of chances for both Chisholm and Grant, he netted hat-tricks in the 7–1 Welsh Cup win at Bangor in March 1951 and in a 6–1 win against the Jersey Saturday League in a friendly two months later. When he decided to leave

the game in 1955 he was still Cardiff's first-choice left-winger and playing well. Broadcaster and contributor to a Sunday newspaper, he was later invited to join the Ninian Park club's board of directors, a position he held for almost 30 years.

EDWARDS Leonard Trevor

Full-back

Born: Rhondda, 24 January 1937.
Career: Charlton Athletic 1956. Cardiff City 1960. Hakoah (Australia).

■ Trevor Edwards had appeared in just a handful of Football League matches for Charlton Athletic when he was selected by Wales as a replacement for Alf Sherwood. After appearing in two full international matches, he took part in Wales's first-ever Under-23 match. Edwards, a nephew of Dai Astley, was a quick-tackling defender, whose pace enabled him to cover well, and he could play in either full-back position and distribute the ball well. His consistent performances in the Addicks defence attracted attention from Liverpool but nothing came of it. Edwards had appeared in 64 games for Charlton when, in the summer of 1960, he was transferred to Cardiff City. While he was with the Bluebirds, he had a spell in the forward line, scoring three goals, but after appearing in 73 League games for

the Ninian Park club he lost his place through injury. Unable to regain his first-team spot, he decided to emigrate to Australia, where he continued his soccer career playing for Hakoah.

EGAN Henry (Harry)

Forward

Born: Tibshelf, 23 February 1912.
Died: 1979.
Career: Sutton Town. Brighton & Hove Albion 1933. Southend United 1936. Aldershot 1937. Cardiff City 1938.

■ Having begun his career with non-League Sutton Town, Harry Egan was given a chance at League level with Brighton & Hove Albion. Unable to hold down a regular place, he joined Southend United, but after just a handful of appearances he moved to Aldershot. It was here that his career blossomed, and in 1937–38 he was the Shots leading scorer with 13 goals in 41 games. Having taken his tally of goals to 19 in 59 games, he impressed playing for Aldershot against Cardiff, and this prompted City boss Bill Jennings to pay £1,500 for his services. Unhappily for Egan, who scored on his debut in a 1–1 draw at Exeter and had scored nine goals in 17 games, World War Two brought an end to his career. He 'guested' for both Notts County and Derby County during the hostilities but was not re-signed by Cardiff in 1945.

ELLIOTT Anthony Robert

Goalkeeper

Born: Nuneaton, 30 November 1969.
Career: Birmingham City 1986. Hereford United 1988. Huddersfield Town 1992. Carlisle United 1993. Cardiff City 1996. Scarborough 1998.

■ A goalkeeper, whose only appearance for his first club Birmingham City was in the League Cup, Tony Elliott, who had won England Youth international honours, joined Hereford United. He spent two seasons at Edgar Street before, following spells with Huddersfield Town and Carlisle United, he joined the Bluebirds in July 1996. He started superbly well at Ninian Park, keeping four clean sheets in the opening five games of 1996–97, before back and

calf injuries limited his appearances. Possessing an ability to react quickly, he found on his return to full fitness that he was the club's second choice after City had signed Jon Hallworth. He then left to play for Scarborough and made an immediate impression when he broke the club record by going 353 minutes without conceding a goal. Sadly, the following season, he suffered another serious back injury, which ultimately led to him having to retire from the game prematurely.

ELLIOTT Richard Mark

Midfield

Born: Rhondda, 20 March 1959.
Career: Merthyr Tydfil. Brighton & Hove Albion. Cardiff City 1979. Bournemouth (loan) 1980. Ton Pentre. Wimbledon 1982.

■ Mark Elliott began his career with Merthyr Tydfil where his impressive displays attracted a number of League clubs to Penydarren. Brighton & Hove Albion eventually secured his services, but he found his chances at the Goldstone Ground extremely limited and in 1979 Richie Morgan brought him to Cardiff on a free transfer. After making his City debut in a 1–1 draw at Watford, Elliott played in only a handful of games before moving on to Bournemouth on loan. He then moved into non-League football with Ton Pentre before joining Wimbledon, where he scored his only first-team goal.

ELLIS Keith Duncan

Centre-forward

Born: Sheffield, 6 November 1935.
Career: Sheffield Wednesday 1955. Scunthorpe United 1964. Cardiff City 1964. Lincoln City 1965.

■ A prolific scorer for Sheffield Wednesday, Keith Ellis's early opportunities at Hillsborough were limited due to the fine form of Roy Shiner. Having made his Wednesday debut against Preston North End in March 1955, he didn't play at all the following season and made just six appearances in 1956–57, though he did net a hat-trick against Birmingham City. It was only when Harry Catterick

became manager that Ellis was given a chance, and in 1960–61 he scored 19 goals in 37 games including another treble in a 7–2 win against Manchester United at Old Trafford! After falling out of favour, he moved on to Scunthorpe United, but a few months later Jimmy Scoular exchanged Dick Scott for him. In a short stay at Ninian Park, Ellis netted nine goals in 23 games before moving on to Lincoln City where he ended his career.

ELSEY Karl William

Midfield

Born: Swansea, 20 November 1958.
Career: Pembroke Borough. Queen's Park Rangers 1979. Newport County 1980. Cardiff City 1983. Gillingham 1985. Reading 1988. Maidstone United 1989. Gillingham 1991.

■ Impressive displays for Pembroke Borough led to Queen's Park Rangers giving Karl Elsey his chance at League level. A versatile player, his stay at Loftus Road was not a productive one, and in the summer of 1980 he joined Newport County. He was an important member of the Somerton Park club's squad for three years, scoring 15 goals in 123 League games before being involved in the startling five-man transfer deal

between County and the Bluebirds, which took both him and Nigel Vaughan to Ninian Park. Len Ashurst used him at full-back, but both Jimmy Goodfellow and Alan Durban played him in midfield. Following the club's relegation to the Third Division in 1984–85, he was given a free transfer and snapped up by Gillingham. A regular in the Kent club side, he later played for Reading and Maidstone United in their first season in the Football League before returning to the Priestfield Stadium, where he took his tally of goals to 16 in 155 League appearances before parting company with the Gills.

EMMERSON George Arthur Heads

Outside-right

Born: Bishop Auckland, 15 May 1906.
Died: 1966.
Career: Jarrow. Middlesbrough 1928. Cardiff City 1930. Queen's Park Rangers 1933. Rochdale 1935. Tunbridge Wells Rangers. Gillingham 1937.

■ Winger George Emmerson was spotted playing for Jarrow in his native North East by Middlesbrough and was

offered the chance to play in the Football League. Cardiff City were alerted to his abilities, and manager Fred Stewart brought him to South Wales in June 1930. He stayed with the Bluebirds for three seasons, being ever present in 1931–32 when he scored 10 goals in the League and four more in Cup games. In the summer of 1933 he was involved in a swap deal for Eddie Marcroft of Queen's Park Rangers. Emmerson spent a couple of seasons at Loftus Road before joining Rochdale and later played for Gillingham, this after a spell with Tunbridge Wells Rangers. On hanging up his boots, he resumed his trade as a plumber.

ENDERSBY Scott Ian Glenn

Goalkeeper

Born: Lewisham, 20 February 1962.
Career: Ipswich Town 1979. Tranmere Rovers 1981. Swindon Town 1983. Carlisle United 1985. York City 1987. Cardiff City (loan) 1987.

■ England Youth international goalkeeper Scott Endersby began his career with Ipswich Town but, due to the outstanding form of Paul Cooper, moved on to Tranmere Rovers. He was the Wirral club's first-choice 'keeper for two seasons before, in the summer of 1983, he joined Swindon Town. Some outstanding displays between the posts had the top-flight club scouts flocking to the County Ground, but when he did move it was on to Carlisle United followed by York City. While at Bootham Crescent, he suffered from injuries, and it was after recovering from one of these that he joined Cardiff on loan. Keeping a clean sheet on his debut as City beat his former club Tranmere Rovers 3–0, he made four appearances midway through what was the promotion-winning season of 1987–88, before returning to York City to end his professional career.

ENGLAND Harold Michael

Centre-half

Born: Holywell, 2 December 1941.
Career: Blackburn Rovers 1959. Tottenham Hotspur 1966. Cardiff City 1975. New England Teamen.

Division Three runner-up 1975–76.

■ One of the few Welshmen to have both played for and managed his country, Mike England began his career

Mike England

with Blackburn Rovers, whom he helped win the FA Youth Cup in 1959. He played for Rovers in a variety of positions before settling in central defence, where his height made him dominant in the air, while on the ground his strength and speed made him a daunting prospect for even the quickest of opposition forwards. Eventually, though, he became disenchanted with the Ewood Park club who, it seemed, lacked ambition, as they let a number of their better players join top clubs. England made a series of transfer requests, and in August 1966, having scored 21 goals in 184 games, he left Blackburn to join Tottenham Hotspur for £95,000 – a British transfer record fee for a defender. It wasn't long before he became a great favourite at White Hart Lane. In his first season he helped Spurs lift the FA Cup, and, despite missing the 1971 League Cup Final with an ankle injury, he helped them win the 1972 UEFA Cup and 1973 League Cup. He also appeared and scored in the 1974 UEFA Cup Final. In March 1975, after being troubled by ankle problems, he suddenly announced his retirement after scoring 20 goals in 434 games for Spurs. However, he re-emerged the following August to play for one season with Cardiff. Scoring his only goal in the 1–1 draw at Halifax, he helped the Bluebirds win promotion from the Third Division and then spent the next few summers playing for the New England Teamen. On hanging up his boots, England, who won 44 caps for Wales, became Welsh team manager, taking them close to qualification for both the World Cup and European Championships.

ESLOR John (Jack)

Left-back

Born: Edinburgh.
Career: Heart of Midlothian. Cardiff City 1936. Workington.

■ Full-back Jack Eslor joined the Bluebirds from Heart of Midlothian in December 1936, this after his impressive displays for the Tynecastle club had alerted others in the Football League. After a good debut in a goalless draw at Gillingham, Eslor made just two more

starts before leaving Ninian Park in the close season to continue his career with Workington.

EVANS Anthony

Forward

Born: Liverpool, 11 January 1954.
Career: Formby. Blackpool 1973. Cardiff City 1975. Birmingham City 1979. Crystal Palace 1983. Wolverhampton Wanderers 1984. Bolton Wanderers (loan) 1985. Swindon Town 1985.

Division Three runner-up 1975–76.
Welsh Cup winner 1975–76.

■ A former electrician, Tony Evans began his Football League career with Blackpool but never made his mark at Bloomfield Road, and in the summer of 1975 he joined Cardiff City. In 1975–76 Evans scored 31 goals in 57 matches and topped the club's League goalscoring charts with 21 strikes as the Bluebirds won promotion to Division Two. The club also won the Welsh Cup that season with Vans, and Evans, who netted a hat-trick in a 5–0 win over Sully, scored in both legs of the Final against Hereford United. The following season, Evans was again the club's leading scorer with 24 goals in 57 games, including all four in the 4–4 draw at Bristol Rovers in a League Cup first-round, second-leg tie. In 1977–78 Evans was hampered by a thigh injury, and, though he returned to first-team action in readiness for the 1978–79 campaign, he left Ninian Park at the end of that season to join Birmingham City. Evans, who cost the

Midlands club £120,000, scored 28 goals in 66 League games for them before later playing for Crystal Palace, Wolverhampton Wanderers, Bolton Wanderers (on loan) and Swindon Town.

EVANS Albert H.

Wing-half/inside-forward.

Born: Cardiff.
Career: Cardiff City 1931. Dundalk.

■ In two seasons at Ninian Park Albert Evans, who fluctuated between the wing-half and inside-forward positions, appeared in 22 games without finding the net. Having made his Cardiff debut in a 3–1 defeat at Exeter City, he never appeared in the side on a regular basis, a run of nine consecutive matches in 1932–33 being his best. Disappointed at not being able to secure a regular first-team spot, he left the club to continue his career in Irish football with Dundalk.

EVANS David Andrew

Forward

Born: Aberystwyth, 25 November 1975.
Career: Cardiff City 1994. Merthyr Tydfil.

■ With a lot of enthusiasm added to his natural game, Andy Evans looked a good prospect after making his Bluebirds debut in the final game of the 1993–94 season at Bradford City. The following term he put together 15 first-team appearances, five of them as a starter, but failed to find the net. In 1995–96 Evans proved himself a prolific scorer in the club's junior side, but he made only one appearance in the League side as a last minute replacement for Carl Dale at Cambridge. In February 1996 he became yet another of the players released in the economy drive, joining Cambridge United on trial, but, being injured on his first day of training, he returned to South Wales and Merthyr Tydfil.

EVANS Elfed

Inside-forward

Born: Ferndale, 28 August 1926.
Died: 1988.
Career: Treharris. Cardiff City 1949.

Torquay United (loan) 1951. West Bromwich Albion 1952. Wrexham 1955. Southport 1956.

■ Elfed Evans joined the Bluebirds from Treharris Athletic in May 1949 at a time when the Ninian Park club were having trouble scoring goals. He didn't have too long to wait to make his League debut, playing in a 1–1 draw at Sheffield Wednesday. Though he only played in 20 games in that 1949–50 season, he was the club's top scorer with eight goals, including four in successive games. The following season he had a brief loan spell with Torquay United before later signing for West Bromwich Albion. Evans had impressed Albion officials when scoring against them in the previous season's FA Cup, but he struggled at the Hawthorns and moved on to Wrexham. In 1955–56, his only season at the Racecourse Ground, he was their top scorer, but midway through the following season he left to end his career with Southport.

EVANS Herbert Price (Herbie)

Right-half

Born: Llandaff, 30 August 1894.
Died: 1982.
Career: Cardiff Corinthians. Cardiff City 1920. Tranmere Rovers 1926.

Welsh Cup winner 1921–22, 1922–23. Division One runner-up 1923–24.

■ Herbie Evans was playing as an amateur for Cardiff Corries when he signed for the Bluebirds during their first season of League football. Originally an inside-forward, City converted him to a wing-half. He remained an amateur with City long enough to win an amateur cap against England in 1922. Also a keen cricketer, it was around this time that he had two seasons playing for Glamorgan. After turning professional, he won full international honours, but shortly afterwards he broke his left leg and a difficult recovery meant a two-year absence from first-team football. Losing his place to Harry Wake, Evans moved to Tranmere Rovers, but fate struck again in 1927 when he broke his right-leg, and that cruel blow ended his career.

EVANS John Hugh (Jack)

Outside-left

Born: Bala, 31 January 1889.
Died: 1971.
Career: Bala Wanderers. Welshpool. Wrexham. Cwmparc. Treorchy. Rhondda. Cardiff City 1910. Bristol Rovers 1926.

Division Two runner-up 1920–21. Welsh Cup winner 1921–22, 1922–23. Division One runner-up 1923–24. FA Cup finalist 1924–25.

■ As a youngster Jack Evans, an apprentice printer, turned out for Bala Wanderers rather than Bala Press, the team that featured his three older brothers. After joining Wrexham he sustained a serious shoulder injury and was told his football career was at an end. Deciding to move to South Wales to continue his work as a printer, he played junior football and was soon noticed by Cardiff City. In his first season he scored his side's first goal in the friendly against Aston Villa to mark the opening of Ninian Park on 1 September 1910. Two years later he was the first Cardiff City player to be capped when he was called up as a late substitute for Ted Vizard against Ireland. Standing supreme on the left-wing and with his cannonball shot, he was a consistent scorer – 52 goals in 170 Southern League appearances – until Cardiff's entry to the Football League, when he adopted a more orthodox role. Following Army service he returned to

Ninian Park and scored on his League debut – the club's inaugural game against Stockport County. Nicknamed the 'Bala bang' on account of his fearsome shooting power, Jack Evans once broke the wrist of one goalkeeper and once knocked Sharpe of Manchester City out cold! Evans's career at Ninian Park ended in 1926, and he linked up with Joe Clennell, his former City colleague at Bristol Rovers, before finally retiring from football to become a full-time print compositor.

EVANS Kevin

Midfield

Born: Carmarthen, 16 December 1980.
Career: Leeds United 1998. Swansea City (loan) 2000. Cardiff City 2000. Boston United.

Division Three runner-up 2000–01.

■ When he started out with Leeds United, Kevin Evans was a central-defender, and it was in this position that he played when loaned out to Swansea City. On his return to Elland Road the Welsh Under-21 international was unable to win a first-team spot, and in the summer of 2000 he joined Cardiff City. Bluebirds boss Bobby Gould switched him to a midfield role, and the move was so effective that he stayed in that position. Although he spent much of the 2000–01 season on a learning curve, he featured regularly for the club without really finding consistent form, though he did score some vital goals. Midway through the following season he was allowed to leave Ninian Park and joined Boston United.

EVANS Leslie Norman

Outside-left

Born: Kingswinford, 13 October 1929.
Career: Brierley Hill Alliance. Cardiff City 1950. Plymouth Argyle 1952.

■ Signed from non-League Brierley Hill Alliance, Les Evans found his progress at Ninian Park blocked by the consistency of George Edwards. In two seasons with the club he only made three League appearances, though he did score in a 3–0 home win over Barnsley in March 1952 as City went on to win promotion to Division One. Before the Bluebirds embarked on their campaign in the top flight, Evans had moved on to Plymouth Argyle but was unable to break into the Pilgrims side.

EVANS Paul Alan

Forward

Born: Brentwood, 14 September 1964.
Career: Cardiff City 1982. Brecon Corries. Newport County 1987.

■ After working his way up through the ranks, Paul Evans made his City debut as a substitute for Wayne Matthews in a 1–0 home defeat by Blackburn Rovers in December 1983. He wore the number-12 shirt the following week, again coming off the bench in a 5–2 defeat at Sheffield Wednesday. Unable to make much headway, he joined Brecon Corries before being given another chance at Football League level by Newport County.

EVANS Roland (Rollo)

Left-half

Born: Cardiff.
Career: Bradford City 1930. Bristol Rovers 1931. Cardiff City 1932.

■ Wing-half Rollo Evans had seen service with both Bradford City and Bristol Rovers, without breaking into either club's first team, before joining Cardiff City in September 1932. Strong in the tackle and a good passer of the ball, he made just one appearance for the club, providing the through ball for Stan Cribb to score the winner in a 2–1 defeat of Brentford. He then returned to the club's reserve side before moving into the local non-League scene.

EVANS Sidney John Vivian Leonard (Len)

Goalkeeper

Born: Llandaff, 20 May 1903.
Died: 1977.
Career: Cardiff Corinthians. Aberdare Athletic 1926. Merthyr Town 1927. Cardiff Corinthians. Lovells Athletic. Barry Town. Cardiff City 1930. Birmingham 1933. Svenborg.

■ As a goalkeeper, Len Evans was something of a latter day Leigh Roose – cool and unorthodox!

He was known as a risk taker who made simple shots look difficult, but nonetheless he was a classy and reliable custodian. Perhaps his one weakness, especially in his early days with Cardiff Corries and Aberdare Athletic, was a tendency to be haphazard in clearing a ball. He remained amateur almost throughout, only turning professional in the last six months or so of his career. Between 1925 and 1933 he won a record 12 amateur caps. He made his first full international appearance when Dan Lewis of Arsenal was unable to play – Ted Robbins was struggling to recruit a team to play the Scots, and Len Evans was a natural choice in goal. He kept a clean sheet on his Cardiff City debut in a goalless draw against Preston North End, but, like other goalkeepers before him, he found his progress barred by the indomitable Tom Farquharson. On leaving Ninian Park he became a member of the Barry Police Force but later left to become a PT instructor. He was also one of the first Welshmen to play soccer on the continent when he 'guested' for Svenborg of Sweden.

EVANS Sidney T. (Sid)

Outside-right

Born: Darlaston.
Career: Darlaston. Cardiff City 1920. Manchester United 1923.

■ Signed by manager Fred Stewart from non-League Darlaston, winger Sid Evans made his Cardiff debut in a 1–0 defeat of Leeds United in 1920–21, the club's first season in the Football League. His only goal for the Bluebirds came on his next appearance at Ninian Park as Nottingham Forest were beaten 3–0. Having helped City win promotion to the First Division, he was unable to win a regular place in 1921–22 due to the consistency of Billy Grimshaw, and in the close season he moved to Manchester United, where he ended his first-class career.

EVANS Terry

Right-back

Born: Pontypridd, 8 January 1976.
Career: Cardiff City 1994.

■ Playing in defence, predominantly at

right-back, Terry Evans made his Cardiff debut in a 2–1 defeat at Bristol Rovers in January 1994, and though he played in a handful of games towards the end of the season it was 1994–95 before he played on a more regular basis. Giving a number of encouraging displays, he was rewarded with three Welsh Under-21 caps. It was thought that if he maintained his current rate of progress he would become one of the cornerstones that the Ninian Park club would build on. However, Evans became another of the Cardiff youngsters who left the club due to the economy drive. The reliable full-back was despatched to play Abacus League football despite the fact that he was a Welsh Under-21 international.

EVANS Trevor John

Outside-left

Born: South Wales.
Career: Caerau Athletic. Cardiff City 1937. Brighton & Hove Albion 1938.

■ Winger Trevor Evans joined the Bluebirds from Welsh League Caerau Athletic and played his one and only game for the club on the final day of the 1937–38 season in a 1–0 defeat at Northampton Town. Unable to force his way into the club's first team, he spent a season playing reserve-team football before joining Brighton & Hove Albion prior to the outbreak of World War Two.

EVEREST John (Jack)

Left-back/centre-forward

Born: Kilcullen, 20 July 1908.
Died: 1979.
Career: Dunnington. Heslington. York City. Stockport County 1928. Rochdale 1930. Blackpool 1931. Cardiff City 1934. Southend United 1936. Barnsley 1937.

■ Unable to make much headway at York City, Jack Everest joined Stockport County and in two seasons at Edgeley Park scored seven goals in seven games. Four of these came midway through the 1929–30 season in a 7–1 defeat of Carlisle United. Everest then joined Rochdale, later remaining in the North West with Blackpool. While with the Seasiders, he was converted from centre-forward to left-back before joining

Cardiff City on the recommendation of former favourite George Blackburn, player-manager of Cheltenham Town who had just lost to Blackpool in the FA Cup. Everest was ever present for the Bluebirds in 1934–35 and, despite injuries, played in most of the games the following season. On leaving Ninian Park he had a spell with Southend United and later Barnsley, helping them win the Third Division North Championship in 1938–39.

FAERBER Winston

Midfield

Born: Surinam, 27 March 1971.
Career: ADO Den Haag (Holland).
Cardiff City 1999. FC Den Bosch
(Holland) 2000.

FAW Invitation Cup finalist 1999–2000.

■ A right-sided wing-back, Winston Faerber joined Cardiff from Dutch club Den Haag under the Bosman ruling before the start of the 1999–2000 season. He made his debut in a 1–1 home draw against Millwall on the opening day of the campaign and, though he was physically strong and crossed the ball well, he found it difficult to settle into British football. This was partly due to the fact that his family were homesick. Although born in Surinam, he was brought up in the Netherlands, and Faerber, whose only goal for the club came on his second appearance in a 3–2 win at Oxford United, was allowed to return to play for FC Den Bosch of Holland, even though he had only served half of his two-year contract.

FARQUHARSON Thomas G. (Tom)

Goalkeeper

Born: Dublin, 4 December 1900.
Died: 1970.
Career: Abertillery. Cardiff City 1921.

Welsh Cup winner 1922–23, 1926–27, 1927–28, 1929–30. Division One runner-up 1923–24. FA Cup finalist 1924–25. FA Cup winner 1926–27. FA Charity Shield winner 1927–28. Welsh Cup finalist 1928–29.

■ Without doubt, Farquharson is the greatest goalkeeper in the history of the club. Legend has it that the Dublin-born 'keeper had arrived in the valleys in search of work and was watching a local game at Oakdale when he was persuaded to make up the numbers by appearing in goal. A natural athlete who had played Rugby Union, he was such a success that he was soon playing for Abertillery, and it was from there that his road led to Ninian Park! He made his debut for City in a 3–1 home win over Manchester United on the final day of the 1921–22 season, and, after sharing the goalkeeping duties the following season with Ben Davies, he became the club's first-choice 'keeper in 1923–24. Also this season he won the first of seven caps for Northern Ireland when he played against Scotland, and six seasons later he won the first of his caps for the Republic of Ireland. He was in goal when City lost 1–0 to Sheffield United in the FA Cup Final of 1925 and when they beat Arsenal, also at Wembley, in 1927. The law that made sure goalkeepers' feet remained on the goal line when a penalty-kick was being taken is down to the antics of Tom Farquharson. He would quite often advance from the back of the net as the penalty taker came in to take the kick! Farquharson, who went on to play in 481 League and Cup games for Cardiff City, later returned to his original trade of painter and decorator before eventually emigrating to Canada to join his daughter.

FARRELL Gregory James Philip

Outside-right

Born: Motherwell, 19 March 1944.
Career: Birmingham City 1961. Cardiff City 1964. Bury 1967.

■ A clever ball player, Greg Farrell's chances at Birmingham City were few and far between, owing to the form of Hellawell and Auld, and in March 1964 he was signed by Cardiff manager George Swindin for a moderate fee. Considered by many Bluebirds fans to be an exasperating winger, he could be outstanding on his day, and without doubt his finest display came in a vital relegation battle with Middlesbrough in

May 1966 when he scored from the penalty spot and created the other four goals in a 5–3 win for City. Within a year, though, he had been sold to Bury and did well for the Gigg Lane club before emigrating to South Africa.

FARRINGTON John Robert

Winger

Born: Lynemouth, 19 June 1947.
Career: Wolverhampton Wanderers 1965.
Leicester City 1969. Cardiff City 1973.
Northampton Town 1974.

Welsh Cup winner 1973–74.

■ A direct winger, he made his Football League debut for Wolves while still an apprentice and later laid on several goals for Derek Dougan before being transferred to Leicester City in October 1969. Foxes manager Frank O'Farrell had Farrington on the right and Glover on the left, and so Leicester's quick-break style was based on an attack of genuine width and pace, helping them win the Second Division Championship in 1970–71. Having scored 27 goals in 145 games, he left Filbert Street to be reunited with O'Farrell after the former Leicester boss had taken charge at Cardiff. Farrington cost a club record £62,000 fee but, though he netted a hat-trick in a 4–1 defeat of Sunderland, his stay at Ninian Park lasted less than a year. Then former Leicester coach Bill

Dodgin took him to Northampton where a 232 game spell ended his 15-year League career. He later managed non-League clubs AP Leamington and Shepshed Charterhouse.

FARRINGTON Mark Anthony

Forward

Born: Liverpool, 15 June 1965.
Career: Everton. Norwich City 1983. Cambridge United (loan) 1985. Cardiff City 1985. Feyenoord (Holland). Brighton & Hove Albion 1991. AIF (Norway). Hereford United 1994.

■ A junior with Everton before joining Norwich City, versatile forward Mark Farrington had limited opportunities at Carrow Road, and in the summer of 1985 he joined Cardiff on a free transfer. Farrington scored on his debut in a 4–1 win at Notts County; however, he suffered in a poor City team doomed to relegation from the Third Division. Before the season had ended, Farrington was 'sacked' by Alan Durban for a breach of club discipline and moved abroad to play for Feyenoord in Holland. On returning to the UK, he played for Brighton & Hove Albion before playing for AIF of Norway prior to ending his career with a substitute appearance for Hereford United.

FELGATE David Wynne

Goalkeeper

Born: Blaenau Ffestiniog, 4 March 1960.
Career: Bolton Wanderers 1978. Rochdale (loan) 1978. Crewe Alexandra (loan) 1979. Rochdale (loan) 1980. Lincoln City 1980. Cardiff City (loan) 1984. Grimsby Town 1985. Bolton Wanderers (loan) 1986. Bolton Wanderers 1987. Wolverhampton Wanderers 1993. Chester City 1993. Wigan Athletic 1995. Leigh RMI.

■ Though he began his career with Bolton Wanderers, he couldn't force his way into the club's first team and was loaned out to Rochdale and Crewe Alexandra to gain experience. Still unable to break into the side, he was transferred to Lincoln City. It was while he was at Sincil Bank that he won full international honours when he replaced

Neville Southall at half-time during Wales's 5–0 hammering of Romania. He went on to play in 198 League games for Lincoln, and in December 1984 he had a four-match loan spell at City. Never on the winning side, he was in goal for three home defeats and a 1–1 draw at Crystal Palace. In the summer of 1985 he joined Grimsby Town, but early the following year he returned to Burnden Park to make his long-awaited Bolton debut. He helped the Wanderers reach the Freight Rover Trophy Final, only to miss out on a Wembley appearance as his loan spell had expired. After joining the Lancashire club on a permanent basis, he was ever present in 1987–88 as the club won promotion to the Third Division. He won a winners' medal in the 1989 Sherpa Van Trophy Final and went on to appear in 300 games before brief spells with Bury and Wolves. His next League appearances came with Chester before he ended his first-team career with Wigan Athletic. He then signed for Unibond League side Leigh RMI and was a regular in their promotion-winning side.

FEREDAY Wayne

Winger

Born: Warley, 16 June 1963.
Career: Queen's Park Rangers 1980. Newcastle United 1989. Bournemouth

1990. West Bromwich Albion 1991. Cardiff City 1994. Merthyr Tydfil. Telford United.

■ It was during 1980–81 that Wayne Fereday made a name for himself as a new teenage star for Queen's Park Rangers when he scored twice on his debut in a 4–0 win over Bristol Rovers. However, it was 1984–85 before he won a regular place in the Rangers side, when he proved himself to be one of the fastest players on the circuit. Able to take on defenders and get in dangerous crosses, Fereday made five appearances for England at Under-21 level. After scoring 25 goals in 242 games, he was transferred to Newcastle United for £300,000. He did not do his reputation justice on Tyneside and spent much of his time in the treatment room. In November 1990 he joined Bournemouth as part of the deal that took Gavin Peacock to St James' Park. After a spell at West Bromwich Albion, he joined the Bluebirds. He was a first-team regular for the two seasons he spent at Ninian Park, but he couldn't prevent City's relegation to Division Three in 1994–95. He then left to play for Merthyr Tydfil before ending his career with Telford United.

FERGUSON Hugh

Centre-forward

*Born: Motherwell, 2 March 1898.
Died: 1930.
Career: Parkhead. Motherwell 1916.
Cardiff City 1925. Dundee 1929.*

*FA Cup winner 1926–27. FA Charity
Shield winner 1927–28. Welsh Cup
winner 1927–28. Welsh Cup finalist
1928–29.*

■ Hughie Ferguson had signed for his
home-town club Motherwell in 1916,
and over the next few seasons he
scored an incredible 362 goals for the
Fir Park club. His transfer to Cardiff
City in November 1925 is still among
the most sensational in the history of a
club, better known for its selling of
players rather than buying! City paid
Motherwell £5,000 for his signature
and at the same time paid Clyde £2,000
for George McLachlan. What a debut
they had, Ferguson scoring one of
City's goals in a 5–2 defeat of Leicester
City. He ended the season with 19 goals
in 26 games, including a hat-trick in a
4–2 win at Notts County. In 1926–27
he established a new club scoring
record with 26 goals in 39 games. Also
that season, he netted six FA Cup goals,
including being credited with the
winning goal in the Wembley Final win
over Arsenal. The following season he
scored 18 goals in 32 games and scored
both goals in the Welsh Cup Final
when the Bluebirds beat Bangor City
2–0. In 1928–29, when the club were
relegated from the First Division,
Ferguson was injured for most of the
season but still managed 14 goals,
including five in a 7–0 rout of Burnley.
He had scored 87 goals in 131 League
and Cup games for Cardiff when
Dundee made an offer the club could
not refuse, but his transfer was to end
in tragedy. Unable to shake off an
injury, he found it difficult to find the
net and was heckled by the Dundee
supporters, who expected more from
him. Hughie Ferguson was a sensitive
person, and on 9 January 1930 the
player who had put the Bluebirds into
football history committed suicide
after a training session at Dens Park –
he was just 32 years old.

FERGUSON Robert Burnett

Full-back

*Born: Dudley, Northumberland, 8
January 1938.
Career: Newcastle United 1955. Derby
County 1962. Cardiff City 1965. Barry
Town. Newport County 1969.*

Welsh Cup winner 1966–67, 1967–68.

■ Bobby Ferguson came from a
footballing family, his father having
played for West Bromwich Albion and
his uncle for Chelsea. A tough-tackling
defender, he began his career with
Newcastle United but his 12
appearances for the Magpies were
spread over nine seasons as he tended
to understudy Alf McMichael. He
moved to Derby County in 1962, and
in a little over three years at the
Baseball Ground he made 129
appearances. On New Year's Eve 1965,
Jimmy Scoular paid £5,000 to bring
Ferguson to Ninian Park, and he soon
settled into the Bluebirds side. A
regular for three years until he was
released by City, he joined Barry Town
as player-manager before coming back
into League football with Newport
County. After a torrid time at
Somerton Park, Ferguson was
dismissed and in 1971 linked up with
Bobby Robson at Ipswich Town.
Eventually graduating to the manager's
post at Portman Road, he helped
Ipswich reach the semi-finals of the
League Cup in 1984–85, but the
following season they were relegated.
The club reached the Second Division
play-offs in 1986–87, but after losing to
Charlton Ferguson had the sad
distinction of being the first manager
to be sacked by Ipswich Town.

FERRETTI Andreas

Forward

*Born: Italy, 18 September 1986.
Career: Parma (Italy). Cardiff City 2005.*

■ Cardiff City signed the former Parma
youngster Andreas Ferretti on a two-
year contract after he impressed while
on trial with the Bluebirds. The 18-year-
old came highly recommended by
Manchester United boss Sir Alex
Ferguson. He showed impressive form
for Cardiff's reserve side and was their
leading scorer with 14 goals. His
displays led to him making four League
appearances for the Bluebirds first team
but all from the bench. He, and the
Cardiff fans, will be hoping that he can
make the transition more permanent
next season.

FIELDING William (Bill)

Goalkeeper

*Born: Broadhurst, 17 June 1915.
Career: Hurst. Cardiff City 1936. Bolton
Wanderers 1945. Manchester United
1946.*

■ Goalkeeper Bill Fielding arrived at
Ninian Park after two seasons playing
for non-League Hurst. During the
1936–37 season, his first with the club,
he had to contest the number-one jersey
with George Poland but then the
following season completely lost out to
Bob Jones, the veteran 'keeper who had
joined the club from Bolton Wanderers.
Midway through the 1938–39 season
Fielding came back into the City first
team and kept his place until the
outbreak of World War Two. During the
fighting Fielding played for Stockport
County and Bolton Wanderers, with
whom he won a League Cup North
medal in 1944–45. He remained with
the Wanderers until January 1947 when
he joined Manchester United for £3,000.
Though he only made six appearances
for the Reds, United fans recall a
somewhat adventurous goalkeeper!

FINLAY James (Jim)

Outside-right

*Born: Glasgow.
Career: Bute Athletic. Cardiff City 1937.*

■ A speedy winger, able to play on
either flank, he joined Cardiff from
Scottish junior club Bute Athletic in
November 1937. After some promising
displays in Cardiff's reserve side, he was
given his League debut in the Third
Division South match at Notts County,
which the Bluebirds lost 2–0. It turned
out to be his only first-team appearance,
and he later returned to his native
Scotland to continue his career.

FINNIESTON Stephen James

Forward

Born: Edinburgh, 30 November 1954.
Career: Chelsea 1971. Cardiff City (loan) 1974. Sheffield United 1978.

■ A strong and determined target man, Steve Finnieston could shield the ball and lay it off to colleagues effectively, but in his early days at Stamford Bridge he couldn't hold down a first-team place. Cardiff signed him on loan in October 1974, and in a season in which the Bluebirds lost their Second Division status he scored twice in nine League appearances. He returned to Chelsea and in 1976–77 he scored 24 League goals in 39 matches as Eddie McCreadie's young side returned the London club to the top flight. Finnieston rounded off this successful season with a hat-trick in the last match at Hull but missed four months of the next campaign with Achilles trouble. When he returned to action, he had lost a lot of his old sharpness and was allowed to move to Sheffield United, who paid £80,000 for him. Sadly, another injury forced him to give up League football.

FLACK Steven Richard

Forward

Born: Cambridge, 29 May 1971.
Career: Cambridge City. Cardiff City 1995. Exeter City 1996.

■ A big, bustling centre-forward, Steve Flack joined the Bluebirds from non-League Cambridge City in the autumn of 1995, though initially he was used mainly as a late substitute. He netted his first goal for the club in the 88th minute of a 3–1 defeat at Wigan towards the end of his first season with the club, but during the early part of the 1996–97 season he was allowed to join Exeter City for £10,000. He soon made an impression with his presence in the air and set pieces, and in 1997–98 he scored 14 goals in 37 starts. Continuing to find the net for the Grecians, he scored in five consecutive matches to equal a club record. The former professional boxer stayed at St James's Park to become the club's longest-serving player, and

though Exeter lost their Football League status Flack remained with the club, taking his tally of goals to 70 in 305 games.

FLEETWOOD Stuart

Striker

Born: Gloucester, 23 April 1986.
Career: Cardiff City 2004.

■ After an impressive pre-season tour to Scandinavia in the summer of 2003,

striker Stuart Fleetwood made his senior debut as a substitute in the Carling Cup match against Leyton Orient. Often included in the first-team squad, he added two further appearances from the bench in the League against Watford and Wimbledon before the end of the season.

FLEMING Haydn Valentine

Right-back

Born: Islington, 14 March 1978.
Career: Cardiff City 1995. Cable Tel (loan) 1996. Merthyr Tydfil 1997.

■ A full-back with attacking ambitions, he made his City debut against Plymouth Argyle in November 1995, and over the course of that 1995–96 season had games where he was inspired

but then showed that he had a lot to learn still in others! Still a trainee during his first season, he turned professional in the summer of 1996 before being loaned out to Cable Tel, where he suffered a terrible knee injury. This brought his career to a halt and resulted in him being freed and joining Merthyr Tydfil.

FLYNN Brian

Midfield

Born: Port Talbot, 12 October 1955.
Career: Burnley 1972. Leeds United 1977. Burnley (loan) 1982. Burnley 1982. Cardiff City 1984. Doncaster Rovers 1985. Bury 1986. Limerick 1987. Doncaster Rovers 1987. Wrexham 1988.

■ Brian Flynn was first spotted playing for Neath Boys by Cardiff City, but the Bluebirds let him slip through the net when, in 1972, he signed for Burnley. He made his League debut for the Clarets against Arsenal in February 1974, but it was 1974–75 before he began to establish himself as a first-team regular. In fact, that season he was just 19 when he won the first of his 66 Welsh caps against Luxembourg at the Vetch. Following Burnley's relegation to Division Two in 1976, it was always going to be difficult for the club to hold on to its stars. In November 1977 Flynn left the Clarets to join Leeds United for a fee of £175,000. Forging a superb midfield partnership with Tony Currie, Flynn's voracious appetite for work and his variety of defence-splitting passes caught the eye. Flynn returned to Turf Moor in 1982, taking his tally of goals to 27 in 254 League and Cup games, before leaving to play for Cardiff City in November 1984. Sadly for the Bluebirds, Flynn struggled to lift an ailing team, and after looking like a shadow of his former self he left to have spells with Doncaster Rovers and Bury. There followed a period as Limerick's player-manager before he took over a similar position with Wrexham. After the Robins had finished bottom of the Fourth Division in 1990–91, Flynn began to turn things around, and in 1992–93 they won promotion to the new Second Division. He stayed at the Racecourse Ground until 2001 before

parting company with the club. He later managed Swansea and, against all the odds, kept them in the Football League before later losing out to Kenny Jackett.

FOGGON Alan

Winger

Born: Chester-le-Street, 23 February 1950.
Career: Newcastle United 1967. Cardiff City 1971. Middlesbrough 1972. Manchester United 1976. Sunderland 1976. Southend United 1977. Hartlepool United (loan) 1978. Consett.

Welsh Cup finalist 1971–72.

■ An England Youth international, Alan Foggon came through the junior ranks with Newcastle United, and when he made the first team he became part of the Magpies side that won the Fairs Cup in 1969. In fact, Foggon scored one of the goals in the second leg of the Final against Ujpest Dozsa. After netting 16 goals in 80 games for Newcastle, he left

St James' Park to join Cardiff City for £25,000. His stay at Ninian Park was short-lived as he did little to impress manager Jimmy Scoular, who accused him of being constantly overweight. Therefore, it came as no surprise when, in October 1972, he returned to the North East with Middlesbrough. Foggon's arrival at Ayresome Park coincided with him being midway through a three-week suspension. When 'Boro won the Second Division Championship in 1973–74, Foggon was the club's leading scorer with 19 goals in 41 games. He continued to find the net the following season, topping the club's scoring charts with 16 goals as they finished seventh in the top flight. Foggon went on to score 49 goals in 136 games for 'Boro before joining Manchester United for £27,000. Unable to make much impression at Old Trafford, he then had spells with Sunderland, Southend United and Hartlepool before going into non-League football with Consett.

FOLEY William

Forward

Born: Bellshill, 25 June 1960.
Career: Swansea City 1986. Frickley Athletic 1986. Cardiff City 1986. Frickley Athletic 1986. Brecon Corries 1987.

■ Will Foley joined Swansea City from Welsh League football, and although he scored twice in four starts for the Swans he was released in February 1986. After a brief spell with Frickley Athletic, he joined the Bluebirds, but he couldn't prevent the club's relegation, and, when not offered a contract, he rejoined Frickley. He later had a spell in New Zealand before joining Brecon Corries for the 1987–88 season.

FORD Francis Martin

Defender

Born: Bridgend, 3 February 1967.
Career: Cardiff City 1985. Afan Lido.

■ A young defender whose only appearances for the Bluebirds were fleeting, he had trials with Oxford United and Exeter City after being released by Cardiff. He was unable to make the grade with either club and

returned to Wales to play Welsh League football with Afan Lido.

FORD Louis

Full-back

Born: Cardiff, 18 May 1914.
Died: 1980.
Career: Cardiff City 1936.

■ A local amateur, he made a good impression when he joined the Bluebirds in 1936. His ability to play at either right or left-back was a distinct advantage, but in three seasons with the club he was unable to maintain a regular place in the City side. Sadly, his first-team career came to an end following the outbreak of World War Two.

FORD Michael Paul

Defender

Born: Bristol, 9 February 1966.
Career: Leicester City 1984. Devizes Town 1984. Cardiff City 1984. Oxford United 1988.

Division Four runner-up 1987–88. Welsh Cup winner 1987–88. Division Three Promotion 1998–99.

■ The son of Tony Ford, who was a full-back with both Bristol clubs, he served his apprenticeship with Leicester City before becoming a full-time professional at the age of 18. After being released by the Foxes, he moved into the Western League with Devizes Town, but within a matter of months he joined Cardiff City and made his debut in a 1–1 draw at Leeds United. He proved himself to be a fine utility player at Ninian Park, appearing at full-back, central-defence and in midfield. In the club's promotion-winning season of 1987–88 he scored seven goals in 45 appearances and was one of the mainstays of the Bluebirds team. Ford later left the club to join Oxford United. During his early days at the Manor Ground he suffered a spate of injuries before being made club captain. He spent 10 seasons with the club, scoring 22 goals in 338 games before being released in the summer of 1998. Returning to Ninian Park, he was Frank Burrows's most crucial signing and was soon named captain. His ability to lead, organise and inspire made him the key

figure in City's promotion campaign. In 1999–2000 he had a problem with a disc in his back, which eventually forced his retirement from the game. He was set to complete his UEFA 'A' coaching course during the summer of 2000, but having been appointed youth-team manager at Oxford he was forced back into action during an injury crisis and then later was appointed caretaker manager.

FORD Trevor

Centre-forward

Born: Swansea, 1 October 1923.
Died: 29 May 2003.
Career: Swansea Town 1942. Aston Villa 1947. Sunderland 1950. Cardiff City 1953. PSV Eindhoven (Holland). Newport County 1960. Romford.

Welsh Cup winner 1955–56.

■ Trevor Ford was one of the leading forwards of his day. He became Wales's leading goalscorer of all time, also netting a hat-trick in a 5–1 win over Belgium and two goals against England at Wembley in 1952. Having signed for his home-town team Swansea in 1942, Ford graduated into the Swans first team during the latter stages of the hostilities. In 1945–46 he scored 44 goals in 41 games and, not surprisingly, a number of First Division clubs began to show an interest in him. After scoring nine goals in the opening six games of the 1946–47 season, he joined Aston Villa for £12,000. He scored 18 goals in each of the next two seasons, while in December 1948 he scored four goals as Villa beat local rivals Wolverhampton Wanderers 5–1. While with Villa, Ford received offers to go and play in both Colombia and Portugal but turned them down. However, in October 1950 Ford did leave Villa Park and joined Sunderland for a fee of £30,000. He netted a hat-trick on his home debut against Sheffield Wednesday and top scored for the Wearsiders for the next two seasons, netting three further hat-tricks and four goals in a 5–2 win at Manchester City. Having scored 70 goals in 117 games, he joined Cardiff City for what was then their record fee of £30,000. Ford became a firm favourite with the Cardiff supporters. Though not as prolific a scorer as in his early playing

Division Three runner-up 2000–01. FAW Premier Cup winner 2001–02. Division Two promotion 2002–03.

■ Signed by Gillingham from Stevenage Borough in June 1995 in return for £5,000, a fee paid by the Gills supporters' club, he finished his first season, 1995–96, as the club's top scorer with 15 goals and helped the Kent club win promotion to Division Two. The following season he broke his ankle and was loaned to Leyton Orient, but on his return to the Priestfield Stadium he couldn't get back in the side and was

sold to Lincoln. Unable to find his form, he had a loan spell with Rotherham United before Brentford paid £60,000 for his services. Surprisingly used mainly as a substitute, a move to Rotherham put him out of his misery, and he repaid the Millers by top scoring and helping them win promotion in 1999–2000. Just days into the new season Cardiff City paid £300,000 to take him to Ninian Park where he again proved how useful he is at disrupting lower Division defences. Netting 12 goals in 28 starts, he helped City win promotion to Division Two – his total including a hat-trick in a 3–3 draw at York City. He was a prominent figure the following season when the Bluebirds came close to a second promotion and again in 2002–03 when City did succeed in winning promotion. Having scored 28 goals in 113 games, he left to join

days, he did net four goals in two Welsh Cup games as Pembroke Borough were beaten 7–0 in 1954–55 and 9–0 in 1955–56. He had scored 59 goals in 119 outings for the Bluebirds when he fell out with Trevor Morris following the City manager's decision to play him at inside-right. After leaving Ninian Park, Ford was banned sine die by the Football League following his revelations about Sunderland FC in his autobiography *I lead the attack*, which was serialised in a Sunday newspaper. He went abroad and had three

successful years with PSV Eindhoven, where, in 1957–58, he scored a remarkable 51 goals. Returning to these shores after the ban was lifted, he played for Newport County and non-League Romford until a knee injury ended his career.

FORTUNE-WEST Leopold Paul Osborne (Leo)

Striker

Born: Stratford, 9 April 1971.
Career: Stevenage Borough. Gillingham

Doncaster Rovers where he became a member of a promotion-winning side for the fifth time.

FOWLER Jason Kenneth George

Midfield

Born: Bristol, 20 August 1974.
Career: Bristol City 1993. Cardiff City 1996. Torquay United 2001.

FAW Invitation Cup finalist 1997–98, 1999–2000. Division Three promotion 1998–99.

■ A left-sided midfield player, Jason Fowler began his career with Bristol City but was released by the Ashton Gate club in the summer of 1996. Joining Cardiff City, he started the 1996–97 season as a regular, and although he lost

his place on a couple of occasions when loan signings were brought in he always came back strongly. He scored six goals from midfield, including one to no avail in the second leg of the play-off semi-finals at Northampton. He soon proved himself capable of producing top-quality displays and scored a number of spectacular goals. A key component of the promotion-winning season of 1998–99, he was always a threat to the opposition and it was no surprise that he was selected by his fellow professionals to grace the award-winning PFA Third Division side. Badly hampered by injuries the following season, he struggled to find consistency and then in 2000–01 he was diagnosed as suffering from an over-active thyroid. This long-term illness led to him losing his place in the Cardiff side, and he left to make a fresh start with Torquay United.

FRANCIS Gerald Charles James (Gerry)

Midfield

Born: Chiswick, 6 December 1951.
Career: Queen's Park Rangers 1969. Crystal Palace 1979. Queen's Park Rangers 1981. Coventry City 1982. Exeter City 1983. Cardiff City 1984. Swansea City 1984. Portsmouth 1984. Bristol Rovers 1985.

■ Having established himself as a first-team regular at Queen's Park Rangers, Gerry Francis was the only ever present when the Loftus Road club won promotion to the First Division in 1972–73. After an impressive first season in the top flight, Francis won the first of his 12 England caps. He was later made captain of the national side and in 1975–76 helped Rangers finish as runners-up to Liverpool. He then suffered an injury that ended his international career and restricted his appearances for Rangers, but after regaining full fitness he joined Crystal Palace in July 1979 for a fee of £465,000. His stay at Selhurst Park was brief, and he rejoined Rangers for a cut-price fee of £150,000. He had taken his tally of goals in his two spells to 65 in 354 games when he left Loftus Road again, this time to join Coventry City. Francis

was only 32 when he became player-manager of Exeter City, but he lost his job when the Grecians finished bottom of the Third Division. He joined Cardiff in the summer of 1984 as a non-contract player but was on the losing side in six of his seven appearances at the start of a campaign in which the club were relegated. After spells with Swansea and Portsmouth, he managed Bristol Rovers to the Third Division Championship. He later managed Queen's Park Rangers and Tottenham Hotspur before ending his involvement in the game with a second spell in charge at Loftus Road.

FRANCOMBE Peter

Defender

Born: Cardiff, 4 August 1963.
Career: Crystal Palace. Cardiff City 1981. Bridgend.

■ An apprentice with Crystal Palace, local-born defender Peter Francombe joined the Ninian Park club in September 1981. A hard-tackling full-back, he made his debut in a 2–1 home defeat at the hands of Rotherham United, and though he impressed he found himself back in the reserves. Recalled for the game at Bolton, he was again on the losing side – it was a season in which Cardiff were relegated to the Third Division. Not retained at the end of the season, he went to play non-League football for Bridgend.

FRASER Gordon

Centre-forward

Born: Elgin, 27 November 1943.
Career: Forres Mechanics. Cardiff City 1961. Millwall 1963. Barry Town. Newport County 1966.

■ Elgin-born centre-forward Gordon Fraser joined the Bluebirds from Scottish junior football and was a prolific scorer in the club's reserve team. Eventually he was given his first-team debut but failed to impress in a dour goalless draw at Norwich City. He made four starts during the course of that 1962–63 season, but having failed to make an impact at League level he was allowed to join Millwall. It was a similar story at The Den, and he returned to South Wales for a short spell with Barry Town before signing for Newport County. Though he managed to score his first goals at senior level, he couldn't hold down a regular place and again drifted into non-League football.

FRIDAY Robin

Forward

Born: Hammersmith, 27 July 1952. Died: 1991.
Career: Hayes. Reading 1974. Cardiff City 1976.

Welsh Cup finalist 1976–77.

■ One of the game's most colourful characters, Robin Friday made his name at Reading after being signed from Hayes. In three seasons at Elm Park, in which he helped the club win promotion to the Third Division in 1975–76, Friday scored 46 goals in 121 games. With the loss of Adrian Alston to America, City manager Jimmy Andrews paid £28,000 to bring Friday to Ninian Park. After scoring twice on his debut in a 3–0 defeat of Fulham, Friday's Cardiff career plummeted with a series of episodes involving club discipline on and off the field – this included several periods of going missing plus two sendings off and a series of bookings. Not surprisingly, his contract was eventually terminated and in later years unsavoury rumours surrounded both his whereabouts and activities – Friday was just 39 when he died, a sad loss of someone with unquestioned ability.

FRIEND Harold

Left-half

Born: Cardiff.
Career: Cardiff Corinthians. Cardiff City 1933.

■ Left-half Harold Friend was playing as an amateur with Cardiff Corries when he was drafted in to the City side during an injury crisis in the club's re-election season of 1933–34. After making his debut in a 2–1 home defeat at the hands of Clapton Orient, Friend appeared in a further two games, the last a 6–3 mauling at Swindon Town.

FROWEN John

Defender

Born: Trelewis, 11 October 1931.
Career: Nelson. Cardiff City 1951. Bristol Rovers 1958. Newport County 1963.

■ Centre-half John Frowen joined City from non-League Nelson and, after graduating through the junior teams, made his debut at right-back in a 1–0 defeat at West Bromwich Albion in September 1952. He could never command a regular place in his more accustomed role due to the fine form of Stan Montgomery and then later following the arrival of Danny Malloy from Dundee in 1955. He left Cardiff in the summer of 1958 to become a regular member of Bristol Rovers' defence before, in March 1963, moving to end his career with Newport County.

FRY Christopher David (Chris)

Winger

Born: Cardiff, 23 October 1969.
Career: Cardiff City 1988. Hereford United 1991. Colchester United 1993. Exeter City 1997. Barry Town 1999.

■ A great crosser of the ball, winger Chris Fry played his way into the

Cardiff side towards the end of the 1988–89 season. Over the next couple of seasons (City were relegated in 1989–90) Chris Fry found himself in and out of the Bluebirds side, though more than half of his 55 League appearances saw him come off the bench. Fry, whose only goal for Cardiff came in a 2–2 draw against Brentford in that relegation season, left for Hereford United in August 1991. In a little over two seasons at Edgar Street, he scored 10 goals in 108 games before signing for Colchester United. Always seeming to pop up with a vital goal, he was very much a crowd favourite at Layer Road, where in 1996–97 he was voted the club's Player of the Year. He went on to appear in 154 games for Colchester before moving to Exeter in the summer of 1997. Surprisingly given a free transfer after two seasons with the Devon club, he returned to South Wales to play for Barry Town.

FURSLAND Sydney Albert (Syd)

Left-half/outside-left

Born: Llwynpia, 31 July 1914.
Career: Cardiff City 1934. Bangor City. Stoke City 1935.

■ Left-half Syd Fursland started his football career with his home village team Llwynpia, where he was a collier, before signing professional forms for Cardiff City. He made just two appearances for the Bluebirds when they were severely restricted with injured players at the start of the 1934–35 season. On leaving Ninian Park he spent just nine days with Bangor City before Stoke pounced for his signature. Most of his time at the Victoria Ground was spent in the reserves, and he parted company with the club prior to the outbreak of war.

GABBIDON Daniel Leon (Danny)

Defender

Born: Cwmbran, 8 August 1979.
Career: West Bromwich Albion 1998. Cardiff City 2000. West Ham United 2005.

Division Three runner-up 2000–01. Division Two promotion 2002–03.

■ Danny Gabbidon started out with West Bromwich Albion when, in his first couple of seasons at the Hawthorns, he was a regular for Wales at Under-21 level. Following his League debut against Ipswich Town midway through the 1998–99 season, he won a regular pace in the Baggies side. After falling victim to a niggling shin injury, he couldn't win back his place and joined Cardiff City for a fee of £175,000. He immediately established himself in the Bluebirds first team, playing in every position across the club's back four. A quality defender, Gabbidon made an impressive debut in the first of 12 internationals against the Czech Republic at the Millennium Stadium in 2002. A virtual ever present in his first two seasons at Ninian Park, he made a disappointing start to the 2002–03 season when he missed over four months of the campaign with a back injury. He returned to the side in April and ended the season on a high note as City beat Queen's Park Rangers

1–0 in the Second Division play-off final. He is a regular in the Welsh side and is one of his country's unsung heroes, and he was selected for the PFA First Division team. Due to the club's financial situation, Gabbidon was allowed to leave Ninian Park and joined West Ham United. His impressive displays in the Hammers defence, helped the club to a respectable mid-table placing in the top flight and to an FA Cup Final date with Liverpool at the Millennium Stadium.

GALBRAITH John McDonald (Jack)

Wing-half

Born: Renton, 4 April 1898.
Career: Vale of Leven Juniors. Shawfield. Clapton Orient 1921. Cardiff City 1931. Milford United 1935.

■ Jack Galbraith started out in Scottish junior football with Vale of Leven and then Shawfield before signing for Clapton Orient in 1921. A tough-tackling wing-half, he spent a decade with the O's, making 280 first-team appearances until joining Cardiff City in February 1931 for a nominal fee. Although he was entering the veteran stage, Galbraith was the player who replaced the great Fred Keenor, and as the Bluebirds plummeted towards the foot of the Third Division South he seldom missed a match. Giving good service for almost four years, Galbraith left City in 1935 to manage Milford United. A few years later he returned to his beloved Orient as coach.

GALE Colin Maurice

Centre-half

Born: Pontypridd, 31 August 1932.
Career: Cardiff City 1950. Northampton Town 1956.

■ Due to the wealth of talent at Ninian Park in the 1950s, centre-half Colin Gale had to wait almost four years before making his League debut for the Bluebirds. An injury crisis forced his appearance at right-back in a 3–0 home defeat at the hands of Manchester City in January 1954. The last of his 12 appearances for Cardiff came in September 1955 as City lost 9–1 at home to Wolves! In March 1956 he joined Northampton Town and became a first-team regular for five years, making 212 League appearances and helping the Cobblers win promotion to Division Three in 1960–61, his last season with the club.

GAMMON Stephen George

Wing-half

Born: Swansea, 24 September 1939.
Career: Cardiff City 1958. Kettering Town 1965.

Welsh Cup winner 1958–59. Division Two runners-up 1959–60. Welsh Cup finalist 1959–60.

■ Spotted playing for Mumbles Boys Club as a 16-year-old, Steve Gammon was offered a professional contract on his 17th birthday and took little time breaking into Cardiff's League side. After making his debut alongside fellow debutant Derek Tapscott in a 4–1 defeat of Grimsby Town in September 1958, Gammon won international recognition when he was selected for Wales at Under-23 level. During City's promotion-winning season of 1959–60, he scored his only goal for the club in a 4–4 home draw with Stoke City. However, in February 1961 he suffered a broken leg following a clash with Denis Law in the match against Manchester City. His career was virtually in ruins after the injury and he broke the leg on another two occasions over the following three seasons. Though he made the occasional appearance, his League career was over, and he joined Kettering Town in the Southern League.

GARDNER James

Winger

Born: Dunfermline, 27 September 1967.
Career: Queen's Park. Motherwell. St Mirren. Scarborough 1995. Cardiff City 1995. Exeter City 1997. Stirling Albion 1999.

■ Orthodox winger Jimmy Gardner played Scottish League football for Queen's Park, Motherwell and St Mirren, but at all of those clubs he never quite fulfilled his potential. Able to play on either flank, he was eventually freed by the Love Street club and joined Scarborough. After only a handful of games for the Yorkshire club – one of them against Cardiff where he impressed – he signed for the Bluebirds in the summer of 1995. He proved to be a fine crosser of the ball but injury and loss of confidence meant he was dropped. Unable to win back his place, he moved to Exeter City where he had two good seasons before moving back to Scotland to continue his career with Stirling Albion.

GAULT William Ernest (Ernie)

Forward

Born: Wallsend, 20 September 1889.
Died: 1980.
Career: Jarrow Caledonians. Everton 1912. Stockport County 1913. Everton 1919. Cardiff City 1920. Stockport County 1920. New Brighton.

■ Ernie Gault began his career with Everton, joining the Goodison club in 1912. He had just forced his way into the Everton side when his career was interrupted by World War One. In 1919–20 he scored 12 goals in 21 games but was then allowed to leave and joined Cardiff City. He made little impression at Ninian Park, failing to dislodge George West, and soon left to play for Stockport County, where he scored 12 goals in 41 games before deciding to retire.

GIBBINS Roger Graeme

Midfield/central-defender

Born: Enfield, 6 September 1955.
Career: Tottenham Hotspur 1972. Oxford United 1975. Norwich City 1976. New England (America). Cambridge United 1979. Cardiff City 1982. Swansea City 1985. Newport County 1986. Torquay United 1988. Newport County 1988. Cardiff City 1989.

Division Three runner-up 1982–83. Welsh Cup winner 1991–92. Division Three champion 1992–93.

■ After playing his early football for Tottenham Hotspur, the Enfield-born midfielder joined Oxford United in the summer of 1975, but after one season at the Manor Ground he moved on to Norwich City. He scored 12 goals in 48 games for the Canaries before going to play in America for the New England Teamen. He returned to these shores in September 1979 and joined Cambridge United. A regular member of the side, he spent three seasons at the Abbey Stadium, scoring 12 goals in his 100 League outings. At the end of the 1981–82 season he was given a free transfer and joined Cardiff City, making his debut against Wrexham on the opening day of the 1982–83 campaign. That season he was the club's only ever present and scored eight League goals as the Bluebirds won promotion. He was ever present again in 1983–84 and played in 91 consecutive League matches from his debut. In October 1985 he joined Swansea City in exchange for Chris Marustik, but after

just one season at the Vetch he left for Newport County. When they lost their League status, he moved to Torquay United before, in March 1989, returning to Ninian Park for a second spell. After taking his total of League and Cup appearances, in which he scored 32 goals, to 324, he remained at Ninian Park as coach until June 1994.

GIBSON Colin Hayward

Outside-right

Born: Middlesbrough, 16 September 1923. Died: 1992.
Career: Penarth Pontoons. Cardiff City 1944. Newcastle United 1948. Aston Villa 1949. Lincoln City 1956.

Division Three South champion 1946–47.

■ A former dockyard engineer, Colin Gibson was playing for Penarth Pontoons when he came to the attention of Cardiff City in 1944. Gibson became the only regular English player in the Bluebirds' marvellous Third Division South Championship-winning team in 1946–47. The fair-haired, dashing winger, a perfect foil for Roy Clarke on the other flank, netted 10 goals in 38 games, including a hat-trick in a 5–0 defeat of Swindon Town. Soon the top-flight clubs were after his talents, and in July 1948, after two seasons as a regular, he was sold to Newcastle United for £15,000. He had made just 23 appearances for the Magpies before he was sold to Aston Villa in February 1949 for £17,000. At the end of his first season at Villa Park he was chosen for the FA party to tour Scandinavia, after playing for England 'B' against Holland earlier in the campaign. He stayed at Villa Park for the next six years, scoring 26 goals in 167 games before moving on to Lincoln City in January 1956, later ending his first-team career with the Sincil Bank club.

GIBSON Ian Stewart

Midfield

Born: Newton Stewart, 30 March 1943.
Career: Accrington Stanley 1958. Bradford Park Avenue 1960. Middlesbrough 1962. Coventry City 1966. Cardiff City 1970. Bournemouth 1972.

Welsh Cup winner 1970–71. Welsh Cup finalist 1971–72.

■ Ian Gibson was just 15 years old when he made his League debut for Accrington Stanley, but after just nine games he was transferred to Bradford Park Avenue, another club that was to lose its League status. Gibson spent two years at Park Avenue, scoring 18 goals in 88 League games before Middlesbrough paid £30,000 for his services in March 1962. A former Scottish Schoolboy international, he was capped at Under-23 level while at Ayresome Park but could do nothing to halt 'Boro's slide into Division Three. He had scored 44 goals in 168 games for the Teeside club when Coventry City paid £40,000 to take Gibson to Highfield Road. After helping the Sky Blues win promotion to the First Division, he joined Cardiff City in the summer of 1970 for £35,000 and made his debut in a 1–0 win at Leicester City on the opening day of the 1970–71 season. Providing many of the goals for Clark, Toshack and Warboys, he also netted twice himself in a 3–1 Welsh Cup Final win over Wrexham. The 1971–72 season was spent helping City avoid relegation to the Third Division, but in October 1972 he left Ninian Park to join Bournemouth in a £100,000 deal. Within months of his arrival at Dean Court, he was forced to quit the game through injury.

GILBERT Timothy Hew

Full-back

Born: South Shields, 28 August 1958. Died: 31 May 1995.
Career: Sunderland 1976. Cardiff City 1981. Darlington 1982.

Welsh Cup finalist 1981–82.

■ Full-back Tim Gilbert began his League career with Sunderland, helping the Wearsiders win promotion to the First Division in 1979–80 before Richie Morgan brought him to Ninian Park in February 1981. Following his debut against Notts County, injuries restricted his appearances, and in 1981–82, when City were relegated, Gilbert netted his only goal for the club in a 2–1 reversal at Norwich City. In the close season he returned to his native North East to end his career with Darlington.

GILCHRIST Alexander

Outside-right

Born: Motherwell, 28 September 1923. Died: 1989.
Career: Cardiff City 1948. Barry Town. Raith Rovers 1949.

■ Motherwell-born winger Alex Gilchrist joined Cardiff in the summer of 1948 and played in the opening game of the 1948–49 season, a match City lost 3–0 at Bradford Park Avenue. It turned out to be his only first-team appearance for the Bluebirds, and after later being released he joined Barry Town. In 1949 he returned to Scotland to see out his career with Raith Rovers.

GILES David Charles

Winger

Born: Cardiff, 21 September 1956.
Career: Cardiff City 1974. Wrexham 1978. Swansea City 1979. Leyton Orient (loan) 1981. Crystal Palace 1982. Birmingham City 1984. Newport County 1984. Cardiff City 1985. Barry Town.

Welsh Cup finalist 1974–75, 1976–77. Division Three runner-up 1975–76. Welsh Cup winner 1975–76.

■ David Giles was a Welsh Schoolboy international when he joined Cardiff City, playing his first game for the Bluebirds in a goalless draw at Nottingham Forest in February 1975. Finding himself in and out of the City side, he left Ninian Park in December

1978, joining Wrexham for a fee of £20,000. He spent two seasons at the Racecourse Ground before Swansea paid £40,000 for his services. At the Vetch he helped the Swans win promotion to the First Division and won nine of his 12 international caps. Despite his success with Swansea, he was loaned out to Orient before moving on to Crystal Palace. He continued to represent Wales while at Selhurst Park, but eventually he was on the move again to Birmingham City and then Newport County. He rejoined the Bluebirds in September 1985, ending his first-class career where he'd started it. Unable to secure a permanent contract as City were relegated from the Third Division, he went to play on a part-time basis for Barry Town. After a spell as a double-glazing salesman, Giles, who is the only player to have played for all four Welsh clubs in the Football League, entered management with Ebbw Vale.

GILES Martyn

Midfield

Born: Cardiff, 10 April 1983.
Career: Cardiff City 2001.

■ A member of the Bluebirds side that won the Welsh Youth Cup, he made his League debut as a substitute for Matt Brazier in the game against Hull City in March 2001, a season in which he also featured for the Wales Under-17 side against Italy. In 2001–02, his first season as a professional, he netted his first goal in the 7–1 LDV Vans Trophy win over Rushden and Diamonds. A talented left-sided player, he failed to make any more first-team appearances and was released.

GILES Paul Anthony

Winger

Born: Cardiff, 21 February 1961.
Career: Cardiff City 1979. Exeter City (loan) 1982. Excelsior (Holland). Newport County (loan) 1984. Merthyr Tydfil (loan). Newport County 1987.

■ Younger brother of David, Paul Giles was a Welsh Under-21 international who was unable to make the most of his

limited chances at Ninian Park. After four frustrating years with the club, Giles, whose only goal for City came in a 2–2 draw at Luton Town in January 1981, moved to Exeter City on loan before having a spell in Holland with Excelsior. On his return to Wales he had loan spells with Newport County and Merthyr Tydfil before being given a second chance by the Somerton Park club.

GILL Gary

Midfield

Born: Middlesbrough, 28 November 1964.
Career: Middlesbrough 1982. Hull City (loan) 1983. Darlington 1989. Cardiff City 1992.

Welsh Cup winner 1991–92.

■ After working his way up through the ranks of his home-town team Middlesbrough, midfielder Gary Gill helped the then Ayresome Park club to win promotion from the Third to the First Division in successive seasons. On parting company with 'Boro, Gill made the short journey to Feethams, the home of Darlington, and in his first season helped them win the GM Vauxhall Conference title before, in 1990–91, being instrumental in them winning the Fourth Division Championship. Towards the end of the following season he signed for Cardiff City, and although he scored in the penultimate game of the campaign in a 3–1 win at Wrexham he wasn't retained at the end of the season.

GILL James J. (Jimmy)

Inside-right/outside-left

Born: Sheffield, 9 November 1894.
Career: Sheffield Wednesday 1913. Cardiff City 1920. Blackpool 1925. Derby County 1925. Crystal Palace 1928.

Division Two runner-up 1920–21. Welsh Cup winner 1921–22. 1922–23. Division One runner-up 1923–24. FA Cup finalist 1924–25.

■ The scorer of Cardiff City's first goal in League football, Jimmy Gill began his career with his home-town club Sheffield Wednesday, but with the Yorkshire club experiencing financial difficulties he was sold to Cardiff City for £750 in 1920. He scored twice on his debut as the Bluebirds won 5–2 at Stockport County in what was the club's first-ever League match. He ended the season as City's leading scorer with 19 goals as the club won promotion to the

First Division as runners-up to Birmingham. In 1921–22 he again topped the club's League goalscoring charts with 20 goals including five 'doubles'. Also that season he won a Welsh Cup-winners' medal, scoring in the Final in a 2–0 win over Ton Pentre. The following season Gill scored 17 League goals including a hat-trick in a 5–0 home win over Blackburn Rovers. The Bluebirds retained the Welsh Cup, and as well as scoring in the Final again in a 3–2 defeat of Aberdare Athletic he netted two hat-tricks in the earlier rounds of the competition as Rhymney were beaten 7–0 and Oswestry 10–0. He continued to find the net in 1923–24 and notched his second League hat-trick in a 4–0 home win over Arsenal. He was in the City team that lost 1–0 to Sheffield United in the 1925 FA Cup Final but left Ninian Park the following year to play for Blackpool. One of the club's greatest players, scoring 94 goals in 212 League and Cup games, he later played for Derby County for a couple of seasons before ending his career with Crystal Palace.

GILLIGAN James Martin

Forward

Born: Hammersmith, 24 January 1964.
Career: Watford 1981. Lincoln City (loan) 1982. Grimsby Town 1985. Swindon Town 1986. Newport County (loan) 1987. Lincoln City 1987. Cardiff City 1987. Portsmouth 1989. Swansea City 1990.

Division Four runner-up 1987–88.
Welsh Cup winner 1987–88.

■ A former England Youth international, Jimmy Gilligan started out with Watford, but in six years at Vicarage Road the bustling centre-forward scored just six goals in 27 League appearances. After a loan spell at Lincoln City he joined Grimsby Town for £100,000, but within 12 months he had left Blundell Park to sign for Swindon Town. Gilligan was soon on the move again, this time to Lincoln City after a loan spell with Newport County. When the Sincil Bank club lost their League status in 1987, Gilligan moved to Cardiff City for what proved a bargain fee of £17,500. He scored City's goal on his debut in a 1–1 home draw

against Leyton Orient and ended the season as the club's top scorer with 20 League goals as the Bluebirds won promotion to the Third Division. One of two ever presents in that 1987–88 season, he also won a Welsh Cup medal, scoring the second goal in a 2–0 win over Wrexham. He was ever present again the following season and the club's top scorer with 14 League goals, while in the European Cup-Winners' Cup he netted a hat-trick in a 4–0 home win over Derry City. Early the following season he followed former Cardiff manager Frank Burrows to Portsmouth before returning to South Wales to end his League career with Swansea City, where, once again, he scored regularly.

GODFREY Clifford (Cliff)

Wing-half

Born: Baildon, 17 February 1909.
Career: Guiseley. Bradford Park Avenue 1928. Cardiff City 1935. Walsall 1938.

■ Wing-half Cliff Godfrey was a miner who played Yorkshire League football for Guiseley prior to being given a chance at Football League level with Bradford Park Avenue. Though he was with the Yorkshire club for six seasons,

he was in and out of the side that challenged consistently for promotion to the top flight. In July 1935 he was transferred to Cardiff City and over the next few seasons was probably the most consistent player. Ever present in 1936–37 when he captained the team on a number of occasions, his only goal for the club came early the following season in a 4–1 home win over Northampton Town. In 1938 he moved to Walsall and after a good first season continued to play for the Saddlers during World War Two.

GODWIN Donald John

Outside-left

Born: Aberbargoed, 5 July 1932.
Career: Bargoed. Cardiff City 1953. Merthyr Tydfil.

■ Signed as a part-time professional from local junior football in 1953, Don Godwin was later released by the club while he completed his apprenticeship as a draughtsman. He was re-engaged by the Bluebirds in 1956 and scored goals in abundance for the club's reserve side while playing on both flanks and at centre-forward. He was eventually given his League debut at outside-left and created goals for Hitchens and Reynolds in a 2–1 win at West Bromwich Albion. Though he retained his place for the club's next game against Leeds United, it was his last appearance as City won just one of their last 14 games before being relegated to Division Two.

GOLDSMITH Martin Sidney

Forward

Born: Carmarthen, 25 May 1962.
Career: Carmarthen Town. Cambridge United 1980. Cardiff City 1984. Merthyr Tydfil. Barry Town.

■ Martin Goldsmith was a trainee hairdresser who played Welsh League football for his home-town team, Carmarthen Town. Having scored seven goals in a Welsh Cup tie for Carmarthen, he was signed by Cambridge United, but in three years at the Abbey Stadium he didn't really establish himself, and in January 1984 he arrived at Ninian Park on trial. He flirted briefly with the Bluebirds first team but was not offered a contract. He then joined Merthyr Tydfil, where he proved to be a prolific goalscorer. He later moved to Barry Town and helped them to successive Welsh League Championships.

GORDON Dean Dwight

Full-back

Born: Croydon, 10 February 1973. Career: Crystal Palace 1991. Middlesbrough 1998. Cardiff City (loan) 2001. Coventry City 2002. Reading (loan) 2004. Grimsby Town 2004. Macclesfield 2005. Apoel Nicosia (Cyprus).

■ England Under-21 international defender Dean Gordon began his career with Crystal Palace where, in his early days, he showed that he could perform equally well either on the left wing, at left-back or in the centre of defence. A strong tackler, adept at hitting long balls behind defenders, he helped Palace win the First Division Championship in 1993–94. In 1995–96 he scored a rare hat-trick at West Bromwich Albion, although two of the goals were penalties! Selected in the PFA award-winning Division One XI, he then suffered with a series of injuries before, in 1996–97, helping the Eagles return to the Premiership following their 1–0 defeat of Sheffield United in the Wembley play-off final. However, after Palace were again relegated after just one season of top-flight football, Gordon, who had scored 23 goals in 241 games for the Selhurst Park club, joined Middlesbrough for a fee of £900,000. Known affectionately as the 'flying wing-back', he was ever present in his first season at the Riverside – his aggression and enthusiasm, however, meant that he picked up a serious knee injury and was ruled out for the whole of the following campaign. The 2000–01 season saw Gordon again blighted by injuries and his absences coincided with the worst of 'Boro's performances. In November 2001 he joined Cardiff on loan, and during his time at Ninian Park he scored with two cracking free-kicks against Blackpool and Stoke City. He returned to the Riverside for a brief spell before joining Coventry City on a

free transfer. He later had a loan spell with Reading after the veteran full-back found himself out in the cold at Highfield Road. He joined Grimsby on a weekly contract as cover for early season injuries but then lost out and after a brief spell with Macclesfield opted to play for Apoel Nicosia of Cyprus.

GORDON Kenyatta Gavin

Striker

Born: Manchester, 24 June 1979. Career: Hull City 1996. Lincoln City 1997. Cardiff City 2000. Oxford United (loan) 2002. Notts County 2004.

Division Three runner-up 2000–01. Division Two promotion 2002–03.

■ Gavin Gordon became Hull City's second-youngest player when, at 16 years 88 days, he came off the bench in the Coca-Cola Cup tie at Premiership Coventry City. Despite showing plenty of promise, with his speed and power causing problems for defences, he was

allowed to join Lincoln City in November 1997, the Imps paying £30,000 for his services. He made good progress at Sincil Bank and his partnership with Lee Thorpe proved one of the most effective in the Third Division. Having scored 31 goals in 110 games for Lincoln, he was transferred to Cardiff City for £275,000 in December 2000. Following a couple of appearances as a substitute, he made the starting line-up for the game with Exeter City on New Year's Day and netted with a header in a 6–1 win. He then spent much of the remainder of the campaign on the treatment table. In 2001–02 he suffered a frustrating time with posture problems, but there is little doubt that the highlight of his campaign was the five goals he scored in City's 7–1 LDV Vans Trophy win over Rushden! After a loan spell with Oxford United, this brave, agile and pacy striker eventually broke into the first team, but at the end of the 2003–04 season he was released by the Ninian Park club. Gordon then joined Notts County where he led the front line well. He scored a number of vital goals and created chances for his teammates until his season was brought to a premature close by injury.

GORIN Edward Rosser (Ted)

Centre-forward

Born: Cardiff, 2 March 1924. Career: Grange Albion. Cardiff City 1948. Scunthorpe United 1950. Shrewsbury Town 1951.

■ A prolific scorer with Grange Albion, centre-forward Ted Gorin joined the Ninian Park staff in October 1948 and made his debut the following month in a 1–0 win at Coventry City. On his next appearance in a Cardiff shirt, he netted a late equaliser in a 2–2 draw at Leicester City, though most of his two seasons with the Bluebirds were spent in the reserves. Gorin, who netted on his last first-team appearance on the final day of the 1949–50 season, was transferred to Scunthorpe United in the close season. He managed a goal every other game for the Irons before moving to Shrewsbury Town where he ended his League career.

GORMAN Andrew David

Defender

Born: Cardiff, 13 September 1974.
Career: Cardiff City 1991. Yeovil Town.

■ Though he only made one League appearance for the Bluebirds during their Third Division Championship-winning season of 1992–93, after playing in 11 games the previous season, defender Andy Gorman netted one of Cardiff's goals in a 3–3 home draw with York City. It proved to be the former YTS player's last game for the club, and shortly afterwards he left to continue his career with non-League Yeovil Town.

GRAHAM Benjamin

Defender

Born: Pontypool, 23 September 1975.
Career: Cardiff City 1994. Bath City.

■ YTS defender Ben Graham's only League appearance for the Bluebirds was as a substitute in the final game of the 1993–94 season at Bradford City – a match Cardiff lost 2–0. During the close season he left Ninian Park to continue his career with non-League Bath City.

GRANT David

Left-back

Born: Sheffield, 2 June 1960.
Career: Sheffield Wednesday 1978. Oxford

United 1982. Chesterfield (loan) 1983. Cardiff City 1984. Rochdale 1985.

■ After working his way up through the ranks at Sheffield Wednesday, David Grant, under new manager Jack Charlton, proved himself to be a very capable full-back, strong in the tackle and a good distributor of the ball. When Wednesday won promotion from the Third Division in 1979–80, Grant missed just three games and was a regular member of the Owls side in their first season back in Division Two. On losing his place to Charlie Williamson, he moved to Oxford United from where he later went on loan to Chesterfield. In March 1984 he signed for Cardiff City but after a year at Ninian Park, he returned north to end his playing days with Rochdale.

GRANT Wilfred (Wilf)

Centre-forward

Born: Ashington, 31 August 1920.
Died: 1990.
Career: Morpeth Town. Manchester City 1943. Southampton 1946. Cardiff City 1950. Ipswich Town 1954.
Welsh Cup finalist 1950–51. Division Two runner-up 1951–52.

■ A Geordie who had been on the books of Manchester City, Wilf Grant moved to Southampton, scoring 11 goals in 61 games for the Saints before Cyril Spiers brought him to Ninian Park in exchange for Ernie Stevenson. Within months of his arrival, both Grant's career and City's future were to be changed forever when Mike Tiddy was signed and Grant moved from the wing to centre-forward. Using his speed through the middle, Grant netted 14 goals from just 25 League games, including a hat-trick in a 5–2 home defeat of Grimsby Town. When the club were promoted to the First Division the following season Grant was the club's only ever present and top scored with 26 League goals. He continued to score on a regular basis in the top flight and his form won him an England 'B' cap. Following the signing of Trevor Ford, Grant reverted to his wing position, but, after scoring 67 goals in 159 League and Cup games, he left Cardiff in October 1954 to join Ipswich Town. In his

second season at Portman Road he scored 16 goals in 35 games, including hat-tricks in two successive games – Millwall (home 6–2) and Reading (away 5–1). He netted another treble against Millwall in the return game. On hanging up his boots, he received an invitation from Cardiff manager Bill Jones to become a member of the club's coaching staff. He then spent five years with City during their rise and fall from the First Division in the early 1960s.

GRANVILLE Arthur

Right-back/right-half

Born: Llwynypia, 15 November 1912.
Died: 1987.
Career: Porth United. Cardiff City 1934.

■ Arthur Granville joined Cardiff from Porth United in the mid-1930s and, after a hesitant start, made the number-two shirt his own, although he occasionally turned out at right-half. In the years leading up to World War Two Granville was a virtual ever present in the City side. An imposing figure in the Cardiff defence, all his six goals for the club came from the penalty spot, but, like so many others, his career was cut short by the hostilities. During the war he stayed at Ninian Park and helped nurture the young talent that abounded in City's teams at that time. When League football resumed in 1946, Granville decided to retire from playing and coached local amateurs.

GRAPES Stephen Philip

Midfield

Born: Norwich, 25 February 1953.
Career: Norwich City 1970.
Bournemouth (loan) 1976. Cardiff City 1976. Torquay United 1982. Merthyr Tydfil.

Welsh Cup finalist 1976–77.

■ Steve Grapes started out with his home-town club, Norwich City, and although he spent six years at Carrow Road he never really established himself in the Canaries first team. Following a brief loan spell with Bournemouth, Grapes joined Cardiff City with Bluebirds boss Jimmy Andrews paying £7,000 to bring him to Ninian Park. His early games for the club were as an orthodox winger and though he laid on a number of chances for his inside-men, he was later moved into midfield. It was here that he played the bulk of his

games, though towards the end of his time at the club he even had the occasional outing at full-back. For much of his time at Ninian Park City were struggling in the lower reaches of Division Two, culminating in their relegation in 1981–82. At the end of that campaign Grapes moved to Torquay United, later returning to South Wales to see out his career with Merthyr Tydfil.

GRAY Alexander David (Alick)

Full-back

Born: Arbroath, 7 November 1936.
Career: Dundee Violet. Burnley 1954. Arbroath 1955. Cardiff City 1957. Worcester City.

■ Full-back Alick Gray was spotted by Burnley manager Frank Hill playing for Dundee Violet, but, although he impressed in the club's Central League side, he failed to break into the first team. He returned north of the border to play for his home-town team Arbroath before, in March 1957, joining Cardiff City. While with the Bluebirds, he did his National Service with the Welch Regiment. He hardly missed a game at reserve-team level, but his only Football League appearance came in a 3–2 defeat at Barnsley when he replaced the injured Ron Stitfall.

GRAY Julian Raymond

Winger

Born: Lewisham, 21 September 1979.
Career: Arsenal 1998. Crystal Palace 2000. Cardiff City (loan) 2003. Birmingham City 2004.

■ A tall, versatile left-sided player, Julian Gray made his first-team debut for Arsenal as a substitute in their final Premiership game of the 1999–2000 season. Possessing plenty of speed and a good crosser of the ball, he was rather surprisingly allowed to leave Highbury in the close season and joined Crystal Palace for a fee of £250,000. Featuring regularly for the Eagles in the first half of the following season, he was then switched to the left wing where he not only caused opponents problems but scored a number of spectacular goals.

Surprisingly transfer listed by Palace in the summer of 2003, he had trials with a number of Premiership clubs before being loaned out to Cardiff in October. He spent a month getting fit and then after a second month, in which he made nine appearances, he returned to Selhurst Park. He then went on to transform the Eagles' season as they rose from the relegation zone to the play-offs and eventually clinched a place in the Premiership. On parting company with Crystal Palace, Gray joined Birmingham City and was a big success during his first full season in the Premiership. His form down the left side was so good that he was considered for an England call-up, though in 2005–06 he struggled to hold down a regular pace as the St Andrew's club struggled in the lower reaches of the top flight.

GREEN Ryan Michael

Right-back

Born: Cardiff, 20 October 1980.
Career: Wolverhampton Wanderers 1997. Torquay United (loan) 2001. Millwall 2001. Cardiff City 2002. Sheffield Wednesday 2002. Hereford United 2003.

■ Wales's youngest ever debutant in 1998, Ryan Green had played twice for his country by the age of 17, yet he had not even been close to a Wolves debut!

He eventually got his chance at Molineux when Kevin Muscat was suspended in November 1998. Unable to win a regular place in the side, he linked up with former boss Colin Lee at Torquay United, but once his loan period expired he joined Millwall, managed by another former Wolves boss, Mark McGhee. Eventually finding himself out of favour, he joined Cardiff City, but after just one substitute appearance against Exeter City in the LDV Vans Trophy he moved on to Sheffield Wednesday before later moving into the Conference with Hereford United.

GREENACRE Christopher Mark (Chris)

Striker

Born: Halifax, 23 December 1977.
Career: Manchester City 1995. Cardiff City (loan) 1997. Blackpool (loan) 1998. Scarborough (loan) 1998. Mansfield Town 1999. Stoke City 2002.

■ One of the many young professionals on Manchester City's books, he was unable to hold down a regular place, and at the start of the 1997–98 season he was loaned out to Cardiff City. He appeared regularly for the Bluebirds, scoring twice and gaining vital experience. Following a brief return to Maine Road he went out on loan again, this time to Blackpool. Placed on Manchester City's transfer list, he had another loan spell with Scarborough before moving to Mansfield Town. A speedy, attacking player with an eye for goals, he netted for the Stags from the centre-circle at Cheltenham and scored a hat-trick against Halifax Town, and his goalscoring exploits attracted a lot of scouts to Field Mill. Selected for the PFA Division Three side in 2001–02, he had scored 58 goals for Mansfield in 131 games when he joined Stoke City. Injuries have disrupted his progress at the Britannia Stadium and he has yet to show his true form.

GREENE David Michael

Central-defender

Born: Luton, 26 October 1973.
Career: Luton Town 1991. Colchester
United (loan) 1995. Brentford (loan) 1996. Colchester United 1996. Cardiff City 2000. Cambridge United 2001.

■ A Republic of Ireland Under-21 international, he worked his way up through the ranks at Luton Town, but due to the presence of Trevor Peake and Marvin Johnson at the heart of the Hatters defence he had loan spells with Colchester United and Brentford before moving on to play for the Layer Road club on a permanent basis. Only missing games through suspension, his presence was vital in a Colchester rearguard, and he contributed the aggregate equaliser against Barnet in the 1997–98 play-off semi-final before putting in a towering display at Wembley. The following season he deservedly claimed a clean sweep of all the 'Player of the Year' awards, but then injuries began to restrict his first-team appearances and in July 2000, after scoring 17 goals in 180 games for Colchester, he joined Cardiff on a free transfer. Signing a three-year deal, he featured regularly in the early season games, but after new owner Sam Hammam arrived and brought in a number of new faces he was allowed to leave and moved to Cambridge United where he ended his first-team career.

GREW Mark Stuart

Goalkeeper

Born: Bilston, 15 February 1958.
Career: West Bromwich Albion 1976. Wigan Athletic (loan) 1978. Leicester City 1983. Oldham Athletic (loan) 1983. Ipswich Town 1984. Fulham (loan) 1985. West Bromwich Albion (loan) 1986. Port Vale 1986. Blackburn Rovers (loan) 1990. Cardiff City 1992. Stafford Rangers. Hednesford Town.

Division Three Champion 1992–93.

■ Mark Grew's debut for West Bromwich Albion was a real oddity for the time – coming on as a substitute goalkeeper in a 1978–79 UEFA Cup tie against Galatasaray! Following a loan spell with Wigan Athletic during the Latics' first season in the Football League, he joined Leicester City and then Ipswich Town, but at both clubs he failed to break into the side on a regular basis. There followed loan spells at
Fulham and West Bromwich Albion before, in the summer of 1986, he joined Port Vale. He suffered a serious knee injury early in his Vale career but returned to perform heroically in both their 1988 Cup run and their 1989 promotion-winning campaign. Twice voted the club's 'Player of the Year', he ended his League career with Cardiff City. After playing in the club's opening 10 games of their Third Division Championship-winning season he suffered an injury that kept him out of action until the following season. After spells at non-League Stafford Rangers and Hednesford Town, Grew returned to Vale Park as the club's Youth Development Officer being appointed assistant manager.

GRIFFITH Cohen

Winger

Born: Guyana, 26 December 1962.
Career: Kettering Town. Cardiff City 1989. Barry Town.

Welsh Cup winner 1991–92, 1992–93. Division Three champion 1992–93. Welsh Cup finalist 1993–94.

■ The Bluebirds paid Kettering Town £60,000 for the services of Cohen Griffith in October 1989, and he scored after just 19 minutes of his first-team debut as City won 3–2 at Huddersfield Town. He ended the season with 10 goals in 38 League games, but City were relegated. He continued to find the back of the net the following season and scored in each of the club's four Football League Cup games. In 1991–92 he was moved into more of a defensive midfield role and, after helping the club win promotion the following season, went on to score 48 goals in 275 League and Cup games before being given a free transfer and leaving to play Welsh League football for Barry Town.

GRIFFITHS Philip Henry

Outside-right

Born: Tylorstown, 25 October 1908.
Died: 1978.
Career: Wattstown. Stoke City 1925. Port Vale 1926. Everton 1931. West Bromwich Albion 1933. Cardiff City 1934. Folkestone.

■ A prolific goalscorer for Wattstown where he scored 79 goals in the 1925–26 season, he was invited to Stoke for a trial but ended up signing for neighbours Port Vale. He soon became a regular for the Valiants and was a member of their Third Division North Championship-winning side of 1929–30. The right-winger, who possessed a powerful shot, joined Everton in May 1931 but did not live up to expectations in his time at Goodison, although he did win full international honours for Wales against Scotland. He then had a spell with West Bromwich Albion before signing for Cardiff in the summer of 1934. After making his City debut in a 2–1 home win over Charlton Athletic on the opening day of the 1934–35 season, he then scored the only goal of the game two days later against Luton Town. Despite some good displays, he lost his place to Reggie Pugh,and at the end of the season he moved into non-League football with Folkestone.

GRIFFITHS Stanley (Stan)

Inside-left/outside-left

Born: Pentre, 20 June 1911.
Career: Cardiff City 1931. Chester 1932. Gillingham 1933. Cardiff City 1934. Dundalk.

■ Stan Griffiths started out with Cardiff City, but after being unable to break into the club's League side he left to play for Chester. He underwent a similar experience with the Cestrians, and it was only when he signed for Gillingham that he first played League football. He rejoined Cardiff in the summer of 1934, and although he only made two appearances he had the unusual experience of scoring against Reading in what turned out to be his last appearance. On leaving Ninian Park he crossed the water to end his career with Dundalk.

GRIFFITHS Wyn Rhys

Goalkeeper

Born: Blaelgwynfi, 17 October 1919.
Career: Cardiff City 1947. Newport County 1952.

■ Goalkeeper Wyn Griffiths was an amateur with Derby County before World War Two and came to Ninian Park during the hostilities. He 'guested' for Arsenal and in 1945 was in their team that entertained Moscow Dynamo. His solitary League appearance for the Bluebirds came in April 1948 in a 1–1 home draw against Newcastle United, but as he was unable to oust Danny Canning and later Phil Joslin he joined his former teammate Fred Stansfield at Newport County where he finished his career.

GRIMSHAW William (Billy)

Outside-right

Born: Burnley, 30 April 1892.
Career: Burnley 1910. Colne. Bradford City 1912. Cardiff City 1919. Sunderland 1923.

Division Two runner-up 1920–21. Welsh Cup winner 1921–22, 1922–23. Division One runner-up 1923–24.

■ Unable to force his way into his home-town team, Burnley, winger Billy Grimshaw had a spell playing for Colne before signing for Bradford City in 1912. An important member of their League side up until the outbreak of World War One, he then left Valley Parade at the end of the hostilities and signed for Cardiff City. He had a full season in City's successful Southern League side, scoring 14 goals in 32

games, mainly at inside-right. Following the arrival of Jimmy Gill, Grimshaw reverted to the flank and scored on his League debut in the club's inaugural game at Stockport County, which the Bluebirds won 5–2. Grimshaw, who was a virtual ever present over the next three seasons of League football, won Football League representative honours before losing his place to Denis Lawson, signed from St Mirren. Transferred to Sunderland, he made 70 appearances for the Wearsiders before hanging up his boots and becoming a licensee in Bradford.

GROTIER Peter David

Goalkeeper

Born: Stratford, 18 October 1950.
Career: West Ham United 1968. Cardiff City (loan) 1973. Lincoln City 1974. Cardiff City 1979. Grimsby Town 1982.

■ Goalkeeper Peter Grotier began his League career with West Ham United. Although for much of his time at Upton Park he was understudy to Bobby Ferguson, he still managed 50 appearances before joining Cardiff on loan prior to signing for Lincoln City. He stayed for five years at Sincil Bank, helping the Imps win the Fourth Division Championship in 1975–76. Having appeared in 233 League games for Lincoln, he then joined Cardiff City in December 1979 after Richie Morgan had paid £25,000 to bring him to Ninian Park. During much of his time with the Bluebirds he found himself sharing the goalkeeping duties with Ron Healey, and in March 1982 he moved to Grimsby Town as player-coach. A few years later he was appointed assistant manager of the Mariners.

GUMMER Jason Craig

Midfield

Born: Tredegar, 27 October 1967.
Career: Cardiff City 1985. Torquay United (loan) 1989.

■ A Welsh Youth international, midfielder, Jason Gummer progressed through the ranks at Ninian Park to make his League debut in a 1–1 draw at York City in September 1985. He was unfortunate that injury and illness then

held him back as his career looked set to take off, and in October 1987 a mixture of disagreement and disillusionment led to Gummer walking out on the club despite being under contract. He later returned to Ninian Park, but after a loan spell with Torquay United he decided to part company with the club on a permanent basis.

HAGAN Alfred (Alfie)

Inside-forward

Born: Usworth, 10 November 1895.
Died: 1980.
Career: Washington Colliery. Newcastle United 1919. Cardiff City 1923. Tranmere Rovers 1926.

■ Without having a great deal of height or build, Alfie Hagan, who joined Newcastle United from Washington Colliery, relied on his considerable ball skills, which at times delighted the Tyneside crowd. Appearing for the Magpies during the immediate seasons after World War One, he was the father of Jimmy Hagan, a noted player for Sheffield United and England during the 1950s. Hagan left St James' Park in the summer of 1923 and joined Cardiff but had to wait until Boxing Day before making his debut in a 3–1 defeat of

Sheffield United. Though he stayed at Ninian Park for three seasons, he found it difficult to hold down a first-team place, and in July 1926 he and Herbie Evans joined Tranmere Rovers. He later returned to his native North East to play local football.

HAIG Richard Neil

Forward

Born: Pontypridd, 29 December 1970.
Career: Cardiff City 1989. Merthyr Tydfil.

■ Having come off the bench at Brentford towards the end of the 1988–89 season, forward Richard Haig made three more appearances as a substitute during the club's relegation season of 1989–90. Eventually, he made his only start for the club at Shrewsbury Town in a match that failed to produce a goal. Not retained at the end of the season, he left to play for Merthyr Tydfil.

HALLIDAY Thomas

Centre-forward

Born: Ardrossan, 28 April 1940.
Career: Dumbarton. Cardiff City 1963. Dumbarton 1965.

■ The chunkily-built Scotsman had built up a good reputation as a part-timer with Dumbarton, prior to Cardiff manager George Swindin paying £5,000 for his services in October 1963. After making his debut in the South Wales derby as City drew 1–1 at home to Swansea, Halliday enjoyed a lengthy run in the team, scoring in successive defeats at Southampton and Norwich before losing out to Derek Tapscott. He later rejoined Dumbarton where he rediscovered his shooting boots!

HALLWORTH Jonathan Geoffrey (Jon)

Goalkeeper

Born: Stockport, 26 October 1965.
Career: Ipswich Town 1983. Bristol Rovers (loan) 1985. Oldham Athletic 1989. Cardiff City 1997.

FAW Invitation Cup finalist 1997–98.
Division Three promotion 1998–99.

■ Jon Hallworth made his Football League debut for Bristol Rovers before

returning to Portman Road and playing his first game for Ipswich Town. Prior to 1987–88 he spent most of his time at the Suffolk club deputising for Paul Cooper but started that season as first choice before making way for Craig Forrest. He never played for Town's first team again and in February 1989 was transferred to Oldham Athletic. He appeared in every game of Oldham's 1990–91 Second Division Championship-winning season, and in the top flight the following season was again consistent to a fault, missing only the final game. In 1992–93 he damaged his wrist diving at the feet of Mark Hughes but carried on playing, not realising his wrist was broken in three places! On regaining full fitness he found that he had to share the goalkeeping duties with Paul Gerrard and then Gary Kelly. Having appeared in 217 games for the Latics, he was given a free transfer, and in the summer of 1997 he joined Cardiff City. He had an outstanding first season at Ninian Park and won every Player of the Year award available. The fans firmly believed he was the best 'keeper in the Third Division and could not understand why he was not named in the PFA Divisional team. However, in 1998–99 his displays led to the Bluebirds winning promotion to Division Two, and he was included in the PFA award-winning Third Division side! Unfortunately in 1999–2000 he suffered a knee problem and gradually lost confidence. Though he had come to the end of his three-year contract, he was offered new terms and stayed at the club as cover for Mark Walton before deciding to retire.

HAMILTON David

Midfield

Born: South Shields, 7 November 1960.
Career: Sunderland 1978. Blackburn Rovers 1981. Cardiff City (loan) 1985. Wigan Athletic 1986. Chester City 1989. Burnley 1990. Chorley. Barrow. Accrington.

■ After winning England Youth international honours, David Hamilton signed as a professional with Sunderland. Unable to break into the Black Cats first team, he joined

Blackburn Rovers on a free transfer. He was never quite a regular in his time at Ewood Park and in March 1985 joined Cardiff City on loan. After making his Bluebirds debut in a 2–2 draw at Manchester City, he played in the last 10 games of the 1984–85 season, and though he performed creditably in a defensive midfield role he couldn't prevent Cardiff's relegation to the Third Division. After another season with Blackburn he signed for Wigan Athletic, and in his first season at Springfield Park he helped the Latics reach the play-offs and the sixth round of the FA Cup. Despite being voted Wigan's Player of the Year in 1987–88, he was later allowed to join Chester City. Hamilton ended his first-team career with Burnley before playing non-League football for Chorley, Barrow and Accrington. He later spent some time on the coaching staff of both Preston and Rochdale.

HAMILTON Derrick Vivian (Des)

Midfield
Born: Bradford, 15 August 1976.

Career: Bradford City 1994. Newcastle United 1997. Sheffield United (loan) 1998. Huddersfield Town (loan) 1999. Norwich City (loan) 2000. Tranmere Rovers (loan) 2000. Cardiff City 2001. Grimsby Town 2003. Barnet.

■ A strong, aggressive and hard-running midfielder, he began his career with Bradford City, and in 1995–96 he scored in both the semi-final and final stages of the play-offs to help the Bantams into the First Division. The following season he was moved to the right wing-back position and became a revelation. Such was his form that he was selected for the Nationwide Under-21 League side against the Italian League and was eventually sold to Newcastle United for £1.5 million. He had yet to make his debut for the Magpies when his newly-found status saw him honoured at England Under-21 level. After playing in a handful of games for United, he was hampered by injury, and, following the appointment of Ruud Gullit, he was loaned out to Sheffield United, Huddersfield Town and Norwich City. Having lost none of his relish for the engine-room battle, he then had two separate loan spells with Tranmere Rovers before signing for the Bluebirds in the summer of 2001. Frustrated by injuries, including a thigh strain that kept him out of the Second Division play-offs and a spate of injuries in 2002–03, which forced him to miss more games than he started, he left to join Grimsby Town. Unable to win a regular place, he later signed non-contract forms for Barnet.

HAMPSON Thomas (Tommy)

Goalkeeper

Born: Bury, 2 May 1898.
Career: South Shields. Walker Celtic. West Ham United 1920. Blackburn Rovers 1925. Burnley 1925. West Stanley. Darlington 1926. Cardiff City 1926. Notts County 1929.

■ Unable to make the grade with South Shields, goalkeeper Tommy Hampson was signed by West Ham United in 1920 as understudy to the Hammers great custodian Ted Hufton. In five years at Upton Park Tommy Hampson proved a more than capable deputy by making 70 appearances until a move to Blackburn Rovers in 1925. After a spell with Burnley, Hampson moved into non-League football with West Stanley on the understanding that if a League club wanted him then he would be free to negotiate. He joined Darlington in December 1926. Cardiff brought Hampson to Ninian Park, but with Tom Farquharson at his peak Hampson found his chances extremely limited and moved on to end his career with Notts County.

HANSBURY Roger

Goalkeeper

Born: Barnsley, 26 January 1955.
Career: Norwich City 1973. Cambridge United (loan) 1977. Eastern Athletic (Hong Kong). Burnley 1983. Cambridge United 1985. Birmingham City 1986. Sheffield United (loan) 1987. Wolverhampton Wanderers (loan) 1989. Colchester United (loan) 1989. Cardiff City 1989.

Welsh Cup winner 1991–92.

■ One of a number of players who seemed to follow John Bond around from club to club, goalkeeper Roger Hansbury started out with Norwich City. While at Carrow Road, he had a loan spell with Cambridge United, helping the U's win promotion to the Second Division in 1977–78. After a spell in Hong Kong playing for Eastern Athletic he joined Burnley, but after finding himself sharing the goalkeeping duties with Joe Neenan he was released and rejoined Cambridge. As United were heading towards an application for re-election, Hansbury left to team up with John Bond yet again, this time at Birmingham City. After understudying David Seaman, he stepped up to become a first-team regular, but later drifted around the League, completing loan spells at numerous clubs until signing for Cardiff, his last League club, in October 1989. Though City were relegated in his first season at Ninian Park, Hansbury was a virtual ever present in his time there, and, while he wouldn't claim to be the best goalkeeper ever, he worked hard at his game and made the most of the ability he had.

HARDING Paul John

Midfield

Born: Mitcham, 6 March 1964.
Career: Carshalton Athletic. Dulwich Hamlet. Enfield. Barnet. Notts County 1990. Southend United (loan) 1993. Watford (loan) 1993. Birmingham City 1993. Cardiff City 1995. Worcester City.

■ A midfielder who didn't play League football until he was 26, he became one of many players signed more than once by Barry Fry. Having played non-League football for Carshalton Athletic, Dulwich Hamlet and Enfield, he was with Barnet when Notts County paid £60,000 for him in the summer of 1990. While with the Meadow Lane club, he had loan spells with Southend United and Watford, and within a few weeks he played at Roots Hall as a substitute against Watford and then for the Hornets as a substitute against Southend! In December 1993 he signed for Birmingham City but failed to hold down a regular place and, in the summer of 1995, joined Cardiff. Seen as an inspirational signing, he was immediately made club captain, but in a side that struggled all through the 1995–96 season he failed to stamp his authority on the team and left to play non-League football for Worcester City.

HARDY William (Billy)

Left-half

Born: Bedlington,18 April 1891.
Died: 1981.
Career: Bedlington United. Heart of Midlothian. Stockport County 1910. Cardiff City 1911. Bradford Park Avenue 1932.

Division Two runner-up 1920–21. Welsh Cup winner 1921–22, 1926–27, 1927–28. Division One runner-up 1923–24. FA Cup finalist 1924–25. FA Cup winner 1926–27. FA Charity Shield winner 1927–28.

■ Whenever the great days of the Bluebirds are recalled, Billy Hardy's name remains synonymous with the club. After beginning his career with his home-town Bedlington United in 1910, left-half Hardy went to play Scottish League football with Heart of Midlothian before returning to England

to play for Stockport County. Hardy arrived at Ninian Park for the start of the club's 1911–12 Southern League season, and, during their time in that competition, he was a virtual ever present, appearing in 144 matches before the club attained Football League status in 1920. Hardy, who made his League debut against his former club Stockport on the opening day of the 1920–21 season, was the club's only ever present as they won promotion to the First Division. Hardy appeared in both of City's FA Cup Finals, and it was often thought he was denied an international cap because he was with a Welsh club. He was selected to represent the Football League in 1927–28. Not including wartime games and friendlies, Billy Hardy appeared in a phenomenal 585 first-team games for Cardiff City, a total that includes 354 Football League matches. His last game in Cardiff colours came at the age of 41 in a 1–0 home win over Gillingham in March 1932. After leaving Ninian Park, he managed Bradford Park Avenue for four seasons, later working as a chief scout for the Yorkshire club.

HARKIN John Terence (Terry)

Centre-forward

Born: Derry, Northern Ireland, 14 September 1941.
Career: Derry City. Coleraine. Port Vale 1962. Crewe Alexandra 1964. Cardiff City 1965. Notts County 1966. Southport 1967. Shrewsbury Town 1969. Finn Harps. Dundalk.

■ Northern Ireland international Terry Harkin played for Derry City and Coleraine before moving into the Football League with Port Vale in September 1962. Only selected periodically, he was allowed to join Crewe Alexandra and in 1964–65 scored 34 goals in 42 League games, including four in a 6–2 win over Barrow. This form prompted Jimmy Scoular to pay £12,000 to bring Harkin to Ninian Park. He scored on his debut in a 2–1 defeat of Derby County and, in fact, scored seven goals in his first eight games. But the goals dried up and after making fleeting appearances after that he moved on to Notts County. Within a year he was on the move again, this time to Southport, where he rediscovered his goalscoring touch. He then had a spell with Shrewsbury Town before returning to Ireland to play for Finn Harps and later Dundalk.

HARPER Alan

Defender/midfield

Born: Liverpool, 1 November 1960.
Career: Liverpool 1978. Everton 1983. Sheffield Wednesday 1988. Manchester City 1989. Everton 1991. Luton Town 1993. Burnley 1994. Cardiff City (loan) 1995.

■ England Youth international Alan Harper began his career with Liverpool, but in five years with the Reds he never got beyond the Central League side and, in June 1983, joined Merseyside rivals Everton for £100,000. Though he immediately won a first-team place, he missed out on Everton's FA Cup triumph against Watford through injury but picked up a runners'-up medal in the League Cup against Liverpool after a replay. He was on the fringe of the Everton team during the club's League Championship and European Cup-Winners' Cup winning season but missed out on the silverware. He did, however, win a League Championship medal in 1987 as the title came to Goodison Park for the second time in three years. In the summer of 1988

Harper moved to Sheffield Wednesday for £275,000 and then again at Christmas 1989 as Manchester City paid £150,000 for his services. He returned to Goodison in August 1991 but moved out of the top flight for the first time in his 10-year League career when he joined Luton. He then played for Burnley before joining Cardiff on loan in November 1995. The last of his five League appearances saw the Bluebirds beaten 5–0 at Preston North End, and he returned to Turf Moor to work as youth coach following the departure of Jimmy Mullen.

HARPER James Alan John (Jamie)

Midfield

Born: Chelmsford, 9 November 1980.
Career: Arsenal 1999. Cardiff City (loan) 2000. Reading 2001.

■ Unable to break into the senior team at Highbury, this talented youngster joined Cardiff City on loan in December 2000 with a view to a permanent transfer. No deal could be reached, and after three games he returned to Arsenal before moving on to Reading for £400,000 shortly afterwards. He scored on his debut and began to play with an assured arrogance and determination and to fulfil his potential as a creative and industrious midfield player. Voted the Royals Player of the Season in 2002–03, he attracted the attention of Premiership clubs but is still at the Madejski Stadium, having now appeared in 129 games.

HARRINGTON Alan Charles

Full-back

Born: Penarth, 17 November 1933.
Career: Cardiff Nomads. Cardiff City 1951.

Welsh Cup winner 1955–56. Division Two runner-up 1959–60. Welsh Cup finalist 1959–60.

■ One of the club's all-time greats, he joined the Bluebirds from local side Cardiff Nomads in the autumn of 1951, but he had to wait until midway through the 1952–53 season before being given a chance in the City side. Playing at wing-half he made an impressive debut in a goalless draw against Tottenham Hotspur at Ninian Park. He went on to make 10 League appearances that season, and in his first six matches for Cardiff the opposition failed to score. However, it

was in the 1954–55 season that Alan Harrington established himself as a first-team regular and, with the exception of the entire 1963–64 campaign because of a broken leg, he was a virtual ever present in the Cardiff side for the next 12 seasons. Harrington was strong in the tackle and a good distributor of the ball. He had played in 405 first-team games for the Ninian Park outfit when he was forced to give up the game following

another broken leg, sustained in a 1–1 draw against Leyton Orient at Brisbane Road in January 1966. He later managed the newly-founded Sully to Welsh League honours.

HARRIS Brian

Wing-half

Born: Bebington, 16 May 1935.
Career: Port Sunlight. Everton 1954. Cardiff City 1966. Newport County 1971.

Welsh Cup winner 1966–67, 1967–68, 1968–69, 1969–70.

■ One of the game's most underrated footballers, Brian Harris was a winger when he joined Everton from non-League Port Sunlight in January 1954. However, he only began to develop his full potential after he'd been converted to wing-half. His skill and vision were supplemented by a ferocious tackle, good aerial ability and a powerful shot. Playing in a deep-lying role, he was an important part of Everton's transformation from a club struggling at the foot of Division One to one of the major powers in British football. He helped the Goodison club win the League Championship in 1962–63 and then the FA Cup in 1966. In the 11 years he was with Everton, Harris played in every position except goalkeeper for the first team. Having scored 27 goals in

346 games, he left Everton in the October, following the Final, to join Cardiff City for £10,000. His debut for the Bluebirds was in stark contrast to his glory days on Merseyside as Cardiff were beaten 7–1 by Plymouth Argyle! No stranger to European soccer, having played in Everton's early European Cup and Fairs games, he played in all nine of Cardiff's 1967–68 European Cup-Winners' Cup games when they just missed out on reaching the Final. While at Ninian Park, he helped the club develop into a good Second Division outfit, but in the summer of 1971 he left to become player-manager of Newport County. He later returned to Ninian Park as assistant manager to Richie Morgan, a post he held for two years.

HARRIS Francis (Frank)

Right-half/inside-right

Born: Catshill, 5 April 1908.
Career: Cradley Heath. Bromsgrove Rovers. Cardiff City 1928. Charlton Athletic 1933. Brierley Hill Alliance.

■ A mechanic who played his early football with Cradley Heath and Bromsgrove Rovers and toured the United States with the Worcestershire FA before signing for City in 1928, Frank Harris was initially an inside-forward before switching to wing-half. He scored on his home debut in a 2–1 defeat by Leicester City but, thereafter, suffered with a spate of niggling injuries before, in 1931–32, being absent for just two games – one of which was a 5–1 defeat at Reading. He had scored 12 goals in 135 League and Cup games when, in 1933, he was surprisingly transferred to Charlton Athletic. The Addicks, like City, had dropped from the First to the Third Division in quick-time, but with Harris in their side the London club won successive promotions to regain their place in the top flight. Without this exciting talent the Bluebirds continued to struggle.

HARRIS Gary Wayne

Winger

Born: Birmingham, 31 May 1959.
Career: Cardiff City 1977. Trowbridge Town.

■ Having joined the Bluebirds on junior forms, winger Gary Harris did well enough in reserve football to earn an early League baptism, but with City playing badly Bristol Rovers ran out winners in the Eastville encounter 4–2. Harris played in the last three matches of the following season, 1979–80, but was not retained and moved into non-League football with Trowbridge Town.

HARRIS Gordon William

Full-back

Born: Campmuir 19 February 1945.
Career: Luncerty. Forfar Athletic. Cardiff City 1965.

■ Full-back Gordon Harris played Scottish junior football for Luncerty before signing as a part-timer with Forfar Athletic. His form for the Loons was so impressive that the scouts of top clubs in the Football League were alerted. In March 1965 Jimmy Scoular paid £2,000 to bring him to Ninian Park, and Harris was drafted into the City side immediately on his arrival. Despite his size and strength, he did not have the required pace to make any impact, his last appearance coming in the 5–0 defeat of Swansea the following month. On leaving City he stayed in Cardiff to continue his studies as a trainee architect.

HARRIS Mark Andrew

Central-defender

Born: Reading, 15 July 1963.
Career: Wokingham Town. Crystal Palace 1988. Burnley (loan) 1989. Swansea City 1989. Gillingham 1995. Cardiff City 1997. Kingstonian.

FAW Invitation Cup finalist 1997–98.

■ Defender Mark Harris was a late entrant into League football, signing for Crystal Palace in 1988, aged 24, from Wokingham Town of the Vauxhall Opel League. After a brief introduction to First Division football, he joined Burnley on loan before being transferred to Swansea City for £22,500. A fixture in the Swans defence during his six years at the Vetch Field, he was ever present in 1993–94, a campaign in which he helped them to victory in the Autoglass Trophy at Wembley. Huddersfield were finally overcome in a penalty shoot-out following a 1–1 draw after extra-time. In September 1995 he moved to Gillingham and was a regular in the side promoted from Division Three. He joined the Bluebirds prior to the start of the 1997–98 season to act as cover for Jeff Eckhardt and Scott Young, but with the former suspended and then suffering a number of injuries Harris stepped in and played for most of the season. His only goal was a magnificent volley against the eventual Third Division champions Notts County, but because of his age he was given a free transfer and joined non-League Kingstonian.

HARRIS Neil

Forward

Born: Orsett, 12 July 1977.
Career: Chelmsford. Millwall 1998. Cardiff City (loan) 2004. Nottingham Forest 2004. Gillingham 2005.

■ Spotted in non-League football as a regular goalscorer for Chelmsford, Neil Harris signed for Millwall on transfer deadline day in March 1998. In his first full season he was the Lions leading scorer with 15 League goals, and it was no surprise when the supporters voted him Player of the Year. Known as 'Bomber', he again top scored in 1999–2000, the quick-footed forward netting 25 times and attracting the attention of a number of Premiership clubs. Remaining at the New Den, he continued his prolific goalscoring with 27 strikes, including an amazing tally of three hat-tricks. Harris, who was one of three Millwall players selected for the PFA's Second Division team at the end of the season, then had a frustrating campaign. But after recovering from a serious illness he was back to his best, and in 2002–03 he was the club's leading scorer in the First Division. He continued to feature regularly for Millwall the following season, though many of his appearances came from the substitutes' bench. A member of the Millwall side that lost to Manchester United in the 2004 FA Cup Final, he had just beaten Teddy Sheringham's Millwall club goalscoring record when he joined Cardiff on loan. He came off the bench to replace Cameron Jerome, who had scored one of City's goals in a 3–1 defeat of Gillingham, before, following another substitute appearance, he started the game against Sheffield United. He repaid Lennie Lawrence's faith by scoring in the Bramall Lane encounter, but the Blades won 2–1. However, terms between the two clubs couldn't be agreed, and Harris moved on to Nottingham Forest but was unable to prevent their relegation. Having failed to add to his career tally of goals, Harris left the City Ground to continue his career with Gillingham.

HARRISON Gerald Randall (Gerry)

Defender/midfield

Born: Lambeth, 15 April 1972.
Career: Watford 1989. Bristol City 1991. Cardiff City (loan) 1992. Hereford United (loan) 1993. Bath City (loan) 1993. Huddersfield Town 1994. Burnley 1994. Sunderland 1998. Luton Town (loan) 1998. Hull City (loan) 1999. Halifax Town 1999. Leigh RMI.

■ After signing as a professional with Watford, Gerry Harrison played a handful of games in the Hornets midfield before being transferred to Bristol City in the summer of 1991. A loan period at Cardiff in 1991–92 saw Harrison make 10 appearances for the

Bluebirds, with his only goal coming in a 2–2 draw at Hereford United. It was only when he returned to Ashton Gate that he enjoyed his first taste of regular first-team football. However, after loan spells at Hereford and Bath City, Harrison joined Huddersfield Town but was released without making an appearance in the first team. He then joined Burnley, where his uncompromising style frequently got him into trouble with referees. His total commitment was never in doubt though, and he went on to appear in 146 games for the Clarets before being out of contract and joining Sunderland. Further loan spells, this time at Luton Town and Hull City, followed before he was released by the Wearsiders. After ending his first-class career with Halifax Town, he moved into non-League circles with Leigh RMI.

HARRISON James

Inside-left

Born: Bolton.
Career: Hibernian. Cardiff City 1937. Chorley.

■ Inside-forward James Harrison began his career north of the border playing for Hibernian. Unable to settle at Easter Road, he signed for Cardiff City in March 1938. His only first-team appearance for the Bluebirds came the following month on Good Friday when he created the goal for Jimmy Collins in a 1–1 draw with Bristol Rovers. In the close season he left Ninian Park and returned to his native North West to play non-League football for Chorley.

HATTON Robert James (Bob)

Forward

Born: Hull, 10 April 1947.
Career: Wolverhampton Wanderers 1964. Bolton Wanderers 1967. Northampton Town 1968. Carlisle United 1969. Birmingham City 1971. Blackpool 1976. Luton Town 1978. Sheffield United 1980. Cardiff City 1982. Dundalk.

Division Three runner-up 1982–83.

■ A consistent goalscorer wherever he played, Bob Hatton began his career

with Wolverhampton Wanderers before moving on to Bolton, Northampton Town and Carlisle United. In October 1971 Hatton joined Birmingham City for a club-record fee of £82,500. He spent five years at St Andrew's, his longest spell with any one club. In his first season he helped Birmingham win promotion to the First Division, scoring 15 goals in 26 games, and netted some important goals in the club's run to the FA Cup semi-finals. Thriving on the pinpoint crosses of Gordon Taylor, he was Birmingham's leading scorer for the next three seasons, but in the summer of 1976, after scoring 73 goals in 218 games, he left to join Blackpool. Following two seasons at Bloomfield Road he moved to Luton Town, where he formed a prolific strike partnership with David Moss. He later played for Sheffield United before, in November 1982, joining Cardiff City. Signed by Len Ashurst to aid the Bluebirds promotion push, Hatton scored on his home debut against Chesterfield and in the next four games, finishing with nine goals in 29 League outings, as City finished runners-up in the Third Division. He then had a spell in the League of Ireland with Dundalk before going into the insurance business in the Midlands.

HAWORTH Simon Owen

Striker

Born: Cardiff, 30 March 1977.
Career: Cardiff City 1995. Coventry City 1997. Wigan Athletic 1998. Tranmere Rovers 2002.

■ Simon Haworth was pitched into the Bluebirds side following an injury crisis at the start of the 1995–96 season. However, it was midway through the following campaign before he established himself as a first-team regular, scoring some superb goals. A proposed transfer to Norwich City on deadline day fell through, but after winning full international honours for Wales he left Ninian Park to join Coventry City for £500,000. Although he scored on his Sky Blues debut, his subsequent performances were not so impressive, and in October 1998 he moved to Wigan Athletic for £600,000, then the club's record signing. He helped the Latics win the Autowindscreens Shield and scored the club's first-ever goal at the new JJB Stadium. He finished the 1999–2000 season with 20 goals and netted in the Wembley play-off final. Haworth topped the club's scoring charts the following season, netting his first ever hat-trick against Colchester United. Having scored 58 goals in 141 games, he left Wigan for Tranmere Rovers in February

2002. Resuming his old striking partnership with Stuart Barlow, he ended his first season at Prenton Park as the Wirral club's top scorer with 22 goals. Sadly, this keen racing fan, who owns a racehorse with teammate Gareth Roberts, suffered a double fracture of his right leg early in 2004. Though he tried a comeback in November 2004, he was in considerable pain and further investigation showed that the break had not completely healed. He then decided to call, at least temporarily, a halt to his football career to concentrate on his partnership in a sports hospitality business.

HAZLETT George

Outside-right

Born: Glasgow, 10 March 1923.
Career: Belfast Celtic. Bury 1949. Cardiff City 1952. Millwall 1953.

■ A fast-raiding winger who joined Bury from Belfast Celtic in 1949, George Hazlett was a regular in the Shakers side for three seasons prior to appearing in Cardiff City's pre-season trial in 1952. He impressed so much that City manager Cyril Spiers offered him terms, and he made his debut at Middlesbrough in the second game of the 1952–53 season. Though he scored on his home debut in a 4–0 defeat of Sheffield Wednesday – the club's first win on their return to the top flight – he was allowed to join Millwall at the end of the season. He gave the Lions four years' service, scoring 10 goals in 131 League games.

HEALEY Ronald

Goalkeeper

Born: Manchester, 30 August 1952.
Career: Manchester City 1969. Coventry City (loan) 1971. Preston North End (loan) 1973. Cardiff City 1974.

Division Three runners-up 1975–76. Welsh Cup winner 1975–76. Welsh Cup finalist 1976–77.

■ Beginning his career with Manchester City, goalkeeper Ron Healey was understudy to Joe Corrigan at Maine Road. Opportunities for him to demonstrate his skills were, thus, limited, and in almost four seasons with

the club he played in just 30 First Division fixtures. He gained valuable experiences with loan spells at Coventry City and Preston North End before, in March 1974, he was also loaned to Cardiff City. Making his debut in a 2–2 draw at West Bromwich Albion and assisting the club in their fight against relegation, the move soon became permanent. Initially he had to share the goalkeeping duties with Bill Irwin, but he then became the club's first-choice 'keeper for five seasons. During that time he helped City win promotion back to Division Two in 1975–76 and won two full international caps for the Republic of Ireland, including keeping a clean sheet on his debut against Poland. Injury finally ended his career in 1982, whereupon he moved back to Manchester and worked at the local airport.

HEARD Timothy Patrick (Pat)

Midfield

Born: Hull, 17 March 1960.
Career: Everton 1978. Aston Villa 1979. Sheffield Wednesday 1983. Newcastle United 1984. Middlesbrough 1985. Hull City 1986. Rotherham United 1988. Cardiff City 1990. Hull City 1992.

■ Much-travelled midfielder Pat Heard began his long career with Everton before Aston Villa paid £100,000 for his services in October 1979. He was unable to claim a regular spot with Villa but was on the bench when they lifted the European Cup against Bayern Munich. There followed a spell at Sheffield Wednesday before Jack Charlton took him to Tyneside to reinforce Newcastle's midfield following the departure of Terry McDermott. The former England Youth international then played for Middlesbrough and Hull City before joining Rotherham United. In his first season at Millmoor he helped the Yorkshire club to win the Fourth Division Championship before, in August 1990, he arrived at Ninian Park on a free transfer. He missed very few games in 1990–91 but was hampered by injuries the following season and later rejoined Hull City for a second spell as a non-contract player.

HEARTY Hugh

Left-back

Born: Edinburgh, 16 January 1912.
Career: Heart of Midlothian. Cardiff City 1935. Clapton Orient 1936.

■ Hugh Hearty had made 37 appearances for Heart of Midlothian before being released by the Tynecastle club in the summer of 1935. Able to play in both full-back positions, Hearty joined the Bluebirds and, though he faced stiff competition from Jack Everest, Arthur Glanville and even Billy Bassett managed to appear in 18 games during the 1935–36 season. Within a month of the season ending Hearty had joined Clapton Orient and played for the O's up until the outbreak of World War Two.

HEATH Philip Adrian

Left-winger

Born: Stoke, 24 November 1964.
Career: Stoke City 1982. Oxford United 1988. Cardiff City 1991. Aldershot 1991.

■ Left-winger Phil Heath's impressive performances for his home-town team Stoke City's reserve side earned him a call to the Potters League side in 1982–83. Over the next six seasons Heath missed very few games and had scored 17 goals in 156 League games when he was transferred to Oxford United in the summer of 1988. Injuries

hampered his time at the Manor Ground, and in March 1991 Cardiff boss Len Ashurst brought him to Ninian Park. He played in the last 11 games of the season, scoring City's goal in a 1–1 draw at Doncaster Rovers, but following a change of manager – Ashurst being replaced by Eddie May – he was allowed to leave and joined Aldershot.

HELSBY Thomas (Tom)

Wing-half

Born: Runcorn, 2 October 1904.
Died: 1961.
Career: Rhyl Athletic. Wigan Borough 1925. Runcorn. Cardiff City 1928. Bradford City 1931. Swindon Town 1933. Hull City 1934. Newport County 1935.

Welsh Cup winner 1929–30.

■ Having gained experience with Rhyl Athletic, wing-half Tom Helsby joined Wigan Borough but later returned to non-League football with his home-town team Runcorn. In April 1928 he joined Cardiff City but was unable to win a regular place as City tumbled out of the First Division. He fared no better in 1929–30, but the following season, in which the club were relegated to the Third Division South, he played in the majority of games. On leaving Ninian Park he signed for Bradford City, where it was discovered that he had heart trouble. However, after two years at Valley Parade he had spells with Swindon Town and Hull City before returning to South Wales to finish his career with Newport County.

HEMMERMAN Jeffrey Lawrence

Forward

Born: Hull, 25 February 1955.
Career: Hull City 1973. Scunthorpe United (loan) 1975. Port Vale 1977. Portsmouth 1978. Cardiff City 1982.

Division Three runner-up 1982–83.

■ A forward who made his League debut for his home-town club Hull City, he found it difficult to establish himself and had a loan spell with Scunthorpe United before joining Port Vale in 1977.

A year later he joined Portsmouth on a free transfer, and in that 1978–79 season he top scored with 16 goals, including a hat-trick against Crewe Alexandra. Hemmerman continued to find the net during the following campaign, as Pompey were promoted to Division Three. Surprisingly dropped in 1982, he moved to Cardiff City and in a fairytale season, 1982–83, scored 22 goals to help the Bluebirds win promotion to Division Two. He also found the net in four Cup games but ended the season at Bristol Rovers with severe knee ligament damage. He tried an abortive comeback the following term, but he had lost his old sharpness and retired. He trained as a physiotherapist, assisting Cardiff City until setting up his own practice in Newport.

HENDERSON Michael Robert

Right-back/midfield

Born: Newcastle, 31 March 1956.
Career: Sunderland 1974. Watford 1979. Cardiff City 1982. Sheffield United 1982. Chesterfield 1985. Matlock Town.

Welsh Cup finalist 1981–82.

■ Able to play at right-back or in midfield, Mick Henderson started out with Sunderland and later played for Watford prior to joining Cardiff City in March 1982. At Vicarage Road he had been an ever present from the time of his signing until the arrival of Pat Rice. Bluebirds manager Len Ashurst brought the experienced Henderson to Ninian Park, but after the club were relegated he left to continue his career with Sheffield United. He spent two and a half seasons at Bramall Lane before moving to his final League club, Chesterfield. Hugely popular with the Spireites fans, he became the Saltergate club's player-coach before ending his playing days with non-League Matlock Town. Henderson later joined the Sheffield police force.

HENDERSON William James (Jim)

Centre-forward
Born: Kilbirnie.

Career: Penicuik Athletic. Cardiff City 1932.

■ Jim Henderson joined the Bluebirds from Penicuik Athletic and scored on his debut in a 2–1 home win over Aldershot in February 1933. Though the club just avoided relegation after a number of heavy defeats, Henderson proved his opportunism in front of goal, netting a hat-trick in a 7–3 defeat at Brentford. Towards the end of that 1932–33 campaign, he equalled the feats of Hughie Ferguson and Walter Robbins when he scored five of the club's goals in a 6–0 home win over Northampton Town to end the season with 12 goals in 16 League games. In 1933–34 City finished bottom of the Third Division South and had to seek re-election, even though Henderson continued to find the net and was the club's second highest scorer with 12 goals in 28 League outings. Henderson, who once scored six goals in a friendly match for the Ninian Park club, was one of the players released by manager Watts-Jones prior to the 1934–35 season.

HEWITT Ronald

Inside-forward

Born: Flint, 21 June 1928.
Died: 23 September 2001.

Career: Wolverhampton Wanderers 1948. Walsall 1949. Darlington 1950. Wrexham 1951. Cardiff City 1957. Wrexham 1959. Coventry City 1960. Chester City 1962. Hereford United. Northwich Victoria. Witton Albion. Caernarvon.

■ After failing to make the grade with Wolverhampton Wanderers, Ron Hewitt had spells with Walsall and Darlington before, in 1951, joining Wrexham. He was the Robins leading scorer in three of the next six seasons with a best of 22 in just 31 appearances in 1956–57 – a total that saw him score hat-tricks against Barrow and Carlisle United. That campaign also saw him represent the Third Division North team against the South, but in the summer of 1957 he left the Racecourse Ground to join Cardiff City for £7,000. Within months of his arrival at Ninian Park, Hewitt won the first of his five Welsh caps in the World Cup play-off second leg against Israel. Hewitt led the Bluebirds goalscoring charts for two successive seasons, with a best of 14 in 1957–58, and netted a hat-trick in a 4–3 home win over Blackburn Rovers in March 1958. He returned to Wrexham in 1959, but after a further season, in which he took his total of goals for the Robins to 111 in 267 first-team games, he joined Coventry City. He later ended his League career with Chester before playing non-League football for Hereford United, Northwich Victoria, Witton Albion and Caernarvon.

HILL Charles John (Midge)

Inside-forward

Born: Cardiff, 6 September 1918.
Died: 22 December 1998.
Career: Cardiff City 1938. Torquay United 1947. Queen's Park Rangers 1949. Swindon Town 1950.

Welsh Cup finalist 1938–39.

■ Signed by the Bluebirds, his home-town club, in 1938, Charlie 'Midge' Hill appeared for the club both before and after World War Two. However, in 1946–47, when the club won the Third Division South Championship, he only appeared in a handful of games, and at the end of the season he joined Torquay United. In two seasons at Plainmoor he netted 15 goals in 63 games. Exchanged

for Don Mills, he then had a season with Queen's Park Rangers before completing is first-team playing career with Swindon Town.

HILL Daniel Ronald (Danny)

Midfield

Born: Enfield, 1 October 1974.
Career: Tottenham Hotspur 1992. Birmingham City (loan) 1995. Watford (loan) 1996. Cardiff City (loan) 1998. Oxford United 1998. Cardiff City 1998. Dagenham and Redbridge.

Division Three promotion 1998–99.
FAW Invitation Cup finalist 1999–2000.
Division Three runner-up 2000–01.

■ England Under-21 midfielder Danny Hill began his career with Tottenham Hotspur, where his passing ability saw him spraying the ball all over the field. Unable to make much of a mark at White Hart Lane, he had loan spells with Birmingham and Watford prior to joining Cardiff, also on loan, in February 1998. He had a major impact on City's midfield. With him in the side the Bluebirds lost just once in seven games, but after he left they managed only two wins in 10 games – both against Merthyr Tydfil in the FAW Invitation Cup. City tried to extend his loan spell but when that failed they almost succeeded in agreeing a brand new loan deal with him. However, a slight back injury sustained in moving furniture ended that possibility! Hill eventually joined Oxford United but joined Cardiff midway through 1998–99 to help their promotion push. With the Bluebirds back in Division Two, Hill looked impressive but then injury intervened. Offered new terms, he lost his place early the following campaign, and with no recognised reserve team at Ninian Park he moved into non-League football with Dagenham and Redbridge.

HILL Fred A. (Freddie)

Inside-right/outside-left

Born: Cardiff, 20 June 1914.
Career: Cardiff City 1932.

■ Recruited from local football, inside-forward Freddie Hill had the misfortune to play in some poor Cardiff City sides during the mid-1930s. His best season in terms of goals scored was 1934–35 when he netted eight times in 23 League outings, including two spells of three goals in four games. The following season he switched from inside-right to outside-left, but midway through the campaign he lost his place and in the close season parted company with the club.

HILLIER Ernest John Guy (Joe)

Goalkeeper

Born: Bridgend, 10 April 1907.
Career: Bridgend Town. Swansea Town 1926. Cardiff City 1927. Middlesbrough 1929. Newport County 1936.

■ A butcher by trade, goalkeeper Joe Hillier had started out with his home-town team Bridgend prior to a trial with Swansea. However, it was with Cardiff City that he turned professional, and after some good displays in the club's reserve side he made his League debut against Everton in December 1927. In the Toffees side that day was the prolific-scoring Dixie Dean, but he failed to beat Hillier who kept a clean sheet in a 2–0 win. He appeared in four more games that season, without being on the winning side, and in a similar number over the next couple of campaigns. Allowed to join Middlesbrough, he was the north-east club's first-choice 'keeper for most of his time on Teeside, though he later returned to South Wales to see out his career with Newport County.

HILLS Joseph John (Joe)

Goalkeeper

Born: Plumstead, 14 October 1897.
Died: 1969.
Career: Northfleet. Cardiff City 1924. Swansea Town 1926. Fulham 1927.

■ A county cricketer with both Kent and Glamorgan, goalkeeper Joe Hills arrived at Ninian Park from non-League Northfleet in 1924. Due to the consistency of the great Tom Farquharson, Hills found his first-team opportunities limited and eventually moved on to Swansea Town. Unable to hold down a regular spot at the Vetch Field, he had a spell with Fulham but

was unable to break into the Craven Cottage club's side. On retirement he turned to umpiring and was on the first-class list until 1956.

HITCHENS Gerald Archibald (Gerry)

Centre-forward

Born: Cannock, 8 October 1934.
Died: 1983.
Career: Kidderminster Harriers. Cardiff City 1955. Aston Villa 1957. Inter Milan 1961. Torino. Atalanta. Cagliari. Worcester City. Merthyr Tydfil.

Welsh Cup winner 1955–56.

■ Gerry Hitchens began his Football League career with Cardiff City, whom he joined from Kidderminster Harriers in January 1955. Within three weeks he was in City's first team, scoring on his debut against Wolverhampton Wanderers – a match the Bluebirds won 3–2 and so avoided relegation. The following season he was Cardiff's leading scorer with 28 goals in all competitions – a total that included five in a 7–0 Welsh Cup win at Oswestry and hat-tricks in previous round victories over Pembroke Borough and Wrexham. He was the club's leading scorer again in 1956–57, but, after netting 41 goals in 99 League and Cup games, he was transferred to Aston Villa for £22,500. He soon gave notice of his goalscoring ability and the following season netted 10 goals over three matches, including five in the 11–1 thrashing of Charlton Athletic. That season he topped the club's scoring charts with 23 goals as they won the Second Division Championship. In 1960–61 he achieved the feat again with 29 goals. He also helped Villa to the League Cup Final, scoring in every round of the competition. Despite those 11 goals, he missed the Final against Rotherham United because it had been put back to the start of the following season, and by that time he had joined Italian giants Inter Milan. Just before his move he won the first of seven England caps, scoring with his first kick against Mexico. He also netted twice in his next appearance against Italy. A most popular player, Hitchens stayed in Italy for eight years, playing for Torino,

Atalanta and Cagliari after his Inter days were over. He returned to England in 1969 to play for Worcester City and then retired after a short spell with Merthyr Tydfil. Gerry Hitchens was only 48 years old when, playing in a charity match in North Wales, he was tragically struck down by a heart attack from which he died.

HOGG Derek

Outside-left

Born: Stockton, 4 November 1930.
Career: Chorley. Leicester City 1952. West Bromwich Albion 1958. Cardiff City 1960. Kettering Town.

■ Outside-left Derek Hogg was playing for Lancashire Combination side Chorley when Leicester City secured his services in October 1952. Hugely popular at Filbert Street, his usually effective but occasionally over-elaborate close-dribbling skills earned him a call-up for the Football League against the Scottish League. A key contributor to Leicester's 1956–57 Division Two Championship effort, working in harmony with Arthur Rowley, he left the Foxes in April 1958 when West Bromwich Albion invested £20,000 in Hogg's talent. But after two seasons at the Hawthorns he moved on to Cardiff City. Hogg made a goalscoring debut for the Bluebirds in a 2–1 defeat of his first club Leicester City, curling a shot past

future England goalkeeping legend Gordon Banks. Hogg, who spent two seasons with Cardiff, netted a number of spectacular goals, the best of which was undoubtedly the one in the 3–2 defeat of double-winning Spurs when he ran half the length of Ninian Park before scoring past Bill Brown with a marvellous shot. On leaving the Bluebirds he then saw out his career with non-League Kettering Town.

HOGG Graham Stuart

Forward

Born: Neath, 15 January 1922.
Career: Cardiff Corries. Cardiff City 1948. Scunthorpe United. Lovells Athletic.

■ A Welsh amateur international, he joined the Ninian Park club from Cardiff Corries. He helped to make a couple of the City goals on his debut, as the Bluebirds beat Bury 3–0 at Gigg Lane, but it proved to be his only first-team appearance. He left the club in the summer of 1949 for a brief spell with Scunthorpe United prior to continuing his career with Lovells Athletic.

HOLE Barrington Gerard (Barrie)

Wing-half

Born: Swansea, 16 September 1942.
Career: Cardiff City 1959. Blackburn Rovers 1966. Aston Villa 1968. Swansea City 1970.

Welsh Cup winner 1963–64, 1964–65.

■ Barrie Hole's father, Billy, a Swansea Town player, had been a pre-war Welsh international winger. His older brothers, Colin and Alan, both followed in their father's footsteps and played for their home-town club. Barrie, however, did not follow the family tradition, preferring to join rivals Cardiff City. He made his League debut for the Bluebirds as a 17-year-old in a 4–3 win at Leyton Orient in February 1960, a season in which Cardiff won promotion to the First Division. He soon established himself as a creative wing-half and inside-forward, although occasionally he turned out at centre-forward in an injury crisis. Hole rarely missed a game, being ever present in 1964–65. While at Ninian Park, Hole won the first of his 30

full international caps, but during the summer of 1966, by which time he was a regular in the Welsh side, he was transferred to Blackburn Rovers for a fee of £40,000. Tall and slight in build, Hole was an extraordinarily gifted ball player. His intelligent positioning and constructive use of the ball made him one of the most exciting midfield players of his era. Not affected by pre-match nerves, he had the ability to ghost into the opposing penalty area completely unmarked, enabling him to score a number of important goals. In September 1968 Hole was on the move again, this time to Aston Villa for £60,000. His time at Villa Park was not a happy one, and he quit the game to go into his father's business. However, Roy Bentley, the Swansea manager, persuaded him to join the Vetch Field club, and he was an important member of their midfield for a couple of seasons.

HOLLYMAN Kenneth Charles

Wing-half

Born: Cardiff, 18 November 1922.
Career: Cardiff Nomads. Cardiff City 1942. Newport County 1953. Ton Pentre.

Division Three South champion 1946–47. Welsh Cup finalist 1950–51. Division Two runner-up 1951–52.

■ A versatile player, Ken Hollyman joined the Bluebirds from Cardiff Nomads in 1942 and scored 13 goals in 81 wartime appearances before making his League debut at Norwich City on the opening day of the 1946–47 season. Although on the small side, Hollyman was strong in the tackle and had an outstanding work rate. He missed very few games in the immediate seasons following the hostilities and was the

club's only ever present in 1950–51 when City finished third in Division Two. He went on to play in 202 League and Cup games for the club, but after 11 years at Ninian Park he left to join Newport County. He was a great favourite at Somerton Park as he had been at Cardiff, playing in 231 League games before becoming player-coach at the valleys club Ton Pentre.

HOLMES Matthew Jason (Matty)

Midfield

Born: Luton, 1 August 1969.
Career: Bournemouth 1988. Cardiff City (loan) 1989. West Ham United 1992.

Blackburn Rovers 1995. Charlton Athletic 1997.

■ Though he started his career down on the south coast with Bournemouth, Matty Holmes actually made his Football League debut while on loan at Cardiff City, coming on as a substitute in the Bluebirds home game against Aldershot in March 1989. It was his only appearance for City as he returned to Dean Court, where he soon won a regular place in the Cherries team. Having played in 136 games, he expressed a desire to find a new club, and he followed recently resigned Harry Redknapp to West Ham United. Though he proved dangerous at set pieces, he couldn't hold down a regular place in the Hammers side, and, after three seasons at Upton Park, he joined Blackburn Rovers for £1.2 million. Hampered by a series of injuries, he moved to Charlton Athletic where, shortly after putting pen to paper, a dreadful tackle in the FA Cup replay at Molineux broke his leg. He later attempted a comeback but needed further surgery and played no further part in the season, eventually being forced to retire.

HOLT Stanley

Centre-half

Born: Manchester.
Career: Manchester City 1927. Altrincham. Ashton National. Macclesfield. Cardiff City 1931. Berne (Switzerland).

■ Centre-half Stan Holt began his career with Manchester City but was unable to force his way into the League side. Drifting into the local non-League scene, he played for Altrincham, Ashton National and Macclesfield before signing for the Bluebirds in June 1931. During his time at Ninian Park Holt found his way in the first team barred by Jack Galbraith and only made a couple of appearances before leaving to play for Swiss club Berne.

HONOR Christian Robert

Defender

Born: Bristol, 5 June 1968.
Career: Bristol City 1986. Torquay United (loan) 1986. Hereford United (loan) 1989. Swansea City (loan) 1991. Airdrieonians. Cardiff City 1995. Bath City. Slough Town.

■ Versatile defender Chris Honor featured in Bristol City's 1989–90 promotion campaign after helping the Robins to reach the promotion play-offs in 1987–88 and Littlewoods Cup semi-final in 1988–89 – his sole goal for the club coming in a 5–0 defeat of Swansea City. Following loan spells with Torquay United, Hereford United and Swansea City, Honor joined Airdrieonians for £20,000 and played in the 1992 Scottish Cup Final as well as gaining European Cup-Winners' Cup experience. During a protracted dispute he signed for Cardiff City but made just 10 League appearances during the club's relegation season of 1994–95. He later played for Bath City and Slough Town.

HOOPER Peter John

Outside-left

Born: Teignmouth, 2 February 1933.
Career: Dawlish. Bristol Rovers 1953. Cardiff City 1962. Bristol City 1963. Worcester City.

■ Peter Hooper was a player with an explosive trademark – in his prime he

possessed what was probably the hardest shot in professional football. He began his career with Bristol Rovers and it wasn't long before it became apparent that the then Eastville club had acquired a potential match winner. Playing alongside Alfie Biggs, Geoff Bradford and Dai Ward, calls mounted for international recognition, and in 1960 he was selected for the Football League. By this time the Pirates were struggling, and when they were relegated two years later, the popular winger moved to Cardiff City for a fee of £7,000. Though he only stayed at Ninian Park for one season – 1962–63 – he left many marvellous memories of his wing play. Netting an impressive 22 goals, he was the Bluebirds leading scorer, his total including a goal on his debut in a 4–4 home draw with Newcastle United and a hat-trick in a 3–2 win at Luton Town. However, during the course of the season, Hooper, due to his dissatisfaction over wages, asked for a transfer on three occasions. He was sold to Bristol City for £11,000, and after overcoming an illness he performed creditably enough, but without ever recapturing the golden touch of his early days. On leaving Ashton Gate there followed a short Southern League stint with Worcester City before returning to Devon, first to run a pub and then to work for the probation service.

HORRIX Dean Victor

Forward

Born: Maidenhead, 21 November 1961.
Died: 1990.
Career: Millwall 1979. Gillingham 1983. Reading 1983. Cardiff City (loan) 1987. Millwall 1988. Bristol City 1990.

■ Dean Horrix had graduated through the ranks at Millwall before going on to score 19 goals in 72 League games for the Lions. After a brief spell with Gillingham, he moved to Reading where he became an important member of their successful team in 1985–86. When he lost his place, Cardiff boss Frank Burrows invited him to Ninian Park, with Nigel Vaughan going in the opposite direction. A projected exchange deal did not materialise, and, after Horrix had scored twice in nine games, he returned to Reading. He then had a brief second spell with Millwall before joining Bristol City. After only a few weeks at Ashton Gate, he was tragically killed in a car crash.

HORTON Ralph

Inside-right

Born: Cardiff.
Career: Lovells Athletic. Cardiff City 1932.

■ Signed from Lovells Athletic, inside-right Ralph Horton made just one appearance for the Bluebirds in December 1932. Despite laying on the pass for Les Jones to score Cardiff's goal in a 1–1 home draw with Bristol City, he returned to the local non-League scene in the close season.

HOUSTON David

Wing-half

Born: Glasgow, 7 July 1948.
Career: Cardiff City 1965. Crystal Palace 1967. Margate.

■ One of a number of Scottish juniors given a trial by Cardiff boss Jimmy Scoular, David Houston looked a terrific prospect as he burst into the Bluebirds first team at only 17. Though his

physique and strength seemed to earmark him for great things, he fell away, and in 1967 he moved to Crystal Palace. Unable to make an impact, he drifted into non-League football with Margate.

HOWELLS Ronald Gilbert

Goalkeeper

Born: Llanelli, 12 January 1927.
Career: Swansea Town 1948. Barry Town. Cardiff City 1950. Worcester City. Chester City 1958.

Division Two runner-up 1951–52.

■ It was his consistent displays between the posts for Cardiff City, where he was a first-team regular for six years, that earned Ron Howells two full caps for

Wales – however, he conceded seven goals in those two games! He began his career with his home-town club Swansea, but after just eight appearances he was released and joined non-League Barry Town. His performances for the Welsh League side led to Cardiff City signing the 'keeper in the summer of 1950. With Iowerth Hughes as the club's first-choice 'keeper, he had to wait until Boxing Day 1951 before making his first-team debut. He gave a near-faultless display in a 3–0 home win over

his former club. After that, apart from the odd game when a young Graham Vearncombe was drafted in, he was a virtual ever present for the next six seasons. On leaving Ninian Park in 1957 he joined Worcester City, but he returned to League action the following year with Chester City and went on to appear in 80 games for the Cestrians.

HOY Roger Ernest

Defender/midfield

Born: Bow, 6 December 1946.
Career: Tottenham Hotspur 1964. Crystal Palace 1968. Luton Town 1970. Cardiff City 1971. Palm Beach (Australia). Bath City 1974.

■ When Roger Hoy joined Spurs in the summer of 1964 he was a full-back but was converted to centre-half before signing professional forms. Though he played in a number of games when Laurie Brown was injured, he fell down the pecking order following the signing of Mike England. He spent a further two years deputising for England but was never in the same class as the Welsh international. Finding himself surplus to requirements, he moved on to Crystal Palace and later played for Luton Town before Jimmy Scoular paid £25,000 for his services in August 1971. He didn't have the best of debuts as Cardiff lost 4–1 at Orient, with Ian Bowyer netting a hat-trick for the O's. Shortly afterwards, Hoy severely damaged a knee and this kept him out of action for long spells. In fact, he soon became a forgotten man, the injury ending his League career in 1973. On his departure from Ninian Park he emigrated to Australia, where he played for the Palm Beach club. In January 1974 he returned to play for Bath City and successfully sued Cardiff City for wrongful dismissal after the club had cancelled his contract on medical grounds.

HUDSON Colin Arthur Richard

Outside-right

Born: Chepstow, 5 October 1935.
Career: Undy United. Newport County 1954. Cardiff City 1957. Brighton & Hove Albion 1961. Newport County 1962.

Welsh Cup winner 1958–59. Division Two runner-up 1959–60. Welsh Cup finalist 1959–60.

■ Winger Colin Hudson played his early football for Undy United before joining Newport County in April 1954. Over the next three seasons Hudson, who completed his National Service, scored 21 goals in 81 League games for the Somerton Park club. In the summer of 1957 Cardiff tempted County into parting with Hudson by offering Cecil Dixon, Neil O'Halloran and Johnny McSeveney in exchange. For the next four years 'Rock', as he was named, after the famous actor, was in and out of the City side with irritating irregularity. His head-down, straight ahead approach did not leave much room for subtlety, although his effort was always appreciated by the Bluebirds faithful. On his wedding day in December 1957 he blasted the opening goal in a 6–1 defeat of Liverpool, and he scored the goal that gave City their first ever League victory at Swansea. He later had a season with Brighton before returning to Newport County for a second spell. In later years Hudson continued playing in non-League and local League football.

HUGHES Byron Wayne

Midfield

Born: Port Talbot, 8 March 1958.
Career: West Bromwich Albion 1976. Tulsa Roughnecks (USA). Cardiff City 1979. Bath City.

■ Welsh Under-21 international midfielder Wayne Hughes captained West Bromwich Albion's youth team before making a handful of League appearances for the Baggies. Progress at the Hawthorns was slow, and he moved to America and Tulsa Roughnecks. It was from Tulsa that Hughes joined Cardiff City in October 1979 when Richie Morgan paid £70,000 for his services. The move wasn't a huge success, with Hughes often struggling to keep his place in an ordinary City side. At the end of the 1981–82 season City manager Len Ashurst released him. After playing for Bath City he became involved in a country club near Port Talbot.

HUGHES Edward Michael (Blodwyn)

Wing-half

Born: Llaniloes, 3 September 1940.
Career: Cardiff City 1958. Exeter City 1961. Chesterfield 1963.

■ Mike 'Blodwyn' Hughes was a promising youngster who found the

wealth of half-back talent at Ninian Park too great an obstacle to overcome, despite his consistent displays in the Bluebirds reserve side. Having made just one appearance in a 2–1 defeat of Sunderland, he moved on to Exeter City, where he stayed for a couple of seasons. In the summer of 1963 Hughes signed for Chesterfield, and in six seasons with the Saltergate club he became one of their most influential players as they challenged for promotion from the Fourth Division, eventually succeeding the season after Hughes hung up his boots!

HUGHES Iowerth (Iorrie)

Goalkeeper

Born: Abergele 26 May 1925.
Died: 1993
Career: Llandudno. Luton Town 1949. Cardiff City 1951. Worcester City. Newport County 1953. Hastings United.

Division Two runner-up 1951–52.

■ A Welsh amateur international with Llandudno, Iorrie Hughes's brilliant goalkeeping displays led to a three-month chase by Luton Town for his signature. Although he was in the company of England internationals Ron Baynham and Bernard Streten, Hughes won four full caps for Wales while with the Hatters, though he almost missed his first with an ankle injury. In two seasons at Kenilworth Road he made 36 appearances before, in August 1951, joining Cardiff City for what was then a reputed £15,000 record fee for a goalkeeper. Going straight into the City side, he kept a clean sheet in a 4–0 home win over Leicester City, but unfortunately injuries restricted his first-team appearances in a season that the club won promotion to the First Division. Unable to win back his place from the replacement Ron Howells, he played reserve-team football until 1953 when, after a brief spell with Worcester City, he joined Newport county. He made 106 appearances for the Somerton Park club before moving to Hastings United, where a broken arm prompted him to retire from the game to concentrate on his work as an electronics engineer.

HUGHES Jamie Joseph

Striker

Born: Liverpool, 5 April 1977.
Career: Tranmere Rovers 1995. Connah's
Quay Nomads. Cardiff City 1999.
Cwmbran Town (loan). Bangor City.

■ Unable to make the grade with
Tranmere Rovers, he had drifted into
non-League football with Connah's
Quay Nomads when City paid £20,000
for his services in the summer of 1999.
He scored in each of his first two
appearances for Cardiff, both as a
substitute. He netted the winner at
Queen's Park Rangers in the
Worthington Cup and scored a late
equaliser in the League against
Scunthorpe less than a week later. It was
a spectacular start, but he got few
further chances and spent most of the
campaign on loan with League of Wales
side Cwmbran Town. Though they
reached the Welsh Cup Final, his loan
spell ended the week before the match!
Released by the Ninian Park club in the
close season, he left to play for Bangor
City.

HUGHES Robert David

Central-defender

Born: Wrexham, 1 February 1978.
Career: Aston Villa 1996. Carlisle United
(loan) 1998. Shrewsbury Town 1999.
Cardiff City 2001.

Division Three runner-up 2000–01.
FAW Premier Cup winner 2001–02.

■ Welsh Under-21 international centre-
back David Hughes began his career
with Aston Villa, where he had a run of
games as replacement for the injured
Steve Staunton during the 1996–97
season. Niggling injuries hampered his
progress the following season, and after
a loan spell with Carlisle United he
returned to Villa Park, later playing for
the Welsh 'B' side that met its Scottish
counterparts. With first-team
opportunities at Villa Park limited,
Hughes joined Shrewsbury Town where
he was guaranteed regular first-team
football. However, in February 2001 he
moved on to Cardiff City for a fee of
£450,000 as the Bluebirds sought to firm
up their defence in the run-up to their
promotion challenge. A commanding

defender with a powerful long throw, he
took a little time to settle into his new
surroundings, but then in 2001–02 he
spent much of his time battling against
injuries and was released by the club.

HULLETT William Alexander (Bill)

Centre-forward

Born: Liverpool, 19 November 1915.
Died: 1982.
Career: Everton 1935. New Brighton
1936. Plymouth Argyle 1937. Manchester
United 1939. Merthyr Tydfil. Cardiff City
1947. Nottingham Forest 1948. Merthyr
Tydfil. Worcester City.

■ Centre-forward Bill Hullett turned
professional with Everton, but on being
unable to force his way into the Toffees
side he moved to nearby New Brighton.
He had scored eight goals in 13 games
when he was transferred to Plymouth
Argyle, where his prolific goalscoring
continued. Hullett had netted 20 goals
in 29 League games when Manchester
United secured his services. His progress
at Old Trafford was hampered by World
War Two, during which he played for
the RAF in the Middle East, Palestine

and Egypt. After the hostilities, he
joined Merthyr Tydfil where his
performances alerted Cardiff City. He
soon proved that goalscoring was no
problem for him as, after netting the
only goal of the game at Bradford Park
Avenue on his second outing, he
proceeded to find the net in five
consecutive games, including braces in
the defeats of Nottingham Forest before
being appointed player-manager of
Merthyr Tydfil. This heralded the
greatest period in the history of the
Penydarren Park club, with Hullett's
goalscoring exploits becoming
legendary.

HUMPHREYS Richard John (Richie)

Midfield/forward

Born: Sheffield, 30 November 197.
Career: Sheffield Wednesday 1996.
Scunthorpe United (loan) 1999. Cardiff
City (loan) 1999. Cambridge United
2001. Hartlepool United 2001.

■ Richie Humphreys began his career
with his home-town team, Sheffield
Wednesday, and after making a handful
of starts in 1995–96 had a great start to
the following season, scoring three goals
in his first four games. Though he
eventually lost his place to a fit again
England striker David Hirst, he
continued to be a regular member of
the Owls squad, his form earning him a
call up to the England Under-21 side.
Unable to impress new Wednesday
manager Ron Atkinson, he was still
highly thought of by the fans, but after a
loan spell with Scunthorpe he joined the
Bluebirds on a similar basis. He started
in outstanding fashion with two goals in
a 3–0 win at Colchester United but,
thereafter, couldn't find the goals Cardiff
needed and returned to Hillsborough.
Still on the fringes of the first team, he
opted for a move to Cambridge United,
but after an impressive start he broke his
foot and missed the rest of the
campaign. In July 2001 he moved to
Hartlepool United and was the only
player to feature in all 51 first-team
games during the season. In 2002–03 he
helped Hartlepool win promotion from
Division Three and scored a memorable
hat-trick against Swansea. Named in the

PFA Third Division side, he began the following season as an author – his book *From Tears to Cheers* selling well in the town where he remains a great favourite with the Pool fans.

HUMPHRIES Stephen Rodney

Goalkeeper

Born: Hull, 29 May 1961.
Career: Leicester City 1978. Doncaster Rovers 1981. Cardiff City 1982. Wrexham 1982. Oldham Athletic 1982. Leicester City 1983. Barnet.

■ An England semi-professional goalkeeper, Steve Humphries had a spell at Leicester City before joining Doncaster Rovers, where he played in 16 games in the 1981–82 season. Signed by the Bluebirds on a trial basis at the start of the following campaign, his only appearance came in a 2–1 home defeat by Wrexham, the club he joined after leaving Ninian Park. That season, in which City won promotion to Division Two, Humphries was the first of five 'keepers used by the club. After leaving Wrexham, he had spells with Oldham and Leicester, without making any League appearances, before playing non-League football for Barnet.

HUTCHINSON Alexander (Alex)

Outside-left

Born: Musselburgh, 4 October 1908.
Career: Bo'ness. Burnley 1929. Blackpool 1930. Bo'ness. Cardiff City 1933. Bo'ness.

■ A former Powderhall sprint

champion, winger Alex Hutchinson had played for Lancashire clubs Burnley and Blackpool prior to arriving at Ninian Park at the start of the disastrous 1933–34 season. He made the best possible debut by netting both City's goals in a 2–1 win at Watford on the opening day of the season. But the rest of the campaign went downhill, and after the Bluebirds had finished bottom of the Third Division South he left and returned to his native Scotland for a third spell with Bo'ness.

IMPEY John Edward

Central-defender

Born: Exeter, 11 August 1954.
Career: Cardiff City 1972. Bournemouth 1975. Torquay United 1983. Exeter City 1985. Torquay United 1986.

Welsh Cup winner 1973–74.

■ Centre-half John Impey was regarded as a major signing when Cardiff boss Jimmy Scoular persuaded the England Schoolboy international to come to Ninian Park in the summer of 1972. Further honours at Youth level followed as City's youth side of the period reached the FA Youth Cup Final against Arsenal. However, with Don Murray and Richie Morgan blocking his progress at Ninian Park, he moved on to Bournemouth. He spent seven seasons at Dean Court, clocking up 284 League appearances, and in 1981–82 he helped the Cherries win promotion to the Third Division. He later had spells with Torquay United and Exeter City before returning to Plainmoor to end his first-class career.

INAMOTO Junichi

Midfielder

Born: Kagashima, Japan, 18 September 1979.
Career: Gamba Osaka (Japan). Arsenal (loan) 2001. Fulham (loan) 2002. West Bromwich Albion 2004. Cardiff City (loan) 2004.

■ A hard-tackling, all-action Japanese international midfield player, Junichi Inamoto joined Arsenal in a loan deal in the summer of 2001. Though he had a disappointing first season at Highbury,

rarely featuring in manager Arsene Wenger's first-team plans, he went on to prove a revelation for Japan in the World Cup Finals. In July 2002 he joined Fulham, also on loan, from J-League side Gamba Osaka, where at 17 he had become the youngest player in the competition's history when he made his debut against Sanfrecce Hiroshima.

He proved a big hit in the early stages of the season for Fulham, especially in the Intertoto Cup Final against Bologna. Following a magnificent goal in Italy, he netted a hat-trick in the home leg. Though he faded a little as the campaign unfolded, he continued to win selection for Japan. An industrious player, always in the thick of the action, he won his 50th international cap while with the Cottagers, but in August 2004 he was transferred to West Bromwich Albion. Having broken his ankle in the international against England, he was not match fit when he arrived at the Hawthorns and hadn't appeared at first-team level when he joined Cardiff on loan. He made his debut off the bench against Wolves, and as Lennie Lawrence extended his loan and each match passed his contribution to the team's improvement increased. Recalled by West Bromwich Albion manager Bryan Robson, Inamoto played more of a part in Albion's 2005–06 season as they struggled to retain their place in the Premiership.

INGRAM Christopher David

Winger

Born: Cardiff, 5 December 1976.
Career: Cardiff City 1995. Merthyr Tydfil.

■ One of a number of Cardiff

youngsters who were called upon during the 1995–96 season, he made his debut as a substitute for Tony Bird in a 2–1 defeat at Hartlepool United. He kept his place in the side and netted the first goal in a 3–0 win over Mansfield Town. Used sparingly thereafter, Ingram, who started less than half a dozen games, was released the following summer and joined Merthyr Tydfil.

INGRAM Godfrey Patrick

Forward

Born: Luton, 26 October 1959.
Career: Luton Town 1977. Northampton Town (loan) 1980. San Jose (USA). Cardiff City 1982. San Jose (USA). St Louis (USA). Peterborough United 1992.

■ England Youth international Godfrey Ingram began his career with his home-town club Luton Town, but he couldn't sustain a regular place in the Hatters side and went on loan to Northampton Town. In 1981 Ingram went to America to play for San Jose Earthquakes, and in September 1982 it was announced that Cardiff City had paid a staggering £200,000 record fee to bring him to Ninian Park. Though he scored in wins over Gillingham and Preston North End, he stayed only nine weeks before rejoining San Jose Earthquakes – the fee, amazingly, the same £200,000. He later made a substitute appearance as a non-contract player for Peterborough United.

IRVING Samuel Johnstone (Sam)

Right-half/inside-right

Born: Belfast, 28 August 1894.
Died: 1969.
Career: Shildon Athletic. Newcastle United 1911. Galashiels United. Esh Winning. Bristol City 1913. Dundee. Blyth Spartans. Shildon Athletic. Dundee. Partick Thistle. New York Centrals (US). Cardiff City 1926. Chelsea 1927. Bristol Rovers 1932.

FA Cup winner 1926–27. Welsh Cup winner 1926–27. FA Charity Shield winner 1927–28.

■ After an unsuccessful trial with Newcastle United, Sam Irving joined Bristol City, but after just one season at Ashton Gate he moved north of the border to play for Dundee. While in Scotland, he also appeared for Partick Thistle and had a loan spell with Blyth Spartans. In July 1926 he joined Cardiff City in exchange for Joe 'Trooper' Cassidy and made his debut in a goalless draw at Leeds United in the second game of the 1926–27 season. He soon became an automatic member of the City side at right-half but was later switched to inside-right to accommodate Fred Keenor. Capped 18 times by Ireland, Sam Irving won an FA Cup medal while with Cardiff, but in March 1928 he moved on to Chelsea. A year later he helped the Stamford Bridge club win promotion to the top flight and was a regular in their side for three seasons. He then joined Bristol Rovers where he ended his League career, before returning to Dundee where he managed a billiard's salon.

IRWIN William (Bill)

Goalkeeper

Born: Newtonards, Northern Ireland, 23 July 1951.
Career: Bangor City. Cardiff City 1971. Washington Diplomats (US).

Welsh Cup finalist 1971–72, 1974–75. Welsh Cup winner 1972–73, 1973–74, 1975–76. Division Three runner-up 1975–76.

■ Irish amateur international goalkeeper Bill Irwin began his career with Irish League club Bangor before joining Cardiff City in October 1971. Replacing the disappointing Frank Parsons, he was pitched straight into the City side in Division Two and coped admirably. During his early days with the Bluebirds he made a number of outstanding saves, perhaps none more so than in Cardiff's 2–0 fifth-round FA Cup defeat at home to Leeds United in February 1972, which won him the BBC Save of the Season award. Irwin was the club's first-choice 'keeper for four seasons, beating off Parsons, Eadie and Grotier, until the arrival of Ron Healey. During the Welsh Cup Final of 1972–73 Irwin had the unenviable distinction of being the first

Cardiff City goalkeeper to be sent off when he received his marching orders against Bangor City. He went on to appear in 210 League and Cup games before leaving to play in the NASL with Washington Diplomats.

JACKSON William (Billy)

Winger

Born: Farnworth, Bolton, 15 July 1902.
Died: 1974.
Career: Leyland. Altrincham. Darwen. Sunderland 1924. Leeds United 1925. West Ham United 1927. Chelsea 1927. Leicester City 1931. Ashford Town. Bristol Rovers 1932. Cardiff City 1934. Watford 1934. Chorley. Netherfield.

■ Winger Billy Jackson played non-League football for Leyland, Altrincham and Darwen before being transferred to Sunderland in May 1924. Unable to make a breakthrough at Roker Park, he joined Leeds United and was their first-choice left-winger for most of the 1925–26 season, until forced out by the brilliance of Tom Mitchell. He then left for West Ham United before moving across London to join Chelsea. After three seasons at Stamford Bridge he was on the move again, this time to Leicester City. Again he failed to settle and moved to Bristol Rovers where he found a more regular slot. Jackson joined Cardiff City at the start of the 1934–35 season and made his 12 League appearances at the beginning of the campaign, before losing his place to Fred Hill. He then played for Watford before returning to non-League football with Chorley and Netherfield. The brother of Bury's Robert Jackson, his aggregate career figures of only 123 League games for seven clubs across 11 years rather aptly indexed his in-and-out status.

JACOBSON Joseph

Defender

Career: Cardiff City 2005.

■ Another of the club's academy players to make it into the League side, Joe Jacobson made his only appearance for the Bluebirds from the bench after 81 minutes of the home game against Norwich City towards the end of the 2005–06 season. Wearing the number-42 shirt, he replaced Chris Barker at left-back but was unable to pull the game back, Robbie Earnshaw's strike winning the game for the Canaries.

JAMES Robert Mark (Robbie)

Forward/midfield

Born: Swansea, 23 March 1957.
Died: 18 February 1998.
Career: Swansea City 1974. Stoke City 1983. Queen's Park Rangers 1984. Leicester City 1987. Swansea City 1988. Bradford City 1990. Cardiff City 1992. Merthyr Tydfil. Barry Town. Llanelli.

Division Three Champions 1992–93. Welsh Cup winner 1992–93.

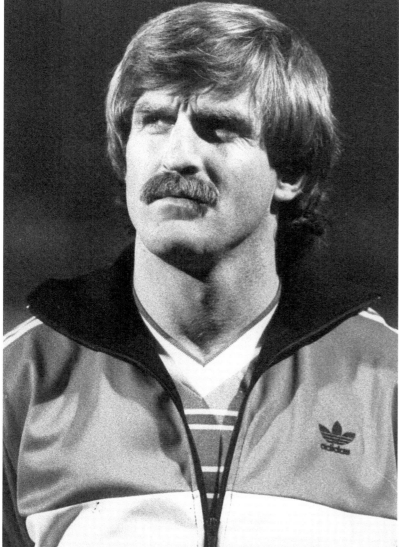

■ After impressing in Welsh League and Football Combination games for Swansea, Robbie James was just 16 when he starred on his League debut in a 2–1 defeat of Charlton Athletic in the final match of the 1972–73 season. The driving midfielder was instrumental in the Swan's rise from the Fourth to the First Division, and in October 1978 his outstanding form resulted in him winning the first of 47 caps for Wales in a 7–0 rout of Malta. Within the space of 12 months, during the Swans' successive promotions, he netted three hat-tricks. James was also an integral member of the Swansea side that took the First Division by storm in 1981–82. He finished the season as the club's leading scorer with 14 goals as they finished the campaign in sixth place. James had scored 99 goals in 394 League games for Swansea when, in July 1983, after they'd lost their place in the top flight, he joined Stoke City. Unable to settle at the Victoria Ground, he had spells with Queen's Park Rangers and Leicester City before returning to the Vetch. Immediately assuming the captaincy, he led the Swans to promotion from the Fourth Division via the play-offs. A year later he was transferred to Bradford City before, in 1992, signing for Cardiff City. He made his debut in the goalless home draw against Darlington on the opening day of the 1992–93 season, going on to play in every game as the Bluebirds won the Third Division Championship – he also picked up his fifth Welsh Cup medal. His move to non-League Merthyr Tydfil as the club's player-manager prompted the first instance of the FAW convening a transfer tribunal to set the £10,000 fee. After playing for Barry Town, Robbie James joined Llanelli, for whom he was playing in a Welsh League game when he collapsed and died, aged just 40.

JAMES William John (Billy)

Centre-forward

Born: Cardiff, 18 October 1921.
Died: 1980.
Career: Cardiff Corries. Cardiff City 1939.

■ In 1940 it was said that Billy James had a brilliant future in the game. Indeed, in November of that year he netted eight goals for Cardiff City against an Army XI. Capped for Wales in early wartime internationals, he joined the Army at 18. He proceeded with his regiment, the 77th overseas, ostensibly for North Africa but, on passage, the events in Pearl Harbour took place and Britain were at war with Japan. The 77th Regiment, with other units, were landed in Java, with the consequence of the whole British force being taken prisoner for four years. James played in only a handful of League games for Cardiff in peacetime football – scoring on his debut in a 2–1 defeat of Notts County and then in his next game as Bournemouth were beaten 2–0. Sadly he was soon forced to give up

His performances during that campaign led to his form being noted by a number of Premiership clubs, but, though the club refused a couple of offers, Jarman wasn't perhaps quite as commanding over the following campaign. Good in the air, he is equally competent on the ground and really came into his own following the appointment of Frank Burrows as manager. Switched to right-back, he began to show far more aggression and consistency and was even appointed captain when David Penney was injured. Once described by former City manager Kenny Hibbitt as 'the best footballer at Cardiff City', a sudden loss of form led to his release midway through the 1999–2000 season. After trials with Carlisle, Brentford and other clubs, he had a spell with Merthyr Tydfil before joining Exeter City on a weekly contract in March 2000. Released in the close season, he signed for Oxford United on a one-year deal. A regular for the U's before the turn of the year, he then fell out of favour and left to play non-League football for Barry Town.

JEANNE Leon Charles

Winger

Born: Cardiff, 17 November 1980.
Career: Queen's Park Rangers 1997.
Cardiff City 2001. Newport County 2002.

FAW Premier Cup winner 2001–02.

■ Welsh Under-21 international Leon Jeanne began his career with Queen's

Park Rangers, making his League debut as a substitute in the match against Watford in February 1999. After some impressive performances he suffered a serious knee injury, and his first-team appearances thereafter became somewhat limited. In the summer of 2001 he joined his home-town club on a free transfer, but, although he made a couple of early season appearances for the Bluebirds, he spent much of the campaign battling against well publicised off-the-field problems! After impressing in the club's reserve side, he returned to first-team action, putting in a useful display to help City to a 1–0 win over Swansea in the FAW Premier Cup Final. Yet, in spite of this, he was allowed to leave Ninian Park in the close season, signing for Newport County.

JENKINS Brian

Winger

Born: Treherbert, 1 August 1935.
Career: Cwmparc. Cardiff City 1957.
Exeter City 1961. Bristol Rovers 1963.
Merthyr Tydfil.

Welsh Cup finalist 1959–60.

■ Winger Brian Jenkins joined the Bluebirds from Cwmparc and didn't

the game because of failing eyesight, a legacy of his time in the camps. He was awarded a benefit in May 1950, while in later years James coached youngsters in the Cardiff area before scouting for the Ninian Park club for many years.

JARMAN Lee

Central-defender

Born: Cardiff, 16 December 1977.
Career: Cardiff City 1995. Merthyr Tydfil.
Exeter City 2000. Oxford United 2000.
Barry Town.

FAW Invitation Cup finalist 1997–98.
Division Three promotion 1998–99.

■ Welsh Under-21 international defender Lee Jarman was blooded during the early part of the 1995–96 season due to an injury to Lee Baddeley.

take long to make a good impression in the club's reserve side. A small, quick-dribbling player with an eye for an opening, Jenkins's best run in the City side came during the 1958–59 season when he not only helped the club finish ninth in Division Two, but he just missed out on full Welsh international honours. However, after that he was unable to dislodge Johnny Watkins and left to spend two seasons with Exeter City prior to a spell with Bristol Rovers. During the mid-1960s Brian Jenkins was a prolific goalscorer with non-League Merthyr Tydfil.

JENKINS Edwin Jonathan (Eddie)

Full-back/wing-half

Born: Cardiff, 16 July 1909.
Career: Cardiff East. Cardiff City 1930. Bristol City 1934. Newport County 1935.

■ A milkman and a local League player with Cardiff East, Eddie Jenkins came to Ninian Park with the unenviable task of filling the gap made by Fred Keenor's move to Crewe Alexandra. After making his debut at Bradford City in February 1931, Jenkins had several long runs in Cardiff's first team over the next three seasons before moving on to Bristol City. He spent just one season at Ashton Gate before moving to Newport County, where he wound down his League career.

JENKINS Edwin Samuel (Eddie)

Defender

Born: Cardiff, 6 July 1895.
Died: 1976.
Career: Cardiff Corinthians. Cardiff City 1921. Lovells Athletic. Cardiff City 1925. Bristol City 1926. Lovells Athletic.

■ The most accomplished Welsh amateur of the 1920s, Eddie Jenkins was a virtual ever present for the Welsh Amateur XI over a decade, usually skippering the side. In all, he appeared in 14 amateur internationals in 11 years, missing just one game. However, he was only called into the senior side against England in 1925. The Bluebirds had lost their first six games in Division One in 1921–22 when Eddie Jenkins was called up for his League debut against Middlesbrough – this coinciding with a 3–1 victory, City's first in the top flight. Although he spent three seasons at Ninian Park, most of his football was played in the club's reserve side, though he did later make a few appearances for Bristol City. In 1926 he overcame a bad illness and returned to play at Rexville for Lovells Athletic, later becoming their manager.

JENKINS Stephen Robert (Steve)

Defender/midfield

Born: Merthyr Tydfil, 16 July 1972.
Career: Swansea City 1990. Huddersfield Town 1995. Birmingham City (loan) 2000. Cardiff City 2003. Notts County 2003. Peterborough United 2004.

■ Beginning his career with Swansea City, Steve Jenkins played in midfield but was later converted into a right-back. In just over five seasons at the Vetch Jenkins played in 215 first-team games, his only goal coming in a 1–1 draw against Hartlepool United in January 1991. Having won Welsh Youth and Under-21 honours, he made his full international debut against Germany at Ninian Park in March 1995, but shortly afterwards he left Swansea to join Huddersfield Town for a tribunal-fixed fee of £275,000. While with the Yorkshire club, he established himself at international level and was appointed captain. Following a loan spell with Birmingham City, it seemed likely that he would join the St Andrew's club, but he returned to the McAlpine Stadium to take his total number of appearances for Huddersfield to 295 before leaving to join Cardiff City in February 2003. He made his debut at Stockport County on St David's Day after Rhys Weston hurt his back in the pre-match warm up! He was then carried off following a clash of heads when he 'swallowed' his tongue. Thanks to the speedy actions of physio Clive Goodyear he recovered and appeared in three more games. He then moved on to play for Notts County and later Peterborough but spent most of his time on the bench.

JENNINGS John (Jack)

Full-back/right-half

Born: Platt Bridge, 27 August 1902.
Died: 1997.
Career: Wigan Borough 1923. Cardiff City 1925. Middlesbrough 1929. Preston North End 1936. Bradford City 1937.

Welsh Cup winner 1927–28. Welsh Cup finalist 1928–29.

■ A railway fireman, Jack Jennings started out with Wigan Borough before signing for Cardiff in 1925. He played his first game for the Bluebirds at right-half but, due to the wealth of international defenders at the club, seldom got a first-team game. In 1926 he was chosen to tour Canada by the FA, and then in 1927–28 he grabbed the opportunity of a full-back berth with City. He remained a virtual ever present in the Cardiff side until 1930 when he figured in the surprising triple transfer with Joe Hillier and Freddie Warren that took all three players to Middlesbrough. Jennings went on to become a first-team regular at Ayresome Park for the next six seasons and, in fact, captained 'Boro for much of that time before handing over the leadership duties to Tom Griffiths following his arrival from Bolton Wanderers. Having played in 205 games for 'Boro, he left to join Preston North End before ending his League career with Northampton Town. He stayed with the Cobblers as their trainer, while he later worked as a masseur for Northamptonshire County Cricket Club and assisted the Indian tourists in 1946. He also coached the England amateur international side and a number of British athletes.

JENNINGS Walter Henry (Wally)

Wing-half/full-back

Born: Bristol, 1 April 1909.
Died: 4 November 1993.
Career: Bristol Rovers 1926. Blackburn Rovers 1927. South Bristol COB. Bristol City 1929. Cheltenham Town. Cardiff City 1934. Bristol St George. Bath City.

■ Following trials with Bristol Rovers and Blackburn Rovers, Wally Jennings, a versatile wing-half, joined Alex Raisbeck's Bristol City in 1929. Over the next few seasons, following a switch to full-back, Jennings missed very few games. His only goal in 98 appearances came in a 4–1 win at Swindon Town. In June 1934 Jennings joined struggling Cardiff and was one of eight debutants for the Bluebirds as they beat Charlton Athletic 2–1 on the opening day of the 1934–35 season. During his time in South Wales, Jennings played at both wing-half and full-back, but after losing his first-team place to Arthur Granville he moved into non-League football with Bath City, this after a brief spell with Bristol St George. He was subsequently chief scout for Everton, Bristol Rovers and Bath City.

JEROME Cameron

Forward

Born: Huddersfield, 14 August 1986.
Career: Huddersfield Town. Cardiff City 2003. Birmingham City 2006.

■ Cameron Jerome, who was previously a junior with Huddersfield Town, had trial spells with a number of clubs before turning professional with Cardiff City. Reserve-team coach Paul

Cameron Jerome

Wilkinson had knowledge of his capabilities, and it was he who suggested to Lennie Lawrence that he should come to Ninian Park. After some impressive displays for the club's reserves, he came off the bench to replace Andy Campbell in the goalless home draw against Leeds United in October 2004. Jerome went on to make eight consecutive appearances from the bench, scoring in the Carling Cup tie at Bournemouth and in the 2–1 defeat at Reading. He then won a place in the starting line up and, in the match against Gillingham, scored after just 13 minutes of what was his first full debut. Later, he was brought down and received a penalty, converted by Peter Thorne, in a 3–1 win for the Bluebirds. In 2005–06 Jerome was handed his first international when he was capped by England at Under-21 level. Throughout the campaign the 19-year-old proved a real handful for opposition defences and was Cardiff's leading scorer with 20 goals in all competitions. Not surprisingly, his displays have led to a number of top-flight clubs showing an interest in buying the sensational striker in the close season – but he has recently signed for relegated Birmingham City for £4 million.

JOHN Dilwyn

Goalkeeper

Born: Rhondda, 3 June 1944.
Career: Cardiff City 1961. Swansea City 1967. Hereford United. Merthyr Tydfil.

■ Goalkeeper Dilwyn John was only 17 years old when Cardiff manager Bill Jones gave him his debut in a First Division match at Chelsea in September 1961. He had an outstanding match in a 3–2 win for the Bluebirds, but, despite this, he found himself in and out of the Cardiff side. An acrobatic 'keeper, John was a little on the light side, and, although he won Welsh Under-23 caps while at Ninian Park, his physique prevented him from developing into one of Cardiff's better goalkeepers. In March 1967 he left Ninian Park and joined Swansea. Initially, he helped stem the flow of goals that the Swansea defence had been leaking, but despite some heroic performances he couldn't prevent

the club's relegation to Division Four. However, he helped the club win promotion in 1969–70 before leaving to play non-League football for both Hereford United and Merthyr Tydfil. During the 1980s he became the Welsh amateur snooker champion.

JOHN Emlyn James

Centre-half/left-back

Born: Tonypandy, 4 March 1907.
Career: Mid-Rhondda United. Cardiff City 1928. Newport County 1932. Barry Town.

Welsh Cup winner 1929–30.

■ Emlyn John joined the Ninian Park staff from Welsh League Mid-Rhondda United in April 1928 and stayed with the Bluebirds for four years. Much of that time was spent in the club's reserves as City slipped from the First Division to the Third Division South. In the summer of 1932 John moved to Newport County, and though they were struggling at the wrong end of the Third Division South he was a virtual ever present for two seasons. He then left Somerton Park to play non-League football for Barry Town.

JOHNSON Glenn Paul

Forward

Born: Sydney, Australia, 16 July 1972.

Career: Blacktown City (Australia). Cardiff City 1996. Blacktown City (Australia).

■ Striker Glenn Johnson was signed in a blaze of publicity in transfer deadline week 1996 from Australian club Blacktown City, having been attracted to the Bluebirds by his boyhood hero Phil Neal. He made an immediate impact by scoring in two run-outs before coming off the bench regularly. Great things were expected of him during the 1996–97 season, yet, surprisingly, he was allowed to part company with the club, rejoining Blacktown City.

JOHNSTON George

Forward

Born: Glasgow, 21 March 1947.
Career: Cardiff City 1964. Arsenal 1967. Birmingham City 1969. Walsall (loan) 1970. Fulham 1970. Hereford United 1972. Newport County 1973.

Welsh Cup winner 1964–65.

■ Often described as a former 'tea boy with Glasgow Corporation', George Johnston came to Ninian Park in 1964. He made a quick breakthrough as a winger towards the end of the 1964–65 season when only 17, but it was the following campaign that his career really took off. Playing alongside the

likes of John Charles and John Toshack, he could not stop scoring, and in 1965–66 he netted 17 goals in 36 League outings. He also scored six Cup goals, including a League Cup hat-trick in a 5–1 defeat of Reading. Two goals at Highbury in a match against Arsenal to aid the victims of the Aberfan Disaster prompted the Gunners to offer £20,000 for Johnston's services in March 1967. Unfortunately, he could not maintain a regular place in the Arsenal side, and after that his career went steadily downhill with brief spells at Birmingham City, Walsall (on loan), Fulham, Hereford United and Newport County before the 26-year-old Scot was on the scrap-heap.

JONES Bernard

Inside-forward

Born: Coventry, 10 April 1934.
Career: Northampton Town 1952. Cardiff City 1956. Shrewsbury Town 1957.

■ Inside-forward Bernard Jones made a name for himself at Northampton Town where, in his first season at the County Ground, his goals almost took the Cobblers into the Second Division. In March 1956 City boss Trevor Morris brought him to Ninian Park, but he struggled in the top flight and after just nine appearances spread over a year he returned to the lower Divisions with Shrewsbury Town. In his last season of League football he helped the Gay Meadow club win promotion to the Third Division.

JONES Brynley

Midfield

Born: Llandrindod, Wells, 8 February 1948.
Career: Cardiff City 1966. Newport County (loan) 1969. Bristol Rovers 1969.

■ A Welsh Schoolboy international, Bryn Jones failed to establish himself at Ninian Park, the highlight of his brief career with the Bluebirds being an appearance against Moscow Torpedo in 1968. The midfielder had a loan spell with Newport County, but in the summer of 1969 he joined Bristol Rovers. Capped by Wales at Under-23 level, Jones had a useful stint with the

Pirates, going on to play until 1974 when he parted company with the club.

JONES Barrie Spencer

Outside-right

Born: Swansea, 10 October 1941.
Career: Swansea Town 1959. Plymouth Argyle 1964. Cardiff City 1967. Yeovil Town.

Welsh Cup winner 1966–67. 1967–68. 1968–69.

■ A winger in the traditional mould, Barrie Jones began his career with his home-town club Swansea, winning the first of 15 international caps when he played against Scotland at Ninian Park in October 1962. Possessing pace and a powerful shot, he had scored 23 goals in 166 games when he was transferred to Plymouth Argyle for £45,000 in September 1964. It was the Devon club's highest-ever payment for a player. It was Jones's exceptional ball control that manager Malcolm Allison was seeking to incorporate into his team plans, but after three seasons at Home Park the fair-haired winger returned to South Wales and Cardiff City for a fee of £25,000. Shortly after his arrival at Ninian Park he switched from the wing to midfield. His play improved so much that he went on to win a further seven international caps while with the Bluebirds. He was ever present in the 1967–68 and 1968–69 seasons, playing in 107 consecutive League games from his debut. On 4 October 1969 he broke his leg in the last minute of Cardiff's 3–2 defeat at Blackpool. Although he attempted a number of comebacks in the club's reserves, he never regained full fitness and had to hang up his boots at League level. Though never a prolific scorer – 20 goals in 115 League and Cup games for City – he did once score a hat-trick in the club's 5–0 win over Mauritius in May 1969. He then had a number of seasons playing non-League football before going into business in the Swansea area.

JONES Charles (Charlie)

Outside-left/right-half

Born: Troedyrhiw, 12 December 1899.
Died: 1966.
Career: Cardiff City 1920. Stockport County 1921. Oldham Athletic 1922. Nottingham Forest 1925. Arsenal 1928.

■ Charlie Jones started his footballing career with Cardiff City and had made just one League appearance – a 1–0 home defeat at the hands of Stoke – when he was injured. But with Grimshaw and Evans playing so well he was unable to regain his place. He then joined Stockport County where his exceptional displays led to much recrimination in Cardiff about the decision to release him. While at Edgeley Park, Jones scored the goal in the Third Division Championship decider against Darlington. After a spell playing for Oldham Athletic, he joined Nottingham Forest, where he produced some brilliant form. While at the City ground he won the first of seven Welsh caps, but in May 1928 he was transferred to Arsenal. While with the North London club, Jones won three League Championship medals and helped the Gunners beat Newcastle United in the 1932 FA Cup Final. On retiring in the summer of 1934 he became manager of Notts County, but after just a matter of months he turned his back on football and became a very successful businessman.

JONES David Gwilym (Dai)

Outside-left/centre-half

Born: Ynysddu, 10 June 1914.
Died: 1988.

Career: Ynysddu. Newport County 1930. Tottenham Hotspur 1931. Northfleet. Cardiff City 1934. Fulham 1934. Newport County 1935. Wigan Athletic. Manchester United 1937. Swindon Town 1938. Cheltenham Town.

■ Dai Jones had spells with both Newport County and Spurs, without making a first-team appearance, before joining the Bluebirds in 1934. In that 1934–35 season he appeared at both left-half and outside-left, but at the end of a disappointing campaign he left to join Newport County. After one season at Somerton Park, in which he scored his only League goal, he had spells with Wigan Athletic and Manchester United before joining Swindon Town and finally Cheltenham.

JONES Glyn

Inside-left

Born: Cardiff, 16 June 1916.
Career: Cardiff City 1935.

■ Able to play in any of the forward positions, Glyn Jones joined Cardiff City from local amateur football, where he gained a good reputation. Despite laying on the only goal of the game for Danny Williams in a 1–0 home win over Brighton, it was his only appearance for the first team. Despite some promising performances over the remainder of the campaign for City's reserve side, he was released in the close season.

JONES Islwyn

Wing-half

Born: Merthyr Tydfil, 8 April 1935.
Career: Cardiff City 1952.

■ Islwyn Jones spent over two seasons in Cardiff's reserve side before being drafted into the City team in place of the injured Billy Baker at Sheffield United in September 1954. He had an impressive debut in a 3–1 win and kept his place for the next eight games – only two of which were lost – not a bad record in a season that the Bluebirds finished 20th in Division One. Jones found himself in and out of the side for the next year or so, but with the talent within the club at half-back he decided to move into local League football.

JONES Ian Michael

Full-back

Born: Germany, 26 August 1976.
Career: Cardiff City 1993. Merthyr Tydfil.

■ German-born Welsh Youth international full-back Ian Jones was just 17 years and 23 days old when he made his Cardiff debut at Blackpool in September 1993. The last of his three appearances came two seasons later, before Jones, who had played in three defeats in which Cardiff also failed to score, moved on to play for Merthyr Tydfil.

JONES James (Jimmy)

Centre-forward

Born: Treorchy, 28 July 1901.
Died: 1977.
Career: Ton Pentre. Cardiff City 1922. Wrexham 1924. Aberdare Athletic 1926. Torquay United 1927. Worcester City.

Division One runner-up 1923–24.

■ Welsh international centre-forward Jimmy Jones began his career with Ton Pentre and 'guested' for Portsmouth in World War One before joining Cardiff in 1922. Signed primarily as cover for Len Davies and Ken McDonald, his excellent form for the club's reserve side thrust him into the side for the run-in for the League Championship in 1923–24, which they missed narrowly on goal average. Despite scoring in the wins over Spurs and Birmingham, he moved on to Wrexham where, for a couple of seasons, he was a prolific scorer. He returned to South Wales to Aberdare Athletic before ending his League career with Torquay United and a brief spell with Worcester City. After hanging up his boots he owned a confectionery shop in Cardiff.

JONES John Alan

Goalkeeper

Born: Wrexham, 12 September 1939.
Career: Druids. Cardiff City 1957. Exeter City 1959. Norwich City 1962. Wrexham 1963.

■ Goalkeeper Alan Jones played for one of Wales's oldest clubs, Druids, before signing for Cardiff City. Nearly all of his time at Ninian Park was spent in the reserves as he made just one appearance – a 3–1 defeat at Rotherham in April 1958 – before he moved to Exeter City. He spent three seasons with the Grecians as their first-choice custodian before spending the 1962–63 campaign with Norwich City. His last club was Wrexham, Jones joining the Robins as part of the deal that took Kevin Keelan to Carrow Road.

JONES Kenneth

Goalkeeper

Born: Aberdare, 2 January 1936.
Career: Cardiff City 1953. Scunthorpe United 1958. Charlton Athletic 1964. Exeter City 1966.

■ Capped by Wales at Under-23 level, goalkeeper Ken Jones was quite a character, whose long kicking often threatened the other goal. He was once dropped by Cardiff manager Trevor Morris for arriving late to play in the game against Bristol Rovers at Ninian Park in March 1958. City lost that match 2–0, and Jones found himself in the Welsh League side the following Saturday, where he scored from the penalty spot and reputedly burst the ball! In December 1958 he moved to Scunthorpe United, having lost his place to Ron Nicholls, and became a popular figure at the Old Show Ground, making 168 League appearances in six years. He later had a spell with Charlton Athletic before winding down his career at Exeter City.

JONES Kenneth

Full-back

Born: Havercroft, 26 June 1944.
Career: Monckton Colliery. Bradford Park Avenue 1961. Southampton 1965. Cardiff City 1971. Bath City.

■ Ken Jones joined Bradford Park Avenue from Monckton Colliery in September 1961, and in his 100 games for the Yorkshire club he gained a reputation as the best full-back in Division Four. Southampton paid £15,000 for him in the summer of 1965, but he found the transition to the First Division difficult and in five seasons at The Dell he never established a regular place. A small fee brought him to Ninian Park in July 1971 but a mixture of poor form and injury restricted him to only six League games, and at the end of the season he left to play for Bath City.

JONES Linden

Right-back/midfield

Born: New Tredegar, 5 March 1961.
Career: Cardiff City 1979. Newport County 1983. Reading 1987.

Welsh Cup finalist 1981–82. Division Three runner-up 1982–83.

■ After impressing in the club's junior teams, full-back Linden Jones was promoted to the first team following the winter freeze-up of 1978–79, making his debut in a 1–0 win over Orient, along with Colin Sullivan and Ronnie Moore. Four days later, on 28 February 1979, he achieved the unenviable record of being the youngest player in the history of Cardiff City to be sent off when he received his marching orders in the club's 4–1 win at Blackburn Rovers. He missed very few games over the next five seasons, and in 1982–83 he was outstanding as the club won promotion to Division Two. In September 1983 he was involved in the remarkable exchange deal with Newport County when himself, John Lewis and Tarki Micallef moved to Somerton Park, with Karl Elsey and Nigel Vaughan coming to Cardiff. He was a regular with County until 1987 when the club faced closure, and he joined Reading, where a spate of niggling injuries forced him into premature retirement.

JONES Leslie Jenkin (Les)

Inside-forward

Born: Aberdare, 1 July 1911.
Died: 1981.
Career: Aberdare Athletic. Cardiff City 1929. Coventry City 1933. Arsenal 1937. Swansea Town 1946. Barry Town. Brighton & Hove Albion 1948.

Welsh Cup winner 1929–30.

■ Les Jones joined Cardiff City in 1929 from his home-town club Aberdare, where he had combined his playing career with an apprenticeship in his father's butchers shop. After making his

City debut in a 1–0 defeat by Swansea in the South Wales derby, Jones formed a formidable left-wing partnership with Walter Robbins. Though the Bluebirds plunged into the Third Division South, Jones carried on in a poor City team until, in January 1934, he left to play for Coventry. In his first full season at Highfield Road he scored 27 goals and won the first of 11 full international caps for Wales. In 1935–36 he won a Third Division South Championship medal and netted his sixth hat-trick for the club against Queen's Park Rangers. Coventry resisted a £7,000 bid from Spurs but could not refuse Arsenal's offer in 1937, and, after scoring 74 goals in 144 games, Jones moved to Highbury. He helped the Gunners win the League Championship in 1937–38, and in the last season before World War Two he won an FA Charity Shield medal against Preston North End. During the hostilities he continued to play for the North London club and won five wartime caps. On the return of peace, he was granted a free transfer and moved to Swansea Town as player-coach. His stay at the Vetch was short-lived, and he became player-manager of Barry Town before returning to League football with Brighton. He later managed Scunthorpe United.

JONES Mark

Midfield

Born: Berinsfield, Oxon, 26 September 1961.
Career: Oxford United 1979. Swindon Town 1986. Cardiff City 1990. Farnborough Town.

■ Midfielder Mark Jones was a prominent member of the successful Oxford United side of the 1980s, helping them win the Third Division Championship of 1983–84 and the Second Division title the following season. In 1985–86 Oxford won the League Cup Final, beating Queen's Park Rangers 3–0, but shortly after that success Jones, who had played in 129 League games, left the Manor Ground club to play for Swindon Town. In his first season at the County Ground he helped the Robins win promotion to Division Two but, thereafter, struggled with injuries. In the summer of 1990 Jones joined Cardiff, but in two seasons of Fourth Division football with the Bluebirds he was again hampered by injuries, and in May 1992 he left to play non-League football for Farnborough Town.

JONES Robert H. (Bob)

Goalkeeper

Born: Everton, 9 January 1902.
Died: 1989.
Career: Ferndale. Everton 1924. Southport 1926. Bolton Wanderers 1929. Cardiff City 1937. Southport 1939.

■ Goalkeeper Bob Jones made a handful of appearances for both Everton and Southport before joining Bolton Wanderers as a replacement for their legendary 'keeper Dick Pym. Establishing himself as the club's first-choice 'keeper in 1930–31, he missed very few games until, in February 1933, he was struck down by appendicitis. He recovered to become a member of the Wanderers team that won promotion from the Second Division and reached the FA Cup semi-final in 1935. After making 244 first-team appearances, he came under threat from Stan Hanson, and in July 1937 he joined Cardiff City on a free transfer. Despite being 35 years old, he was an ever present in his first

season at Ninian Park but eventually lost his place to Bill Fielding, who ironically was to later move to Bolton, after 58 consecutive League appearances. He then joined Southport as the club's first-team trainer, a position he continued to hold for a further eight seasons after the war was over.

JONES Thomas Gethin

Defender

Born: Llanbyther, 8 August 1981.
Career: Carmarthen Town. Cardiff City 2000. Weymouth.

■ Gethin Jones followed in the footsteps of Welsh international full-back Mark Delaney when he joined the Bluebirds from League of Wales club Carmarthen Town in the summer of 2000. He made an immediate impact at Ninian Park, making his senior debut in the Worthington Cup tie against Crystal Palace soon after putting pen to paper. He then made a couple of appearances from the substitutes' bench but had the misfortune of suffering a broken leg in a reserve game against Plymouth Argyle. Despite this setback, he was offered a 12-month contract by owner Sam Hammam. Though he spent most of the 2001–02 season in the reserve side in the Avon Insurance Combination, he came off the bench in the club's remarkable 7–1 victory at Oldham and appeared in two LDV Vans Trophy ties. Unable to force his way into the side on a regular basis, he moved back into non-League football with Weymouth.

JONES Vaughan

Defender

Born: Tonyrefail, 8 September 1959.
Career: Bristol Rovers 1977. Newport County 1982. Cardiff City 1984. Bristol Rovers 1984.

■ Vaughan Jones is living proof that you can't keep a good man down. The versatile defender was sacked by Bristol Rovers, dumped by Newport County and discarded by Cardiff City – and all by the age of 25! He was freed by Bristol Rovers manager Bobby Gould, this after a season in which he played really well. Playing at right-back, he had missed only a handful of matches following his debut – his move to Newport came as a great surprise. Jones spent two seasons at Somerton Park before joining Cardiff City on a free transfer in the summer of 1984. A Welsh Under-21 international, he didn't have the best of debuts as City crashed 3–0 at home to Charlton Athletic. Though he played in 11 of the first 13 matches of the 1984–85 season, he was only on the winning side twice, and it wasn't long after the last of his appearances that he returned to Bristol Rovers. Back at Eastville he became a key figure in the Pirates resurgence and skippered them through the most triumphant campaign in their history as they won the Third Division Championship and reached the Final of the Leyland Daf Cup.

JONES Vincent Wellfield (Vince)

Wing-half/outside-left

Born: Carmarthen, 4 March 1900.
Died: 1950.
Career: Cardiff City 1922. Merthyr Town 1923. Ebbw Vale. Millwall 1927. Luton Town 1931. Norwich City 1932. Newport County 1933. Cardiff City 1934.

■ Carmarthen-born utility player Vince Jones joined the Bluebirds on trial in 1922, making his only first-team appearance as a replacement for the injured Len Davies in a 1–0 home win over Sheffield United. Unable to make much headway at Ninian Park, he moved on to Merthyr Town and Ebbw Vale before joining Millwall. It was with the Lions that he played his best football, later playing for Luton Town and Newport County before returning to Ninian Park. However, his best days were behind him, and he failed to break into the side.

JORDAN Andrew Joseph (Andy)

Central-defender

Born: Manchester, 14 December 1979.
Career: Bristol City 1997. Cardiff City 2000. Hartlepool United 2003.

■ The son of former Scottish international Joe Jordan, he displays

many of the qualities of his father, being very strong in the air and in the tackle. Having started out with Bristol City, where injuries hampered his progress after he had shown early promise and won Scottish Under-21 honours, he joined Cardiff City for £30,000 in October 2000. However, after a brief run in the first team at Ninian Park he lost his place, and after suffering badly with injuries, not playing any first-team football in 2002–03, he left to play for Hartlepool United.

JOSLIN Philip James

Goalkeeper

Born: Kingsteignton, 1 September 1916.
Died: 1981.
Career: Plymouth Argyle. Torquay United 1936. Cardiff City 1948.

Welsh Cup finalist 1950–51.

■ After an unsuccessful trial with Plymouth Argyle, goalkeeper Phil Joslin joined Torquay United and, before the outbreak of World War Two, appeared in 135 League games for the Devon side. During the hostilities he joined the RASC and, in fact, played many games for his Division as a centre-forward. Stationed in London, he also 'guested' for a number of clubs including Arsenal, Fulham and Spurs. When League football resumed after the war he played for Torquay for a further two seasons, building up a fine reputation

before signing for Cardiff. During the 1948–49 season he kept 15 clean sheets in 38 games, including four in successive matches on two occasions. A virtual ever present for three seasons at Ninian Park, he had played in 117 League and Cup games for City when he broke his leg in a goalmouth collision with Wilf Grant during a public trial match prior to the 1951–52 season. Sadly, the injury brought an end to the popular 'keeper's career.

JUDGE Alan Graham

Goalkeeper

Born: Kingsbury, 14 May 1960.
Career: Luton Town 1978. Reading 1982. Oxford United 1984. Lincoln City (loan) 1985. Cardiff City (loan) 1987. Hereford United 1991.

■ Goalkeeper Alan Judge started out with Luton Town, but, on being unable to command a regular place in the Hatters side, went on loan to Reading before making the move a permanent one. During his time at Elm Park he helped Reading win promotion to the Third Division, but in December 1984 he left to play for Oxford United. He helped the U's win the Second Division Championship in his first season at the Manor Ground and was a member of the Oxford side that won the Milk Cup Final in 1986. Unable to hold down a first-team place, he had a loan spell with Lincoln before joining Cardiff in a similar capacity after Graham Moseley had broken his arm. On the losing side only once in eight games as City went on to win promotion, he later ended his career with 105 appearances for Hereford United.

KAVANAGH Graham Anthony

Midfield

Born: Dublin, 2 December 1973.
Career: Home Farm. Middlesbrough 1991. Darlington (loan) 1994. Stoke City 1996. Cardiff City 2001. Wigan Athletic 2005.

FAW Premier Cup winner 2001–02.
Division Two promotion 2002–03.

■ Republic of Ireland international Graham Kavanagh joined

Middlesbrough from Home Farm in the summer of 1991. Somewhat eclipsed by all the big names arriving at the Riverside, he had a loan spell with Darlington prior to signing for Stoke City for £250,000 in September 1996. Possessing one of the hardest shots in football, Kavanagh can, on his day, run a game from the centre of the park. Selected by his fellow professionals for the 1998–99 PFA award-winning Second Division side, he let himself down with disciplinary issues that saw him sent off twice and booked much too often. The following season he helped Stoke to win the Autowindscreens Shield Final at Wembley and retained his place in the PFA side. His displays helped the Potters reach the 2000–01 play-offs, but after winning selection for the Divisional side

for a third time, Kavanagh, who scored 46 goals in 245 games, left Stoke for Cardiff for £1 million. The big money signing lived up to his reputation in 2001–02 with 15 goals, several of which were magnificent strikes, and won selection for the PFA Divisional team for the fourth year in succession. The following season he led the Bluebirds to victory against Queen's Park Rangers in the play-off final and was once again selected for the PFA Division Two team of the season. Since then, the Cardiff skipper has been in excellent form, although he missed part of the 2003–04 season after requiring surgery on his ankle. He was transferred to Wigan Athletic in March 2005. The midfielder played an important part in the Latics making such a good start in the

Premiership, but then injuries saw him lose his place and as the Latics slipped into a mid-table position.

KEATING Albert Edward

Inside-forward

Born: Swillington Common, 28 June 1902.
Died: 1984.
Career: Prudhoe Castle. Newcastle United 1923. Bristol City 1925. Blackburn Rovers 1928. Cardiff City 1930. Bristol City 1932. North Shields.

■ Albert Keating joined Newcastle United from Prudhoe Castle, but in two years at St James' Park he made only 12 appearances. In November 1925 he joined Bristol City and scored twice on his debut in a 5–1 defeat of Luton Town. Forming a prolific goalscoring partnership with 'Tot' Walsh in 1926–27, he helped the club win the Third Division South Championship. His total of 23 goals included hat-tricks against Crystal Palace and Luton. He was the club's leading scorer in 1927–28, netting another treble, this time against Clapton Orient. It was this kind of form that prompted FA Cup winners Blackburn Rovers to pay £4,000 for his services in May 1928. Struggling to hold down a first-team spot – 17 games in three seasons – he joined Cardiff City. Though he had a disappointing first term at Ninian Park, he scored 23 goals in 38 games in 1931–32 including a hat-trick in an 8–0 FA Cup win over Enfield. After a few appearances during the early stages of the following season, he rejoined Bristol City, taking his tally of goals in his two spells to 54 in 104 games before leaving to play non-League football with North Shields.

KEATING Reginald E. (Reg)

Forward

Born: Halton, 14 May 1904.
Died: 1961.
Career: Annfield Plain. Scotswood United. Newcastle United 1926. Lincoln City 1927. Gainsborough Trinity. Scarborough. Stockport County 1930. Birmingham 1931. Norwich City 1932.

North Shields. Bath City. Cardiff City 1933. Doncaster Rovers 1936. Bournemouth 1936. Carlisle United 1937.

■ The brother of Albert Keating, he had an unusual career as he alternated between the Football League and non-League. He began his first-team career with Newcastle United but left St James' Park without playing a game for them and had spells with Gainsborough Trinity and Scarborough before joining Stockport County. It was for the Edgeley Park club that he made his Football League debut, but his stay at County was brief, as were his spells with his next two clubs Birmingham and Norwich City. Reg Keating played his first match for the Bluebirds in March 1934 as they beat Queen's Park Rangers 3–1 and the following month netted his first hat-trick for the club at Aldershot. The following season he was the club's leading scorer with 20 League goals, helping City to avoid finishing bottom of the Third Division South. In the penultimate match of the campaign he netted four goals in a 5–0 home win over Exeter City. He was the club's top scorer again in 1935–36 with 10 League goals, including his third treble in a 4–2 win at Millwall. He later played for Doncaster Rovers and Bournemouth before winding down his career with Carlisle United.

KEENOR Frederick Charles (Fred)

Centre-half/right-half

Born: Cardiff, 31 July 1894.
Died: 1972.
Career: Roath Wednesday. Cardiff City 1912. Crewe Alexandra 1931. Oswestry Town. Tunbridge Wells Rangers.

Division Two runner-up 1920–21. Welsh Cup winner 1922–23, 1926–27, 1927–28, 1929–30. Division One runner-up 1923–24. FA Cup finalist 1924–25. FA Cup winner 1926–27. FA Charity Shield winner 1927–28. Welsh Cup finalist 1928–29.

■ Fred Keenor joined Cardiff City in the pre-World War One Southern League days as an amateur inside-forward, having been capped at outside-right in 1907 in the first Schoolboy

international between Wales and England. He turned professional in 1913, but at the outbreak of war he joined the 'Footballers Battalion' (17th Middlesex) and was twice wounded in action. At the end of the hostilities, he returned to Cardiff and made his first appearance for Wales in the Victory internationals. When City entered the Football League, he scored in the club's first League game in a 5–2 win at Stockport County. Succeeding Charlie Brittan as captain, he led both his club and country to success. He led Wales to the Home International Championships in 1924, took Cardiff to an unsuccessful 1925 FA Cup Final but in 1927 returned to Wembley in the 1–0 defeat of Arsenal. Keenor, who made 32 appearances for his country, was an inspirational captain. His will to win, coupled with his uncompromising tackling, made him a tough opponent. He went on to appear in 414 League and Cup games for a club he had done much to establish before leaving to join Crewe Alexandra after 19 years at Ninian Park. In three years at Gresty Road he made 121 first-team appearances before going into non-League football, first with Oswestry and then as player-manager of Tunbridge

Wells Rangers. A serious illness ended the career of a man who had become a legend in Welsh football.

KELLOCK William (Billy)

Midfield

Born: Glasgow, 7 February 1954.
Career: Aston Villa. Cardiff City 1971. Norwich City 1973. Millwall 1974. Kettering Town. Peterborough United 1979. Luton Town 1982. Wolverhampton Wanderers 1983. Southend United 1983. Port Vale 1984. Halifax Town 1985. Kettering Town.

Welsh Cup finalist 1971–72. Welsh Cup winner 1972–73.

■ Much-travelled midfielder Billy Kellock served with 10 League clubs, amassed over 350 appearances and scored close on 100 goals. A Scottish Schoolboy international on Aston Villa's books, Kellock was released by the Midlands club, and Jimmy Scoular brought him to Ninian Park where he became a member of Cardiff's successful youth team of 1971. He made his League debut five days after his 18th birthday and did well in a City team undergoing some traumatic times. Norwich City spotted his potential, but he made little impact at Carrow Road and moved on to Millwall. While at the Den he dropped into non-League football with Kettering Town before re-entering League football with Peterborough United. He helped keep Posh challenging for promotion for three seasons, scoring 43 goals in 134 League outings. There then followed spells with Luton, Wolves, Southend United and Port Vale before he ended his League career with Halifax Town, later returning to the non-League scene with Kettering Town.

KELLY George Lawson

Inside-forward

Born: Aberdeen, 29 June 1933.
Career: Aberdeen. Stoke City 1956. Cardiff City 1958. Stockport County 1959.

■ A tall, rangy Scot, George Kelly left his home-town club Aberdeen to join Stoke City in February 1956. In two years at the Victoria Ground Kelly

earned a good reputation as a goalscoring inside-forward, finding the net 35 times in 67 games. In May 1958 Trevor Morris brought him to Ninian Park, and he looked a good signing for the Bluebirds. Unfortunately City made a poor start to the 1958–59 season, and though he scored twice against Sheffield United he lost his place after six games following the arrival of Derek Tapscott. He later scored another brace in a 3–1 derby win over Swansea, but in the close season he was transferred to Stockport County where he later ended his League career.

KELLY Mark David

Midfield

Born: Blackpool, 7 October 1966.
Career: Shrewsbury Town 1985. Cardiff City 1987. Fulham 1990.

Division Four runner-up 1987–88. Welsh Cup winner 1987–88.

■ Frank Burrows's first signing of the 1987 close season, Mark Kelly came to Ninian Park on a free transfer from Shrewsbury Town. Kelly, who had spent two years at Gay Meadow without making a League appearance, made his Football League debut with the Bluebirds in a 1–1 draw with Leyton Orient on the opening day of the 1987–88 season. He appeared in 36 games that campaign as City won promotion from the Fourth Division

and was a regular for the two seasons that followed. In June 1990 Kelly joined Fulham and spent three seasons at Craven Cottage before parting company with the London club.

KELLY Nyree Anthony Okpara (Tony)

Winger

Born: Meriden, 14 February 1968.
Career: Bristol City 1982. Dulwich Hamlet. Cheshunt. Enfield. St Albans City. Stoke City 1990. Hull City (loan) 1992. Cardiff City (loan) 1992. Bury 1993. Leyton Orient 1995. Colchester United (loan) 1996. St Albans City.

■ A winger who could play on either flank, Tony Kelly possessed incredible pace and ball control when on top of his game. Unable to make much progress with his first club Bristol City, he played non-League football for a number of clubs, including Dulwich Hamlet, Cheshunt, Enfield and St Albans City, before signing for Stoke City for £25,000. While with the Potters, Kelly had loan spells with Hull City and Cardiff – his spell at Ninian Park saw the Bluebirds win all their three home games with Kelly scoring on his debut in a 3–0 defeat of Scunthorpe United. Having played in 73 games for Stoke, Kelly joined Bury in the summer of 1993, although niggling injuries saw him out of the Gigg Lane side more often than not, and after two seasons in the North West he signed for Leyton Orient for a fee of £30,000. Again he was beset by injury problems, and, after a loan spell with Colchester, he was released by the O's and rejoined St Albans.

KELLY Seamus

Goalkeeper

Born: Tullamore, Eire, 6 May 1974.
Career: UCD Dublin. Cardiff City 1998. St Patrick's Athletic.

Division Three promotion 1998–99. FAW Invitation Cup finalist 1999–2000.

■ Goalkeeper Seamus Kelly moved to Cardiff City just before the start of the 1998–99 season having been spotted playing for University College, Dublin, in the League of Ireland. He then stepped into the City side at a crucial stage – five games from the end of their promotion campaign after regular 'keeper Jon Hallworth had broken two ribs in the game at Leyton Orient. Making his debut four days later, he kept a clean sheet in a 1–0 defeat of Southend United. Indeed, he conceded just one goal in his first four appearances as the Bluebirds clinched promotion before the final match of the season at Mansfield, which City lost 3–0. He then returned to his home town of Tullamore for a well-earned holiday! He was next called into action as the 1999–2000 campaign neared its tense climax, plunged into the fray once again after Hallworth had been injured six matches from the end of the season. This time the outcome was different as City were relegated. Released at the end of the season, he returned to Ireland to play for St Patrick's Athletic.

KELSO James (Jimmy)

Full-back/left-half

Born: Cardross, 8 December 1910.
Died: 1987.
Career: Helensburgh. Dumbarton. Bradford Park Avenue 1933. Port Vale 1934. Newport County 1935. Cardiff City 1938. Swindon Town 1945. Ebbw Vale.

Welsh Cup finalist 1938–39.

■ A fast, left-sided defender, he played for Helenburgh and Dumbarton before coming south of the border to play for Bradford Park Avenue. His stay with the Yorkshire club was brief, and in 1934 he joined Port Vale before moving on to Newport County. Ever present in 1935–36, he missed just a handful of games in three seasons at Somerton Park before, in June 1938, Cardiff City paid £1,000 for his services. Unluckily for him, he missed out on County's promotion to the Second Division but also the outbreak of World War Two meant that the Bluebirds were robbed of a fine full-back who was at his peak. During the fighting he 'guested' for Bristol City, Bath, Liverpool and Swansea Town before, in 1945, signing for Swindon Town. He later played for Ebbw Vale and scouted for Blackpool.

KERR Andrew Alphonso

Central-defender

Born: West Bromwich, 7 April 1966.
Career: Shrewsbury Town 1984. Cardiff City 1986. Telford United. Wycombe Wanderers 1988.

■ Spotted by Luton Town when playing junior football in Birmingham, defender Andy Kerr turned to Shrewsbury Town when the Hatters interest cooled. Though he had to wait two years before making his League debut for the Gay Meadow club, he had made just 10 appearances when Shrewsbury decided to release him. In the summer of 1986 Kerr joined the Bluebirds and the following season played in 31 games, his only goal coming in a 3–1 win at Scunthorpe United. On leaving Ninian Park he joined non-League Telford United before returning to League action with Wycombe Wanderers prior to retiring.

KETTERIDGE Stephen Jack

Midfield

Born: Stevenage, 7 November 1959.
Career: Derby County. Wimbledon 1978. Crystal Palace 1985. Leyton Orient 1987. Cardiff City (loan) 1988.

■ Steve Ketteridge was an apprentice on Derby County's books when Dario Gradi brought him to Wimbledon in April 1978. In his first season with the Dons the then Plough Lane club won promotion and Ketteridge showed his

versatility by playing in a number of different positions. One of the unsung heroes of the Wimbledon side, he helped them win promotion for a second time in 1980–81, following their relegation after just one season of Third Division football. Despite the club being relegated again, Ketteridge was an important member of the side that won the Fourth Division Championship in 1982–83 and won immediate promotion to Division Two after finishing as runners-up to Oxford United. Ketteridge, who had scored 36 goals in 269 games, left Wimbledon to join Crystal Palace, but after two seasons with the Eagles he was transferred to Leyton Orient. Unable to command a regular place at Brisbane Road, he was loaned out to Cardiff City and scored in the games against Mansfield Town and Bury during his six-match spell, before returning to Orient.

KEVAN David John

Midfield

Born: Wigtown, 31 August 1968.
Career: Notts County 1986. Cardiff City (loan) 1989. Stoke City 1990. Maidstone United (loan) 1991. Bournemouth 1994.

■ A Scottish Under-21 international, whose progress at Notts County was interrupted when Neil Warnock became manager, he had a loan spell with the Bluebirds during the early part of the club's relegation season of 1989–90 before Stoke manager Alan Ball swooped to sign him for £75,000. Unable to settle at the Victoria Ground, he went on loan to Maidstone United until the arrival of Lou Macari as Stoke boss transformed his career. Switched to right-back, he went on to win a medal in the Autoglass Trophy Final at Wembley before later ending his career with a brief spell at Bournemouth.

KING Gerald Henry (Gerry)

Winger

Born: Radnor, 7 April 1947.
Career: Cardiff City 1964. Torquay United 1965. Luton Town 1966. Newport County 1967.

■ A former Welsh Schoolboy international, all Gerry King's first-team appearances for the Bluebirds came in the early part of the 1964–65 season when he was only 17 years old. Though he created a number of goals for Ivor Allchurch, King was never on the winning side in his six League outings for City. He lost his place when Jimmy Scoular switched Bernard Lewis from the right to the left wing, and within a year he had moved to Torquay United. He later had a spell with Luton Town before returning to South Wales to play out his career with Newport County.

KING John (Jake)

Right-back

Born: Glasgow, 29 January 1955.
Career: Shrewsbury Town 1972.
Wrexham 1982. Cardiff City 1984.
Limerick.

■ Glasgow-born right-back Jake King played in schools football in his native city, but it was Shrewsbury Town with whom he began his professional career. Between 1972 and 1982 he made 306 appearances for the Shrews, scoring 20 goals. After being released King had offers from a number of clubs but chose Wrexham because of the chance of playing European football. Despite the Robins suffering relegation to Division Four during his time at the Racecourse, he did get his wish of playing in Europe when he popped up twice to score against FC Porto. In November 1984 he teamed up with Alan Durban again, at Cardiff but failed to prevent City's relegation to Division Three. Injury the following season curtailed his League career, but he did have a spell with Limerick prior to running a wine bar in Shrewsbury.

KING John William

Centre-forward

Born: Wrenbury, 9 August 1932.
Career: Crewe Alexandra 1949. Stoke City 1953. Cardiff City 1961. Crewe Alexandra 1962.

■ Centre-forward Johnny King, who began his career with Crewe Alexandra, was deceptively quick over a short distance, and it wasn't long before his

displays for the Railwaymen alerted higher Division clubs. In September 1953 he moved down the road to Stoke City and, in eight years with the Potters, King scored 105 goals in 284 League games, including a quickfire Christmas Day hat-trick in 1954 as Stoke beat Bury 3–2. King came to Ninian Park in the summer of 1961 and in a single season of First Division football often demonstrated neat skills and sharpness around the penalty area. When City were relegated, King's career came full circle when he rejoined Crewe. In his first season back at Gresty Road he helped the Railwaymen win promotion to Division Three and went on to score 60 goals in 226 League games in his two spells with the club.

KING Peter Charles

Forward

Born: Worcester, 3 April 1943.
Career: Worcester City. Cardiff City 1960.

Welsh Cup winner 1963–64, 1964–65, 1966–67, 1967–68, 1968–69, 1969–70, 1970–71. Welsh Cup finalist 1971–72.

■ One of Cardiff City's most loyal clubmen, Peter King played his early football for his home-town team

Worcester City before joining the Bluebirds in 1960. He made his League debut at Burnley in October 1961 as a right-winger and, after overcoming a chest illness early in his career, continued in the position until Jimmy Scoular decided to utilise his workrate in a midfield role. In 1963–64, having fully recovered from his illness, he scored both Cardiff's goals in a 2–0 Welsh Cup Final replay win over Bangor City. The following season King scored his only Football League hat-trick for the club in a 6–1 home defeat of Middlesbrough and netted their first goal in Europe when he scored the only goal of the two-leg tie against Esjberg. He missed very few games over the next few seasons and in 1967–68 was ever present and the club's leading scorer with 12 League goals and six more in Cup competitions. In 1970–71 he missed just one game as Cardiff finished third in Division Two, but an Achilles tendon injury forced him to quit the game in 1974 after he had scored 89 goals in 431 League and Cup games in 13 seasons at Ninian Park.

KIRTLEY John Harold (Harry)

Inside-forward

Born: Washington, 23 May 1930.
Career: Fatfield Juniors. Sunderland

1948. Cardiff City 195. Gateshead 1957.
Welsh Cup winner 1955–56.

■ Having played his early football with Fatfield Juniors, Harry Kirtley signed for Sunderland in May 1948. Although he could never command a regular place in the Wearsiders team, he scored 18 goals in 95 games over the next seven years with the north-east club. In the summer of 1955 Harry Kirtley, Johnny McSeveney and Howard Sheppeard all joined Cardiff from Sunderland, and both Kirtley and McSeveney made their Bluebirds debuts against their former club – City beating Sunderland 3–1. He was virtually an ever present for Cardiff in 1955–56 but had the misfortune to break a leg in the 3–2 defeat of Swansea in the end of season Welsh Cup Final. Despite regaining fitness, he did not play in City's first team again and moved to Gateshead in the Third Division North, playing for them until they lost their League status.

KITCHEN Michael Peter

Forward

Born: Mexborough, 16 February 1952.
Career: Doncaster Rovers 1970. Leyton Orient 197. Fulham 1979. Cardiff City 1980. Happy Valley (Hong Kong). Leyton Orient 1982. Dagenham. Chester City 1985.

■ After scoring 89 goals in 228 League games for Doncaster Rovers, Peter Kitchen became one of the prized assets of the lower Divisions, and it came as no surprise when Orient paid £40,000 to take him to Brisbane Road in the summer of 1977. He continued to find the net for Orient, 28 in 65 games, including the only goal of the final game of the 1977–78 season, to save the London club from relegation. He moved across the capital to play for Fulham, but he failed to settle at Craven Cottage and in the 1980 close season he joined Cardiff City for £100,000. He made his debut against one of his former clubs Orient but failed to score in a 4–2 win for the Bluebirds. He ended the season as top scorer with 13 League goals and netted five in a 6–0 Welsh Cup win over Cardiff Corinthians. Sadly, he lost form midway through the following season and left to play for Orient again, after a

spell in Hong Kong, before ending his career with Dagenham and Chester

KITE Philip David

Goalkeeper

Born: Bristol, 26 October 1962.
Career: Bristol Rovers 1980. Southampton 1984. Middlesbrough (loan) 1986. Gillingham 1987. Bournemouth 1989. Sheffield United 1990. Mansfield Town (loan) 1991. Plymouth Argyle (loan) 1992. Rotherham United (loan) 1992. Crewe Alexandra (loan) 1992. Stockport County (loan) 1993. Cardiff City 1993. Bristol City 1994. Bristol Rovers 1996.

■ An England Youth international goalkeeper, Phil Kite started out with his home-town club Bristol Rovers, where his displays between the posts prompted Southampton to sign him as cover for Peter Shilton. The move, however, was not a great success, and he was loaned out to Middlesbrough and Gillingham, later signing for the Kent club on a permanent basis. After two years at the Priestfield Stadium, he moved to Bournemouth as understudy to Gerry Peyton. His next port of call was Sheffield United, and though he performed well during his early days at Bramall Lane he was always second-choice behind a variety of 'keepers including Simon Tracey and Alan Kelly. There followed loan spells at Mansfield Town, Plymouth Argyle, Rotherham United, Crewe Alexandra and Stockport County before in May 1993 he arrived at Ninian Park. In 1993–94, his only season with the club, he shared the goalkeeping duties with Mark Grew and moved on to play for Bristol City before ending his career with his first club Bristol Rovers.

KNEESHAW Herbert Justin (Jack)

Goalkeeper

Born: Beckhill, 1883.
Died: 1955.
Career: Heaton. Bradford City 1903. St Cuthbert's. Guiseley Celtic. Bradford City 1907. Colne Town. Cardiff City 1912.

Division Two runner-up 1920–21.

■ Goalkeeper Jack Kneeshaw was a loyal servant of Cardiff City Football Club, both as a player and after his career had ended. After failing to make much impression with his local club Bradford City, he tried his luck with both Guiseley and Colne, and it was from the latter club that City manager Fred Stewart signed him in the summer of 1912. After making his Southern League debut in a 1–1 draw at Swansea on the opening day of the 1912–13 season, Kneeshaw went on to be a virtual ever present, playing in 111 games in four seasons. He was still the club's first-choice 'keeper when the Bluebirds entered the Football League for the 1920–21 season and played in the club's first-ever match at Stockport County. After losing his place to Ben Davies, he gave up playing to become a member of the club's training staff and in the late 1930s was appointed as Cardiff's coach. Despite being replaced by Ernie Blenkinsop, he stayed at Ninian Park working behind the scenes.

KNILL Alan Richard

Central-defender

Born: Eton, 8 October 1964.
Career: Southampton 1982. Halifax

Town 1984. Swansea City 1987. Bury 1989. Cardiff City (loan) 1993. Scunthorpe United 1993. Rotherham United 1997.

■ After failing to make the grade with Southampton, Alan Knill joined Halifax Town, and in three seasons with the Shaymen he was a virtual ever present. In the summer of 1987 he joined Swansea City for a tribunal-fixed fee of £15,000. At the Vetch he formed an effective central-defensive partnership with Andy Melville and, in his first season with the club, helped them win promotion to the Third Division via the play-offs. His performances in 1988–89 led to him winning full international honours for Wales against Holland in a World Cup qualifier. Claiming that Swansea lacked ambition, Knill left for Bury, the Gigg Lane club paying £95,000 for his services. In four seasons with the Shakers, Knill played in two consecutive play-off finals, suffered relegation to the League's basement and then appeared in another play-off match! After a four-match loan spell with Cardiff, where he was never on the winning side and played in a 5–0 defeat at York, he joined Scunthorpe United, later ending his career with Rotherham United.

KNOWLES Harold Frederick (Harry)

Outside-left

Born: Hednesford, 6 September 1932.

Career: Excelsior. Walsall 1950. Kidderminster Harriers. Worcester City. Cardiff City 1959. Worcester City.

■ Unable to make much headway at Walsall, Harry Knowles drifted into non-League football, but by becoming a prolific scorer for both Kidderminster Harriers and Worcester City he rebuilt his career. Bill Jones brought Knowles to Ninian Park in 1959, but try as he might the bustling winger could not hit the target in first-team games but scored in abundance for the reserves. In 1961 he rejoined Worcester City in exchange for Peter King, while in later years, after hanging up his boots, he worked in the building trade in Cornwall.

KOSKELA Toni

Midfielder

Born: Helsinki, Finland, 16 February 1983.

Career: HJK Helsinki. Jokerit (Helsinki) FC. KTP (Finland). Cardiff City 2005.

■ Finnish Under-21 international midfielder Toni Koskela had played for a number of clubs in his homeland prior to coming to Ninian Park on trial during the early part of the 2004–05 season. However, it was early in January 2005 before he signed on for the remainder of the season. He made his debut as a substitute against Ipswich Town in mid-March, and though he failed to force his way into the Bluebirds side on a regular basis he may well be a player for the future.

KOUMAS Jason

Midfield

Born: Wrexham, 25 September 1979. Career: Tranmere Rovers 1997. West Bromwich Albion 2002. Cardiff City (loan) 2005.

■ Welsh international Jason Koumas made his Football League debut for Tranmere Rovers midway through the 1998–99 season when he came on as a substitute at Sunderland. Two weeks later he scored the first of a number of unstoppable thunderbolts against Huddersfield Town at Prenton Park. Although he had only made 11 starts, his form was such that he attracted

scouts from a number of top clubs. A hard-running, creative midfield player, Koumas demonstrated good all-round skills in dribbling, passing and shooting. Although Tranmere struggled in 2000–01, Koumas developed into the main focus for the Rovers attack and ended the campaign as the club's leading scorer with 10 goals. At the beginning of June 2001, he made his debut in international football for Wales when he came off the bench in the closing stages of the World Cup qualifier against Ukraine. The following season he was rewarded with a place in the PFA award-winning Second Division side. Although he was the subject of much transfer speculation, he remained at Prenton Park until August 2002 when West Bromwich Albion paid £2.5 million to take him to the Hawthorns. He quickly became a great favourite with the Baggies fans, and in 2003–04 he helped Albion return to the top flight at the first time of asking. Having been selected for the PFA First Division side, he surprisingly did not figure in either Gary Megson or Bryan Robson's plans for West Bromwich Albion in 2004–05. In fact, he started in only five Premiership games, and after a disagreement with manager Robson he joined Cardiff on a season-long loan. It was a grave mistake by the Albion boss as they went on to lose their Premiership status while Koumas looked like the Premiership star he had shown himself to be before the fall out. With his driving runs from midfield and his powerful shooting, he scored a number of stunning goals, including a splendid effort at Leeds which helped Cardiff return from Elland Road with three points. Koumas, who dominated most of the games in which he played, was quite deservedly selected for the PFA award-winning Championship side. It remains to be seen where the classy midfielder will be playing his football in 2006–07.

LAMIE Robert (Bob)

Inside-forward

Born: Newarthill, 28 December 1928.
Career: Stonehouse Violet. Cardiff City 1949. Swansea Town 1951. Lincoln City.

■ A player with a powerful shot, Bob Lamie joined the Bluebirds from Scottish junior club Stonehouse Violet in October 1949. After making his debut the following month in a 1–0 home defeat at the hands of West Ham United, he found his first-team opportunities restricted by the form of George Edwards and Mike Tiddy. Making just three League appearances in each of his two seasons at Ninian Park, he did get on the score sheet in a 2–2 draw against Bury at the start of the 1950–51 season. The following spring he joined Swansea Town, but after just a couple of first-team games he moved to Lincoln City where he later hung up his boots without having made the side.

LANE Edward

Right-back

Born: Birmingham, 1908.
Career: West Bromwich Albion 1932. Notts County 1933. Cardiff City 1934.

■ After spells with both West Bromwich Albion and Notts County, full-back Edward Lane joined the Bluebirds in readiness for the 1934–35 season. Despite a 4–0 reversal at Luton on his debut, Lane became a regular member of City's defence, but at the end of the campaign in which he had made 30 League appearances he was not retained and moved into local League football.

LANGLEY Richard Barrington Michael

Midfielder

Born: Harlsden, 27 December 1979.
Career: Queen's Park Rangers 1996. Cardiff City 2003. Queen's Park Rangers 2005.

■ A Jamaican international, he scored after just eight minutes of his full debut for Queen's Park Rangers before suffering a serious leg injury that kept him out of action for most of the 1998–99 season. One of the successes of the Queen's Park Rangers youth academy, he soon began to make progress and was one of the very few players to hold down a regular place in the side. Unfortunately, he suffered a cruciate ligament injury and this put him out of acton until midway through the 2001–02 season. Once fully

recovered he again became a regular in the Rangers side, only missing games when suspended, and though not a prolific scorer he did net a hat-trick in the London club's 3–1 win at Blackpool. He had scored 21 goals in 148 games for the Loftus Road side when, in August 2003, he joined Cardiff City for a fee of £250,000. He took a little time to settle in at Ninian Park, but he showed flashes of real ability as the 2003–04 season wore on. Injured after a good start to the following campaign, Langley was out of action until Boxing Day when he came off the bench against Wolves. Thereafter, he won a regular place in the side as City began to string a run of good results together. Following the appointment of Dave Jones, Langley left Cardiff to rejoin Queen's Park Rangers, where he has continued to display his undoubted talents, this despite the club struggling at the foot of the Championship.

LARMOUR Albert Andrew James

Central-defender

Born: Belfast, 23 August 1977.
Career: Linfield. Cardiff City 1972. Torquay United 1979.

Welsh Cup winner 1972–73, 1973–74,. 1975–76. Welsh Cup finalist 1974–75, 1976–7. Division Three runner-up 1975–76.

■ Signed by Jimmy Scoular from Irish League club Linfield for a fee of £12,000 in the summer of 1972, Belfast-born defender Albert Larmour didn't really establish himself until 1974–75. That was the season he scored his only goal for the club in the second leg of the Welsh Cup Final, which City lost 5–2 on aggregate to Wrexham. In 1975–76 he played an important role as sweeper as the club won promotion to Division Two. Losing his place midway through the 1978–79 season when the Bluebirds paid £65,000 to sign Dave Roberts from Hull City, he left to play for Torquay United. Appointed the Devon club's captain, he spent two seasons at Plainmoor before parting company with the club.

LATHOM George

Wing-half/centre-half

Born: Newtown, 1 January 1881.
Died: 1939.
Career: Newtown. Liverpool 1902. Caledonian (South Africa). Southport Central. Stoke. Cardiff City 1921.

■ The oldest League debutant in Cardiff City's history was their legendary trainer George Lathom, who was forced into first-team action at the age of 41 at Blackburn Rovers – a match the Bluebirds won 3–1. George Lathom's name is now, perhaps, associated only with Lathom Park, home of Newtown FC, but in the inter-war years he was one of the great characters of Welsh soccer. It was not until Lathom returned from the Boer War that he took up soccer seriously. A trial with Everton ended with the match being abandoned, and it was with Liverpool in 1902 that he began his career. In six seasons at Anfield he was never a first-team regular but was thought good enough to play for Wales on eight occasions. Lathom, who later played for Southport Central and Stoke, became Cardiff trainer and was in charge of the City sides for the 1925 and 1927 FA Cup Finals. In 1932 he moved to Chester but soon came back to Cardiff where, midway through the decade, he was badly injured in a bicycle accident. Ill-health later forced him to retire to his beloved Newtown where he died a few months before the outbreak of World War Two.

LAWSON Denis

Outside-right

Born: Lennoxtown, 11 December 1897.
Career: Kilsyth Emmett Rovers. St Mirren. Cardiff City 1923. Springfield Babes (US). Providence Clamdiggers (US). Wigan Borough 1927. Clyde 1928.

■ After gaining experience in Army football, Scottish-born winger Denis Lawson played for Kilsyth Emmett before joining St Mirren. His form for the Love Street club, where he won full international honours for Scotland, alerted Cardiff City, and in November 1923 the Bluebirds paid £3,400 for his services. Initially he replaced Billy Grimshaw, but a year later he had to make way for Willie Davies and missed the 1925 FA Cup Final as a result. Lawson, whose only City goal came in a 3–0 home win over Leeds United in September 1924, got back into the team but later had a disagreement with the board. Unable to get a transfer request accepted, he went to America and had spells with Springfield Babes and Providence Clamdiggers. On his return to these shores he couldn't join anyone as City still held his registration. Eventually they relented, and he left to play for Wigan Borough. In 1928 he returned north of the border to end his career with Clyde.

LAYTON Arthur Edmund D.

Full-back

Born: Gornal, 14 February 1885.
Died: 1959.
Career: Royston United. Sheffield United 1905. South Kirby. Rotherham Town. Aston Villa 1908. Middlesbrough 1911. Whitby Town (loan). Cardiff City 1914. Stockport County 1920.

■ Unable to make the grade with Sheffield United, full-back Arthur Layton joined Aston Villa in 1908 and spent a couple of seasons at Villa Park before switching to Middlesbrough. While with 'Boro, he had a loan spell with non-League Whitby Town before signing for Cardiff in 1914. He immediately stepped into the Bluebirds Southern League team and remained with the club until their football League entry. He had made just two League appearances when, following the arrival of Jimmy Blair in November 1920, he moved to Stockport County, whom he helped win the Third Division North Championship in 1921–22.

LEA Leslie

Winger

Born: Manchester, 5 October 1942.
Career: Blackpool 1959. Cardiff City 1967. Barnsley 1970.

Welsh Cup winner 1967–68, 1968–69, 1969–70.

■ After beginning his career at Blackpool where he played alongside the great Stanley Matthews, Leslie Lea suffered a spate of injuries and a loss of form, and it wasn't until midway through the 1962–63 season that he regained his place. He then formed an exciting right-wing pairing with Pat Quinn before the emergence of future England World Cup winner Alan ball restricted his appearances. A very talented player, he had scored 16 goals in 179 games for the Seasiders when Cardiff boss Jimmy Scoular made a successful £15,000 offer for him in December 1967. An administrative error prevented Lea from making his City debut at Plymouth, and they had to draft in Gary Bell and play the match, which they drew 0–0 without a substitute! Scoular switched Lea from the wing to a floating midfield role, and he went on to have three successful seasons at Ninian Park. One of the club's most popular players, he had scored seven goals in 76 League games when, in August 1970, he was sold along with Frank Sharp to Barnsley for £20,000. Lea spent six seasons at Oakwell, scoring 32 goals in 205 games, before retiring to become a gardener with Barnsley Council.

LECKIE John T. (Jock)

Goalkeeper

Born: Alva, 3 March 1906.
Career: Alva Albion. Alloa Athletic. St Johnstone. Raith Rovers. Bray Unknowns. Port Vale 1931. Stockport County 1933. Cardiff City 1934. Walsall 1936. Carlisle United 1937.

■ Despite his nickname 'Jock', Leckie was a much-travelled Irishman, who, after playing for Alva Albion, turned out for Scottish clubs Alloa Athletic, St Johnstone and Raith Rovers before returning to Ireland to play for Bray Unknowns. In March 1932 Leckie came into the Football League with Port Vale but injuries restricted his first-team appearances, and he moved onto Stockport County. Leckie, who was seen as a replacement for Tom Farquharson, signed for Cardiff City in 1934, but in the face of competition from Jack Deighton and George Poland he failed to win a regular place. A little on the short side to be a competent 'keeper, he later played for Walsall and Carlisle United.

LEDLEY Joseph

Midfielder

Born: Cardiff, 21 January 1987.
Career: Cardiff City 2004.

■ Welsh Under-21 international midfielder Joe Ledley was a schoolboy trainee with the Bluebirds before working his way up through the ranks to make his debut in the Carling Cup second-round tie against the MK Dons, which City won 4–1. His first League appearance, also off the bench, came in the League basement battle against Rotherham United – a match that saw the Bluebirds win 2–0. He kept his place in the side for the following game and was a regular member for the remainder of the season, scoring a number of vital goals including the only goal of the game against Sheffield United. During the 2005–06 season, Joe Ledley was very impressive, missing very few games in a campaign which saw Cardiff push for a place in the play-offs. His mature decision making coupled with quick feet are the main features of his game, and he has been called up for international duty for Wales.

LEE Alan Desmond

Striker

Born: Galway, 21 August 1978.
Career: Aston Villa 1995. Torquay United (loan) 1998. Port Vale (loan) 1999. Burnley 1999. Rotherham United 2000. Cardiff City 2003. Ipswich Town 2005.

■ Unable to get a game at Aston Villa, this big, strong striker went on loan to Torquay United and Port Vale to gain League experience and on both occasions scored vital goals for the respective clubs. Shortly after returning to Villa Park, he joined Burnley in a £150,000 deal but had little chance to make his mark in his first season at Turf Moor, due to the consistency of the Clarets' regular front two. Allowed to leave the club for a similar fee, he moved to Rotherham United and soon netted his first Football League hat-trick in a 3–1 home defeat of Cambridge United. Having helped the Millers win promotion to the First Division, he adjusted well to life in the higher Division, and though he wasn't as

prolific he did score some vital goals in the battle against relegation. In 2002–03 he was soon into double figures in terms of goals and thoroughly deserved his call-up into the full Republic of Ireland side. He had scored 41 goals in 122 games for the Yorkshire club when he joined Cardiff for a Millers club record fee of £850,000. Although troubled by injury at Ninian Park, he was a regular in the Bluebirds side in the closing stages of the 2003–04 season and scored three goals. Most of Alan Lee's appearances during the first half of the 2005–06 season were from the bench, and it came as no surprise when he was allowed to leave Ninian Park to join Joe Royle's Ipswich Town side. His performances for the Tractor Boys in the latter stages of the campaign were very impressive as he continued to represent the Republic of Ireland on the international stage.

LEE Trevor Carl

Forward

Born: Lewisham, 3 July 1954.
Career: Epsom and Ewell. Millwall 1975. Colchester United 1978. Gillingham 1981. Leyton Orient (loan) 1982. Bournemouth 1982. Cardiff City 1983. Northampton Town 1984. Fulham 1985.

■ Trevor Lee was signed from non-League Epsom and Ewell by Millwall in

October 1975, along with another forward, Phil Walker. They both went on to become regular members of the Millwall attack and attracted other clubs. Lee had scored 22 goals in 108 games when, in November 1978, he was transferred to Colchester United for £15,000. He continued to find the net with great regularity in three years at Layer Road – 35 in 96 League outings – before a £90,000 cheque took him to Gillingham in January 1981. While with the Kent club he had a loan spell with Orient before moving on to Bournemouth. It was from the Cherries that Cardiff signed him in December 1983. He scored on his debut in a 3–2 derby win over Swansea City, and whenever he scored – five in 21 games – City were never beaten! He later played for Northampton Town before ending his League career with a single appearance for Fulham.

LEGG Andrew (Andy)

Full-back. Midfield

Born: Neath, 28 July 1966.
Career: Britton Ferry. Swansea City 1988. Notts County 1993. Birmingham City 1996. Ipswich Town (loan) 1997. Reading 1998. Peterborough United (loan) 1998. Cardiff City 1998. Peterborough United 2003.

Division Three promotion 1998–99.

FAW Invitation Cup finalist 1999–2000. Division Three runner-up 2000–01. FAW Premier Cup winner 2001–02. Division Two promotion 2002–03.

■ Fast and skilful, Andy Legg started out with Britton Ferry before joining Swansea in August 1988. He was an important member of the Swans side for five seasons, scoring 38 goals in 207 games before Notts County paid £275,000 to take him to Meadow Lane. Two and a half seasons later he was on the move again, this time to Birmingham City where he soon settled down on the left side of the club's midfield. His form with Birmingham was such that he won full international honours for Wales but midway through the 1997–98 season this long-throw specialist – whose world record throw of 44.54 metres was beaten by Tranmere's Dave Challinor – had a loan spell with Ipswich before joining Reading. Failing to impress the manager, he spent a month on loan with Peterborough before signing for the Bluebirds. He was given a great reception by City fans when showing total commitment to the team and an ability to take on the opposition. He won the 1999–2000 season Player of the Year award. Reportedly taking a big pay cut to join the Ninian Park club, he switched to playing as a sweeper the following season and again won the club's Player of the Year award. Legg was also made club captain, and although many thought his playing days were coming to an end he played an important part in Cardiff's promotion to the First Division in 2002–03. Having scored 12 goals in 209 first-team outings, he returned to Peterborough United as the London Road club's player-coach.

LEONARD Carleton Craig

Full-back

Born: Oswestry, 3 February 1958. Career: Shrewsbury Town 1975. Hereford United 1983. Cardiff City 1985. Oswestry Town.

■ Oswestry-born full-back Carleton Leonard turned professional with Shrewsbury Town in 1975 and went on to become one of the Gay Meadow club's finest post-war defenders, making

227 League appearances. During that time he helped the Shrews to the 1978–79 Third Division Championship, but in the summer of 1983 he joined Hereford United, doubling as a player and physiotherapist. It was in this capacity that he joined his former Shrewsbury boss Alan Durban at Ninian Park in 1985, but these were troubled times at the club and his stay was brief. On leaving the Bluebirds he returned to play for his home-town club Oswestry Town.

LEVER Arthur Richard

Full-back

Born: Cardiff, 25 March 1920. Died: 20 August 2004. Career: Cardiff City 1943. Leicester City 1950. Newport County 1954.

Division Three South champion 1946–47.

■ Full-back Arthur Lever, popularly known as 'Buller', joined Cardiff City during World War Two and made 104 wartime appearances for the club before making his League debut in a 2–1 reversal at Norwich City on the opening day of the 1946–47 season. He went on to become the club's only ever present that season as the Bluebirds won the Third Division South Championship. He was ever present again the following season when he scored in both matches against the Second Division runners-up

Newcastle United from his position at right-back. Lever went on to make 114 consecutive appearances from his debut until he was injured in City's 1–0 win at Spurs in March 1949. The popular full-back had made 165 League and Cup appearances for the Ninian Park club when, in September 1950, he joined Leicester City for a fee of £17,000. At Filbert Street he was entrusted with the team captaincy, his form leading to him winning full international honours when he played against Scotland at the beginning of the 1952–53 season. On parting company with the Foxes, he returned to South Wales to assist Fred Stansfield at Newport before, on retirement, working as a market gardener.

LEWIS Allan

Defender

Born: Pontypridd, 31 May 1971. Career: Cardiff City 1989.

■ YTS player Allan Lewis made his first start for the Bluebirds in a 1–1 home draw with Chester City, though all of his other 10 appearances in that relegation season of 1989–90 were from the bench. Over the next couple of seasons of Fourth Division football, Lewis was a regular member of the Cardiff side until injury forced his retirement from the game, having appeared in 50 League games for the Ninian Park club.

LEWIS Bernard (Bernie)

Outside-left

Born: Merthyr, Tydfil 12 March 1945. Career: Cardiff City 1964. Watford 1967. Southend United 1970. Chelmsford City.

Welsh Cup winner 1963–64. 1964–65.

■ An apprentice motor mechanic, winger Bernie Lewis joined the Bluebirds as a part-time professional and didn't take long to force his way into City's Second Division side. He made his debut in a 2–1 defeat at Rotherham United in January 1964 as a right-winger, though the following season he was switched to the left flank. Lewis, who won five Welsh Under-23 caps, was sold to Watford in November 1967 for a fee of £7,000 and on his debut for the Hornets had a hand in all

but one of the goals in a 7–1 rout of
Grimsby Town. He had frequent bursts
of first-team action but later left
Vicarage Road to end his League career
with Southend United, prior to playing
non-League football for Chelmsford
City.

LEWIS David B.

Inside-right

Born: Cardiff.
Career: Cardiff City 1934.

■ Local product David Lewis was
drafted into the City side towards the
end of the 1934–35 season, making his
debut in a 1–0 defeat at Gillingham.
However, with City struggling near the
foot of the Third Division South, he
made just one more League appearance
before parting company with the
Bluebirds.

LEWIS Ernest G.

Inside-left

Born: Cardiff.
Career: Cardiff City 1933.

■ Local League player Ernest Lewis
made his Cardiff debut at inside-
forward in a 3–2 defeat at Crystal Palace
during the club's troubled season of
1933–34, when they had to seek re-
election. Lewis played in 14 games that
season, his only goal coming at Swindon

Town when the Bluebirds went down
6–3. Not retained, he returned to the
local League scene.

LEWIS John

Midfield

Born: Tredegar, 15 October 1955.
Career: Pontllanfraith. Cardiff City 1978.
Newport County 1983. Swansea City
1987.

Division Three runner-up 1982–83.

■ Midfielder John Lewis was spotted
playing for Pontllanfraith in a Welsh
League match, and when offered terms
by Cardiff boss Jimmy Andrews he
jumped at the chance. A former clerk
with British Steel, he made his debut for
the Bluebirds in a 2–0 home win over
Blackburn Rovers in September 1978
and for the next five seasons was a
permanent fixture in the City side. In
1982–83, when the club won promotion
to the Second Division, he played in 39
games, scoring five goals. He was a lucky
omen because whenever Lewis scored in
that season the Bluebirds won – one of
his strikes coming in the 2–0 win over
Orient, the game in which the club
clinched promotion. In 1983 Lewis,
along with Linden Jones and Tarki
Micallef, left Ninian Park to play for
Newport County with Nigel Vaughan
and Karl Elsey coming in the opposite
direction. An established member of the
County team, he became the club's
player-manager when Jimmy Mullen
went to Aberdeen in 1986, but he
couldn't prevent their relegation to the
Fourth Division in 1986–87. Sacked by
the Somerton Park club, he then signed
for Swansea as a player and made 25
appearances for the Vetch Field side.

LEWIS James John (Jack 'Ginger')

Left-half/left-back

Born: Newport, 16 January 1902.
Career: Somerton Park Juniors. Newport
County 1922. Cardiff City 1924.
Tranmere Rovers 1925.

■ Nicknamed 'Ginger' for obvious
reasons, he had joined Cardiff City from
his home-town club Newport County,
in 1924, and he had made just one

appearance in a 4–1 defeat at Bury
when the call to play for Wales came. He
was waiting on a Newport station
platform for a train to Birmingham,
where he was due to play for Cardiff,
when he was told to report to Ninian
Park to solve the Welsh selection
problems. Lewis, who would not
normally have been considered for
international duty, was a forceful and
enthusiastic player who couldn't find a
place in the City line-up and joined
Tranmere Rovers. An ever present in his
second season at Prenton Park, he
missed very few games over the next
seven campaigns, going on to make 288
first-team outings before hanging up his
boots at the end of the 1933–34 season.

LEWIS Terence John

Wing-half

Born: Newport, 22 October 1950.
Career: Cardiff City 1968.

■ Defender Terry Lewis was a Welsh
Schoolboy international who was
thought to have a great future in the
game. Yet, in three seasons at Ninian
Park he appeared in just three League
games – the last a 4–2 defeat of Queen's
Park Rangers when John Toshack netted
a hat-trick. Disillusioned with the
professional game, he retired!

LEWIS William (Billy)

Outside-right

Born: Cardiff, 4 July 1923.
Career: Cardiff City 1941. Newport
County 1947.

■ Able to play on either flank, Billy
Lewis made his Cardiff debut on the
right-wing against Northampton Town
in January 1947. His pace and pin-point
crosses led to Bryn Allen netting a hat-
trick in a 6–2 win over the Cobblers.
Despite this start, Lewis lacked the
ability to hold down a regular first-team
place and this ultimately led to him
joining Newport County, where he
scored 11 goals in 49 League games.

LEWIS Wilfred Leslie (Wilf)

Forward

Born: Swansea, 1 July 1903.
Died: 1976.

Career: Baldwins Welfare. Swansea Amateurs. Swansea Town 1925. Huddersfield Town 1928. Derby County 1931. Yeovil and Petters United. Bath City. Cardiff City 1934. Haverfordwest County.

■ Wilf Lewis was another of Swansea's local discoveries in the 1920s who went on to play for Wales. At one stage it looked as if he would not fulfil his early promise, but he eventually settled in the side as Jack Fowler's goalscoring left-wing partner. Hat-tricks against Oldham Athletic and South Shields attracted the attention of Manchester United, but after the clubs failed to agree terms Lewis had another season at the Vetch, taking his tally of goals to 43 in 64 League games before joining First Division Huddersfield Town for £5,000. Although he marked his Town debut against Burnley with two goals, a few days later, at Cardiff, he sustained a knee injury, which troubled him for the remainder of his career. He recovered sufficiently to help Huddersfield reach the 1930 FA Cup Final, but a few days before the match he slipped in training and aggravated his knee injury. Lewis missed the Final and the following year, after further surgery, he was released. A comeback with Derby County was unsuccessful, and he joined Southern League Yeovil, where he hit 65 goals in the 1932–33 season. However, they were short of cash, and he was allowed to join Bath City. In 1934 he returned to the Football League with Cardiff City, making his Bluebirds debut in a 4–0 defeat at Luton Town. His best performance in a Cardiff shirt came towards the end of that season when he netted twice and struck the bar in a 3–1 win over Millwall. Early the following season his injury problems reappeared and, after a few games for Haverfordwest, he decided to retire.

LIEVESLEY Wilfred (Wilf)

Forward

*Born: Staveley, 6 October 1902.
Career: Staveley Old Boys. Derby County 1920. Manchester United 1922. Exeter City 1923. Wigan Borough 1928. Cardiff City 1929.*

■ Part of a footballing family, Joseph Lievesley (Sheffield United and Arsenal) was the father of Leslie (Doncaster Rovers, Manchester United, Chesterfield, Torquay United and Crystal Palace), Wilf and Ernest (Manchester City, Southend, Exeter and Rotherham) were cousins to Les, and he had two older brothers also in football. He first built a solid career in the lower Divisions with Exeter City after brief appearances for Derby County and Manchester United – 40 goals in 97 games – before going north to play for Wigan Borough. Top scorer in his only season at Springfield Park, he joined Cardiff City in 1929 and played in three consecutive games at the start of the 1929–30 season before deciding to retire.

LIGHTBOURNE Kyle Lavince

Centre-forward

*Born: Bermuda, 29 September 1968.
Career: Pembroke Hamilton (Bermuda). Scarborough 1992. Walsall 1993. Coventry City 1997. Fulham (loan) 1998. Stoke City 1998. Swindon Town (loan) 2001. Cardiff City (loan) 2001. Macclesfield Town 2001. Hull City (loan) 2002.*

■ Bermudan international Kyle Lightbourne played a few games for Scarborough before joining Walsall in the summer of 1993. In 1994–95 he was a revelation, his 27 goals, including a hat-trick against Fulham, earning him a place in the PFA Third Division award-winning side. The following season he became the first Walsall player for 10 years to score four goals in a game – a feat he achieved against Wycombe Wanderers in the Autowindscreens Shield. In 1996–97 Lightbourne was the Saddlers leading scorer for the third successive season and this prompted Coventry City to pay £500,000 for his services. Unable to settle at Highfield Road, he had a loan spell at Fulham before joining Stoke City for a similar fee. Illness and injury, plus relegation, made his time with the Potters a difficult one, that is until 1999–2000. He terrorised Second Division defences and helped Stoke win the Final of the Autowindscreens Shield at Wembley.

However, he then lost his place and had loan spells with Swindon and Cardiff. At Ninian Park he was used as cover for Gavin Gordon and Kevin Nugent but received few chances before returning to the Potters. He later signed for Macclesfield and went on loan to Hull City before, on rejoining the Silkmen, netting his 100th Football League goal prior to retiring.

LIVERMORE Douglas Ernest

Midfield

*Born: Prescot, 27 December 1947.
Career: Liverpool 1965. Norwich City 1970. Bournemouth (loan) 1975. Cardiff City 1975. Chester City 1977.*

Division Three runner-up 1975–76. Welsh Cup winner 1975–76. Welsh Cup finalist 1976–7.

■ After being taken on by Liverpool as a junior in 1965, he was handed Ian St John's role when the Scot was axed after the shock FA Cup quarter-final defeat at Watford in February 1970. He enjoyed a 13-match run to the end of the season but wasn't to start another League game

for Liverpool and joined Norwich City in November 1970 for £22,000. In 1971–72 he missed just one game as the Canaries won the Second Division Championship and, though he later had to undergo two cartilage operations, he clocked up 131 appearances before joining Cardiff City in August 1975. He proved to be an inspirational signing for the Bluebirds, anchoring midfield and making a more than useful contribution to the club's promotion in 1975–76. He later joined Chester where he ended his playing career. He returned to Ninian Park as coach under Richie Morgan, but after two years he moved on to Swansea City as assistant to John Toshack in the Swans' glory days. After a short spell coaching Norwich, he joined Spurs and was their caretaker-manager following David Pleat's dismissal until the appointment of Terry Venables. A much respected coach, he was involved with the Welsh national side for eight years.

LLOYD Kevin Gareth

Left-back

Born: Llanidloes, 26 September 1970.
Career: Caersws. Hereford United 1994.
Cardiff City 1996. Oldham Athletic 1999.

■ Spotted while playing for Caersws, left-back Kevin Lloyd joined Hereford United in November 1994. Strong and reliable, he soon established himself in the Edgar Street club side but then suffered a spate of niggling injuries, including an ankle problem. Freed by the Bulls in the summer of 1996, he joined Cardiff where his pace got him into good attacking positions, and from one such move he scored against Carlisle United – his lob beating the stranded 'keeper to put City on their way to the play-offs. Unfortunately, in 1997–98 he suffered a severe back problem, which eventually needed an operation. After quite an horrendous time he was given a free transfer but offered the option to start training with the Bluebirds in 1998–99 to prove his fitness. He eventually went on trial with Oldham but with several clubs in the League of Wales showing an interest he left Boundary Park.

LLOYD Kevin John James

Forward

Born: Wolverhampton, 12 June 1958.
Career: Darlaston. Cardiff City 1979.
Gillingham 1980.

■ Signed from non-League Darlaston, Kevin Lloyd failed to make Cardiff City's starting line-up, his only taste of League football for the Bluebirds coming on the opening day of the 1979–80 season when he came off the bench to replace Ray Bishop in a 4–1 defeat at Notts County. At the end of the season he left Ninian Park to join Gillingham, but again his only game for the Kent club came when he made a brief appearance as a substitute.

LLOYD Robert Clive

Inside-forward

Born: Merthyr Tydfil, 4 September 1945.
Career: Norwich City 1962. Cardiff City 1964. Swindon Town 1965.

■ Clive Lloyd spent two years on junior terms with Norwich City but was released without making the Canaries first team. He spent the 1964–65 season with Cardiff City but, though he impressed in the reserves, manager Jimmy Scoular only gave him two League appearances, against Newcastle United and Northampton Town, who just happened to be the two clubs that won promotion to the top flight! At the end of the season he joined Swindon Town but, on being unable to make the grade, drifted into non-League football.

LOOVENS Glenn

Central-defender

Born: Doertinchem, Holland, 22 September 1983.
Career: Feyenoord (Holland). Cardiff City 2005.

■ Central-defender Glenn Loovens joined Cardiff City from Dutch club Feyenoord in the summer of 2005 on a season's long loan. He impressed with the Bluebirds in 2005–06. Cardiff boss Dave Jones and executive deputy chairman Peter Ridsdale travelled to Rotterdam just after the turn of the year to try and cement a deal for the Holland Under-21 international, who managed

to find the net twice during the course of the campaign and at the end of the season his move became a permanent one.

LOVE Ian James

Forward

Born: Cardiff, 1 March 1958.
Career: Barry Town. Swansea City 1986. Torquay United 1989. Cardiff City 1989. Barry Town 1990.

■ Ian Love's predatory instincts for Barry Town led to Swansea City offering him terms in the summer of 1986. Initially he struggled to come to terms with the higher standard of football, and, though he found the net nine times in 41 League games, he was allowed to leave Vetch Field and join Torquay United. Unable to make much of an impression, he left the Devon club to join Cardiff City during the early stages of the 1989–90 season. Substituted when making his debut at Mansfield Town, his only other appearance was as a substitute later that season at Wigan. His career then went full circle when he left to play for Barry Town.

LOW Joshua David (Josh)

Winger

Born: Bristol, 15 February 1979.
Career: Bristol Rovers 1996. Farnborough (loan). Leyton Orient 1999. Cardiff City 1999. Oldham Athletic 2002. Northampton Town 2003.

Division Three runner-up 2000–01.

■ Welsh Youth and Under-21 international Josh Low made his League debut in the last 90 seconds of the final game of Bristol Rovers' 1995–96 season against Wycombe Wanderers, before an ankle injury early the following season restricted his appearances. During 1997–98 he got more of a look in but was one of four Bristol Rovers players sent off at Wigan, when the club equalled the League record for most team dismissals in a match! After a loan spell with Farnborough, Low turned down the chance to join Rushden and Diamonds in favour of a move to Leyton Orient. Unable to settle in London, he signed for the Bluebirds,

initially on loan. Though his free-running style delighted the fans, he couldn't hold down a first-team place until 2000–01, when he made the right wing-back position his own. Voted the Most Improved Player at Ninian Park, he was also selected for the PFA's Third Division team. Injuries then cost him his place in the team, and after a spell with Oldham he joined Northampton Town where he has become a great favourite with the Cobblers fans.

LYNEX Steven Charles

Winger

Born: West Bromwich, 23 January 1958. Career: West Bromwich Albion 1976. Shamrock Rovers. Birmingham City 1979. Leicester City 1981. Birmingham City (loan) 1986. West Bromwich Albion 1987. Cardiff City 1988. Telford United.

■ Despite having only a limited League career at St Andrew's, where he gained a reputation as 'super sub', Steve Lynex arrived at Leicester City with two Cup-winning medals to his name, having won an FA Youth medal with West Bromwich Albion and an FAI Cup medal with Shamrock Rovers. At Filbert Street he developed quickly with regular top-flight football and was the Foxes' regular penalty-taker. The only orthodox winger on Leicester's books,

he went on to score 60 goals in 240 appearances before, following a loss of form, he rejoined his home-town club West Bromwich Albion. After just over a season back at the Hawthorns he left to play for Cardiff City. Unfortunately, during his stay at Ninian Park the Bluebirds were fighting to avoid relegation to the Fourth Division, and though he showed his versatility by appearing in six different numbered outfield shirts, he couldn't prevent the

club dropping into the League's basement in 1989–90. After a spell playing non-League football for Telford United, he hung up his boots to become a licensee. Sadly, he hit the headlines again in 1994 when he was burned in a Bonfire Night explosion, which proved fatal for one child.

McANUFF Joel Joshua Frederick (Jobi)

Winger

Born: Edmonton, 9 November 1981. Career: Wimbledon 2000. West Ham United 2004. Cardiff City 2004. Crystal Palace 2005.

■ A talented right-winger who possesses lightning speed along with the confidence to take on defenders and get past them, Jobi McAnuff began his career with Wimbledon. He acquitted

himself well in his debut season of 2001–02, so much so that he won full international recognition for Jamaica. The following season saw him show some stunning form for the Dons as time after time he tore opposing defences to ribbons with his pace, control and fierce shooting. Picking up a groin injury, he missed vital games later on and was left out of the side once the club's play-off hopes had gone. It wasn't a surprise when the club's administrators sold him to West Ham United for £300,000. He scored a stunning goal for the Hammers against Crewe, and in the remaining months of the 2003–04 season he continued to excite the Upton Park crowds. Surprisingly allowed to leave West Ham in August 2004, he joined the Bluebirds for a fee of £250,000. McAnuff made his City debut at Ipswich Town and was a virtual ever present for the remainder of the season, scoring his first goal for the club in a 4–1 win over his former club West Ham United. City fans were disappointed to learn during the early part of the close season that he had left Ninian Park to join Championship newcomers Crystal Palace, who had lost their Premiership status. With Cardiff's financial situation being dire, Jobi McAnuff was allowed to leave the club to join Championship rivals Crystal Palace in the summer of 2005. His outstanding displays for the Eagles were instrumental in them reaching the end of season play-offs.

MacAULAY Robert (Bob)

Full-back

Born: Wishaw, 28 August 1904.
Died: 1994.
Career: Carsteel (Montreal). Montreal Grenadier Guards. Providence Clamdiggers. Fall River Marksmen. Glasgow Rangers. Chelsea 1932. Cardiff City 1936. Sligo Rovers. Workington. Raith Rovers.

■ Scottish international full-back Bob MacAulay was a successful defender with Glasgow Rangers, helping the Ibrox club win the Scottish Cup in 1932. Shortly afterwards, he was signed by Chelsea and went on to make 66 appearances for the Stamford Bridge outfit before going on to play for Cardiff City during the latter stages of 1936. MacAulay's debut for the Bluebirds was a disaster for both him and fellow debutant John Mellor in the full-back berths as Luton Town ran riot with Joe Payne grabbing four goals and George Stephenson a hat-trick in an 8–1 win! MacAulay was by now lacking in pace and after just four appearances moved on to Sligo Rovers before eventually returning to Ibrox to become a scout.

MacBENNETT James Congall (Seamus)

Outside-right

Born: Newcastle, Northern Ireland, 16 November 1925.
Died: 1995.
Career: Belfast Celtic. Cardiff City 1947. Tranmere Rovers 1948.

■ A speedy winger, Seamus MacBennett joined Cardiff City from Belfast Celtic in the summer of 1947, and in the second of four first-team appearances for the Bluebirds he scored both the club's goals in a 2–2 draw at Southampton. After losing his place to Colin Gibson, he had to content himself with a year of playing reserve-team football until joining Tranmere Rovers in November 1948. Always on the fringes of the Wirral club's first team, he

spent a season at Prenton Park before moving into local non-League football.

McCAMBRIDGE James (Jimmy)

Forward

Born: Larne, 23 September 1905.
Career: Larne. Ballymena United. Everton 1930. Cardiff City 1930. Bristol Rovers 1933. Exeter City 1935. Sheffield Wednesday 1936. Hartlepool United 1936. Cheltenham Town.

■ Irish-born forward Jimmy McCambridge played his early football with Larne and Ballymena United before a move to Everton brought him into the Football League. At Goodison Park McCambridge spent much of his time as understudy to Dixie Dean. He became a major signing for Cardiff City

in January 1931 and scored twice on his debut in a 3–2 defeat at West Bromwich Albion. He ended that season with nine goals in 18 League games, including a hat-trick in a 3–2 home win over Stoke. In 1931–32 the Irish international established a new club League goalscoring record when he hit 26 League goals, including hat-tricks against Queen's Park Rangers and Clapton Orient. He was the club's leading scorer again the following season with 16 goals after netting 11 in the first 12 games of the campaign. Surprisingly, McCambridge, who had

scored 53 goals in 100 League and Cup games, was allowed to join Bristol Rovers in 1933. He headed their scoring charts in his first season at Eastville and had scored 23 goals in 57 games when he left to play for Exeter City. The prolific marksman again topped the scoring charts with 16 goals in just 23 games before moving to play First Division football with Sheffield Wednesday. His stay at Hillsborough was short, and he moved to Hartlepool United where he ended his first-class career, prior to a spell with Cheltenham Town.

McCARTHY Daniel John Anthony

Winger

Born: Abergavenny, 26 September 1942.
Career: Abergavenny Thistle. Cardiff City 1960. Merthyr Tydfil. Abergavenny Thistle.

■ Winger Danny McCarthy was spotted playing for his home-town club Abergavenny Thistle in the Welsh

League, and at the time they were a leading force. Expected to be a player with a big future, he was given his League baptism during the club's

relegation season of 1961–62, though he was on the winning side on his debut as the Bluebirds beat Manchester City 2–1. Unable to make the most of his opportunity, he was released and had a spell with Merthyr Tydfil before returning to Abergavenny.

McCAUGHEY Cecil

Right-half

Born: Bootle, 1909.
Career: Burscough Rangers. Liverpool 1933. Blackburn Rovers 1934. Coventry City 1935. Cardiff City 1937. Southport 1929.

■ After learning his footballing trade in the Lancashire League with Burscough Rangers, he turned professional and had spells with Liverpool and Blackburn Rovers without breaking into either club's first team. In 1935 he moved to Coventry City and, in his first season with the club, helped them win the Third Division South Championship. A clever, constructive half-back, he joined Cardiff in the summer of 1937 and became a regular team member for the next two seasons, scoring some vital goals. In 1939 he joined Southport but the outbreak of World War Two put an end to his playing career.

McCLELLAND John

Central-defender

Born: Belfast, 7 December 1955.
Career: Portadown. Cardiff City 1974. Bangor City. Mansfield Town 1978. Glasgow Rangers. Watford 1984. Leeds United 1989. Watford (loan) 1990. Notts County (loan) 1992. St Johnstone. Carrick Rangers. Arbroath. Wycombe Wanderers. Yeovil Town. Darlington 1996.

Welsh Cup finalist 1974–75.

■ Multi-capped Northern Ireland international defender John McClelland began his career with Portadown before trying his luck in the Football League with Cardiff City. Coming off the bench on his debut against Bristol Rovers, he scored a late equaliser in a 2–2 draw. Though he appeared in the remaining two games of that 1974–75 season, League football had come to early for the young McClelland, and he joined

Bangor City. Mansfield Town gave him his second chance at League football and in May 1981 his career took off in a big way when he joined Scottish giants Glasgow Rangers for £90,000. After a little over three seasons at Ibrox, First Division Watford paid £225,000 for his services. He played in Northern Ireland's 1982 and 1986 World Cup Final teams and represented the Football League against the Rest of the World at Wembley in August 1987. In the summer of 1989 he joined Leeds United but his time at Elland Road was hampered by injury. After a loan spell with Notts County he joined St Johnstone as player-coach, later being elevated to player-manager. After losing his job with the Saints, he had a brief spell with Carrick Rangers before moving back to Scotland with Arbroath. He then had spells with Wycombe Wanderers, Yeovil Town and Darlington as coach, before becoming assistant manager at Bradford City.

McCULLOCH Andrew

Forward

Born: Northampton, 3 January 1950.
Career: Walton and Hersham. Queen's Park Rangers 1970. Cardiff City 1972. Oxford United 1974. Brentford 1976. Sheffield Wednesday 1979. Crystal Palace 1983. Aldershot 1984.

Welsh Cup winner 1972–73.

■ Son of Adam McCulloch, the prolific centre-forward who played for Northampton, Shrewsbury and Aldershot in the early 1950s, he began his career with Walton and Hersham before joining Queen's Park Rangers in 1970. He failed to become a regular at Loftus Road, and in October 1972 he was transferred to Cardiff City for £42,000 at a time Jimmy Scoular was wheeling and dealing in the transfer market following the club's poor start. After scoring on his debut in a 3–0 defeat of Preston North End, he went on to top the scoring charts with 14 goals in 26 games and keep City out of the relegation places. Though he was again leading scorer in 1973–74, he did not fit into Jimmy Andrew's plans and was sold to Oxford United for £70,000. Injuries hampered his progress at the Manor

Ground, and he moved on to Brentford. In the summer of 1979 he signed for Sheffield Wednesday where he helped the Owls win promotion at the end of his first season with the club. One of the game's bravest strikers, he later played for Crystal Palace and Aldershot, going on to score 140 League goals for his seven clubs.

McCULLOCH Scott Anderson James

Defender

Born: Irvine, 29 November 1975.
Career: Glasgow Rangers 1992. Hamilton Academicals 1995. Dunfermline Athletic 1997. Dundee United 1999. Cardiff City 2000. Airdrie. Forfar Athletic.

Division Three runner-up 2000–01.

■ The burly defender was on the books of Glasgow Rangers, but on being unable to make the grade at Ibrox he joined Hamilton Academicals. He spent a couple of seasons with the Accies before switching to Dunfermline Athletic and later Dundee United. It was from the Tannadice club that Cardiff paid £100,000 to take him to Ninian Park in September 2000. Generally used on the left-hand side of a back three or in a midfield role, he never quite made either position his own, spending much of his time on the bench. Though he showed plenty of ability on the ball and packed a powerful shot, he was placed on the open to offers list and, after a trial period with Airdrie, signed for Forfar Athletic.

McDERMOTT Brian James

Winger

Born: Slough, 8 April 1961.
Career: Arsenal 1979. Fulham (loan) 1983. IFK Norrkoping (loan). Oxford United 1984. Huddersfield Town. (loan) 1986. Cardiff City 1987. Exeter City 1989. Yeovil Town.

Division Four runner-up 1987–88. Welsh Cup winner 1987–88.

■ A prolific scorer for Arsenal's reserve side, England Youth international Brian McDermott failed to establish himself in the Gunners side, and in seven seasons at Highbury he only appeared in 70 League and Cup games. While with the North London club, he had brief loan spells with Fulham and IFK Norrkoping, but in December 1984 he joined Oxford United for a fee of £40,000. In his first season at the Manor Ground he helped Oxford win promotion to the First Division but then lost his way through injury and a loss of form. Following a loan spell at Huddersfield, McDermott joined the Bluebirds in an attempt to rebuild his faltering career. Making his debut against Leyton Orient on the opening day of the 1987–88 season, he missed just one game as City won promotion to the Third Division and the Welsh Cup. The scorer of a number of vital goals, he left Ninian Park during the early part of the following season to join Exeter City, later playing non-League football for Yeovil Town.

McDONAGH Charles

Right-half

Born: Coventry, 1912.
Career: Coventry City 1931. Southampton 1932. Bournemouth 1933. Kidderminster Harriers. Cardiff City 1935. Peterborough United. Southport.

■ Much-travelled wing-half Charles McDonagh saw service with Coventry City, Southampton and Bournemouth in the 1930s but failed to make a first-team appearance with any of those clubs. After a spell playing non-League football for Kidderminster, he joined Cardiff City, making his debut in a 1–1 home draw against Crystal Palace in December 1935. He kept his place in the side for the next game, but after the Bluebirds were beaten 4–1 at Reading he wasn't called upon again. In the close season he joined Peterborough United, later finishing his career with Southport.

McDONALD Curtis

Midfield

Born: Wales.
Career: Cardiff City 2006.

■ Midfielder Curtis McDonald, who had worked his way up through the club's junior and reserve ranks, made his first-team debut for the Bluebirds as a substitute for Guylain N'Dumbu-Nsungu in the 62nd minute of the final match of the 2005–06 season at Coventry City.

McDONALD Kenneth (Ken)

Centre-forward

Born: Llanrwst, 24 April 1898.
Career: Inverness Citadel. Inverness Clachnacuddin. Aberdeen. Caerau. Cardiff City 1921. Manchester United 1922. Bradford Park Avenue 1923. Hull City 1928. Halifax Town 1929. Coleraine. Walker Celtic. Blyth Spartans.

■ Despite his Welsh birthplace, centre-forward Ken McDonald played his early football in the Highland League with Inverness Clachnacuddin before joining Aberdeen prior to the 1920–21 season. On leaving Pittodrie he moved to South Wales and was with Caerau in the Welsh League when he came to the attention of Cardiff manager Fred Stewart. His prolific scoring for City's reserves, plus his goal return in the first team, including one on his debut in a 3–0 defeat of Preston North End, made him a target for other clubs. McDonald left Ninian Park in 1923 and had a brief spell with Manchester United before signing for Bradford Park Avenue. He was a scoring sensation as in four seasons with the Yorkshire club he scored 135 goals in 145 games. His total of 46 in 1925–26 remained a League record for Bradford, and in 1927–28 his goals helped them win the Third Division North Championship. He later continued his prolific scoring with Hull City before ending his League career with Halifax Town. He then had brief spells with Coleraine, Walker Celtic and Blyth Spartans before retiring.

MacDONALD Kevin Duncan

Midfield

Born: Inverness, 22 November 1960.
Career: Inverness Caledonian. Leicester City 1980. Liverpool 1984. Leicester City (loan) 1987. Rangers (loan). Coventry City 1989. Cardiff City (loan) 1991. Walsall 1991.

■ After only two seasons of Highland League football with Inverness Caledonian, Kevin Macdonald was playing First Division football with Leicester City. Once he had mastered his occasionally fiery temper – he was the first Leicester player to be sent off twice – he proved himself with his combativeness and memorable cool defensive work. Macdonald had played in 152 games when Liverpool paid £400,000 for his services. Sadly, at Anfield, injuries cruelly hampered his progress in a formidably strong squad, though he did pick up an FA Cup medal

in 1986. After loan spells with Leicester and Rangers he was eventually freed from Anfield and joined Coventry City. In March 1991 he had a loan spell with Cardiff but then turned down a player-coach role at Ninian Park before moving to Walsall. He retired after their 1992–93 play-off exit and returned to Filbert Street as Leicester's youth coach.

McGORRY Brian Paul

Midfield

Born: Liverpool, 16 April 1970.
Career: Weymouth. Bournemouth 1991. Peterborough United 1994. Wycombe Wanderers 1995. Cardiff City (loan) 1996. Hereford United 1997. Torquay United 1998. Telford United.

■ Midfielder Brian McGorry's impressive displays for non-League Weymouth alerted a number of lower Division League clubs, and in August 1991 Bournemouth paid £30,000 to take him to Dean Court. An industrious player who, on his day, could be a match-winner, he scored 14 goals in 83 games for the Cherries before a £60,000 move to Peterborough in February 1994. Released after two seasons at London Road, he was one of Alan Smith's first signings for Wycombe Wanderers. Frustrated by the lack of first-team action, he joined Cardiff on loan where he impressed as a welcome addition to the City midfield. After another frustrating season with Wycombe, McGorry joined Hereford United. Following the Bulls losing their League status, he signed for Torquay United, but after one season at Plainmoor he went to play non-League football for Telford United.

McGRATH James (Jimmy)

Left-half/winger

Born: Washington, 4 March 1907.
Career: Washington Colliery. Cardiff City 1928. Port Vale 1932. Notts County 1934. Bradford Park Avenue 1934.

■ A left-half who was later converted to a winger, Jimmy McGrath joined Cardiff City from Washington Colliery in December 1929, making his debut in a 1–0 defeat of Charlton Athletic. Unable to make a permanent

breakthrough to City's first team, he moved to Port Vale where for two seasons he was a regular in the Valiants side. He then had a short spell with Notts County before signing for Bradford Park Avenue, where he eventually joined their coaching staff.

McGUCKIN George Kay Whyte

Half-back

Born: Dundee, 11 August 1938.
Career: Dundee Shamrock. Cardiff City 1955.

■ Signed as a 17-year-old from Scottish junior club Dundee Shamrock, wing-half George McGuckin became a regular in Cardiff City's reserve side. Due to the wealth of talent in his position at Ninian Park, his first-team chances were limited and his only League outings came towards the end of the 1957–58 season and, oddly, all were away from home.

McILVENNY Patrick (Paddy)

Outside-right/centre-forward

Born: Belfast, 1900.
Career: Distillery. Cardiff City 1924. Sheffield Wednesday 1925. Shelbourne. Northampton Town 1928. Boston Town. Hinckley United.

■ Irish international forward Paddy McIlvenny joined the Bluebirds from Distillery in 1924. Though his first-team chances were restricted by Len Davies, then at his most prolific, he did score twice in five First Division outings in 1924–25. He left Ninian Park in November 1925 to join Sheffield Wednesday, but after just one appearance for the Owls he was on the move again, this time to Irish club Shelbourne. He later returned to Football League action with Northampton Town before playing non-League football for Boston Town and Hinckley United.

McINCH James Reid (Jimmy)

Forward

Born: Glasgow, 27 June 1953.

Career: Cardiff City 1970. Bath City. Bridgend.

■ Glasgow-born forward Jimmy McInch joined Cardiff as an apprentice and exploded onto the club's youth team with a number of electrifying performances as he forged a most productive partnership with Derek Showers. Unfortunately, McInch never lived up to his early reputation and left Ninian Park to play non-League football for Bath City. He later played for Bridgend for many years.

McINTOSH Alan

Winger

Born: Llandudno, 29 July 1939.
Career: Llandudno Town. Cardiff City 1962.

■ A Welsh amateur international with his home-town club Llandudno, Alan McIntosh, a qualified teacher, played his first two games for Cardiff City as an amateur in the First Division season of 1961–62. After signing professional terms in the close season, he switched from the left-wing to the right with good results as he played in all but one

game of the 1962–63 campaign. Midway through the following season he suffered a badly broken leg in an FA Cup third-round tie against Leeds United. Sadly, the injury was severe enough to end a blossoming career.

McJENNETT John James (Jack)

Right-back

Born: Cardiff, 1906.
Career: Cardiff City 1929. Exeter City 1932.

■ Defender Jack McJennett worked his way up through the ranks at Cardiff City to make his first-team debut at Bradford City in February 1930. However, his handful of League appearances were spread over three seasons, and in June 1932 he moved to Exeter City. During his time at St James's Park he was hampered by injury and illness and failed to make a first-team appearance for the Grecians.

McKENZIE John D. (James)

Inside-forward

Born: Sudbrook, 1914.
Career: Chepstow. Gloucester City. Bristol Rovers 1933. Leicester City 1934. Cardiff City 1935. Notts County 1939.

■ After some good displays for non-League clubs Chepstow and Gloucester City, James McKenzie had trials with Bristol Rovers and Leicester City before being given a chance at League level with Cardiff City. After making his debut at Clapton Orient in the final game of the 1935–36 season, McKenzie failed to make his mark the following campaign, and the arrival of Jimmy Collins condemned him to reserve-team football. He later moved to Notts County where the outbreak of World War Two put an end to his footballing career.

McLACHLAN George Herbert

Outside-left/left-half

Born: Glasgow, 21 September 1902.
Career: Crosshill Amateurs. Parkhead Juniors. Rutherglen Glencairn. Queen's Park Strollers. Clyde. King's Park Strollers. Cardiff City 1925. Manchester United 1929. Chester 1933. Le Havre.

FA Cup winner 1926–27. Welsh Cup winner 1926–27, 1927–28. FA Charity Shield winner 1927–28. Welsh Cup finalist 1928–29.

■ George McLachlan was one of a small number of footballers to have enjoyed playing League football with English, Scottish and Welsh clubs. He began his career by playing junior football with a number of clubs, including Rutherglen, before joining Clyde for the 1922–23 season. His performances for the Bully Wee led to a number of Football League clubs making enquiries about the ball-playing left-winger. In November 1925 McLachlan joined Cardiff City for a fee of £2,000 and made his debut in a 5–2 home win over Leicester City. Despite breaking his leg in 1926, McLachlan bounced back to star in City's 1927 FA Cup-winning team, the first and only time the trophy has been won by a non-English club. He was ever present in 1927–28, but as the Bluebirds dropped towards Division Two in 1929–30 McLachlan joined Manchester United to continue his career in the First Division. He spent four seasons at Old Trafford before moving on to join Third Division North club Chester. After just one season he had a brief spell with French club Le Havre before returning to Scotland to become manager of Queen of the South.

McLAREN Robert (Bobby)

Inside-forward

Born: Glasgow, 5 August 1929.
Career: Barry Town. Cardiff City 1950. Barry Town. Scunthorpe United 1951.

■ Glasgow-born inside-forward Bobby McLaren joined the Bluebirds from Barry Town but, despite starring for the club's reserve side, his first-team opportunities were limited to a single League game against Luton Town in March 1950. Despite all his promptings, City couldn't break down the Hatters defence and the game ended goalless. After a brief spell back with Barry Town, he signed for Scunthorpe United where he later ended his playing career.

McLAUGHLIN Robert (Bobby)

Wing-half/inside-forward

Born: Belfast, 6 December 1925.
Career: Distillery. Wrexham 1950. Cardiff City 1950. Southampton 1953. Headington United. Salisbury.

Welsh Cup finalist 1950–51. Division Two runner-up 1951–52.

■ Bobby McLaughlin played his early football in his native Ireland for Distillery before moving to Wales to play for Wrexham in January 1950. Four months later he had left the Racecourse Ground to sign for Cardiff City. Converted from wing-half to inside-forward, McLaughlin didn't make his first-team debut until the start of the following season and, in 1951–52, was part of the side that won promotion to the First Division. After just three games in the top flight, McLaughlin lost his place and opted for a move to Southampton. He gave the Saints six seasons' loyal service, clocking up 177 League and Cup appearances before, on being given a free transfer, he played non-League football for Headington United and later Salisbury.

McLEAN Ian

Central-defender

Born: Paisley, 13 August 1966.
Career: Metro Ford (Canada). Bristol Rovers 1993. Cardiff City (loan) 1994. Rotherham United (loan) 1996.

■ Canadian international central-defender Ian McLean began his League career with Bristol Rovers, whom he joined from Metro Ford of Canada in September 1993. In January 1995, after some good displays at the heart of the Rovers defence, he managed to make his full international debut for the country he emigrated to as a youngster. However, on his return to Twerton Park he was unable to hold down a regular place in the Rovers side and, during the course of the 1994–95 season, spent two separate loan periods at Cardiff. Still finding it difficult to establish a regular place in the Pirates line-up, he joined Second Division rivals Rotherham United on loan. During his time with the Millers he received his marching orders in the match against Chesterfield. Released by Bristol Rovers in the summer of 1996, he then drifted into non-League football.

McLOUGHLIN Paul Brendan

Midfield/forward

Born: Bristol, 23 December 1963.
Career: Yeovil Town. Gisborne (New Zealand). Cardiff City 1984. Oster Vaxjo (Sweden). Bristol City 1987. Hereford United 1987. Wolverhampton Wanderers 1989. Walsall (loan) 1991. York City (loan) 1992. Mansfield Town 1992.

■ A good footballing midfielder who could also fill in as an emergency striker, Paul McLoughlin failed to make the grade with his home-town clubs Bristol City and Bristol Rovers and so joined non-League Yeovil Town. Along with Kevin Meacock, he went to play in New Zealand for Gisborne City, where he won several domestic honours before returning to these shores and successfully applying to the Bluebirds for a trial. He became a fairly regular first-team member, even occasionally playing as an experimental full-back, but following City's relegation to the

Fourth Division he was freed. He tried his luck in Sweden with Oster Vaxjo before joining Bristol City. Again he failed to make a first-team appearance for the Robins and moved on to Hereford United. While with his next club Wolves, he had loan spells with Walsall and York City before ending his career with Mansfield Town.

McMILLAN John Shaw

Outside-right

Born: Renton, 14 April 1937.
Career: Dumbarton. Cardiff City 1958. Exeter City 1961.

■ Winger John McMillan played Scottish League football for Dumbarton prior to Cardiff City manager Trevor Morris bringing him to Ninian Park in February 1958. He spent three seasons in City's reserve side before making a couple of appearances towards the end of the 1960–61 season – both heavy defeats. In October 1961 he joined Exeter City, spending a couple of seasons with the Grecians before ending his involvement with the game.

McNALLY Owen

Centre-forward/inside-right

Born: Denny, 20 June 1906.
Died: 1973.
Career: Denny Hibernian. Celtic. Arthurlie (loan). Hamilton Academicals (loan). Bray Unknowns. Cardiff City 1931. Bray Unknowns. Norwich City 1932. Lausanne (Switzerland). Sligo Rovers. Distillery. Leicester City 1935. Racing Club de Paris (France). Shamrock Rovers.

■ A frustrated reserve to record scorer Jimmy McGrory at Celtic, he was loaned out to Arthurlie and in a Scottish Second Division match netted eight of his side's goals in a 10–0 defeat of Armadale. After that he started collecting clubs and countries in almost equal proportion! A loan spell with Hamilton Academicals followed before he crossed the water to play for Bray Unknowns. It was from here that he joined Cardiff City for the start of the 1931–32 season, but after appearing in five consecutive games he lost his place to Albert Keating. After returning for

another spell with Bray, he tried his luck in Switzerland with Lausanne, but after that didn't work out he played on both sides of the Irish border for Sligo Rovers and Distillery. While playing for Distillery, he made a scoring appearance for the victorious Irish League against the Football League at Blackpool's Bloomfield Road ground. There followed spells with Leicester City and Racing de Paris before he top-scored for League of Ireland Champions Shamrock Rovers in 1938–39.

McSEVENEY John Haddon

Outside-left

Born: Shotts, 8 February 1931.
Career: Hamilton Academicals. Sunderland 1951. Cardiff City 1955. Newport County 1957. Hull City 1961.

Welsh Cup winner 1955–56.

■ Johnny McSeveney began his career north of the border with Hamilton Academicals, but in 1951 he joined Sunderland. In four seasons at Roker Park he struggled to hold down a first-team spot, making just 35 appearances, and when the opportunity of a move came along he jumped at the chance. McSeveney joined Cardiff City in a triple deal that also brought Harry Kirtley and Howard Sheppeard to Ninian Park. He made a sensational home debut for the Bluebirds when he scored twice against his former club Sunderland in a 3–1 win. In 1956 he scored the winning goal in the Welsh Cup Final when City beat Swansea 3–2, while in 1956–57, operating at inside-right, he scored 13 goals in 34 League appearances. Following the club's relegation, though, he left to play for Newport County in a deal that brought Colin Hudson to Ninian Park. In four seasons at Somerton Park, McSeveney scored 51 goals in 172 League games before moving to Hull City, where he continued to score on a regular basis, netting 60 goals in 161 League outings. After retiring, he coached the Tigers before becoming manager of Barnsley. He later had a spell as Guyana's national coach and led them to their first win in 29 years before becoming assistant manager to Ian Porterfield at both Rotherham and Sheffield United.

McSTAY Raymond

Midfield

Born: Hamilton, 26 November 1961.
Career: Celtic. Hamilton Academicals. Hereford United (loan). East Stirling (loan). Cardiff City 1996.

■ Unable to make the grade with Celtic, the creative midfielder joined Hamilton Academicals. Finding himself in and out of the Accies side, he had brief loan spells with Hereford United and East Stirling before joining the Bluebirds on non-contract terms towards the end of 1996. Though he showed himself to be a tidy passer of the ball, he never really settled, playing just once in the 2–1 home defeat by Mansfield Town before returning north of the border.

MADDY Paul Michael

Midfield

Born: Cwmcarn, Monmouthshire, 17 August 1962.
Career: Cardiff City 1980. Hereford United (loan) 1983. Swansea City 1983. Hereford United 1984. Brentford 1986. Chester City 1987. Hereford United 1988.

■ After making his Bluebirds debut just a month after his 18th birthday, much

was expected of midfielder Paul Maddy. But he was frustratingly inconsistent, and after a loan spell with Hereford United he was transferred to rivals Swansea City in August 1983. Before the following season was over, Maddy had moved to Hereford on a permanent basis. He became a first-team regular at Edgar Street until, in the summer of 1986, Brentford paid £7,000 for his services. He later had a brief spell with Chester City before signing for Hereford for a third time and taking his tally of goals to 18 in 121 games for the Bulls.

MAHON Alan Joseph

Midfield

Born: Dublin, 4 April 1978.
Career: Tranmere Rovers 1995. Sporting Lisbon (Portugal). Blackburn Rovers 2000. Cardiff City (loan) 2003. Ipswich Town (loan) 2003. Wigan Athletic 2004.

■ An attacking midfielder who burst onto the Football League scene with Tranmere Rovers in 1995–96, the Irish Youth international also made his debut for the Republic of Ireland's Under-21 side during the course of that campaign. Over the next couple of seasons, he developed a probing and tricky style of play and rumours began to circulate about a big money move to the Premiership, but in the summer of 2000, after making his full international debut for the Republic against Greece, he chose to move to Sporting Lisbon. He found it difficult to break into the

side, though he did appear in a European Champions League game against Real Madrid. In December 2000 he joined Blackburn Rovers and helped them win promotion to the Premiership, but then, with the exception of UEFA Cup ties, he was never in the frame. In January 2003 he joined Cardiff City on loan. Though he provided the width that had been missing all season, he returned to Ewood Park shortly before the end of the season, thus missing out on the play-off excitement. In January 2004 Wigan paid £250,000 for Mahon's services, and he went on to play his part in their promotion to the top flight.

MAIDMENT Thomas (Tom)

Inside-right/right-half

Born: Monkwearmouth, 4 November 1905.
Died: 1971.
Career: St Columba. Robert Thompson's. Sunderland 1925. Lincoln City 1925. Portsmouth 1931. Workington. Cardiff City 1932. Blyth Spartans. South Shields.

■ Unable to make much headway with Sunderland, Tom Maidment joined Lincoln City. In five years with the Sincil Bank club, he developed into a more than useful player, netting 43 goals in 126 games and helping the imps finish

as runners-up in the Third Division North in 1927–28. He joined Portsmouth but failed to settle on the south coast, moving into non-League football with Workington.

MAIN Walter Gay (Bill)

Left-half

Born: St Monance, 30 November 1915. Died: 1969.
Career: St Monance Juniors. Raith Rovers. Cardiff City 1936. Colchester United.

■ Wing-half Bill Main had begun his career north of the border with Raith Rovers prior to joining Cardiff city in December 1936. Making his debut in a 1–0 Christmas Day defeat at Torquay United, Main made just a handful of League appearances before returning to the club's reserve side. Just before the start of the aborted 1939–40 season, he joined Colchester United.

MALLORY Richard James Leroy (Dick)

Outside-left

Born: Bermuda, 10 August 1942.
Career: Bermuda. Cardiff City 1963. Bermuda.

■ Bermudan winger Dick Mallory was one of a number of players given the chance to show their worth in Cardiff's League side at the start of the 1963–64 season, when eight of the club's first-team squad were struck down by injury. Mallory, whose main asset was his pace, was never on the losing side in any of his four League and Cup appearances but was only on the winning side once! He then spent the rest of the season in the reserves before returning to Bermuda, where he later became a steward at an exclusive yacht club.

MALLOY Daniel (Danny)

Centre-half

Born: Loanhead, 6 November 1930.
Career: Dundee. Cardiff City 1953. Doncaster Rovers 1961.

Welsh Cup winner 1955–56, 1958–59. Division Two runner-up 1959–60. Welsh Cup finalist 1959–60.

■ Following the departure of Stan Montgomery, Cardiff manager Trevor Morris signed Dundee centre-half Danny Malloy, who had already been capped by Scotland at 'B' international level for a fee of £17,500. He made his debut in a 3–1 home win over Charlton Athletic, a match in which Neil O'Halloran, also making his debut, netted a hat-trick. Malloy was ever present in 1956–57, a campaign in which he scored his only League goal from the penalty spot in a 3–1 defeat at

Manchester United. Malloy, who went on to appear in 69 consecutive League games from his debut, was also ever present in 1958–59 and 1960–61 and missed just one game in 1959–60. During that season, Malloy was captain and led the club back to the top flight as runners-up to Aston Villa. That campaign also saw the Scottish defender score two own goals in the opening match when City beat Liverpool 3–2. In the summer of 1961, Malloy, who had appeared in 242 League and Cup games, failed to agree terms for the coming season and left to become player-coach of Doncaster Rovers.

MANSELL John (Jack)

Full-back

Born: Salford, 22 August 1927.
Career: Manchester United. Brighton &

Hove Albion 1949. Cardiff City 1952. Portsmouth 1953.

■ Jack Mansell was an amateur with Manchester United after World War Two but turned professional on joining Brighton & Hove Albion in March 1949. In three seasons with the Seagulls he developed into an exciting left-back who could operate anywhere along the left flank. Having scored nine goals in 116 games for Brighton, he joined Cardiff in October 1952 – a surprise capture considering the full-backs already on the Ninian Park staff. He spent a year with City, appearing in 24 First Division games before leaving to play for Portsmouth. At Fratton Park he gained England 'B' and Football League honours and, in 1954–55, helped Pompey finish third in Division One. On leaving Portsmouth he went into coaching with Telstar and later Ajax of Holland before managing Rotherham United and Reading, where he gained a reputation for producing sides which tried to play with First Division style in the lower Divisions.

MARCHANT Marwood Godfrey

Inside-forward

Born: Milford Haven, 19 June 1922.
Career: Milford United. Cardiff City 1951. Torquay United 1951.

■ Recruited from Welsh League side Milford United in January 1951, 'Mars' Marchant was a regular scorer for Cardiff's reserve side and, when given his opportunity in the League side the following month, netted in a 3–0 defeat of Chesterfield. He also scored within four minutes of his home debut against Leicester City but failed to maintain his impressive start and in November 1951 trod the well-worn path to join Torquay United, where he scored 19 goals in 40 League games.

MARCROFT Edward Hollows (Ted)

Winger

Born: Rochdale, 13 April 1910.
Career: Bacup Borough. Great Harwood. Middlesborough 1931. Queen's Park Rangers 1932. Cardiff City 1933.

Accrington Stanley 1934. Bacup Borough. Rochdale 1936. Macclesfield.

■ A winger whose impressive form for Lancashire League clubs Bacup Borough and Great Harwood prompted Middlesbrough to give him a chance in the Football League. Later, he made his mark with Queen's Park Rangers. In the summer of 1933 he joined Cardiff City in exchange for George Emmerson – it was a deal in which the Loftus Road club got the better end as Marcroft was not retained by the Bluebirds at the end of the 1933–34 season. He returned to the North West to play for Accrington Stanley and later Rochdale, before he ended his career with Macclesfield.

MARDENBOROUGH Stephen Alexander (Steve)

Winger. Forward

Born: Birmingham, 11 September 1964.
Career: Coventry City 1982. Wolverhampton Wanderers 1983. Cambridge United (loan) 1984. Swansea City 1984. Newport County 1985. Cardiff City 1987. Hereford United 1988. IFK Ostersund. Cheltenham Town. Darlington 1990. Lincoln City 1993.

Scarborough 1995. Stafford Rangers. Colchester United 1995. Swansea City 1995.

Division Four runner-up 1987–88.

■ Much-travelled striker Steve Mardenborough was released by Coventry after serving his apprenticeship and joined Wolves, for whom he once scored at Anfield. While at Molineux he had a loan spell with Cambridge United before in July 1984 signing for Swansea City. Despite being a favourite of the Vetch faithful, he was released in a clear-out and joined Newport County. Just before transfer deadline day in March 1987 he jumped at the chance of joining Cardiff, but his only goal during his time with the club came shortly after his arrival in a 3–1 defeat of Torquay United. On leaving Ninian Park he played for Hereford United before trying his luck abroad with IFK Ostersund. He then played for Cheltenham Town before linking up with Darlington, whom he helped win the GM Vauxhall Conference the following season. He then had spells with Lincoln, Scarborough and Colchester United before being released on economic grounds from another spell with Swansea.

MARGETSON Martyn Walter

Goalkeeper

Born: Neath, 8 September 1971.
Career: Manchester City 1990. Bristol Rovers (loan) 1993. Southend United 1998. Huddersfield Town 1999. Cardiff City 2002.

■ Welsh international goalkeeper Martyn Margetson began his career with Manchester City and made his League debut in the local derby against Manchester United at Old Trafford in May 1991, a game United won 1–0. Tony Coton and Andy Dibble restricted his appearances at Maine Road, and he had a loan spell with Bristol Rovers before moving to Southend United. A regular during his only season at Roots Hall, he switched to Huddersfield Town in the summer of 1999 but found his appearances limited due to the fine form of Nico Vaesen. With the Belgian

'keeper moving to Birmingham, Margetson grabbed his opportunity with both hands and became the McAlpine Stadium club's first-choice 'keeper. However, in the summer of 2002 he moved to Cardiff City as back-up to Neil Alexander and filled that role superbly. When he was called upon, he gave some high-quality displays, and in 2003–04 he made great strides, replacing Alexander in the Bluebirds line-up. He kept his place in the side for the remainder of the campaign, though he finished up playing with a broken finger. His form led to him coming off the bench for Wales as a second-half substitute in the friendly international against Canada in May 2004.

MARRIOTT Paul William

Forward

Born: Liverpool, 26 September 1973.
Career: Cardiff City 1991.

■ Paul Marriott was on a YTS at Ninian Park when he made what transpired to be his only Football League appearance. At least he was involved in a memorable game as he came off the bench to replace goalscorer Carl Dale in a 5–0 trouncing of Wrexham in October 1991.

MARSHALL Ernest (Ernie)

Left-half/inside-right

Born: Dinnington, 23 May 1918.
Died: 1983.
Career: Dinnington Athletic.

Huddersfield Town 1934. Sheffield United 1936. Cardiff City 1939. Yeovil Town.

■ Ernie Marshall spent three seasons with Sheffield United before signing for the Bluebirds in the summer of 1939. Like a number of players, his career was blighted by World War Two. Having played in the opening three games of the aborted 1939–40 season, he joined the armed forces while the club held his registration. After the war he played in just one game, a 2–1 win over Notts County, before leaving to end his career playing non-League football for Yeovil Town.

MARSHALSEY William Henry Gray (Bill)

Right-half

Born: Fife, 18 April 1910.
Died: 1977.
Career: Denbeath Star. St Bernard's. Heart of Midlothian. St Bernard's (loan). Cardiff City 1933.

■ A Scot who played junior football with Fife club Dunbeath Star before joining St Bernard's, wing-half Bill Marshalsey's displays led to him signing for Hearts in 1930. However, he failed to settle at Tynecastle and was loaned back to St Bernard's while being transfer listed by Hearts. There were no takers even though the fee being asked was reduced from £600 to £300, and in 1933 he joined Cardiff City on a free transfer. Though he scored at Torquay United, he failed to get a regular place in the Cardiff side that finished bottom of the Third Division South and left Ninian Park.

MARTIN Michael Paul (Mick)

Midfield

Born: Dublin, 9 July 1951.
Career: Home Farm. Bohemians. Manchester United 1973. West Bromwich Albion 1975. Newcastle United 1978. Vancouver Whitecaps (Canada). Cardiff City 1984. Peterborough United 1985. Rotherham United 1985. Preston North End 1985.

■ Mick Martin is the son of Con Martin, the former Republic of Ireland international who won caps as a goalkeeper, defender and midfielder in the 1940s and 50s. Like his father, Mick Martin was a versatile player. Martin began in Ireland with Home Farm and Bohemians and was already a full international when Manchester United took him to Old Trafford in January 1973 for a fee of £20,000 – a record receipt for a League of Ireland club at the time. After a good first season, but following relegation to Division Two, he was sold to West Bromwich Albion. He walked straight into their team and didn't miss a match for the rest of that 1975–76 promotion-winning season. However, on their return to the top flight he found himself out in the cold and was sold to newly relegated Newcastle United for £100,000. He became captain at St James' Park and in six years with the Magpies made 147 League appearances. On parting company with the north-east club he played for Vancouver Whitecaps in the NASL before returning to Football League action with Cardiff City, after accepting Alan Durban's offer of a monthly contract. Even though the Bluebirds beat Carlisle United 2–1 on his debut, it was the only time he was on the winning side, and after only seven League appearances he moved on to have brief spells with Peterborough, Rotherham United and Preston North End before coaching Glasgow Celtic.

MARUSTIK Christopher (Chris)

Midfield

Born: Swansea, 10 August 1961.
Career: Swansea City 1978. Cardiff City 1985. Barry Town.

■ The son of a Czech immigrant, Chris Marustik caught the eye of Swansea City's Harry Griffiths while playing for the town's schoolboy side. Signed as an apprentice at the Vetch, he later turned professional and made his first-team debut as a substitute in the second round of the League Cup as the Swans drew 2–2 at home to Tottenham Hotspur in August 1978. However, his full League debut didn't come until seven months later when the Swans visited Peterborough United. Quick and very versatile, Marustik's talent was nurtured by John Toshack, John Mahoney and Les Chappell. Over the next six seasons at the Vetch Marustik scored 11 goals in 153 games before leaving to join Cardiff City in exchange for Roger Gibbins in October 1985. Marustik made his Bluebirds debut at Gillingham before scoring what proved to be his only goal for the club on his home debut as City beat Wigan Athletic 3–1. Capped seven times by Wales, he was not only on the winning side in each of his last three appearances, but he also helped to keep consecutive clean sheets. Sadly, injuries marred his progress at Ninian Park, and after two years he left to play non-League football for Barry Town. He later ran a bar with his brother.

MASON Frederick Oliver (Frank)

Full-back

Born: Solihull, 1 August 1901.
Career: Coventry City 1921. Cardiff City 1922. Rochdale 1924. Merthyr Town 1927. Dundalk.

■ Signed by Cardiff City from Coventry in the summer of 1921, Frank Mason spent three years as understudy to the great Jimmy Blair. His only game for the Bluebirds during that time was against Sheffield United in April 1923 when, due to calls on international players, he was one of six reserves drafted in for the First Division game. It was testimony to the wealth of talent at Ninian Park that City won 1–0. A year later Mason moved on to play for Rochdale in the Third Division North. He had appeared in 49 games for the Spotland club before ending his League career with Merthyr Town. He later crossed the Irish Sea and spent a season playing for Dundalk.

MATSON Francis Robert (Frank)

Outside-right/inside-right

Born: Reading, 21 November 1905.
Died: 1985.
Career: Cardiff Corinthians. Reading 1925. Cardiff City 1926. Newport County 1930. Southampton 1931.

Welsh Cup finalist 1928–29.

■ Frank Matson's impressive form with Cardiff Corries brought him to Ninian Park during the club's 'Golden Era'. Yet the speedy right-winger, who spent five years with City, found first-team opportunities hard to come by, and in 1930 he moved to Newport County. After scoring on his debut on the opening day of the 1930–31 season, he left to end his career on the south coast with Southampton.

MATTHEWS Neil Peter

Right-back/midfield

*Born: Manchester, 3 December 1967.
Career: Blackpool 1985. Cardiff City 1990. Rochdale 1993.*

**Division Two Champion 1992–93.
Welsh Cup winner 1992–93.**

■ Having played for Northern Ireland at Youth, Under-21 and 'B' international level, Neil Matthews, who had begun his career with Blackpool, playing 76 League games for the Seasiders, joined Cardiff in the summer of 1990. A versatile performer, he wore eight different numbered shirts in two seasons of Fourth Division football with the Bluebirds before leaving to play for Chinese side Songdal in May 1992. In December of that year he rejoined Cardiff and helped them win the Third Division Championship before moving on to Rochdale. Injuries hampered his time at Spotland though he did manage the honour of being Dale's first international representative of any kind for 75 years when turning out for Northern Ireland 'B'.

MATTHEWS Wayne John

Midfield

*Born: Cardiff, 11 September 1964.
Career: Cardiff City 1983. Ton Pentre.*

■ Local winger Wayne Matthews was on Cardiff City's staff for a number of years, always seeming to be on the fringe of the club's first team without making any significant impact. Most of his appearances were as a substitute, and at the end of the 1983–84 season he dropped into non-League football with Ton Pentre, being a member of their successful 1986–87 side.

MAXWELL Layton Jonathan

Midfield

*Born: Rhyl, 3 October 1979.
Career: Liverpool 1997. Stockport County (Loan) 2000. Cardiff City 2001. Swansea City 2004.*

**FAW Premier Cup winner 2001–02.
Division Two promotion 2002–03.**

■ A product of the Liverpool Academy, Layton Maxwell is an orthodox winger, capable of beating players and getting crosses into the box. A Welsh Youth international, he scored on his first-team debut for Liverpool in a 4–2 Worthington Cup win over Hull City. His displays in the Anfield club's reserve side earned him selection for the Wales Under-21 side, but he then joined Stockport County on a 12-month loan deal. He made an immediate impact with a goal on his debut at Gillingham but then faded from the picture. In the summer of 2001 he joined Cardiff City, but initially he found it difficult to win a place in the starting line-up. Developing into a busy, bustling midfield player, he was still unable to break the midfield dominance of Graham Kavanagh and Willie Boland, and though he was told he could find another club he opted to stay and fight for a place. But midway through the 2003–04 campaign he joined Swansea City in a short-term deal, but after damaging his ankle on his first day at the Vetch he suffered other injuries and was released by the Swans in the summer.

MAY Harry

Full-back

*Born: Glasgow, 15 October 1928.
Career: Thorniewood United. Cardiff City 1948. Swindon Town 1950. Barnsley 1952. Southend United 1955.*

■ Hard tackling full-back Harry May arrived at Ninian Park from Scottish junior club Thorniewood United in the summer of 1948, but his only appearance for City came as a stop-gap replacement in the forward line at Leicester City, a match the Bluebirds lost 1–0. Unable to force his way into the reckoning, he moved to Swindon Town and it was at the County Ground, where he made 78 appearances, that he established himself as a League player. In May 1952 he was transferred to Barnsley and was an ever present in 1954–55 when the Oakwell club won the Third Division North Championship. May had appeared in 106 League games for the Colliers when a disagreement over wages led to him leaving to end his playing career with Southend United.

MAYO Alfred C.

Centre-forward

*Born: Cardiff.
Career: Cardiff City 1930.*

■ Little is known about this Bluebirds forward, although he is believed to be a local amateur. With City already relegated to the Third Division South, he made his only appearance in the Football League in the final game of the 1930–31 season, a match Cardiff lost 3–1 at home to Bury.

MEACOCK Kevin Michael

Forward

*Born: Bristol, 16 September 1963.
Career: Gisborne City (New Zealand). Devizes Town. Cardiff City 1984. Gisborne City.*

■ Kevin Meacock joined Cardiff City, together with Paul McLoughlin, in 1984 on a trial basis after playing in New Zealand with Gisborne City and later Western League club Devizes Town. Pitched straight into the Bluebirds relegation fight, Meacock showed plenty of enthusiasm, but his lack of experience reduced his confidence as the team plummeted into Division Three. Released in the close season, he returned to New Zealand and rejoined Gisborne City.

MELANIPHY Eugene Michael Joseph Patrick (Ted)

Forward

Born: Westport, 5 February 1913.
Career: Redhill. Finchley Town. Plymouth Argyle 1931. Cardiff City 1936. Worcester City. Northampton Town 1939.

■ An Irish law student who played non-League football for Redhill and Finchley Town before joining Plymouth Argyle in 1931, Ted Melaniphy stayed at Home Park for five years. Although never a regular during his time with the Pilgrims, his return of 33 goals in 68 League games prompted Cardiff boss Ben Watts-Jones to bring him to Ninian Park in June 1936. He looked a good signing, but he failed to hold down a first-team place and joined non-League Worcester City prior to ending his League career at Northampton Town.

MELLOR John

Full-back

Born: Oldham
Career: Witton Albion. Manchester United 1930. Cardiff City 1936.

■ John Mellor switched codes from Oldham Rugby Union to play non-League football for Witton Albion before being signed by Manchester United in September 1930. At the time, United faced a full-back crisis in the middle of a run of 12 consecutive defeats – the worst ever start to a season by a League club. They were relegated but Mellor was to remain a mainstay of their defence for the next six seasons, helping them win promotion back to the top flight in 1935–36. The last of his 122 appearances for the Red Devils was in a 6–2 defeat at Grimsby Town, but that was nothing compared to his next match. He made his Bluebirds debut in the 8–1 massacre at Luton Town. Mellor stayed at Ninian Park for two seasons before injury forced his retirement.

MELVILLE James

Left-back

Born: Dykehead.
Career: Partick Thistle. Clyde. Cardiff City 1921. East Stirling. Beith.

■ Scottish-born defender James Melville had played his early football north of the border for Partick Thistle and Clyde before joining Cardiff City for their first season in Division One. He didn't have the best of debuts as City lost 4–1 at Spurs, and then, after failing to force his way into the side, he returned to Scotland to play first for East Stirling and later Beith.

MENZIES Adam Ross

Half-back

Born: Rutherglen, 31 October 1934.
Career: Glasgow Rangers. Cardiff City 1957.

■ A Scottish Schoolboy international, half-back Ross Menzies was on the books of Glasgow Rangers, but on being unable to make much impact with the Ibrox club he joined Cardiff City. Much of his time at Ninian Park was spent in the club's Football Combination and Welsh League sides, and his only appearance for the City first team came in the Second Division in February 1958 when the Bluebirds lost 3–1 at Charlton Athletic. He remained with City until the end of the following season before returning north of the border.

MERRY William (Bill)

Inside-right

Born: Fishguard, 14 December 1910.
Career: Fishguard Sports. Cardiff City 1930. Drumcondra. Manchester United 1934. Halifax Town 1935. St James' Gate.

■ Signed from his local side Fishguard Sports in 1930, inside-forward Bill Merry played in eight games towards the end of the 1930–31 season – only one of which was won – as City crashed out of Division Two. He had a spell with Drumcondra before joining Manchester United but, after failing to break into their League side, moved on to end his first-team career with Halifax Town.

MICALLEF Constantinous (Tarki)

Midfield

Born: Cardiff, 24 January 1961.
Career: Cardiff City 1978. Newport County 1983. Gillingham 1984. Cardiff City 1984. Bristol Rovers 1986. Barry Town.

Welsh Cup finalist 1981–82. Division Three runner-up 1982–83.

■ A Welsh Schoolboy international, Tarki Micallef joined Cardiff City as an apprentice and worked his way through the ranks before making his first-team debut at Sheffield United in December 1978. That was his only appearance in the Bluebirds first team that season, and though he showed exciting touches it was not until the 1981–82 season that he established himself as a regular in the City side. In September 1983 Micallef was part of the five-man transfer swap with Newport County, but within 12 months he had moved on to Gillingham. His stay at the Priestfield Stadium was short, and he rejoined Cardiff, but made only a handful of appearances as the Bluebirds were relegated to the Third Division. At the end of the 1985–86 season he joined Bristol Rovers before later turning to non-League football with Barry Town.

MICHAEL James David

Winger

Born: Pontypridd, 28 October 1978.
Career: Cardiff City 1996. Newport AFC.

■ Still a trainee, Welsh Youth international James Michael was given a run out with the Cardiff first team against Mansfield Town at Ninian Park in December 1996, when he came off the bench after 75 minutes to directly replace an off-key Jimmy Gardner on the left flank. A good crosser of the ball, he showed himself to be both skilful and quick. Able to play on either flank, there were hopes that he would have got further opportunities in the Bluebirds first team, but it wasn't to be and he moved on to Newport.

MIDDLETON Craig Dean

Midfield

Born: Nuneaton, 10 September 1970.
Career: Coventry City 1989. Cambridge United 1993. Cardiff City 1996. Plymouth Argyle (loan) 2000. Halifax Town 2000. Bedworth United.

FAW Invitation Cup finalist 1997–98. Division Three promotion 1998–99.

■ Both Craig and his twin brother Lee began their career with Coventry City – Craig left Highfield Road to join Cambridge United in the summer of 1993. After a good first season, he missed the entire 1994–95 campaign through injury, prior to returning to action in 1995–96. Unfortunately, his time at Cambridge ended prematurely with a shoulder injury, and, on being released, he joined the Bluebirds. Remaining a regular in the City side, he quickly got on the score sheet, scoring four goals in eight outings before drying up. In 1997–98 he played in a variety of positions, and though his aggression occasionally got him into trouble with referees he was named Most Improved Player by Cardiff City Supporters' Club. Strong running and athletic, he continued to be an important member of the City side until 1999–2000 when he was in and out of the team. After a loan spell with Plymouth, he joined Halifax Town with many Cardiff fans being disappointed to see him leave. Almost single-handedly, he kept the Shaymen in the Football League before leaving to play for Bedworth United.

MILES Albert Edwin

Centre-forward

Born: Treorchy, 1903.
Career: Bridgend Town. Mid-Rhondda United. Luton Town 1925. Derby County 1926. Cardiff City 1927. Crystal Palace 1930. Yeovil and Petters United.

Welsh Cup winner 1929–30.

■ Having played his early football for Bridgend Town and Mid-Rhondda United, Welsh amateur international Albert Miles had trials with Luton Town and Derby County prior to arriving at Ninian Park in 1927. A prolific scorer for the reserves, his highlight at Football League level came in November 1929 when, in one of his rare first-team outings, he netted a hat-trick in a 5–0 win over Oldham Athletic. Later, he moved to Crystal Palace but couldn't force his way into their side and joined non-League Yeovil.

MILES Idris

Outside-right

Born: Neath, 2 August 1908.
Died: 1983.
Career: Cardiff City 1930. Yeovil and Petters United. Leicester City 1932. Clapton Orient 1934. Exeter City 1937. Worcester City.

■ Winger Idris Miles had been spotted playing for Radnor Road FC when Cardiff signed him in October 1930. He made his debut at the end of that month in a 1–1 home draw against Nottingham Forest, but had only appeared in three League games when he left to play non-League football for Yeovil. A year later he returned to League football with Leicester City, and though he scored on his Foxes debut at Everton he suffered appalling fortune in twice breaking his collarbone during the course of his first season at Filbert Street. In May 1934 he signed for Clapton Orient and was a regular with the London club for the next three seasons. He then had spells with Exeter City and Worcester as they switched from the Birmingham League to the Southern League.

MILLAR William Paul

Midfield/forward

Born: Belfast, 16 November 1966.
Career: Glentoran. Portadown. Port Vale 1988. Hereford United (loan) 1990. Cardiff City 1991. Linfield.

Welsh Cup winner 1991–92. Division Three Champion 1992–93. Welsh Cup finalist 1993–94.

■ A striker who was chosen as the Irish Young Footballer of the Year in 1986, he became a Northern Ireland Youth and Under-21 international and played for Glentoran and Portadown before signing for Port Vale for £20,000 in December 1988. He seriously damaged his knee ligaments in training and didn't make his League debut until October 1989. Unable to win a regular place, he was loaned to Hereford United before Cardiff manager Eddie May paid £60,000 for him in August 1991. After finding himself in and out of the City side in his first season at Ninian Park, Millar played an important part in the Bluebirds winning the Third Division title, while, in 1993–94, he netted a hat-trick for City (including two penalties) in a 5–3 win at Brighton. However, following the club's relegation the following season, Millar returned to Irish football with Linfield.

MILLS Donald (Don)

Inside-forward

Born: Maltby, 17 August 1926.
Died: 1994.
Career: Queen's Park Rangers 1946. Torquay United 1949. Queen's Park Rangers 1950. Cardiff City 1951. Leeds United 1951. Torquay United 1952.

■ Inside-forward Don Mills began his career with Queen's Park Rangers immediately after World War Two but, on being unable to win a regular spot, was loaned out to Torquay United. So popular was he at Plainmoor that the fans tried to buy him! He returned to Loftus Road prior to Cardiff acquiring his services in exchange for Charlie 'Midge' Hill in February 1951. Though the Bluebirds had splashed out £12,500 on his signature, he appeared in just one game for the Ninian Park club, a 1–1 home draw with Barnsley. Later that year he joined Leeds United before leaving for a second spell with Torquay. Regarded as the Devon club's greatest-ever player, he spent a decade at Plainmoor, scoring 81 goals in 342 games, before later becoming Torquay's coach and chief scout.

MILNE Alexander Soutar (Alec)

Full-back

Born: Dundee, 4 June 1937.
Career: Arbroath. Cardiff City 1957. Barry Town.

Welsh Cup winner 1958–59.
Division Two runner-up 1959–60.

■ Full-back Alec Milne joined Cardiff from Arbroath in the summer of 1957. By the end of the 1957–58 season he had established himself as a first-team regular and the following season, when City finished ninth in Division Two, he was ever present. In 1959–60 Milne turned in a number of resolute performances as the club won promotion to the First Division. He was ever present again in 1961–62, the club's last season in the top flight, scoring the only League goal of his career in a 3–2 home defeat by Wolves. After that he began to suffer from injuries and played the last of his 188 League and Cup games against Plymouth Argyle in

August 1964. He later emigrated to New Zealand, and when the Bluebirds toured the sub-continent in the summer of 1968 the Dundee-born defender played against his former club!

MILSOM Paul Jason

Forward

Born: Bristol, 5 October 1974.
Career: Bristol City 1993. Cardiff City 1995. Oxford United. Gloucester City.

■ Striker Paul Milsom began his career with his home-town club Bristol City, playing his first game for the Ashton Gate side in 1993–94. Unable to build on his early displays, he was given a free transfer, and in March 1995 he joined Cardiff City. After a couple of appearances as a substitute, he made his first start against Bristol Rovers, and though he came close to scoring on a couple of occasions City lost 1–0. Surprisingly released during the close season, he signed for Oxford United, but after just one appearance from the bench in an Autowindscreens Shield game he left to play non-League football for Gloucester City.

MITCHELL Graham Lee

Central-defender

Born: Shipley, 16 February 1968.
Career: Huddersfield Town 1986. Bournemouth (loan) 1993. Bradford City 1994. Raith Rovers 1996. Cardiff City 1998. Halifax Town 1999. Bradford Park Avenue.

Division Three promotion 1998–99.

■ Graham Mitchell began his career with Huddersfield Town where his performances in defence, midfield or in a striking role made him a firm favourite with the Yorkshire club supporters. In eight seasons with the then Leeds Road outfit Mitchell made 310 appearances before being signed by Bradford City as part of a deal that took Lee Sinnott to Huddersfield. A versatile player, he helped the Bantams win promotion to the First Division via the play-offs, but midway through the 1996–97 season he left Valley Parade to join Scottish Premier League side Raith Rovers. After one season at Stark's Park Mitchell signed for the Bluebirds and,

after a rusty start, became the club's most consistent player in 1998–99. Always composed and cool in possession, he made many crucial interceptions at the heart of the City defence, yet he was allowed to leave Ninian Park in the close season! He returned to his native Yorkshire to captain Halifax Town, whom he helped narrowly avoid relegation to the Conference. During his time at the Shay he helped out with coaching duties but later left to play for Bradford Park Avenue.

MITCHELL James William (Jimmy)

Outside-right/inside-right

Born: Barry, 1 September 1918.
Career: Cardiff City 1937. Barry Town.

■ Despite some impressive displays for Cardiff's reserve side, winger Jimmy Mitchell couldn't dislodge Reggie Pugh and, in the seasons leading up to World War Two, made just three League appearances. He joined the armed services during the hostilities, serving in Germany, and though he re-signed for the club in 1946 he made no further appearances and joined Barry Town.

MOKONE Stephen Madi (Steve)

Outside-right

Born: Pretoria, South Africa, 23 March 1932.
Career: Pretoria (South Africa). Coventry City 1956. PSV Eindhoven (Holland). Cardiff City 1959. Barnsley.

■ Steve Mokone began his playing career in his native South Africa, whom he represented at international level before coming to England to play for Coventry City. He failed to settle at Highfield Road and went to play in the Dutch League for PSV Eindhoven. After two seasons he joined Cardiff City and, after playing well in the public trial, made a sensational debut in the opening game of the season against Liverpool, scoring after just five minutes in a 3–2 win. Though the Bluebirds went on to win promotion that season, his physique did not help him, and he was soon in the club's reserve side. Later that season he was one of three players to be sent off in a Welsh Cup tie at Swansea when the Bluebirds fielded their Football Combination side and won 2–1! On leaving Ninian Park, Mokone joined Barnsley but, on being unable to break into the League side, returned to South Africa.

MOLLOY Peter (Paddy)

Wing-half

Born: Haslingden, 20 April 1909.
Died: 1993.
Career: Accrington Stanley 1930. Fulham 1931. Bristol Rovers 1933. Cardiff City 1933. Queen's Park Rangers 1935. Stockport County 1936. Carlisle United 1937. Bradford City 1938. Belfast Distillery. Accrington Stanley 1945. Kettering Town. Notts County 1947.

■ One of football's mercenaries during the decade leading up to World War Two, he made appearances for no fewer than seven clubs! After starting out with Accrington Stanley, where he failed to make a first-team appearance, he had brief spells with Fulham and Bristol Rovers before signing for Cardiff in February 1934. Unable to prevent the Bluebirds finishing bottom of the Third Division South, he had done enough to prevent him being one of the players released in the close season and stayed on for 1934–35. On leaving City, he had spells with Queen's Park Rangers, Stockport County, Carlisle United and Bradford City before war broke out. During the hostilities he played for Distillery and represented the Irish League before ending his career after the war with Notts County.

MONTGOMERY Stanley William (Stan)

Centre-half

Born: Silvertown, 7 July 1920.
Died: 6 October 2000.
Career: Romford. Hull City 1944. Southend United 1946. Cardiff City 1948. Worcester City. Newport County 1955. Ton Pentre.

Division Two runner-up 1951–52.

■ The son-in-law of Jimmy Nelson, he began his career with non-League

Romford before joining Hull City during World War Two. After 'guesting' for Southend United during the 1945–46 season, he returned to Boothferry Park for the first peacetime Football League campaign in 1946–47. After just a handful of games he moved to Southend on a permanent basis. After spending two seasons at Roots Hall, Montgomery, on the recommendation of Jimmy Nelson, joined Cardiff City for a fee of £6,000. The giant centre-half scored on his debut in a 2–2 draw at Grimsby Town in January 1949 and then played in the remaining 17 games – being on the losing side only twice as City finished fourth in Division Two. Over the next six seasons Montgomery missed very few matches and was a tower of strength in the club's promotion-winning season of 1951–52, when his only goal of the campaign secured a point in a 1–1 draw at Notts County. He had played in 243 League and Cup games for the Bluebirds when, in the summer of 1955, he joined non-League Worcester City. After just nine appearances he was back in League football with Newport County before a spell with Ton Pentre. He later returned to Ninian Park as the club's trainer before becoming Bristol Rovers' South Wales scout, a position he held for a good number of years. He then became

involved with the Bluebirds again when Alan Durban asked him to take charge of the club's trialists.

MOORE Graham

Midfield

Born: Hengoed, 7 March 1941.
Career: Cardiff City 1958. Chelsea 1961. Manchester United 1963. Northampton Town 1965. Charlton Athletic 1967. Doncaster Rovers 1971.

Welsh Cup winner 1958–59. Division Two runner-up 1959–60. Welsh Cup finalist 1959–60.

■ Graham Moore won the first of his 21 Welsh caps against England at Ninian Park in October 1959, when he scored with a last-minute header to earn his side a 1–1 draw. Having joined the Bluebirds in 1957, he spent a season in the reserves before making his first-team debut at Brighton & Hove Albion in September 1958 and scoring a last-minute equaliser to make the score 2–2. In 1959–60 Moore scored in the opening three games of the season and went on to find the net 13 times in 41 League outings as the club won

promotion to the First Division. The following season he had the misfortune to break a leg but recovered to score four of City's goals in their 16–0 Welsh Cup win over Knighton. In December 1961 Chelsea manager Tommy Docherty paid £35,000 to take Moore, the 'Golden Boy' of Welsh football, to Stamford Bridge. He had scored 32 goals in 101 first-team outings for Cardiff, but in his first few weeks with Chelsea he struggled to find his form as the club were relegated. He led them back to the top flight in 1962–63, but in November 1963 he was transferred to Manchester United, also for £35,000. Unable to make an impression at Old Trafford, he moved on to Northampton Town before playing for Charlton Athletic and Doncaster Rovers.

MOORE John Frederick Beriah

Outside-left

Born: Cardiff, 25 December 1919.
Career: Bangor City. Cardiff City 1941. Bangor City. Newport County 1950. Caernarfon Town.

■ An amateur with Bangor City, Beriah Moore became a part-time professional with the Bluebirds during the 1940–41 season and was a prolific scorer during wartime competitions. During that period he scored 111 goals in 182 games, but perhaps his most notable moment came in November 1945. He was brought in for the match against Moscow Dynamos because Billy Rees was injured and had the distinction of scoring City's consolation goal in a 10–1 defeat! Moore returned to North Wales at the end of the hostilities to have another season with Bangor City before returning to Ninian Park in 1947. He made a two-goal League debut for the Bluebirds in a 5–1 defeat of Southampton and had scored four goals in six games when, rather surprisingly, he rejoined Bangor. Moore later joined his former Cardiff captain Fred Stansfield at Newport County and, in 121 League games, scored 45 goals. He then returned to non-League football with Caernarfon Town where, in 1956–57, he helped the club to one of its most successful post-war seasons.

MOORE Patrick (Paddy)

Centre-half

Born: Ballybough, 1909.
Died: 1951.
Career: Richmond Rovers. Shamrock Rovers. Cardiff City 1929. Merthyr Town 1929. Tranmere Rovers 1930. Shamrock Rovers. Aberdeen. Shamrock Rovers. Shelbourne. Brideville. Shamrock Rovers.

■ Having played his early football for Richmond Rovers, Republic of Ireland international Paddy Moore was turning out for Shamrock Rovers prior to joining Cardiff in the summer of 1929. The strong-tackling defender replaced Harry Wake in the opening game of the 1929–30 season, a 4–1 defeat at Charlton Athletic, but never made the first team again. He then had brief spells with Merthyr Town and Tranmere Rovers before signing for Aberdeen, where he played in the forward line and became a prolific scorer! He eventually returned to Ireland and had spells with a number of clubs, including a fourth with Shamrock Rovers, before hanging up his boots.

MOORE Ronald David (Ronnie)

Forward/central-defender

Born: Liverpool, 29 January 1953.
Career: Tranmere Rovers 1971. Cardiff City 1979. Rotherham United 1980. Charlton Athletic 1983. Rochdale 1985. Tranmere Rovers 1986.

■ In his early days at Tranmere Rovers, Ronnie Moore was played at both centre-half and centre-forward until he eventually settled in an attacking role to become one of the lower Divisions leading scorers. In the Wirral club's promotion-winning season of 1975–76, Moore scored 37 goals in 50 games, including three matches (two in succession) when he scored four goals! He topped the club's scoring charts again in 1977–78 with 17 goals and in 1978–79 was joint top scorer, netting another hat-trick against Chester. It took £100,000 for Richie Morgan to prise him away from Prenton Park, but once he arrived at Cardiff the goals dried up. Moore was hugely popular with Bluebirds fans for his honest endeavour, but he seemed fated never to get the goals his workrate deserved. He was sold to Rotherham for a similar fee in 1980, and he scored profusely as the Millers won promotion from the Third Division in 1980–81. He later played for Charlton Athletic, but when the London club hit their cash crisis in 1984 he moved to Rochdale and later Tranmere to take his career full circle. Having scored 86 goals in 372 games in his two spells, he later became the club's coach before becoming manager of another of his former clubs, Rotherham United. He has recently taken over as manager of Tranmere Rovers.

MOORE William Albert (Billy)

Left-half

Born: Llanbradach, 14 October 1912.
Career: Cardiff City 1934. Southampton 1935. Wolverhampton Wanderers 1936.

■ In the mid-1930s Cardiff City often recruited local amateurs to supplement their professional staff. Wing-half Billy Moore was one of these, and in 1934–35 he not only appeared in 11 League games but became a Welsh amateur international. After a season of reserve-team football, he joined Southampton and later Wolverhampton Wanderers but failed to register a first-team appearance with either club.

MORGAN Jonathan Peter (Jon)

Midfield

Born: Cardiff, 10 July 1970.
Career: Cardiff City 1988. Merthyr Tydfil.

■ A Welsh Youth international midfielder, Jon Morgan was a YTS with the Bluebirds before making his debut in a 2–1 home defeat at the hands of Reading in October 1988. Unable to win a regular place, it was the following season, as City were relegated, that Morgan established himself in the side. A versatile player, he appeared in six different numbered shirts for Cardiff during his three seasons in the side before leaving to play non-League football for Merthyr Tydfil.

MORGAN Peter William

Defender

Born: Cardiff, 28 October 1951.
Career: Cardiff City 1969. Hereford United 1974. Newport County 1976.

■ The younger brother of Richie Morgan did not make much of an impression at Ninian Park and found Albert Larmour barring his way. The Morgan brothers did play together four times during the 1972–73 season, when the club just avoided relegation from Division Two. At the end of the following season Peter Morgan joined Hereford United, later playing for Newport County before joining the local non-League scene.

MORGAN Richard Leslie (Richie)

Central-defender

Born: Cardiff, 3 October 1946.
Career: Cardiff Corries. Cardiff City 1966.

Welsh Cup finalist 1971–72.

■ A Welsh Schoolboy international, Richie Morgan's long association with the Bluebirds began when he joined them in 1966 from Welsh League Cardiff Corries. Though much of his playing career at Ninian Park was spent in the shadow of Don Murray, whenever pressed into service, whether it be League, Cup or European action, he proved a most capable deputy. When his playing career was over, he continued at Ninian Park on the club's administrative staff, until in 1978 he was appointed manager following the dismissal of Jimmy Andrews. Richie Morgan left Cardiff City under a cloud but later established himself as an outstanding manager with Welsh League Barry Town.

MORRIS Edwin (Ted)

Goalkeeper

Born: Pontypool, 6 May 1921.
Career: Bewdley. Cardiff City 1948. Barry Town.

■ Goalkeeper Ted Morris was signed from Bewdley in the Kidderminster League. He became understudy to the

club's regular 'keeper Phil Joslin, and his eight appearances in City's League side were spread over three seasons. When he came into the side he never let anyone down, only being on the losing side on his last appearance, a 1–0 defeat at Swansea. He left the Bluebirds in 1951 to play non-League football for Barry Town.

MORRIS Eric Lewis

Right-back

Born: Cardiff.
Career: Cardiff City 1931.

■ Full-back Eric Morris was a local League player who joined Cardiff City in 1931. His first three games for the club were extraordinary. After making his debut in a 5–0 defeat of Northampton Town in January 1932, he was on the losing side at Reading as City lost 5–1 but then played in the 9–2 hammering of Thames Association! His next two games also produced high-scoring results and, all told, in those five matches a total of 34 goals were scored! At the end of the following season Morris retired to become a Local Government Officer.

MORT Enoch F.

Centre-half

Born: Ogmore Vale, 1912.
Career: Gilfach Goch. Cardiff City 1933. Carlisle United 1938.

■ Signed from local side Gilfach Goch, Enoch Mort played in the final 13

games of the 1933–34 re-election season. He avoided the mass, close season clear-out but then found his way into the first team blocked by new signing Bill Bassett. The tough-tackling centre-half had to content himself with understudy, which eventually yielded him a 20-match consecutive run in 1935–36. In the summer of 1938 Mort joined Carlisle United but struggled to make much impact in a side that hovered around the foot of the Third Division North.

MOSELEY Graham

Goalkeeper

Born: Manchester, 16 November 1953.
Career: Blackburn Rovers 1970. Derby County 1971. Aston Villa (loan) 1974. Walsall (loan) 1977. Brighton & Hove Albion 1977. Cardiff City 1986.

Division Four runner-up 1987–88.

■ Goalkeeper Graham Moseley began his career as an apprentice with Blackburn Rovers in 1971, but he didn't make the first team there and was signed by Derby County a year later. He earned an England Youth cap when at the Baseball ground but spent much of his time as understudy to Colin Boulton. While with Derby he had loan spells at Aston Villa and Walsall. In 1977 Moseley joined Brighton, and when the Seagulls won promotion to the First Division in 1978–79 he shared the goalkeeping duties with Eric Steele. Moseley became the south-coast club's first-choice 'keeper the following season, but, after appearing for Brighton in the 1983 FA Cup Final matches against Manchester United, he began to be hampered by injury. Having played in 224 games for Brighton, he moved to play for Cardiff City in what was their first season in the Fourth Division. In 1987–88 he played in the club's opening 13 games before injury forced his retirement – a season in which City won promotion as runners-up to Wolves.

MOSS Frank

Wing-half
Born: Aston, 17 April 1895.
Died: 1965.
Career: Aston Manor. Walsall. Aston Villa

1914. Cardiff City 1928. Bromsgrove Rovers. Worcester City.

■ Joining Aston Villa in 1914, Frank Moss appeared in just two League games before World War One interrupted his career. During the war he served with the 4th Lincolnshire Regiment but was severely wounded in his left knee and sent home. After becoming a PE instructor, his wound healed and, when football resumed in 1919, he was back at Villa Park. At the end of his first full season he replaced the injured Jimmy Harrop in the FA Cup Final win over Huddersfield Town, blotting out the Terriers twin-strike force of Mann and Taylor. He won five full caps for England, the first being against Scotland at Villa Park in April 1922. He continued to play for Villa until 1929 when, after appearing in 283 first-team games, he joined Cardiff City. The Bluebirds had just suffered their worst defeat in an FA Cup tie – 6–1 at Aston Villa – and they paid £2,500 for Frank Moss. Though the England wing-half was past his best, his class still shone through, but when City were relegated from the First Division he moved on to become player-manager of Bromsgrove Rovers.

MOUNTAIN Patrick Douglas

Goalkeeper

Born: Pontypridd, 1 August 1976.
Career: Barry Town. Cardiff City 1996. Barry Town.

■ Having starred for Barry Town in their historic UEFA Cup win over Budapest of Hungary, Patrick Mountain joined the Bluebirds on non-contract terms, prior to the start of the 1996–97 season, to provide goalkeeping cover in the event of an emergency. Following an injury to Tony Elliott, Mountain was called into the side for the match against Mansfield Town, a game the visitors won 2–1, but kept his place for the next five League and Cup games. Producing some good displays, he was twice capped for the Welsh Under-21 side when appearing against Holland and Turkey, yet was still released in the close season and returned to Barry.

MUGGLETON Carl David

Goalkeeper

Born: Leicester, 13 September 1968.
Career: Leicester City 1986. Chesterfield (loan) 1987. Blackpool (loan) 1988. Hartlepool United (loan) 1988. Stockport County (loan) 1990. Stoke City (loan) 1993. Glasgow Celtic. Stoke City 1994. Rotherham United (loan) 1995. Sheffield United (loan) 1996. Mansfield Town (loan) 1999. Chesterfield (loan) 1999. Cardiff City (loan) 2001. Cheltenham Town 2001. Bradford City (loan) 2001. Chesterfield 2002.

■ Unable, initially, to break into the Leicester City side due to the fine form of Ian Andrews and Paul Cooper, he had loan spells with Chesterfield, Blackpool, Hartlepool, Stockport and Stoke before winning a place in the Fixes side. Having represented England at Under-21 level, he became the first Leicester City goalkeeper to be sent off after conceding a penalty against Charlton in March 1991. In the First Division play-off final against Blackburn Muggleton saved Mike Newell's second penalty. In January 1994 Celtic paid £150,000 for his signature, but a change of management at Parkhead saw the 'keeper return to the Football League with Stoke. Axed after a shake-up following the club's poor start to the 1995–96 season, he went on loan to Rotherham and Sheffield United before returning to the Potteries club to fight for his place. There followed more loan spells with Mansfield and Chesterfield prior to him joining Cardiff, also on loan. He appeared in six games towards the end of the club's 2000–01 promotion-winning season, keeping a clean sheet in a 1–0 defeat of Barnet on his debut before returning to the Britannia Stadium. He later played for Cheltenham Town and Bradford City before joining Chesterfield for a third time.

MULLEN James (Jimmy)

Central-defender

Born: Jarrow, 8 November 1952.
Career: Sheffield Wednesday 1970. Rotherham United 1980. Preston North End (loan) 1981. Cardiff City 1982. Newport County 1986.

Welsh Cup finalist 1981–82. Division Three runner-up 1982–83.

■ Jimmy Mullen began his career with Sheffield Wednesday and stayed with the Owls for 10 years, during which time they suffered a couple of relegations. Mullen, though, captained them to promotion from the Third Division in 1979–80. Having appeared in over 250 first-team games, he joined Rotherham United and in 1980–81 captained the Millers to the Third Division Championship. In March 1982 he joined Cardiff on loan, later making the move a permanent one. Though he turned in some impressive performances in his 12 outings at the end of that season, he failed to prevent the Bluebirds being relegated. In 1982–83 he completed a unique treble by captaining his third club to promotion from the Third Division. After a spell as joint-manager with Jimmy Goodfellow, Mullen became Alan Durban's assistant before being appointed manager on a temporary basis in May 1986. However, after failing to secure the job permanently he joined Newport County as player-manager. Five months later he joined Aberdeen as assistant manager to Ian Porterfield before being appointed manager of Blackpool, but his only season at

Bloomfield Road ended in relegation. In August 1990 he was made manager of Burnley. In 1991–92 he led the Clarets to the Fourth Division Championship and, two years later, to promotion from the new Second Division, but after the club lost their First Division status he left Turf Moor.

MULRYNE Phillip Patrick

Midfield

Born: Belfast, 1 January 1978.
Career: Manchester United 1995.
Norwich City 1999. Cardiff City 2005.

■ A member of Manchester United's FA Youth Cup-winning side of 1994–95, he made a promising start to his senior career at Old Trafford with an excellent performance against Norwich in the Coca-Cola Cup in October 1997. Already a full international, having scored on his Northern Ireland debut against Belgium, Phil Mulryne looked to have a bright future ahead of him. Yet, after just a handful of appearances for United he was allowed to join Norwich City for £500,000 in March 1999. Sadly at the start of the 1999–2000 season he had the misfortune to suffer a double compound fracture of the right leg, which resulted in over seven months on the sidelines. It was 2001–02 before he completed his first season of regular first-team football and became an integral member of Nigel Worthington's side. Steering clear of injuries, he became one of the game's best playmakers outside of the Premiership. Having then helped the Canaries into the top flight, he remained a vital cog for both club and country, but after Norwich lost their top-flight status he was allowed to join Cardiff. His first season with the Bluebirds was a most frustrating one as he made just one start and three appearances from the bench. Desperate for first-team football, it seems inevitable that he will be leaving Ninian Park in the close season.

MUNRO James Auchterlonie (Jim)

Centre-forward

Born: Glasgow, 20 May 1905.
Died: 1978.

Career: St Johnstone. Cardiff City 1928. Millwall 1929. St Johnstone.

■ A prolific goalscoring centre-forward with St Johnstone, Jim Munro joined the Bluebirds in February 1929 as a replacement for Hughie Ferguson, who had left Ninian Park for his ill-fated move to Dundee. Though he netted twice in the final few games of the season, he couldn't prevent City from being relegated to Division Two. Midway through the following season he lost his place to Ralph Williams and moved on to Millwall. Unable to force his way into the Lions side on a regular basis, he returned north of the border to play for St Johnstone again.

MURPHY Jeremiah (Jerry)

Inside-forward

Born: Dowlais, 1907.
Career: Merthyr Town 1925. Cardiff City 1927. Fulham 1929. Crystal Palace 1931. Barry Town. Merthyr Town. Troedyrhiw. Dolphin.

■ Signed from Merthyr Town, inside-forward Jerry Murphy replaced the injured Hughie Ferguson for the match at Arsenal towards the end of the 1927–28 season. It was his only appearance for the Bluebirds, and after a season in the reserves he moved on to Fulham. After two seasons at Craven Cottage he spent a similar time with Crystal Palace before playing for a number of Welsh League clubs, including Barry Town, Merthyr and Troedyrhiw.

MURPHY Patrick

Half-back

Born: Merthyr Tydfil, 19 December 1947.
Career: Cardiff City 1965. Merthyr Tydfil.

■ A highly-rated youngster, Pat Murphy's only appearance for the Ninian Park club was as a substitute for the injured Alan Harrington in a 1–1 draw at Leyton Orient in January 1966 – the match that ended the Welsh international's career. Unable to force his way into the Cardiff side in any more games, Murphy left to continue his career with his home-town club Merthyr Tydfil.

MURRAY Donald James (Don)

Central-defender

Born: Elgin, 18 January 1946.
Career: Cardiff City 1963. Swansea City (loan) 1974. Heart of Midlothian 1975. Newport County 1976.

Welsh Cup winner 1963–64, 1964–65, 1966–67, 1967–68, 1968–69, 1969–70, 1970–71, 1972–73, 1973–74. Welsh Cup finalist 1971–72.

■ One of the greatest centre-halves in the club's history, Don Murray was just 17 years and 113 days old when he made his first-team debut for the Bluebirds at Middlesbrough in May 1963. After playing in half of the club's games the following season, he established himself as the club's first-choice pivot at the start of the 1964–65 campaign, a position he held for 10 seasons. He was ever present for three consecutive seasons, 1968–69 to 1970–71, and holds the club record for the most consecutive appearances at Football League level, when he played in 146 games from 4 May 1968 to 20 November 1971. Despite often being in trouble with referees during the early stages of his career, he became a player who led by example and gave his all. The winner of nine Welsh Cup medals

during his time at Ninian Park, he was also instrumental in the club reaching the semi-final of the European Cup-Winners' Cup in 1967–68. His performances around this time led to offers from the game's top clubs, but Murray remained loyal to Cardiff and, though his play was often worthy of full international honours, the Scottish-born centre-half had to be content with just one Under-23 cap. In October 1974, after appearing in 483 League and Cup games for City, he had a five-match loan spell with Swansea before returning north of the border to play for a season with Hearts. He then returned to South Wales to see out his career with Newport County, where former Cardiff boss Jimmy Scoular was in charge.

NARDIELLO Gerardo (Gerry)

Forward

Born: Warley, 5 May 1966.
Career: Shrewsbury Town 1984. Cardiff City (loan) 1986. Torquay United 1986.

■ Brother of Welsh international Donato Nardiello, who was capped twice in the mid-1970s, Gerry Nardiello was born in the Midlands and, after being taken on as a member of the groundstaff at Shrewsbury, represented England at Youth international level. Unable to win a regular place at Gay Meadow, he joined Cardiff on loan near the end of the dismal 1985–86 season. He did well with four goals in seven games, including both strikes in a 2–0 win at Doncaster Rovers, but City were still relegated. Alan Durban was sacked and Nardiello returned to Shrewsbury before later moving to Torquay United on a free transfer.

NASH Harold Edward (Harry)

Left-half/inside-left

Born: Fishponds, 10 April 1892.
Died: 1970.
Career: Brislington United. Mardy. Aberdare. Abertillery. Pontypridd. Aston Villa 1914. Coventry City 1920. Cardiff City 1920. Merthyr Town 1923. Aberbargoed. Ystrad Mynach.

Division Two runner-up 1920–21.

■ Having played for a number of Welsh sides, including Aberdare, Abertillery and Pontypridd, Harry Nash began his League career with Aston Villa prior to joining Coventry City. On leaving Highfield Road midway through the 1920–21 season Nash joined Cardiff, scoring on his debut in a 2–0 win at Barnsley. Though most of his time at Ninian Park was spent in the reserves, he was always a dependable deputy when called upon. In May 1923 he joined Merthyr Town, then a League club, before playing for Welsh League club Aberbargoed and later Ystrad Mynach.

N'DUMBU-NSUNGU Guylain

Forward

Born: Kinshasa, DR Congo, 26 December 1982.
Career: Amiens (France). Sheffield Wednesday 2003. Preston North End (loan) 2004. Colchester United 2005. Cardiff City 2005.

■ Signed from French club Amiens, pacy striker Guylain N'Dumbu-Nsungu arrived at Sheffield Wednesday on loan but was quickly signed up on a permanent contract. He went on to finish the 2003–04 season as the club's leading scorer, registering 10 goals in all competitions. The following season he struggled to match his form, and after a loan spell with Preston North End he joined Colchester United on short-term contract. Released by the Layer Road club, he joined Darlington and had scored 11 goals in 23 games, including five in his last five matches, when in January 2006 he joined Cardiff City. Since his arrival he has struggled to make much of an impact, with most of his appearances coming from the bench.

NELSON James (Jimmy)

Right-back

Born: Greenock, 7 January 1901.
Died: 1965.
Career: St Paul's. Glenavon. Crusaders. Cardiff City 1921. Newcastle United 1930. Southend United 1935.

Welsh Cup winner 1922–23, 1926–27, 1927–28, 1929–30. Division One

runner-up 1923–24. FA Cup finalist 1924–25. FA Cup winner 1926–27. FA Charity Shield winner 1927–28.

■ One of the greatest of all Cardiff City full-backs and a member of the famous Scotland 'Wembley Wizards' team, Jimmy Nelson was born in Greenock but moved to Ireland with his family. He began his football career with the amateurs of Belfast Crusaders and captained the Irish Alliance XI that played an England team. He was on the verge of full honours when the Irish found that he was a Scot by birth! He joined Cardiff midway through the 1922–23 season and, after playing at Sunderland, was a virtual fixture in the Bluebirds team for the next six seasons. He was ever present in 1923–24 when the club were runners-up in Division One. In the opening match of the 1925–26 season Nelson made an unwanted piece of Cardiff City history when he became the first Bluebirds player to be sent off in a League match. Playing at Maine Road, he became involved in a last-minute altercation with Manchester City winger Johnson. The referee awarded a penalty to the home side, dismissed Nelson and Cardiff went down 3–2. He appeared in both of City's FA Cup Finals and went on to play in 271 games before the Cardiff board accepted an offer of £7,000 for him from Newcastle United in the summer of 1930. He was soon back at Wembley as captain of the Magpies 1932 FA Cup-winning team. He went on to appear in 159 League games for Newcastle before joining Southend United in June 1935. He played at Roots Hall up until the outbreak of World War Two. Capped four times by Scotland, he assisted Southend for a number of years, where his son, Tony, an amateur international, played, later returning to Cardiff to become licensee of the Greyhound Inn.

NEWTON Edward John Ikem (Eddie)

Midfield

Born: Hammersmith, 13 December 1971.
Career: Chelsea 1990. Cardiff City (loan) 1992. Birmingham City 1999. Oxford United 2000. Barnet 2000. Hayes.

■ Having played in a variety of positions in Chelsea's youth and reserve teams, he was loaned out to Cardiff City in January 1992, making his League debut in a 4–0 win against Chesterfield. He played a major role in launching the Bluebirds promotion challenge with his dynamic midfield performances plus four crucial goals. Sadly, it was not quite enough as City finished three points short of a play-off place. At the end of his three-month loan period he returned to Stamford Bridge and, after establishing himself in the side, collided with his own goalkeeper Kevin Hitchcock and broke his right shin. An England Under-21 international, he must have come close to full international recognition in a Chelsea career that saw him score one of his side's goals in a 2–0 1997 FA Cup Final win over Middlesbrough, erasing the painful memories of the 1994 Final when a penalty was awarded against him. The following season, despite suffering a number of injuries, he helped Chelsea win the Coca-Cola Cup and the European Cup-Winners' Cup against VFB Stuttgart in Stockholm. More injuries followed for 'Steady Eddie', and in July 1999, after appearing in 213 games for Chelsea, he joined Birmingham City. He had a disappointing time at St Andrew's and was soon on his way to Oxford United

before joining Barnet. Unable to impress manager John Still, he signed for Hayes in the Conference before going to play in Singapore.

NEWTON William (Billy)

Right-half

Born: Cramlington, 14 May 1893.
Died: 1973.
Career: Blyth Spartans. Hartford Colliery. Newcastle United 1919. Cardiff City 1920. Leicester City 1923. Grimsby Town 1926. Stockport County 1927. Hull City 1931. Stockport County 1932.

■ At the age of 16, Billy Newton moved to Blyth to work in the shipyards and began his career with Blyth Spartans. A terrier-like wing-half, his qualities soon attracted a number of League clubs, and in 1919 he joined Newcastle United. With his chances of first-team football at St James' Park limited, he joined Cardiff City. After making his debut in a 2–0 win at Barnsley in February 1921, Newton found it difficult to win a regular place due to the form of Charlie Brittan, Jimmy Blair and Jack Page, and so after two seasons at Ninian Park he moved to Leicester City. During four seasons at Filbert Street he made 95 appearances before moving on to Grimsby Town. Unable to settle at Blundell Park, he joined Stockport County, a move that began a 40-year association with the Edgeley Park club. He spent four years as a player, clocking up 160 appearances, before having a brief spell with Hull City. On his return to Stockport, he became the club's player-coach then trainer, a position he held for 30 years.

NIBLOE Joseph (Joe)

Full-back

Born: Glasgow, 10 December 1926.
Career: Clydebank Juniors. Cardiff City 1948.

■ Tough tackling left-back Joe Nibloe was playing for Clydebank Juniors when Cardiff City manager Cyril Spiers persuaded him to join the Bluebirds in the summer of 1948. Though he gave some good performances in defence for City's reserve side, when he did get a chance in the club's League side it was at

outside-left! A goalless draw at Lincoln City was his only appearance for Cardiff, and he drifted into local football.

NICHOLLS John

Inside-forward

Born: Wolverhampton, 3 April 1931.
Died: 1 April 1995.
Career: Wolverhampton Wanderers. Heath Town. West Bromwich Albion 1951. Cardiff City 1957. Exeter City 1957. Worcester City. Wellington Town.

■ After an early association with his home-town club, Johnny Nicholls moved to West Bromwich Albion, spending his first season at the Hawthorns flitting in and out of the side. However, his form at the start of the 1953–54 season was outstanding, as he formed a deadly partnership with Ronnie Allen, and he went on to score 28 goals. That season Albion won the FA Cup and finished third in Division One, and Nicholls won two caps for England, scoring on his debut in a 4–2 win over Scotland. During the early part of the following season, Nicholls developed an ankle problem and was transferred to Cardiff City. His stay at Ninian Park was both brief and unhappy, and it was only when he moved on to Exeter City that he rediscovered his scoring form. Subsequently, after drifting through the non-League scene with Worcester and Wellington Town, he decided to retire. He died of a heart attack while returning home from an Albion game in April 1995.

NICHOLLS John Barry L. (Jack)

Inside-right

Born: Cardiff, 14 February 1898.
Died: 1970.
Career: Ton Pentre. Cardiff Corinthians. Pontypridd. Bridgend Town. Newport County 1923. Cardiff City 1924. Swansea Town 1925. Cardiff Corinthians.

■ Jack Nicholls was the son of Syd Nicholls, a Cardiff City director and FAW vice-president. During the 1923–24 season he enjoyed a startling rise, making his League debut for

Newport County and then becoming the Somerton Park club's first Welsh international player. He had earlier been capped at amateur level against England and went on to make a further nine appearances for the Welsh amateur side. Employed by the Cardiff City Water Board, his work commitments limited his appearances for Newport, and at the end of the season he was released. He then had a brief spell with Cardiff City, making the first of two appearances in a 2–1 win at Newcastle United in October 1924 before joining Cardiff Corries. He served on that club's committee for many years and in 1939 was their manager when they agreed to become City's nursery.

NICHOLLS Ronald Bernard (Ron)

Goalkeeper

Born: Berkeley, 4 December 1933.
Died: 1994.
Career: Fulham. Bristol Rovers 1954. Cardiff City 1958. Bristol City 1961.

■ Footballing cricketer Ron Nicholls was an amateur with Fulham before turning professional with Bristol Rovers in November 1954. While at Eastville, he shared the goalkeeping duties with Howard Radford, but Nicholls was in goal in the 1955–56 FA Cup third-round tie when Rovers beat Manchester United 4–0. Along with fellow county cricketer Barrie Meyer, he had a disagreement with Rovers about the overlap of the two sports, with the result that Meyer was allowed to join Plymouth Argyle, while Nicholls signed for Cardiff City. With Graham Vearncombe in the Merchant Navy, Nicholls was the club's first-choice 'keeper in 1958–59, but the following season when City won promotion to the First Division he only appeared in five games towards the end of the campaign. In 1960–61 he played in the 3–2 victory over the Spurs double-winning team, but in the close season he signed for Bristol City, later ending his football career with Cheltenham Town. An opening batsman for Gloucestershire, he scored 23,612 runs in 534 matches during his 24-year county career.

NICHOLLS Ryan Rhys

Winger

Born: Cardiff, 10 May 1973.
Career: Leeds United 1991. Cardiff City 1995. Merthyr Tydfil.

■ A former Welsh Schoolboy international, Ryan Nicholls joined Leeds United, where he turned professional, during the 1991 close season. Unfortunately, most of his time at Elland Road was spent on the treatment table, and he was unable to break into the Yorkshire club's first team. Released by Leeds in January 1995, he joined Cardiff on a non-contact basis. Nicholls made an encouraging debut against Blackpool, a match the Bluebirds lost 1–0, before picking up an injury. An excellent dribbler and passer of the ball, he was surprisingly allowed to leave Ninian Park to join non-League Merthyr Tydfil at the end of the season.

NICHOLSON George

Wing-half

Born: Pelaw, 12 May 1905.
Career: Pelaw. South Shields 1929. Washington Colliery. Bolton Wanderers 1931. Cardiff City 1936. Oldham Athletic 1939.

Welsh Cup finalist 1938–39.

■ George Nicholson, an ex-miner, was a latecomer to League football, joining Bolton Wanderers when he was 25. The Bolton scout had actually been checking up on another player when he spotted the wing-half playing for Washington Colliery. Having made his debut in a 2–2 draw at Liverpool in September 1931, he remained a regular for the next couple of seasons until losing his place to Harry Goslin. After languishing in the club's reserves for more than a season, Nicholson jumped at the chance of joining Cardiff City in the summer of 1936. One of seven new faces in the Bluebirds side, he missed just three games in 1936–37. A great favourite with the Ninian Park crowd, he was instrumental in City's revival and improvement in their League position before moving to Oldham Athletic. War then broke out, and he failed to make an appearance for the Latics.

NICHOLSON Joseph Robinson (Joe)

Wing-half.

Born: Ryhope, 4 June 1898.
Died: 1974.
Career: Ryhope Colliery. Clapton Orient 1919. Cardiff City 1924. Aston Villa 1926. Bangor City. Spennymoor United.

FA Cup finalist 1924–25.

■ One of football's most aggressive players, Joe Nicholson gained League experience in the Second Division with Clapton Orient, where he was a regular for five years, making 145 appearances. Arriving at Ninian Park in 1924, he competed with Harry Wake for the right-half position, but before the end of the season he had switched to centre-forward in place of the injured Len Davies. His displays in attack helped City reach the 1925 FA Cup Final, and he scored in the 3–1 semi-final defeat of Blackburn Rovers. At the end of the following season he went to Aston Villa in exchange for George Blackburn but injury cut short his Villa Park career.

NOCK A. Jack

Inside-left

Born: Stourbridge, 1899.
Career: Leicester Fosse 1914. Merthyr Town. Nuneaton Town. Tamworth Castle. Cradley Heath. Cardiff City 1921. Wrexham 1924. Burton United. Worcester City. Flint Town. Oswestry Town.

■ Inside-forward Jack Nock played for Leicester Fosse and Merthyr Town around the time of World War One before, in 1919, joining non-League Cradley Heath. In 1921 he returned to League football with Cardiff City but, despite being on the fringe of the first team, made only three appearances. In November 1924 Wrexham offered him the chance of regular first-team football and he accepted. He netted a hat-trick against Wigan Borough and, at the end of the 1924–25 season, won a Welsh Cup medal. The following season he was again a consistent goalscorer, but in the summer of 1926, having scored 26 goals in 73 games, he was allowed to leave and joined Burton United before having spells with Worcester City, Flint Town and Oswestry.

NOGAN Kurt

Forward

Born: Cardiff, 9 September 1970.
Career: Luton Town 1989. Brighton &
Hove Albion 1992. Burnley 1995. Preston
North End 1997. Cardiff City 2000.

Division Three runner-up 2000–01.

■ Though he won international recognition for Wales at Under-21 level during his time with Luton Town, he failed to hold down a regular first-team place at Kenilworth Road, and following a trial with Peterborough United he joined Brighton in October 1992. The goals soon started to flow, and in 1993–94 he was the Seagulls leading scorer with 26 League and Cup strikes. After a bright start to the following season, the goals began to dry up, and he moved to Burnley for a fee of £300,000. He rediscovered his goalscoring touch with the Clarets, netting 27 in all competitions in 1995–96. Midway through the next season his Burnley career fell apart with a much-publicised contractual dispute. Signed by Preston for a knock-down fee, he soon found his form. He netted twice against Arsenal in a televised FA

Cup game and hit his 100th League goal against his first club Luton Town. Capped by Wales at 'B' level, he left Deepdale in March 2000. The Bluebirds fans had helped raise the £100,000 fee to bring Nogan back to South Wales, but the expectations aroused by his arrival were unfortunately unrealistic. Nogan had injury problems from the onset and never looked fully fit. The 2000–01 season was just as frustrating as he failed to start a match in the club's promotion-winning season, though he did come off the bench 12 times, scoring in the 3–2 defeat of Hartlepool. Shortly afterwards, though, he parted company with the club.

NORMAN Albert Griffith (Griff)

Half-back

Born: Cardiff, 20 February 1926.
Career: Cardiff City 1950. Torquay
United 1952.

■ Though he spent two years at Ninian Park, half-back Griff Norman could only manage a solitary League appearance for the Bluebirds, that in a 1–1 draw at Southampton in September 1951. He then took the familiar route that a number of fringe players took and joined Torquay United. He spent five seasons at Plainmoor, making 216 League appearances and helping the Devon club finish runners-up in the Third Division South in 1956–57.

NORTHCOTT Thomas Theodore (Tommy)

Inside-forward

Born: Torquay, 5 December 1931.
Career: Torquay United 1948. Cardiff
City 1952. Lincoln City 1955. Torquay
United 1957.

■ Tommy Northcott began his career with his home-town club Torquay United, where he earned England Youth honours. Under the arrangement between the Bluebirds and the Devon club, in which City had first call on good prospects in exchange for loan players, Tommy Northcott came to Ninian Park in October 1952. At the time he was a National Serviceman, and

he went straight into the Cardiff side. Over the next three years he developed into a very useful utility forward, scoring some vital goals in matches against some of the First Division's best defences. In July 1955 he left to play for Lincoln City and did well for the Imps, with 34 goals in 94 games, before he rejoined Torquay in November 1957. Over the next decade Tommy Northcott developed into one of the Plainmoor club's greatest servants. He helped them win promotion to the Third Division in 1959–60 and went on to score 136 goals in 410 games before hanging up his boots.

NUGENT Kevin Patrick

Striker

Born: Edmonton, 10 April 1969.
Career: Leyton Orient 1987. Cork City
(loan) 1989. Plymouth Argyle 1992.
Bristol City 1995. Cardiff City 1997.
Leyton Orient 2002. Swansea City 2003.

Division Three promotion 1998–99.
FAW Invitation Cup finalist 1999–2000.
Division Three runner-up 2000–01.

■ A former Leyton Orient trainee, he signed professional terms under Frank Clark, but in his early days at Brisbane Road he couldn't command a regular place and went on loan to Cork City, for whom he played in the 1989 FAI Cup Final. After finishing the 1991–92 season as the O's leading marksman, he was transferred to Peter Shilton's Plymouth Argyle for £200,000. He was outstanding as the Pilgrims reached the Second Division play-offs in 1993–94, but after the Pilgrims were surprisingly relegated the following season he left to play for Bristol City as Joe Jordan signed him in exchange for Ian Baird plus £75,000 in September 1995. One of the Ashton Gate club's unsung heroes, he joined Cardiff for £65,000 in the summer of 1997. Sadly, he was scarcely fit all season, carrying a number of niggling injuries, and he was desperately frustrated by his run of bad luck. The 1998–99 season was completely different as he was voted Cardiff's Player of the Year. Leading the line with great skill, he scored 18 goals in all competitions, and it was a surprise for many when he missed out on being named in the PFA award-winning Third Division team. He finished the 1999–2000 season as Bluebirds captain and was also joint top scorer with Jason Bowen with 17 goals. In November 2000 Nugent had the misfortune to suffer a major Achilles problem, which kept him out for the remainder of the club's promotion-winning season. On regaining fitness he rejoined Leyton Orient after a 10-year absence, but his stay was short-lived, and in January 2003 he signed for Swansea. After scoring three goals in his first four appearances, he forged a useful partnership with Lee Trundle and on occasions captained the side.

NUGENT William Clifford (Cliff)

Outside-left

Born: Islington, 3 March 1929.
Career: Headington United. Cardiff City 1951. Mansfield Town 1958.

■ Utility forward Cliff Nugent was playing his football with Headington United when Cardiff manager Cyril Spiers brought him to Ninian Park in January 1951. Though he made his debut the following season in a 1–0 defeat of Hull City, it was 1953–54 before he won a regular place in the Bluebirds side. Playing predominantly at inside-right, he scored three League

goals in 22 games, his first for City coming against Wolves in January 1954. The following season he showed his versatility by playing at outside-left, scoring four goals in 24 games as the club just avoided relegation by beating Wolves 3–2 in their final home game. He missed all but one game of the 1955–56 season through injury before returning for the following campaign, when he netted a well-struck hat-trick in a 7–0 home win over Barnsley. In November 1958 Nugent left South Wales to play for Mansfield Town, having scored 20 goals in 122 League and Cup games spread over eight seasons.

NUTT Gordon Edward

Winger

Born: Birmingham, 8 November 1932.
Career: Coventry City 1949. Cardiff City 1954. Arsenal 1955. Southend United 1960. PSV Eindhoven (Holland). Hereford United. Rugby Town. Bexley United. Sydney Corinthians (Australia).

■ Gordon Nutt started his career with Coventry City where, after working his way up through the ranks, he became a regular in the side. The winger built up a good reputation, and in December 1954 he joined Cardiff City, the Bluebirds paying £12,000 for his services. He slotted into City's First Division team, turning in some fine performances and scoring some spectacular goals. However, in September 1955 Arsenal offered Brian Walsh and a cash adjustment to take Mike Tiddy and Nutt to Highbury. The offer was accepted, but within a fortnight he broke an ankle at Everton and was out of action for a couple of months. Nutt spent five years with the Gunners but could never hold down a regular first-team spot, leaving to play for Southend United in October 1960. There followed spells with PSV Eindhoven, Hereford United, Rugby Town and Bexley United before he went to Australia to play for Corinthians of Sydney.

OAKLEY Kenneth (Ken)

Centre-forward

Born: Rhymney, 9 May 1929

Career: Ebbw Vale. Cardiff City 1950. Northampton Town 1954. Ebbw Vale.

■ Spotted playing junior football, he began the 1950–51 season as leader of Cardiff City's Second Division attack, but after only five games he lost his place. At the end of the season he returned to Welsh League football with Ebbw Vale, but two years later he was re-signed and played twice in the First Division in 1953–54. Unlucky with injury and the arrival of Trevor Ford, Oakley departed for Northampton Town but, after scoring six goals in 13 games, returned to Ebbw Vale where, for many years after, he was a prolific scorer.

OATWAY Anthony Philip David Terry Frank Donald Stanley Gerry Gordon Stephen James (Charlie)

Midfield

Born: Hammersmith, 28 November 1973.
Career: Yeading. Cardiff City 1994. Coleraine (loan). Torquay United 1995. Brentford 1997. Lincoln City (loan) 1998. Brighton & Hove Albion 1999.

■ Signed from non-League Yeading in the summer of 1994, he made a good impression in midfield during pre-season friendlies with his terrier-like workrate. Making his League debut on the opening day of the 1994–95 season against Stockport County, he was an instant hit with the fans. Unfortunate to be involved in a non-football related problem, he was out of the game for several months. On regaining full fitness he had a loan spell with Coleraine before, on his return to Ninian Park, being discarded by Cardiff's new management team. Transferred to Torquay United, he was voted the club's Player of the Year in his first season at Plainmoor. He later joined Brentford where his boss was the former Torquay manager Eddie May. After suffering a series of injuries he was loaned to Lincoln City before returning to Griffin Park and helping the Bees win the Third Division Championship. Allowed to join Brighton, he won another Third Division title medal in 2000–01 and then, the following season, this most popular of players helped the Seagulls win the Second Division Champion-ship. Still with the south-coast club, he owes his plethora of names to the fact that he was named after the Queen's Park Rangers players of the early 1970s!

O'CONNOR Timothy Daniel (Tim)

Midfield

Born: Neath, 3 October 1967.
Career: Afan Lido. Cardiff City 1985. Afan Lido.

■ Midfielder Tim O'Connor was spotted playing for Afan Lido when signed by manager Alan Durban in the summer of 1985. After a number of impressive performances for the club's youth and reserve sides, he made his debut in a 2–1 reversal at Bristol Rovers before coming on as a substitute for Paul Wheeler at home to Gillingham towards the end of the 1985–86 season. Released at the end of the campaign, he then rejoined Afan Lido.

O'HALLORAN Keith James

Midfield

Born: Dublin, 10 November 1975.
Career: Cherry Orchard BC. Middlesbrough 1994. Scunthorpe United (loan) 1996. Cardiff City (loan) 1996.

■ Equally at home at full-back or in midfield, Keith O'Halloran made his League debut for Middlesbrough against Derby County in March 1995. Early the following season he won international recognition for the Republic of Ireland at Under-21 level but couldn't hold down a first-team place at 'Boro and joined Scunthorpe United on loan. His first-team chances were even more limited following the influx of foreign players to Teeside, and in November 1996 he joined the Bluebirds on loan. Strong and determined and a good tackler, he started well, but he wasn't really suited to the Third Division and returned to the Riverside before leaving to play in the Republic.

O'HALLORAN Neil

Centre-forward

Born: Cardiff, 27 June 1933.
Died: 1995.

Career: Cardiff City 1954. Newport County 1957. Merthyr Tydfil. Barry Town.

■ Neil O'Halloran made the most spectacular debut of any player in Cardiff City's history when, in December 1955, he netted a hat-trick in a 3–1 defeat of Charlton Athletic. A boilermaker and part-time professional, he had graduated through City's junior sides in a variety of positions, but despite the historic start he failed to win a regular place in the Cardiff side, and at the end of the 1956–57 season he joined Newport County as part of the deal that brought Colin Hudson to Ninian Park. It was a similar story at Somerton Park, and he left to become a prolific marksman with both Merthyr Tydfil and Barry Town, for whom he was later chairman.

O'NEIL Gary Paul

Midfielder

Born: Bromley, 18 May 1983
Career: Portsmouth 2000. Walsall (loan) 2003. Cardiff City (loan) 2004.

■ One of the finest prospects to emerge from the Portsmouth youth system in recent seasons, Gary O'Neil is an exciting midfield player with fine vision, composure and an ability to create space for himself. In his third season at Fratton Park the talented youngster found his first-team appearances restricted as manager Harry Redknapp opted for experience. Continuing to be left waiting in the wings for Pompey, he had a loan spell at Walsall where he demonstrated plenty of energy and commitment in the Saddler's midfield.

The England Under-21 captain, he joined the Bluebirds on loan in September 2004 and made his debut when coming off the bench to replace Jobi McAnuff in a 3–2 win at Wolves. After that he played in nine Championship games, scoring his only goal in a 2–2 draw at Millwall. However, in the goalless home draw against Leicester City he hit the inside of the post on two occasions, each time seeing the ball rebound to safety. During his spell at Ninian Park, City lost just once and Bluebirds fans were devastated when he was recalled to Fratton Park to help Pompey in their fight for Premiership survival. In 2005–06 Gary O'Neil was an influential member of the Portsmouth midfield and though the club were again struggling near the foot of the top flight for most of the campaign, he continued to give some sterling performances.

O'NEILL Harold (Harry)

Full-back/centre-forward

Born: Castle Ward, Newcastle, 15 November 1894.
Career: Wallsend. Sheffield Wednesday 1919. Bristol Rovers 1922. Swindon Town 1923. Runcorn. Cardiff City 1931. Berne (Switzerland).

■ After beginning his career as a full-back, first with Sheffield Wednesday and then Bristol Rovers, Harry O'Neill

joined Swindon Town where, towards the end of his stay at the County Ground, he was converted to centre-forward. After moving into non-League football with Runcorn, O'Neill signed for Cardiff City in July 1931. He scored on his home debut in a 1–1 draw with Brighton and netted against one of his former clubs Bristol Rovers in another drawn match, but by the turn of the year he had made his last appearance for the club. On leaving Ninian Park he went to play for Swiss club Berne.

OSMAN Russell Charles

Central-defender

Born: Ilkeston, 14 February 1959.
Career: Ipswich Town 1976. Leicester City 1985. Southampton 1988. Bristol City 1991. Plymouth Argyle 1994. Brighton & Hove Albion 1995. Cardiff City 1996.

■ Russell Osman started out with Ipswich Town, where, under the management of Bobby Robson, he formed an excellent central-defensive

partnership with Terry Butcher. In 1975 he won an FA Youth Cup medal, though he had to wait until September 1977 before making his first-team debut. In May 1980 he won the first of 11 caps for England when he played against Australia. Osman twice came close to a

League Championship medal, the club finishing runners-up in the First Division in 1980–81 and 1981–82. He also helped Town win the UEFA Cup in 1981, when they beat AZ67 Alkmaar 5–4 on aggregate. He had played in 384 games for Ipswich when, in the summer of 1985, he joined Leicester City for £240,000. He made 108 appearances for the Foxes before moving on to Southampton. Osman's first managerial role was with Bristol City, where he was initially caretaker manager, but in 1994 he lost his job. He then joined the Bluebirds and appeared in 15 games towards the end of the 1995–96 season. He became Cardiff manager in November 1996 but the following month gave way to Kenny Hibbitt. He then returned to Ashton Gate as Bristol City's coach.

O'SULLIVAN Wayne St John

Midfield

Born: Cyprus, 25 February 1974.
Career: Swindon Town 1993. Cardiff City 1997. Plymouth Argyle 1999.

FAW Invitation Cup finalist 1997–98. Division Three promotion 1998–99.

■ Cyprus-born slightly built midfielder Wayne O'Sullivan came through the ranks at Swindon Town under the watchful eye of former full-back John Trollope. Having helped the Robins win the Second Division Championship in 1995–96, he was selected by the Republic of Ireland at Under-21 level. Having appeared in 109 games for the Wiltshire club, he joined Cardiff for £75,000 in the summer of 1997. He made an immediate impact with some tricky runs down the right and then played a full part in City's promotion in 1998–99. However, following the departure of Mark Delaney his game suffered. Out of contract in the summer of 1999, he was offered terms but opted to join Plymouth Argyle, where he proved a consistent and reliable player. Always giving his best, he was the Player of the Year in 2000–01 but then turned down a new contract to go and play in Australia instead.

OVENSTONE David Guthrie (Davie)

Outside-left

Born: St Monance, 17 June 1913.
Died: 1983.
Career: St Monance Swifts. Rosslyn Juniors. Raith Rovers 1932. Bristol Rovers 1934. Queen's Park Rangers 1935. Cardiff City 1936. Watford 1937. Southport 1937. Barry Town. Ebbw Vale. Broughly Ex-Service. Forthill Athletic.

■ Having played Scottish junior football for St Monance Swifts and Rosslyn Juniors, Davie Ovenstone soon came to the attention of Raith Rovers, signing for the Stark's Park club in 1932. After a fruitless spell with Bristol Rovers, he had his first taste of League football with Queen's Park Rangers, but after one season he moved to Cardiff City. The left-winger also spent just one season with the Bluebirds in 1936–37, and though the club finished 18th in the Third Division South he was not on the losing side in the four games in which he scored. His next club were Watford before he again left after one season to end his League career with Southport. After spells with Barry Town and Ebbw Vale, he returned to his native Scotland to end his career in his country's lower Leagues.

OWEN Gordon

Right-winger

Born: Barnsley, 14 June 1959.
Career: Sheffield Wednesday 1976. Rotherham United (loan) 1980. Doncaster Rovers (loan) 1982. Chesterfield (loan) 1983. Cardiff City 1983. Barnsley 1984. Bristol City 1986. Hull City (loan) 1987. Mansfield Town 1988. Blackpool 1989. Carlisle United (loan) 1990. Exeter City (loan) 1990. Frickley Athletic.

■ Much-travelled right-winger Gordon Owen began his career with Sheffield Wednesday, where he featured in the 1979–80 promotion success under Jack Charlton. Following loan spells at Rotherham, Doncaster and Chesterfield, he moved to Cardiff City on a free transfer in August 1983. His speedy wing play and powerful shooting made him a huge favourite with the Ninian

Park faithful, and in 1983–84 he was City's leading scorer with 14 League goals. Sadly, he wanted to return north, and in the close season he joined Barnsley for £27,000 – the fee being fixed by a tribunal. He proved quite a hit with his home-town club, finishing his first season at Oakwell as their leading scorer. After starting the following season in fine form, he moved to Bristol City. Later, after a loan spell with Hull, he joined Freight Rover Trophy holders Mansfield Town. Sold to Blackpool, he had loan spells with Carlisle and Exeter while at Bloomfield Road before moving into non-League football with Frickley Athletic.

PAGE John (Jack)

Right-back

Born: Liverpool, 24 March 1886.
Died: 1951.
Career: Rochdale. Everton 1913. Cardiff City 1920. Merthyr Town 1926.

■ The brother of England international Louis Page, full-back Jack Page started out with Rochdale before signing for Everton in 1913. Though he was with the Goodison Park club until 1920, he made only nine League appearances. Cardiff manager Fred Stewart saw his

experience and ability to play in either full-back position an asset to his team on their entry into the Football League. Though he was never a regular, when called upon, due to the absence of Charlie Brittan, Jimmy Blair or Jimmy Nelson, he performed extremely well. In 1926 Page moved to Merthyr Town where, as well as making 100 League appearances, he scored his one and only goal in the competition.

PAGE Robert John

Central-defender

Born: Llwynpia, 3 September 1974.
Career: Watford 1993. Sheffield United 2001. Cardiff City 2004.

■ Robert Page began his career with Watford where, in his first season in the Hornet's side, he won representative honours for Wales at Under-21 level. Strong in the tackle and dominant in the air, he was made Watford club captain at the start of the 1996–97 season, aged only 21. That season he gained personal reward when he won his first full Welsh cap against Turkey. In 1997–98 he had the unusual distinction

of playing for Wales against Brazil and for Watford against Barnet in the same week, before winning a Second Division Championship medal. In the Premiership, Page was voted Watford's Player of the Year and continued to provide inspirational leadership until, in the summer of 2001, after making 252 appearances, he was placed on the open to offers list. Sheffield United paid £350,000 and immediately appointed him captain. Although injury restricted his appearances at Bramall Lane, he had played in 128 games prior to joining Cardiff for the start of the 2004–05 season.

PAGET William Sidney Thomas (Tommy)

Forward

Born: Cardiff, 4 March 1909.
Career: Cardiff City 1932. Newport County 1934. Clapton Orient 1935. Barry Town.

■ Tommy Paget was on Cardiff City's books for two trouble-torn seasons, though during the course of that time he only made six League appearances and was only on the winning side once. On leaving City, he joined Newport County but stayed just one season before moving on to Clapton Orient. Unable to break into the London club's side, he returned to South Wales to play non-League football for Barry Town.

PAGNAM Frederick (Fred)

Forward

Born: Poulton-le-Fylde, 4 September 1891.
Died: 1962.
Career: Lytham. Blackpool Wednesday. Huddersfield Town 1910. Doncaster Rovers. Southport Central. Blackpool 1912. Gainsborough Trinity. Liverpool 1914. Arsenal 1919. Cardiff City 1920. Watford 1921.

Division Two runner-up 1920–21.

■ Fred Pagnam was a prolific goalscoring forward who had played junior football in his native Lancashire for Lytham and Blackpool Wednesday before joining Huddersfield Town in 1910. He spent two seasons at Leeds

Road without playing a League game and then one season with Southport Central before signing for Blackpool. He made little progress with the Seasiders and, in 1914, joined Liverpool. In that last season prior to the outbreak of World War One, he was Liverpool's leading scorer when netting 24 times in

29 League games. In wartime games he netted 42 goals in 48 games before, in October 1919, joining Arsenal for £1,500. In his first season at Highbury he played in 25 games, scoring a goal every other game, while in 1920–21 he was their top scorer with 14 goals – this in spite of leaving for Cardiff City midway through the campaign. He scored on his Bluebirds debut in a 3–2 defeat of Barnsley and went on to net six times in 14 outings as the club won promotion to the First Division. He found life in the top flight much harder, and after losing his place he joined Watford – the Hornets paying out their first-ever four-figure fee. He stayed for five seasons at Vicarage Road, scoring 75 goals in 150 first-team games including being the leading scorer in the Third Division South in 1922–23. He later managed Watford before coaching in both Turkey and Holland.

PARFITT Henry Edward (Harry)

Full-back

Born: Cardiff, 26 September 1929.
Career: Cardiff City 1949. Torquay United 1952. Worcester City.

■ Local born full-back Harry Parfitt joined Cardiff in the summer of 1949,

but despite some solid displays in the club's second string he couldn't break into the City side and was loaned out to Torquay United. Parfitt spent two seasons at Plainmoor, appearing in 58 League games for the Devon club before returning to Ninian Park. Eventually he made his League debut for Cardiff in a 3–0 defeat at Bolton Wanderers, but it was his only appearance in a City shirt, and in the close season he left to play non-League football for FA Cup giantkillers Worcester City.

PARKER Reginald Ernest Arundel (Reg)

Centre-forward

Born: Llantrisant, 10 June 1921.
Career: Cardiff City 1941. Newport County 1948.

■ Reg Parker came to Ninian Park during the early years of World War Two and was a regular scorer until entering the armed forces. After the hostilities had ended he rejoined the Bluebirds but found Stan Richards in possession of the number-nine jersey. He made a couple of appearances towards the end of the 1947–48 season, but then the following summer he joined Newport County in exchange for Bryn Allen, who had gone to Somerton Park the previous year. In five years with County he developed into a consistent goalscorer, netting 99 goals in 201 League games.

PARRY Paul Ian

Midfield

Born: Newport, 19 August 1980.
Career: Hereford United 1998. Cardiff City 2004.

■ Midfielder Paul Parry began his career with Hereford United, joining them as a trainee in the summer of 1998. After establishing himself with the Nationwide Conference side, he soon began to score a number of vital goals and netted 10 in the 2002–03 campaign. Early the following season he had just netted a well-taken hat-trick in a 7–1 win at Forest Green when Cardiff manager Lennie Lawrence paid £75,000 to take him to Ninian Park. He made his Bluebirds debut in a 3–2 defeat of

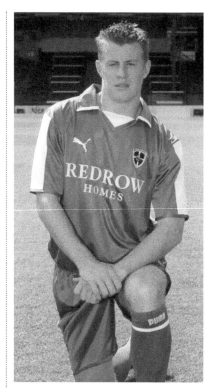

Rotherham United and had played in only five First Division games when Mark Hughes gave him his full international debut against Scotland. Parry continued to hold down a regular place for Cardiff and, at the end of the season, scored the only goal of the game as Wales beat Canada 1–0. Despite his success on the international stage, he couldn't hold down a regular place in the Cardiff side in 2005–06, with the majority of his first-team appearances coming from the bench.

PARSONS Frank Ronald

Goalkeeper

Born: Amersham, 29 October 1947.
Career: Crystal Palace 1965. Cardiff City 1970. Reading 1974. Wokingham.

■ Goalkeeper Frank Parsons had made just a handful of first-team appearances for Crystal Palace when City manager Jimmy Scoular, seeking a replacement for Fred Davies, paid £17,000 to bring him to Ninian Park. After an encouraging debut in a 1–0 win at Leicester City, Parsons made a number of costly mistakes, which became more and more highlighted. It all came to a head in the home match against

Middlesbrough in October 1970 as, with City 3–1 up and having saved a penalty, he let in some dreadful goals and 'Boro won 4–3. After that he only played the odd game, and his final appearance for the club came on the last day of the 1971–72 season when he was carried off injured at Queen's Park Rangers! On parting company with the Bluebirds, he had a brief spell with Reading before playing non-League football for Wokingham.

PARSONS John Stuart

Forward

Born: Cardiff, 10 December 1950.
Career: Cardiff City 1968. Bournemouth 1973. Newport County 1975.

■ John Parsons certainly qualified for the tag of 'super sub' as he scored two goals after coming off the bench in wins over Oxford United and Sunderland in February 1971, before making his full League debut. A prolific goalscorer for City's reserve side, his lack of size was against him at first-team level, for these were the days of Brian Clark, Alan Warboys and John Toshack, and Parsons didn't seem to fit into manager Jimmy Scoular's plans. He left Ninian Park in February 1973 to play for Bournemouth, but his stay at Dean Court was hampered by a spate of injuries, and it wasn't until he moved to Newport County in March 1975 that he rediscovered his shooting boots. Parsons scored 23 goals in 60 games for County before drifting into non-League football, where he still retained the gift of scoring goals.

PARTRIDGE Scott Malcolm

Winger

Born: Leicester, 13 October 1974.
Career: Bradford City 1992. Bristol City 1994. Torquay United (loan) 1995. Plymouth Argyle (loan) 1996. Scarborough (loan) 1996. Cardiff City 1997. Torquay United 1998. Brentford 1999. Rushden and Diamonds 2001. Exeter City (loan) 2002. Shrewsbury Town 2003. Weymouth.

■ The son of former Grimsby favourite Malcolm, he made a handful of appearances for Bradford City prior to

linking up with Bristol City in February 1994. A skilful, two-footed player, reminiscent of an old-fashioned inside-forward, he was unable to get a run in the team in 1995–96 and had loan spells with Torquay, Plymouth and Scarborough before, in February 1997, joining the Bluebirds for £50,000. A welcome addition to the City squad, his probing runs down the left and incisive passing helped pave the way for a successful climax that ended in the play-offs. The following season he found it hard to discover his best form and in March 1998 left to join Torquay United. He had a wonderful season in 1998–99 with 15 goals and this prompted Brentford to pay a six-figure fee for his services. In his first season with the Bees he helped them win the Third Division Championship, then won a runners-up medal in the LDV Vans Trophy Final against Port Vale at the Millennium Stadium before leaving to play for Rushden and Diamonds. There followed a loan spell with Exeter before he joined Shrewsbury, but after failing to prevent their drop into the Conference he left to play for Weymouth.

PATERSON Scott

Midfield/central-defender

Born: Aberdeen, 13 May 1972.
Career: Cove Rangers. Liverpool 1992. Bristol City 1994. Cardiff City (loan) 1997. Carlisle United 1998. Cambridge United 1999. Plymouth Argyle 2000. Peterhead.

■ Freed by Liverpool, Scott Paterson signed for Bristol City during the 1994 close season and made a number of promising appearances during the following campaign. The skilful midfield player looked set to have a lengthy run in the Ashton Gate club's side before injury intervened. On his return to fitness, he switched to a central-defensive role. His ability both on the ground and in the air, together with an overall air of assurance, prompted Cardiff to take him on loan in November 1997. He impressed greatly during his month at Ninian Park, and if the Bluebirds could have persuaded Bristol City to part with the player at the right price there is no

doubt he would have been snapped up. After returning to Ashton Gate, he was surprisingly given a free transfer and in the summer of 1998 he joined Carlisle United. His progress with the Cumbrian club was hampered by injury, and he was released during the close season. There followed spells as a non-contract player with Cambridge United and Plymouth Argyle before he went north of the border to play for Peterhead.

PEARSON John Stuart

Forward

Born: Sheffield, 1 September 1963.
Career: Sheffield Wednesday 1981. Charlton Athletic 1985. Leeds United 1987. Rotherham United (loan) 1991. Barnsley 1991. Hull City (loan) 1992. Carlisle United 1993. Mansfield Town 1994. Cardiff City 1995. Merthyr Tydfil (loan). Chorley.

■ Beginning his career with his home-town club Sheffield Wednesday, John Pearson scored on his Owls debut and won England Youth honours in 1981 and 1982. He was often used as a substitute by Wednesday and in the summer of 1985 he was sold to Charlton Athletic for £100,000. He finished his first season at The Valley, as the Addicks won promotion to Division One, as their top scorer, but after losing form he returned to Yorkshire to play for Leeds United. Injuries hampered his progress at Elland Road, and after a loan spell with Rotherham United he joined Barnsley. Again injuries meant that he didn't do himself justice, and he went on loan to Hull City before signing for Carlisle United. A qualified coach, he then had a spell at Mansfield before joining the Bluebirds in February 1995. He appeared in 12 games without scoring a goal as City were relegated from Division Two. After succumbing to a neck injury, he spent a month on loan to Merthyr Tydfil before finally playing for Chorley.

PECK Dennis Trevor

Full-back

Born: Llanelli, 25 May 1938.
Career: Llanelli. Cardiff City 1958. Worcester City.

■ Versatile defender Trevor Peck signed for Cardiff from Southern League Llanelli in February 1958 and soon became a useful acquisition to the playing staff. While on City's books, he did his National Service and so didn't play in a League game for two years – his first game after being a 1–0 win at Stoke in April 1960. Most of Peck's football was played for the reserves and his 42 League appearances were spread over six seasons. Peck left Ninian Park in the summer of 1965 to play non-League football for Worcester City.

PEMBREY Gordon Dennis

Outside-left/wing-half

Born: Cardiff, 10 October 1926.
Career: Cardiff Nomads. Norwich City 1947. Cardiff City 1948. Torquay United 1950. Charlton Athletic 1952. Swindon Town 1956.

■ Discovered playing for Cardiff Nomads, Gordon Pembrey was signed by Norwich City but made a solitary League appearance for the Canaries before being released and signing for his home-town club. Able to play at wing-half or outside-left, it was in the latter position that he played his only game for Cardiff in a 1–0 defeat of Plymouth Argyle in December 1949. He joined the exodus to Torquay United where he was a regular in the side before signing for Charlton Athletic. Most of his time at The Valley was spent in the Addicks reserve side before he left to end his career with Swindon Town.

PENNEY David Mark

Midfield

Born: Wakefield, 17 August 1964.
Career: Pontefract Colliery. Derby County 1985. Oxford United 1989. Swansea City (loan) 1991. Swansea City 1994. Cardiff City 1997. Doncaster Rovers.

FAW Invitation Cup finalist 1997–98.

■ Derby County gave midfielder David Penney his break into League Football, but his first-team opportunities were limited with the Rams, and in the summer of 1989 Oxford United paid £175,000 for him. He had made 129 appearances for the Manor Ground club when, following an earlier one-month loan period with Swansea, he joined the Vetch Field club on a permanent basis. Capable of scoring from long range, it was an ability that brought a new dimension to the Swans midfield. Appointed club captain, he ended the 1996–97 season as the club's leading scorer. Surprisingly, after scoring 26 goals in 144 games, he was allowed to leave and joined the Bluebirds, where on his arrival he was appointed captain. After an impressive 1997–98 campaign, Penney, a qualified FA coach, left Ninian Park to join Doncaster Rovers. Appointed manager in 2002, he led them out of the Conference to a successful League return, the first club in any Division to gain promotion in 2003–04 as champions of the Third Division.

PERKS Henry (Harry)

Outside-left

Born: Cardiff, 1912.
Career: Cardiff City 1933. Newport County 1934. Barry Town.

■ Local born winger Harry Perks spent just one season at Ninian Park – the re-election campaign of 1933–34 – where he found Alex Hutchinson in possession of the number-11 shirt for most of the time. Perks, whose only goal came in a 2–1 home defeat at the hands of Aldershot, moved on to Newport County for the following season before ending his playing days at Barry Town.

PERRETT Russell (Russ)

Central-defender

Born: Barton-on-Sea, 18 June 1973.
Career: Lymington. Portsmouth 1995. Cardiff City 1999. Luton Town 2001.

■ After being released by Portsmouth as a youngster in 1991, Russ Perrett rejoined the Fratton Park club for the start of the 1995–96 season, and though he was sent off in his second game he bounced back with a string of good performances. Forming a solid partnership with Andy Awford, the ball-playing central-defender was outstanding until injury cost him his place in the side. In the summer of 1999 he joined Cardiff for £10,000, but in his early days at Ninian Park he was hit by a series of relatively minor knocks, including a kick to the knee, which forced him to miss the run-in to the season. The 2000–01 season was even worse as injuries kept him out for virtually the entire campaign, at the end of which he moved to Luton. The Hatters took a bit of a gamble in signing him, but he made a full recovery to appear in almost every match in 2001–02 for the Kenilworth Road club. However, the last few seasons have seen this popular defender once again hampered by injuries.

PERRY Jason

Central-defender

Born: Caerphilly, 2 April 1970.
Career: Cardiff City 1987. Bristol Rovers

1997. Lincoln City 1998. Hull City 1998. Newport County.

Welsh Cup winner 1991–92, 1992–93. Division Three champion 1992–93. Welsh Cup finalist 1993–94.

■ Jason Perry began his League career with Cardiff City, making his Bluebirds debut in a goalless draw at home to

Exeter City in March 1987. But it was 1989–90 before he established himself as a first-team regular. After helping the club win the Third Division Championship in 1992–93, he hardly missed a game until 1995–96 when he suffered the worst injury crisis of his career. He bounced back the following season, missing very few games and helping the club reach the play-offs. His tigerish tacking and commanding presence were sorely missed when, in the summer of 1997, after almost 10 years and 344 first-team appearances, he was allowed to join Bristol Rovers. The all-action defender became a cult figure among Rovers fans, but suspensions ruined his run of appearances and he was eventually freed. He then had brief spells with Lincoln and Hull City, and, after turning down a move to Chester City, he returned to South Wales to play non-League football for Newport County.

PETHARD Frederick James (Freddie)

Full-back

Born: Glasgow, 7 October 1950.
Career: Glasgow Celtic. Cardiff City 1969. Torquay United 1979.

Welsh Cup winner 1973–74, 1975–76. Welsh Cup finalist 1974–75, 1976–77. Division Three runner-up 1975–76.

■ Released by Glasgow Celtic, Freddie Pethard made the long journey to Ninian Park, joining the Bluebirds in the summer of 1969. Able to play in both full-back berths, he was initially understudy to both David Carver and Gary Bell before winning a regular place in the side. Pethard played regularly for City throughout the seventies – except for 1975–76 when Clive Charles wore the number-three shirt. Pethard, who overcame a number of minor injuries during his 10 years with the club, left the Bluebirds to join Torquay United in August 1979, this following the signing of Colin Sullivan. Pethard was at Plainmoor for three seasons, clocking up another 105 League appearances before hanging up his boots.

PHILLIPS Joseph Roy

Full-back

Born: Cardiff, 8 July 1923.
Died: 1992.
Career: Cardiff Corries. Cardiff City 1942.

■ Originally with Cardiff Corries, full-back Joe Phillips came to Ninian Park during World War Two. When League football resumed in 1946–47, he found himself in the club's reserve side but did appear twice in City's first team during the course of that Third Division South Championship-winning campaign – his debut coming in a 2–2 draw against eventual runners-up Queen's Park Rangers, a game that attracted 44,010 to Ninian Park.

PHILLIPS Lee

Central-defender

Born: Aberdare, 18 March 1979.
Career: Cardiff City 1997. Barry Town 2000.

FAW Invitation Cup finalist 1997–98.

■ Lee Phillips came into the Cardiff side when Scott Young was unavailable, making his League debut in a 3–2 win at Hartlepool United in February 1997. He played twice more before going back to the reserves for further experience. Showing great composure for a youngster, his displays were quickly recognised by a call up to the Welsh Under-21 squad. Following the arrival of new manager Frank Burrows, Phillips was given further opportunities, playing in the last seven matches of 1997–98. Yet it was a frustrating season for him as he spent most of the time in the stands as Cardiff did not have a reserve team. Injuries then began to hamper his progress, and although he was named in the starting line-up against Wrexham in the FAW Premier Cup semi-final he was harshly sent off for two bookable offences. Given only a handful of chances the following season, he left the club in the summer of 2000 to play for Barry Town.

PHILLIPS Leighton

Central-defender/midfield

Born: Neath, 25 September 1949.

Career: Cardiff City 1967. Aston Villa 1974. Swansea City 1978. Charlton Athletic 1981. Exeter City 1983.

Welsh Cup winner 1970–71, 1972–73, 1973–74. Welsh Cup finalist 1971–72.

■ After winning Welsh Schoolboy international honours, Leighton Phillips joined the groundstaff of Cardiff City. He worked his way through the club's junior and reserve teams, making his League debut as a substitute in a 2–2 home draw against Rotherham United in January 1968. He scored with his first touch of the ball to level the scores after City had been 2–0 down. At Ninian Park, Phillips had plenty of opportunities to show his versatility, appearing as a striker, defender and in midfield, before succeeding Brian Harris in the role of sweeper. His performances led to him winning Welsh Under-21 and Under-23 caps before he won the first of 58 full caps against Czechoslovakia in 1971. In September 1974, having appeared in 216 first-team games for the Bluebirds, he became dissatisfied with Cardiff's lack of success and left to play for Aston Villa, who paid £80,000 for his services. Phillips went on to captain the club and help them win promotion to the First Division in his first season at Villa Park. He won a League Cup-winners' medal in 1977 as Villa beat Everton. A defender of real pace and determination, he made 175 League and Cup appearances for Villa before returning to South Wales in November 1978 to play for Swansea City. The Swans record signing at £70,000, he helped them win promotion to the Second Division in his first season at the Vetch and then into the top flight before later playing for Charlton Athletic and Exeter City.

PHILLISKIRK Anthony (Tony)

Forward

Born: Sunderland, 10 February 1965. Career: Sheffield United 1983. Rotherham United (loan) 1986. Oldham Athletic 1988. Preston North End 1989. Bolton Wanderers 1989. Peterborough United 1992. Burnley 1994. Carlisle United (loan) 1995. Cardiff City 1995. Macclesfield (loan) 1998.

■ A former England Schoolboy international, Tony Philliskirk started out with Sheffield United, his goals in the 1983–84 season helping the Blades to win promotion from the Third Division. Falling out of favour at Bramall Lane, he joined Oldham Athletic, but after just 10 appearances for the Latics he moved to Preston, where his stay was even shorter. In June 1989 he signed for Bolton Wanderers for £50,000 and formed a partnership with David Reeves that would give him the most prolific period of his career. He netted after just four minutes of his Bolton debut in a 2–0 win at Cardiff City! The club's regular penalty-taker, he topped the scoring charts in his three full seasons with the club, helping them reach the play-offs in 1990–91. The arrival of John McGinlay put pressure on Philliskirk, and after scoring 75 goals in 182 games he joined Peterborough United for £80,000. He scored 11 goals in their First Division campaign before signing for Burnley. There followed a loan spell with Carlisle United before Cardiff City paid £60,000 for his services in December 1995. At Ninian Park, he switched from the forward line to a central-defensive role, often playing as a sweeper. Having been a regular with the Bluebirds in 1996–97 when they reached the Third Division play-offs, he was mystified why he was not in the running for a first-team place the following season. Loaned out to Macclesfield Town, who had just come up from the Conference, he then began to look to his future in the game by taking refereeing examinations. Philliskirk is now assistant manager to Brian Talbot at Oldham Athletic.

PICKRELL Anthony David (Tony)

Outside-left

Born: Neath, 3 November 1942. Career: Cardiff City 1960.

■ Left-winger Tony Pickrell had a brief career with Cardiff City that was to end tragically. During the club's relegation season of 1961–62, Pickrell scored four times in 16 games, including a brace in an 8–3 defeat at Everton in the penultimate game of the campaign. Just

when it seemed as if he was going to make a big impact at Ninian Park, he contracted a chest illness that put an immediate end to his playing days. Pickrell later made a career in the world of art and design.

PIKE Christopher (Chris)

Forward

Born: Cardiff, 19 October 1961. Career: Maesteg. Barry Town. Fulham 1985. Cardiff City (loan) 1986. Cardiff City 1989. Hereford United 1993. Gillingham 1994.

Welsh Cup winner 1991–92, 1992–93. Division Three champion 1992–93.

■ Chris Pike played his early football in the Cardiff Combination League before playing Welsh League football, first for Maesteg and then Barry Town. After some impressive performances he was given his chance in the Football League by Fulham. He did well in his first season at Craven Cottage but then, after an injury, failed to regain his place. He joined his home-town team Cardiff on loan, but after a satisfactory spell at Ninian Park he rejoined Fulham as they were beset by injury problems. He later joined the Bluebirds on a permanent basis, becoming a much more prolific scorer than he had been with the Cottagers. In 1989–90, despite the club being relegated, he scored 18 goals in 41 League games – he also scored five goals in Cup games. He continued to find the net during his stay with Cardiff and in 1991–92 had his best season in terms of goals scored with 21 in 40 League

outings, including a hat-trick in a 5–0 home win over Wrexham. Having helped City win the Third Division Championship in 1992–93, he left for a spell with Hereford United before ending his League career with Gillingham.

PINXTON Albert Edward

Inside-right

Born: Shelton, 1912.
Career: Stoke City 1931. Stoke St Peters. Nantwich. Blackburn Rovers 1935. Cardiff City 1936. Torquay United 1937.

■ Inside-forward Albert Pinxton arrived at Ninian Park in a double deal with Les Talbot from Blackburn Rovers prior to the start of the 1936–37 season. One of seven newcomers to join Cardiff, he had originally been on Stoke's books

without playing in their first team, and though he started well, finding the net in early games against Bristol City and Southend United, he lacked consistency and moved on to Torquay United, where he made just a handful of appearances.

PIRIE Thomas S. (Tom)

Centre-half

Born: Aberdeen, 9 December 1900.
Career: Battlefield Juniors. Bathgate. Queen's Park. Manchester United 1923. Queen's Park. Aberdeen. Cardiff City 1926. Bristol Rovers 1928. Brighton & Hove Albion 1929.

■ A civil engineer by profession, Tom Pirie played his early football with Queen's Park before having a trial with Manchester United. Unable to impress the Old Trafford hierarchy, he joined Aberdeen and was a regular member of the Pittodrie club's side when Fred Stewart signed him for the Bluebirds in 1926. Normally a centre-half, he made his debut in a 2–0 defeat against Manchester United at centre-forward, but sadly his one and only season at Ninian Park was beset by injury and illness. He even spent time in a nursing home before he reappeared in the first team towards the end of the 1926–27 season. He then tried his luck with Bristol Rovers and later Brighton, but injury put an end to his unlucky career and he returned to Aberdeen to work for a firm of contractors.

PLATNAUER Nicholas Robert (Nicky)

Left-back/midfield

Born: Leicester, 10 June 1961.
Career: Bedford Town. Bristol Rovers 1982. Coventry City 1983. Birmingham City 1984. Reading (loan) 1986. Cardiff City 1986. Notts County 1989. Port Vale (loan) 1991. Leicester City 1991. Scunthorpe United 1993. Mansfield Town 1993. Lincoln City 1994. Bedworth United.

Division Four runner-up 1987–88.
Welsh Cup winner 1987–88.

■ Nicky Platnauer was working as a bank clerk when Bedford Town folded,

and he was surprisingly signed by Bristol Rovers. He impressed them so much that boss Bobby Gould took him to Coventry City when he became manager at Highfield Road. Platnauer proved a disappointment in the First Division, and Ron Saunders bought him to play wide on the left in Birmingham City's bid for promotion. Things didn't work out for him at St Andrew's, and after a loan spell at Reading he joined Cardiff City in September 1986. Having made his debut in a 1–1 draw at Halifax, Platnauer went on to be a virtual ever present for the club over the next three seasons, helping City win promotion to the Third Division and the Welsh Cup in 1987–88. After leaving Cardiff, he played for Notts County before joining Port Vale on loan. He later had spells with Leicester, Scunthorpe, Mansfield and Lincoln before ending his playing days with non-League Bedworth United.

PLATT James Archibald (Jim)

Goalkeeper

Born: Ballymoney, Northern Ireland, 26 January 1952.
Career: Ballymena. Middlesbrough 1970. Hartlepool United (loan) 1978. Cardiff City (loan) 1978. Ballymena.

■ Northern Ireland international goalkeeper Jim Platt began his career with Ballymena, where his form led to Liverpool offering him a trial, but they had just signed Ray Clemence from Scunthorpe and didn't offer Platt terms. He returned to Ballymena where he won Irish amateur caps and an Irish FA Cup runners'-up medal before joining

Middlesbrough in 1970. In 12 seasons at Ayresome Park Platt missed very few games. In 1973–74, when 'Boro won the Second Division Championship, he was in tremendous form, conceding just 28 goals in 40 appearances. His form led to him winning the first of 23 caps for his country. Midway through the 1978–79 season Platt found himself out of favour following a well publicised row with Jack Charlton and was loaned out to both Hartlepool and Cardiff City. At Ninian Park, Platt was never on the winning side in the four games he played and returned to Teeside where he won back his first-team place. He went on to play in 481 games for 'Boro before returning to Ireland to become player-manager of Ballymena. He later returned to the North East to become manager of Darlington and then Gateshead.

PLUMLEY Gary Edward

Goalkeeper

Born: Birmingham, 24 March 1956.
Career: Leicester City 1974. Newport County 1976. Happy Valley (Hong Kong) 1982. Hereford United 1982. Newport County 1982. Happy Valley (Hong Kong) 1983. Cardiff City 1983. Newport County

(loan) 1984. Ebbw Vale 1985. Newport County 1987.

■ It was while he was an apprentice with Leicester City that goalkeeper Gary Plumley was spotted by Jimmy Scoular, then managing Newport County. With Plumley in goal, County improved beyond all recognition, and in 1979–80 they won promotion to the Third Division and the Welsh Cup. After a spell in Hong Kong with Happy Valley, he joined Hereford United before going into semi-retirement and opening a wine bar in Caerleon. In the summer of 1983 he accepted Len Ashurst's offer of becoming understudy to Andy Dibble but only stayed for two seasons, the latter of which saw City relegated. Plumley, who while on loan with Newport County took his total of League appearances for the Somerton Park club to 187, then joined Welsh League side Ebbw Vale. In March 1987 he answered Watford's distress call for a 'keeper to play in their FA Cup semi-final against Spurs at Villa Park. The fairytale ended there as Spurs won 4–1, and Plumley returned to the Welsh League.

POLAND George

Goalkeeper

Born: Penarth, 21 September 1913.
Died: 1988.
Career: Cardiff City 1935. Wrexham 1938. Liverpool 1939. Cardiff City 1946.

■ When he began his career, George Poland was a goalscoring centre-forward with Penarth Mission before Swindon Town manager Ted Vizard invited him to the County Ground to play as a left-winger. Unable to settle, he joined Cardiff City, who had earlier rejected him as an outfield player. George Poland was thought of as the club's best goalkeeper since Tom Farquharson and, rather unusually, was selected to make his debut at Norwich City after conceding seven goals in a reserve match! On leaving Ninian Park he joined Wrexham, where he did so well that at the end of his first season he was capped by Wales. The watching Liverpool scouts at the Racecourse saw enough for the Anfield club to sign him. During the war he served with the Royal Welch Guards and 'guested' for Brentford. It was during a 'guest' appearance for Leeds United in 1943 that Poland broke his arm. The injury troubled him thereafter, and after rejoining City he managed just two post-war League appearances before being displaced by Danny Canning.

POLLARD Robert (Bob)

Full-back/right-half

Born: Platt Bridge, 25 August 1899.
Career: Plank Lane. Exeter City 1920. Queen's Park Rangers 1929. Cardiff City 1932. St Etienne (France).

■ Full-back Bob Pollard entered the Football League with Exeter City in 1920–21 and played on a regular basis for the Grecians for nine seasons. During that time he amassed 246 League appearances, finding the net on just one occasion. By the time he joined Queen's Park Rangers in 1929, Pollard had gained a reputation for being one of the Third Division South's outstanding defenders. He spent three seasons at Loftus Road before, in June 1932, Cardiff signed the veteran defender. Although he appeared regularly in the City side during the 1932–33 season, he could not shore up a leaky defence that conceded 99 goals! Released at the end of the season, he went to France to play for St Etienne.

POLYCARPOU Andrew (Andy)

Midfield

Born: Islington, 15 August 1958.
Career: Southend United 1976. Cambridge United 1981. Cardiff City 1982.

■ Andy Polycarpou started out with Southend United, and in his five years at Roots Hall he helped the Shrimpers win promotion to the Third Division in 1977–78 and the Fourth Division Championship in 1980–81, this after they had been relegated the previous season. In the close season of 1981 he was transferred to Cambridge United, but, hampered by injuries, he opted for a move to Ninian Park in April 1982. Unable to prevent the Bluebirds from being relegated, he left to continue his career in Greece.

PONTIN Keith

Central-defender

Born: Pontyclun, 14 June 1956.
Career: Cardiff City 1974. Merthyr Tydfil. Barry Town.

Welsh Cup finalist 1976–77, 1981–82.

■ A one club man, central-defender Keith Pontin worked his way up through the ranks before making his debut in a 2–0 win for the Bluebirds at Charlton Athletic on the opening day of the 1976–77 season. But following the arrival of Paul Went from Portsmouth, he went back to playing reserve-team football. He was recalled to Cardiff's first team in September 1977 after Went was moved into the attack. Over the next four seasons Pontin missed very few matches and his form was such that he won two full caps for Wales – the first in a 4–1 defeat of England. During the 1981–82 season, when City were relegated from the Second Division, Keith Pontin played in 40 matches, which was more than anyone else. One of Cardiff's most experienced players at that time, he left Ninian Park during the early part of the following promotion-winning season after an argument with manager Len Ashurst. Pontin, who had played in 231 first-team matches for the Bluebirds, was aged just 26 when he joined Merthyr Tydfil in the Southern League. He later signed for Barry Town, playing out his career with the successful Welsh League club.

POSTIN Eli L.

Inside-right/outside-right

Born: Dudley, 3 June 1905.
Died: 1991.
Career: Cradley Heath. West Bromwich Albion 1931. Dudley Town. Cardiff City 1933. Bristol Rovers 1934. Wrexham 1935. Brierley Hill Alliance.

■ Having learned his footballing trade in the West Midlands with Cradley Heath, Eli Postin joined West Bromwich Albion. Unable to break into the club's League side, he joined Cardiff City in the summer of 1933. Despite the following disastrous season, Postin was the Bluebirds leading scorer with 13 goals from 33 games, but it was still not enough for him to be retained by City,

and he moved on to Bristol Rovers. He made little impression in two seasons at Eastville and moved on to Wrexham prior to ending his playing days with non-League Brierley Hill Alliance.

POWELL Clifford George (Cliff)

Defender

Born: Watford, 21 February 1968.
Career: Watford 1986. Hereford United (loan) 1987. Sheffield United 1988. Doncaster Rovers (loan) 1989. Cardiff City (loan) 1989.

■ Watford-born defender Cliff Powell was unable to break into his home-town club's side, so, following a loan spell with Hereford United, he joined Sheffield United. After a season at Bramall Lane, in which he was in and out of the Blades side, he had loan spells with Doncaster Rovers and Cardiff City, though his only appearance for the Bluebirds was as a substitute for Jon Morgan in a 3–1 home win over Bury in November 1989.

POWELL David

Central-defender

Born: Afon Conwy, 15 October 1944.
Career: Gwydyn Rovers. Wrexham 1963. Sheffield United 1968. Cardiff City 1972.

Welsh Cup winner 1972–73.

■ Central-defender Dave Powell began his playing career with Gwydyn Rovers, and during his spell at the club he was capped by Wales at Youth level. In January 1962 Wrexham took him on their groundstaff, and, after working his way up through the juniors and reserves, he was given his first-team debut while still an amateur. Over the next couple of seasons it became clear that the strong-tackling defender was destined for greater things. Although his only club honour with the Robins was a Welsh Cup runners'-up medal, he gained four Under-23 caps and made his full international debut against West Germany at Ninian Park in May 1968. In September of that year he signed for Sheffield United, where in 1970–71 he was a member of the Blades team that won promotion to the First Division.

During the early part of the 1972–73 season, the Bluebirds were in deep trouble, so manager Jimmy Scoular set up a deal that brought Dave Powell and Gil Reece to Ninian Park and took Alan Warboys to Bramall Lane. Scoring his only goal for the club at Swindon Town in March 1975, he suffered from a series of niggling injuries throughout his two seasons' stay. Sadly he had to finish his career prematurely, and he left the club to join the South Wales Police, working at their training centre at Bridgend.

PRESCOTT James R.

Winger

Born: Waterloo, Lancashire, 1914.
Career: Everton 1932. Southport 1933. Marine. Liverpool 1935. Cardiff City 1936. Hull City 1939. Plymouth Argyle 1945.

■ James Prescott played all his early football in his native North West with Everton, Southport and Liverpool but never made it into any of these club's League sides. Prescott, who also played non-League football for Marine, joined Cardiff City in 1936, and though he stayed for three seasons at Ninian Park, he never established himself as a first-team regular. Nicknamed 'Pluto', James Prescott was also deaf, and the Cardiff crowd could be very cruel to a player who often followed a brilliant move by falling over himself! On leaving Cardiff he had spells, either side of the war, with Hull City and Plymouth Argyle without playing in their League sides.

PRICE Allen Douglas

Defender

Born: Gelligaer, 24 March 1968.
Career: Newport County. Cardiff City 1985.

■ Welsh Youth international defender Allen Price was on the books of Newport County as a junior but was unable to force his way into the Somerton Park club's League side, so he joined the Bluebirds. Some steady performances in the club's reserve side saw him play against Wigan and Doncaster in 1985–86 – both victories for City – but he was still released at the end of the season.

PRICE Cecil

Outside-left

*Born: Cardiff, 2 December 1919.
Career: Cardiff City 1948. Bradford City
1949.*

■ Winger Cecil Price played most of his
football for the Bluebirds in either the
Welsh League or Football Combination
and his only appearance in the City first
team came in a 3–1 defeat at West Ham
United in October 1948. At the end of
the season, Price left Ninian Park and
joined Bradford City, making seven
appearances for the Valley Parade club
before drifting into local football.

PRIOR Spencer Justin

Central-defender

*Born: Southend, 22 April 1971.
Career: Southend United 1989. Norwich
City 1993. Leicester City 1996. Derby
County 1998. Manchester City 2000.
Cardiff City 2001.*

**FAW Premier Cup winner 2001–02.
Division Two promotion 2002–03.**

■ Central-defender Spencer Prior was
17 when he made his League debut for
his home-town team Southend United
against Gillingham in February 1989, a
season in which the Shrimpers were
relegated. Over the next four seasons
Prior helped Southend win two
consecutive promotions, but in the
summer of 1993, having played in 156
games, he joined Norwich City for
£200,000. Initially he struggled to find
his feet, but in 1995–96 was voted the
Canaries Player of the Year. Surprisingly
allowed to join Leicester City for
£600,000, he proved a bargain buy for
Martin O'Neill's side and helped them
win the 1997 Coca-Cola Cup. He then
moved on to Derby County, the Rams
paying £700,000 for his services, and
though he hardly missed a game he was
allowed to move to Manchester City in
March 2000. Though he helped the then
Maine Road club win promotion to the
Premiership, their was a surplus of
central-defenders at the club, and he
was soon on the move again, this time
to Cardiff City for £650,000. Providing
some experience in the club's back four,
he began to struggle for form but
eventually came good and was

outstanding in the 14-match unbeaten
run that took City through to the
Second Division play-offs. He continued
to be a regular in the City side, winning
the ball in the air, getting in tackles and
clearing the ball out of the danger area.
However, in 2003–04 he was only on the
fringes of the Cardiff team and, on
being out of contract, was released by
the Bluebirds.

PUGH Reginald (Reg)

Outside-right

*Born: Aberaman, 28 July 1917.
Career: Aberaman Athletic. Cardiff City
1934.*

Welsh Cup finalist 1938–39.

■ Winger Reg Pugh was, at 17, one of
the club's youngest debutants when he
played for the Bluebirds in a 3–1 win at
Watford in October 1934. He soon
established himself in the City side, and
in 1935–36, when the club finished 20th
in the Third Division South, he was ever
present. Though not a prolific scorer, he
netted five goals in the first seven
matches of the following season and
went on to score 27 goals in 182 games
up until the outbreak of World War
Two. In the last League season prior to
the hostilities Pugh had lost his place to
new signings Albert Rhodes and Tom
Rickards but soon bounced back to such
an effect that both wingers were allowed
to leave Ninian Park! He was only 23 at
the outbreak of war, and he played at
full-back in some of the early wartime
games, then served in Burma with the
South Wales Borderers.

PURSE Darren John

Defender

*Born: Stepney, 14 February 1977.
Career: Leyton Orient 1994. Oxford
United 1996. Birmingham City 1998.
West Bromwich Albion 2004. Cardiff City
2005.*

■ After beginning his career with
Leyton Orient, Darren Purse, at the age
of only 18, was appointed the Brisbane
Road club's captain – at the time the
youngest skipper in the Football
League. Outstanding at the heart of the
Orient defence, although he did play in
a few games up front, he left Orient in
July 1996 to sign for Oxford United.
His impressive form for Oxford led to
him being selected for the Nationwide
squad against the Italian League. His
outstanding form in the early part of
the 1997–98 season led to Birmingham
City paying £800,000 for his services.
His form for the St Andrew's club saw
him capped by England at Under-21
level, playing twice in the Toulon
tournament. He continued to develop
with the Midlands club and in
1999–2000 was voted Birmingham's
Young Player of the Year. He grew in
stature to become an inspirational
figure in the Blues defence. Entrusted
with the vital injury-time penalty in
the Worthington Cup Final against
Liverpool, he kept his nerve to fire the
ball home and then followed up with
another penalty in the shoot out
Having been instrumental in helping
Birmingham reach the play-offs, he
was named as the Blues Player of the
Year. Continuing to impress, he formed
a formidable central-defensive
partnership with Kenny Cunningham
until losing his place to Matthew
Upson. Having played in 200 games for
Birmingham, he signed for
Premiership newcomers West
Bromwich Albion in the summer of
2004. A regular in the side for the first
half of the season, he then dropped out
of contention and was allowed to join
the Bluebirds in the close season of
2005. Appointed club captain, he
missed very few games during his first
season at Ninian Park and scored a
number of vital goals.

RAINFORD John William

Inside-forward

Born: Camden, 11 December 1930.
Career: Crystal Palace 1949. Cardiff City
1953. Brentford 1953.

■ Johnny Rainford began his career at
Crystal Palace in 1948, graduating to the
club's League side a year later. A
scheming inside-forward, he had four
seasons at Selhurst Park before joining
Cardiff City in the summer of 1953. He

played in the opening three games of
the 1953–54 season, but despite scoring
on his home debut as Aston Villa were
beaten 2–1 he found life in the First
Division difficult. Within a matter of
weeks Rainford had returned to London
to play for Brentford, where he enjoyed
a long and successful career, scoring 42
goals in 299 games and helping the Bees
finish runners-up in the 1957–58 Third
Division South Championship.

RAMSEY Paul Christopher

Midfield/right-back

Born: Derry, Northern Ireland, 3
September 1962.
Career: Leicester City 1980. Cardiff City
1991. St Johnstone. Cardiff City (loan)
1994. Telford United. Torquay United
1995.

Welsh Cup winner 1991–92, 1992–93.
Division Three champion 1992–93.

■ Northern Ireland international Paul
Ramsey began his Football League
career with Leicester City, though
injuries and occasional loss of form left
him sidelined from both domestic and
international action. He was also
utilised extensively as a full-back
during the club's Second Division days,
helping the Foxes win promotion in
1982–83. Following the arrival of
David Pleat as Leicester manager,
Ramsey was handed the team
captaincy, but when Pleat was replaced
as boss by Brian Little Ramsey was no
longer assured of first-team football.
Having appeared in 322 games for
them, he left Leicester to join his one
time Foxes reserve coach Eddie May at
Cardiff. As well as winning two Welsh
Cup medals, Ramsey captained the
Bluebirds to the Championship of the
'new' Third Division. He then left to
play for St Johnstone but was unable to
settle. He would have rejoined Cardiff
then, but the Football League invoked a
rule forbidding a transfer back within
12 months. Rules tripped him up again
when, a further year on, he rejoined
the Bluebirds on loan, as he was
ineligible to turn out against Ebbw Vale

in the Welsh Cup, and his team were
unceremoniously ejected from the
1994–95 competition – though legal
arguments eventually won them a
reinstatement!

RANKMORE Frank Edward John

Centre-half

Born: Cardiff, 21 July 1939.
Career: Cardiff Corries. Cardiff City
1957. Peterborough United 1963.
Northampton Town 1968.

■ Signed by Cardiff City from local
club Cardiff Corinthians, centre-half
Frank Rankmore found himself mainly
in the Bluebirds reserve side at Ninian
Park, and at the end of the 1959–60
season he was placed on the transfer list.
However, when the club's regular

centre-half Danny Malloy left the
bluebirds, Rankmore was re-signed and
came off the transfer list. In his first full
season, in which he made 37 League
appearances, Cardiff were relegated to
the Second Division. He was a
powerfully-built defender, full of
determination and enthusiasm.
Rankmore lost his place when John
Charles arrived at Ninian Park and was
sold to Peterborough United for

£10,000. Rankmore was at home in the lower Divisions and in 1966 gained a full international cap when he played against Chile on Wales's tour of South America. In June 1968 he moved to Northampton Town where he became a great crowd favourite, but in 1971 an injury led to his retirement and probably cost the Cobblers promotion to the Third Division.

RATCLIFFE Kevin

Central-defender

Born: Deeside, 12 November 1960.
Career: Everton 1978. Dundee. Everton 1992. Cardiff City 1993. Nottingham Forest 1993. Derby County 1994. Chester City 1994.

Division Three champion 1992–93.

■ The most successful captain in Everton's history, he also captained Wales in many of his 59 internationals. His role in the Everton side, whose game was built on a very sound defensive system, was crucial. The Blues often played a tight and rigid offside game, but if a striker did break through Ratcliffe's speed was such that the danger was snuffed out immediately. In May 1984, after Watford had been beaten 2–0, at the age of 23, Ratcliffe became the youngest man since Bobby Moore 20 years earlier to receive the FA Cup. Within the next year he had led Everton forward to pick up the Charity Shield, the League Championship and the European Cup-Winners' Cup in Rotterdam. Thereafter, he skippered Everton to the runners-up spot in both the League and FA Cup in 1985–86 and to another League title in 1986–87. Despite losing some of his astonishing speed, he continued to retain the style and consistency that made him one of the world's classiest defenders. He had played in 461 League and Cup games when, after losing his place to Martin Keown, he joined Cardiff City in January 1993. He had an outstanding debut, netting an 83rd-minute winner in a 2–1 defeat of Carlisle United at Brunton Park. After that he kept his place in the side for the remainder of the season as the Bluebirds won the Third Division Championship. He later became player-manager of Chester City

before taking charge of Shrewsbury Town, but he parted company with the Gay Meadow club in 2003 after they had lost their League status.

REDWOOD Douglas James (Doug)

Outside-left

Born: Ebbw Vale, 1918.
Career: Ebbw Vale. Cardiff City 1935. Walsall 1937. Rochdale 1939.

■ The Bluebirds had high hopes for left-winger Doug Redwood when they signed him from Welsh League side Ebbw Vale in 1935. But unfortunately, like a number of players who joined the club around this time, the early promise did not develop, and after two seasons at Ninian Park he moved on to Walsall. Though not an automatic in the Saddlers side, he did appear much more regularly than he had with City, but just prior to the outbreak of World War Two he had signed for Rochdale.

REECE Gilbert Ivor (Gil)

Winger

Born: Cardiff, 2 July 1942.
Died: 20 December 2003.
Career: Cardiff City 1961. Ton Pentre (loan). Pembroke Borough. Newport County 1963. Sheffield United 1965. Cardiff City 1972. Swansea City 1976.

Welsh Cup winner 1972–73, 1973–74, 1975–76. Welsh Cup finalist 1974–75 Division Three runner-up 1975–76.

■ Gil Reece joined Cardiff City as a part-timer in May 1961 while continuing his trade as a plumber. He

graduated to the club's reserve side and had a loan spell with Welsh League side Ton Pentre. Towards the end of the 1962–63 season he was released and left to see out the campaign with Pembroke Borough. After some useful displays, he was offered the chance to join Newport County, and in 1964–65 he became one of their most consistent goalscorers. At the end of that season he joined Sheffield United for £10,000, soon winning the first of 29 Welsh caps against England at Ninian Park. Despite breaking a leg while with the Blades, he scored 58 goals in 210 appearances for the Bramall Lane club before leaving to rejoin Cardiff City in September 1972. He became club captain and played in a variety of roles for the Bluebirds. In his first season he scored a hat-trick in a 5–0 Welsh Cup Final second leg win over Bangor City. He repeated the feat the following season when he scored the only goal of the Welsh Cup Final second leg against Stourbridge. Although the club were relegated in 1974–75, Reece was top scorer with nine goals. The following season he helped the Bluebirds win promotion to the Second Division at the first attempt and won his third Welsh Cup medal. He scored 35 goals in 114 games for City before ending his career with a short spell at Swansea.

REED Ebor

Centre-half/left-half

Born: Spennymoor, 30 November 1899.
Died: 1971.
Career: Newcastle United 1924. Cardiff City 1925. Nottingham Forest 1926. Rotherham United 1927. Derry City.

■ Ebor Reed had been on Newcastle United's books without breaking into the Magpies League side prior to signing for Cardiff in 1925. Due to the wealth of talent in his position already at the club, Reed found his first-team appearances were limited. In 1926 he signed for Nottingham Forest but once again struggled to win a regular place, and it was only when he moved to Rotherham United that he played on a regular basis. Reed later crossed the water to end his playing days with Derry City.

REES Melvyn John (Mel)

Goalkeeper

Born: Cardiff, 25 January 1967.
Died: 1993.
Career: Cardiff City 1984. Watford 1987. Crewe Alexandra (loan) 1989. Leyton Orient (loan) 1990. West Bromwich Albion 1990. Sheffield United 1992.

■ One of the first youngsters to be signed by Cardiff City on a YTS scheme, goalkeeper Mel Rees found himself pitched into a Second Division match before he was ready and had a traumatic experience as the Bluebirds went down 4–2 at home to Brighton. He didn't make another League appearance for a year, and in nine games at the start of the 1985–86 season eight ended in defeat! A wrist injury sidelined him for another year, and with Graham Moseley now between the posts Rees joined First Division Watford for £60,000. After three years understudying Tony Coton, he looked set for a run in the Hornets first team until superseded by David James. While with Watford, Rees had loan spells with Crewe and Leyton Orient before joining West Bromwich Albion. Before he was 21 he'd played in all four Divisions of the Football League, but after later joining Sheffield United and having fought off one attack of cancer he succumbed to a recurrence at the age of 26.

REES Nigel Richard

Winger

Born: Bridgend, 11 July 1953.
Career: Cardiff City 1970. Bridgend.

■ A member of Cardiff City's successful youth side that reached the FA Youth Cup Final in 1971 and a Welsh Youth international, Nigel Rees looked to have the world at his feet when he made his City debut as a 17-year-old in a 4–0 defeat of Sheffield Wednesday. It was Nigel Rees who provided the centre for Brian Clark's header to beat Real Madrid 1–0 in that epic European Cup-Winners' Cup quarter-final tie in that 1970–71 season. However, as Cardiff struggled the following season Rees lost his way and was eventually released. He played for many years at Bridgend and even came back to Ninian Park for a trial when Jimmy Andrews was manager, but nothing ever came of it.

REES William (Billy)

Inside-forward

Born: Blaengarw, 10 March 1924.
Died: 27 July 1996.
Career: Caernarvon Rovers. Cardiff City 1944. Tottenham Hotspur 1949. Leyton Orient 1950. Headington United. Kettering Town.

Division Three South champion 1946–47.

■ Billy Rees, a coal miner for over seven years, was playing for Caernarvon Rovers when he was spotted by Cardiff

City manager Cyril Spiers. Principally an inside-forward, he turned out regularly for the Bluebirds during the war years, scoring 74 goals in 83 games and playing for Wales against England in a wartime international in May 1945. Rees was a regular member of the Cardiff side that won the Third Division South Championship in 1946–47, scoring 16 goals in 35 games. He was the club's top scorer the following season with 11 goals, but in the summer of 1949 he left Ninian Park to join Tottenham Hotspur. Just before he left the Bluebirds he won the first of four Welsh caps against Northern Ireland. Early on at White Hart Lane he suffered a number of minor injuries and this, coupled with a loss of form, restricted his first-team appearances. Spurs recouped their outlay in 1950 when he was allowed to join Leyton Orient for £14,500. At Brisbane Road he netted 66 goals in 198 games, before entering non-League circles with Headington United and Kettering Town. He later worked as a plant operator and then for a pharmaceutical company in Bridgend.

REID George Hull (Paddy)

Forward

Born: 16 January 1896.
Career: Distillery. Blackpool 1920.

Walsall 1921. Cardiff City 1922. Fulham 1923. Stockport County 1924. Rotherham County 1924. Mid-Rhondda United.

■ Northern Ireland international forward 'Paddy' Reid was a much-travelled player who began his League career with Blackpool after joining the Seasiders from Distillery. However, it was only when he moved to Walsall in 1921 that his talent for scoring goals emerged. He was the Saddlers leading scorer in 1921–22 with 22 goals in 34 games and had scored nine in 13 games the following season when, in December 1922, he signed for Cardiff City. Although Reid scored on his Cardiff debut, the Bluebirds were beaten 5–1 by Manchester City, and though he played well when selected he eventually lost his place to Len Davies. He then had a brief spell with Fulham before playing for both Stockport and Rotherham County. Reid later returned to South Wales to finish his career with Mid-Rhondda United.

REYNOLDS Arthur Brayley

Centre-forward

Born: Blackwood, 30 May 1935.
Career: Lovells Athletic. Cardiff City 1956. Swansea City 1959. Worcester City.

■ Brayley Reynolds came to Cardiff City's attention when playing for Lovells Athletic in the Southern League, and after some impressive displays in City's reserve side he made his League debut in a 4–1 defeat of Leeds United in October1956. Though on the smallish

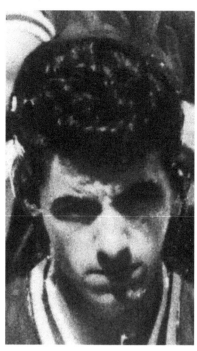

side for a centre-forward, he scored 15 goals in 57 League and Cup games, but his three years with the club were littered with a series of injuries. In May 1959 he signed for Swansea, and in his first season at the Vetch he scored 16 goals in 37 games. However, his best season in terms of goals scored for the Swans was 1961–62, when he found the net 18 times in 33 matches. Included in this total was a hat-trick in a 5–1 defeat of Plymouth Argyle. He went on to score 57 goals in 151 League games for the Swans before leaving to play non-League football for Worcester City.

RHODES Albert (Arthur)

Inside-right/outside-right

Born: Devon.
Career: Stockport County 1936. Bournemouth 1937. Torquay United 1938. Cardiff City 1938.

■ Disappointed not to make the grade with Stockport County, Arthur Rhodes moved south to Bournemouth, but despite scoring three goals in six games he was allowed to move to Torquay United. In his first season at Plainmoor Rhodes had an outstanding game against the Bluebirds in December 1938, and within a matter of days City manager Bill Jennings had secured his services. Rhodes went straight into the

Cardiff team ahead of Reggie Pugh and Tom Rickards, but he was dropped after a handful of games and released at the end of the season.

RICHARDS Leonard George (Len)

Left-back

Born: Barry, 13 April 1911.
Died: 1985.
Career: Tottenham Hotspur 1931. Cardiff City 1932. Dundalk. Newport County 1938.

■ Len Richards joined Cardiff from Spurs, but the young amateur could not have had a worse debut as, along with Bob Macaulay and John Mellor, he was part of the Bluebirds side that were beaten 8–1 at Luton Town in October 1932. On leaving Ninian Park in the close season, he played for Irish club Dundalk before returning to South Wales to play for Newport County. The tough-tackling left-back made 33 League appearances for the Ironsides before the outbreak of World War Two curtailed his career.

RICHARDS Percy

Outside-left

Born: Merthyr Tydfil, 1907.
Career: Merthyr Vale. Cardiff City 1926. Chesterfield 1927. Tranmere Rovers 1928. Newport County 1929. Merthyr Town. Leicester City 1930. Coventry City 1932. Bath City. Brierley Hill Alliance. Hereford United.

■ Recruited from local football in Merthyr Vale, left-winger Percy Richards replaced George McLachlan – one of a number of players to lose their place after a 5–0 defeat at Newcastle in December 1926. He appeared in just a handful of games before the experienced McLachlan was restored to the Bluebirds side. Richards left Ninian Park in 1927 to join Chesterfield, but after failing to break into their League side he had brief spells with Tranmere and Newport before finding himself back in the Welsh League with Merthyr. His hard-up club visited Filbert Street, the then home of Leicester City, explicitly as a 'shop window' for their saleable talent, and Richards was offered another chance in the top flight before later ending his first-team career with Coventry City. He then had spells at a number of non-League clubs including Bath City, Brierley Hill Alliance and Hereford United.

RICHARDS Stanley Verdun

Centre-forward

Born: Cardiff, 21 January 1917.
Died: 1987.
Career: Tufnell Park. Cardiff City 1946. Swansea Town 1948.

Division Three South champions 1946–47.

■ Although he was born in Cardiff, Stan Richards played his early football in London with Tufnell Park before returning to South Wales to play for the Bluebirds. He scored on his Football League debut in a 2–1 defeat at Norwich City, the first of 30 League goals in that 1946–47 season. His total, which included a hat-trick in a 6–1 home win over the Canaries on 28 December 1946, was a club record for the most League goals by an individual in a season, until 2002–03 when it was beaten by Rob Earnshaw. He was a great favourite with the Cardiff crowd, who would often chant 'Open the score Richards and nod one in', illustrating the impact he had made in such a short space of time. Surprisingly, he won only one Welsh cap, hearing about his selection for the game against England in November 1946 in a telephone call to a Cardiff cinema. When he arrived at Maine Road he found that in a rush to pack his kit he had forgotten his boots! In 1947–48 he suffered a spate of niggling injuries an,d having scored 40 goals in just 57 League games, he was allowed to join his former manager Billy McCandless at Swansea. Although still experiencing problems with his knee, Richards made a magnificent contribution to Swansea's Third Division South Championship-winning season of 1948–49, scoring 26 goals in 32 games, including all the goals in a 4–0 defeat of Swindon Town. Despite periods when his knees were so bad that he couldn't even train, Richards scored 35 goals in 65 games for the Swans before being forced to retire.

RICHARDSON Nicholas John (Nick)

Midfield

Born: Halifax, 11 April 1967.
Career: Emley. Halifax Town 1988. Cardiff City 1992. Wrexham (loan) 1994. Chester City (loan) 1994. Bury 1995. Chester City 1995. York City 2001. Harrogate Town.

Division Three champion 1992–93. Welsh Cup winner 1992–93. Welsh Cup finalist 1993–94.

■ Having played non-League football for Emley, midfielder Nick Richardson joined Halifax Town and was a regular for three and a half seasons at The Shay, scoring 21 goals in 120 games before being transferred to Cardiff City for £35,000. In 1992–93, his first season with the Bluebirds, he won a Third Division Championship medal and helped City win the Welsh Cup, beating Rhyl 5–0 in the Final. Injuries and a loss of form over the next couple of seasons saw him have loan spells with Wrexham and Chester City before joining Bury in the summer of 1995. Having made just six appearances for the Shakers in a month, he left Gigg Lane to join Chester City. In his second season with the Cestrians, he suffered an horrendous knee injury and had to undergo a lengthy rehabilitation programme. After battling to win back his first-team place, he was voted the club's Player of the Year in 1997–98. He went on to play in 200 games, until the club lost its League status, and then joined York City before playing non-League football for Harrogate Town.

RICKARDS Charles Thomas (Tom 'Tex')

Inside-right/outside-right

Born: Giltbrook, 19 February 1915.
Died: 1980.
Career: Johnson and Barnes. Notts County 1932. Cardiff City 1938. Scunthorpe United.

■ A regular for Notts County where he scored 22 goals in 110 games, he joined the Bluebirds in the summer of 1938 amid much publicity as he was challenging local hero Reggie Pugh for

the right-wing position, which he had held for four years. After playing some games at inside-right, Rickards finally dislodged Pugh, but by the end of the 1938–39 season he too was out of the side and on his way to Scunthorpe. World War Two curtailed his first-class career, though during the hostilities he 'guested' for Leicester City – netting a hat-trick against Port Vale – Notts County, Crewe, Stockport County, Derby County and Chesterfield.

RICKETTS Michael Barrington

Forward

Born: Birmingham, 4 December 1978.
Career: Walsall 1996. Bolton Wanderers 2000. Middlesbrough 2003. Leeds United 2004. Stoke City (loan) 2005. Cardiff City (loan) 2005. Burnley (loan) 2006.

■ Michael Ricketts made a sensational entrance onto the Football League stage when, in Walsall's final game of the 1995–96 season, he calmly chipped the Brighton 'keeper within three minutes of coming on as a substitute. Possessing an excellent football brain and good feet, coupled with aerial ability, Ricketts soon made the grade with the Saddlers, and though injuries hampered his progress he was Walsall's leading scorer in 1999–2000. Unsettled at the Bescot Stadium, he left to join Bolton Wanderers in July 2000, the Trotters paying £500,000 for his services. Ricketts scored on his Bolton debut and continued to find the net for the remainder of the campaign, finishing with 24 goals in all competitions. After the Wanderers won promotion to the top flight via the play-offs, he made an immediate impression on the Premiership stage, scoring some fantastic goals. His form led to him winning full international honours for England against Holland, but after that the goals dried up and he went almost a year before scoring again from open play. Hoping to resurrect his goalscoring touch, he joined Middlesbrough in a £3.5 million deal, but things didn't work out for him at the Riverside and he joined Leeds United on a free transfer. Struggling with the pace of the game at Elland Road, he had a spell on loan with

Stoke before arriving at Ninian Park on a four-month loan deal in the early stages of the 2005–06 season. Ricketts impressed and scored some vital goals, including the only one of the game against high-flying Crystal Palace. He scored three in five games during his stay with the club but later returned to Elland Road before joining Burnley, also on loan.

RILEY Harold (Harry)

Inside-forward

Born: Hollinwood, 22 November 1909.
Died: 1982.
Career: Altrincham. Hurst. Birmingham 1928. Ashton National. Accrington Stanley 1930. Lincoln City 1931. Notts County 1933. Cardiff City 1934. Northampton Town 1936. Exeter City 1938. Ruston Bucyrus.

■ Having started his career with Altrincham and then Hurst, he moved into League football with Birmingham where, surprisingly, they played the inside-forward link man on the right-wing. It was an odd choice as Riley was naturally left-footed. On leaving St Andrew's he had a brief spell with Ashton National before signing for Accrington Stanley. He scored 18 goals in 32 games for the Lancashire club before joining Lincoln City, where he proved to be a quite prolific goalscorer with 25 in 57 outings. Following a short spell with Notts County, Riley arrived at Ninian Park in the summer of 1934 and was one of eight debutants in a rebuilt Cardiff City team after re-election. He scored on his debut as the Bluebirds beat Charlton Athletic 2–1. A regular in the City side for two seasons, he later played for Northampton Town and Exeter City before playing local League football.

ROBBINS Walter William

Outside-left/inside-left

Born: Cardiff, 24 November 1910.
Died: 1979.
Career: Ely Brewery. Ely United. Cardiff City 1928. West Bromwich Albion 1931. Newport County 1939.

■ Walter Robbins worked for a local brewery in Cardiff before taking a

motor engineering apprenticeship, but he made a name for himself by hitting 70 goals in one season for Ely United in the Cardiff and District League. Robbins joined Cardiff City as a 16-year-old amateur and was taken under George Lathom's wing. He made his Cardiff debut in the club's only away win of 1928–29 at Portsmouth and then scored on his home debut the following week in a 1–1 draw with Bolton Wanderers. Following the departures of McLachlan, Warren and Richards, Walter Robbins took full advantage, playing at both inside and outside-left. His form led to an invitation to join the FAW tourists to Canada in 1929 and this, in turn, marked him out as a future international. Robbins, who had netted hat-tricks against Millwall (home 4–4) in December 1930 and Reading (home 5–1) in September 1931, then scored five of City's goals in the club's record 9–2 League win over the ill-fated Thames. In 1932 Robbins was transferred to West Bromwich Albion for a substantial fee, and though he spent seven seasons at the Hawthorns there was stiff competition for places, and he found himself in and out of the side. After World War Two he returned to Ninian Park as the club's trainer, later holding a similar post with Newport County. He then moved to Swansea where he filled a variety of jobs at the Vetch, and on one occasion he turned down the opportunity to manage the Swans.

ROBERTS Christian John (Chris)

Forward

Born: Cardiff, 22 October 1979.
Career: Cardiff City 1997. Hereford United (loan). Drogheda (loan). Exeter City 2000. Bristol City 2002.

FAW Invitation Cup finalist 1997–98.

■ Chris Roberts made his debut for Cardiff while still a trainee. At the age of 17 he went on as a substitute in the match against Rochdale in September 1997 and sparked a recovery in an outstanding display, laying on goals for Steve White and Jeff Eckhardt in a 2–1 win. Unfortunately, he then twisted a knee in training and needed an operation before coming back into the side towards the end of the season. Though he struggled to win a regular first-team place, in 1998–99, having had a loan spell with Hereford, he did make an appearance off the bench for the Welsh Under-21 side. Following another loan spell, this time with Irish club Drogheda, he was unable to persuade manager Billy Ayre that he was worth a new contract and left to join Exeter City. He appeared in almost every game for the Grecians and in 2000–01 was the Devon club's top scorer. Later transferred to Bristol City, he scored in both League games against Cardiff in 2002–03 but failed to find the net against his former club in the play-offs. However, his goal the following season took his side through to the promotion play-offs, though this did cost him the chance of a Welsh cap!

ROBERTS David Frazer

Central-defender

Born: Southampton, 26 November 1949.
Career: Fulham 1967. Oxford United 1971. Hull City 1975. Cardiff City 1978. Kettering Town. Barry Town.

■ The Southampton-born central-defender began his career with Fulham, but in four years at Craven Cottage he made just 22 appearances. In February 1971 he joined Oxford United in the hope of playing regular first-team football. He was prompted by his teammates at the Manor Ground to write to the FAW, drawing attention to his eligibility based on parental qualification – his college lecturer father had been born in Anglesey – and he went on to win 17 full caps after making his debut against Poland in 1973. On leaving Oxford United Roberts joined Hull City, but after three seasons at Boothferry Park he signed for Cardiff City. Although not particularly tall for a central-defender, he was, nevertheless, a highly capable player. Injuries, especially in his first season at Ninian Park, prevented him from giving a full return on the £65,000 fee, and he was eventually forced to retire from League football. He made a comeback with non-League Kettering Town before being reunited with former Cardiff boss Richie Morgan at Barry Town. Roberts later became coach at Bridgend Town.

ROBERTS Joseph (Joe)

Outside-left

Born: Birkenhead, 2 October 1900.
Died: 1984.
Career: Oswestry Town. Watford 1926. Queen's Park Rangers 1927. York City. Halifax Town 1929. Southport 1929. Clapton Orient 1931. Luton Town 1932. Millwall 1932. Barrow 1933. Luton Town 1934. Cardiff City 1935. Dartford. Worcester City.

■ Having played his early football with Oswestry Town, Joe Roberts was 26 when he entered League football with Watford. He then roamed extensively in the next 10 years and acquired a remarkable sequence of employers, mostly at Third Division level. On leaving Vicarage Road, he had spells with Queen's Park Rangers, Halifax Town, Southport, Clapton Orient, Luton Town and Barrow before signing for Cardiff City. Though he was only with the club for one season in 1935–36, his return of five goals in 22 games in the number-11 shirt was quite good in a poor Bluebirds team. Roberts later played non-League football for both Dartford and Worcester City.

ROBERTS Jonathan Wesley (Jon)

Goalkeeper

Born: Pontypridd, 30 December 1968.
Career: Cardiff City 1987. Barry Town.

■ Goalkeeper Jon Roberts progressed through the Bluebirds youth and Macbar League teams to play his first three senior matches in different competitions within the space of seven days in November 1987. With Graham Moseley injured and loan signing Alan Judge unavailable, Roberts played in the FA Cup tie at Peterborough and three days later in the embarrassing goalless Welsh Cup match with Ebbw Vale. His League debut at Newport County, where he did well, resulted in a 2–1 win for City. Roberts remained with Cardiff until the end of the following season before joining Barry Town.

ROBERTS William J. (Bill)

Left-back

Born: Birmingham, 1907.
Career: Flint Town United. Cardiff City 1928.

Welsh Cup finalist 1928–29. Welsh Cup winner 1929–30.

■ Recruited from Flint Town United, full-back Bill Roberts joined the Bluebirds in 1928 when they were a First Division club and left them four

years later when they were in the Third Division South. During the club's demise he was a virtual ever present, scoring his only goal in a Second Division game against Southampton in November 1929, a match City won 5–2. An uncompromising defender, he parted company with the club at the end of the 1932–33 season.

ROBINSON John Robert Campbell

Winger

Born: Bulawayo, Rhodesia, 29 August 1971.
Career: Brighton & Hove Albion 1989. Charlton Athletic 1992. Cardiff City 2003.

■ A tricky winger who can play on either side, although predominantly right-footed, he began his career with Brighton & Hove Albion. Having appeared in 73 games for the Seagulls, he left for Charlton Athletic in September 1992 when the Addicks paid £75,000 for his services. His early displays for the London club led to him winning the first of 30 Welsh caps – he retired from international football at the start of the 2002–03 season – and in 1995–96 he was Charlton's Player of the Year. Over the next couple of seasons he scored a number of vital goals for the club, but midway through the 1997–98 campaign he suffered a hairline fracture to his right leg, though he did return as

a substitute in the Wembley play-off final. Recognised by his fellow professionals, he was voted into the PFA First Division select side for the next two seasons and won a First Division Championship medal as Charlton returned to top-flight action. Charlton's most capped international, he left the Valley after making 382 first-team appearances to join Cardiff in the summer of 2003. In what was their first season in the higher Division of football for 18 years, he was a great success, inspiring all those around him with his commitment and enthusiasm. A regular for most of the campaign, he scored in the home games against Sheffield United and Wimbledon towards the end of the season.

ROBINSON Matthew

Inside-forward/wing-half

Born: Felling, 1909.
Career: Pelaw. Cardiff City 1928.
Manchester United 1931. Chester 1931.
Barrow 1932.

■ Taken on trial from North Eastern League club Pelaw in 1928, Matthew Robinson had to wait over a year before making his League debut after being offered a contract. Robinson's debut came in the penultimate game of the 1928–29 season, and though City drew 1–1 with Portsmouth they dropped out

of the top flight. The following season he shared the number-10 shirt with Walter Robbins, but following the arrival of Les Jones he found himself permanently in the reserves. After brief spells with Manchester United and Chester, he joined Barrow, and in six seasons with the Holker Street club, in which he was a virtual ever present, he scored 42 goals in 226 Third Division North games.

ROBSON Keith

Winger

Born: Hetton-le-Hole, 15 November 1953.
Career: Newcastle United 1971. West Ham United 1974. Cardiff City 1977. Norwich City 1978. Leicester City 1981. Carlisle United (loan) 1983.

■ Keith Robson was unlucky to be at Newcastle United at the time of the Macdonald-Tudor partnership and so, with his first-team opportunities limited, he moved on to West Ham United. He scored on his Hammers debut in a 6–2 defeat of Leicester City, and though he was not a prolific scorer he netted with a spectacular effort in the 3–1 semi-final, second leg victory over Eintrackt Frankfurt, ensuring West Ham a place in the 1976 European Cup-Winners' Cup Final. He scored again in the Final as the Hammers lost 4–2 to Anderlecht in Brussels. Something of a temperamental player, having had a number of bust-ups with both

opponents and referees, he was allowed to join Cardiff City in the summer of 1977, after scoring 19 goals in 87 games for West Ham. Signed by manager Jimmy Andrews as cover for the wayward Robin Friday, he showed glimpses of his bustling aggression, but after a well-publicised incident with City coach Alan Sealey in the car park he was on his way to Norwich City. He later had spells with Leicester City and Carlisle United before playing in Hong Kong.

RODGERSON Ian

Winger/right-back

Born: Hereford, 9 April 1966.
Career: Hereford United 1985. Cardiff City 1988. Birmingham City 1991. Sunderland 1993. Cardiff City 1995. Hereford United 1997.

■ Ian Rodgerson suffered an early setback in his career when he was not taken on as an apprentice with his home-town club Hereford United, simply because they had axed their youth team. Later, he was given a second chance by the Bulls and developed into a useful midfielder, playing wide on the

right and being ever eager to support his forwards. Cardiff paid £35,000 for his services in the summer of 1988, and, though his stay at Ninian Park saw the club continually struggling to avoid relegation, he was one of the few City players to turn in consistent displays. In December 1990 he left to play for Birmingham City, making 116 appearances for the St Andrew's club, before joining Sunderland. After suffering from a number of injuries and a loss of form, he was given a free transfer and rejoined Cardiff for a second spell. He took his first-team League and Cup appearances to 191 before being released at the end of the 1996–97 season and rejoining Hereford.

RODON Christopher Peter (Chris)

Forward

Born: Swansea, 5 February 1945.
Career: Pontardawe. Brighton & Hove Albion 1983. Cardiff City (loan) 1983. Haverfordwest.

■ The son of Peter Rodon, who played for Bradford City in the early 1960s, he played his early football for Pontardawe before joining Brighton & Hove Albion in January 1983. Unable to make much progress at the Goldstone Ground, he came to Cardiff on loan and played in the opening four games of the 1983–84 season. Not making much of an impression, he returned to the south coast club before later playing for Haverfordwest.

RODRIGUES Peter Joseph

Right-back

Born: Cardiff, 21 January 1944.
Career: Cardiff City 1961. Leicester City 1966. Sheffield Wednesday 1970. Southampton 1975.

Welsh Cup winner 1963–64.

■ A fast, attacking full-back, Peter Rodrigues enjoyed nothing more than mounting spectacular overlapping raids down the wing. A former Welsh Schoolboy and Youth international, he was almost transferred to Newport County during his early days at Ninian Park. At the time, Rodrigues hadn't

made his League debut for the Bluebirds, but they wisely turned down the £500 offer from the Somerton Park club. After making his City debut in a 3–3 draw at Sunderland in September 1963, Rodrigues was a virtual ever present in the Bluebirds side for the next three seasons, appearing in both full-back positions. However, the Ninian Park club were unable to offer him the standard of football he required, and in January 1966 they sold him to Leicester City for a fee of £42,500. Rodrigues, who had won the first of 40 Welsh caps earlier that year, won a Second Division Championship medal and reached the 1969 FA Cup Final with the Foxes before, in October 1970, Danny Williams paid £50,000 to take him to Sheffield Wednesday. Within three months Williams had been sacked, but Rodrigues remained to serve two more successors, Dooley and Burtenshaw. Unable to halt the Owls slide, he probably felt he had achieved all he could in the game when he joined Lawrie McMenemy's Southampton, yet 12 months later he captained the unfancied south coast club to a shock FA Cup Final win over Manchester United.

ROGERS Alan James

Left-winger

Born: Plymouth, 6 July 1954.

Career: Plymouth Argyle 1972. Portsmouth 1979. Southend United 1984. Cardiff City 1986. Saltash United.

■ Winger Alan Rogers began his career with his home-town club Plymouth Argyle, spending six seasons at Home Park and helping the Pilgrims win promotion to the Second Division in 1974–75. In the summer of 1979 he was involved in a £25,000 move to Portsmouth, where Frank Burrows was in charge, the fee being one of the first to be set by a tribunal. A regular in the Pompey side for five years, he helped them win promotion from the Fourth Division in his first season at the club and then in 1982–83 was instrumental in them winning the Third Division Championship. He had scored 15 goals in 161 games when, in March 1984, he moved to Southend United. In the summer of 1986 he rejoined Frank Burrows at Ninian Park, but, coming towards the end of his successful career, he did not fit in easily with Fourth Division life. As a result his two-year contract was terminated by mutual consent with a year left to run, and he joined Saltash United.

ROGERS Thomas W.

Outside-right

Born: Cardiff, 1914.
Career: Cardiff City 1933.

■ Winger Tom Rogers was one of the innumerable players drafted into the Cardiff City side during the dreadful 1933–34 season when short-term signings and local amateurs were used. Despite scoring on his debut in a 4–1 win over Watford, he played in only one more League match before being released.

ROLLO James Stuart

Defender/midfield

Born: Wisbech, 22 May 1976.
Career: Walsall 1995. Bath City. Cardiff City 1997. Forest Green Rovers.

■ Starting his career with Walsall, utility player James Rollo was released by the Saddlers after just one substitute appearance in the Autowindscreens Shield, and after a brief spell with Bath City he joined the Bluebirds on a non-contract basis. A real livewire of a player, who was used in a number of positions including wing-back, he created a good impression. In 1997–98 he scored his first ever goal when he sent a bullet-like header into the net for Cardiff against Southend in the Coca-Cola Cup, but unfortunately he could not remember a thing, having collided head on with a Shrimpers defender, and had to be taken to hospital. Yet despite his promise, he was given a free transfer by Frank Burrows and went to play in the Conference for Forest Green Rovers.

RONAN Peter

Wing-half

Born: Dysart, 1911.
Career: Rosslyn Juniors. Cardiff City 1931. East Fife.

■ A miner who had played for Rosslyn Juniors, Peter Ronan came to Ninian Park in 1931 and took over the left-half position from the ageing Billy Hardy. However, Ronan, whose only goal for the club came from the penalty spot in a 2–2 draw at Bristol Rovers in November 1931, was not to be the answer, and at the end of the following season he went to play Scottish League football for East Fife.

RONSON William (Billy)

Midfield

Born: Fleetwood, 22 January 1957.
Career: Blackpool 1974. Cardiff City 1979. Wrexham 1981. Barnsley 1982. Birmingham City (loan) 1985. Blackpool 1986. Baltimore Blasts (US).

■ A diminutive, tigerish midfield player, Billy Ronson began his League career with his local club Blackpool and made his debut against Nottingham Forest in March 1975. After appearing in just a handful of games over the next couple of seasons, he won a regular place in the team. Unable to prevent their relegation to the Third Division in 1977–78, Ronson spent just one more season at Bloomfield Road before Cardiff City paid a club record fee of £130,000 for his services in the summer of 1979. Ronson was certainly a good signing and after missing just one game in his first season was ever present in 1980–81.

Though Bluebirds fans would have liked to have seen him score more goals, he more than made up for that with honest endeavour. Growing disenchanted with City's lack of progress, he moved to Wrexham but after just one season at the Racecourse Ground, in which the Robins were relegated to the Third Division, he signed for Barnsley. Highly rated by the Yorkshire club, he played in 113 League games over the next three seasons before, following a disagreement with manager Allan Clarke and a loan spell with Birmingham, he rejoined Blackpool. Unable to recapture his best form, he left to play for Baltimore Blasts, becoming one of the most successful performers on the American Indoor circuit.

ROPER Harry

Inside-right/left-half

Born: Romiley, 13 April 1910.
Died: 1983.
Career: New Mills. Leeds United 1932. Cardiff City 1935. Stockport County 1937.

■ A former warehouse clerk, Harry Roper played his early football for New Mills before Leeds United snapped him up. Though he had to wait almost three years for his League debut, he marked it with a goal, and though it was only the second game of the 1932–33 season he

was not picked again that term. Bedevilled by cartilage problems, he moved to Cardiff City. Fluctuating between the inside-right and half-back positions, he scored twice during his first few appearances, but, though he spent two seasons at Ninian Park, he was never an automatic choice. In October 1937 Roper left the Bluebirds to end his first-class career with Stockport county but was plagued by knee trouble and failed to make a first-team appearance for the club.

ROSS William Bernard

Outside-right

Born: Swansea, 8 November 1924.
Career: Towey United. Cardiff City 1943. Sheffield United 1948. Southport 1949.

■ Bernard Ross joined the Bluebirds from Towey United towards the end of World War Two, but when League football resumed in 1946–47 he found himself confined to a place in the club's reserve side. He eventually made his League debut towards the end of that season in a 2–0 win at Exeter City before scoring twice a week later in a 3–2 defeat of Queen's Park Rangers. After a handful of games the following season, he joined Sheffield United but failed to settle at Bramall Lane. Ross then moved to Southport, scoring 13 goals in 46 games for the Sandgrounders.

ROWLAND Alfred (Alf)

Centre-half

Born: Stokesley, 2 September 1920.
Died: 1997.
Career: Stockton. Aldershot 1946. Cardiff City 1949. Stockton.

■ Having played with non-League Stockton before World War Two, Alf Rowland then served in the Middle East with the Green Howards. Unfortunately he was captured, which meant four years as a prisoner of war. In 1946 he joined Aldershot as a part-timer, switching from outside-left to centre-half! After appearing in 93 games for the Shots and having an outstanding match against Tommy Lawton, Rowland joined Cardiff City. Deputising for the injured Fred Stansfield, he made just three appearances and, with his chances of

first-team football limited, his career turned full circle when he left to play for Stockton and concentrate on his market gardening business.

RUSSELL George Henry

Full-back

Born: Atherstone, 11 August 1902. Career: Atherstone Town. Portsmouth 1925. Watford 1926. Northampton Town 1927. Bristol Rovers 1930. Atherstone

Town. Cardiff City 1932. Sheffield United 1933. Newport County 1934. Stafford Rangers. Bangor City.

■ Though he was on Portsmouth's books, George Russell gained his first League experience with Watford before signing for Northampton Town. Unable to hold down a regular place in the Cobblers side, he left to continue his career with Bristol Rovers. As with Northampton, he had made 55 appearances for the Eastville club when he left to sign for Cardiff City. Able to play in either full-back position, he became a regular in the Bluebirds side, where the only goal in his time with the club came in a 3–1 defeat at Bristol City in April 1933. Given a free transfer in the close season, he moved to Newport County before playing for Stafford Rangers and becoming player-manager of Bangor City.

RUSSELL Kevin John

Forward/winger

Born: Portsmouth, 6 December 1966. Career: Brighton & Hove Albion. Portsmouth 1984. Wrexham 1987. Leicester City 1989. Peterborough United (loan) 1990. Cardiff City (loan) 1991. Hereford United (loan) 1991. Stoke City (loan) 1992. Stoke City 1992. Burnley 1993. Bournemouth 1994. Notts County 1995. Wrexham 1995.

■ Kevin 'Rooster' Russell served his apprenticeship at Brighton before joining Portsmouth in 1984. Playing only occasionally for the first team, in the summer of 1987 he was transferred to Wrexham. In 1987–88, his first full season of League football, he netted 25 goals for the Robins, and they reached that season's play-offs, but they failed to win promotion from the Fourth Division. Within weeks he was on his way to Leicester City for £100,000, but, unable to command a regular place, he was loaned out to Peterborough, Cardiff, Hereford and Stoke. At Ninian Park he appeared in three games but failed to get on the scoresheet. Recalled by the Foxes, he scored five goals during their run in to the Second Division play-offs in 1992. He then joined Stoke, helping them win the Championship of the 'new'

Second Division. Russell later had spells with Burnley, Bournemouth and Notts County before returning to Wrexham, his spiritual home. Something of a cult figure at the Racecourse Ground, he had scored 74 goals in 340 games for the Robins when he hung up his boots at the end of the 2002–03 season.

RUTTER Charles Frederick

Full-back

Born: Bromley, 22 December 1927. Career: Taunton Town. Cardiff City 1949. Exeter City 1958.

Welsh Cup finalist 1950–51. Division Two runner-up 1951–52.

■ Full-back Charlie Rutter joined the Bluebirds from non-League Taunton Town in September 1949 but had to

wait over a year before making his League debut in a goalless draw at Doncaster Rovers. Rutter was an important member of the City side that won promotion to the First Division in 1951–52, his outstanding displays earning him a call-up to the England 'B' side. A knee injury sustained in the 1–0 home win over Notts County towards the end of that season kept him out for the whole of the 1952–53 campaign in the top flight. When he had recovered full fitness, he faced stiff competition from Ron Stitfall and, though he remained at Ninian Park until August 1958, he eventually moved on to Exeter City where he ended his first-class career. He later became well known in Cardiff's Central Market with his tropical bird business.

RYDER Derek Francis

Full-back

Born: Leeds, 18 February 1947.
Career: Leeds United 1964. Cardiff City 1966. Rochdale 1968. Southport 1972.

■ After being released by Leeds United without playing a League game, full-back Derek Ryder joined Cardiff City on a free transfer. However, in two seasons at Ninian Park he made just four appearances, and in the summer of 1968 he signed for Rochdale. Ryder was a regular at Spotland for four years, appearing in 168 games and helping them win promotion to the Third Division in his first season with the club. After moving to Southport prior to the start of the 1972–73 season, Ryder was outstanding in helping the Haig Avenue club win the Fourth Division Championship.

SANDER Christopher Andrew (Chris)

Goalkeeper

Born: Swansea, 11 November 1962.
Career: Swansea City 1979. Wrexham (loan) 1984. Cardiff City 1985. Haverfordwest. Cardiff City 1986. Barry Town.

■ Goalkeeper Chris Sander worked his way up through the ranks with Swansea City before appearing in 20 games for the Vetch Field club. While with the Swans, he had a loan spell with Wrexham, but in March 1985, after being released by Swansea, he went to work as a computer programmer while playing Welsh League football for Haverfordwest. Alan Durban signed Sander on part-time terms in the summer of 1985, thus allowing him to continue playing for Haverfordwest

when not required by the Bluebirds. In the game against Walsall at Ninian Park in April 1986 which City drew 1–1, Sander became the first Cardiff 'keeper to save two penalties in a match. Released at the end of that relegation season, he joined Barry Town.

SANDERS Alan John

Midfield

Born: Newport, 29 October 1963
Career: Cardiff City 1981.

■ Youth-team player Alan Sanders had appeared as a substitute against Newcastle United during the early stages of the club's relegation season of 1981–82 before making his only first start under new manager Len Ashurst at Bolton Wanderers. With the club due to start the following season in the Third Division, Sanders was released.

SANDERSON Paul David

Winger

Born: Blackpool, 28 July 1964.
Career: Fleetwood Town. Manchester City 1983. Chester City 1983. Halifax Town 1984. Cardiff City 1987. Walsall 1988.

Division Four runner-up 1987–88.

■ Paul Sanderson began his career with non-League Fleetwood Town before making the big time with a move to Manchester City. Failing to break through at Maine Road, he quickly moved on to Chester City. Sanderson left Sealand Road in the summer of 1984 to join Halifax Town and played in over 100 League games for the Shaymen before arriving at Ninian Park in July 1987. Initially arriving on a three-month trial, this was later extended, but Sanderson, whose only goal was scored in a 2–1 defeat at Scunthorpe United, left City before they were relegated to see out his career with Walsall.

SAUNDERS Dean Nicholas

Forward

Born: Swansea, 21 June 1964.
Career: Swansea City 1982. Cardiff City (loan) 1985. Brighton & Hove Albion 1985. Oxford United 1987. Derby County 1988. Liverpool 1991. Aston Villa 1992. Galatasaray (Turkey). Nottingham Forest

1996. Sheffield United 1997. Benfica (Portugal). Bradford City 1999.

■ The son of Roy, who played for Liverpool and Swansea, Dean Saunders was thrown into League action in October 1983 with the Swans after they had just been relegated from the First Division. Despite scoring more than his fair share of goals, he couldn't prevent Swansea dropping into Division Three, and when John Bond became manager he was loaned out to the Bluebirds. He had netted twice in a 3–2 win for the Swans over Cardiff, but in the brief time he was at Ninian Park he disappointed. Given a free transfer, he joined Brighton and his impressive scoring ratio alerted Oxford United, who paid the hard-up south coast club £60,000 for his services. The 1987–88 campaign was hugely successful for Saunders, whose 21 goals included six in the League Cup and helped Oxford to a second semi-final in three seasons. Later transferred to Derby County for £1 million, he was the club's leading scorer in each of his three seasons at the Baseball Ground. This led to Liverpool paying £2.9 million in the summer of 1991 – a record between two English clubs. Just over a year later he moved to Aston Villa for £2.3 million and his career was resurrected. In his first season at Villa Park he was the club's leading scorer and helped them finish runners-up in the Premiership to Manchester United. After a spell with

Turkish club Galatasaray, he returned to the top flight with Nottingham Forest before later joining Sheffield United. The Welsh international, who won 75 caps, then played for Benfica before ending his playing career with Bradford City. After working alongside Mark Hughes with the national team, he had a spell as assistant manager to Graeme Souness at Newcastle United.

SAVILLE Andrew Victor (Andy)

Forward

Born: Hull, 12 December 1964.
Career: Hull City 1983. Walsall 1989. Barnsley 1990. Hartlepool United 1992. Birmingham City 1993. Burnley (loan) 1994. Preston North End 1995. Wigan Athletic 1996. Cardiff City 1997. Hull City (loan) 1998. Scarborough 1999. Gainsborough Trinity.

■ After signing for his home-town team Hull City, Andy Saville topped the Tigers scoring charts in 1986–87, his first full season in the side. In March 1989 he joined Walsall for £100,000, but within a year he had moved to Barnsley, later playing for Hartlepool United, before a £155,000 move took him to Birmingham City in March 1993. In

1994–95 he helped the St Andrew's club win the Second Division Championship and triumph in the Autowindscreens Shield against Carlisle United at Wembley. Following a loan spell with Burnley, he joined Preston and was an immediate hit with the Deepdale fans, scoring 29 goals as North End won the Third Division title. Only Alan Shearer, with 31 goals, scored more in English football in that 1995–96 season. Unable to rediscover his goalscoring form the following season, he moved to Wigan, and though he never got an extended run in the side he played in enough games to pick up another Third Division Championship medal. In October 1997 he signed for Cardiff City for £75,000, and though he netted a hat-trick for the Bluebirds in a 3–3 draw at Scunthorpe he was never going to figure in Frank Burrows's long-term plans. After a loan spell with Hull he joined Scarborough, but after they lost their League status he was not retained and joined Gainsborough Trinity.

SAYER Peter Anthony

Winger

Born: Cardiff, 2 May 1955.
Career: Cardiff City 1973. Brighton & Hove Albion 1978. Preston North End 1980. Cardiff City (loan) 1981. Chester City 1984. Northwich Victoria.

Division Three runner-up 1975–76. Welsh Cup winner 1975–76. Welsh Cup finalist 1976–77.

■ Cardiff-born Peter Sayer worked his way up through the ranks of his home-town club before making his debut for the Bluebirds against Hull City in September 1974. He went on to play in a further nine games that season, but towards the end of that 1974–75 campaign he broke his ankle in Cardiff's match at Southampton. He recovered to play in a number of matches towards the end of the following season as the club won promotion to the Second Division. In 1976–77 Sayer missed just a handful of matches as the club avoided relegation back to the Third Division. However, his form was such that he won the first of seven full international caps when he played against Czechoslovakia. Though

not a prolific scorer, he found the net six times in six games towards the end of that campaign. Midway through the 1977–78 season he left Ninian Park to join Brighton & Hove Albion for £100,000. In his first full season at the Goldstone Ground he helped the Seagulls win promotion to the First Division before later moving to play for Preston North End. He returned to Cardiff on loan in September 1981 before playing in just four games and scoring in a 3–2 win at Luton Town. He left the Bluebirds after scoring 20 goals in 98 first-team outings and ended his League career with Chester. He later appeared in non-League football for Northwich Victoria.

SCHWINKENDORF Jorn

Defender/midfield

Born: Hamburg, Germany, 27 January 1971.
Career: SC Freiburg (Germany). SV Waldhof (Germany). Cardiff City 1999. Vfl Osnabruck.

■ Having played his early football for SC Freiburg, he was playing for SV Waldhof Mannheim in Germany when City paid £110,000 to bring him to Ninian Park in November 1999. Many Bluebirds fans were confused following his arrival as he was thought to be a centre-half, yet he made little use of his height, rarely winning the ball in the air. Used as a holding midfield player, he never really looked comfortable with the physical, competitive style of Second Division football. He found it difficult to settle in South Wales and at the end of the season the 6ft 5in German returned to his homeland to play for Vfl Osnabrück

SCIMECA Ricardo

Defender/Midfield

Born: Leamington Spa, 13 June 1975. Career: Aston Villa 1993. Nottingham Forest 1999. Leicester City 2003. West Bromwich Albion 2004. Cardiff City 2005.

■ After an impressive first season with Aston Villa, Ricky Scimeca was voted the club's Young Player of the Year and was recognised by England at Under 21 level. He would have hoped to have made more appearances than he did in 1996–97, but the following season he showed his versatility by playing in a number of positions as he established himself as a first-team regular. He also captained the England Under-21 side and was also selected for the England 'B' side against Chile. Comfortable on the ball, with excellent skills and tight control, he became one of David Platt's first signings when he was appointed manager of Nottingham Forest. Appointed club captain, he led the team by example, but it seemed that Platt was never sure of Scimeca's best position, and he was tried at full-back, centre of defence and in central midfield before eventually settling on the right side of midfield. The scorer of some vital goals for Forest, he eventually left the City Ground to join Leicester, where he proved himself an accomplished member of the Foxes side. In the summer of 2004 he joined West Bromwich Albion and played his part in helping the club retain its Premiership status. He joined Cardiff in the 2005 close season, and even though over the last season he struggled with injuries whenever he was called into action he never let the side down.

SCOTT Andrew Michael

Full-back

Born: Manchester, 27 June 1975.

Career: Blackburn Rovers 1993. Cardiff City 1994. Rochdale 1997. Stalybridge Celtic.

■ A full-back with a very good left foot and plenty of pace, he failed to make the grade at his first club Blackburn Rovers, and in July 1994 he moved to Cardiff City. He appeared in 15 games in 1994–95, a season that saw the Bluebirds relegated to Division Three, but then went out of contention due to injury. In fact, he was injured for so long that in 1995–96 he was limited to four appearances on the bench and only got involved once. Unable to do himself justice having suffered from a whole spate of injuries, he was freed by City after playing just three times in 1996–97. He was then given a year's contract by Rochdale, but after being unable to reach full match fitness he was released and moved into non-League football with Stalybridge Celtic.

SCOTT Morrys James

Forward

Born: Swansea, 17 December 1970. Career: Cardiff City 1989. Colchester United. Southend United 1990. Plymouth Argyle 1991. Northampton Town 1992.

■ Though he made eight appearances from the bench, Morrys Scott's only League start for the Bluebirds came in a 3–1 defeat at Leyton Orient during the club's relegation season of 1989–90. After spells with Colchester United and Southend without ever appearing in their League sides, Scott spent a season with Plymouth Argyle before ending his first-class career as a non-contract player with Northampton Town.

SCOTT Richard Sydney Arthur (Dick)

Wing-half/inside-forward

Born: Thetford, 26 October 1941. Career: Norwich City 1958. Cardiff City 1963. Scunthorpe United 1964. Lincoln City 1966.

■ A former apprentice with Norwich City, Dick Scott was signed by manager George Swindin for Cardiff City in the summer of 1963, after he had made 28 appearances for the Canaries. Initially employed at centre-forward, Scott soon

reverted to his more familiar half-back role and, as the club's penalty-taker, had a good first season at Ninian Park. However, following the appointment of Jimmy Scoular as manager, he made just one more appearance before going to Scunthorpe United in exchange for Keith Ellis. After two seasons at the Old Show Ground he wound down his career with Lincoln City.

SCOTT Robert John (Bob)

Wing-half

Born: Dundee, 16 March 1937. Career: Dundee Violet. Cardiff City 1957. Swindon Town 1961. Newport County 1981. Sankeys. Southport 1963.

■ Wing-half Bob Scott was playing for Dundee Violet when Cardiff City manager Trevor Morris signed him in February 1957. He had the unenviable task of having to compete with some fine players at Ninian Park, including Colin Baker, Alan Harrington and Derek Sullivan, and so didn't make his first-team debut until the following November in a 1–1 draw at West Ham United. Scott spent four seasons at Ninian Park, mostly in the reserves, before joining Swindon Town. After less than half a year at the County Ground he was on the move again, this time to Newport County where he made 18 appearances in two seasons with the Somerton Park club. He then ended his first-team career with Southport.

SCOTT William John (Bill)

Full-back

Born: Belfast. Career: Belfast Celtic. Macclesfield. Darlington 1933. Stockport County 1935. Cardiff City 1936. Wigan Athletic.

■ Irish full-back Bill Scott had played his early football with Belfast Celtic and later Macclesfield before joining Darlington in 1933. A regular member of the Quakers side for a couple of seasons, he then had a brief spell with Stockport County before becoming one of seven new signings for Cardiff City prior to the beginning of the 1936–37 season. Scott played in 17 consecutive games from his debut, but after heavy defeats against Bristol Rovers (1–5) and

Swindon Town (2–4) he lost his place. Unable to win back a first-team spot, he joined Wigan Athletic, who were then members of the Cheshire League.

SCULLY Anthony Derek Thomas (Tony)

Midfield

Born: Dublin, 12 June 1976.
Career: Crystal Palace 1993. Bournemouth (loan) 1994. Cardiff City (loan) 1996. Portadown (loan). Manchester City 1997. Stoke City (loan) 1998. Queen's Park Rangers 1998. Cambridge United 2001. Southend United (Loan) 2002. Peterborough United 2003. Dagenham and Redbridge. Barnet. Tamworth. Notts County 2004.

■ A Republic of Ireland Under-21 international, he came through the junior ranks at Crystal Palace, but before he was given his League debut he was loaned out to Bournemouth to gain experience. He finally made his Palace debut, coming off the bench against Charlton, but then in January 1996 he was loaned to Cardiff. Proving to be a busy, ball-winning midfielder in the two months he spent at Ninian Park, Phil Neal was interested in signing him, but it was to no avail as he was recalled to Selhurst Park. Even then he couldn't win a place in the Palace side and had a loan period with Portadown. Eventually he joined Manchester City for £80,000 but again failed to impress and was loaned to Stoke before a £155,000 move to Queen's Park Rangers. While at Loftus Road, he was selected for the Republic of Ireland 'B' side against the Irish National League, but generally found first-team appearances hard to come by and joined Cambridge United. Soon out of favour, he had loan spells with Southend and Peterborough before playing non-League football for Dagenham and Redbridge, Barnet and Tamworth, later earning himself a move to Notts County.

SEARLE Damon Peter

Left-back

Born: Cardiff, 26 October 1971.
Career: Cardiff City 1990. Stockport County 1996. Carlisle United 1998.

Rochdale (loan) 1999. Southend United 2000. Chesterfield 2003. Forest Green Rovers.

Welsh Cup winner 1991–92, 1992–93. Division Three champion 1992–93. Welsh Cup finalist 1993–94.

■ Representing Wales at Youth, Under-21 and 'B' international level, left-back Damon Searle made his Cardiff debut in a 1–1 home draw against Peterborough United in October 1990. He went on to appear in all the remaining 34 games that season before becoming the club's only ever present in 1991–92. That season also saw him score his first goal for the club in a 2–1 home win over Walsall after the Bluebirds had come from behind. In six seasons at Ninian Park Searle was a virtual ever present and appeared in 278 League and Cup games before signing for Stockport County in the summer of 1996. Early on at Edgeley Park he lost his place to Lee Todd, but after the County player signed for Southampton Searle became a first-team regular. Out of contract in 1998, he moved on to Carlisle United, but after a good first season he lost his place and went on loan to Rochdale before signing for Southend United. An ever present in his first season at Roots Hall, he hardly missed a game in three seasons with the club. Released as part of Southend's cost-cutting measures, he had a brief spell with Chesterfield before moving to Conference outfit Forest Green Rovers.

SEASMAN John

Midfield

Born: Liverpool, 21 February 1955.
Career: Tranmere Rovers 1973. Luton Town 1975. Millwall 1976. Rotherham United 1980. Cardiff City 1984. Rochdale (loan) 1984. Chesterfield 1985. Rochdale 1985.

■ Much-travelled midfielder John Seasman began his career with local club Tranmere Rovers before, following a brief spell with Luton Town, he joined Millwall. His career blossomed at The Den, and in his first season he helped them win promotion to Division Two. In four years with the club he scored 35 goals in 158 League games before moving to Rotherham United for a

substantial fee. His first season at Millmoor was a huge success as the Yorkshire club won the Third Division Championship, and Seasman went on to net 25 goals in 100 games before a free transfer brought him to Ninian Park. Unfortunately, he didn't show anything like his true form in his time with the Bluebirds, and after only three months he had gone to Rochdale on loan. After a spell with Chesterfield, he joined Rochdale on a permanent basis but his time spent at Spotland saw the Lancashire club struggling at the foot of the League's basement.

SEMARK Robin Harry

Forward

Born: Portsmouth, 5 September 1972.
Career: Cardiff City 1991. Havant Town.

■ Portsmouth-born forward Robin Semark's impressive displays for Cardiff's reserve side brought him his Football League debut in a 2–1 home defeat by Lincoln City on the opening day of the 1991–92 season. It was the only time he was on the losing side in six games of that Fourth Division campaign, but despite laying on goals for both Dale and Pike he wasn't retained and in the close season returned to his native area to play for Havant Town.

SENDALL Richard Adam

Forward

Born: Stamford, 10 July 1967.
Career: Watford. Blackpool 1985. Carlisle United 1988. Cardiff City (loan) 1989.

■ Initially an apprentice with Watford, Richard Sendall began his Football League career with Blackpool but failed to find the net during his time with the Seasiders, and in July 1988 he joined Carlisle United. A regular member of the Cumbrian club's Fourth Division side, he scored a number of vital goals for them before going on loan to Cardiff City. Never on the winning side in his four games for the Bluebirds – in fact, City scored once during his loan spell – he rejoined Carlisle, taking his tally of goals to 14 in 84 games before moving into the local non-League scene.

SHARP Frank

Winger

Born: Edinburgh, 28 May 1947.
Career: Tynecastle Athletic. Heart of Midlothian. Carlisle United 1967. Cardiff City 1969. Barnsley 1970. Grimsby Town 1973. Port Vale 1974. Northwich Victoria.

Welsh Cup winner 1968–69.

■ Having started out with Edinburgh junior side Tynecastle Athletic, left-winger Frank Sharp then played Scottish League football for Heart of Midlothian prior to a £500 move to Carlisle United. With him unable to hold down a regular place at Brunton Park, City boss Jimmy Scoular paid a similar fee to bring him to Ninian Park. Though he scored in a 1–1 draw at Hull City in March 1970, he was dogged by injury during his time with the club. In the close season he and Leslie Lea went in a £20,000 package deal to Barnsley, and for three seasons he was a regular in the Oakwell club's side, making 125 appearances. Sharp later played for Grimsby Town and Port Vale before opting for non-League football with Northwich Victoria.

SHAW Paul

Forward

Born: Burnham, 4 September 1973.
Career: Arsenal 1991. Burnley (loan) 1995. Cardiff City (loan) 1995. Peterborough United (loan) 1995. Millwall 1997. Gillingham 2000. Sheffield United 2004.

■ An England Youth international, his partnership with Paul Read was quite phenomenal for Arsenal's youth team in the early 1990s. After making his League debut for the Gunners against Nottingham Forest in December 1994, his first-team opportunities became limited, and he had loan spells with Burnley and Cardiff. At Ninian Park he failed to find the net in six starts and, after returning to Highbury, joined Peterborough in a similar capacity. His stay at London Road was more fruitful, but United were quoted a ridiculous fee when they tried to sign him on a permanent basis. Shaw did eventually leave Highbury, joining Millwall for a fee of £250,000, and ended the 1997–98 season as the club's leading scorer with 13 goals. Injuries then hampered his progress, and he left for Gillingham, the Kent club paying £450,000 for his services. After a disappointing start the glows began to flow, but after winning the Gills Player of the Year award he was out of contract and opted for a move to Sheffield United.

SHAW William (Bill)

Forward

Born: Kilnhurst, 3 October 1897.
Career: Frickley Colliery. Bradford City 1921. Chesterfield 1923. Scunthorpe United. Southend United 1925. Gainsborough Trinity. Cardiff City 1928. Gainsborough Trinity. Mansfield Town.

■ A much-travelled footballer, Bill Shaw had played for five clubs in the 1920s before he arrived at Ninian Park in 1928. Starting out with non-League Frickley, he gained League experience with Bradford City before having a brief spell with Chesterfield. He then dropped out of the League for a season, playing for Scunthorpe before returning to League action with Southend United. During the 1925–26 season, Shaw was the Shrimpers

top scorer with 19 goals in 34 games, but at the end of the season he returned to non-League football with Gainsborough Trinity. It was from there that Shaw was recruited by Cardiff City, where he played twice as a replacement for the injured Hughie Ferguson. He later returned to Gainsborough before seeing out his career with Mansfield Town.

SHERLOCK Steven Edward

Left-back

Born: Birmingham, 10 May 1959.
Career: Manchester City 1977. Luton Town 1978. Stockport County 1979. Cardiff City 1986. Newport County (loan) 1986. Newport County 1987.

■ As a young left-back, Steve Sherlock progressed through to the reserve team at Manchester City and was a member of the club's Central League Championship-winning team of 1977–78. Unable to displace Scottish international Willie Donachie, he joined Luton Town, making his Football League debut in a 6–1 win against Oldham Athletic. However, after just one more appearance he moved to the League's other Hatters, Stockport County. Sherlock, who had a powerful shot and was an excellent crosser of the ball, spent seven seasons at Edgeley Park, making 273 League and Cup appearances before moving to Cardiff City in July 1986. His early displays were impressive, but in Cardiff's epic 2–1 Littlewoods Cup defeat of Chelsea he suffered a leg injury, and when fully fit he couldn't force his way back into the side. Loaned to Newport County, he later joined the Somerton Park club on a permanent basis. His final season in League football, 1987–88, was also Newport's last as they were relegated to the Conference. Another bad leg injury in that season's Welsh Cup Final against Merthyr Tydfil forced his retirement.

SHERWOOD Alfred Thomas (Alf)

Full-back

Born: Aberaman, 13 November 1923.
Died: 1990.
Career: Aberaman. Cardiff City 1942. Newport County 1956.

Division Three South champion 1946–47. Division Two runner-up 1951–52.

■ A master of the sliding tackle, Alf Sherwood had pace, tackling ability and positional sense that made him one of the best full-backs in the Football League and the one defender who could subdue the great Stanley Matthews. Sherwood started out with his home-town club Aberaman, alongside wartime greats such as Dai Astley and Bryn Jones. Sherwood played his early football as a wing-half, and it was in that position that he first came to Cardiff City's attention. He was playing against the Bluebirds in a wartime game at Ninian Park and was so impressive that City manager Cyril Spiers signed him there and then. That was in 1942, and over the next few years of wartime football he turned out whenever he could get away from working down the pits. During a game against Lovells Athletic, Cardiff found themselves short at the back. Sherwood agreed to have a go and, after performing as if he'd always played in this position, he stayed

there for the rest of his career. Sherwood played in 140 wartime games for Cardiff. Missing just one game, he helped City win the 1946–47 Third Division South Championship as they finished nine points ahead of runners-up Queen's Park Rangers. Following Fred Stansfield's departure to Newport County, Sherwood's defensive partner at Ninian Park was Ron Stitfall. Sherwood was appointed the Bluebirds captain and in 1951–52 led the side into the top flight as runners-up to Sheffield Wednesday. Sherwood was also the stand-in goalkeeper for both Cardiff and Wales. When the Bluebirds travelled to Anfield for an end-of-season game in April 1954, the home side had to win to keep their First Division status. City were 1–0 up when Sherwood, who'd taken over from the injured Ron Howells, had to face a penalty from Liverpool's Scottish international winger Billy Liddell. He saved it and Liverpool were relegated! Sherwood had appeared in 372 League and Cup games for Cardiff when it became apparent that he was no longer part of manager Trevor Morris's plans. He left Ninian Park in the summer of 1956 to join Newport County where he confounded his critics, not only by playing in 205 games for the Somerton Park club but by taking his tally of Welsh caps to 41. He later had a brief spell as manager of Barry Town before being employed as a security officer with the National Coal Board.

SHOWERS Derek

Forward

Born: Merthyr Tydfil, 28 January 1953. Career: Cardiff City 1970. Bournemouth 1977. Portsmouth 1979. Hereford United 1980. Barry Town.

Welsh Cup winner 1972–73, 1973–74, 1975–76. Welsh Cup finalist 1974–75, 1976–77.

■ Derek Showers, who won two full international caps for Wales in 1975, joined the Cardiff City groundstaff at the age of 15 after being spotted on a coaching course at Whitchurch by John Charles, Colin Baker and Bobby Ferguson. Showers was without doubt a prolific goalscorer at junior level and

this led to his early – arguably premature – baptism into League football at the age of 17. Following John Toshack's transfer to Liverpool, Showers made his debut in a 1–0 defeat at Oxford United in December 1970. He found it hard going, but the Cardiff manager stood by him. Showers always gave maximum effort to the Bluebirds cause, but unfortunately he lacked polish and was made the scapegoat by a section of Cardiff fans when things weren't going well for the Ninian Park club. After seven years with City, he joined Bournemouth, where he soon rediscovered his goalscoring touch and netted a number of important goals for the Cherries before moving along the south coast to Portsmouth. He flitted in and out of the Pompey side before joining Hereford United, where he ended his League career having scored 50 goals in 271 League games for his four clubs. After a spell playing non-League football for Barry Town, he was involved with Cardiff City's junior teams before going to work for the Royal Mail.

SIMMONS Anthony John (Tony)

Forward

Born: Stocksbridge, 9 February 1965. Career: Sheffield Wednesday 1983. Queen's Park Rangers 1983. Rotherham United 1984. Lincoln City 1986. Cardiff City (loan) 1987.

■ An England Youth international, he began his career with Sheffield Wednesday before linking up with Queen's Park Rangers. The spell at Loftus Road was fruitless and four months later he returned to his native South Yorkshire to play for Rotherham United. Given an extended run in the Millers side, he repaid the management team by scoring 27 goals in 96 games before moving on to Lincoln City. Injuries had hampered his progress at Sincil Bank, and he was struggling when he joined Cardiff on loan in February 1987. Though he scored against Tranmere Rovers, his period was not extended, and he returned to Lincoln, who dropped out of the Football League at the end of that season.

SIMPKINS Michael James (Mike)

Defender

*Born: Sheffield, 28 November 1978.
Career: Sheffield Wednesday 1997.
Chesterfield 1998. Cardiff City 2001.
Exeter City (loan) 2002. Cheltenham
Town (loan) 2002. Rochdale 2003.*

■ Mike Simpkins joined Chesterfield in March 1998 from Sheffield Wednesday, after graduating to the professional ranks as a trainee. After some impressive early displays he was laid low by a hernia operation before bouncing back to play an important part in the Spireites promotion in 2000–01. Surprisingly allowed to leave Saltergate, he joined Cardiff, but, though he began tentatively, he gradually began to receive few chances and was loaned out to Exeter and Cheltenham, and soon after returning to Ninian Park he was released from his contract. Simpkins then joined Rochdale but lost his place following the appointment of new manager Steve Parkin.

SLOAN Thomas M. (Tom)

Centre-half

*Born: Portadown, 11 September 1900.
Career: Crusaders. Linfield. Cardiff City
1924. Linfield.*

FA Cup winner 1926–27. Welsh Cup winner 1926–27.

■ Centre-half Tom Sloan played his early football with Belfast Crusaders before joining Irish League side Linfield.

Sloan signed for Cardiff City midway through the 1924–25 season. In his first couple of seasons with the club he was in competition for the number-five shirt with Fred Keenor, but when the Bluebirds won the FA Cup in 1927 both Keenor and Sloan were in the Cardiff side. Also that season he won a Welsh Cup medal when Rhyl were beaten 2–0 in the Final. Though he only made 90 appearances during his five seasons at Ninian Park, he won eight full international caps for Ireland, the first against England in 1925. Sloan's only goal for the Bluebirds came in one of his last appearances as City drew 1–1 with Arsenal. On leaving Ninian Park, he and Tom Watson returned to Ireland to rejoin Linfield, where he added an Irish Cup medal to his collection. On his retirement from playing he became manager of his home-town club Portadown.

SMELT Lee Adrian

Goalkeeper

*Born: Edmonton, 13 March 1958.
Career: Colchester United 1975.
Gravesend and Northfleet. Nottingham
Forest 1980. Peterborough United (loan)
1981. Halifax Town 1981. Cardiff City
1984. Exeter City (loan) 1985. Welling
United.*

■ Goalkeeper Lee Smelt failed to make the grade with Colchester United and

dropped into non-League football with Gravesend and Northfleet. It was from there, in 1979, that he was invited to go on Cardiff City's pre-season tour of Denmark, during which he made several appearances. Nottingham Forest then came in with an offer, and Smelt went to the City Ground as cover for Peter Shilton. Following a loan period with Peterborough United, he signed for Halifax Town and made 119 League appearances for the Shaymen before arriving at Ninian Park on a free transfer in July 1984. Smelt's 37 League appearances for the Bluebirds were spread over the two relegation seasons of 1984–85 and 1985–86 when City dropped from Division Two to Division Four. Following a loan spell with Exeter City, he helped coach Cardiff's youngsters before leaving to play for Welling United.

SMITH Colin Richard

Central-defender

*Born: Ruddington, 3 November 1958.
Career: Nottingham Forest. Norwich City
1982. Caroline Hill (Hong Kong). Cardiff
City 1983. Aldershot 1984.*

■ Defender Colin Smith had spent four years at Nottingham Forest without any chances of first-team football, and a move to Norwich City only produced a handful of first-team appearances. He

then had a spell in Hong Kong with Caroline Hill before being invited to Ninian Park on his return by Len Ashurst. An ability to play in any of the back four positions made him a more than useful player, and he performed creditably until, in November 1984, he moved to Aldershot. He went on to appear in 190 games for the Shots, helping them win promotion to the Third Division via the play-offs in 1986–87.

SMITH Ernest Edwin (Bert)

Centre-half

Born: Donegal, 4 January 1896.
Career: Cardiff City 1919. Middlesbrough 1923. Watford 1925. Emsworth.

Division Two runner-up 1920–21. Welsh Cup winner 1921–22, 1922–23.

■ One of the greatest defenders in the history of Cardiff City, Irish

international Bert Smith played his early football in the Indian Army during World War One before joining the Bluebirds prior to the start of the 1919–20 season. During that campaign he played in more Southern League games than anyone else and was instrumental in the club finishing fourth in that competition's First Division. He made his Football League debut in the club's first-ever game at Stockport County and over the next three seasons was a virtual ever present in the City side. After the club had won promotion at the end of the 1920–21

season, Smith scored the club's first goal in Division One when they went down 2–1 at Aston Villa. Towards the end of the 1923–24 season Smith joined Middlesbrough, but his first-team opportunities were limited and he moved to Watford, where his former Cardiff teammate Fred Pagnam was manager. He appeared in 50 games for the Hornets before playing non-League football for Emsworth.

SMITH Frederick Cecil

Centre-forward

Born: Marchwiel, 30 October 1904.
Died: 1977.
Career: Oswestry. Welshpool. Wrexham 1926. Wigan Borough 1928. Notts County 1930. Macclesfield. Stalybridge Celtic. Burnley 1932. Cardiff City 1936.

■ Having played non-League football with Oswestry and Welshpool, burly centre-forward Cecil Smith came into League football with Wrexham in 1926. In his first season at the Racecourse Ground he was the Robins top scorer, and the following campaign he continued to find the net before moving to Wigan Borough. He scored 23 goals in 38 games for the former League club before spending a season each with non-League Macclesfield and Stalybridge Celtic. At Macclesfield, in 1930–31, he scored 60 goals, while in 1931–32, with Stalybridge, he netted a mammoth 77 goals. This form prompted Burnley, then struggling at the foot of Division Two, to bring him back into League football. Smith had four very productive years at Turf Moor, scoring 49 goals in 106 games, until he lost his place to a 17-year-old called Tommy Lawton. In July 1936 Smith joined Cardiff amid much excitement, but despite scoring on his home debut and five times in his first eight games he soon faded, and at the end of the season he decided to retire.

SMITH George

Midfield

Born: Newcastle, 7 October 1945.
Career: Newcastle United 1963. Barrow 1965. Portsmouth 1967. Middlesbrough 1969. Birmingham City 1971. Cardiff

City 1973. Swansea City 1975. Hartlepool United 1977.

Welsh Cup winner 1973–74.

■ A boyhood fan of Newcastle United, it was his greatest regret that he was released by the Magpies without making the first team during his time at St James' Park. He then rebuilt his League career with Barrow before a £20,000 move to Portsmouth in May 1967. His forceful midfield play resulted in a further move to Middlesbrough and then Birmingham City. His career was interrupted by injuries at St Andrew's, and in the summer of 1973 he was signed by Jimmy Scoular. His early games for City demonstrated his bulldozing style, but after Scoular was dismissed he seemed to lose his drive. Under Jimmy Andrews, he lost his confidence and his place. After hurling his shirt at the bench after being substituted in the match against Sheffield Wednesday in March 1974, he was given a free transfer and joined Swansea City before returning to the North East to see out his career as player-coach with Hartlepool United.

SMITH Harold R.

Wing-half/centre-half

Born: Wealdstone.
Career: Wealdstone. Notts County 1930. Cardiff City 1935.

■ A railway porter at Wealdstone, Harold Smith was playing for the local amateur team before turning professional with Notts County. In 1930–31 he was a member of the County side that won the Third Division South Championship, going on to appear in 117 League games for the Magpies before Ben Watts-Jones snapped him up for Cardiff in the summer of 1935. He became a fairly regular member of the Bluebirds side over the next couple of seasons before deciding to hang up his boots.

SMITH John (Jock)

Full-back

Born: Dalbeattie, 7 December 1898.
Career: Neilston Victoria. Ayr United. Middlesbrough 1926. Cardiff City 1930. Distillery.

■ Having started in junior football with Neilston Victoria, Jock Smith joined Ayr United as an outside-left before being successfully converted into a full-back. While at Somerset Park, he formed a famous full-back partnership with Phil McCloy, the two of them playing for Scotland against England at Wembley in 1924. Also appearing for the Scottish League, he spent six seasons with Ayr before Middlesbrough paid £2,000 for him in 1926. At the end of his first season with 'Boro he had helped them win the Second Division Championship and, though they were immediately relegated, was instrumental in the north-east club winning the Division Two title again in 1928–29. He had played in 113 League games for 'Boro when, in September 1930, he joined Cardiff. The Bluebirds were relegated in Smith's first season at Ninian Park, but he continued to be the club's first-choice right-back until the end of the 1931–32 season when he signed for Distillery, helping them reach the Irish Cup Final in his only season with the club.

SMITH James A.

Centre-half/left-back

Born: Worcester.
Career: Cardiff City 1936. Wrexham 1938.

■ Worcester-born defender James Smith is known to have played Army football when stationed in China, prior

to joining Cardiff in 1936. Though he spent two years in City's colours, making just 15 appearances, he was often in the side when it was on the receiving end of some heavy defeats including: Luton Town (1–8), Queen's Park Rangers (0–6), Bright and Hove Albion (2–7) and Watford (0–4). In 1938 he joined Wrexham, playing for the Robins until the outbreak of World War Two.

SMITH Ritchie

Outside-left

Born: Aberdeen.
Career: Aberdeen Mugiemoss. Aberdeen 1934. Cardiff City 1938. Clyde.

■ A Scottish Schoolboy international winger, Ritchie Smith joined his home-town team Aberdeen from junior side Aberdeen Mugiemoss in 1934. When the Dons visited Ninian Park for a friendly in 1938, Smith gave such an impressive display that City manager Bill Jennings signed him straightaway. He found competition for the left-wing berth too much, and though he had scored in successive home games against Newport County and Bristol City at the turn of the year he was soon released and returned to Scotland to continue his career with Clyde.

SMITH Samuel James William (Sam)

Inside-forward

Born: Stafford, 7 September 1904.
Died: 1988.
Career: Cradley Heath. Cardiff City 1925. Port Vale 1927. Hull City 1928. Millwall 1929.

■ Signed from non-League Cradley Heath, Sam Smith was a rangy inside-forward who had to wait 18 months before making his First Division debut at Aston Villa in October 1925. Smith celebrated with his only goal in a 2–0 win, but found competition for places too fierce and remained in the reserves until his transfer to Port Vale in May 1927. His time with the Valiants was brief, and he was soon on his way to Hull City, before later ending his playing days with Millwall.

SMITH Thomas Potter

Inside-forward

Born: Newcastle, 30 July 1901.
Died: 1978.
Career: St Peters Albion. Merthyr Town 1922. Hull City 1923. Hartlepool United 1924. Merthyr Town 1925. Cardiff City 1925. Brighton & Hove Albion 1929. Crystal Palace 1937. Gloucester City.

Welsh Cup winner 1927–28.

■ A Geordie blacksmith who came to prominence with Merthyr Town in their pre-League days, he attracted the attention of Hull City. His stay with the Tigers was brief, and he had a season with Hartlepool before returning to South Wales for a second spell with Merthyr, then a League club. Cardiff City admired his skills, and towards the end of the 1925–26 season he joined the Bluebirds. Seen as the ideal replacement for Joe Cassidy, he was, unfortunately, to spend long periods sidelined by injury and illness. After four seasons at Ninian Park he left to continue his career with Brighton & Hove Albion, where his promptings created a wealth of scoring opportunities for his side's forwards. Smith later became Brighton captain, but again he was beset by injury problems and allowed to join Crystal Place, where he failed to make a first-team appearance prior to playing non-League football for Gloucester City.

SPRING Andrew John

Full-back

Born: Gateshead, 17 November 1965.
Career: Coventry City 1983. Bristol Rovers 1985. Cardiff City (loan) 1985.

■ Full-back Andy Spring appeared in a handful of games for Coventry City before, in the summer of 1985, joining Bristol Rovers. Though he made a promising start at the then Eastville club, he lost his place and went on loan to Cardiff City. He played in a 2–0 defeat at Gillingham, but then suffered an injury during training and didn't appear in the Bluebirds side again. He rejoined Bristol Rovers and made a few more appearances towards the end of the 1985–86 season before leaving the club.

STANSFIELD Frederick (Fred)

Centre-half

Born: Cardiff, 12 December 1917.
Career: Grange Athletic. Cardiff City 1943. Newport County 1949.

Division Three South champion 1946–47.

■ Centre-half Fred Stansfield might have won more than his solitary cap for Wales against Scotland in October 1948 if not for a broken leg sustained against Barnsley some three months later. Because of World War Two Fred Stansfield did not turn professional with Cardiff City until he was 24 years old. He made his League debut in a 2–1 defeat at Norwich City on the opening day of the 1946–47 season and missed just one game in that campaign as City won the Third Division South Championship. His form the following season, as City pressed for another promotion, was so impressive, and a month after playing for Wales he scored his only League goal for the Bluebirds in a 4–3 home defeat at the hands of Chesterfield. Then came the tragic injury in the match against Barnsley. Unable to get back into the side as the Cardiff manager Cyril Spiers had bought San Montgomery from Southend United, he joined Newport County. On hanging up his boots, he remained at Somerton Park as the club's manager – his best season being 1951–52 when County finished sixth in the Third Division South.

STANT Philip Richard (Phil)

Forward

Born: Bolton, 13 October 1962.
Career: Cambereley Town. Reading 1982. British Army. Hereford United 1986. Notts County 1989. Blackpool (loan) 1990. Lincoln City (loan) 1990. Huddersfield Town (loan) 1991. Fulham 1991. Mansfield Town 1991. Cardiff City 1992. Mansfield Town (loan) 1993. Bury 1995. Northampton Town (loan) 1996. Lincoln City 1996. Brighton & Hove Albion 1997. Worcester City.

Division Three Champion 1992–93. Welsh Cup winner 1992–93. Welsh Cup finalist 1993–94.

■ Much travelled striker 'Corporal Stant', the nickname a throwback to his days as a regular soldier, began his League career with Reading after some impressive displays for Camberley Town. He then joined the Army before returning to League action with Hereford United, where he scored 49 goals in 106 games before a £175,000 move to Notts County. Unable to make the same impression at Meadow Lane, he had loan spells with Blackpool, Huddersfield and Lincoln prior to signing for Fulham. Unable to settle at Craven Cottage, he joined Mansfield, where he rediscovered his scoring touch before signing for the Bluebirds for £100,000 in December 1992. His 11 goals in 24 games helped City win promotion from Division Three, while he netted two hat-tricks in the club's successful Welsh Cup campaign, including a treble in the Final against Rhyl. He continued to score freely in 1993–94, and had scored 13 goals in 19 games the following season, including a hat-trick against Cambridge United, when he was sold to Bury. During his early days at Gigg Lane he netted four in the Shakers 5–1 win at Mansfield and helped them win promotion. He then lost form and moved on to Lincoln, where he eventually became the Imps manager. He then ended his League career with Brighton before moving into non-League football with Worcester City.

STEEL Alfred (Alf)

Goalkeeper

Born: Glasgow, 15 August 1925.
Career: Petershill. Walsall 1947. Cardiff City 1950.

■ Goalkeeper Alf Steel spent three seasons with Walsall, but in that time he made just two League appearances before joining Cardiff in January 1950 as understudy to Phil Joslin. Having made his City debut in a 1–0 defeat at Leicester City within days of putting pen to paper, the remainder of his appearances came in the latter half of the 1949–50 season when Joslin was injured.

STEELE Eric Graham

Goalkeeper

Born: Wallsend, 14 May 1954.
Career: Newcastle United 1972. Peterborough United 1973. Brighton & Hove Albion 1977. Watford 1979. Cardiff City (loan) 1983. Derby County 1984. Southend United 1987. Mansfield Town (loan) 1988.

■ After failing to make the grade with Newcastle United, goalkeeper Eric Steele joined Peterborough United in December 1973. He was Posh's first-choice 'keeper for three seasons, helping them win promotion as Fourth Division Champions in 1973–74. On leaving London Road he played for Brighton and then Watford, but most of his time at Vicarage Road was spent as understudy to Steve Sherwood. He joined Cardiff on loan in March 1983

and kept four clean sheets in his seven appearances to help City win promotion to Division Two as runners-up to Portsmouth. After returning to Watford he joined Derby County, adding more promotions while at the Baseball Ground. At most of his clubs Eric Steele did a great deal of unpublicised charity work. He later worked as a specialist goalkeeping coach with Derby County and recently Aston Villa.

STEPHENS Lee Michael

Forward

Born: Cardiff, 30 September 1971.
Career: Cardiff City 1990.

■ Another YTS product, he made his Football League debut for Cardiff in a 4–0 defeat at Gillingham in November 1990, moving to the bench for the club's next game at Burnley. Stephens's last appearance for the Bluebirds was also as a substitute in a goalless draw at Chesterfield – all his appearances being away from Ninian Park.

STEVENS Gary Martin

Forward/central-defender

Born: Birmingham, 30 August 1954.
Career: Evesham. Cardiff City 1978.
Shrewsbury Town 1982. Brentford 1986.
Hereford United 1987.

Welsh Cup finalist 1981–82.

■ Spotted while playing for West Midlands club Evesham and working in a Herefordshire chicken factory, Gary Stevens joined Cardiff City in the summer of 1978. He made his debut in a 7–1 defeat at Luton Town in September of that year but then went on to score 13 goals in 32 League games, including one on his home debut a week later as Blackburn Rovers were beaten 2–0. In 1978–79 he was the club's joint-top scorer with 11 goals, which included him finding the net in five successive games at the start of the season. Though the club were relegated from the Second Division in 1981–82, Stevens top-scored with 13 goals, including a hat-trick in a 5–4 win over Cambridge United. At the end of the season he left to join Shrewsbury Town for a fee of £20,000. It was a bargain fee for a player who could play at both centre-half and centre-forward, and he went on to score 29 goals in 150 games for the Gay Meadow club. He then joined Brentford before moving to Hereford United to end his career.

STEVENSON Ernest (Ernie)

Inside-forward

Born: Rotherham, 28 December 1923.
Died: 1970.

Career: Wolverhampton Wanderers 1940.
Cardiff City 1948. Southampton 1950.
Leeds United 1951. Wisbech Town.

■ Like so many of his contemporaries, Ernie Stevenson's career was disrupted by World War Two. After playing for Wath Wanderers, Wolves nursery side, he played in the first leg of the League North Cup in 1942 and the War Cup-winners' Cup the following year. In October 1948 he left Molineux to join Cardiff City and ended his first season at Ninian Park as the club's leading scorer. His total of 12 goals in 27 games included 'doubles' in the games against Bradford Park Avenue (home 6–1), West Ham United (home 4–0), Lincoln City (home 3–1) and Coventry City (home 3–0). He continued to find the net during the early stages of the following season, but when the goals dried up he went to Southampton in exchange for Wilf Grant. Unable to find his form at The Dell, he joined Leeds United, where his boss was his old Wolves manager Major Frank Buckley. Unable to make much impression, he drifted into non-League football with Wisbech Town.

STEVENSON Nigel Charles Ashley

Central-defender

Born: Swansea, 2 November 1958.
Career: Swansea City 1976. Cardiff City (loan) 1985. Reading (loan) 1986. Cardiff City 1987.

Division Four runner-up 1987–88.
Welsh Cup winner 1987–88.

■ Tall centre-half Nigel Stevenson began his career with Swansea City and remained with the club during their dramatic rise and fall through the Football League. Having made his debut for the Swans in a Fourth Division match at Southport in 1976, he soon became an established member of the Vetch Field side. After 10 seasons with the Swans, 'Speedy', as he was known, was awarded a testimonial match

against Read Sociedad of Spain, managed by his former boss John Toshack. It was around this time that he lost his place in the side and had loan spells with Cardiff and Reading. His spell at Ninian Park was extended to three months and coincided with the Bluebirds best run of form in that 1985–86 relegation season. On returning to the Vetch, he went on to complete 259 League appearances before, in the summer of 1987, joining the Bluebirds on a free transfer. He played in a further 68 League games for City, helping them win promotion from the Fourth Division before deciding to hang up his boots.

STITFALL Albert Edward

Full-back

Born: Cardiff, 7 July 1924.
Career: Cardiff City 1948. Torquay United 1952.

■ The smallest of the three Stitfall brothers, Albert was another of the boys who joined the Bluebirds straight from school. During World War Two he served in the Navy, and on his return to Ninian park he found it difficult to win a regular first-team place. After making spasmodic appearances in four years with the club, he left to play for Torquay United, later ending his career with the Devon side.

STITFALL Ronald Frederick (Ron)

Full-back

Born: Cardiff, 14 December 1925.
Career: Cardiff City 1947.

Welsh Cup winner 1955–56, 1958–59. Division Two runner-up 1959–60. Welsh Cup finalist 1959–60.

■ In a playing career that spanned two decades, Ron Stitfall joined his home-town club Cardiff City as a schoolboy during World War Two and played his first game for the club in wartime competition when only 14 years of age. He appeared in a number of wartime games for the club before serving in the

Army for four years. It was 1947 when he returned to Ninian Park. In October of that year he made his League debut at left-back in place of Alf Sherwood, who was away on international duty. The match at Brentford ended in a goalless draw thanks to Stitfall's last-minute goal-line clearance. For the next 18 seasons Ron Stitfall was virtually ever present in the Bluebirds side. During his

first few seasons with the club Stitfall played in a variety of positions. In 1949–50 he had a spell playing at centre-forward and scored in each of his first five appearances in the number-nine shirt. Given that he scored only eight goals in the 454 first-team games in which he played, it was a remarkable performance. Much of that time was spent partnering Alf Sherwood, the two of them making the best full-back pairing outside the top flight. After hanging up his boots, Ron Stitfall left Ninian Park and joined Newport County's training staff.

STOCKIN Ronald (Ron)

Inside-forward

Born: Birmingham, 27 June 1931.
Career: West Bromwich Albion. Walsall 1951. Wolverhampton Wanderers 1952. Cardiff City 1954. Grimsby Town 1957. Nuneaton Borough.

■ After playing services football, Ron Stockin was an amateur with West Bromwich Albion and Walsall before turning professional with the Saddlers in January 1952. Yet within five weeks Stockin had left Fellows Park to join Wolves for a fee of £10,000. Unable to maintain a regular first-team spot, he moved to Cardiff City. He appeared regularly in 1954–55, his first season at Ninian park, but injury and the emergence of Gerry Hitchens saw his appearances dwindle. Strangely enough, Ron Stockin is best remembered by Bluebirds fans as having scored the goal against Wolves when City went down 9–1 at home to the Molineux club in September 1955! In the summer of 1956 Stockin was sold to Grimsby Town, later ending his career with Nuneaton Borough.

STOKER Gareth

Midfield/central-defender

Born: Bishop Auckland, 22 February 1973.
Career: Leeds United. Hull City 1991. Bishop Auckland. Hereford United 1995. Cardiff City 1997. Rochdale 1999. Scarborough 2000.

■ A former Leeds United junior, he began his career with Hull City, but

after two seasons with the Tigers, in which he made 38 appearances, he was released and went to play non-League football for his home-town team Bishop Auckland. Towards the end of the 1994–95 season he returned to League action with Hereford United where, despite having to battle hard for places, he made fairly regular appearances. His impressive form led to City paying £80,000 for his services in January 1997 and his gritty displays led to the Bluebirds reaching the play-offs. An enthusiastic member of the City midfield, he needed an operation on cruciate ligament damage and was ruled out for months. Unable to regain his place after the injury, he joined Rochdale on loan before signing on a permanent basis, but after one season at Spotland he joined Scarborough.

SUGRUE Paul Anthony

Forward/midfield

Born: Coventry, 6 November 1960.
Career: Nuneaton Borough. Manchester City 1980. Cardiff City 1981. Kansas City (USA). Middlesbrough 1982. Portsmouth 1984. Northampton Town 1986. Newport County 1986.

■ Paul Sugrue was playing non-League football for Nuneaton Borough when Manchester City manager Malcolm Allison paid out £30,000 to take him to Maine Road. Unable to make much of an impression, he came to Ninian Park on a free transfer in the summer of 1981 but only featured with Cardiff's first team on a few occasions before injury put him out for the rest of the season. After regaining full fitness, he was released by Len Ashurst and went to play in America for Kansas City. On his return to these shores, he signed for Middlesbrough and was a virtual ever present in two seasons at Ayresome Park. He later had brief spells with Portsmouth, Northampton Town and Newport County before injury ended his career.

SULLIVAN Colin John

Left-back

Born: Saltash, 24 June 1951.
Career: Plymouth Argyle 1968. Norwich

City 1974. Cardiff City 1979. Hereford United 1981. Portsmouth 1982. Swansea City 1985.

■ Colin Sullivan had already represented England at Youth international level when he signed for Plymouth Argyle in the summer of 1968. Winning a first-team place almost immediately, he made 230 League appearances for the Devon club and won two England Under-23 caps. In June 1974 Norwich City paid £70,000 to take Sullivan to Carrow Road. In his first season with the club, the Canaries finished third in Division Two. Over the next few seasons, Sullivan, who missed very few games, made 181 appearances before leaving Carrow Road in February 1979 to join Cardiff City. A regular in the Bluebirds side until struck by injury, his only League goal in Cardiff colours came in a 1–1 home draw against Burnley in May 1979. On leaving Ninian Park, he had a brief spell with Hereford United before a move to Portsmouth rebuilt his career. After making almost a century of League appearances for Pompey he returned to South Wales to end his playing days with Swansea City.

SULLIVAN Derrick

Wing-half

Born: Newport, 10 August 1930.
Died: 1983.
Career: Cardiff City 1947. Exeter City

1961. Newport County 1962. Hereford United. Ebbw Vale.

Welsh Cup finalist 1950–51. Division Two runner-up 1951–52, 1959–60. Welsh Cup winner 1955–56.

■ A wholehearted player, Derrick Sullivan was one of the Welsh team that did so well in the 1958 World Cup Finals – he was also one of the most versatile Cardiff City players. He worked his way up through the ranks to make his League debut for the Bluebirds in a 1–1 home draw against Newcastle United in April 1948 at the age of 17 years 243 days. He played on the left wing in that game, but over the next few seasons he played in all the forward

positions before settling into a half-back position in 1952–53. However, he still went on to play in almost every outfield shirt for the Bluebirds in a career that saw him score 21 goals in 305 League and Cup games. His best season in terms of goals scored was the club's promotion-winning season of 1959–60 when he netted eight times in 30 appearances. Sullivan left Ninian Park in September 1961 and joined Exeter City, later returning to South Wales to play for Newport County. Ending his first-class career at Somerton Park, he then had spells playing non-League football for Hereford United and Ebbw Vale.

SUMMERFIELD Kevin

Winger

Born: Walsall, 7 January 1959.
Career: West Bromwich Albion 1975. Birmingham City 1982. Walsall 1982. Cardiff City 1984. Plymouth Argyle 1984. Exeter City (loan) 1990. Shrewsbury Town 1990.

■ Kevin Summerfield had made just a handful of appearances for West Bromwich Albion when he left the Hawthorns and joined Birmingham City in May 1982. He failed to establish himself in the first team at St Andrew's and went on loan to Walsall. But when the teams were drawn together in the FA Cup he was recalled to St Andrew's and, after coming off the bench, scored the match-winning goal! Eventually he

joined the Saddlers on a permanent basis, and after scoring a goal every three games he arrived at Ninian Park on a free transfer in July 1984. However, City were struggling and Summerfield did too, and within months he was allowed to join Plymouth Argyle, whom he helped win promotion to the Second Division in 1985–86. Following a loan spell with Exeter City, Summerfield joined Shrewsbury Town where, after moving into a midfield role, he ended his career.

SUMMERHAYES David Michael

Wing-half

Born: Cardiff, 21 March 1947.
Career: Cardiff City 1965. Hereford United.

■ David Summerhayes will always be remembered for being Cardiff City's first substitute in League football when he came off the bench to replace Colin Baker on the opening day of the 1965–66 season as the Bluebirds beat Bury 1–0. Despite earning Welsh Under-23 honours, Summerhayes found it difficult to progress at Ninian Park, and in 1967 he joined non-League Hereford United where he stayed for several seasons, amassing 133 appearances. His brother Robert was on Cardiff's books and played League football for Newport County.

SUMMERS Christopher (Chris)

Forward

Born: Cardiff, 6 January 1972.
Career: Cardiff City 1990.

■ Welsh Youth international Chris Summers joined Cardiff City as a YTS in the summer of 1990. During the course of the 1990–91 season he came off the bench three times but failed to change the course of events at Maidstone United (lost 0–3) and Gillingham (lost 0–4) before helping the Bluebirds draw 1–1 with Blackpool. Released at the end of the season, he continued to play non-League football in the local Leagues.

SUTTON Melvyn Charles (Mel)

Midfield

Born: Birmingham, 13 February 1946.
Career: Aston Villa. Cardiff City 1967. Wrexham 1972. Crewe Alexandra 1982.

Welsh Cup winner 1969–70, 1970–71.
Welsh Cup finalist 1971–72.

■ Mel Sutton was signed from Aston Villa, where he was an amateur, by Cardiff City manager Jimmy Scoular in December 1967, though he had to wait until the start of the 1968–69 season before making his first-team debut. That came in a 1–0 home defeat by Charlton Athletic in August 1968, after which he missed very few games over the next four seasons. The hard-tackling midfielder was surprisingly allowed to leave Ninian Park in the summer of

1972 to join Wrexham for £15,000. He scored the only goal of the game on his debut for the Robins at Southend United and soon proved to be one of the game's great bargains. In nine seasons as a player at the Racecourse Ground, he appeared in 469 games and in 1977–78, when the club won the Third Division Championship and reached the sixth round of the FA Cup, Sutton played in every game. During that season he became player-assistant manager to Arfon Griffiths and in May 1981, when Griffiths resigned his post, he became manager. He later joined Arfon Griffiths at Crewe Alexandra, but after a short stay at Gresty Road he left the game.

SWAN Maurice Michael George

Goalkeeper

Born: Dublin, 27 September 1938.
Career: Drumcondra. Cardiff City 1960. Hull City 1963. Dundalk. Drumcondra.

■ Republic of Ireland international Maurice Swan was a confident and skilful goalkeeper who signed for First Division newcomers Cardiff City from Drumcondra in the summer of 1960. He had to share the goalkeeping duties at Ninian Park with Ron Nicholls and

Welsh international Graham Vearncombe, and it was Boxing Day 1960 before he made his debut in a 1–1 draw at West Bromwich Albion. That season he appeared in eight games and was only on the losing side twice. The following season he had made just one appearance when a damaged collarbone kept him out of the game for a year. This had first been damaged when diving at the feet of Newcastle United's Len White the previous season. In June 1963 he left to play for Hull City, his agile anticipation, courage and the ability to inspire his colleagues winning him many admirers at Boothferry Park. In 1965–66, while with the Tigers, he won a Third Division Championship medal, but after 103 League appearances he returned to Ireland where he played for Dundalk. By the early 1970s he was back guarding Drumcondra's goal.

TAGGART Robert (Bobby)

Inside-forward

Born: Newmains, 10 March 1927.
Career: Coltness United. Cardiff City 1949. Torquay United 1950. Aldershot 1951.

■ After playing his early football for Coltness United, inside-forward Bobby Taggart joined the Bluebirds. A regular in the club's reserve side, he stepped in for two consecutive games in 1949–50, his only season with the club. In June 1950 he took the road to Torquay and appeared in 14 games for the Plainmoor club before moving to Aldershot, where he ended his career after 16 first-team appearances.

TALBOT Frank Leslie (Les)

Inside-forward

Born: Hednesford, 3 August 1910.
Career: Hednesford Town. Blackburn Rovers 1930. Cardiff City 1936. Walsall 1939.

Welsh Cup finalist 1938–39.

■ Brother of Aston Villa's Alex Talbot, he played non-League football for his home-town team Hednesford Town before being given a chance in the Football League by Blackburn Rovers. Though his opportunities were somewhat limited in his first few years at Ewood Park, he eventually established himself in the Lancashire club's side, and when, in the summer of 1936, he signed for Cardiff City he had scored 20 goals in 90 League games. Talbot arrived at Ninian Park in a double deal with Rovers reserve Albert Pinxton, and he was one of the main reasons for City's improvement in the immediate pre-war years. The scorer of some vital goals, he had spent three seasons with the Bluebirds when, in the summer of 1939, he joined Walsall, where he played in the first three games of the abandoned 1939–40 season. During the war he 'guested' for Bath City, but when peacetime football resumed he returned to Walsall and had one season with the Saddlers. He continued his links with the game over the years and was still coaching in Holland during the 1970s.

TAPSCOTT Derek Robert

Centre-forward

Born: Barry, 30 June 1932.
Career: Barry Town. Arsenal 1953.
Cardiff City 1958. Newport County 1965.
Cinderford Town. Carmarthen.

Welsh Cup winner 1958–59. Division Two runner-up 1959–60. Welsh Cup finalist 1959–60.

■ Derek Tapscott was one of the Football League's most consistent goalscorers of the mid and late 1950s. Tapscott hailed from a family of 17. On leaving school, he had a variety of jobs including working on a building site. He also played football for his home-town side Barry Town, where he built up a reputation as a prolific goalscorer. In October 1953 Arsenal manager Tom Whittaker gave him the chance to sign for one of the most famous teams in the country. He scored twice on his debut as the Gunners beat Liverpool 3–0, and then, following his international debut for Wales, he scored twice at Portsmouth to end the season with five goals in as many matches. He soon established himself as a first-team regular and consistently headed the Arsenal goalscoring charts. His best season in terms of goals scored was 1956–57 when his 25-goal total was Arsenal's highest since Ronnie Rooke

netted 33 in 1947–48. In 1957–58 he had to undergo a cartilage operation and this cost him his place in the Welsh side for the 1958 World Cup Finals. Even when he regained full fitness, Arsenal decided he had no future at Highbury and sold him to Cardiff City for £15,000. He was the Bluebirds leading scorer in 1959–60 with 20 goals as the Ninian Park club won promotion to the First Division. He was top scorer again the following season with 21 goals in 39 games, including his first City hat-trick in a 3–1 win over West Bromwich Albion. Despite Cardiff being relegated in 1961–62, Tapscott netted his second hat-trick for the club in a 3–2 home defeat of Birmingham City. The following season he netted his third treble in a 4–2 win at Charlton Athletic. Tapscott continued to score on a regular basis, and in seven years at Ninian Park he netted 99 goals in 233 first-team games, including six in the 16–0 Welsh Cup defeat of Knighton in 1960–61, still the individual scoring record of any Cardiff player in a first-team fixture. In July 1965 he joined Newport County before later moving into non-League football with Cinderford Town and Carmarthen.

TAYLOR Peter Mark Richard

Left-winger

Born: Hartlepool, 20 November 1964.
Career: Hartlepool United 1982. Crewe Alexandra (loan) 1985. Blackpool 1986. Cardiff City (loan) 1990. Wrexham 1992.

■ After a disagreement with the management at his home-town club, Hartlepool United, and a loan spell with Crewe, Mark Taylor joined Blackpool on a free transfer in the summer of 1986. After making his debut as a winger, he moved to a more central role, backing up Paul Stewart and, after scoring 14 goals in his first season, was top scorer with 21 in 1987–88. Midway through the following season, Taylor suffered a nasty injury at Huddersfield, which sidelined him for almost two years. The injury left him short of pace and he went on loan to Cardiff – three goals in wins over Carlisle United and Halifax Town didn't persuade Len Ashurst to make the deal permanent, and he signed for Wrexham instead. Taylor, who had scored 46 goals in 137 games for Blackpool, never made his mark at the Racecourse Ground and, after qualifying as a physiotherapist, he took such a role with Bolton Wanderers.

TAYLOR Sidney G.

Outside-left
Born: Cardiff.
Career: Cardiff City 1934.

■ Not too much is known about winger Sid Taylor, apart from the fact that as the club were struggling at the wrong end of the Third Division South they drafted him in from local football. Though he helped make one of Reg Keating's goals in a 3–2 defeat at Bristol Rovers, he wasn't called upon again.

TAYLOR William (Billy)

Winger

Born: Langley Green, 15 June 1898.
Career: Langley Green Zion. West Bromwich Albion 1920. Redditch Town. Stourbridge. Cardiff City 1922. Aberdare Athletic 1924. Hull City 1926. Norwich City 1931. Llanelly. Aldershot 1933. Chance & Hunt.

■ Unable to force his way into West

Bromwich Albion's League side, winger Billy Taylor left the Hawthorns to play non-League football for Redditch Town and Stourbridge before joining Cardiff in the summer of 1922. The legendary Jack Evans was in possession of the number 11 shirt and Taylor found himself in the role of understudy. Midway through the 1924–25 season he moved to Aberdare Athletic where he had a productive 18 months with the Welsh Valley team. Taylor's career took an upturn when he joined Hull City in June 1926 as, over the next five seasons, he scored 15 goals in 151 games before following a spell with Norwich City. He ended his playing days with Aldershot.

TENNANT James (Jim)

Outside-right

Born: Glasgow.
Career: Cardiff City 1932. St Johnstone.

■ Winger Jim Tennant came south from his native Scotland to try his luck with Cardiff City during the course of the 1932–33 season. Replacing George Emmerson, he made two League appearances for the Bluebirds before leaving Ninian Park to return north of the border with St Johnstone, whom he helped reach the Scottish Cup semi-final.

THIRLAWAY William J. (Billy)

Winger

Born: New Washington, 10 October 1896.
Died: 1983.
Career: Usworth Colliery. West Ham United 1921. Southend United 1924. Luton Town 1924. South Shields 1925. Birmingham 1926. Cardiff City 1927. Tunbridge Wells Rangers. Usworth Colliery.

FA Charity Shield winner 1927–28. Welsh Cup winner 1927–28. Welsh Cup finalist 1928–29.

■ Billy Thirlaway played his early football with Usworth Colliery before signing for West Ham United and making his League debut for the Hammers in 1921. He then had spells with Southend, Luton and South Shields before joining Birmingham,

who were then a First Division club. Unable to settle at St Andrew's, he joined Cardiff City in March 1927 and made his debut in a 2–2 draw at Sunderland. Having played in an earlier round of the FA Cup with Birmingham, he was unable to face Arsenal in the FA Cup Final, which of course City won 1–0. In 1927–28 he showed outstanding form as City finished sixth in the First Division, scoring nine goals in 40 League games. Also that season he was in the Bluebirds side that beat Corinthians 2–1 to lift the FA Charity Shield. On leaving Cardiff he played non-League football for Tunbridge Wells Rovers.

THOMAS Daniel

Midfielder/forward

Born: Cardiff, 13 May 1985.
Career: Cardiff City 2004. Carmarthen Town 2005.

■ First year professional Danny Thomas's impressive displays for the club's reserve side, including coming off the bench to score two goals in a 3–2 win at Swindon Town, saw him listed among the substitute's for Cardiff's Championship home game against

Preston North End in November 2004. With the Bluebirds trailing 1–0, Thomas replaced Chris Barker as Lennie Lawrence sought to pull the game round. With the exception of the FAW Premier Cup quarter-final against Bangor City, Thomas didn't appear in the City side again but is definitely one to watch for the future. Despite that, he was allowed to leave Ninian Park and left to play Welsh League football for Carmarthen Town.

THOMAS David John (Dai)

Forward

Born: Caerphilly, 26 September 1975.
Career: Swansea City 1994. Watford 1997. Cardiff City 1998. Merthyr Tydfil.

Division Three Promotion 1998–99.

■ Dai Thomas began his career with Swansea City, where his prolific goalscoring displays for the Vetch Field club's reserve side earned him his League debut against Plymouth Argyle towards the end of the 1994–95 season. Unable to hold down a regular place, he was offered a free transfer but decided to stay and fight for his place. In 1996–97 he appeared on a more regular basis and ended the season with 10 goals to his name. This prompted Watford to pay £100,000 for his services in readiness for the start of the new season. Although securing Welsh Under-21 honours, he was unable to command a regular place at Vicarage Road, though he did play in enough games to win a Second Division Championship medal. Signed by Cardiff in the summer of 1998, he spent a disappointing personal season on the fringe of the Bluebirds team. Still, he scored a few crucial goals and after pledging to spend the summer training in order to get fitter hopes were high for a better season in 1999–2000. Sadly, he had another disappointing campaign and his career went sharply downhill following much publicised off the field events in the summer of 2000, and after a spell at Dr Martens League club Merthyr Tydfil he finished the following season playing in the South Wales Amateur League for Bryntirion.

THOMAS Martin Richard

Goalkeeper

Born: Senghenydd, 28 November 1959.
Career: Bristol Rovers 1977. Cardiff City
(loan) 1982. Southend United (loan)
1983. Newcastle United 1983.
Middlesbrough (loan) 1984. Birmingham
City 1988. Cheltenham Town.

■ There was a time when Martin
Thomas seemed set for an illustrious
international future, but the 'keeper,
who was understudy to Dai Davies,
made only one appearance at full
international level. Starting out with
Bristol Rovers, he was their first-choice
'keeper for three and a half seasons
before dislocating a finger and needing
an operation. Unable to regain his place,
he joined the Bluebirds on loan during
the early part of the 1982–83 season, but
after the clubs failed to agree terms he
had another loan spell with Southend.
Thomas then joined Newcastle United,
where he won his long-awaited cap.
Eventually, though, more injuries led to
frustration and a move to Birmingham
City. Thomas's penalty saves against
Swansea in 1991 were instrumental in
the club winning the Leyland Daf Cup.
He then began to suffer a spate of
niggling injuries and in 1993 left the
club to play non-League football for
Cheltenham Town. Later he became a
goalkeeping coach for a number of clubs
and the FA at Lilleshall.

THOMAS Peter John

Outside-right

Born: Pontypridd, 18 October 1932.

Career: Cardiff City 1953. Exeter City
1954. Newport County 1956.

■ Flying winger Peter Thomas replaced
the injured Mike Tiddy in the opening
game of the 1953–54 season and scored
in what was his debut in a 2–1 defeat of
Aston Villa. Unfortunately, he was
unable to maintain his early promise
and drifted back into the reserves before
moving to Exeter City in December
1954. His style of play was hugely
popular with the St James's Park
faithful, but even so he left the Grecians
after 29 appearances to end his League
career with Newport County.

THOMAS Roderick John (Rod)

Full-back

Born: Glyncorrwg, 1 January 1947.
Career: Gloucester City. Swindon Town
1964. Derby County 1973. Cardiff City
1977. Gloucester City. Newport County
1982.

■ A cool, unhurried defender, Rod
Thomas was discovered by Swindon
Town playing for Gloucester City in the
Southern League as an inside-forward.
During his years at the County Ground,
Thomas made the Welsh full-back
position his own, and it was surprising
that he was not signed by a First
Division club earlier than his move to
Derby County. Thomas gave eight
seasons' service to the Wiltshire club
and was a member of the side that won
the League Cup in 1969, a season in
which they also achieved promotion to
the Second Division. Though he joined
Derby in November 1973, he had to
wait to make his mark. An injury to Ron
Webster let him into the side, and he
helped the Rams win the 1974–75
League Championship. Able to play
anywhere in the back four, he joined
Cardiff City in October 1977, when
manager Jimmy Andrews paid £10,000
for his signature. He made his debut in
a 2–0 win over Stoke City and, though
he stayed at Ninian Park for four years,
injury problems curtailed his overall
appearances. However, when he did
appear he continued to demonstrate a
cool head until he left to play for
Gloucester City in 1981. He then had a
short spell with Newport County before

leaving Somerton Park to work for
Francis Lee's paper empire.

THOMAS Walter Keith

Outside-right

Born: Oswestry, 28 July 1929.
Career: Oswestry Town. Sheffield
Wednesday 1950. Cardiff City 1952.
Plymouth Argyle 1953. Exeter City 1956.

■ He began his career with his home-
town club Oswestry Town, where his
impressive displays on the wing
prompted Sheffield Wednesday to offer
him a chance to play in the Football
League. In two years at Hillsborough,
Thomas made just 10 appearances, and
in July 1952 he joined Cardiff City.
Despite scoring on his debut in a 2–1
reversal at home to West Bromwich
Albion, Thomas found the competition
at Ninian Park too great and in
November 1953 moved on to Plymouth
Argyle. He spent three seasons at Home
Park but again couldn't command a
regular place and joined Exeter City,
from where he later drifted into local
non-League football.

THOMPSON Andrew Richard (Andy)

Left-back/midfield

Born: Cannock, 9 November 1967.
Career: West Bromwich Albion 1985.
Wolverhampton Wanderers 1986.

Tranmere Rovers 1997. Cardiff City 2000. Shrewsbury Town 2002.

■ Determined full-back Andy Thompson began his career with West Bromwich Albion but was never given a chance at the Hawthorns, and in November 1986 he joined Wolves along with Steve Bull. In his second season with the club he helped them win the Fourth Division title and lift the Sherpa Van Trophy. He was the only ever present in 1988–89 when the Molineux club won the Third Division Championship, and over the next eight seasons he missed very few games. Awarded a testimonial by the club, he went on to score 45 goals in 451 first-team games before, in July 1997, joining Tranmere Rovers. After a good first season at Prenton Park, he was laid low by a spate of injuries including ligament trouble and after 116 games was given a free transfer. On joining Cardiff City, Thompson, who was more effective as an organiser rather than a creative force, had his season disrupted by injury, tearing his stomach muscles – an injury that required surgery. Later placed on

the open to offers list, he joined Shrewsbury Town, initially on loan, before joining the Gay Meadow club on a permanent basis. Unable to prevent the club being relegated to the Conference, he then retired.

THOMPSON Christopher David (Chris)

Midfield

Born: Walsall, 24 January 1960.
Career: Bolton Wanderers 1977. Lincoln City (loan) 1983. Blackburn Rovers 1983. Wigan Athletic 1986. Blackpool 1988. Cardiff City 1990. Walsall 1991.

■ England Youth international Chris Thompson made his League debut for Bolton Wanderers as a striker in the club's last season in Division One in 1979–80. After switching to midfield, he became a regular in the Trotters side and grabbed some vital goals to prevent the Lancashire club from a second successive relegation. Following a brief loan period at Lincoln, he joined Blackburn Rovers where he reverted to a striking role and in 1984–85 was the club's leading scorer with 15 goals as they just missed out on promotion to

Division One. After suffering a spate of niggling injuries, Thompson joined Wigan Athletic and, in only his fourth game, netted a hat-trick in a 5–1 win over his home-town club Walsall. After helping the Latics almost win promotion and reach the sixth round of the FA Cup, he was again troubled by injuries and decided to sign for Blackpool. He spent just one season at Bloomfield Road before moving to Cardiff City, where he appeared in just a couple of games prior to ending his first-team career with the Saddlers.

THOMPSON Garry Linsey

Forward

Born: Birmingham, 7 October 1959.
Career: Coventry City 1977. West Bromwich Albion 1983. Sheffield Wednesday 1985. Aston Villa 1986. Watford 1988. Crystal Palace 1990. Queen's Park Rangers 1991. Cardiff City 1993. Northampton Town 1995.

Welsh Cup finalist 1993–94.

■ A powerful, athletic centre-forward, Garry Thompson began his long career with Coventry City where he scored 49 goals in 158 games and won selection for England at Under-21 level. In February 1983 he joined former Sky Blues boss Ron Wylie at West Bromwich Albion, the Baggies paying £225,000 for Thompson's services. He teamed up well with Cyrille Regis, scoring 45 goals in 105 games for Albion before signing for Sheffield Wednesday for what was then a club record £450,000. He failed to adapt his style of play to fit in with Wednesday's pattern, and after one season he left to play for Aston Villa. He later had spells with Watford, Crystal Palace and Queen's Park Rangers before arriving at Ninian Park on a free transfer in the summer of 1993. Mainly used as a target man with good aerial strength, he made plenty of chances for others but failed to get as many goals as he would have liked. On leaving City he played for Northampton Town and was later appointed the club's player-coach before being released in the summer of 1997. Having had almost 20 years in the game, he scored 153 goals in 584 games for his nine League clubs.

THOMPSON Steven

Forward

Born: Paisley, 14 October 1978.
Career: Dundee United. Glasgow
Rangers. Cardiff City 2005.

■ Paisley-born forward Steven
Thompson began his career with
Dundee United. In his first couple of
seasons at Tannadice he found himself in
and out of the side, and it was
1999–2000 before he won a regular
place. It was during the course of that
season that Thompson netted his first
senior goal for the club in a 2–0 win over
local rivals Dundee at Dens Park.
Though not a prolific scorer for the
Terrors he had taken his tally to 18 in
133 League games, including six in the
opening 20 games of the 2002–03 season
when Rangers manager Alex McLeish
signed him for the club. Thompson, who
made his full international debut against
France in 2002, scored two vital goals in
the closing stages of the campaign to
help Rangers win the Premier Division
title. A regular member of Berti Vogts
national squad, scoring against Hong
Kong and Canada, he then saw his
international opportunities limited due
to a lack of first-team football with
Rangers. Thompson joined Cardiff for a
fee of £250,000, and during his early
days with the club he impressed,
especially in the game against Burnley
when he scored two goals in the space of
three minutes in the 3–0 defeat of the
Clarets.

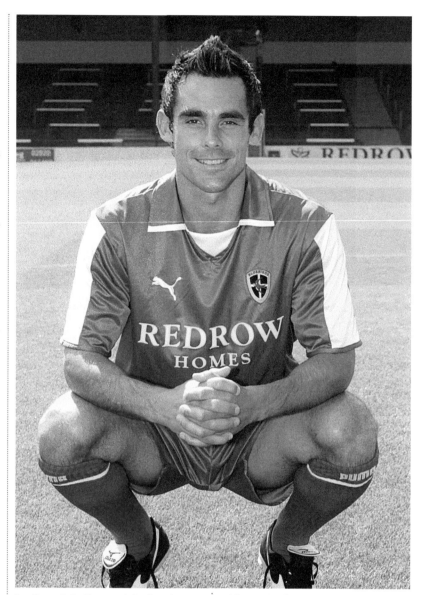

THORNE Peter Lee

Striker

Born: Manchester, 21 June 1973.
Career: Blackburn Rovers 1991. Wigan
Athletic (loan) 1994. Swindon Town
1995. Stoke City 1997. Cardiff City 2001.
Norwich City 2005.

Division Two promotion 2002–03.

■ Though he progressed to Blackburn
Rovers' professional ranks in the
summer of 1991, he was unable to break
into the club's first team, and after a
loan spell with Wigan Athletic he joined
Swindon Town. He was an instant 'hit'
at the County Ground, grabbing two
goals on his debut against Burnley and
another two a week later in Town's first-

leg Coca-Cola Cup semi-final against
Bolton. Though injuries took their toll
the following season, he did enough to
score 11 goals and help the Robins win
the Second Division Championship.
After refusing improved terms, Thorne,
who'd scored 27 goals in 77 League
outings, signed for Stoke City in the
summer of 1997 for a tribunal-fixed fee
of £350,000, rising to a maximum of
£550,000 linked to appearances. Back
and ankle injuries disrupted his first
couple of seasons, but after that he was
a revelation. In 1999–2000 he became
the first Stoke player for some time to
net more than 20 goals in a season, a
total that included four in the home
game against Chesterfield and a hat-

trick at Bristol Rovers. His winning goal
in the Autowindscreens Shield Final
typified his sharpness, answering any
possible doubts about his goalscoring
abilities! Surprisingly, after scoring 65
goals in 158 League games he was sold
to Cardiff City at the start of the
2001–02 season. Injuries kept him out
of action for a significant portion of the
campaign, but he still managed to score
eight times for the Bluebirds. In
2002–03 he teamed up well with Welsh
international Rob Earnshaw, the two of
them scoring 50 goals. Though he didn't
have his best season in front of goal, his
total of 16 helped the Ninian Park club
win promotion to the First Division via
the play-offs. Although he remained a

crucial player in 2003–04, injuries disrupted his progress and he was forced to miss the end of the campaign because he had fractured a bone at the bottom of his foot. Thorne left Cardiff prior to the start of the 2005–06 season, joining Norwich City more out of necessity than choice due to the financial difficulties at Ninian Park. Sadly, injuries disrupted his career at Carrow Road.

TIDDY Michael Douglas

Outside-right

Born: Helston, 4 April 1929.
Career: Torquay United 1946. Cardiff City 1950. Arsenal 1955. Brighton & Hove Albion 1958.

Welsh Cup finalist 1950–51. Division Two runner-up 1951–52.

■ Having joined Torquay United at the end of World War Two, Mike Tiddy had to complete his National Service before winning a regular place in the Devon club side. His potential as a winger of pace was noted, and in November 1950 he joined Cardiff City. For the next five seasons he was a virtual ever present in the Bluebirds side, thrilling the Ninian Park faithful with his speed, bravery and powerful shooting. Tiddy, who was easily identifiable by the distinctive broad grey streak in his dark hair, was one of the club's most popular players

during the early to mid-1950s. A lay-preacher in his spare time, he left Cardiff in September 1955, joining Arsenal along with Gordon Nutt in exchange for Brian Walsh. Unfortunately, much of his time at Highbury was spent on the treatment table, including a cartilage operation, and, on being unable to win back his first-team place following a return to full fitness, he moved to Brighton where he ended his career.

TOBIN Robert (Bobby)

Inside-left

Born: Cardiff, 29 March 1921.
Career: Cardiff Corries. Cardiff City 1940. Barry Town. Newport County 1949.

■ Local boy Bobby Tobin joined the Bluebirds from Cardiff Corries during World War Two and was one of a number of players who lost their best years to the hostilities. He appeared in a couple of games during the 1947–48 season before leaving to play for Barry Town. He later signed for Newport County but couldn't force his way into the Somerton Park club side.

TONG David Joseph

Midfield

Born: Blackpool, 21 September 1955.
Career: Blackpool 1973. Shrewsbury Town 1978. Cardiff City 1982. Rochdale (loan) 1985. Bristol City 1985. Gillingham 1986. Cambridge United 1986. Merthyr Tydfil.

Division Three runner-up 1982–83.

■ Midfielder David Tong joined his home-town club Blackpool, and after making his debut at Norwich City on the opening day of the 1974–75 season he became a regular member of the Seasiders team. In September 1978 he joined Shrewsbury Town, and in four years at Gay Meadow he hardly missed a game. He had scored 11 goals in 199 League and Cup games when, in the summer of 1982, he was surprisingly released. Tong then joined Cardiff City and repaid Len Ashurst's faith in him with a series of consistent displays in that 1982–83 season when the Bluebirds won promotion from Division Three.

Ever present in 1983–84, he was then loaned to Rochdale before joining Bristol City. There followed short spells with Gillingham and Cambridge United before he joined non-League Merthyr Tydfil. In May 1987 he reappeared at Ninian Park at right-back for the Merthyr team who won the Welsh Cup to earn a place in the European Cup-Winners' Cup.

TOSHACK John Benjamin

Forward

Born: Cardiff, 22 March 1949.
Career: Cardiff City 1966. Liverpool 1970. Swansea City 1978.

Welsh Cup winner 1967–68, 1968–69.

■ John Toshack, who once scored a hat-trick for Wales against Scotland, was, at just 16 years 236 days old, the youngest player to appear in a League match for the Bluebirds. Coming off the bench on 13 November 1965, he scored the final goal in a 3–1 win over Leyton Orient. Over the next few seasons he continued to find the net, hitting his first hat-trick for the club in January 1978 as Ebbw

John Toshack

Vale were beaten 8–0 in a Welsh Cup game. After teaming up with Brian Clark he netted 31 goals in 1968–69, including scoring in both legs of the Welsh Cup Final as Swansea were beaten 5–1 on aggregate, and he was the Second Division's leading scorer. In 1969–70 he netted his first League treble for Cardiff in a 4–2 defeat of Queen's Park Rangers and followed it up with another, early the following season, as Hull were beaten 5–1. It wasn't long before Liverpool persuaded Cardiff to part with him, Bill Shankly paying out a then club record fee of £110,000. The partnership he established with Kevin Keegan made the pair the most feared attacking force in the First Division. During their period together, Toshack carried off two UEFA Cup-winners' medals, three League Championships and the FA Cup. Sadly, he was forced to sit out Liverpool's first European Cup victory on the bench. Injuries were limiting Toshack's appearances for the Reds, and in March 1978 he left Liverpool to become player-manager of Swansea City. By the end of his first season at the Vetch he had helped the Swans clinch third place and promotion to the Third Division. In a three-year spell with Toshack at the helm, Swansea climbed from the Fourth Division to the First – a feat unrivalled in League history. Then it all started to go wrong and Toshack moved on to manage, in turn, Sporting Lisbon, Real Sociedad and Real Madrid. He guided the Spanish giants to the League Championship with a record number of points and goals in his first season with the club but it didn't prevent him from being sacked! Later, while managing Deportivo La Coruna and for a second time, John Toshack, who had spent 44 days in charge of the Welsh national side before, was put back in charge of the Welsh team as the replacement boss for Mark Hughes.

TOSHACK Jonathan Cameron

Forward

Born: Cardiff, 7 March 1970.
Career: Swansea City 1988. Bristol City 1989. Cardiff City 1991. Dundee.

■ The son of the legendary Welsh international and current Wales manager, he had spells on the books of both Swansea and Bristol City without making either club's League side. In February 1991 he joined Cardiff City, and after three appearances from the bench – in which City won two and drew one of the games – he made his first and only start at Wrexham, a match Cardiff lost. At the end of the season he tried his luck in Scotland with Dundee.

TOWNSEND Christopher Gordon (Chris)

Forward

Born: Abertillery, 30 March 1966.
Career: Cardiff City 1983.

■ Welsh Youth international Chris Townsend created a little bit of history by becoming the first player employed under the Youth Training Scheme to play in the Football League when he came off the bench in the 2–0 defeat of Carlisle United on 8 October 1983. Townsend had, in fact, scored a goal past Peter Shilton in a friendly against Southampton, which promoted him to the first-team squad. He was not retained after his YTS ran out, and he went to Southampton on trial but was not offered terms.

TUCKER Kenneth John

Winger

Born: Merthyr Tydfil, 15 July 1935.
Career: Aston Villa. Cardiff City 1955. Shrewsbury Town 1958. Northampton Town 1960. Hereford United. Merthyr Tydfil.

■ After a spell on amateur terms with Aston Villa, Ken Tucker joined the Bluebirds in October 1955. A diminutive winger, much of his time at Ninian Park was spent in the reserves, making just 13 appearances in two and a half years. He then joined Shrewsbury Town, and in his first season at Gay Meadow he helped them win promotion to the Third Division. After another season with the Shrews he signed for Northampton Town, but his stay at the County Ground was brief, and after a couple of seasons playing for

Hereford United he returned to his native Merthyr Tydfil to see out his career.

TUPLING Stephen

Midfield

Born: Wensleydale, 11 July 1964.
Career: Middlesbrough 1982. Carlisle United 1984. Darlington 1984. Newport County 1987. Cardiff City 1988. Torquay United (loan) 1988. Exeter City (loan) 1989. Hartlepool United 1989. Darlington 1992.

■ Much-travelled midfielder Steve Tupling had played just one game for Carlisle United prior to joining Darlington in October 1984. In his first season at the Feethams he helped the Quakers win promotion to the Third Division, going on to appear in 111 games before switching to Newport County in the summer of 1987. After just one season at Somerton Park Tupling left to play for Cardiff, the Ironsides having lost their League status. Unable to make much headway at Ninian Park, he made a handful of appearances and had loan spells with Torquay and Exeter before joining

Hartlepool. In 1990–91 he helped them win promotion from the Fourth Division, later ending his first-class career back at Darlington.

TURNBULL William (Billy)

Forward/full-back.

Born: Blyth, 21 December 1900.
Career: New Delavel Villa. Blyth Spartans. West Stanley. Cardiff City 1922. Newport County 1924. Ashington 1925. Manchester City 1926. Chesterfield 1927. Brighton & Hove Albion 1928. Ashington. Blyth Spartans. Wallsend Town. Gateshead 1932. Oldham Athletic 1934.

■ Able to play in any of the forward positions, Billy Turnbull played his early football for Blyth Spartans and West Stanley before joining Cardiff City in 1922. Despite some promising displays in the club's reserve side, he made just one first-team appearance for the Bluebirds as a stand-in for the injured Jimmy Gill against Oldham Athletic in April 1923. Though he failed to get on the scoresheet, he made City's second goal for Joe Clennell in a 2–0 win. He left Ninian Park early the following season to play for Newport County but his most successful spells in League football came later for Ashington and then Chesterfield where he scored a goal every other game. The much-travelled Turnbull later played for Brighton before making his last League appearance for Gateshead.

TURNER Albert (Bert)

Outside-left/inside-left

Born: Sheffield, 3 September 1907.
Career: Ecclesfield United. Halifax Town 1925. Denaby United. Hull City 1928. Walsall 1931. Doncaster Rovers 1933. Cardiff City 1937. Bristol Rovers 1938. Bath City.

■ After playing non-League football with Denaby United, winger Bert Turner stepped up to League level with Hull City. Never an automatic choice for the Tigers, he moved on to Walsall, and in two years at Fellows Park he scored 21 goals in 56 League games. It was this kind of form that led to Doncaster Rovers signing him in the summer of 1933. In his first season for the Belle Vue club he scored 26 goals, including five against New Brighton, as the Yorkshire club went on to win the Third Division Championship. He had scored 52 goals in 119 games when, in 1937, Cardiff City secured his services. After making his debut in a 1–1 draw at Clapton Orient on the opening day of the 1937–38 season, Turner went on to score 19 goals in 40 games, many of them powerfully-struck left-foot drives. Though he netted against Exeter City on the opening day of the following campaign, he then lost his place and moved on to Bristol Rovers before ending his playing days with Bath City.

TURNER Charles

Left-back

Born: Bangor.
Career: Bangor City. Cardiff City 1936. Workington.

■ Formerly with Bangor City where his performances attracted the attention of a number of League clubs, Charles Turner joined Cardiff City in the summer of 1936. Though he only made two first-team appearances, his last game in a Bluebirds shirt saw City lose 8–1 at Southend United! On leaving Ninian Park he moved to Workington.

TURNER Robert Peter (Robbie)

Forward

Born: Durham, 18 September 1966.
Career: Huddersfield Town 1984. Cardiff City 1985. Hartlepool United (loan) 1986. Bristol Rovers 1986. Wimbledon 1987. Bristol City 1989. Plymouth Argyle 1990. Notts County 1992. Shrewsbury Town (loan) 1993. Exeter City 1994. Cambridge United 1995. Hull City (loan) 1996.

■ Much-travelled gangling striker Robbie Turner joined Sunderland straight from school but was offered a trial by Huddersfield Town and signed apprentice forms for them. He graduated to the first team and made a couple of appearances before being involved in an incident concerning Huddersfield's youth team, which led to himself and others being released. He came to Ninian Park and had a reasonable season in the poor 1985–86 team, scoring seven goals in 34 games as City were relegated. After a loan spell at Hartlepool, he discovered he wasn't in Frank Burrows plans and joined Bristol Rovers. He then followed Bobby Gould to Wimbledon before switching to Bristol City, where he formed an excellent partnership with Bob Taylor in the Robins 1989–90 promotion success and FA Cup run. He then signed for Plymouth Argyle, the Pilgrims paying £150,000 for his services, and was the club's leading marksman. After that he played for Notts County, Shrewsbury Town (on loan), Exeter City and Cambridge United, though his final games were spent on loan with Hull City.

TYSOE George Frank

Winger

Born: Northampton, 13 November 1902.
Career: Northampton Town 1920. Birmingham Tramways. Cardiff City 1926. Charlton Athletic 1927. Crewe Alexandra 1929. Derry City.

■ Able to play on either wing, Frank Tysoe started out with his home-town club Northampton Town, but his chances were limited due to the form of Louis Page, and he joined Birmingham Tramways Co, turning out for their football team. He was then given a trial by Cardiff City before signing professional terms for the Bluebirds. However, following the arrival of Billy Thirlaway he spent all but two games in the reserves before, following a brief spell with Charlton Athletic, he joined Crewe Alexandra. He later ended his career across the water playing for Derry City.

UNSWORTH Jamie Jonathan

Right-back

Born: Bury, 1 May 1973.
Career: Cardiff City 1991. Radcliffe Borough.

■ Bury-born full-back Jamie Unsworth arrived at Ninian Park on a YTS and, after some solid displays in the club's reserve side, made his debut in a 2–1 home win over Scarborough when he came off the bench to replace the injured Chris Pike. His only start came in the 2–1 defeat of Doncaster Rovers when the aforementioned Pike scored twice from the penalty spot. Despite his promise, Unsworth was later released and returned to the Bury area to play non-League football for Radcliffe Borough.

UPTON James Edwin Glen

Full-back

Born: Coatbridge, 3 June 1940.
Career: Glasgow Celtic. Cardiff City 1963. Bath City.

■ Versatile defender Jim Upton joined Cardiff on a free transfer from Glasgow Celtic in the summer of 1963. Having been unable to force his way into the Bhoys side, he was quickly pressed into first-team action following the spate of injuries suffered by the Bluebirds during the early part of the 1963–64 season. He lost his place following a 5–2 defeat at Charlton Athletic and spent the rest of the season in the reserves before then moving on to Bath City.

VALENTINE Albert Finch

Centre-forward

Born: Higher Ince, 3 June 1907.
Died: 1990.
Career: Ince St Mary's. Liverpool 1927. Abram Colliery. Horwich RMI. Ince St Mary's. Southport 1928. Cardiff City 1929. Wigan Borough 1931. Chester 1931. Crewe Alexandra 1932. Macclesfield. Halifax Town 1934. Stockport County 1937. Accrington Stanley 1937. Oldham Athletic 1938. Ince St Mary's.

■ A former miner, his early football, following a trial with Liverpool, was played with Abram Colliery and Horwich RMI before he turned professional with Southport. In his only season at Haig Avenue, Valentine scored 17 goals in 21 games, prompting Cardiff City to secure his services in the summer of 1929. He found it difficult to win a regular first-team place at Ninian Park, and, although he got a run of 12 games in 1930–31, when Jim McCambridge and Albert Keating signed he joined Wigan Borough. Before

the end of the 1931–32 season he had moved on to Chester, later having spells with Crewe and Macclesfield before signing for Halifax Town. In 1934–35 he helped the Shaymen finish runners-up in the Third Division South, and in three seasons, in which he was the club's top scorer, he netted 89 goals in 114 games before finishing his career with spells at Accrington Stanley and Oldham Athletic.

VAUGHAN Anthony John (Tony)

Defender

Born: Manchester, 11 October 1975.
Career: Ipswich Town 1994. Manchester City 1997. Cardiff City (loan) 1999. Nottingham Forest 2000. Scunthorpe United (loan) 2002. Mansfield Town (loan) 2002. Motherwell (loan) 2003. Mansfield Town 2003. Barnsley 2004.

■ Versatile defender Tony Vaughan's early career with Ipswich Town saw him serve a number of suspensions, mainly due to arriving slightly late for challenges! Though he also missed a number of matches through injury, he had appeared in 79 games for the Tractor Boys when he signed for Manchester City at a cost of £1.35 million in July 1997. At Maine Road he was moved into a midfield role, but though he looked comfortable on the ball he returned to defence. Despite making a good contribution to Manchester City's promotion to Division One in 1998–99, he became a fringe player the following season, and in September 1999 he joined Cardiff City on loan. In three months at Ninian Park he performed well, and the Bluebirds were keen to sign him and agreed a fee with Manchester City, but the deal fell through. Placed on the transfer list, he joined Nottingham Forest for £350,000 and became a great favourite at the City Ground until falling out with David Pleat. Loaned to Scunthorpe United, Mansfield Town and Motherwell, he eventually joined the Field Mill club on a free transfer before being released by the Stags in the summer of 2004. On leaving Field Mill, Vaughan joined Barnsley where manager Paul Hart made him captain

but sadly his time at Oakwell was disrupted by a series of niggling injuries.

VAUGHAN Nigel Mark

Midfield

Born: Caerleon, 20 May 1959.
Career: Newport County 1977. Cardiff City 1983. Reading (loan) 1987. Wolverhampton Wanderers 1987. Hereford United 1990. Newport County.

■ Nigel Vaughan began his League career with Newport County, and while with the Somerton Park club, where he scored 32 goals in 224 games, he won the first of 10 Welsh caps. In September 1983 he joined Cardiff City as part of an unusual five-man exchange deal between the two clubs. He suffered a disappointing debut as the Bluebirds lost at home to Barnsley 3–0. He then played in all the remaining 36 games of the season as the club finished 15th in Division Two. In 1984–85 the diminutive forward was Cardiff's top scorer with 16 goals, but despite his efforts the club were relegated to

Division Three. He was the club top scorer again the following season but the Bluebirds were relegated for a second successive season and dropped into the League's basement. In 1986–87 he became dissatisfied with Fourth Division football and played on a weekly contract until, after scoring 54 goals in 178 games, he left to join Wolverhampton Wanderers for a fee of £12,000. He actually made his Wolves debut at Ninian Park, coming on as a substitute and scoring in a 3–2 win for the Bluebirds. He later ended his first-team career with Hereford United before becoming player-manager of his first club Newport County.

VAUGHAN Thomas (Tommy)

Inside-right/centre-forward
Born: Cardiff.
Career: Treorchy. Chester 1932. Cardiff City 1934. Folkestone.

■ Having played his early football for Treorchy, Tommy Vaughan had a couple of games for Chester before joining Cardiff. He made his Bluebirds debut against Charlton Athletic on the opening day of the 1934–35 season, when he was one of eight debutants. In and out of the side throughout the season, he was later released and moved on to play non-League football for Folkestone.

VEARNCOMBE Graham

Goalkeeper

Born: Cardiff, 28 March 1934.
Died: 1990.
Career: Cardiff City 1952. Merthyr Tydfil.

Welsh Cup winner 1955–56, 1958–59. 1963–64. Division Two runner-up 1959–60. Welsh Cup finalist 1959–60.

■ Goalkeeper Graham Vearncombe, who was capped twice by Wales, played his first game for the Bluebirds on the final day of the 1952–53 season in a 2–0 defeat at Aston Villa. However, over the next two years he appeared in only 17 League games as he understudied Ron Howells. He eventually became the Ninian Park club's first choice 'keeper midway through the 1955–56 campaign. That season also saw him win a Welsh

Cup medal as Swansea Town were beaten 3–2 in the Final. In 1957–58 he shared the goalkeeping duties with Ken Jones, but the following season he played in only the final game of the campaign as the club's cricketing 'keeper Ron Nicholls took over between the posts. However, he was the club's 'keeper in all bar one of the games in City's run to lifting the Welsh Cup again and won his second medal in that competition as Lovells Athletic were beaten 2–0. Vearncombe became the club's number-one custodian again in 1959–60 as the club won promotion and went on to appear in 238 first-team games, making the last of those appearances in the 2–0 Welsh Cup Final replay win over Bangor City in May 1964 to win his third such medal. Vearncombe left the Bluebirds in the close season to play part-time football for Merthyr Tydfil.

VICK Leigh

Midfield

Born: Cardiff, 8 January 1978.
Career: Cardiff City 1996.

■ Leigh Vick was still a trainee when he made an encouraging League debut in Cardiff's 2–1 home defeat against York City in March 1995. However, after

taking some heavy knocks in his next game against Brighton, a match the Bluebirds drew 0–0, he was rested. In 1995–96 he was only required towards the end of the campaign before City's season petered out to a non-event. Unable to force his way into the side the following season, he parted company with the club.

VIDMAR Anthony (Tony)

Defender

Born: Adelaide, Australia, 15 April 1969.
Career: Ekeren. Adelaide City (Australia). NAC Breda (Holland). Glasgow Rangers 1997. Middlesbrough 2002. Cardiff City 2003.

■ A much-travelled and vastly experienced Australian international, Tony Vidmar joined Glasgow Rangers from NAC Breda of Holland after earlier playing for Australian clubs Ekeren and Adelaide City. At Ibrox the 'play-anywhere' defender helped Rangers to the treble of Premier Division Championship, Scottish Cup and League Cup in 1998–99 and 1999–2000 and to a Scottish Cup and League Cup double in 2001–02. He had scored 11 goals, mainly from set pieces, in 159 games for Rangers when, in September 2002, he signed for Middlesbrough on a one-year contract. The transfer went ahead after the deadline had passed because the player was out of contract.

Finding himself in and out of the 'Boro side, he joined Cardiff in the summer of 2003 and had a very successful first season with the club. Operating at left-back or in the centre of defence, he won just about every award going at City's Player of the Year dinner, being voted top man by sponsors Redrow Homes, Cardiff City Supporters Club and Cardiff Valley RAMS.

VILLARS Anthony Keith (Tony)

Winger

Born: Pontypool, 24 January 1952.
Career: Pontnewydd. Panteg. Cwmbran Town. Cardiff City 1971. Newport County 1976.

Welsh Cup finalist 1971–72, 1974–75. Welsh Cup winner 1973–74. Division Three runner-up 1975–76.

■ Winger Tony Villars was a member of the Newport County groundstaff but left Somerton Park because the pay was so poor. He then took work as an electrician and began playing for Pontnewydd, a side that was so successful that Welsh League South side Panteg signed up the entire team en bloc! After some impressive displays for his next club Cwmbran Town, Cardiff City offered him a second stab at League football. A master at close dribbling, he was soon in the Bluebirds first team, making his debut in a 4–3 defeat at Fulham in November 1971. In 1974 he scored the goal against Crystal Palace that secured Cardiff's place in the Second Division for another season, when all had looked lost. Although an undoubted talent, Villars was an enigmatic player, flawed by inconsistency. He made three full international appearances for Wales while with Cardiff. However, dogged by injury problems, he could no longer hold down a first-team place, and in June 1976 he moved down the M4 to Newport County. His stay at Somerton Park was brief, and in December of the following year his contract was cancelled. Villars was only 25 – two and a half years after gaining international honours – when his career in senior soccer ended in enforced premature retirement. He

then ran his own milk business while occasionally turning out in charity matches.

VINCENT John Victor (Johnny)

Midfield

Born: West Bromwich, 8 February 1947.
Career: Birmingham City 1964. Middlesbrough 1971. Cardiff City 1972. Atherstone Town.

Welsh Cup winner 1972–73, 1973–74.

■ England Youth international Johnny Vincent was in Birmingham City's Football Combination side when only 16, and he had just turned 17 when he made his Football League debut against Blackburn Rovers. However, it was 1966–67 before he won a regular place in the Birmingham side, having developed into an attacking left-sided midfielder. Though he created many goalscoring opportunities for his teammates, he possessed a powerful shot in his left foot, and in 1967–68 he netted 14 times – his best return. Having scored 44 goals in 194 games he left St Andrew's for Middlesbrough for a fee of £40,000. Unable to settle in the North East, he was signed for Cardiff by Jimmy Scoular in October 1972. Ironically, he made a goalscoring debut for the Bluebirds against Middlesbrough, a match City won 2–0, and in his early days with the club he played very well. But the sacking of Jimmy Scoular and some bad injuries affected his form and, in the summer of 1975, he left Ninian Park to go into business in his native West Midlands and play non-League football for Atherstone Town.

WAKE Henry Williamson (Harry)

Right-half/inside-right

Born: Seaton Delaval, 21 January 1901. Died: 1978.
Career: Bigges Main Colliery. Newcastle United 1919. Cardiff City 1923. Mansfield Town 1931. Gateshead 1932.

Division One runner-up 1923–24. FA Cup finalist 1924–25. Welsh Cup finalist 1928–29. Welsh Cup winner 1929–30.

■ Signed from Newcastle United, he made his first-team debut for the Bluebirds in a 1–1 draw at Tottenham Hotspur in February 1924 and went on to play in 12 of the last 14 games of a season that saw City finish runners-up in the First Division. In 1924–25 he faced competition from Joe Nicholson, but Wake's form was such that he played in all of the club's eight FA Cup matches as they reached the Final, but they lost 1–0 to Sheffield United. It was Wake who lost the ball on the edge of the box for Fred Tunstall to net the game's only goal. In the FA Cup competition of 1926–27, he scored one of the goals in the 3–0 semi-final win over Reading but had to miss the Final when he damaged his kidneys in a 3–2 defeat of Sheffield Wednesday. Thankfully, despite a London newspaper reporting his death, he went on to play for Cardiff City until 1931 when he left to play for Mansfield Town, taking part in the Stags first-ever League game.

WALKER Lee

Midfield

Born: Pontypool, 27 June 1978.
Career: Cardiff City 1994.

■ Midfielder Lee Walker was a non-contract player whose only appearance for the Bluebirds was on the final day of the 1993–94 season. It was a disappointing day for the Pontypool-born youngster as Cardiff lost 2–0 at Bradford City, and he was replaced by Andy Evans in the second-half.

WALKER Philip Albert

Forward

Born: Kirkby-in-Ashfield, 27 January 1957.
Career: Mansfield YC. Chesterfield 1977. Rotherham United 1982. Cardiff City (loan) 1983. Chesterfield 1984. Scarborough 1986.

■ Phil Walker started out with Chesterfield and soon became a regular at Saltergate. In six seasons playing for the Spireites Walker scored 38 goals in 166 League games before, in 1982, joining Rotherham United. Unable to hold down a first-team spot, he came to Cardiff on loan, but after just two appearances (he was substituted in the latter) he returned to Millmoor before rejoining Chesterfield. He went on to take his tally of League goals for the Saltergate club to 47 in 204 games before leaving to make one appearance as a substitute for Scarborough on their entry to the Football League.

WALSH Alan

Midfield/forward

Born: Hartlepool, 9 December 1956. Career: Horden Colliery. Middlesbrough 1976. Darlington 1978. Bristol City 1984. Besitkas (Turkey). Walsall 1991. Huddersfield Town 1991. Shrewsbury Town 1992. Cardiff City 1992. Southampton 1993. Backwell United. Hartlepool United 1994.

■ After a series of impressive performances for Horden Colliery, Alan Walsh joined Middlesbrough, but in October 1978, after just three appearances as a substitute, he was allowed to move to Darlington. In six seasons at the Feethams, Walsh scored 90 League goals, still the club record. In the summer of 1984 Walsh left the Quakers to sign for Bristol City, the £18,000 fee being set by a Football League tribunal. In his first season at Ashton Gate he topped the Robins scoring charts with 20 goals. Forming a good understanding up front with Steve Neville, he helped the club reach two Wembley Finals, while in February 1987 he netted his only hat-trick for the club against Doncaster Rovers. He went on to score 88 goals in 257 games before leaving to join Turkish side Besitkas in July 1989. There followed brief non-contract spells with Walsall, Huddersfield and Shrewsbury before he made an appearance for Cardiff City in a goalless draw at Northampton Town in March 1992. He then had a spell at Hartlepool United before becoming Community Development Officer at Bristol Rovers.

WALSH Ian Patrick

Forward

Born: St David's, 4 September 1958. Career: Crystal Palace 1975. Swansea

City 1982. Barnsley 1984. Grimsby Town 1986. Cardiff City 1988.

Division Four runner-up 1987–88.

■ With his club Crystal Palace in the First Division, Ian Walsh became a regular choice for Wales. After scoring on his international debut in a 2–1 win over the Republic of Ireland in September 1979, he went on to find the net seven times in 18 appearances, including scoring both goals in a 2–0 defeat of Scotland in May 1981. Walsh helped Palace juniors win the FA Youth Cup in 1977 and then forced his way into the Eagles League side and became a key member of the Selhurst Park club's 1979 Second Division Championship-winning team. He had scored 23 goals in 117 League outings when, in February 1982, he moved to Swansea, playing in the Vetch Field club's First Division side. He averaged a goal every three games for the Swans but, following their relegation in 1982–83, he left to continue his career with Barnsley. He spent two seasons at Oakwell, netting 15 goals in 33 games in 1986–87. He then joined Grimsby Town and helped the Mariners win promotion in his first season at Blundell Park. Midway through the 1987–88 season Walsh suffered a spate of niggling injuries and was allowed to join Cardiff City. Most of his appearances for the Bluebirds were

from the bench, though he did net three goals in the club's first two home games of the 1988–89 campaign. Forced into premature retirement, he sold insurance but now works in the media and went into financial services.

WALSH John Brian

Winger

Born: Aldershot, 26 March 1932. Career: Arsenal 1949. Cardiff City 1955. Newport County 1961.

Welsh Cup winner 1955–56, 1958–59. Division Two runner-up 1959–60.

■ Winger Brian Walsh was playing for Chase of Chertsey when he joined Arsenal as an amateur in March 1949, turning professional five months later.

He had appeared in youth-team friendly matches for the club when he was called up for National Service in 1950. On his return to Highbury in 1952 he won a regular place in the club's Football Combination side before making his first-team debut against Cardiff City in September 1953. However, over the next two seasons he only made 17 League appearances, and in September 1955 he joined the Bluebirds in the deal that took Gordon Nutt and Mike Tiddy to Highbury. He made his debut in a 2–1 win at Preston North End and went on to thrill the Ninian Park crowd with his brilliant ball play for six seasons, scoring

35 goals in 224 League and Cup games. He won two Welsh Cup medals in 1956 and 1959, scoring two goals in the 3–2 win over Swansea in the first of those Finals. In November 1961 he left Ninian Park to play for Newport County for a fee of £2,000. During his time with the Bluebirds, Walsh qualified as a chartered accountant, and he concentrated on that profession after a season at Somerton Park.

WALTON George

Inside-forward

Born: Burnley, 1911.
Career: Burnley Works XI. Accrington Stanley 1929. Bolton Wanderers 1932. Cardiff City 1936. Walsall 1939.

Welsh Cup finalist 1938–39.

■ Inside-forward George Walton's introduction to League football was with Accrington Stanley in 1929. A fairly regular member of the Stanley side, he had scored 21 goals in 79 games when Bolton Wanderers paid £300 to take him to Burnden Park midway through the 1932–33 season. Despite being a consistent scorer for Bolton's Central League team, he couldn't hold down a regular place in the Wanderers side, and in October 1936 he took the opportunity to follow former Bolton teammate George Nicholson to Ninian Park. He made a substantial contribution to Cardiff's improvement in fortunes before World War Two, netting some vital goals. But of all his goals, by far the most important was the strike with which City knocked First Division Charlton Athletic out of the FA Cup in 1938–39. Walton later appeared for Walsall before the hostilities ended his playing career.

WALTON Mark Andrew

Goalkeeper

Born: Merthyr Tydfil, 1 June 1969.
Career: Luton Town 1987. Colchester United 1987. Norwich City 1989. Wrexham (loan) 1993. Dundee 1993. Bolton Wanderers (loan) 1994. Hong Kong. Barry Town. Merthyr Tydfil. Fulham 1996. Gillingham (loan) 1998. Brighton & Hove Albion 1999. Cardiff City 2000.

Division Three runner-up 2000–01. FAW Premier Cup winner 2001–02.

■ After failing to figure in a League game at Kenilworth Road, goalkeeper Mark Walton joined Colchester United, playing his 40th and final game for them in May 1989 when they beat Torquay 3–1 to avoid the bottom spot in Division Four. Norwich City paid £75,000 for his services, and though most of his time at Carrow Road was spent as understudy to Bryan Gunn he did win Welsh Under-21 honours and help the Canaries reach the 1992 FA Cup semi-final. Following a loan spell with Wrexham he joined Dundee, but following another loan period with

Bolton he drifted out of the League game. After spending some time in Hong Kong he played for both Barry Town and Merthyr Tydfil before returning to League action with Fulham. After helping the Cottagers win promotion from Division Three, he lost his place to Mark Taylor and, following a loan spell with Gillingham, signed for Brighton. In and out of the Seagulls side, he opted for a move to Cardiff City in the summer of 2000. He was an ever present in the Bluebirds goal until the arrival of Carl Muggleton, though he returned to the side for the last few games to help the club clinch promotion to Division Two. After missing the start of the 2001–02 season through injury, he found new signing Neil Alexander had established himself as the club's first-choice 'keeper. He still signed a 12-month contract to remain

at Ninian Park as Alexander's understudy but, following the signing of Martyn Margetson, this accomplished cricketer, who has played for Wales and the Minor Counties, parted company with the club.

WARBOYS Alan

Forward

Born: Goldthorpe, 18 April 1949.
Career: Doncaster Rovers 1967. Sheffield Wednesday 1968. Cardiff City 1970. Sheffield United 1972. Bristol Rovers 1973. Fulham. Hull City 1977. Doncaster Rovers 1979.

Welsh Cup winner 1970–71, 1971–72.

■ Hailing from the coal-mining area of South Yorkshire, Alan Warboys began his career with Doncaster Rovers, and after his first season at Belle Vue, in which he scored 12 goals in 39 games, he was signed by Sheffield Wednesday. The Owls were then a First Division club, but, when they lost their top flight status in 1970, Warboys, who had scored 13 goals in 71 games, was allowed to leave Hillsborough. Cardiff City manager Jimmy Scoular paid £42,000 to take Warboys to Ninian Park, and on his home debut he scored twice against his former club Sheffield Wednesday in a 4–0 win. He ended that 1970–71 season, in which City finished third in Division Two, with 13 goals in 17 League games, including all four in a 4–0 defeat of Carlisle United. He continued to find the net in 1971–72 and scored a hat-trick in the 5–2 home win over Preston North End. Early the following season he returned to Yorkshire to play for Sheffield United in a deal that saw Dave Powell and Gil Reece join the Bluebirds. He was soon on the move again, this time to Bristol Rovers where he had his most successful period, including scoring four in an 8–2 win against Brighton at the Goldstone Ground, a match savoured by millions on TV. Striking up a potent partnership with Bruce Bannister, he went on to score 60 goals in 162 games for the Pirates before a rift with manager Don Megson precipitated a switch to Fulham. He later had a spell with Hull City before ending his career with his first club Doncaster Rovers.

WARD David (Dai)

Inside-forward

Born: Barry, 16 July 1934.
Died: 1996.
Career: Barry Town. Bristol Rovers 1954. Cardiff City 1961. Watford 1962. Brentford 1963.

■ Dai Ward was a born opportunist, an inside-forward of pace, skill and bravery. He started his career with his home-town club Barry Town, where his goalscoring exploits alerted a number of clubs. Ward joined Bristol Rovers, and although he had to wait a couple of years before replacing Geoff Bradford he responded by scoring nine times in eight outings. In December 1956 Ward netted a hat-trick in the space of just four minutes in the match against Doncaster Rovers. Ward's best season for Rovers in terms of goals scored was 1958–59, when he found the net 27 times in 38 matches. This form led to the first of two international caps. After disagreeing on a number of occasions with Bristol Rovers boss Bert Tann, Ward embarked on a bitter battle to leave the club, which he criticised for lack of ambition. At one time he threatened to quit the game and actually took a job as an ice-cream salesman! The unhappy saga eventually ended in February 1961 when he signed for Cardiff City. Predictably he continued to score at a higher level and won a second Wales cap. In 1961–62 he was Cardiff's leading scorer with 17 goals, including doubles in the home wins over Blackpool (3–2) and West Ham United, (3–0) but at the end of the campaign City were relegated. Sadly he fell out of favour at Ninian Park too and saw his playing days out with Watford and Brentford, an anti-climax to a career that could and should have hit the heights.

WARD Gavin John

Goalkeeper

Born: Sutton Coldfield, 30 June 1970.
Career: Aston Villa. Shrewsbury Town 1988. West Bromwich Albion 1989. Cardiff City 1989. Leicester City 1993. Bradford City 1995. Bolton Wanderers 1996. Burnley (loan) 1998. Stoke City 1999. Walsall 2002. Coventry City 2003. Barnsley (loan) 2004. Preston North End 2004.

Division Three Champion 1992–93. Welsh Cup winner 1992–93.

■ After being freed by Aston Villa, goalkeeper Gavin Ward had spells with Shrewsbury Town and West Bromwich Albion without making either club's League side before joining the Bluebirds in October 1989. In his first two seasons at Ninian Park he found himself understudy to Roger Hansbury before winning a regular place in 1991–92. Ward was City's number one when they won the Third Division Championship in 1992–93, keeping 10 clean sheets in his 32 appearances. At the end of that season Leicester City paid £175,000 for his services, but during his time at Filbert Street he found it hard to displace the in-form Kevin Poole between the sticks. Moving on to Bradford City, he proved a huge hit at Valley Parade until joining Bolton as cover for Keith Branagan. He spent three years at Burnden Park, going on loan to Burnley where lack of funds ruled out a permanent signing. In February 1999 he moved to Stoke and helped the Potters win the Autowindscreens Shield Final at Wembley. Hugely popular in the Potteries, Ward suffered a bad back injury that kept him out of action for six months. Further long absences followed, and in the summer of 2002 he moved to Walsall, prior to playing for Coventry City and having a loan spell with Barnsley. He was released by the Highfield Road club in the summer of 2004. Ward then joined Preston North End as back up for the Lilywhites regular 'keeper Andy Lonergan and got his chance when the young 'keeper broke his hand. His displays were so impressive that he won an extension to his contract.

WARDLE George

Outside-right

Born: Kimblesworth, 24 September 1919.
Died: 1991.
Career: Middlesbrough 1937. Exeter City 1939. Cardiff City 1947. Queen's Park Rangers 1949. Darlington 1951.

■ After a single appearance for Middlesbrough, George Wardle joined Exeter City prior to the outbreak of World War Two, though it was the peacetime season of 1946–47 before he played his first game for the Grecians. At the end of that campaign Wardle was signed by Cardiff City to replace the departing Roy Clarke. He scored on his debut in a 3–2 win at Queen's Park Rangers and played in most of the games in 1947–48, scoring 10 goals in 36 outings. On leaving Ninian Park, he spent two years with Queen's Park Rangers before returning to his native North East with Darlington. On hanging up his boots, Wardle became a trainer with several League clubs.

WARE Paul David

Midfield

Born: Congleton, 7 November 1970.
Career: Stoke City 1988. Stockport County 1994. Cardiff City (loan) 1997. Hednesford Town. Macclesfield 1999. Nuneaton Borough (loan). Rochdale 2000. Hednesford Town.

■ Hardworking midfielder Paul Ware worked his way up through the ranks at Stoke City. He will long be remembered as the player who scored the goal that took the Potters to their second Wembley Final in the Autoglass Trophy in 1992 and then tragically hurt his knee and missed out on the big day! Ware, who had scored 14 goals in 142 games for Stoke, joined Stockport County in September 1994. Though his first-team chances were limited at Edgeley Park, he was always a committed player. In January 1997 he joined Cardiff on loan. Although performing well in his five games, his probing passes being a joy to watch, a permanent move failed to materialise, and he rejoined County. There followed a spell with non-League Hednesford Town before signing for Macclesfield. Another loan spell, this time with Nuneaton Borough, was followed by a move to Rochdale. His time at Spotland was hampered by injuries, and he rejoined Hednesford Town.

WARE Thomas (Tom)

Left-back

Born: Cardiff.
Career: Cardiff City 1930.

■ Tough-tackling left-back Tom Ware joined Cardiff from local football and most of his time at Ninian Park was spent as understudy to Bill Roberts. When he eventually got his chance in City's first team, Ware had a disastrous debut as the Bluebirds were beaten 7–0 by Preston North End. However, he kept his place in the side and appeared in 12 consecutive games before returning to the reserves.

WARNER Anthony Randolph (Tony)

Goalkeeper

Born: Liverpool, 11 May 1974.
Career: Liverpool 1994. Swindon Town (loan) 1997. Celtic (loan) 1998. Aberdeen (loan) 1999. Millwall 1999. Cardiff City 2004. Fulham 2005.

■ Goalkeeper Tony Warner joined Swindon Town on loan from Liverpool at a time when all three 'keepers on the Robins books were simultaneously struck down by injury. After returning to Anfield, Warner continued to be denied by the presence of David James

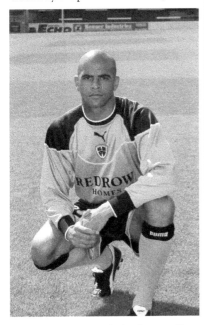

and Brad Friedel, and after loan spells north of the border with Celtic and Aberdeen he joined Millwall prior to the start of the 1999–2000 season. Under the expert guidance of Nigel Spink, he produced a series of inspirational performances to establish himself as a

regular in the side. He had a great season in goal in 2000–01 as Millwall won the Second Division Championship and then the following season developed a talent for saving penalties. An ever present in the Millwall goal for two successive seasons, he was voted the club's Player of the Year for the 2002–03 season and didn't miss a game until January 2004 when a neck injury kept him out of action until the end of the season. Warner had appeared in 225 games for the Lions when, in the summer of 2004, he joined Cardiff City. Initially he was understudy to Martyn Margetson but made his debut in a 3–1 defeat at Ipswich Town. After that, with the exception of Carling Cup matches, he was the club's first–choice 'keeper until losing out to Neil Alexander later in the season. He parted company with the Bluebirds in the summer of 2005, joining Premiership Fulham where he shared the goalkeeping duties with Welsh international Mark Crossley.

WARREN Frederick Windsor (Freddie)

Outside-left

Born: Cardiff, 23 December 1907.
Died: 1986.
Career: Cardiff City 1927. Middlesbrough 1929. Heart of Midlothian 1936. Barry Town.

■ Freddie Warren's first-team career at Ninian Park began in April 1928 after a season as understudy to George McLachlan, and the following season he had several outings in the senior side, culminating in his selection for Wales. In January 1930 Warren was rather controversially allowed to leave Ninian Park to sign for Middlesbrough for £8,000 – a transfer deal that also involved Joe Hillier and Jack Jennings. In his first full season at Ayresome Park, Warren scored 20 goals from the outside-left position and went on to net 50 goals in 162 appearances during his six seasons in the North East. In April 1936 he moved north of the border to play for Heart of Midlothian alongside the gifted forwards Andy Black and Tommy Walker. Though his wife couldn't settle in Edinburgh, Freddie

Warren remained with the Tynecastle club until the outbreak of World War Two, scoring 46 goals in 192 appearances. He then returned to South Wales to assist Barry Town.

WATKINS John Vincent

Outside-left

Born: Bristol, 9 April 1933.
Career: Bristol City 1951. Cardiff City 1959. Bristol Rovers 1961. Chippenham Town. Welton Rovers.

Division Two runner-up 1959–60. Welsh Cup finalist 1959–60.

■ Johnny Watkins spent three seasons at Ashton Gate before establishing himself as a regular in the Bristol City side. His powerful shooting brought him a number of important goals with a best return of 10 in 43 games during the 1957–58 season. The flying winger went on to score 21 goals in 105 games before surprisingly being allowed to join Cardiff City for £2,500 in the summer of 1959. He scored on his debut for the Bluebirds in a 3–2 home win over Liverpool and went on to be City's only ever present as they won promotion to the First Division as runners-up to Aston Villa, scoring 15 goals in his 42 appearances. Halfway through the following season he left Ninian Park to join Bristol Rovers in a deal which saw Dai Ward sign for the Bluebirds. He seemed to lose his form at Eastville and, after making just 23 appearances, drifted into non-League football, first with Chippenham Town and then Welton Rovers.

WATKINS Philip John

Wing-half

Born: Caerphilly, 2 January 1945.
Career: Cardiff City 1962. Barry Town.

■ Wing-half Phil Watkins was an apprentice who made his one and only Football League appearance against Portsmouth at Fratton Park in January 1964. The Bluebirds lost 5–0 in the fifth match of a losing sequence around the turn of the year that saw them concede 21 goals in those matches. Released at the end of the season, Phil Watkins moved into the Welsh League with Barry Town.

WATSON Thomas (Tom)

Left-back

Born: Belfast, 4 October 1902.
Career: Crusaders. Cardiff City 1925.
Linfield 1929.

FA Cup winner 1926–27. Welsh Cup winner 1926–27.

■ One of three Cardiff City's 1927 FA Cup Final winners to have connections with Crusaders (Jimmy nelson and Tom Sloan were the others), Tom Watson took over the left-back spot from Jimmy Blair in 1925. He soon proved himself to be a solid defender and his consistent displays led to him winning full international honours for Northern Ireland. During his time at Ninian Park, Watson was plagued with cartilage trouble, and after only one game of the 1928–29 season he underwent surgery. Unable to regain his place in Cardiff's League side, Watson, along with Tom Sloan, left City and joined Linfield of the Irish League, where they both completed a remarkable hat-trick of Cup medals when they won the FA of Ireland medals to go with the Welsh and English ones they had won while with the Bluebirds.

WATSON William Thomas (Bill)

Full-back

Born: Swansea, 11 June 1918.
Died: 1978.
Career: Preston North End 1946. Cardiff City 1947.

■ Bill Watson was a no-nonsense full-back who played wartime football for Preston North End. When League football resumed in 1946–47, he was still on the Deepdale club's staff and made 15 appearances for the Lilywhites before returning to his native South Wales with Cardiff City. Despite some impressive displays at reserve-team level, he appeared in just one League game for the Bluebirds, a 1–1 home draw against Coventry City in November 1947.

WEALE Robert Henry (Bobby)

Outside-right

Born: Troedyrhiw, 9 November 1903.

Died: 1970.
Career: Troedyrhiw. Luton Town 1924. West Ham United 1925. Swindon Town 1927. Southampton 1928. Guildford City (loan). Cardiff City 1930. Guildford City. Boson. Merthyr Town. Newport County 1932. Wrexham 1932. Glentoran. Cheltenham Town.

■ A junior sprint champion, Bobby Weale also won Welsh Schoolboy international honours before, following a trial with Luton Town, he joined West Ham United. Though he was a regular in their London Combination side, he only made a handful of appearances for the League side before moving on to Swindon Town. He had two seasons at the County Ground before signing for Southampton. In his early games for the Saints, Weale netted a hat-trick in a 4–0 defeat of Notts County, but his goals dried up and he moved into non-League football with Guildford. In 1930 he returned to League action with Cardiff City, but in a season in which the Bluebirds were relegated he made just five League appearances. On leaving Ninian Park, Weale had spells with other Welsh clubs Newport County and Wrexham before ending his playing days with Cheltenham Town.

WELSBY Arthur

Left-half/winger

Born: Downall Green, 17 November 1902.
Died: 1980.
Career: Ashton St Marys. Wigan Borough 1923. Sunderland 1931. Exeter City 1932. Stockport County 1934. Southport 1935. Cardiff City 1936. Mossley.

■ One of football's earliest utility players, although he was more at home when playing at half-back, Arthur Welsby began his long and varied career with his local club, Wigan Borough. Playing his first game for the now defunct club in 1923–24, he spent eight seasons at Springfield Park, scoring 30 goals in 220 games, before his consistency – he was ever present in 1929–30 – prompted First Division Sunderland to take him to Roker Park. Though he scored in a 4–0 win over Blackpool, he made only three appearances in two seasons in

the North East, and in the summer of 1933 he signed for Exeter City. He spent two years with the Grecians before having spells with Stockport County and Southport prior to arriving at Ninian Park in July 1936. He appeared in just three games for the Bluebirds – his last being a 3–1 reversal against one of his former clubs Exeter City. On being released by City he returned to the North West to play for Mossley.

WENT Paul Frank

Central-defender

Born: Bromley-by-Bow, 12 October 1949.
Career: Leyton Orient 1966. Charlton Athletic 1967. Fulham 1972. Portsmouth 1973. Cardiff City 1976. Leyton Orient 1978.

■ England Youth international Paul Went became the second youngest debutant in League history when, at 15 years 327 days of age, he played for Leyton Orient against Preston North End in September 1965. He showed great potential during his time at Brisbane Road, and in 1967 Charlton Athletic paid £27,000 for his services. In five years at The Valley Went established himself as a top-class player, appearing in 163 games for the Addicks. In July 1972 he moved to his third London club when Fulham paid £90,000 for him. His impressive displays led to Portsmouth splashing out a then staggering £160,000 for him. The south coast club were trying to buy success, but this policy backfired on them, and in October 1976 they were forced to accept a bid of £30,000 from Cardiff boss Jimmy Andrews. It took some time for Went to settle at Ninian Park as he conceded penalties in his first two matches. But his experience eventually shone through, and as well as shoring up the defence he also turned out in attack, scoring a number of vital goals. Hugely popular with the Bluebirds fans, he helped out on the commercial front before rejoining Orient. When Cardiff manager Jimmy Andrews was sacked, Went applied for the vacancy but was unsuccessful, though he did later manage Orient.

WEST George

Inside-forward

Born: Wardley.
Career: Wallsend. Cardiff City 1913.
Stockport County 1921.

Division Two runner-up 1920–21.

■ George West was one of a number of players lured to Ninian Park by the persuasive powers of manager Fred

Stewart, and when he arrived in South Wales from Wallsend in 1913 he took over from Jack Burton. In the two seasons of Southern League football, prior to the outbreak of World War One, West was Cardiff's leading scorer, and when he returned after the hostilities to reclaim the inside-left position he not only took his tally of goals to 33 in 79 Southern League games but guided the Cardiff side in their push towards the Football League. Following City's election to Division Two, he played half of the 1920–21 season until losing his place to Harry Nash. After that he had occasional outings, but following the arrival of Joe Clennell West moved to Stockport County where he ended his career.

WEST Joseph (Joe)

Centre-forward

Born: Walker, 1910.
Died: 1965.
Career: Walker Park. Newcastle United

1932. Cardiff City 1933. Darlington 1934.

■ Though he was on the books of Newcastle United for a couple of seasons, Joe West failed to make a first-team appearance for the Magpies, and midway through Cardiff's re-election season of 1933–34 he arrived at Ninian Park. During the course of this campaign, City used a multitude of players, and though West scored twice in his six League outings and was retained at the end of the season he was on his way to Darlington after a few weeks of the 1934–35 campaign.

WESTON Rhys David

Full-back

Born: Kingston, 27 October 1980.
Career: Arsenal 1999. Cardiff City 2000.

Division Three runner-up 2000–01.
FAW Premier Cup winner 2001–02.
Division Two promotion 2002–03.

■ Starting out with Arsenal, Rhys Weston, who is a good tackler and strong in the air, made his Gunners debut on the final day of the 1999–2000 season against Newcastle United, acquitting himself well in his duel with an in-form Alan Shearer. Having been capped by England at Under-16 level, it came as a surprise when he was given his full international debut by Wales

against Portugal in the summer of 2000. After a couple of appearances in Arsenal's League Cup side, he left Highbury to join Cardiff City, the Bluebirds paying £300,000 for his services. He had a mixed first season at Ninian Park, showing moments of real quality at times but on other occasions losing concentration. He did, however, show his versatility, appearing in defence, at wing-back and in midfield, as the club won promotion from the Third Division. Gradually his performances won over the Cardiff fans, and he scored the first goals of his senior career in successive matches against Tranmere Rovers and Peterborough United, and though he has failed to add to that tally he remains a regular in the Bluebirds side. In 2005–06, Weston appeared on a more regular basis and gave a series of solid displays as City embarked on a much more successful campaign.

WHALLEY Gareth

Midfield

Born: Manchester, 19 December 1973.
Career: Crewe Alexandra 1992. Bradford City 1998. Crewe Alexandra (loan) 2002. Cardiff City 2002.

Division Two promotion 2002–03.

■ One of a number of talented youngsters to have come through Crewe Alexandra's YT Scheme, Gareth Whalley soon became the Gresty Road club's captain and represented the Endsleigh Under-21 side against an Italian Serie B XI. Selected by his fellow professionals in the 1996–97 PFA award-winning Second Division side, Whalley was assessed by both Liverpool and Spurs before moving to Bradford City for £600,000 in the summer of 1998. Whalley, who made 231 appearances for the Railwaymen, saw his early days at Valley Parade hampered by injuries. After a loan spell back at Crewe, he joined Cardiff on a free transfer in July 2002. As early as November he was taken off on a stretcher after suffering a knee ligament injury. He was out for almost five months before returning for the run-in and played a huge role in the Bluebirds earning promotion via the play-offs. It was Gareth Whalley's lofted

pass that set Andy Campbell free for the only goal of the game against Queen's Park Rangers at the Millennium Stadium. He struggled a little to hold down a regular place in 2003–04 but is a player who can unlock the tightest of defences.

WHEELER Paul

Midfield/forward

Born: Caerphilly, 3 January 1965.
Career: Bristol Rovers 1983. Taff's Well. Aberaman. Cardiff City 1985. Hull City 1989. Hereford United 1990. Stockport County 1991. Scarborough (loan) 1992. Chester City 1993.

Division Four runner-up 1987–88.
Welsh Cup winner 1987–88.

■ Spotted by Stan Montgomery scouting for Bristol Rovers in South Wales, Paul Wheeler went to Eastville on apprentice terms. He was released after two years and returned to South Wales to take up a caretaker job at Cyncoed College in Cardiff and play Welsh League football for Taff's Well and Aberaman. After impressing in a match against Cardiff's reserves, he was invited to Ninian Park for a trial and eventually Alan Durban offered him a contract. Wheeler soon became a regular member of the Cardiff side, and though they were relegated in his first season he helped them win promotion from the Fourth Division in 1987–88, though, to be fair, more than half of his appearances were after he had come off the bench! After a brief non-contract spell with Hull City, Wheeler played for Hereford United, Stockport County and

Scarborough before signing for Chester City. He was a regular in the Cestrians side until they lost their Football League status at the end of the 1992–93 season.

WHITE Stephen James (Steve)

Forward

Born: Chipping Sodbury, 2 January 1959. Career: Mangotsfield United. Bristol Rovers. Luton Town 1979. Charlton Athletic 1982. Lincoln City (loan) 1983. Luton Town (loan) 1983. Bristol Rovers 1983. Swindon Town 1986. Hereford United 1994. Cardiff City 1996. Bath City.

FAW Invitation Cup finalist 1997–98.

■ An England Schoolboy international, Steve White was spotted by Bristol Rovers while playing for Mangotsfield in the Western League, and though he scored almost a goal every other game – 24 in 5 games – he was not an automatic choice. In December 1979 he was sold to Luton Town for £200,000 but struggled to make an impact until 1981–82, when he top scored with 18 goals as the Hatters won the Second Division Championship. Inexplicably sold to Charlton Athletic for less than Luton paid for him, he was dropped, despite leading the club's scoring charts, and after a loan spell with Lincoln he rejoined Bristol Rovers. After three seasons, in which he took his goals tally to 53 in 177 games, he joined Swindon Town. Top scorer in his first season at the County Ground, he also netted both goals against Gillingham in the play-off final. After that, White became Town's most reliable and frequent goalscorer, with a best return of 23 goals in 1989–90. He helped the Robins reach the Premier League, but, having scored 111 goals in 312 first-team matches, he left to play for Hereford United. In 1995–96 he scored 32 goals, including four against Cambridge United, to help the Edgar Street club reach the play-offs. White was 38 years old when he joined Cardiff City, and in 1996–97 he top scored with 14 goals, including doubles in the wins over Cambridge, Exeter and Fulham. Most of his time the following season was spent on the bench, and he decided to leave the first-class game.

Then the oldest outfield player in the Nationwide League, he had taken his tally of League goals to 223 in 646 appearances for his seven clubs before joining Bath City.

WHITHAM Jack

Forward

Born: Burnley, 8 December 1946. Career: Sheffield Wednesday 1964. Liverpool 1970. Cardiff City 1974. Reading 1975.

Welsh Cup winner 1973–74.

■ After being turned down by his home-town club Burnley, Jack Whitham joined Sheffield Wednesday in November 1964. His debut was against the Clarets when he came off the bench to score twice in a 7–0 rout of the Turf Moor club. Though he possessed the instincts of a natural goalscorer, he was seldom able to shake off injuries and enjoy a long run in the side. However, he is ensured of a lasting place in the club's history for his hat-trick in one of the most unforgettable matches ever played at Hillsborough – when the Owls beat European Cup holders Manchester United 5–4. He had scored 31 goals in 71 games when he was surprisingly sold to Liverpool for £57,000 in May 1970. He appeared in only 16 games for the Anfield club, yet scored a powerfully struck hat-trick against Derby County. After spending several years trying to regain full fitness, his contract was cancelled by mutual consent, and Frank O'Farrell invited him to Ninian Park for a trial. Though he was offered a contract and stayed a year with the Bluebirds, his appearances were spasmodic. He later ended his career with Reading.

WHITLEY Jeffrey

Midfield

Born: Zambia, 28 January 1979. Career: Manchester City 1996. Wrexham (loan) 1999. Notts County (loan) 2002. Sunderland 2003. Cardiff City 2005.

■ Zambian born but with mixed parentage, he opted to play for Northern Ireland and made his international debut against Belgium. Starting out with Manchester City, he found it difficult to hold down a regular place and went on loan to Wrexham. It was whilst at the Racecourse Ground that he contributed to Wrexham's good run in the Autowindscreens Shield, which saw them reach the Northern Section Final. He returned to Maine Road to help City win promotion from the Second Division via the play-offs and was selected for the starting line-up for the start of the 1999–2000 season. Appointed captain of the Northern Ireland Under-21 side, though he continued to play for the senior side, he missed very few games for City that season before being replaced by new signing Alfie Haaland. Back in the side for the start of the 2001–02 season, he then broke his ankle and on recovery joined Notts County on loan. After helping them avoid relegation, he returned to City before being released on a free transfer. Having joined Sunderland, he enjoyed a good first season with the Black Cats before helping them win the First Division Championship in 2004–05. Surprisingly released by Sunderland's then manager Mick McCarthy, the Northern Ireland international joined Cardiff City and in a season when the club were expected to struggle to avoid relegation, he was a revelation in the club's midfield.

WHITLOW Frederick William James (Fred)

Centre-forward
Born: Bristol, 3 September 1904.
Died: 1978.
Career: Barry Town. Dundee. Charlton Athletic 1927. Exeter City 1931. Cardiff City 1934. Barry Town.

■ Fred Whitlow began his career as an amateur with Barry Town before trying his luck in Scotland with Dundee. On leaving Dens Park, he turned professional with Charlton Athletic and in 1928–29 was a member of the side that won the Third Division South Championship. Whitlow was a prolific scorer at The Valley, finding the net 60 times in 95 League games, and was twice the club's top scorer. In 1931 Whitlow moved to Exeter City and continued to find the net with great regularity. In 1932–33 he helped the Grecians finish runners-up in the Third

Division South, while the following season he scored a remarkable 34 goals in 33 games! When he joined Cardiff City in 1934 he was past his prime and his only goal for the club was a 1–0 winner at Clapton Orient. He soon left Ninian Park and rejoined Barry Town where his career had begun.

WIGG Nathan Marlow

Midfield
Born: Newport, 27 September 1974.
Career: Cardiff City 1993. Dundalk.

■ Midfielder Nathan Wigg improved immensely after making his City debut as a substitute for Derek Brazil in a 2–2 draw against Brighton in August 1993. Though it was only towards the end of that season that he won a regular place in the side, in 1994–95, when the club were relegated from Division Two, it was Wigg more than anyone else who relished the battles for points on the run in. Wigg's only goal for Cardiff came against neighbours Swansea in a 4–1 defeat at the Vetch towards the end of that campaign. Despite his enthusiasm, biting tackle and competitive tendencies, he was allowed to leave and joined Dundalk.

WILLIAMS Christopher Robert (Chris)

Forward
Born: Brecon, 25 December 1955.
Career: Talgarth. Cardiff City 1977. Bridgend. Merthyr Tydfil. Barry Town.

■ Centre-forward Chris Williams came to Ninian Park from Brecon League side Talgarth and had a brief run in Cardiff's Second Division team. A hard-working player, he was released after three first-team appearances and continued playing in South Wales as a popular figure with Bridgend, Merthyr Tydfil and Barry Town.

WILLIAMS Daniel J.

Centre-forward
Born: Cardiff.
Career: Cardiff City 1935.

■ Local-born centre-forward Danny Williams burst into the Bluebirds' first

team midway through the 1935–36 season, making his debut in a 2–0 derby defeat of Newport County. Keeping his place in the side, he then scored twice in a 4–0 home win over Gillingham and went on to score a goal every other game in 18 appearances. Surprisingly, he was only called upon twice the following season, scoring in his comeback game against Queen's Park Rangers as City relied heavily on new signings Cecil Smith and George Walton. Unable to force his way into the side despite his enthusiastic displays for the reserves, he drifted into the local non-League scene.

WILLIAMS Darren

Full-back
Born: Middlesbrough, 28 April 197
Career: York City 1995. Sunderland 1996. Cardiff City 2004. Hartlepool United 2005.

■ A member of the York City side that beat Manchester United in the 1995–96 League Cup competition, Darren Williams began his career as an industrious midfield player before joining Sunderland for £50,000 in October 1996. Unable to prevent their relegation from the Premiership, he was then moved into a central-defensive position, with his performances earning him international recognition for England at Under 21 and 'B' level. In 1998–99 he picked up a First Division Championship medal with Sunderland, but back in the top flight he found himself appearing in a variety of positions – right-back, midfield and outside-right. Williams then signed a five-year extension to his contract, and no matter what position he played he always contributed 100% to the team's cause. Sunderland's longest-serving player, he became the last surviving link on the playing staff from the Roker Park days, taking his tally of appearances to almost 250 before deciding to join Cardiff City, initially on loan. He made his debut in the 3–2 win at Molineux and kept his place in the side until shortly after the move became a permanent one when injury forced him to miss the return match with Wolves. Williams left Cardiff in the close season and, like Lee Bullock, signed for Hartlepool United where he soon became a Victoria Ground favourite.

WILLIAMS David Peter

Goalkeeper

Born: Liverpool, 18 September 1968. Career: Oldham Athletic 1987. Burnley 1988. Rochdale (loan) 1991. Cardiff City 1994. Linfield.

■ After failing to make the first team at Oldham, goalkeeper David Williams joined Burnley as cover for Chris Pearce. He made his League debut for the Clarets following the infamous training ground incident between Pearce and George Oghani but played only infrequently during his time at Turf Moor. He had a loan spell with Rochdale before, in August 1994, leaving to play for Cardiff City. At Ninian Park he immediately established a regular first-team place, and at the end of his first season he was voted Player of the Year. David Williams was the club's first-choice 'keeper until the latter end of the 1995–96 season when he lost out to his namesake Steve Williams at Scunthorpe and left soon afterwards to play for Linfield.

WILLIAMS Donald Roland (Roley)

Inside-forward

Born: Swansea, 10 July 1927. Career: Milford United. Cardiff City 1949. Northampton Town 1956. Bath City. Lovells Athletic.

Division Two runner-up 1951–52.

■ Swansea-born inside-forward Roley Williams was playing for Milford United in the Welsh League when Cyril Spiers moved in to sign him in February 1949, before his home-town club could offer him terms. Equally at home at outside and inside-right, he soon became a regular member of the City side, this in spite of him suffering some niggling injuries. Williams, who gave the club seven years' service, provided many of the crosses for Wilf Grant to top score, with 26 goals in 1951–52, as the Bluebirds won promotion to the First Division, though he did score in the

opening two games of the campaign himself. He never played a full season due to injuries and left Ninian Park in 1956 to join Northampton Town. His stay at the County ground was brief, and he went into non-League football with Bath City. He later played for Lovells Athletic and played against the Bluebirds in the Welsh Cup Final of 1959, which City won 2–0 with goals from Bonson and Hudson.

WILLIAMS Gareth Cyril

Midfield

Born: Hendon, 30 October 1941. Career: Cardiff City 1961. Bolton Wanderers 1967. Bury 1971.

Welsh Cup winner 1963–64. 1964–65. 1966–67.

■ Gareth Williams was born a stone's throw from Wembley, but his family returned to Hengoed where he developed in local schools football along with another player who was to make the grade, Graham Moore. Williams was signed by Cardiff City in the summer of 1961 and gained a regular spot in the Bluebirds midfield during the 1962–63 season. By 1964 he was the club captain and over the next three seasons he missed very few games. He had scored

15 goals in 190 League and Cup games when, in October 1967, he joined Bolton Wanderers for £45,000. Despite becoming club captain at Burnden Park, he suffered a loss of form which was not helped by a poor disciplinary record. During November 1969 he was suspended by the club for refusing to train while claiming that he was being made the scapegoat for Bolton's poor

results. He never recaptured the form of his Ninian Park days, and in October 1971 he joined Bury. After leaving the Shakers he worked in the prison service, managed a Fylde coast hotel and finally moved to the Gran Canaria where he ran a bar.

WILLIAMS Glyndwr James John (Glyn)

Right-back

Born: Maesteg, 3 November 1918. Career: Caerau. Cardiff City 1946.

Welsh Cup finalist 1950–51. Division Two runner-up 1951–52.

■ A hard-tackling defender, Glyn Williams began his career with Caerau and in 1946 helped them win the Welsh Amateur Cup. Even though he had only played a handful of games, his form had been impressive and Cardiff had no hesitation in signing him. He made his

debut for the Bluebirds in a 1–0 win at Aldershot in January 1947, during the club's Third Division South Championship-winning season. In the seven games in which he played in that campaign, the opposition failed to score in five of them. Since he was able to play in either full-back position or at wing-half, he missed very few games over the five seasons. In 1950–51, as Cardiff just failed in their bid for promotion to the First Division, his form led to him being selected for Wales's close season tour, during which he won his only full international cap against Switzerland. In 1951–52 he played his part in helping the Bluebirds reach the top flight, but at the end of the following season he was released and returned to junior football. Although he failed to score at Football League level, he did get on the scoresheet in an FA Cup third-round tie against West Bromwich Albion in January 1950.

WILLIAMS John Nelson

Winger

Born: Birmingham, 11 May 1968.
Career: Cradley Town. Swansea City 1991. Coventry City 1992. Notts County (loan) 1994. Stoke City (loan) 1994. Swansea City (loan) 1995. Wycombe Wanderers 1995. Hereford United 1997. Walsall 1997. Exeter City 1997. Cardiff City 1998. York City 1999. Darlington 2000. Swansea City 2001. Kidderminster Harriers 2003.

Division Three promotion 1998–99.

■ A relatively late starter in League football at the age of 23, John Williams achieved fame by winning the televised sprints to find the 'fastest man in football', in only his first season. He was playing for Cradley Town of the West Midlands League when, in August 1991, he was signed by Swansea. In his first season with the Swans he netted a hat-trick in a 6–4 win at Bradford City, a remarkable result as the Vetch Field club were struggling at the foot of the table. Finishing the season as the club's top scorer, he joined Coventry City for £250,000. After scoring on his Sky Blues debut, the lightning fast striker suffered a number of injuries and had loan spells with Swansea, Notts County and Stoke. On his return to Highfield Road he took his tally of goals to 11 in 86 games before a £150,000 move to Wycombe Wanderers. Known as 'The Flying Postman', Williams's next move was to Hereford United before spells with Walsall and Exeter City. In the summer of 1998 he joined Cardiff City and became a cult hero with the Ninian Park faithful. He scored 18 goals in all competitions, helping the club win promotion from the Third Division, with his best being the winner at Southend United. Remarkably, he parted company with the Bluebirds and continued his career with York City and later Darlington. In July 2001 he signed for Swansea and, after a major fitness drive, began to show his old sharpness, prior to a move to his 12th club, Kidderminster Harriers.

WILLIAMS Ralph Shirley

Centre-forward/inside-left

Born: Aberaman, 2 October 1905.
Died: 1985.
Career: Aberdare Athletic 1923. Aberavon. Brentford 1924. Aberaman Athletic. Poole Town. Chesterfield 1927. Manchester Central. Colwyn Bay United. Cardiff City 1929. Crewe Alexandra 1931. Southport 1932. Rochdale 1932. Merthyr Town. Lovells Athletic. Aberdare Town. Bangor City. Rhyl. Aberdare Town.

■ A natural goalscorer, Ralph Williams began his career with Aberdare Athletic before later playing for Brentford, prior to non-League spells with Aberaman Athletic and Poole. With these clubs, he began rattling in the goals and this prompted Chesterfield to take him to Saltergate. He was their top scorer in 1927–28 with 15 goals in 31 games, but within a year he had joined Manchester Central, Billy Meredith's team of all-stars playing outside the Football League at Belle Vue. He then had a short spell at Colwyn Bay before signing for Cardiff in December 1929. In the 16 games that remained, Williams scored 11 goals, including a hat-trick on the final day of the season in a 5–1 defeat of Bury. He was leading the way the following season when he left to follow Fred Keenor to Crewe. On leaving Gresty Road he had spells with Southport and Rochdale before playing non-League football for a number of clubs. In one season with Merthyr Town he netted 10 hat-tricks, and though he wasn't as prolific with Lovells Athletic, Bangor City, Rhyl or Aberdare Town, where damaged knee ligaments ended his football career, he was a prolific batsman in South Wales cricket until well into his 50s.

WILLIAMS Steven David

Goalkeeper

Born: Aberystwyth, 16 October 1974.
Career: Coventry City. Cardiff City 1993. Merthyr (Loan) 1996. Dundalk.

Welsh Cup finalist 1993–94.

■ Goalkeeper Steve Williams joined the Bluebirds from Coventry City juniors and was given his first-team debut at York City in October 1993. It proved to be a disastrous first match for him as the Minstermen won 5–0. Though he was given an extended run in the side later in the season, his appearances over the following campaigns were few and far between. However, he came good in the Welsh Cup semi-final of 1995 when brought off the bench, and he saved a Steve Torpey penalty in the match against Swansea. In 1996–97 he was loaned out to Merthyr but was recalled by City towards the end of the campaign following an injury to Tony Elliott and did his bit in getting the Bluebirds into the play-offs. Released in the close season, he went to play for Dundalk.

WILLIAMS Thomas P.

Centre-half

Born: Cardiff, 1915.
Career: Cardiff City 1937.

■ A player for whom a bright future was predicted, centre-half Tom Williams spent the two seasons prior to the outbreak of World War Two as understudy to Bill Bassett. Though the hostilities put paid to his better years, Tom Williams was retained for the 1946–47 season of League football but didn't make the Bluebirds first team due to the presence of Fred Stansfield.

WILLIAMS William John

Central-defender

Born: Liverpool, 3 October 1960.
Career: Tranmere Rovers 1979. Port Vale 1985. Bournemouth 1986. Wigan Athletic (loan) 1991. Cardiff City 1991.

■ Tall central-defender John Williams soon established himself at the heart of the Tranmere Rovers defence, and in five seasons from 1980–81 he missed very few games. Dangerous at set pieces, he went on to score 13 goals in 201 League and Cup games before leaving Prenton Park in July 1985 to join Port Vale for £12,000. In his first season at Vale Park he helped the club win promotion to the Third Division, but after losing form the following season he was allowed to join Bournemouth. An important member of the Dean Court side, he suffered a bad knee injury, and on regaining fitness he had a loan spell with Wigan Athletic before joining Cardiff City in December 1991. He appeared in five games for the Bluebirds and the only time he was on the losing side was on New Year's Day when City crashed to a 5–0 home defeat at the hands of Maidstone. He later returned to Bournemouth as the club's Community Development Officer before becoming the Cherries assistant manager.

WILSON Robert John (Bob)

Goalkeeper

Born: Birmingham, 23 May 1943.
Career: Aston Villa 1961. Cardiff City 1964. Bristol City (loan) 1969. Exeter City 1970.

Welsh Cup winner 1964–65, 1966–67.

■ Aston Villa goalkeeper Bob Wilson became Jimmy Scoular's first signing in August 1964, when the City manager paid just £2,000 to bring him to Ninian Park. It proved to be money well spent as Wilson played well for several seasons when the rest of the Cardiff side were not playing so well, and though he did lose confidence on occasions, losing his place to both Dilwyn John and Lyn Davies, he

always fought back to reclaim his place. During 1964–65, his first season with the club, he won a Welsh Cup medal and played in the European Cup-Winners' Cup quarter-final against Real Zaragosa. The following season he played his part in helping City reach the semi-finals of the Football League Cup but lost his place after conceding five goals at West Ham in the first leg. The Hammers then proceeded to hit five in the second leg past Wilson's stand-in! He won another Welsh Cup medal in 1966–67 and played in all of the club's nine European Cup-Winners' Cup matches. His performances in this competition helped the Bluebirds reach the semi-final, but after making

some outstanding saves in the first leg in Hamburg he made a costly error at Ninian Park that allowed the Germans to win 3–2 on the night and 4–3 on aggregate. Leaving Cardiff in January 1970 following a loan spell with Bristol City, Wilson moved to Exeter where he played consistently well for a further six seasons, making 204 League appearances.

WILSON Thomas Henry (Tom)

Centre-half/centre-forward

Born: Walthamstow, 9 December 1902.
Career: Walthamstow Avenue. Charlton Athletic 1924. Wigan Borough 1926. Cardiff City 1930. Charlton Athletic 1931. Southend United 1932.

■ Able to play at both centre-half and centre-forward, Tom Wilson began his career with Charlton Athletic, but, finding it difficult to establish himself fully, he moved north to play with Wigan Borough. Then a League club, he gave them great service, appearing in 109 games before joining the Bluebirds in 1930. His only appearance came in a 4–2 defeat at Oldham Athletic when he was deemed to be at fault for two of the Latics goals. City finished bottom of the First Division and were relegated. He then resumed his career with Charlton before ending his involvement with the game with a brief spell at Southend.

WIMBLETON Paul Philip

Midfield

Born: Havant, 13 November 1964.
Career: Portsmouth 1982. Cardiff City 1986. Bristol City 1989. Shrewsbury Town 1990. Maidstone United (loan) 1991. Exeter City 1991. Swansea City 1992.

Division Four runner-up 1987–88.

■ England Schoolboy international Paul Wimbleton started out with Portsmouth, making his debut for the south coast club midway through the 1981–82 season. A knee injury sustained during the early part of the following campaign did not heal properly and let him down again when he tried to make a comeback, with the result that Wimbleton had to undergo delicate surgery and a lengthy recuperation period in order to rebuild his career. Portsmouth released him, and in July 1986 Frank Burrows brought him to Ninian Park. The hard-running midfielder repaid Burrows's faith in him by becoming Cardiff's leading scorer and an ever present in 1986–87. He was an important member of the City side that won promotion to the Third Division in 1987–88 when he scored twice in the 4–1 win at champions Wolves. Wimbleton had another season with Cardiff and then went on his travels playing for Bristol City, Shrewsbury Town, Maidstone United (loan), Exeter City and Swansea.

WINSPEAR John (Jack)

Outside-right

Born: Leeds, 24 December 1946.
Career: Leeds United 1964. Cardiff City 1966. Rochdale 1967.

■ Having been unable to break into Leeds United's first team, Jack Winspear left Elland Road to join Cardiff City in June 1966. Though he was quite prolific for the club's reserve side, when he did get his chance at first-team level he was a little out of his depth in a 4–0 defeat for the Bluebirds at Preston North End. At the end of the season he was transferred to Rochdale where he scored three goals in 16 League outings.

WITHEY Graham Alfred

Forward

Born: Bristol, 11 June 1960.
Career: Bath City. Bristol Rovers 1982. Coventry City 1983. Cardiff City 1984. Bath City. Bristol City 1986. Cheltenham Town. Exeter City 1988.

■ Graham Withey was playing non-League football for Bath City when given a League chance by Bristol Rovers in 1982. He had scored 10 goals in 22 games for the Pirates when he followed manager Bobby Gould to Coventry City. After a good start in the First Division he fell away and in December 1984 came to Ninian Park on loan, prior to the move being made permanent. Withey failed to live up to his early promise and was allowed to leave Cardiff for Bath City, leaving the Bluebirds regretting their decision to pay £20,000 for his services. Withey

tried League comebacks with Bristol City and Exeter either side of a spell at non-League Cheltenham Town but to no avail.

WOOD George

Goalkeeper

Born: Douglas, Lanarkshire, 26 September 1952.
Career: East Stirling. Blackpool 1972. Everton 1977. Arsenal 1980. Crystal Palace 1983. Cardiff City 1988. Blackpool (Loan) 1990. Hereford United 1990. Merthyr Tydfil. Inter Cardiff.

Division Four runner-up 1987–88.
Welsh Cup winner 1987–88.

■ Goalkeeper George Wood joined Blackpool during the 1971–72 season from East Stirling. Signed primarily as cover for John Burridge, he spent his first four seasons at Bloomfield Road vying for the number-one spot with Burridge before establishing himself in 1975–76. Having appeared in 144 games for the Seasiders, he was transferred to Everton for £150,000 in August 1977. An ever present in his first two seasons at Goodison, his performances led to him winning full international honours for Scotland. Midway through the 1979–80 season he lost his place to Martin Hodge, and at the end of the campaign he was allowed to join Arsenal for £150,000. In three seasons at Highbury he made 70 League and Cup appearances before leaving to play for Crystal Palace. A big favourite at Selhurst Park, he spent a further five

seasons playing for the Eagles before, in January 1988, joining Cardiff City. He made his debut for the Bluebirds in a 4–0 home win over Cambridge United and went on to keep nine clean sheets in 13 appearances in helping the club win promotion from the Fourth Division. That season he also won a Welsh Cup medal as City beat Wrexham 2–0 in the Final. Wood went on to play in 86 first-team games before being granted a free transfer and joining Hereford United after a brief loan period back at Blackpool. He later played for Merthyr Tydfil and Inter-Cardiff where he was manager.

WOOD Terence Laurence (Terry)

Wing-half

Born: Newport, 3 September 1920.
Career: Newport Docks. Cardiff City 1946.

■ A Welsh amateur international, half-back Terry Wood joined Cardiff City from the Newport Docks team during World War Two. When the Bluebirds were beaten 10–1 by Moscow Dynamo in November 1945, Wood played at inside-left, and during the war years he scored 29 goals in 76 games for the Ninian Park club. He made a handful of appearances during the club's Third Division South Championship-winning season of 1946–47 before returning to junior football.

WOODRUFF Robert William (Bobby)

Midfield/forward

Born: Highworth, 9 November 1940.
Career: Swindon Town 1958. Wolverhampton Wanderers 1964. Crystal Palace 1966. Cardiff City 1969. Newport County 1974.

Welsh Cup winner 1969–70, 1970–71, 1972–73, 1973–74.

■ A member of Swindon Town's successful young side that gained promotion to the Second Division in 1962–63, Bobby Woodruff was a versatile player who soon established himself as a first-team regular. He had scored 20 goals in 180 games for the

Robins when, in March 1964, he was transferred to Wolverhampton Wanderers for £40,000. Known for his long-throw 'specials', Woodruff, who had netted a hat-trick in a 3–0 defeat of Sunderland, left Molineux in the summer of 1966, after scoring 21 goals in 72 games. The midfielder then joined Crystal Palace and in 1968–69 helped them win promotion to Division One. He had only played a few games in the top flight when he left to play for Cardiff City for a fee of £25,000. Signed as a replacement for the injured Barrie Jones, he turned out to be a shrewd investment, rarely missing a match in five years and always proving to be a

reliable player. Once, when asked to play centre-forward, he scored six goals in six games. Released in the summer of 1974, he linked up with Brian Harris at Newport County before finishing his career playing for a number of clubs in the Welsh League.

WOODS Jonathan Paul (Jon)

Forward

Born: Blackwood, 5 October 1966.
Career: Arsenal. Cardiff City 1984. Ebbw Vale. Brecon Corries.

■ Released by Arsenal, Cardiff City took on Jon Woods as a YTS youngster. His only taste of first-team action came in a 4–2 home defeat at the hands of Brighton in September 1984 when he came off the bench to replace Roger Gibbins. He later left Ninian Park to play Welsh League football with Ebbw Vale and then Brecon Corries.

WOOF William (Billy)

Forward

Born: Gateshead, 16 August 1956.
Career: Middlesbrough 1974. Peterborough United (loan) 1977. Blyth Spartans. Cardiff City 1982. Gateshead. Hull City 1983.

■ Billy Woof began his career with Middlesbrough, but in six years at Ayresome Park he found progress slow. Unable to hold down a regular place, he had a loan spell with Peterborough United before moving into non-League football with Blyth Spartans. He came to Cardiff City on trial in September 1982 and made a sensational debut with the winning goal in a 3–2 defeat of Wigan Athletic just two minutes from time. Sadly, Woof then had a disagreement with manager Len Ashurst and returned to the North East to play for his home-town team Gateshead. He later returned to League action with Hull City before hanging up his boots.

YOUDS Edward Paul (Eddie)

Central-defender/midfield

Born: Liverpool, 3 May 1970.
Career: Everton 1988. Cardiff City (loan) 1989. Wrexham (loan) 1990. Ipswich Town 1991. Bradford City 1995. Charlton Athletic 1998. Huddersfield Town 2002. Grays Athletic.

■ Unable to hold down a first-team spot at Everton, Eddie Youds had loan spells with Welsh clubs Cardiff City and Wrexham, though his solitary League appearance for the Bluebirds was as a substitute in a 3–1 defeat at Bolton after replacing Gareth Abraham. He also appeared after coming off the bench in an earlier FA Cup third-round replay at Queen's Park Rangers. In November 1991 he joined Ipswich Town, but during four years at Portman Road he made just 50 League appearances. He signed for Bradford City, becoming the Valley Parade club captain and leading them to promotion to the First Division in 1995–96. He then missed the whole of the following season with serious knee injuries before returning to take his tally of appearances for the Bantams to 99 before Charlton Athletic paid £550,000 for his services. A no-nonsense central-defender, he continued to make his presence felt in the opposition penalty area and in 1999–2000 helped the Addicks win the First Division Championship. Injuries then hampered his progress at The Valley, and in the summer of 2002 he joined Huddersfield Town, later becoming the Terriers captain before entering non-League football with Grays Athletic.

YOUNG Scott

Central-defender

Born: Pontypridd, 14 January 1976.
Career: Cardiff City 1994.

FAW Invitation Cup finalist 1997–98, 1999–2000. Division Three promotion 1998–99. Division Three runner-up 2000–01. Division Two promotion 2002–03.

■ Dependable and solid, good on the ground and in the air, central-defender Scott Young played in a variety of positions during his early days with the club. He played at centre-half, right-back, in a more forward role, just behind midfield and in midfield in 1997–98, a season in which he won Wales 'B' honours as well as adding to his appearances at Under-21 level. A hernia operation disrupted his progress, and though he returned to action in 1999–2000 it was a disappointing season as his home-town club were relegated. However, in 2000–01 he bounced back with a series of powerful performances for the Bluebirds. Missing just one League game, he revealed his hidden talents as a goalscorer, scoring 10 times and so doubling his previous career total! Despite a niggling groin injury, Young battled on, his performances earning him a Wales call-up, although he was only on the bench for the match against the Czech Republic. He again suffered with injuries in 2002–03 but showed his

delight at promotion when he raced onto the pitch to hug teammates as the final whistle blew. As the club's longest-serving player, he was awarded a deserved testimonial in 2003–04.

ZHIYI Fan

Central-defender

Born: Shanghai, China, 6 November 1969.
Career: Shanghai Shenhua (China). Crystal Palace 1998. Dundee 2001. Shanghai Zhongyuan Huili (loan). Cardiff City 2002.

■ Captain of the Chinese international team, Fan Zhiyi was brought to Selhurst Park with Sun Jihai by Terry Venables in September 1998. Capable of playing on the left side of midfield or up front, he became the first Chinese international to play in the Football League. Although he lost quite a chunk of the season due to international duty and injury, he came back strongly to show excellent form. In 1999–2000 he suffered a cracked rib against Birmingham, this after missing the first five games because of a suspension! He also missed most of January when called up for

China's Asian Cup matches. Having been moved into the centre of defence at Palace, he was voted as the Eagles Player of the Year in 2000–01. Having appeared in 102 games for Palace, Zhiyi was rather surprisingly sold to Scottish club Dundee for a substantial fee. After one season at Dens Park, he spent the summer on loan in China with Shanghai Zhongyuan Huili and with the national team at the World Cup Finals. Capped 109 times, he made a surprise move to Cardiff City in November 2002 but never really established himself. Hampered by a foot injury, he never managed to settle, though he did manage a spectacular 40-yard volleyed goal for the reserves! Released at the end of the season, he returned to China.

ZOIS Peter

Goalkeeper

Born: Australia, 21 April 1978.
Career: Purfleet. Cardiff City 1998.

■ Australian goalkeeper Peter Zois arrived at Ninian Park one February evening in 1998 to replace the injured Jon Hallworth against Rotherham United at home. Having earlier had trials with Spurs and West Ham, Zois was playing non-League football for Purfleet. On the night the Australian didn't look too happy and his eccentric goalkeeping in a game that ended all-square at 2–2 led to manager Frank Burrows ending his trial period immediately!

Cardiff City Managers

Fred Stewart

May 1911 – May 1933

Division Two runner-up 1920–21. Welsh Cup winner 1921–22, 1922–23, 1926–27, 1927–28, 1929–30. Division One runner-up 1923–24. FA Cup finalist 1924–25. FA Cup winner 1926–27. FA Charity Shield winner 1927–28. Welsh Cup finalist 1928–29.

Fred Stewart was appointed secretary-manager of Stockport County just after they had been elected to the Football League in August 1900 and remained in that post until May 1911, when he moved to Cardiff City in a similar post.

Stewart was Cardiff's first-ever secretary-manager, and he brought a wealth of experience and knowledge with him to Ninian Park. Within two seasons Cardiff moved from the Second to the First Division of the Southern League, but it was on the resumption of professional football after the war that City's golden era began. Following election to the Football League in 1920, they were promoted to Division One in their first season, finishing second on goal average to champions Birmingham. In the same season they reached the FA Cup semi-finals, losing the all-Second Division tie to Wolves 3–1 in a replay at Old Trafford. Cardiff reached the quarter-finals in two of the next three seasons before Stewart at last took Cardiff to the Cup Final in 1925. Although they lost 1–0 to Sheffield United, they returned to Wembley in

1927 when a Hughie Ferguson goal beat Arsenal to take the FA Cup out of England for the one and only time. Stewart was cruelly deprived of the League Championship on the last day of the 1923–24 season. If Cardiff could win at Birmingham the title was theirs, if they drew Huddersfield Town, their closest rivals, had to beat Nottingham Forest 3–0 to take the title. Huddersfield did beat Forest 3–0, while City were held to a goalless draw at St Andrew's. Cardiff even missed a late penalty and were denied the Championship by 0.02 of a goal! City could never repeat this form, and in 1929, two years after their historic Cup win, they were relegated to Division Two before, two years later, being relegated to the Third Division South. When Cardiff finished in a miserable 19th place in 1933, Fred Stewart retired after a long and eventful career. He remained in Cardiff to concentrate on his businesses and died in 1954.

Bartley Wilson

May 1933 – February 1934

Bartley Wilson helped to form Cardiff City and was appointed their secretary in 1910. Wilson, who had to get about on crutches, had a great knowledge of soccer. A sound judge of a player and of tactics, he saw the Cardiff club grow from the pioneering days of Riverside Cricket Club to a First Division side.

With the retirement of manager Fred Stewart, he stepped into the breach but it proved a disastrous period for the club anchored to the foot of the Third Division South. Wilson was no doubt relieved to give up the managers post to Ben Watts-Jones. A lithographic artist, he remained in a backroom capacity with his beloved Cardiff City for many years.

Ben Watts-Jones

February 1934 – April 1937

Ben Watts-Jones became a director then chairman of Swansea in their pioneering

days. He helped them gain admission to the Football League in 1921 and also served on the selection committee of the Welsh FA. He took over at Ninian Park in 1934 with City at its lowest ebb after years of success. Watts-Jones released all but five of the club's professional staff and brought in 17 new players as City embarked on the 1934–35 season. He had a constant battle with low attendances and little cash to spend. He did, by 1936, start to bring in better players and Bill Jennings as coach before making way for the former Bolton player to manage the club in 1937. Watts-Jones reverted to his place on the board of directors where he remained until the outbreak of World War Two.

Bill Jennings

April 1937 – April 1939

Bill Jennings was still playing for Bolton's reserves when he won the first of 11 caps for Wales in 1914. He went on to make 287 appearances for the Wanderers and suffered a great deal from injuries during his career. He played in the first FA Cup Final at Wembley and also gained a medal three years later with Bolton. Jennings retired in 1931 and two years after became coach at Notts County. In 1936 Jennings was appointed by Cardiff City as chief coach and his connection with the North West helped bring former Bolton players Bob Jones, George Nicholson and George Walton to Ninian Park, while Blackburn Rovers' Albert Pinxton and Les Talbot also joined the Bluebirds. In April 1937 Jennings was appointed secretary-manager, but he had a difficult time, with little money to spend and a fire at the ground shortly after he took over. Jennings, who had employed former England full-back Ernie Blenkinsop as coach, was replaced in favour of Cyril Spiers.

Cyril Spiers

April 1939 – June 1946 and November 1947 – May 1954

Welsh Cup finalist 1938–39, 1950–51. Division Two runner-up 1951–52.

An agile and brave goalkeeper, he began his career with Aston Villa. He had made over 100 appearances when he was injured towards the end of the 1926–27 season, and Villa decided he would not be fit to play again and released him. He underwent an experimental operation during the close season and was signed by Spurs. At White Hart Lane he represented the Football League and played in the international trial match of 1931, but after 186 games for Spurs he was given a free transfer. He then became assistant manager to Major Frank Buckley at Wolves before, in April 1939, he accepted the secretary-manager post at Cardiff City. Sadly, the outbreak of World War Two cut short his rebuilding programme, but Spiers remained with City throughout the hostilities, setting

up nursery teams such as Cardiff Nomads and encouraging much of the local talent to come to Ninian Park. A disagreement over money led to Spiers joining Norwich City in 1946, and he adopted Cardiff Nomads for the East Anglian club. Within two years and following the departure of Billy McCandless Spiers had returned to Ninian Park. He immediately carried on his policy of grooming local talent to augment several imports from other clubs. He took Cardiff City into the First Division as runners-up in Division Two in 1951–52, but two years later he left. He accepted an offer to manage Crystal Palace in September 1954. At Palace he discovered Johnny Byrne, but they languished near the bottom of the Third Division South. He later scouted for Leicester City and had a brief spell in charge of Exeter City.

Billy McCandless

June 1946 – November 1947

Division Three South champion 1946–47.

One of the game's great characters, Billy McCandless has a unique record, having taken separate South Wales sides to the Third Division South Championship. As a player he gained honours galore at Linfield and Glasgow Rangers and carried on in the same vein when he

became a manager. McCandless, who gained nine international caps for Ireland, won seven League Championship medals in the great Rangers side of that time. In 1930 he left Ibrox to become player-manager of Ballymena United, while in 1934 he took over the reins at Dundee. Though they held their own in Scottish League Division One without ever looking like winning anything, McCandless lost his job at Dens Park in May 1937. Later that year he became the manager of Newport County. His astute and inspiring leadership soon developed

County into an outstanding combination, and in their Championship-winning season of 1938–39 he used only 13 players. The war years decimated the Newport side, and in June 1946 he took over as manager of Cardiff City. In 1946–47 City ran away with the Third Division South title, finishing seven points clear of nearest rivals Queen's Park Rangers. This included 30 wins, and they scored 93 goals. In November 1947 McCandless moved to Swansea, and in 1948–49 the Vetch Field club took the Southern Section title. McCandless stayed with the Swans until his death in the summer of 1955. He left behind a wealth of talent at Vetch Field, including some of the greatest players to have played for the club.

Trevor Morris

April 1954 – July 1958

Welsh Cup winner 1955–56.

Trevor Morris's playing career was ended by a broken leg in a wartime Cup game against Bristol City in 1942, at a time when he was 'guesting' for Cardiff City. Morris, who piloted the lead aircraft of a squadron of Lancaster

bombers on D-Day and flew more than 40 missions over enemy territory, was awarded the Distinguished Flying Medal. After joining Cardiff City as assistant-secretary he was appointed secretary-manager following Cyril Spiers's resignation. It was not a good period for City, and in 1956–57 the Bluebirds lost their top-flight status. A year later Morris had been appointed general manager of Swansea, and though he worked the transfer market feverishly he found he could not replace the stars he sold with adequate replacements. A year after reaching the FA Cup semi-final, Swansea dropped into the Third Division and, after securing a lucrative severance payment, Morris resigned. He had a brief spell as general manager of Newport County before accepting the post of secretary to the FA of Wales – a position he held for 11 years before leaving because of a heart complaint.

Bill Jones

September 1958 – September 1962

Welsh Cup winner 1958–59. Division Two runner-up 1959–60. Welsh Cup finalist 1959–60.

Bill Jones made only a handful of Football League appearances for Newport County before moving into non-League football with Barry Town. He later became chief scout for Ipswich Town and in 1950 was appointed manager of Barry Town, where he discovered both Derek Tapscott and Dai Ward. In 1954 Jones became manager of Worcester City before, three years later, arriving at Ninian Park as assistant manager and chief scout to Trevor Morris, whom he succeeded a year later. Jones took Cardiff City into the First Division in 1959–60 and produced some exciting talents such as Alan Durban, Graham Moore, Barrie Hole and Frank Rankmore. However, the Bluebirds were relegated in 1961–62 and after a bad start to the following season Jones was dismissed and rejoined Worcester City.

George Swindin

November 1962 – April 1964

Welsh Cup winner 1963–64.

One of Arsenal's best-ever goalkeepers, George Swindin moved to Highbury after just 26 League games for Bradford City and gained a League

Championship medal in 1937–38, despite playing in only 17 games for the club. Unlucky not to win international honours, he was ever present when Arsenal were again champions in 1947–48 and played 14 games when they won it again in 1952–53. Swindin played in two FA Cup Finals for the Gunners, picking up a medal in 1950 when they beat Liverpool 2–0. In 1954 he joined non-League Peterborough United as player-manager, leading them to three Midland League titles before returning to Highbury as manager. Unable to find much success there, he had a brief spell in charge of Norwich

City before being appointed manager of Cardiff City in November 1962. His stay at Ninian Park was not a particularly happy one as City suffered one of their worst injury crises in 1963–64 after signing John Charles from Roma against Swindin's wishes. City did win the Welsh Cup and entered Europe for the first time, but even so Swindin was sacked after 18 months of struggle.

Jimmy Scoular

June 1964 – November 1973

Welsh Cup winner 1964–65, 1966–67, 1967–68, 1968–69, 1969–70, 1970–71, 1972–73. Welsh Cup finalist 1971–72.

An inspiring captain, Jimmy Scoular was a well-built half-back who was renowned for his hard and relentless tackling, although he was an intelligent distributor and could produce delicate touches when needed. A permanent fixture in the Portsmouth side, he helped the south coast club to successive League Championships in 1948–49 and 1949–50 before, in June 1953, joining Newcastle United for a club record fee of £22,500. He captained the Magpies to success in the 1955 FA Cup Final and went on to play the same number of games – 247 – as he had for Pompey. He then appeared over 100 times for Bradford Park Avenue as player-manager, discovering such talents as Ian

Gibson, Kevin Hector and Jim Fryatt, but was sacked in May 1964. A month later he was appointed manager of Cardiff City – an association that was to last nine years. He was very unlucky not to win anything other than seven Welsh Cup Finals at Ninian Park. The Bluebirds reached the semi-finals of the European Cup-Winners' Cup in 1967–68, losing 4–3 on aggregate to SV Hamburg, and Scoular turned Cardiff into one of the best sides in Division Two before being sacked following boardroom changes at Ninian Park. He later managed Newport County before acting as scout for both Swansea and Newcastle United.

Frank O'Farrell

November 1973 – April 1974

A regular in the West Ham United side for six years, Frank O'Farrell soon gained international recognition, winning the first of nine caps for the Republic of Ireland against Austria in 1952. Having made 210 appearances for the Hammers, he joined Preston North End in a straight exchange for Eddie Lewis. After a comparatively short association with the Deepdale club, he moved to non-League Weymouth as player-manager in May 1961. He proved to be a success at the south coast club, steering them to the Southern League Championship before taking over at Torquay United, where he gained the club promotion at the end of his first season. At Leicester City he led the club to the FA Cup Final and promotion to the First Division before taking over at Manchester United. He found it difficult to follow in the footsteps of Matt Busby and left Old Trafford a bitter man. O'Farrell was brought to Ninian Park by David Goldstone to succeed Jimmy Scoular, but he accepted a lucrative offer from the Middle East and left the club after just 158 days in office! After managing the Iran national team he returned to Britain and had a second spell in charge of Torquay United

Jimmy Andrews

May 1974 – November 1978

Welsh Cup winner 1973–74, 1975–76.
Welsh Cup finalist 1974–75, 1976–77.
Division Three runner-up 1975–76.

A small, quick dribbling winger, Jimmy Andrews played Scottish League football for Dundee before joining West Ham United in November 1951. Proving a most worthwhile investment, he scored 21 goals in 114 League games before signing for Leyton Orient and later ending his playing career with Queen's Park Rangers. He built up a good

reputation as a coach with the Loftus Road club and went on to work in a similar capacity with Chelsea, Luton Town, Coventry City, Spurs and eventually Cardiff to work alongside Frank O'Farrell. On O'Farrell's departure to Iran, Andrews took over as caretaker-manager, but when City avoided relegation he was appointed permanently. The following season the Bluebirds dropped into Division Three but Andrews brought them straight back up again in 1975–76, playing brilliant football and with a new board of directors. He had put the club back on its feet again and there was a harvest of goals from Adrian Alston and Tony Evans. However, back in Division Two Cardiff struggled, narrowly avoiding relegation in 1976–77. They also had a run in the European Cup-Winners' Cup, but there was still a high turnover of players, and in 1978, following the unsuccessful coaching appointment of Micky Burns, Andrews felt the wrath of the City fans when results went against him. Sacked in November 1978, he later acted as a scout for Southampton.

Richie Morgan

November 1978 – November 1981

After a long playing career with his home-town club, primarily as understudy to Don Murray, Richie Morgan was the surprise choice as

manager in November 1978. After surrounding himself with an excellent backroom staff of Brian Harris, Dave Elliott and Doug Livermore, Morgan spent large amounts of money on players like Dave Bennett, Peter Kitchen, Ronnie Moore and Colin Sullivan but sadly found little success. City plunged down the table after they brought in Graham Williams as team manager with Morgan as general manager. Both were eventually sacked, though Morgan went on to have outstanding success as manager of Barry Town, who won the Welsh League Championship on a number of occasions.

Graham Williams

November 1981 – February 1982

Welsh international Graham Williams joined West Bromwich Albion as a left-winger but was soon converted to left-back. A stout-hearted defender, he went

on to make 360 appearances for Albion, playing in two League Cup Finals for the club. In 1968 he skippered Albion to an FA Cup Final victory over Everton before, in the 1970s, he managed Weymouth and Poole Town as well as coaching abroad in Kuwait and Greece. When he was appointed by Cardiff City, he was officially classed as chief coach, not manager, but in three months in charge, the Bluebirds won just one of the 11 games and he was sacked, along with Richie Morgan.

Len Ashurst

March 1982 – March 1984 and August 1989 – May 1991

Welsh Cup finalist 1981–82. Division Three runner-up 1982–83.

A steady constructive full-back, Len Ashurst made 410 League appearances for Sunderland before moving to Hartlepool United in March 1971 as player-manager. The highspot of the England Under-23 international's career was helping the Wearsiders back into the First Division in 1963–64. Ashurst had spells as manager at Gillingham and Sheffield Wednesday where he built the foundations for future success. Even though he was unable to get the Owls promoted out of the Third Division, he made a number of important signings and also developed some fine youngsters. When Ashurst took over at Newport County in 1978 they were near the bottom of the Fourth Division. He soon pulled them round, and in

1979–80 they won promotion and, in lifting the Welsh Cup, entry into Europe. They failed by the narrowest of margins in reaching the semi-final of the European Cup-Winners' Cup. A month after being replaced by Colin Addison in February 1982, Ashurst joined Cardiff. He was unable to prevent the Bluebirds dropping into the Third Division, but the following season they won promotion back again. He then had an unhappy spell at his former club Sunderland, who lost in the League Cup Final and were relegated to Division Two. He was sacked soon afterwards and, after spells coaching in Kuwait and Qatar, became assistant manager of Blackpool, before taking charge again at Ninian Park. City were relegated to the Fourth Division in 1989–90 and, after another poor season, he was sacked.

Jimmy Goodfellow

March 1984 – September 1984

Jimmy Goodfellow had won a reputation as a goalscorer with Bishop Auckland when he was signed by Port Vale in 1966 but was converted into a more defensive role at Vale Park. He made almost 200 appearances for his next club Workington and then, with Rotherham United, took his total of League appearances for his three clubs, in which he scored 34 goals, to 479. After being assistant manager to Len

Ashurst at Newport County he followed him to Cardiff City in 1982. Goodfellow was made caretaker-manager after Ashurst's departure in 1984 and had a very short period officially in charge at the start of the 1984–85 season. With little backing from the board of directors, he was eventually replaced by Alan Durban. Two years later Goodfellow returned to Ninian Park as the club's physiotherapist.

Alan Durban

September 1984 – May 1986

A skilful midfield player, Alan Durban joined Derby County from Cardiff City

when the Rams were a moderate Second Division side, but was one of the players that blossomed following the arrival of Brian Clough as manager at the Baseball Ground. Under Clough he won a Second Division Championship medal in 1968–69 and a League Championship medal in 1971–72. He went on to score 112 goals in 403 games for Derby before moving on to Shrewsbury Town as player-manager. He steered the club out of the Fourth Division in 1974–75 and later into the Second Division and to Welsh Cup success. There followed a managerial spell at Stoke City, during which they were promoted to Division One in 1978–79. Durban left for Sunderland after a more tempting offer but was sacked after three troubled years at Roker Park. Six months later he was brought back into management by Cardiff City, but it proved a bad move. His spell at Ninian Park was a disaster with the club plummeting from the Second to the Fourth Division. In 1986 Durban left football to run an indoor tennis club in Telford.

Frank Burrows

May 1986 – August 1989 and February 1998 – January 2000

Division Four runner-up 1987–88. Welsh Cup winner 1987–88. FAW Invitation Cup finalist 1997–98. Division Three promotion 1998–99.

A tough, uncompromising defender, Frank Burrows began his career with Raith Rovers before entering the Football League with Scunthorpe United. After over 100 League appearances for the Irons he joined Swindon Town in July 1968 and, with the exception of a short loan spell with Mansfield, was a virtual ever present in the Robins side for eight seasons. After 345 appearances he became Swindon's assistant manager before later going into coaching with Portsmouth. Burrows later succeeded Jimmy Dickinson as Pompey's manager and the club won promotion to the Third Division in his first season in charge at Fratton Park. He later coached Southampton and Sunderland before returning to management with Cardiff City as they entered the Fourth Division

for the first time. The Bluebirds finished runners-up in 1987–88 but shortly afterwards Burrows left to work as assistant to John Gregory at Portsmouth. When Gregory moved on Burrows took control at the club for a second time. Lack of good results and general disenchantment throughout the club led to Burrows resigning as manager. In 1991 he took over the reins at Swansea, and in 1992–93 the Swans reached the Second Division play-offs. He lost his job in 1995 and three years later returned to Ninian Park for a second spell as manager, helping the Bluebirds win promotion to the Second Division in 1998–99. Burrows parted company with the club in January 2000 and is now assistant manager at West Bromwich Albion.

Eddie May

July 1991 – November 1994 and March 1995 – May 1995

Division Three champion 1992–93. Welsh Cup winner 1992–93. Welsh Cup finalist 1993–94.

A solid and useful defender, Eddie May made over 500 League appearances in his career, including 333 in which he scored 34 goals for Wrexham. He helped Wrexham to promotion to Division Three in 1969–70 and to two Welsh Cup successes. He was coach at Leicester City when they won the Second Division

Championship in 1979–80 and for three years was assistant manager under Lennie Lawrence at Charlton Athletic. After coaching in Saudi Arabia and Iceland, May was manager at Newport County for just a month! Officially chief coach in charge of team affairs at Ninian

Park, he saw the Bluebirds narrowly miss the Fourth Division play-offs in 1991–92 but with a large increase in support. In 1992–93 big crowds returned to Ninian Park as City took the Third Division title with 83 points. They also won the Welsh Cup, beating Rhyl 5–0 in the Final at Cardiff Arms Park to gain entry into the European Cup-Winners' Cup. The only blight on the campaign was a first round FA Cup defeat against non-League Bath City. After finishing 19th in Division Two, City lost to non-League Enfield in the following season's FA Cup competition, and in November 1994 May was sacked. Four months later, following the departure of Terry Yorath, May returned to take charge of the Bluebirds for a second time but couldn't prevent their relegation. He left Ninian Park to manage Torquay United, later taking charge of Brentford.

Terry Yorath

November 1994 – March 1995

An often under-appreciated member of the great Leeds United side of the late 1960s and early 1970s, the rugged blond Welsh international, who won 59 caps, left Elland Road in August 1976 to join Coventry City. Three years later he

moved to Spurs and had an outstanding first season at White Hart Lane. Hampered by injuries, he had a spell playing for Vancouver Whitecaps before being appointed assistant to Trevor Cherry at Bradford City. He was then appointed Swansea's manager and took the Vetch Field club to promotion to the Third Division in 1987–88 but then left the club in controversial circumstances to return to Valley Parade. He paid £18,000 out of his own pocket to honour his contract with the Swans. He did not last long at Bradford and was dismissed after a string of disappointing results. In a bizarre turn of events he returned to Swansea but was later sacked. After being appointed Wales national manager he took them close to

qualification to the 1992 European Championships, before taking charge at Cardiff City following the sacking of Eddie May. Yorath, who was also a director as well as team manager and a member of a consortium trying to buy the club, resigned in March 1995 as City ended the campaign in one of the Second Division relegation places. He later worked in Beirut as the Lebanese national team manager before taking charge of Bradford City and Sheffield Wednesday. He is currently at Huddersfield Town as the Yorkshire club's assistant manager.

Kenny Hibbitt

July 1995 – January 1996 and December 1996 – February 1998

Elegant midfielder Kenny Hibbitt, who

won Under-23 honours for England, played the bulk of his football for Wolverhampton Wanderers. He was on the winning side twice with Wolves in League Cup Finals, and in the 1974 victory over Manchester City he scored one of the goals in a 2–1 win. Hibbitt also gained promotion twice to Division One with Wolves, gaining a Second Division Championship medal in

1976–77. After retiring from playing he became Gerry Francis's assistant at Bristol Rovers before taking up his first management post at Walsall. He took over too late to prevent the club from being relegated for the second successive season. Walsall moved into the new Bescot Stadium, but they continued to struggle on the pitch despite Hibbitt's efforts. On leaving the Saddlers, Hibbitt took charge at Ninian Park, but midway through the 1995–96 season he made way for Phil Neal and took on the title of director of football development. Following the departure of Neal and the short tenure of Russell Osman, Hibbitt again assumed control, leading the Bluebirds to a creditable seventh in Division Three in 1996–97. However, he wasn't as successful the following season and made way for the return of Frank Burrows, Hibbitt reverting to his original post as director of football development.

Phil Neal

January 1996 – October 1996

After beginning his League career with Northampton Town, Phil Neal made 206 first-team appearances for the Cobblers before joining Liverpool for £65,000 in October 1974. From his second appearance for the club in December 1974 until injury caused him to miss Liverpool's game with Sunderland in October 1983, Phil Neal played in 366 consecutive League games. The winner of 50 full England caps, Neal won almost every honour while playing for Liverpool. He won seven League Championship medals and was on the winning side in four League Cup Finals. He won a UEFA Cup medal and four European Cup medals – only an FA Cup medal eluded him. Halfway through the 1985–86 season he left Anfield to join Bolton Wanderers as player-manager. He led the Trotters to promotion from the Fourth Division and to success in the Sherpa Van Trophy, but he left the Lancashire club at the end of the 1991–92 season. After a period of involvement with the England management team, he took charge of Coventry City before becoming manager of Cardiff City in January

1996. He couldn't wave a magic wand, and the Bluebirds finished 22nd in the Third Division. After an indifferent start to the following season he was replaced by Russell Osman and went to Manchester City, where he became caretaker-manager following Alan Ball's departure but was soon replaced by Frank Clark.

Russell Osman

November 1996 – December 1996

Russell Osman began his Football League career with Ipswich Town, where he formed an excellent central-defensive partnership with Terry Butcher under the managership of Bobby Robson. Capped 11 times by England, Osman went close to a League Championship medal in seasons 1980–81 and 1981–82 when Town finished runners-up in the First Division. He also helped the club win the UEFA Cup in 1981 when they

beat AZ Alkmaar 5–4 on aggregate. Having played in 384 League games, he left Portman Road in the summer of 1985 to join Leicester City, later playing for Southampton. Osman's first managerial role was with Bristol City, where he was initially caretaker-manager, but in 1994 he lost his job. In November 1996 he became manager of Cardiff City, but after just over a month in charge, in which the Bluebirds won two and lost three matches, he was replaced by Kenny Hibbitt. Osman later returned to Ashton Gate as coach after spells with Plymouth Argyle, Sudbury Town and Brighton.

Billy Ayre

February 2000 – August 2000

FAW Invitation Cup finalist 1999–2000.

As a player, Billy Ayre had spells with Hartlepool United, Halifax Town and Mansfield Town before rejoining the Shaymen as assistant manager to Mick Jones. He was a popular choice to

succeed Jones – Halifax being on the brink of bankruptcy when Ayre took over. He could not have had a tougher baptism in football management. He won a reputation as a team boss who could produce good young players, but in March 1990, with the club in imminent danger of dropping out of the Football League, he resigned his post. Two months later he joined Blackpool as assistant manager to

Graham Carr, replacing Carr in the hot-seat following his departure. Almost immediately he began to turn things around, the Seasiders only losing to Torquay United in a penalty shoot-out in the play-off final at Wembley. In 1991–92 the club again reached the play-off final but this time won promotion, beating Scunthorpe United on penalties. After two disappointing seasons Ayre lost his job and managed Scarborough before taking over the reins of Vauxhall Conference side Southport. After a spell as assistant manager of Swansea City he took charge of Cardiff City in February 2000 but couldn't prevent their relegation from Division Two. Following the arrival of new owner Sam Hammam, Ayre lost his job, being replaced by Bobby Gould.

Bobby Gould

August 2000 – October 2000

The much-travelled striker and great-hearted competitor Bobby Gould began his career with his home-town club Coventry City. After helping the Sky

Blues win promotion to the First Division, he joined Arsenal and was in the side that lost to Third Division Swindon Town in the 1969 League Cup Final. He joined Wolves in the summer of 1970 and ended his first season at Molineux as top scorer with 24 goals. His next move was to West Bromwich Albion before later playing for Bristol City and West Ham United. In December 1975 he rejoined Wolves and then had spells with Bristol Rovers and Coventry City before being appointed manager of Wimbledon in July 1987. The Dons finished seventh in Division One but beat mighty Liverpool 1–0 in

the 1988 FA Cup Final. Gould went on to enjoy three years in charge of the Dons but parted company with the club in the summer of 1990. He moved back to Highfield Road in 1992 after an unhappy spell in charge of West Bromwich Albion. Gould later took charge of the Welsh national side before resigning his post in the summer of 1999. In August 2000 Gould made a surprise return to club management by linking up with Sam Hammam, Cardiff's new owner. Two months later, after City had lost two games in succession following their nine-game unbeaten start to the 2000–01 season, Gould was replaced by Alan Cork, though he retained the title of club manager.

Alan Cork

October 2000 – February 2002

Division Three runner-up 2000–01.

Initially with Derby County where he failed to make the grade, he had a loan spell with Lincoln City before joining Wimbledon in February 1978. In his first full season with the club he netted 25 goals including four against Torquay United and a hat-trick in the defeat of Northampton Town. In the Dons promotion season of 1980–81, Cork was again top scorer with 26 goals including another treble against Crewe. A broken leg then kept him out of first-team action for almost two years, but in 1983–84 he returned to top score with 33 goals, including another hat-trick against Newport County, as the Dons won promotion to Division Two. Another treble followed in the game against Blackburn Rovers in 1985–86, as Wimbledon finished third in Division Two. He won an FA Cup medal in 1988 but after that spent his last few years at the club as a squad player. In March 1992, after scoring 168 goals in 501 games, he followed his manager Dave Bassett to Sheffield United. On leaving the Blades he joined Fulham, taking charge of the youth team before being appointed first-team coach. After becoming the Swans assistant manager, he replaced Micky Adams as the Vetch club boss in October 1997 but was later replaced himself by John Hollins. Cork replaced Bobby Gould as Cardiff boss in

October 2000 and led the Bluebirds to promotion from the Third Division as runners-up to Brighton & Hove Albion. The club were having a fairly good season in Division Two, but in February 2002 Cork resigned his post.

Lennie Lawrence

February 2002 – May 2005

FAW Premier Cup winner 2001–02. Division Two promotion 2002–03.

In his eight years as manager of Charlton Athletic Lennie Lawrence experienced just about everything. As well as promotion and relegation, the London club nearly went bankrupt, lost their Valley ground, shared with Crystal Palace and won an exciting play-off match to avoid relegation. In June 1991, with Charlton on the point of returning to The Valley, Lawrence resigned to take the manager job at Middlesbrough. He took the then Ayresome Park club to promotion to the newly formed Premiership at the end of his first season in charge. They finished runners-up to Ipswich and also reached the semi-finals of the League Cup. Relegated in 1992–93, Lawrence lost his job in May 1994 after the club had ended the

campaign in ninth place in the First Division. Three weeks later he was appointed manager of Bradford City. Feeling that he had to recruit new players, he spent £1.5 million but City finished 14th following a disastrous end to the season when they won just one of their last 12 games. In November 1995 Lawrence lost his job but the following month took charge of Luton Town, leading the Hatters to the Second

Division play-offs in 1996–97. There then followed three seasons of mid-table placings before he left to manage Grimsby Town. An abysmal run of results – the Mariners winning 16 of their 69 games under Lawrence's leadership, saw the Grimsby boss lose his job. In February 2002 Lawrence was appointed manager of Cardiff City following the resignation of Alan Cork. The Bluebirds reached the play-offs but went down to Stoke City. In 2002–03 Lawrence took City to the play-offs again, but this time, after beating Bristol City, they defeated Queen's Park Rangers in the play-off final in front of a Millennium Stadium crowd of 66,096. After finishing mid-table in 2003–04, the following season, with Lawrence still at the helm, the club finished the First Division campaign below mid-table and he was sacked in May 2005.

Dave Jones

May 2005 –

The former defender began his career as a player with Everton and spent seven years at the club, suffering a potentially threatening injury, before moving on to Coventry City. After a spell in Hong Kong with Seiko, he returned to England and Preston North End. A start in management came at Southport and he also took charge of Moseley and Morecambe before moving into League football with Stockport County. His first role at Edgeley Park was youth coach before being promoted to first-team coach and eventually manager. Jones enjoyed two very successful seasons at Edgeley Park, guiding the club to a ninth-place finish in his first full season in charge. The dream of promotion to the First Division became a reality in 1997 as he led the team to the runners-up spot and automatic promotion. Jones also took the club to the semi-finals of the League Cup that season, where they were eliminated by Middlesbrough when so close to a Wembley Final as a Second Division club. His Premiership management potential was recognised by Southampton when in the summer of 1997 he succeeded Graeme Souness. It was always going to be a test for the

Liverpudlian with the Saints perennial strugglers in the top flight. His time at The Dell was traumatic, mainly due to off-the-field affairs, which eventually led to him being replaced. In January 2000, Southampton chose to 'suspend' their manager on full pay for 12 months while he fought to clear his name. It was obvious he would not return as Glenn Hoddle had been installed as 'interim' manager. After nearly a year out of the game, he was appointed manager of Wolverhampton Wanderers, and in his first full season after persuading owner Sir Jack Hayward to invest more of his millions into the club Wolves finished third in the Division and lost to Norwich in the play-off semi-final. The following season saw Wolves again reach the play-offs, and after defeating Reading in the semi-finals they blew away Sheffield United to end their 19-year absence from the top flight. But the Premiership stay was a short one, as Wolves went straight back down. That

pressure proved too much, and with the club languishing near the foot of the Championship he was sacked. In May 2005 Jones was confirmed as the new manager of Cardiff City, a club with financial problems which had narrowly avoided relegation to League One. The Bluebirds were reportedly £30 million in debt and had been relying on the PFA to meet a crippling £600,000-a-month wage bill. The pundits were again tipping the club for a relegation battle in 2005–06, and Jones knew that his first task would be to keep the Bluebirds in the Championship prior to work beginning on the club's long-awaited new stadium. Jones's tactical acumen and shrewd transfer-market business proved to be the difference once again, and Cardiff finished just outside the play-off places. Given time and the right backing, Dave Jones may well be the man to lead the club into the Premiership.

Bluebirds Internationals

Wales

Aizlewood M. 1994–95 v Bulgaria (1).

Allchurch I.J. 1962–63 v Scotland, England, Northern Ireland, Holland (2); 1963–64 v England; 1964–65 v Scotland, England, Northern Ireland Greece, Italy, Russia (12).

Baker C.W. 1957–58 v Mexico; 1959–60 v Scotland, Northern Ireland; 1960–61 v Scotland, England, Republic of Ireland; 1961–62 v Scotland (7).

Baker W.G. 1947–48 v Northern Ireland (1).

Beadles G.H. 1924–25 v England, Scotland (2).

Charles M. 1961–62 v Brazil, Northern Ireland; 1962–63 v Scotland, Holland (4).

Charles W.J. 1963–64 v Scotland; 1964–65 v Scotland, Russia (3).

Collins J.M. 2003–04 v Norway, Canada (2).

Curtis A. 1986–87 v Russia (1).

Curtis E.R. 1927–28 v Scotland (10).

Davies L.S. 1921–22 v England, Scotland, Northern Ireland; 1922–23 v England, Scotland, Northern Ireland; 1923–24 v England, Scotland, Northern Ireland; 1924–25 v Scotland, Northern Ireland; 1925–26 v England, Northern Ireland; 1926–27 v England, Northern Ireland; 1927–28 v Scotland, Northern Ireland, England; 1928–29 v Scotland, Northern Ireland, England; 1929–30 v England, Scotland (23).

Davies W. 1924–25 v England, Scotland, Northern Ireland; 1925–26 v England, Scotland, Northern Ireland; 1926–27 v Scotland; 1927–28 v Northern Ireland (8).

Derrett S.C. 1968–69 v Scotland, West Germany; 1969–70 v Italy; 1970–71 v Finland (4).

Dwyer P. 1977–78 v Iran, England, Scotland, Northern Ireland; 1978–79 v Turkey, Scotland, England, Northern Ireland, Malta; 1979–80 v West Germany (10).

Earnshaw R. 2001–02 v Germany; 2002–03 v Croatia, Azerbaijan, Bosnia; 2003–04 v Serbia (2) Italy, Finland, Russia, Scotland, Hungary, Norway, Canada (13).

Edwards G. 1948–49 v Northern Ireland, Portugal, Belgium, Switzerland; 1949–50 v England, Scotland (6).

Evans H.P. 1921–22 v England, Scotland, Northern Ireland; 1923–24 v England, Scotland, Northern Ireland (6).

Evans J. 1911–12 v Northern Ireland; 1912–13 v Northern Ireland; 1913–14 v Scotland; 1919–20 v Scotland, Northern Ireland; 1921–22 v Northern Ireland; 1922–23 v England, Northern Ireland (8).

Evans L. 1930–31 v England, Scotland (2).

Ford T. 1953–54 v Austria; 1954–55 v Scotland, England, Northern Ireland, Yugoslavia; 1955–56 v Scotland, Northern Ireland, England, Austria; 1956–57 v Scotland (10).

Gabbidon D.L. 2001–02 v Czech Republic; 2002–03 v Croatia, Finland, Italy; 2003–04 v Serbia (2) Russia (2) Scotland, Hungary, Norway, Canada (12).

Harrington A.C. 1955–56 v Northern Ireland; 1956–57 v England, Scotland; 1957–58 v Scotland, Northern Ireland, Israel (2); 1960–61 v Scotland, England; 1961–62 v England, Scotland (11).

Haworth S.O. 1996–97 v Scotland (1).

Hewitt R. 1957–58 v Northern Ireland, Israel, Sweden, Holland, Brazil (5).

Hole B.G. 1962–63 v Northern Ireland; 1963–64 v Northern Ireland; 1964–65 v Scotland, England, Northern Ireland, Denmark, Greece (2), Russia, Italy; 1965–66 v England, Scotland, Northern Ireland, Russia, Denmark, Brazil (2) Chile (18).

Howells R.G. 1953–54 v England, Scotland (2).

Jones B.S. 1968–69 v Scotland, England, Northern Ireland, Italy, West Germany, East Germany, Rest of UK (7).

Jones L.J. 1932–33 v France (1).

Keenor F.C. 1919–20 v England, Northern Ireland; 1920–21 v England, Northern Ireland, Scotland; 1921–22 v Northern Ireland; 1922–23 v England, Northern Ireland, Scotland; 1923–24 v England, Northern Ireland, Scotland; 1924–25 v England, Northern Ireland, Scotland; 1925–26 v Scotland; 1926–27 v England, Northern Ireland, Scotland; 1927–28 v England, Northern Ireland, Scotland; 1928–29 v England, Northern Ireland, Scotland; 1929–30 v England, Northern Ireland, Scotland; 1930–31 v England, Northern Ireland, Scotland (31).

Latham G. 1912–13 v Northern Ireland (1).

Legg A. 1998–99 v Denmark; 2000–01 v Armenia (2).

Lewis J. 1925–26 v Scotland (1).

Margetson M.W. 2003–04 v Canada (1).

Moore G. 1959–60 v Scotland, England, Northern Ireland; 1960–61 v Republic of Ireland, Spain (5).

Nicholls J. 1924–25 v England, Scotland (2).

Parry P.I. 2003–04 v Scotland, Norway, Canada (3).

Perry J. 1993–94 v Norway (1).

Phillips L. 1970–71 v Czechoslovakia, Scotland, England, Northern Ireland; 1971–72 v Czechoslovakia, Romania, Scotland, Northern Ireland; 1972–73 v England; 1973–74 v Poland, Northern Ireland; 1974–75 v Austria (12).

Pontin K. 1979–80 v England, Scotland (2).

Ratcliffe K. 1992–93 v Belgium (1).

Reece G.I. 1972–73 v England, Northern Ireland; 1973–74 v Poland, England, Scotland, Northern Ireland; 1974–75 v Austria, Holland (2), Luxembourg (2) Scotland, Northern Ireland (13).

Rees W. 1948–49 v Northern Ireland, Belgium, Switzerland (3).

Richards S.V. 1946–47 v England (1).

Robbins W.W. 1930–31 v England, Scotland; 1931–32 v England, Northern Ireland, Scotland (5).

Rodrigues P.J. 1964–65 v Northern Ireland, Greece (2); 1965–66 v Russia, England, Scotland, Denmark (7).

Sayer P. 1976–77 v Czechoslovakia, Scotland, England, Northern Ireland; 1977–78 v Kuwait (2) v Scotland (7).

Sherwood A.T. 1946–47 v England, Northern Ireland; 1947–48 v Scotland, Northern Ireland; 1948–49 v England, Scotland, Northern Ireland, Portugal, Switzerland; 1949–50 v England, Scotland, Northern Ireland, Belgium; 1950–51 v England,

Scotland, Northern Ireland, Portugal, Switzerland; 1951–52 v England, Scotland, Northern Ireland, Rest of UK; 1952–53 v Scotland, England, Northern Ireland, France, Yugoslavia; 1953–54 v England, Scotland, Northern Ireland, Austria; 1954–55 v Scotland, England, Yugoslavia, Northern Ireland; 1955–56 v England, Scotland, Northern Ireland, Austria (39).
Showers D. 1974–75 v England, Northern Ireland (2).
Stansfield F. 1948–49 v Scotland (1).
Stitfall R.F. 1952–53 v England; 1956–57 v Czechoslovakia (2).
Sullivan D. 1952–53 v Northern Ireland, France, Yugoslavia; 1953–54 v Northern Ireland; 1954–55 v England, Northern Ireland; 1956–57 v England, Scotland; 1957–58 v Sweden, Brazil, Northern Ireland, Holland (2); 1958–59 v Scotland, Northern Ireland; 1959–60 v England, Scotland (17).
Tapscott D.R. 1958–59 v England, Northern Ireland (2).
Thomas R.J. 1977–78 v Czechoslovakia (1).
Toshack J.B. 1968–69 v Scotland, England, Northern Ireland, West Germany, East Germany, Rest of UK; 1969–70 v East Germany, Italy (8).
Vaughan N. 1983–84 v Romania, Bulgaria, Yugoslavia, Northern Ireland, Norway, Israel; 1984–85 v Spain (7).
Vearncombe G. 1957–58 v East Germany; 1960–61 v Republic of Ireland (2).
Villars A.K. 1973–74 v England, Scotland, Northern Ireland (3).
Ward D. 1961–62 v England (1).
Warren F.W. 1928–29 v Northern Ireland (1).
Weston R.D. 2002–03 v Croatia, Azerbaijan, Bosnia; 2003–04 v Finland, Serbia (5).
Williams G.J.J. 1950–51 v Switzerland (1).

Scotland
Blair J. 1920–21 v England; 1921–22 v England; 1922–23 v England, Wales, Northern Ireland; 1923–24 v Wales (6).
Nelson J. 1924–25 v Wales, Northern Ireland; 1927–28 v England; 1929–30 v France (4).

Northern Ireland
Farquharson T.G. 1922–23 v Scotland, Wales; 1923–24 v England, Scotland, Wales; 1924–25 v England, Scotland (7).
Irving S.J. 1926–27 v Scotland, England, Wales; 1927–28 v Scotland, England Wales (6).
McCambridge J. 1930–31 v Wales; 1931–32 v England (2).
Reid G.H. 1922–23 v Scotland (1).
Sloan T. 1925–26 v Scotland, Wales, England; 1926–27 v Wales, Scotland; 1927–28 v England, Wales; 1928–29 v England (8).
Smith E.E. 1920–21 v Scotland; 1922–23 v Wales, England; 1923–24 v England (4).
Watson T. 1925–26 v Scotland (1).

Republic of Ireland
Farquharson T.G. 1928–29 v Belgium; 1929–30 v Belgium; 1930–31 v Spain; 1931–32 v Spain (4).
Healey R. 1976–7 v Poland; 1979–80 v England (2).
Kavanagh G.A. 2003–04 v Canada, Brazil (2).
Lee A.D. 2003–04 v Czech Republic, Poland, Nigeria, Jamaica, Holland (5).

Other Appearances by Competitions

FA Charity Shield (1927–28)
G.Blackburn, E.Curtis, L.Davies, T.Farquharson, H.Ferguson, W.Hardy, S.Irving, F.Keenor, G.McLachlan, J.Nelson, W.Thirlaway.
Goalscorers: H.Ferguson 1, L.Davies 1.

Division Three South Cup (1933–34 to 1938–39)
R.Pugh 4, J.Collins 3, A.Granville 3, R.Jones 3, E.Mort 3, F.Talbot 3, G.Walton 3, B.Bassett 2, J.Everest 2, J.Galbraith 2, J.Leckie 2, C.McCaughey 2, W.Main 2, G.Nicholson 2, A.Turner 2, W.Ballsom 1, A.Brown 1, R.Calder 1, W.Corkhill 1, E.Curtis 1, J.Diamond 1, F.Duthie 1, T.Farquharson 1, W.Fielding 1, L.Ford 1, C.Godfrey 1, J.Harrison 1, W.Henderson 1, C.Hill 1, F.Hill 1, W.Jackson 1, W.Jennings 1, G.Jones 1, L.Jones 1, R.Keating 1, J.Kelso 1, E.Lane 1, D.McKenzie 1, W.Marshalsey 1, J.Mellor 1, J.Mitchell 1, P.Molloy 1, D.Ovenstone 1, A.Pinxton 1, E.Postin 1, H.Riley 1, T.Rogers 1, H.Roper 1, G.Russell 1, W.Scott 1, H.Smith 1, T.Vaughan 1, F.Whitlow 1.
Goalscorers: J.Collins 1, J.Diamond 1, A.Turner 1, T.Vaughan 1.

Anglo-French Friendship Cup (1961–62)
A.Harrington 2, J.King 2, P.King 2, A.Milne 2, D.Tapscott 2, C.Baker 1, M.Charles 1, L.Edwards 1, S.Gammon 1, B.Hole 1, D.John 1, G.Moore 1, T.Peck 1, D.Pickrell 1, F.Rankmore 1, G.Vearncombe 1, D.Ward 1.
Goalscorers: P.King 2, M.Charles 1, J.King 1, G.Moore 1, D.Tapscott 1.

European Cup Winners Cup (1964–65 to 1993–94)
D.Murray 33, P.King 31, J.Toshack 19, B.Harris 18, G.Bell 16, B.Clark 14, M.Sutton 14, D.Carver 13, B.S.Jones 13, B.Wilson 13, L.Phillips 11, B.Woodruff 10, G.Williams 9, R.Bird 8, M.Clarke 8, G.Farrell 8, B.Ferguson 8, I.Gibson 8, B.Hole 8, P.Rodrigues 8, D.Showers 8, J.Charles 7, L.Lea 7, B.Lewis 7, F.Pethard 7, G.Coldrick 6, F.Davies 6, S.Derrett 6, P.Dwyer 6, J.Eadie 6, A.Evans 6, A.Harrington 6, B.Irwin 6, D.Livermore 6, W.Anderson 5, A.Campbell 5, C.Charles 5, A.Larmour 5, P.Sayer 5, D.Tapscott 5, A.Alston 4, B.Attley 4, L.Baddeley 4, B.Bartlett 4, A.Bird 4, T.Boyle 4, J.Buchanan 4, A.Curtis 4,

N.Dean 4, J.Gilligan 4, C.Griffith 4, R.Healey 4, D.John 4, M.Kelly 4, B.McDermott 4, R.Morgan 4, N.Platnauer 4, D.Searle 4, A.Villars 4, P.Wimbleton 4, G.Wood 4, G.Abraham 3, P.Bater 3, N.Blake 3, B.Brown 3, R.James 3, K.Pontin 3, N.Stevenson 3, J.Vincent 3, S.Allan 2, I.Allchurch 2, D.Brazil 2, G.Byrne 2, C.Dale 2, J.Farrington 2, D.Giles 2, M.Grew 2, T.Harkin 2, J.Impey 2, G.Johnson 2, K.Jones 2, A.McCulloch 2, F.Parsons 2, T.Peck 2, J.Perry 2, C.Pike 2, D.Powell 2, P.Ramsey 2, K.Ratcliffe 2, G.Reece 2, N.Rees 2, I.Rodgerson 2, G.Smith 2, P.Stant 2, A.Warboys 2, P.Went 2, R.Bishop 1, M.Charles 1, A.Foggon 1, A.Gorman 1, S.Grapes 1, J.Gummer 1, T.Halliday 1, B.H.Jones 1, P.Kite 1, T.Lewis 1, S.Lynex 1, R.McInch 1, P.Millar 1, P.Morgan 1, N.Richardson 1, F.Sharp 1, D.Summerhayes 1, G.Thompson 1, I.Walsh 1, N.Wigg 1, S.Williams 1.

Goalscorers: J.Toshack 11, P.King 9, B.Clark 7, S.Allan 3, N.Dean 3, I.Gibson 3, J.Gilligan 3, A.Bird 2, R.Bird 2, B.Brown 2, B.S.Jones 2, M.Sutton 2, A.Alston 1, M.Clarke 1, P.Dwyer 1, A.Evans 1, G.Farrell 1, B.Harris 1, R.James 1, G.Johnston 1, L.Lea 1, B.McDermott 1, L.Phillips 1, C.Pike 1, D.Showers 1, D.Tapscott 1, A.Villars 1, G.Williams 1, B.Woodruff 1.

Anglo-Scottish Cup (1978–79)

R.Bishop 3, J.Buchanan 3, A.Campbell 3, P.Dwyer 3, D.Giles 3, F.Pethard 3, K.Ponton 3, R.Thomas 3, J.Davies 2, A.Larmour 2, P.Went 2, M.Burns 1, S.Grapes 1, G.Harris 1.

Goalscorers: P.Dwyer 1.

Associate Members' Trophy

Freight Rover Trophy 1985–86 and 1986–87. Sherpa Van Trophy 1987–88 and 1988–89. Leyland Daf Cup 1989–90 and 1990–91. Autoglass Trophy 1991–92, 1992–93 and 1993–94. Autowindscreens Shield 1994–95, 1995–96, 1996–97, 1997–98, 1998–99 and 1999–2000. LDV Vans Trophy 2000–01, 2001–02 and 2002–03.

D.Searle 18, J.Perry 15, L.Baddeley 13, N.Blake 12, C.Dale 12, C.Griffith 12, S.Young 10, P.Millar 8, N.Platnauer 8, N.Richardson 8, I.Rodgerson 8, K.Bartlett 7, A.Bird 7, D.Brazil 7, M.Ford 7, C.Pike 7, P.Ramsey 7, G.Ward 7, P.Wimbleton 7, M.Bonner 6, T.Boyle 6, R.Gibbins 6, J.Gilligan 6, A.Lewis 6, P.Wheeler 6, D.Adams 5, M.Aizlewood 5, P.Bater 5, J.Collins 5, A.Curtis 5, L.Jarman 5, M.Kelly 5, N.Matthews 5, N.Wigg 5, D.P.Williams 5, G.Abraham 4, J.Gardner 4, D.Hamilton 4, J.Low 4, S.Lynex 4, C.Middleton 4, J.Morgan 4, P.Stant 4, G.Thompson 4, N.Vaughan 4, L.Barnard 3, J.Bowen 3, J.Eckhardt 3, A.Evans 3, D.Giles 3, J.Gummer 3, R.Hansbury 3, D.Hill 3, C.Marustik 3, G.Moseley 3, P.Sanderson 3, N.Stevenson 3, A.Thompson 3, S.White 3, G.Wood 3, M.Brazier 2, P.Brignull 2, G.R.Davies 2, C.Fry 2, G.Gordon 2, J.Hallworth 2, P.Harding 2, A.Harper 2, S.Haworth 2, P.Heard 2, C.Ingram 2, R.James 2, M.Jones 2, S.McCulloch 2, B.McDermott 2, P.McLoughlin 2, S.Mardenborough 2, J.Mitchell 2, P.Mountain 2, J.Mullen 2, C.Oatway 2, N.O'Halloran 2, W.O'Sullivan 2, T.Philliskirk 2, C.Roberts 2, J.W.Roberts 2, A.Rogers 2, C.Sander 2, M.Walton 2, R.Weston 2, S.Williams 2, C.Allen 1, M.Bennett 1, W.Boland 1, P.Brayson 1, D.Burton 1, N.Cadette 1, R.Carpenter 1, A.Carss 1, J.Chandler 1,

D.Christie 1, G.Crowe 1, M.Curtis 1, R.Daniel 1, R.Earnshaw 1, A.Elliott 1, D.Evans 1, K.Evans 1, W.Faeber 1, M.Farrington 1, W.Fereday 1, H.Fleming 1, J.Fowler 1, A.Gorman 1, D.Greene 1, M.Grew 1, R.Haig 1, M.Harriott 1, A.Judge 1, A.Kerr 1, P.Kite 1, K.Lloyd 1, M.Miethig 1, G.Mitchell 1, K.Nogan 1, S.Partridge 1, R.Perrett 1, Lee Phillips 1, C.Powell 1, K.Ratcliffe 1, J.Rollo 1, M.Scott 1, R.Semark 1, L.Stephens 1, G.Stoker 1, C.Summers 1, D.Thomas 1, P.Thorne 1, C.Toshack 1, R.Turner 1, J.Unsworth 1, A.Vaughan 1, J.Williams 1, G.Withey 1.

Goalscorers: C.Dale 12, G.Gordon 6, C.Griffith 4, J.Gilligan 3, P.Stant 3, P.Wimbleton 2, D.Adams 1, G.Abraham 1, L.Barnard 1, N.Blake 1, M.Bonner 1, J.Bowen 1, Andy Campbell 1, A.Curtis 1, J.Eckhardt 1, L.Fortune-West 1, M.Giles 1, B.McDermott 1, P.Millar 1, K.Nugent 1, C.Pike 1, P.Ramsey 1, N.Richardson 1, G.Thompson 1, P.Wheeler 1, S.Young 1.

Over 100 Consecutive Appearances
League

146	Don Murray	May 1968 to November 1971
126	Damon Searle	October 1990 to September 1993
117	David Carver	October 1968 to September 1971
114	Arthur Lever	August 1946 to March 1949
108	Roger Gibbins	August 1982 to December 1984
103	Danny Malloy	November 1957 to August 1960
101	Terry Boyle	August 1986 to October 1988

All Matches

154	David Carver	October 1968 to September 1972
152	Don Murray	January 1969 to November 1971
152	Damon Searle	October 1990 to August 1993
132	Jimmy Gilligan	August 1987 to September 1989
129	Gary Bell	September 1969 to December 1971
129	Roger Gibbins	August 1982 to December 1984
123	Arthur Lever	August 1946 to March 1949
114	Colin Baker	October 1960 to December 1962
111	Fred Davies	April 1967 to March 1970
109	Reg Pugh	October 1934 to January 1937
108	Peter King	December 1966 to October 1969
107	Danny Malloy	November 1957 to January 1960
105	Keith Pontin	September 1979 to October 1981

Ever Presents in a Football League Season

Season	Games	
1920–21	42	W.Hardy
1923–24	42	J.Nelson
1927–28	42	G.McLachlan
1928–29	42	J.Jennings
1931–32	42	G.Emmerson, W.Roberts
1934–35	42	J.Everest
1935–36	42	C.Godfrey, R.Pugh
1937–38	42	R.Jones
1946–47	42	A.Lever
1947–48	42	A.Lever
1949–50	42	A.Sherwood

1950–51	42	K.Hollyman
1951–52	42	W.Grant
1956–57	42	D.Malloy
1958–59	42	D.Malloy, A.Milne
1959–60	42	J.Watkins
1960–61	42	D.Malloy
1961–62	42	C.Baker, A.Milne
1964–65	42	B.Hole
1967–68	42	B.S.Jones, P.King
1968–69	42	F.Davies, B.S.Jones, D.Murray
1969–70	42	D.Carver, B.Clark, D.Murray
1970–71	42	G.Bell, D.Carver, P.King, D.Murray
1971–72	42	B.Clark
1972–73	42	L.Phillips
1973–74	42	P.Dwyer
1979–80	42	A.Campbell
1980–81	42	K.Pontin, W.Ronson
1982–83	46	R.Gibbins
1983–84	42	P.Dwyer, R.Gibbins, D.Tong
1986–87	46	T.Boyle, P.Wimbleton
1987–88	46	T.Boyle, J.Gilligan
1988–89	46	J.Gilligan
1990–91	46	R.Hansbury
1991–92	42	D.Searle
1992–93	42	R.James, D.Searle
1997–98	46	C.Beech
1998–99	42	G.Mitchell
2001–02	42	N.Alexander
2002–03	42	R.Earnshaw, P.Thorne
2003–04	42	R.Earnshaw

Most Ever Present Seasons

3   D.Malloy, D.Murray.

2   T.Boyle, P.Dwyer, R.Earnshaw, R.Gibbins, J.Gilligan, B.S.Jones, P.King, A.Lever, A.Milne, D.Searle.

1   N.Alexander, C.Baker, C.Beech, G.Bell, A.Campbell, D.Carver, B.Clark, F.Davies, G.Emmerson, J.Everest, C.Godfrey, W.Grant, R.Hansbury, W.Hardy, B.Hole, K.Hollyman, R.James, J.Jennings, R.Jones, G.McLachlan, G.Mitchell, J.Nelson, L.Phillips, K.Pontin, R.Pugh, W.Roberts, W.Ronson, A.Sherwood, D.Thorne, D.Tong, J.Watkins, P.Wimbleton.

Progressive Scoring Record

Jimmy Gill set the first target in Cardiff City's opening League season, scoring 19 League goals and adding another in the FA Cup. This chart shows how individual scoring records have been equalled and beaten since then.

Season	Football League		All Matches	
1920–21	Jimmy Gill	19	Jimmy Gill	20
1921–22	Jimmy Gill	20	Len Davies	30
1923–24	Len Davies	23		
1926–27	Hughie Ferguson	25	Hughie Ferguson	31

1931–32	Jim McCambridge	26		
1946–47	Stan Richards	30		
1968–69			John Toshack	31
2002–03	Robert Earnshaw	31	Robert Earnshaw	35

Individual Scoring Feats

Six goals in a game

D.Tapscott v Knighton (h) Welsh Cup	28	Jan	1961

Five goals in a game

H.Ferguson v Burnley (h) Division One	1	Sep	1928
W.Robbins v Thames Association (h) Division Three South	6	Feb	1931
W.Henderson v Northampton Town (h) Division Three South	22	Apr	1933
G.Hitchens v Oswestry (a) Welsh Cup	17	Mar	1956
B.Clark v Barmouth and Dyffryn (h) Welsh Cup	21	Jan	1970
P.Kitchen v Cardiff Corinthians (h) Welsh Cup	3	Dec	1980
G.Gordon v Rushden and Diamonds (h) LDV VT	16	Oct	2001

Four goals in a game

L.Davies v Newport County (h) Welsh Cup	18	Jan	1922
L.Davies v West Bromwich Albion (a) Division Two	10	Nov	1923
R.Keating v Exeter City (h) Division Three South	27	Apr	1935
L.Evans v Barry Town (h) Welsh Cup	31	Jan	1951
T.Ford v Pembroke (a) Welsh Cup	12	Jan	1955
T.Ford v Pembroke (h) Welsh Cup	8	Feb	1956
G.Moore v Knighton (h) Welsh Cup	28	Jan	1961
A.Warboys v Carlisle United (h) Division Two	6	Mar	1971
T.Evans v Bristol Rovers (a) League Cup	17	Aug	1976
C.Dale v Caerau (a) Welsh Cup	5	Dec	1992
R.Earnshaw v Gillingham (h) Division One	13	Sep	2003

Three goals in a game

7 times	L.Davies
6	R.Earnshaw
4	J.Gill
3	J.McCambridge W.Robbins P.Stant D.Tapscott J.Toshack
2	I.Allchurch J.Collins W.Grant G.Hitchens R.Keating C.Pike
1	A.Allan, B.Allen, A.Alston, R.Bird, N.Blake, J.Buchanan, A.Campbell, J.Farrington, H.Ferguson, L.Fortune-West, C.Gibson, J.Gilligan, J.Henderson, R.Hewitt, P.Hooper, G.Johnston, A.Keating, P.King, P.Kitchen, H.Knowles, A.Miles, P.Millar, C.Nugent, N.O'Halloran, G.Reece, E.Reid, S.Richards, A.Saville, G.Stevens, W.Thirlaway, D.Thomas, P.Thorne, A.Warboys, R.Williams.

Leading Scorers

Season	League		Overall	
1920–21	J.Gill	19	J.Gill	20
1921–22	J.Gill	20	L.Davies	30
1922–23	L.Davies	19	L.Davies	28
1923–24	L.Davies	23	L.Davies	24
1924–25	L.Davies	20	L.Davies	22
1925–26	H.Ferguson	19	H.Ferguson	21
1926–27	H.Ferguson	25	H.Ferguson	31
1927–28	H.Ferguson	18	H.Ferguson	25
1928–29	H.Ferguson	14	H.Ferguson	15
1929–30	R.S.Williams	11	L.Davies	15
1930–31	W.Robbins	11	W.Robbins	12
1931–32	J.McCambridge	26	J.McCambridge	28
1932–33	J.McCambridge	17	J.McCambridge	18
1933–34	E.Postin	13	J.Henderson/E.Postin	13
1934–35	R.Keating	19	R.Keating	19
1935–36	R.Keating	10	R.Keating	11
1936–37	C.Smith	8	G.Walton	9
1937–38	J.Collins	23	J.Collins	28
1938–39	J.Collins	18	J.Collins	21
1946–47	S.Richards	30	S.Richards	30
1947–48	W.Rees	11	W.Rees	12
1948–49	E.Stevenson	12	E.Stevenson	14
1949–50	E.Evans	8	E.Evans	12
1950–51	W.Grant	14	W.Grant	18
1951–52	W.Grant	26	W.Grant	27
1952–53	K.Chisholm	13	K.Chisholm	15
1953–54	K.Chisholm/W.Grant	12	W.Grant	15
1954–55	T.Ford	19	T.Ford	24
1955–56	G.Hitchens	15	G.Hitchens	28
1956–57	G.Hitchens	21	G.Hitchens	25
1957–58	R.Hewitt	14	R.Hewitt	15
1958–59	R.Hewitt	13	R.Hewitt	17
1959–60	D.Tapscott	20	D.Tapscott	21
1960–61	D.Tapscott	21	D.Tapscott	30
1961–62	D.Ward	17	D.Ward	21
1962–63	P.Hooper	22	P.Hooper	24
1963–64	I.Allchurch	12	M.Charles	17
1964–65	I.Allchurch	15	I.Allchurch	19
1965–66	G.Johnston	17	G.Johnston	23
1966–67	R.Brown	14	R.Brown	17
1967–68	P.King	12	P.King	18
1968–69	J.Toshack	22	J.Toshack	31
1969–70	B.Clark	18	B.Clark	28
1970–71	B.Clark	15	B.Clark	22
1971–72	B.Clark	21	B.Clark	27
1972–73	A.McCulloch	14	A.McCulloch	19
1973–74	A.McCulloch	10	A.McCulloch	14
1974–75	G.Reece	9	G.Reece	10
1975–76	A.Evans	21	A.Evans	29
1976–77	A.Evans	15	A.Evans	24
1977–78	J.Buchanan	10	J.Buchanan	14
1978–79	J.Buchanan	16	J.Buchanan	18
1979–80	R.Bishop/G.Stevens	11	R.Bishop/G.Stevens	11
1980–81	P.Kitchen	13	P.Kitchen	19
1981–82	G.Stevens	13	G.Stevens	18
1982–83	J.Hemmerman	22	J.Hemmerman	26
1983–84	G.Owen	14	G.Owen	18
1984–85	N.Vaughan	15	N.Vaughan	17
1985–86	N.Vaughan	12	N.Vaughan	17
1986–87	P.Wimbleton	8	P.Wimbleton	11
1987–88	J.Gilligan	19	J.Gilligan	25
1988–89	J.Gilligan	14	J.Gilligan	23
1989–90	C.Pike	18	C.Pike	23
1990–91	C.Pike	14	C.Pike	16
1991–92	C.Dale	22	C.Dale/C.Pike	28
1992–93	C.Pike	12	P.Stant	18
1993–94	N.Blake	14	P.Stant	22
1994–95	P.Stant	13	P.Stant	15
1995–96	C.Dale	21	C.Dale	30
1996–97	S.White	13	S.White	14
1997–98	A.Saville	11	A.Saville	14
1998–99	K.Nugent	15	K.Nugent	22
1999–2000	J.Bowen	12	J.Bowen/K.Nugent	17
2000–01	R.Earnshaw	19	R.Earnshaw	25
2001–02	G.Kavanagh	13	G.Kavanagh	16
2002–03	R.Earnshaw	31	R.Earnshaw	35
2003–04	R.Earnshaw	21	R.Earnshaw	26
2004–05	P.Thorne	12	P.Thorne	14
2005–06	C.Jerome	18	C.Jerome	20

Top 20 Scorers

	All Matches			League Matches	
1	Len Davies	148	1	Len Davies	128
2	Robert Earnshaw	103	2	Robert Earnshaw	84
3=	Carl Dale	94	3	Jimmy Gill	82
	Jimmy Gill	94	4=	Brian Clark	79
5	Brian Clark	91		Derek Tapscott	79
6	Peter King	89	6	Hughie Ferguson	77
7=	Hughie Ferguson	87	7	John Toshack	74
	John Toshack	87	8	Carl Dale	71
9	Derek Tapscott	86	9=	Peter King	67
10	Chris Pike	74		Chris Pike	67
11	Wilf Grant	67	11	Wilf Grant	65
12	John Buchanan	61	12	John Buchanan	54
13	Tony Evans	58	13	Jim McCambridge	51
14	Jim McCambridge	53	14	Tony Evans	47
15	Cohen Griffith	50	15	Gary Stevens	44
16	Gary Stevens	47	16	Trevor Ford	42
17=	Jimmy Collins	46	17=	Jimmy Collins	41
	Jimmy Gilligan	46		Phil Dwyer	41
19=	Phil Dwyer	45		Nigel Vaughan	41
	Trevor Ford	45	20	Gerry Hitchens	40

Totals include League, FA Cup, League Cup, play-offs, FA Charity Shield, European Cup-Winners' Cup, Anglo-Scottish Cup, Anglo-French Friendship Cup, Freight Rover Trophy, Sherpa Van Trophy, Leyland Daf Cup, Autoglass Trophy, Autowindscreens Shield and LDV Vans Trophy games.

Top 20 Appearances

	All Matches			League Matches	
1	Phil Dwyer	525 /6	1	Phil Dwyer	466 /5
2	Don Murray	483	2	Tom Farquharson	445
3	Tom Farquharson	481	3	Don Murray	406
4	Peter King	426 /5	4	Ron Stitfall	398
5	Ron Stitfall	421	5	Fred Keenor	371
6	Fred Keenor	414	6	Peter King	352 /3
7	Billy Hardy	408	7=	Billy Hardy	354
8	Alan Harrington	381		Alf Sherwood	354
9	Alf Sherwood	372	9	Alan Harrington	348
10=	Len Davies	338	10	Len Davies	305
	Jason Perry	334 /4	11	Colin Baker	298
12	Scott Young	308 /25	12	Billy Baker	292
13	Colin Baker	328	13=	Roger Gibbins	267 /14
14	Roger Gibbins	309 /15		Jason Perry	278 /3
15	Billy Baker	308	15	Scott Young	257 /20
16	Derrick Sullivan	285	16	Derrick Sullivan	275
17	Damon Searle	276 /2	17	Jimmy Nelson	240
18	Cohen Griffith	241 /31	18=	Cohen Griffith	205 /29
19	Jimmy Nelson	271		Damon Searle	232 /2
20	Gary Bell	264 /1	20	John Buchanan	217 /14

Totals include League, FA Cup, League Cup, play-offs, FA Charity Shield, European Cup-Winners' Cup, Anglo-Scottish Cup, Anglo-French Friendship Cup, Freight Rover Trophy, Sherpa Van Trophy, Leyland Daf Cup, Autoglass Trophy, Autowindscreens Shield and LDV Vans Trophy games.

Career Records

Below are the career records (League, FA Cup and League Cup) of every Bluebirds first-team player since the club's first Football League game on 28 August 1920. The years given are the first years of the seasons, thus 1946 means 1946–47. In the 'Others' list are all the competitions not accounted for in the rest of the table. This list contains figures for the FA Charity Shield, the Division Three South Cup, the Anglo-French Friendship Cup, the European Cup-Winners' Cup, the Anglo-Scottish Cup and the Associate Members' Cup which includes all games in the Freight Rover Trophy, Sherpa Van Trophy, Leyland Daf Cup, Autoglass Trophy, Autowindscreens Shield and LDV Vans Trophy.

Player	Played	LEAGUE A	G	FA CUP A	G	FL CUP A	G	OTHERS A	G	TOTAL A	G
Abraham G.	1987–92	82/5	4	8	0	7	0	7	1	104/5	5
Abram R.L.	1920	1	0	0	0	0	0	0	0	1	0
Adams D.S.	1993–95	21/12	4	2	0	1/2	0	4/1	2	28/15	6
Adams R.J.	1932–33	11	0	2	0	0	0	0	0	13	0
Adlam L.W.	1933	4	0	0	0	0	0	0	0	4	0
Ainsworth G.	2002	9	0	0	0	0	0	0	0	9	0
Aitken F.McK.	1922	2	0	0	0	0	0	0	0	2	0
Aizlewood M.	1993–94	39	3	6/1	0	1	0	5	0	51/1	3
Alexander N.	2001–06	173/1	0	9	0	5	0	6	0	193/1	0
Allan A.B.	1967–69	8/1	1	1	0	0	0	2	3	11/1	4
Allchurch I.J.	1962–64	103	39	2	0	5	0	2	0	112	39
Allen B.W.	1946–48	58	21	6	2	0	0	0	0	64	23
Allen C.A.	1998	3/1	0	0	0	0	0	1	0	4/1	0
Alston A.	1975–76	44/4	16	4	4	3	1	4	1	55/4	22
Anderson F.	1921	1	0	0	0	0	0	0	0	1	0
Anderson R.S.	1938	2	1	0	0	0	0	0	0	2	1
Anderson W.J.	1972–76	122/4	12	6	0	5	0	3/2	0	136/6	12
Andrews G.	1965–66	43	21	0	0	5	4	0	0	48	25
Ardley N.C.	2004–06	30/8	1	1	0	1/1	0	0	0	32/9	1
Ashton R.W.	1947	1	0	0	0	0	0	0	0	1	0
Attley B.R.	1974–78	73/6	1	5	0	6/1	0	3	0	87/7	1
Attley L.J.	1934–35	12	2	0	0	0	0	0	0	12	2
Baddeley L.M.	1990–96	112/21	1	8	0	4/2	0	16/1	0	140/24	1
Baillie J.	1926–27	5	0	0	0	0	0	0	0	5	0
Baird I.J.	1983	12	6	0	0	0	0	0	0	12	6
Baker C.W.	1953–65	298	18	17	0	12	0	1	0	328	18
Baker W.G.	1938–54	292	5	16	1	0	0	0	0	308	6
Ballsom W.G.	1938	34	0	6	0	0	0	1	0	41	0
Bannon P.A.	1984	3/1	0	0	0	0	0	0	0	3/1	0
Barber K.	1978	2	0	0	0	0	0	0	0	2	0
Barker C.A.	2002–06	144/15	0	8	0	9	0	4	0	165/15	0
Barnard L.K.	1989–90	61/2	9	7	0	4	0	3	1	75/2	10
Barnett A.	1920–21	17	1	8	0	0	0	0	0	25	1
Bartlett J.	1933	1	0	0	0	0	0	0	0	1	0
Bartlett K.F	1986–88	60/22	25	8	3	2/2	0	9/2	0	79/26	28
Bassett W.E.G.	1934–38	154	2	14	0	0	0	2	0	170	2
Bater P.T.	1987–88	67/9	0	1/1	0	1	0	6/2	0	75/12	0
Beadles G.H.	1920	31	14	8	2	0	0	0	0	39	16
Beare G.	1920	23	3	11	3	0	0	0	0	34	6
Beech C.	1997	45	1	6	0	2	0	0	0	53	1
Bell G.	1966–73	222/1	10	17	0	9	2	16	0	264/1	12
Bellamy G.	1991	9	0	0	0	0	0	0	0	9	0
Bennett D.A.	1981–82	75/2	18	4	0	4	1	0	0	83/2	19
Bennett G.E.	1981–83	85/2	11	3	0	6	1	0	0	94/2	12
Bennett M.R.	1996	5/9	1	1/1	0	2	0	0/1	0	8/11	1
Best T.H.	1948–49	28	11	0	0	0	0	0	0	28	11

Player	Played	LEAGUE		FA CUP		FL CUP		OTHERS		TOTAL	
		A	G	A	G	A	G	A	G	A	G
Bird A.	1992–95	44/31	13	4/2	1	8	2	7/4	2	63/37	18
Bird D.W.C.	1929–30	13	4	0	0	0	0	0	0	13	4
Bird R.P.	1965–70	97/11	25	8	1	2/2	0	7/1	2	114/14	28
Bishop R.J.	1977–80	92/9	26	4	0	7/2	3	3/1	0	106/12	29
Blackburn G.F	1926–30	115	1	3	0	0	0	1	0	119	1
Blair D.	1947–53	204	30	12	0	0	0	0	0	216	30
Blair J.	1920–25	177	0	31	0	0	0	0	0	208	0
Blake D.	2005–06	0/1	0	0	0	0	0	0	0	0/1	0
Blake N.A.	1989–93	113/18	35	10	4	6/2	0	13/2	1	142/22	40
Blakemore R.G.	1930	1	0	0	0	0	0	0	0	1	0
Bland W.H.	1934	8	0	0	0	0	0	0	0	8	0
Blenkinsop E.	1937	10	0	1	0	0	0	0	0	11	0
Bodin P.J.	1982–84	68/7	4	4	0	11	0	0	0	83/7	4
Boland W.J.	1999–2006	187/22	3	11/4	1	12/1	0	6	0	216/27	4
Bolesan M.	1995	1	0	0	0	0	0	0	0	1	0
Bonner M.	1998–2003	113/30	2	7/1	0	8	0	8/3	1	136/34	3
Bonson J.	1957–59	72	36	7	4	0	0	0	0	79	40
Boulding M.	2004–05	0/4	0	0	0	0	0	0	0	0/4	0
Bowen J.P.	1998–2003	105/29	34	15/2	0	6	2	2/2	1	128/33	37
Boyle T.D.J.	1986–88	126/2	7	10	0	10	2	10	0	156/2	9
Brack A.H.B.	1962–63	1	0	0	0	1	0	0	0	2	0
Brayson P.	1999–2001	48/36	19	3/4	1	2	0	1	0	54/40	20
Brazier M.R.	1998–2001	43/13	3	5/1	1	2/3	1	2	0	52/17	5
Brazil D.M.	1992–95	109/6	1	9	0	8	0	8/1	0	134/7	1
Brignull P.A.	1985–86	44	0	6	0	4	0	2	0	56	0
Brittan R.C.	1920–22	75	0	10	0	0	0	0	0	85	0
Brock K.S.	1993	14	2	0	0	0	0	0	0	14	2
Brown A.R.	1936–37	2	0	0	0	0	0	1	0	3	0
Brown J.G.	1982	3	0	0	0	0	0	0	0	3	0
Brown R.H.	1966–67	50	23	4	0	2	2	3	2	59	27
Brown T.H.	1921	2	0	0	0	0	0	0	0	2	0
Buchanan J.	1974–81	217/14	54	10/1	2	14/1	5	7	0	248/16	61
Bullock L.	2003–06	12/20	6	0/1	0	3/1	2	0	0	15/22	8
Burke M.	1983	3	0	1	0	0	0	0	0	4	0
Burns M.E.	1978	6	0	0	0	2	0	1	0	9	0
Burton D.J.	1996	5	2	0	0	0	0	1	0	6	2
Byrne G.	1977–78	11/4	0	0	0	1	0	2	0	14/4	0
Cadette N.D.	1997–98	0/4	0	0/1	0	0	0	0/1	0	0/6	0
Calder R.	1933	37	0	2	0	0	0	1	0	40	0
Callan D.	1955	1	0	0	0	0	0	0	0	1	0
Campbell A.J.	1975–80	165/2	2	4	0	14	0	8	0	191/2	2
Campbell A.P.	2001–06	30/43	12	2/5	2	3/3	1	2/5	2	37/56	17
Campbell H.	1936	1	0	0	0	0	0	0	0	1	0
Canning L.D.	1946–47	80	0	2	0	0	0	0	0	82	0
Carless E.F	1932	1	0	0	0	0	0	0	0	1	0
Carlin W.	1973	22	1	0	0	0	0	0	0	22	1
Carpenter R.	1998–99	69/6	2	8/1	0	3/1	0	1	0	81/8	2
Carss A.J.	1997	35/6	1	5/1	0	2	0	1	0	43/7	1
Carver D.F	1965–72	210	1	13/1	1	6	0	13	0	242/1	2
Carver J.W.	1985	13	0	0	0	2	0	0	0	15	0
Cashmore A.A.	1920–21	30	10	7	2	0	0	0	0	37	12
Cassidy J.	1925	24	6	3	1	0	0	0	0	27	7
Castle F.R.	1926–27	3	0	0	0	0	0	0	0	3	0
Chandler J.G.	1989–90	21/4	0	3	0	0/2	0	1	0	25/6	0
Charles C.M.	1973–77	75/2	5	4	0	7	0	5	0	91/2	5

Player	Played	LEAGUE A	LEAGUE G	FA CUP A	FA CUP G	FL CUP A	FL CUP G	OTHERS A	OTHERS G	TOTAL A	TOTAL G
Charles M.	1961–64	79	25	2	0	3	1	2	1	86	27
Charles W.J.	1963–65	68	18	1	0	3	0	7	0	79	18
Chisholm K.	1951–53	62	33	1	0	0	0	0	0	63	33
Christie D.H.M.	1985	18/1	2	1	0	0	0	1	0	20/1	2
Clark B.D.	1967–72 & 1975	196/8	79	12/1	2	9	3	13/1	7	230/10	91
Clark J.W.	1920–21	14	0	3	0	0	0	0	0	17	0
Clarke M.McQ.	1967–68	44/2	3	1	0	2	0	8	1	55/2	4
Clarke R.J.	1946	39	10	3	0	0	0	0	0	42	10
Clennell J.	1921–24	118	36	17	5	0	0	0	0	135	41
Coldicott S.	1996	6	0	0	0	0	0	0	0	6	0
Coldrick G.G.	1963–69	91/5	2	6/1	0	9	1	5/1	0	111/7	3
Collins J.	1932	7	0	0	0	0	0	0	0	7	0
Collins J.H.	1937–38	76	41	10	4	0	0	3	1	89	46
Collins J.M.	2000–06	59/17	3	4/5	3	5	0	4/2	0	72/24	6
Collins W.E.	1923–26	12	0	0	0	0	0	0	0	12	0
Cooper K.	2005–06	31/5	2	1	0	1	0	0	0	33/5	2
Corkhill W.G.	1938	23	0	0	0	0	0	1	0	24	0
Corner D.E.	1985	6	0	0	0	0	0	0	0	6	0
Cornforth J.M.	1999	6/4	1	0	0	1/2	0	0	0	7/6	1
Cornwell J.A.	1993	5	2	0	0	1	0	0	0	6	2
Couch A.	1971–72	7/4	0	0/1	0	0	0	0	0	7/5	0
Court H.J.	1938	1	0	0	0	0	0	0	0	1	0
Cox N.	2005-06	21/6	2	1	0	1	0	0	0	23/6	2
Crawford A.	1983	6	1	0	0	3	2	0	0	9	3
Cribb S.R.	1932	27	11	2	0	0	0	0	0	29	11
Croft G.	2001–06	65/12	3	3/2	0	2	0	2/2	0	72/16	3
Crowe G.M.	1997	7/1	1	0	0	0	0	1	0	8/1	1
Curtis A.T.	1986–89	122/3	10	8	0	11/1	2	8/1	1	149/5	13
Curtis E.R.	1926–27 & 1933	62	14	6	1	0	0	2	0	70	15
Curtis M.W.	1985	24/3	2	0	0	0	0	1	0	25/3	2
Dale C.	1991–97	187/25	71	14	6	10/1	5	15/1	12	226/27	94
Daniel R.C.	1989–90	56	1	5	0	5	0	1	0	67	1
Daniel W.R.	1957	6	0	0	0	0	0	0	0	6	0
Darlington J.	2005–06	7/2	0	0	0	0	0	0	0	7/2	0
Davies A.B.	1935–37	9	0	1	0	0	0	0	0	10	0
Davies B.E.	1920–22	73	0	16	0	0	0	0	0	89	0
Davies D.L.	1965–66	16	0	2	0	1	0	0	0	19	0
Davies F.	1967–69	98	0	5	0	2	0	6	0	111	0
Davies G.M.	1996	6	2	0	0	0	0	0	0	6	2
Davies G.R.	1986	1/1	0	0/1	0	0	0	1/1	0	2/3	0
Davies J.G.	1978–79	7	0	0	0	0	0	2	0	9	0
Davies L.S.	1920–30	305	128	33	19	0	0	1	1	339	148
Davies P.A.	1979–80	1/1	0	0	0	0	0	0	0	1/1	0
Davies R.T.	1955–57	32	3	0	0	0	0	0	0	32	3
Davies S.C.	1928	14	2	0	0	0	0	0	0	14	2
Davies W.	1924–27	87	17	9	2	0	0	0	0	96	19
Davies W.J.	1938	1	0	0	0	0	0	0	0	1	0
Dean N.	1966–68	20/1	3	0	0	1	0	4	3	25/1	6
Deighton J.	1935	18	0	1	0	0	0	0	0	19	0
Delaney M.A.	1998	28	0	5/1	0	2	0	0	0	35/1	0
Demange K.J.P.P.	1990	15	0	0	0	0	0	0	0	15	0
Derrett S.C.	1967–71	61/5	1	4/1	0	1	0	6	0	72/6	1
Diamond J.J.	1935	18	9	1	0	0	0	1	1	20	10
Dibble A.G.	1981–83	62	0	4	0	4	0	0	0	70	0

Player	Played	LEAGUE A	G	FA CUP A	G	FL CUP A	G	OTHERS A	G	TOTAL A	G
Dixon C.H.	1954–56	21	1	0	0	0	0	0	0	21	1
Dobbs G.F	1995	3	0	0	0	1	0	0	0	4	0
Donnelly P.	1960–61	31	8	0	0	1	1	0	0	32	9
Downing K.G.	1995	3/1	0	0	0	0/1	0	0	0	3/2	0
Dudley F.E.	1953	5	1	0	0	0	0	0	0	5	1
Durban W.A.	1959–62	52	9	1	0	5	2	0	0	58	11
Durkan J.	1933	6	0	0	0	0	0	0	0	6	0
Durrell J.T.	1975	2	0	0	0	1	0	0	0	3	0
Duthie J.F	1933	13	0	1	0	0	0	1	0	15	0
Dwyer P.J.	1972–84	466/5	41	23	0	28	2	9	2	526/5	45
Eadie J.	1969–71	43	0	2	0	2	0	6	0	53	0
Earnshaw R.	1997–2004	141/37	85	11/2	9	6/2	10	5/1	1	163/42	105
Eckhardt J.E.	1996–2000	129/11	14	11/1	1	5/2	1	5	1	150/14	17
Edgley B.K.	1960	10	1	0	0	0	0	0	0	10	1
Edwards G.	1948–54	195	36	14	1	0	0	0	0	209	37
Edwards L.T.	1960–63	73	3	2	0	3	1	0	0	78	4
Egan H.	1938	17	9	1	0	0	0	0	0	18	9
Elliott A.R.	1996–97	38/1	0	2	0	2	0	1	0	43/1	0
Elliott R.M.	1979	5/2	0	0	0	1	0	0	0	6/2	0
Ellis K.D.	1964	22	9	1	0	0	0	0	0	23	9
Elsey K.W.	1983–84	59	5	2	0	4	0	0	0	65	5
Emmerson G.A.H.	1930–32	120	16	7	3	0	0	0	0	127	19
Endersby S.IG.	1987	4	0	0	0	0	0	0	0	4	0
England H.M.	1975	40	1	3	0	2	0	0	0	45	1
Eslor J.	1936	3	0	0	0	0	0	0	0	3	0
Evans A.	1975–78	120/4	47	8	4	6/1	6	6	1	140/5	58
Evans A.H.	1931–32	22	0	0	0	0	0	0	0	22	0
Evans D.A.	1994–95	5/9	0	0/1	0	0/2	0	0/1	0	5/13	0
Evans E.	1949–51	44	16	7	4	0	0	0	0	51	20
Evans H.P.	1920–25	93	1	16	1	0	0	0	0	109	2
Evans J.H.	1920–25	184	6	42	6	0	0	0	0	226	12
Evans K.	2000	24/6	3	3	2	1	0	0/1	0	28/7	5
Evans L.N.	1950–51	3	1	0	0	0	0	0	0	3	1
Evans P.A.	1983	0/2	1	1	0	0	0	0	0	1/2	1
Evans R.	1932	1	0	0	0	0	0	0	0	1	0
Evans S.J.V.L.	1930–32	8	0	0	0	0	0	0	0	8	0
Evans S.T.	1920–22	9	1	0	0	0	0	0	0	9	1
Evans T.	1993–95	12/2	0	1	0	2	0	2/1	0	17/3	0
Evans T.J.	1937	1	0	0	0	0	0	0	0	1	0
Everest J.	1934–35	73	5	2	0	0	0	2	0	77	5
Faerber W.	1999	31/2	1	4/1	0	4	0	1	0	40/3	1
Farquharson T.G.	1921–34	445	0	34	0	0	0	2	0	481	0
Farrell G.J.P.	1963–66	93/1	8	5	0	6	0	8	1	112/1	9
Farrington J.F.	1973–74	23	6	1	0	0	0	1/1	0	25/1	6
Farrington M.A.	1985	24/7	3	0	0	2	1	1	0	27/7	4
Felgate D.W.	1984	4	0	0	0	0	0	0	0	4	0
Fereday W.	1993–94	43/1	2	0	0	1	0	1	0	45/1	2
Ferguson H.	1925–28	117	77	13	9	0	0	1	1	131	87
Ferguson R.B.	1965–68	88/1	0	7	0	4	0	8	0	107/1	0
Ferretti A.	2005–06	0/4	0	0	0	0/3	0	0	0	0/7	0
Fielding W.	1936–38	50	0	7	0	0	0	1	0	58	0
Finlay J.	1937	1	0	0	0	0	0	0	0	1	0
Finnieston S.J.	1974	9	2	0	0	0	0	0	0	9	2
Flack S.R.	1995–96	6/5	1	0	0	0	0	0	0	6/5	1
Fleetwood S.	2003–06	1/7	0	0	0	1/3	0	1	0	3/10	0

Player	Played	LEAGUE A	LEAGUE G	FA CUP A	FA CUP G	FL CUP A	FL CUP G	OTHERS A	OTHERS G	TOTAL A	TOTAL G
Fleming H.V.	1995–96	29/3	0	2	0	0	0	1	0	32/3	0
Flynn B.	1984–85	32	0	1	0	2	2	0	0	35	2
Foggon A.	1971–72	14/3	1	4	0	3	1	0/1	0	21/4	2
Foley W.	1985	10/2	1	0	0	0	0	0	0	10/2	1
Ford F.M.	1984	1/1	0	0	0	0	0	0	0	1/1	0
Ford L.	1936–38	35	0	2	0	0	0	2	0	39	0
Ford M.P.	1984–87										
	& 1998–99	192/4	13	19	1	10	0	7	0	228/4	14
Ford T.	1953–56	96	42	5	3	0	0	0	0	101	45
Fortune-West L.	2000–02	53/39	23	7/6	3	2/1	0	5	2	67/46	28
Fowler J.K.G.	1996–2000	137/7	14	12/2	4	8	1	3	1	160/9	20
Francis G.C.J.	1984	7	0	0	0	0	0	0	0	7	0
Francombe P.	1981	2/1	0	0	0	0	0	0	0	2/1	0
Fraser G.	1962	4	0	0	0	0	0	0	0	4	0
Friday R.	1976–77	20/1	6	0	0	0	0	0	0	20/1	6
Friend H.	1933	3	0	0	0	0	0	0	0	3	0
Frowen J.	1952–57	35	0	0	0	0	0	0	0	35	0
Fry C.D.	1988–90	22/33	1	0/2	0	1/2	0	0/2	0	23/39	1
Fursland S.A.	1934	2	0	0	0	0	0	0	0	2	0
Gabbidon D.L.	2000–06	194/3	10	11	0	8	0	3	0	216/3	10
Galbraith J.	1930–34	143	2	7	0	0	0	2	0	152	2
Gale C.M.	1953–55	13	0	1	0	0	0	0	0	14	0
Gammon S.G.	1958–64	66	1	3	0	1	0	1	0	71	1
Gardner J.	1995–96	51/12	5	3	0	0/1	0	4/1	0	58/14	5
Gault W.E.	1920	2	0	0	0	0	0	0	0	2	0
Gibbins R.G.	1982–85										
	& 1988–92	267/14	25	14	1	22/1	6	6	0	309/15	32
Gibson C.H.	1946–47	71	16	3	0	0	0	0	0	74	16
Gibson I.S.	1970–72	90	11	6	0	5	0	8	3	109	14
Gilbert T.H.	1980–81	33	1	0	0	0	0	0	0	33	1
Gilchrist A.	1948	1	0	0	0	0	0	0	0	1	0
Giles D.C.	1974–78										
	& 1985–86	101/8	3	6	1	8	2	7/1	0	122/9	6
Giles M.	2000–01	1/4	0	0	0	0	0	0/2	1	1/6	1
Giles P.A.	1980–82	17/7	1	1/1	0	0	0	0	0	18/8	1
Gill G.	1991	3/3	1	0	0	0	0	0	0	3/3	1
Gill J.J.	1920–25	184	82	28	12	0	0	0	0	212	94
Gilligan J.M.	1987–89	99	34	4	4	8	1	10	7	121	46
Godfrey C.	1935–37	104	1	6	0	0	0	2	0	112	1
Godwin D.J.	1956	2	0	0	0	0	0	0	0	2	0
Goldsmith M.S.	1983	3/6	2	0	0	0	0	0	0	3/6	2
Gordon D.D.	2001	7	2	0	0	0	0	0	0	7	2
Gordon K.G.	2000–03	26/24	5	2	1	0/2	0	1/1	6	29/27	12
Gorin E.R.	1948–49	6	2	0	0	0	0	0	0	6	2
Gorman A.D.	1991–92	8/4	1	0	0	0	0	0/2	0	8/6	1
Graham B.	1993	0/1	0	0	0	0	0	0	0	0/1	0
Grant D.	1983–84	25	0	0	0	4	1	0	0	29	1
Grant W.	1949–54	154	65	5	2	0	0	0	0	159	67
Granville A.	1934–38	98	6	5	1	0	0	3	0	106	7
Grapes S.P.	1976–81	138/9	6	4/1	0	11/1	0	1/1	0	154/12	6
Gray A.D.	1958	2	0	0	0	0	0	0	0	2	0
Gray J.R.	2003	5/4	0	0	0	0	0	0	0	5/4	0
Greenacre C.M.	1997	11	2	0	0	0	0	0	0	11	2
Greene D.M.	2000	10	0	0	0	2	0	1	0	13	0
Grew M.S.	1992–93	21	0	6	0	2	0	3	0	32	0
Griffith C.	1989–94	205/29	39	14/2	0	9	5	15/1	4	243/32	48

Player	Played	LEAGUE		FA CUP		FL CUP		OTHERS		TOTAL	
		A	G	A	G	A	G	A	G	A	G
Griffiths P.H.	1934	12	1	0	0	0	0	0	0	12	1
Griffiths S.	1934	2	2	0	0	0	0	0	0	2	2
Griffiths W.R.	1947	1	0	0	0	0	0	0	0	1	0
Grimshaw W.	1920–23	108	17	16	0	0	0	0	0	124	17
Grotier P.D.	1973 & 1979–81	40	0	0	0	5	0	0	0	45	0
Gummer J.C.	1985–89	28/6	5	1	0	2/2	0	4	0	35/8	5
Hagan A.	1923–25	9	2	0	0	0	0	0	0	9	2
Haig R.N.	1988–89	1/4	0	0/1	0	0	0	1	0	2/5	0
Halliday T.	1963–64	16	2	0	0	0	0	1	0	17	2
Hallworth J.G.	1997–99	122	0	15	0	8	0	2	0	147	0
Hamilton D.	1984	10	0	0	0	0	0	0	0	10	0
Hamilton D.V	2001–02	16/9	0	4/1	1	0/1	0	4	0	24/11	1
Hampson T.	1926–28	8	0	1	0	0	0	0	0	9	0
Hansbury R.	1989–91	99	0	5	0	6	0	3	0	113	0
Harding P.J.	1995	36	0	1	0	4	0	2	0	43	0
Hardy W.	1920–31	354	6	53	0	0	0	1	0	408	6
Harkin J.T.	1965–66	20	10	2	0	7	3	2	0	31	13
Harper A.	1995	5	0	0	0	0	0	1	0	6	0
Harper J.A.J.	2000	3	0	0	0	0	0	0	0	3	0
Harrington A.C.	1952–65	348	6	14	1	11	0	8	0	381	7
Harris B.	1966–70	146/3	0	9	0	5	0	17/1	1	177/4	1
Harris F.	1928–32	130	10	5	2	0	0	0	0	135	12
Harris G.W.	1978–79	4	0	0	0	0	0	1	0	5	0
Harris G.W.	1964	5	0	0	0	0	0	0	0	5	0
Harris M.A.	1997	37	1	6	0	2	0	0	0	45	1
Harris N.	2004–05	1/2	1	0	0	0	0	0	0	1/2	1
Harrison G.R.	1991	10	1	0	0	0	0	0	0	10	1
Harrison J.	1937	1	0	0	0	0	0	0	0	1	0
Hatton R.J.	1982	29/1	9	0	0	0	0	0	0	29/1	9
Haworth S.O.	1995–96	27/10	9	0/1	0	4	0	4	1	35/11	10
Hazlett G.	1952	7	1	0	0	0	0	0	0	7	1
Healey R.	1973–81	216	0	9	0	12	0	4	0	241	0
Heard T.P.	1990–91	45/1	4	0	0	6	0	2	0	53/1	4
Hearty H.	1935	18	0	0	0	0	0	0	0	18	0
Heath P.A.	1990	11	1	0	0	0	0	0	0	11	1
Helsby T.	1928–30	46	2	3	1	0	0	0	0	49	3
Hemmerman J.L.	1982–83	54/1	22	3	2	4	2	0	0	61/1	26
Henderson M.R.	1981	11	0	0	0	0	0	0	0	11	0
Henderson W.J.	1932–33	43	25	2	0	0	0	1	0	46	25
Hewitt R.	1957–58	65	27	6	3	0	0	0	0	71	30
Hill C.J.	1938–46	19	3	0	0	0	0	1	0	20	3
Hill D.R.	1997–2000	40/25	4	3/3	0	2	0	3	0	48/28	4
Hill F.A.	1932–35	67	15	5	1	0	0	1	0	73	16
Hillier E.J.G.	1927–29	9	0	0	0	0	0	0	0	9	0
Hills J.J.	1924–25	14	0	3	0	0	0	0	0	17	0
Hitchens G.A.	1954–57	95	40	4	1	0	0	0	0	99	41
Hogg D.	1960–61	41	7	3	0	1	0	0	0	45	7
Hogg G.S.	1948	1	0	1	0	0	0	0	0	2	0
Hole B.G.	1959–65	208	16	6	1	18	1	9	0	241	18
Hollyman K.C.	1946–53	189	8	13	3	0	0	0	0	202	11
Holmes M.J.	1988	0/1	0	0	0	0	0	0	0	0/1	0
Holt S.	1931	2	0	0	0	0	0	0	0	2	0
Honor C.R.	1994	10	0	0	0	0	0	0	0	10	0
Hooper P.J.	1962	40	22	1	0	2	1	0	0	43	23

Player	Played	LEAGUE		FA CUP		FL CUP		OTHERS		TOTAL	
		A	G	A	G	A	G	A	G	A	G
Horrix D.V.	1986	9	3	0	0	0	0	0	0	9	3
Horton R.	1932	1	0	0	0	0	0	0	0	1	0
Houston D.	1965–66	17/1	0	0	0	3	0	0	0	20/1	0
Howells R.G.	1951–56	155	0	8	0	0	0	0	0	163	0
Hoy R.E.	1971–72	14/2	0	1	0	0	0	0	0	15/2	0
Hudson C.A.R.	1957–60	60	9	4	0	2	1	0	0	66	10
Hughes B.W.	1979–81	42/4	1	2	0	0/2	0	0	0	44/6	1
Hughes E.M.	1958	1	0	0	0	0	0	0	0	1	0
Hughes I.	1951	26	0	0	0	0	0	0	0	26	0
Hughes J.J.	1999	0/2	1	0	0	0/3	1	0	0	0/5	2
Hughes R.D.	2000–01	12/2	0	0	0	1	0	2	0	15/2	0
Hullett W.A.	1947–48	27	15	0	0	0	0	0	0	27	15
Humphreys R.J.	1999	8/1	2	1	0	0	0	1	0	10/1	2
Humphries S.R.	1982	1	0	0	0	0	0	0	0	1	0
Hutchinson A.	1933	23	4	1	0	0	0	0	0	24	4
Impey J.E.	1972–74	13/8	0	1	1	0/2	0	0/2	0	14/12	1
Inamoto J.	2004–05	13/1	0	2	0	0	0	0	0	15/1	0
Ingram C.D.	1995	4/4	1	0	0	1	0	1/1	0	6/5	1
Ingram G.P.	1982	7/4	2	1/1	1	0/1	0	0	0	8/6	3
Irving S.J.	1926–27	47	3	9	1	0	0	1	0	57	4
Irwin W.	1971–77	180	0	15	0	9	0	6	0	210	0
Jackson W.	1934	12	0	0	0	0	0	1	0	13	0
Jacobson J.	2005–06	0/1	0	0	0	0	0	0	0	0/1	0
James R.M.	1992–93	51	2	1	0	4	0	6	1	62	3
James W.J.	1946	6	3	0	0	0	0	0	0	6	3
Jarman L.	1995–99	77/16	1	3/3	1	3/2	0	5/2	0	88/23	2
Jeanne L.C.	2001	0/2	0	0	0	0	0	0	0	0/2	0
Jenkins B.	1956–60	29	7	0	0	0	0	0	0	29	7
Jenkins E.J.	1930–33	77	0	3	0	0	0	0	0	80	0
Jenkins E.S.	1921–23	12	0	1	0	0	0	0	0	13	0
Jenkins S.R.	2002	4	0	0	0	0	0	0	0	4	0
Jennings J.	1925–29	94	0	3	0	0	0	0	0	97	0
Jennings W.H.	1934–35	30	0	2	0	0	0	1	0	33	0
Jerome C.	2004–06	65/8	24	2	1	2	1	0	0	69/8	26
John D.	1961–66	88	0	1	0	10	0	5	0	104	0
John E.J.	1928–31	15	0	0	0	0	0	0	0	15	0
Johnson G.P.	1995	1/4	0	0	0	0	0	0	0	1/4	0
Johnston G.	1964–66	57/2	20	6	2	7	3	2	1	72/2	26
Jones B.	1955–56	9	0	0	0	0	0	0	0	9	0
Jones B.H.	1966–67	0/2	0	0	0	0	0	1	0	1/2	0
Jones B.S.	1966–69	108	19	3	1	4	0	12/1	2	127/1	22
Jones C.	1920	1	0	0	0	0	0	0	0	1	0
Jones D.G.	1934	9	0	0	0	0	0	1	0	10	0
Jones G.	1934–35	1	0	0	0	0	0	0	0	1	0
Jones I.	1954–55	26	0	1	0	0	0	0	0	27	0
Jones I.M.	1993–95	3	0	0	0	0	0	0	0	3	0
Jones J.	1923	12	2	0	0	0	0	0	0	12	2
Jones J.A.	1957	1	0	0	0	0	0	0	0	1	0
Jones K.	1957–58	24	0	4	0	0	0	0	0	28	0
Jones K.	1971	6	0	0	0	2	0	2	0	10	0
Jones L.	1978–83	142/3	2	4	1	11	0	2	0	159/3	3
Jones L.J.	1929–33	142	31	6	1	0	0	1	0	149	32
Jones M.	1990–91	33/3	2	2	0	6	1	2	0	43/3	3
Jones R.H.	1937–38	58	0	4	0	0	0	3	0	65	0
Jones T.G.	2000–01	0/3	0	0	0	1	0	2	0	3/3	0
Jones V.	1984	11	1	0	0	4	0	0	0	15	1

Player	Played	LEAGUE		FA CUP		FL CUP		OTHERS		TOTAL	
		A	G	A	G	A	G	A	G	A	G
Jones V.W.	1922	1	0	0	0	0	0	0	0	1	0
Jordan A.J.	2000	3/2	0	1	0	0	0	0	0	4/2	0
Joslin P.J.	1948–50	108	0	9	0	0	0	0	0	117	0
Judge A.G.	1987	8	0	0	0	0	0	1	0	9	0
Kavanagh G.	2001–04	140/2	28	11	3	6/1	0	5	0	162/3	31
Keating A.E.	1930–32	45	22	3	4	0	0	0	0	48	26
Keating R.E.	1933–35	70	35	1	0	0	0	1	0	72	35
Keenor F.C.	1920–30	371	13	42	1	0	0	1	0	414	14
Kellock W.	1971–72	33/2	2	7	3	0	0	0	0	40/2	5
Kelly G.L.	1958	8	4	0	0	0	0	0	0	8	4
Kelly M.D.	1987–89	93/12	2	6/1	0	7	0	9	0	115/13	2
Kelly N.A.O.	1992	5	1	0	0	0	0	0	0	5	1
Kelly S.	1998–99	12/1	0	0	0	0	0	0	0	12/1	0
Kelso J.	1938	41	0	6	0	0	0	1	0	48	0
Kerr A.A.	1986	31	1	3/1	0	4	0	0/1	0	38/2	1
Ketteridge S.J.	1988	6	2	0	0	0	0	0	0	6	2
Kevan D.J.	1989	6/1	0	0	0	0	0	0	0	6/1	0
King G.H.	1964	6	0	0	0	0	0	0	0	6	0
King J.	1984–85	30	0	1	0	1	0	0	0	32	0
King J.W.	1961	33	6	1	0	4	2	2	1	40	9
King P.C.	1960–73	351/5	67	20	5	22	6	32/1	11	425/6	89
Kirtley J.H.	1955	38	4	2	0	0	0	0	0	40	4
Kitchen M.P.	1980–81	64/3	21	1	0	4	1	0	0	69/3	22
Kite P.D.	1993	17/1	0	0/1	0	2	0	2	0	21/2	0
Kneeshaw H.J.	1920–23	34	0	7	0	0	0	0	0	41	0
Knill A.R.	1993	4	0	0	0	0	0	0	0	4	0
Knowles H.F	1958–59	8	0	0	0	0	0	0	0	8	0
Koskela T.	2004–06	0/2	0	0/1	0	0	0	1	0	1/3	0
Koumaas J.	2005–06	42/2	12	0	0	2/1	1	0	0	44/3	13
Lamie R.	1949–50	6	1	0	0	0	0	0	0	6	1
Lane E.	1934	30	0	1	0	0	0	1	0	32	0
Langley R.	2004–05	63/6	8	3	0	0	0	0	0	66/6	8
Larmour A.J.J.	1972–78	152/2	0	10	0	11	0	5	0	178/2	0
Lathom G.	1921	1	0	0	0	0	0	0	0	1	0
Lawson D.	1923–25	64	2	13	0	0	0	0	0	77	2
Layton A.E.D.	1920	2	0	4	0	0	0	0	0	6	0
Lea L.	1967–69	75/1	6	2	0	1	0	6/1	1	84/2	7
Leckie J.T.	1934–35	46	0	1	0	0	0	2	0	49	0
Ledley J	2004–06	62/8	6	2	0	4/1	1	0	0	68/9	7
Lee A.D.	2003–06	50/40	10	2/1	1	3	1	0	0	55/41	12
Lee T.C.	1983	21	5	0	0	0	0	0	0	21	5
Legg A.	1998–2002	152/23	12	17/4	0	8/1	0	4	0	181/28	12
Leonard C.C.	1985	4	0	1	0	1	0	0	0	6	0
Lever A.R.	1946–50	155	9	10	0	0	0	0	0	165	9
Lewis A.	1988–91	27/23	0	2	0	1/2	0	5/1	0	35/26	0
Lewis B.	1963–67	87/1	7	4	0	6	3	7	0	104/1	10
Lewis D.B.	1934	2	0	0	0	0	0	0	0	2	0
Lewis E.G.	1933	14	1	0	0	0	0	0	0	14	1
Lewis J.	1978–83	135/5	9	8	0	12	1	0	0	155/5	10
Lewis J.J.	1924	1	0	0	0	0	0	0	0	1	0
Lewis T.J.	1968–69	3	0	0	0	0	0	1	0	4	0
Lewis W.	1946–47	10	0	0	0	0	0	0	0	10	0
Lewis W.L.	1934–35	35	6	1	1	0	0	0	0	36	7
Lievesley W.	1929	3	0	0	0	0	0	0	0	3	0
Lightbourne K.L.	2000	2/1	0	0	0	0	0	0	0	2/1	0

Player	Played	LEAGUE		FA CUP		FL CUP		OTHERS		TOTAL	
		A	G	A	G	A	G	A	G	A	G
Livermore D.E.	1975–77	84/4	5	7	0	6	0	5/1	0	102/5	5
Lloyd K.G.	1996–97	27/6	1	0	0	2/2	0	3	0	32/8	1
Lloyd K.J.J.	1979	0/1	0	0	0	0	0	0	0	0/1	0
Lloyd R.C.	1964	2	0	0	0	1	0	0	0	3	0
Loovens G.	2005–06	32/1	2	1	0	2	0	0	0	35/1	2
Love I.J.	1989	2	0	0	0	0	0	0	0	2	0
Low J.D.	1999–2001	54/21	6	2/3	0	1/1	0	3/1	0	60/26	6
Lynex S.C.	1988–89	56/6	2	4/2	1	4/1	1	5	0	69/9	4
McAnuff J.	2004–05	42/1	2	2	1	3	0	0	0	47/1	3
MacAulay R.	1936	4	0	0	0	0	0	0	0	4	0
MacBennett J.C.	1947	4	2	0	0	0	0	0	0	4	2
McCambridge J.	1930–32	95	51	5	2	0	0	0	0	100	53
McCarthy D.J.A.	1961	7	0	0	0	2	0	0	0	9	0
McCaughey C.	1937–38	66	5	10	0	0	0	2	0	78	5
McClelland J.	1974	1/3	1	0	0	0	0	0	0	1/3	1
McCulloch A.	1972–73	58	24	5	3	3	3	2	0	68	30
McCulloch S.A.J.	2000–01	9/12	1	3	0	1	0	2	0	15/12	1
McDermott B.J.	1987–88	50/1	8	1	0	3	0	5/1	2	59/2	10
McDonagh C.	1935	2	0	0	0	0	0	0	0	2	0
McDonald C.	2005–06	0/1	0	0	0	0	0	0	0	0/1	0
McDonald K.	1921–22	11	7	1	0	0	0	0	0	12	7
MacDonald K.D.	1990	8	0	0	0	0	0	0	0	8	0
McGorry B.P.	1995	7	0	0	0	0	0	0	0	7	0
McGrath J.	1928–31	33	0	4	0	0	0	0	0	37	0
McGuckin G.K.W.	1957	4	0	0	0	0	0	0	0	4	0
McIlvenny P.	1924	5	2	0	0	0	0	0	0	5	2
McInch J.R.	1972–74	11/2	0	0	0	1	1	1	0	13/2	1
McIntosh A.	1961–63	64	11	2	0	4	0	0	0	70	11
McJennett J.J.	1929–31	5	0	2	0	0	0	0	0	7	0
McKenzie J.D.	1935–38	35	6	1	0	0	0	1	0	37	6
McLachlan G.H.	1925–29	140	22	13	2	0	0	1	0	154	24
McLaren R.	1949	1	0	0	0	0	0	0	0	1	0
McLaughlin R.	1950–53	48	3	2	0	0	0	0	0	50	3
McLean I.	1994	4	0	0	0	0	0	0	0	4	0
McLoughlin P.B.	1984–85	40/9	4	0/1	0	2	0	2	0	44/10	4
McMillan J.S.	1960	2	0	0	0	0	0	0	0	2	0
McNally O.	1931	6	0	0	0	0	0	0	0	6	0
McSeveney J.H.	1955–56	75	19	4	2	0	0	0	0	79	21
McStay R.	1996	1	0	0	0	0	0	0	0	1	0
Maddy P.M.	1980–82	35/8	3	1	1	0	0	0	0	36/8	4
Mahon A.J.	2002	13/2	2	0	0	0	0	0	0	13/2	2
Maidment T.	1932–33	44	8	2	0	0	0	0	0	46	8
Main W.G.	1936–38	6	0	0	0	0	0	2	0	8	0
Mallory R.J.L.	1963	3	0	0	0	1	0	0	0	4	0
Malloy D.	1955–60	226	1	14	0	2	0	0	0	242	1
Mansell J.	1952–53	25	0	1	0	0	0	0	0	26	0
Marchant M.G.	1950	12	3	0	0	0	0	0	0	12	3
Marcroft E.H.	1933	28	2	2	0	0	0	0	0	30	2
Mardenboro' S.A.	1986–87	18/14	1	0/1	0	1	0	1/1	0	20/16	1
Margetson M.W.	2002–06	31/1	0	2	0	5	0	2	0	40/1	0
Marriott P.W.	1991	0/1	0	0	0	0	0	0	0	0/1	0
Marshall E.	1946	1	0	0	0	0	0	0	0	1	0
Marshalsey W.H.G.	1933	7	1	0	0	0	0	1	0	8	1
Martin M.P.	1984	7	0	0	0	0	0	0	0	7	0
Marustik C.	1985–86	43	1	7	3	1	0	3	0	54	4
Mason F.O.	1922	1	0	0	0	0	0	0	0	1	0

Player	Played	LEAGUE		FA CUP		FL CUP		OTHERS		TOTAL	
		A	G	A	G	A	G	A	G	A	G
Matson F.R.	1926–29	27	3	0	0	0	0	0	0	27	3
Matthews N.P.	1990–92	59/7	2	4	0	3	0	5	0	71/7	2
Matthews W.J.	1983	4/10	0	0	0	2/1	0	0	0	6/11	0
Maxwell L.J.	2001–03	10/24	1	1/3	0	2/1	0	3/1	0	16/29	1
May H.	1949	1	0	0	0	0	0	0	0	1	0
Mayo A.C.	1930	1	0	0	0	0	0	0	0	1	0
Meacock K.M.	1984–85	20/5	3	1	0	1	0	0	0	22/5	3
Melaniphy E.M.J.P.	1936–37	20	8	1	1	0	0	0	0	21	9
Mellor J.	1936–37	28	0	2	0	0	0	1	0	31	0
Melville J.	1921	1	0	0	0	0	0	0	0	1	0
Menzies A.R.	1957	1	0	0	0	0	0	0	0	1	0
Merry W.	1930	8	0	0	0	0	0	0	0	8	0
Micallef C.	1978–82 & 1984–85	93/28	12	3/3	0	7/2	0	2	0	105/33	12
Michael J.D.	1996	0/1	0	0	0	0	0	0	0	0/1	0
Middleton C.D.	1996–99	94/24	8	13/1	3	3/1	0	4/2	0	114/28	11
Miles A.E.	1927–29	16	8	1	0	0	0	0	0	17	8
Miles I.	1930	3	0	0	0	0	0	0	0	3	0
Millar W.P.	1991–94	91/29	17	8/1	1	7/1	1	7/2	1	113/33	20
Mills D.	1950	1	0	0	0	0	0	0	0	1	0
Milne A.S.	1957–64	172	1	8	0	6	0	2	0	188	1
Milsom P.J.	1994	1/2	0	0	0	0	0	0	0	1/2	0
Mitchell G.L.	1998	46	0	5	0	2	0	1	0	54	0
Mitchell J.W.	1937–38	3	0	0	0	0	0	1	0	4	0
Mokone S.M.	1959	3	1	0	0	0	0	0	0	3	1
Molloy P.	1933–34	23	0	0	0	0	0	1	0	24	0
Montgomery S.W.	1948–54	230	4	13	0	0	0	0	0	243	4
Moore G.	1958–61	85	23	4	0	1	1	1	1	91	25
Moore J.F.B.	1947–48	6	4	1	0	0	0	0	0	7	4
Moore P.	1929	1	0	0	0	0	0	0	0	1	0
Moore R.D.	1978–79	54/2	6	2	0	2	0	0	0	58/2	6
Moore W.A.	1934	11	0	1	0	0	0	0	0	12	0
Morgan J.P.	1988–90	43/12	3	5	0	3/2	0	2/3	0	53/17	3
Morgan P.W.	1972	16	0	1	0	0	0	0	0	17	0
Morgan R.L.	1967–76	68	0	5	0	2	0	4	0	79	0
Morris E.	1948–50	8	0	0	0	0	0	0	0	8	0
Morris E.L.	1931–32	16	0	2	0	0	0	0	0	18	0
Mort E.F	1933–37	43	0	1	0	0	0	3	0	47	0
Moseley G.	1986–87	38	0	3	0	4	0	3	0	48	0
Moss F.	1928	9	0	0	0	0	0	0	0	9	0
Mountain P.D.	1996	5	0	1	0	0	0	2	0	8	0
Muggleton C.D.	2000	6	0	0	0	0	0	0	0	6	0
Mullen J.	1981–85	128/5	12	5	0	8/1	0	2	0	143/6	12
Mulryne P.	2005–06	1/3	0	0	0	0	0	0	0	1/3	0
Munro J.A.	1928–29	14	3	2	0	0	0	0	0	16	3
Murphy J.	1927	1	0	0	0	0	0	0	0	1	0
Murphy P.	1965	0/1	0	0	0	0	0	0	0	0/1	0
Murray D.J.	1962–74	406	6	23	1	21	0	33	0	483	7
Nardiello G.	1985	7	4	0	0	0	0	0	0	7	4
Nash H.E.	1920–22	30	6	1	1	0	0	0	0	31	7
N'Dumbu Nsungu G.	2005–06	4/7	0	0	0	0	0	0	0	4/7	0
Nelson J.	1921–29	240	2	30	1	0	0	1	0	271	3
Newton E.J.I.	1991	18	4	0	0	0	0	0	0	18	4
Newton W.	1920–21	6	0	0	0	0	0	0	0	6	0
Nibloe J.	1948	1	0	0	0	0	0	0	0	1	0

Player	Played	LEAGUE A	G	FA CUP A	G	FL CUP A	G	OTHERS A	G	TOTAL A	G
Nicholls J.	1957	8	2	0	0	0	0	0	0	8	2
Nicholls J.B.L.	1924	2	0	0	0	0	0	0	0	2	0
Nicholls R.B.	1958–60	51	0	2	0	1	0	0	0	54	0
Nicholls R.R.	1994	6/6	1	0	0	0	0	0	0	6/6	1
Nicholson G.	1936–38	98	0	13	0	0	0	2	0	113	0
Nicholson J.R.	1924–25	47	12	8	2	0	0	0	0	55	14
Nock A.J.	1921–22	3	0	0	0	0	0	0	0	3	0
Nogan K.	1999–2000	4/14	1	0/1	0	1	0	1	0	6/15	1
Norman A.G.	1951	1	0	0	0	0	0	0	0	1	0
Northcott T.T.	1952–54	76	13	3	1	0	0	0	0	79	14
Nugent K.P.	1997–2001	93/5	29	9	6	8/1	1	1/1	1	111/7	37
Nugent W.C.	1951–58	113	19	9	1	0	0	0	0	122	20
Nutt G.E.	1954–55	17	4	0	0	0	0	0	0	17	4
Oakley K.	1950–53	7	1	0	0	0	0	0	0	7	1
Oatway A.P.D.	1994–95	29/3	0	1/1	0	2	1	2	0	34/4	1
O'Connor T.D.	1985	1/1	0	0	0	0	0	0	0	1/1	0
O'Halloran K.J.	1996	8	0	0	0	0	0	2	0	10	0
O'Halloran N.	1955–56	10	4	0	0	0	0	0	0	10	4
O'Neil G.	2004–05	8/1	1	0	0	0	0	0	0	8/1	1
O'Neill H.	1931	9	2	2	2	0	0	0	0	11	4
Osman R.C.	1995	14/1	0	0	0	0	0	0	0	14/1	0
O'Sullivan W.S.	1997–98	78/7	4	10	1	1/2	0	2	0	91/9	5
Ovenstone D.G.	1936	21	4	0	0	0	0	1	0	22	4
Owen G.	1983	38/1	14	1	0	4	1	0	0	43/1	15
Page J.	1920–25	71	0	8	0	0	0	0	0	79	0
Page R.J.	2004–06	8/1	0	0	0	0	0	0	0	8/1	0
Paget W.S.T.	1932–33	6	0	0	0	0	0	0	0	6	0
Pagnam F.	1920–21	27	8	0	0	0	0	0	0	27	8
Parfitt H.E.	1953	1	0	0	0	0	0	0	0	1	0
Parker R.E.A.	1947	2	0	0	0	0	0	0	0	2	0
Parry P.I.	2003–06	37/31	6	0	0	5/2	0	0	0	42/33	6
Parsons F.R.	1970–72	17	0	0	0	1	0	2	0	20	0
Parsons J.S.	1970–72	7/8	6	0	0	1	1	0	0	8/8	7
Partridge S.M.	1996–97	28/8	2	2	0	2	0	1	0	33/8	2
Paterson S.	1997	5	0	0	0	0	0	0	0	5	0
Pearson J.S.	1994	12	0	0	0	0	0	0	0	12	0
Peck D.T.	1959–64	42	0	0	0	1	0	3	0	46	0
Pembrey G.D.	1949	1	0	0	0	0	0	0	0	1	0
Penney D.M.	1997–98	33/2	5	6	0	2	0	0	0	41/2	5
Perks H.	1933	9	1	0	0	0	0	0	0	9	1
Perrett R.	1999–2000	28/1	1	5	1	0	0	1	0	34/1	2
Perry J.	1986–96	278/3	5	14/1	0	22	0	19/1	0	333/5	5
Pethard F.J.	1971–78	161/10	0	3	0	7	0	10	0	181/10	0
Phillips J.R.	1946	2	0	0	0	0	0	0	0	2	0
Phillips L.	1996–99	11/5	0	0	0	2/1	0	0/1	0	13/7	0
Phillips L.	1966–74	169/13	11	12	2	8	0	8/3	1	197/16	14
Philliskirk A.	1995–96	55/6	5	2	0	2	0	0/2	0	59/8	5
Pickrell A.D.	1960–61	18	4	1	0	1	0	1	0	21	4
Pike C.	1986 & 1989–92	140/14	67	8/2	3	6/2	2	9	2	163/18	74
Pinxton A.E.	1936	20	3	2	0	0	0	1	0	23	3
Pirie T.S.	1926	5	0	0	0	0	0	0	0	5	0
Platnauer N.R.	1986–88	110/5	7	9	0	6	2	12	0	137/5	9
Platt J.A.	1978	4	0	0	0	0	0	0	0	4	0
Plumley G.E.	1983–84	25	0	0	0	1	0	0	0	26	0

Player	Played	LEAGUE		FA CUP		FL CUP		OTHERS		TOTAL	
		A	G	A	G	A	G	A	G	A	G
Poland G.	1935–36										
	& 1946	26	0	2	0	0	0	0	0	28	0
Pollard R.	1932	31	0	0	0	0	0	0	0	31	0
Polycarpou A.	1981	7	0	0	0	0	0	0	0	7	0
Pontin K.	1976–82	193	5	6	0	13 /1	0	5 /1	0	217 /2	5
Postin E.L.	1933	33	13	2	0	0	0	1	0	36	13
Powell C.G.	1989	0 /1	0	0	0	0	0	0 /1	0	0 /2	0
Powell D.	1972–74	36	1	3	0	0 /1	0	2	0	41 /1	1
Prescott J.R.	1936–38	31	7	4	3	0	0	0	0	35	10
Price A.D.	1985	2	0	0	0	0	0	0	0	2	0
Price C.	1948	1	0	0	0	0	0	0	0	1	0
Prior S.J.	2001–03	72 /9	2	8	0	2	0	5	0	87 /9	2
Pugh R.	1934–38	166	25	12	2	0	0	4	0	182	27
Purse D.	2005–06	39	5	1	0	3	1	0	0	43	6
Rainford J.W.	1953	3	1	0	0	0	0	0	0	3	1
Ramsey P.C.	1991–92										
	& 1994	80	7	3	0	2	0	9	1	94	8
Rankmore F.E.J.	1961–62	67	0	1	0	5	0	1	0	74	0
Ratcliffe K.	1992–93	25	1	0	0	1	0	3	0	29	1
Redwood D.J.	1935–36	13	0	0	0	0	0	0	0	13	0
Reece G.I.	1972–75	94 /6	23	8 /1	2	5	1	1 /1	0	108 /8	26
Reed E.	1925	6	0	0	0	0	0	0	0	6	0
Rees M.J.	1984–86	31	0	3	0	3	0	0	0	37	0
Rees N.R.	1970–72	21 /6	1	3 /2	0	0	0	2	0	26 /8	1
Rees W.	1946–48	101	34	6	2	0	0	0	0	107	36
Reid G.H.	1922	7	4	0	0	0	0	0	0	7	4
Reynolds A.B.	1956–58	55	14	2	1	0	0	0	0	57	15
Rhodes A.	1938	5	0	0	0	0	0	0	0	5	0
Ricahrds L.G.	1932	1	0	0	0	0	0	0	0	1	0
Richards P.	1926	3	0	1	0	0	0	0	0	4	0
Richards S.V	1946–47	57	39	2	0	0	0	0	0	59	39
Richardson N.J.	1992–94	106 /5	13	6	0	4	0	8 /1	1	124 /6	14
Rickards C.T.	1938	20	5	2	0	0	0	0	0	22	5
Ricketts M.	2005–06	17	5	0	0	0	0	0	0	17	5
Riley H.	1934–35	61	13	2	0	0	0	1	0	64	13
Robbins W.W.	1928–31	86	38	6	1	0	0	0	0	92	39
Roberts C.J.	1997–99	6 /17	3	2 /3	0	2	0	0 /2	0	10 /22	3
Roberts D.F	1978–80	40 /1	2	1	0	4	0	0	0	45 /1	2
Roberts J.	1935	22	5	1	0	0	0	0	0	23	5
Roberts J.W.	1987–89	9	0	1	0	0	0	1 /1	0	11 /1	0
Roberts W.J.	1928–32	130	1	5	0	0	0	0	0	135	1
Robinson J.R.C.	2003–06	39 /3	3	0	0	0 /1	0	0	0	39 /4	3
Robinson M.	1928–30	18	2	2	0	0	0	0	0	20	2
Robson K.	1977	21	5	0	0	1	0	0	0	22	5
Rodgerson I.	1988–90										
	& 1995–96	141 /12	5	14	0	13 /1	1	9 /1	0	177 /14	6
Rodon C.P.	1983	4	0	0	0	2	0	0	0	6	0
Rodrigues P.J.	1963–65	85	2	2	0	8	0	8	0	103	2
Rogers A.J.	1986	25 /2	1	2	0	2 /1	0	2	0	31 /3	1
Rogers T.W.	1933	2	1	0	0	0	0	1	0	3	1
Rollo J.S.	1996–97	6 /9	0	0 /2	0	0 /1	1	1 /1	0	7 /13	1
Ronan P.	1931–32	30	1	5	0	0	0	0	0	35	1
Ronson W.	1979–81	90	4	3	0	9	0	0	0	102	4
Roper H.	1935–36	31	2	0	0	0	0	1	0	32	2
Ross W.B.	1946–47	8	2	0	0	0	0	0	0	8	2

Player	Played	LEAGUE A	LEAGUE G	FA CUP A	FA CUP G	FL CUP A	FL CUP G	OTHERS A	OTHERS G	TOTAL A	TOTAL G
Rowland A.	1948–49	3	0	0	0	0	0	0	0	3	0
Russell G.H.	1932–33	56	1	2	0	0	0	1	0	59	1
Russell K.J.	1990	3	0	0	0	0	0	0	0	3	0
Rutter C.F	1950–57	118	0	7	0	0	0	0	0	125	0
Ryder D.F	1966	4	0	0	0	0	0	0	0	4	0
Sander C.A.	1985	13	0	0	0	1	0	0	0	14	0
Sanders A.J.	1981	1/1	0	0	0	0	0	0	0	1/1	0
Sanderson P.D.	1987	8/13	1	0/1	0	2	1	1/2	0	11/16	2
Saunders D.N.	1984	4	0	0	0	0	0	0	0	4	0
Saville A.V	1997–98	35	12	4/1	2	1	0	0	0	40/1	14
Sayer P.A.	1973–81	74/12	15	4	2	7	2	3/2	0	88/14	19
Schwinkendorf J.	1999	5	0	1	0	0	0	0	0	6	0
Scimeca R.	2005–06	17/1	1	0	0	0	0	0	0	17/1	1
Scott A.M.	1994–96	15/1	1	1	0	0/1	0	0	0	16/2	1
Scott M.J.	1989	1/8	0	2	3	0	0	1	0	4/8	3
Scott R.SA.	1963–64	37	5	0	0	2	0	0	0	39	5
Scott R.J.	1957	3	0	0	0	0	0	0	0	3	0
Scott W.J.	1936	17	0	2	0	0	0	1	0	20	0
Scully A.D.T.	1995	13/1	0	0	0	0	0	0	0	13/1	0
Searle D.B.	1989–95	232/2	3	13	0	9	1	22	0	276/2	4
Seasman J.	1984	10/2	2	0	0	4	0	0	0	14/2	2
Semark R.H.	1991	4/2	0	0	0	0	0	1	0	5/2	0
Sendall R.A.	1989	3/1	0	0	0	0	0	0	0	3/1	0
Sharp F.	1968–69	14/1	1	0	0	0	0	1	0	15/1	1
Shaw P.	1995	6	0	0	0	0	0	0	0	6	0
Shaw W.	1928	2	0	0	0	0	0	0	0	2	0
Sherlock S.E.	1986	14/1	0	0	0	3	0	0	0	17/1	0
Sherwood A.T.	1946–55	354	14	18	1	0	0	0	0	372	15
Showers D.	1970–76	77/6	10	2	1	7	1	7/1	1	93/7	13
Simmons A.J.	1986	4/1	1	0	0	0	0	0	0	4/1	1
Simpkins M.J.	2001–02	13/4	0	0	0	1	0	2	0	16/4	0
Sloan T.M.	1924–28	79	1	11	0	0	0	0	0	90	1
Smelt L.A.	1984–85	37	0	2	0	3	0	2	0	44	0
Smith C.R.	1983–84	50	3	0	0	5	0	0	0	55	3
Smith E.E.	1920–23	105	2	18	1	0	0	0	0	123	3
Smith F.C.	1936	16	8	0	0	0	0	0	0	16	8
Smith G.	1973–74	43/2	1	1	0	3	0	2	0	49/2	1
Smith H.R.	1935–36	50	3	1	0	0	0	1	0	52	3
Smith J.	1930–31	61	0	4	0	0	0	0	0	65	0
Smith J.A.	1936–37	13	0	0	0	0	0	0	0	13	0
Smith R.	1938	11	2	5	0	0	0	0	0	16	2
Smith S.JW.	1925–26	4	0	1	0	0	0	0	0	5	0
Smith T.P.	1925–28	42	7	0	0	0	0	0	0	42	7
Spring A.J.	1985	1	0	0	0	0	0	0	0	1	0
Stansfield F.	1946–48	106	1	5	0	0	0	0	0	111	1
Stant P.R.	1992–94	77/2	34	6/1	4	2	2	8	3	93/3	43
Steel A.	1949	10	0	0	0	0	0	0	0	10	0
Steele E.G.	1982	7	0	0	0	0	0	0	0	7	0
Stephens L.M.	1990	1/2	0	0	0	0	0	1	0	2/2	0
Stevens G.M.	1978–81	138/12	44	2/2	0	9	3	0	0	149/14	47
Stevenson E.	1948–49	50	15	3	1	0	0	0	0	53	16
Stevenson N.C.A.	1985 & 1987–88	80/2	2	2	1	5	0	6	0	93/2	3
Stitfall A.E.	1948–50	7	1	0	0	0	0	0	0	7	1
Stitfall R.F.	1947–63	398	8	20	0	3	0	0	0	421	8
Stockin R.	1954–56	57	16	3	1	0	0	0	0	60	17

Player	Played	LEAGUE A	LEAGUE G	FA CUP A	FA CUP G	FL CUP A	FL CUP G	OTHERS A	OTHERS G	TOTAL A	TOTAL G
Stoker G.	1996–97	28/8	4	2/2	0	1/1	0	3	0	34/11	4
Sugrue P.A.	1981	2/3	0	0/1	0	1	1	0	0	3/4	1
Sullivan C.J.	1978–81	61/2	1	2	0	4	0	0	0	67/2	1
Sullivan D.	1947–60	275	19	10	0	0	0	0	0	285	19
Summerfield K.	1984	10	1	0	0	2	0	0	0	12	1
Summerhayes D.M.	1965–67	7/6	0	0	0	1	0	1	0	9/6	0
Summers C.	1990	0/3	0	0	0	0	0	0/1	0	0/4	0
Sutton M.C.	1968–71	135/3	5	8	0	5	0	14	2	162/3	7
Swan M.M.G.	1960–62	15	0	3	0	1	0	0	0	19	0
Taggart R.	1949	2	0	0	0	0	0	0	0	2	0
Talbot F.L.	1936–38	94	21	13	2	0	0	3	0	110	23
Tapscott D.R.	1958–64	193	79	9	2	5	3	7	2	214	86
Taylor P.M.R.	1990	6	3	0	0	0	0	0	0	6	3
Taylor S.G.	1934	1	0	0	0	0	0	0	0	1	0
Taylor W.	1922–24	6	0	0	0	0	0	0	0	6	0
Tennant J.	1932	2	0	0	0	0	0	0	0	2	0
Thirlaway W.J.	1926–29	108	22	6	0	0	0	1	0	115	22
Thomas D.	2004–06	0/1	0	0	0	0	0	1	0	1/1	0
Thomas D.J.	1998–2000	21/10	5	0/3	0	0/1	0	1	0	22/14	5
Thomas M.R.	1982	15	0	0	0	4	0	0	0	19	0
Thomas P.J.	1953	4	1	1	0	0	0	0	0	5	1
Thomas R.J.	1977–81	89/7	0	4	0	3/1	0	3	0	99/8	0
Thomas W.K.	1952–53	9	4	0	0	0	0	0	0	9	4
Thompson A.R.	2000–01	5/2	0	0/1	0	0	0	2/1	0	7/4	0
Thompson C.D.	1989	1/1	0	0	0	0	0	0	0	1/1	0
Thompson G.L.	1993–94	39/4	5	5/2	1	2	0	4/2	1	50/8	7
Thompson S.	2005–06	14	4	0	0	0	0	0	0	14	4
Thorne P.L.	2001–06	116/10	46	6/1	1	4	3	6	1	132/11	51
Tiddy M.D.	1950–54	146	20	4	0	0	0	0	0	150	20
Tobin R.	1947	2	0	0	0	0	0	0	0	2	0
Tong D.J.	1982–85	119/1	3	5	1	12	0	0	0	136/1	4
Toshack J.B.	1965–70	159/3	74	6	1	6	1	19	11	190/3	87
Toshack J.C.	1990–91	1/4	0	0	0	0	0	0/1	0	1/5	0
Townsend C.G.	1983	2/3	0	0	0	1/1	0	0	0	3/4	0
Tucker K.J.	1956–57	13	0	0	0	0	0	0	0	13	0
Tupling S.	1988–89	3/2	0	1/1	1	0	0	0	0	4/3	1
Turnbull W.	1922	1	0	0	0	0	0	0	0	1	0
Turner A.	1937–38	42	20	4	1	0	0	2	1	48	22
Turner C.	1936	2	0	0	0	0	0	0	0	2	0
Turner R.P.	1985–86	34/5	8	1	0	3	1	1	0	39/5	9
Tysoe F.G.	1926	2	0	0	0	0	0	0	0	2	0
Unsworth J.J.	1990–91	1/3	0	0	0	0	0	0/1	0	1/4	0
Upton J.E.G.	1963	5	0	0	0	2	0	0	0	7	0
Valentine A.F.	1929–30	16	3	2	1	0	0	0	0	18	4
Vaughan A.J.	1999	14	0	0	0	0	0	1	0	15	0
Vaughan N.M.	1983–86	144/5	41	7	1	9	2	4	0	164/5	44
Vaughan T.	1934	12	3	1	0	0	0	1	1	14	4
Vearncombe G.	1952–63	207	0	5	0	3	0	1	0	216	0
Vick L.	1994–95	2/2	0	0	0	0	0	0	0	2/2	0
Vidmar A.	2003–06	68/5	2	1/1	0	6	0	0	0	75/6	2
Villars A.K.	1971–75	66/7	4	2/1	0	4	0	4	1	76/8	5
Vincent J.V	1972–74	59/7	11	5	0	3	1	3	0	70/7	12
Wake H.W.	1923–30	149	9	17	1	0	0	0	0	166	10
Walker L.	1993	1	0	0	0	0	0	0	0	1	0
Walker P.A.	1983	2	0	0	0	0	0	0	0	2	0

Player	Played	LEAGUE A	LEAGUE G	FA CUP A	FA CUP G	FL CUP A	FL CUP G	OTHERS A	OTHERS G	TOTAL A	TOTAL G
Walsh A.	1991	1	0	0	0	0	0	0	0	1	0
Walsh I.P.	1987–88	5/12	4	0	0	0/1	0	1	0	6/13	4
Walsh J.B.	1955–61	206	33	14	1	4	1	0	0	224	35
Walton G.	1936–38	84	16	11	2	0	0	3	0	98	18
Walton M.A.	2000–01	40	0	4	0	2	0	2	0	48	0
Warboys A.	1970–72	57/4	27	3/2	0	4	0	2	0	66/6	27
Ward D.	1960–61	34	18	1	0	3	2	1	0	39	20
Ward G.J.	1989–92	58/1	0	1	0	0	0	7	0	66/1	0
Wardle G.	1946–48	40	11	1	0	0	0	0	0	41	11
Ware P.D.	1996	5	0	0	0	0	0	0	0	5	0
Ware T.	1930	12	0	2	0	0	0	0	0	14	0
Warner T.	2004–06	26	0	2	0	2	0	0	0	30	0
Warren F.W.	1927–29	37	8	1	0	0	0	0	0	38	8
Watkins J.V.	1959–60	65	17	4	0	0	0	0	0	69	17
Watkins P.J.	1963	1	0	0	0	1	0	0	0	2	0
Watson T.	1925–28	85	0	11	0	0	0	0	0	96	0
Watson W.T.	1947	1	0	0	0	0	0	0	0	1	0
Weale R.H.	1930	5	0	0	0	0	0	0	0	5	0
Welsby A.	1936	3	0	0	0	0	0	0	0	3	0
Went P.F.	1976–78	71/1	11	4	0	4	0	4	0	83/1	11
West G.	1920–21	25	5	5	1	0	0	0	0	30	6
West J.	1933	6	2	0	0	0	0	0	0	6	2
Weston R.D.	2000–06	170/12	2	14/1	0	9	0	7	0	200/13	2
Whalley G.	2002–06	33/8	2	1	0	2	0	3	0	39/8	2
Wheeler P.	1985–88	72/29	10	3/1	1	5/2	2	4/2	1	84/34	14
White S.J.	1996–97	43/23	15	1/2	2	4	0	4/1	0	52/26	17
Whitham J.	1973–74	12/2	3	1	0	0	0	0	0	13/2	3
Whitley J.	2005–06	32/2	1	1	0	3	0	0	0	36/2	1
Whitlow F.W.J.	1934	7	1	0	0	0	0	1	0	8	1
Wigg N.M.	1993–95	40/19	1	1/2	0	3	0	2/1	0	46/22	1
Williams C.R.	1977	3	0	0	0	0	0	0	0	3	0
Williams D.	2004–06	17/3	0	0	0	0	0	0	0	17/3	0
Williams D.J.	1935–36	20	10	0	0	0	0	0	0	20	10
Williams D.P.	1994–95	82	0	3	0	6	0	5	0	96	0
Williams D.R.	1948–55	138	19	1	0	0	0	0	0	139	19
Williams G.C.	1961–67	161	13	8	1	12	0	9	1	190	15
Williams G.J.J.	1946–52	144	0	6	1	0	0	0	0	150	1
Williams J.N.	1998	26/17	12	5	3	2	1	1	0	34/17	16
Williams R.S.	1929–30	30	17	2	0	0	0	0	0	32	17
Williams S.C.	1992–96	33/1	0	1	0	0	0	5	0	39/1	0
Williams T.P.	1937–38	6	0	0	0	0	0	0	0	6	0
Williams W.J.	1991	5	0	0	0	0	0	0	0	5	0
Wilson R.J.	1964–67	115	0	5	0	7	0	13	0	140	0
Wilson T.H.	1930	1	0	0	0	0	0	0	0	1	0
Wimbleton P.P.	1986–88	118/1	17	8/1	4	6	0	11	2	143/2	23
Winspear J.	1966	1	0	0	0	0	0	0	0	1	0
Withey G.A.	1984–85	27	7	1	1	0	0	0/1	0	28/1	8
Wood G.	1987–89	67	0	6	0	6	0	7	0	86	0
Wood T.L.	1946	4	0	2	0	0	0	0	0	6	0
Woodruff R.W.	1969–73	141/9	22	11/1	2	5	1	10	1	167/10	26
Woods J.P.	1984	0/1	0	0	0	0	0	0	0	0/1	0
Woof W.	1982	1	1	0	0	0	0	0	0	1	1
Youds E.P.	1989	0/1	0	0/1	0	0	0	0	0	0/2	0
Young S.	1993–2003	257/20	22	21/1	2	13/1	1	17/3	1	308/25	26
Zhiyi F.	2002	6	0	0	0	0	0	1	0	7	0
Zois P.	1997	1	0	0	0	0	0	0	0	1	0

ND - #0352 - 270225 - C0 - 260/195/16 - PB - 9781780911519 - Gloss Lamination